LIBERATION IN THE PALM OF YOUR HAND

PABONGKA RINPOCHE

Liberation in the Palm of Your Hand

A Concise Discourse on the Path to Enlightenment

NEW REVISED EDITION

Pabongka Rinpoche

Edited in the Tibetan by Trijang Rinpoche

Translated into English by Michael Richards

Including a memoir of Pabongka Rinpoche by Rilbur Rinpoche

Wisdom Publications • Boston

Wisdom Publications, Inc.
199 Elm Street
Somerville, MA 02144 USA
www.wisdompubs.org

First Edition, 1991
Revised Edition, 1993
New Revised Edition, 2006

Text © Michael Richards 1991, 2006
Illustrations pp. 2 & 246 © Robert Beer 1991; all others © Eva van Dam 1991
All rights reserved.

No part of this book may be reproduced in any form or by any means, electronic or mechanical, including photography, recording, or by any information storage and retrieval system or technologies now known or later developed, without permission in writing from the publisher.

Library of Congress Cataloging in Publication Data

Pha-boṅ-kha-pa Byams-pa-bstan-'dzin-'phrin-las-rgya-mtsho, 1878–1941.
[Rnam sgrol lag bcaṅs su... English]
Liberation in the palm of your hand: a concise discourse on the path to enlightenment / Pabongka Rinpoche; edited in the Tibetan by Trijang Rinpoche; translated into English by Michael Richards.
p. cm.
Includes bibliographical references and index.
ISBN 0-86171-500-4 (pbk. : alk. paper)
1. Lam-rim. I. Richards, Michael, 1950– II. Title.
BQ7645.L35P4613 2006
294.3'923—dc22 2006022542

ISBN 9780861715008; eBook ISBN 9780861719457
14 13
5 4 3

Cover and interior designed by Gopa&Ted2. Set in Adobe Garamond 10.9/13.7

Wisdom Publications' books are printed on acid-free paper and meet the guidelines for the permanence and durability of the Committee on Production Guidelines for Book Longevity of the Council on Library Resources.

Printed in the United States of America.

This book was produced with environmental mindfulness. For more information, please visit our website, www.wisdompubs.org. This paper is also FSC certified. For more information, please visit www.fscus.org.

CONTENTS

PART THREE: THE FOUNDATIONS OF THE PATH

PART FOUR: THE SMALL SCOPE

PART FIVE: THE MEDIUM SCOPE

PART SIX: THE GREAT SCOPE

APPENDIXES

LIST OF ILLUSTRATIONS

TRANSLATOR'S INTRODUCTION

In 1921, some seven hundred Tibetan monks, nuns, and lay people gathered at Chuzang Hermitage, near Lhasa, to receive a *lamrim* discourse from the renowned teacher, Kyabje Pabongka Rinpoche. For the next twenty-four days they listened to what has become one of the most famous teachings ever given in Tibet.

The term *lamrim*—steps on the path to enlightenment—refers to a group of teachings that have developed in Tibet over the past millennium based on the concise, seminal text, *A Lamp on the Path,* by the great Indian master Atiśha (Dīpaṃkara Śhrījñāna, 982–1054). In some ways, *Liberation in the Palm of Your Hand* represents the culmination of the lamrim tradition in Tibet.

Over 2,500 years ago, Śhākyamuni Buddha spent about forty-five years giving a vast array of teachings to an enormous variety of people. He did not teach from some predetermined syllabus but according to the spiritual needs of his listeners. Hence any individual studying the Buddha's collected works would find it extremely difficult to discern a clear path that he or she could put into practice. The importance of Atiśha's lamrim was that he put the Buddha's teachings into logical order, delineating a step-by-step arrangement that could be understood and practiced by whoever wanted to follow the Buddhist path, irrespective of his or her level of development.

Not only did Atiśha rely on what the Buddha himself taught, he also brought with him to Tibet the still-living oral traditions of those teachings—the unbroken lineages of both method and wisdom, which had passed from the Buddha to Maitreya and Mañjuśhrī respectively, and then on down through Asaṅga, Nāgārjuna and many other great Indian scholar-yogis to Atiśha's own spiritual masters. Thus as well as writing the first lamrim text, Atiśha also conveyed these extremely important oral traditions, which still exist today, and are being transmitted to Westerners through contemporary lamas such as His Holiness the Fourteenth Dalai Lama.

Atiśha's disciples formed a school known as the Kadam, most of whose traditions were absorbed into the Gelug school of Tibetan Buddhism, which was founded by the great Tsongkapa (1357–1419). Many Kadam and Gelug lamas wrote lamrim commentaries, and the most famous was Tsongkapa's master work, the *Great Stages of the Path (Lamrim Chenmo).* Pabongka Rinpoche followed the general outline of this text in the 1921 discourse that was to become *Liberation in the Palm of Your Hand.* However, while Tsongkapa's work has a more scholarly emphasis, Kyabje Pabongka's focuses on the needs of practitioners. It goes into great detail on such such subjects as how to prepare for meditation, guru yoga, and the development of *bodhichitta.* Thus *Liberation* is a highly practical text.

Among those present in 1921 was Kyabje Trijang Dorje Chang (1901–81), one of Pabongka Rinpoche's closest disciples, and later Junior Tutor to the Fourteenth Dalai Lama and root guru of many of the Gelug lamas who fled Tibet in 1959. Trijang Rinpoche took notes at the teachings, and over the next thirty-seven years edited them painstakingly until they were ready to be published in Tibetan as *Liberation in the Palm of Your Hand (rNam grol lag bcangs).*

Pabongka Rinpoche was probably the most influential Gelug lama of this century, holding all the important lineages of sūtra and tantra and passing them on to most of the important Gelug lamas of the next two generations; the list of his oral discourses is vast in depth and breadth. He was also the root guru of Kyabje Ling Rinpoche (1903–83), Senior Tutor of the Dalai Lama, Trijang Rinpoche, and many other highly respected teachers. His collected works occupy fifteen large volumes and cover every aspect of Buddhism. If you have ever received a teaching from a Gelug lama, you have been influenced by Pabongka Rinpoche.

There are four main schools of Tibetan Buddhism, and all have lamrim-style teachings, but the Nyingma, Sakya and Kagyu schools do not emphasize the lamrim as does the Gelug. Although generally in the Gelug monastic curriculum the lamrim is not taught to the monks until quite late in their careers, it is often the first teaching given to Westerners. And *Liberation* has been the lamrim that Gelug masters teach most.

In his brief introduction, Kyabje Trijang Rinpoche conveys a strong sense of what it was like to be there. Indeed, this text is unusual among Tibetan works in that it is the edited transcript of an oral discourse, not a literary composition. Hence not only do we receive some very precious teachings—the essence of the eight key lamrims—but we also gain insight into how such discourses were given in Tibet. The points that detail the special features of this teaching may be found in Trijang Rinpoche's introduction and at the end of Day 1.

Each chapter corresponds to a day's teaching and usually begins with a short talk to set the motivation of the listeners. In the book, the motivations have been abbreviated in favor of new material, but the remarkable first chapter, Day 1, is both an elaborate motivation and an excellent glance meditation on the entire lamrim. In a sense, the rest of the book is a commentary on this chapter. As Pabongka Rinpoche makes clear throughout, dedicating ourselves to the development of bodhichitta is the most meaningful way of directing our lives, and the graded realizations summarized in Day 1 lead us to that goal. At the end of the book, Pabongka Rinpoche says, "Practice whatever you can so that my teachings will not have been in vain... But above all, make bodhichitta your main practice."

These teachings contain much that is new and unfamiliar, especially for Westerners, but as with any meaningful pursuit, study and reflection lead to clarity and understanding.

A NOTE ON THIS TRANSLATION

I have tried to make this translation as readable as possible without sacrificing accuracy, but since Trijang Rinpoche was a poet of renown, there can be no doubt that some of the beauty of the Tibetan text has been lost. To help Western readers, I have presented the structural hierarchy of the material in a way that Tibetan books do not: the outline of these headings and subheadings is clearly displayed in appendix 1 and serves as an elaborate table of contents.

I have not translated all the technical terms, preferring to leave the Sanskrit word where there is no suitable English equivalent. This is preferable to concocting some English term that may be even less familiar to the reader than the Sanskrit, and new Sanskrit Buddhist words are entering English dictionaries all the time.

In the main body of the text, all Tibetan words and proper names are in phonetics only; their transliterations are in the glossary. Sanskrit transliteration is standard except that *ś* is written as *śh*, *ṣ* as *ṣh*, *c* as *ch*, *ṛ* as *ṛi*, and *ḷ* and *ḷi* to assist readers in pronunciation.

ACKNOWLEDGMENTS

Heartfelt thanks go to my precious root guru, Gen Rinpoche Geshe Ngawang Dhargyey, for teaching this text at the Library of Tibetan Works and Archives and for giving me the complete oral transmission in 1979. I am also deeply grateful to the Venerable Amchok Rinpoche, who worked so long and hard over five years, going through the entire text with me and improving my translation with his excellent suggestions. Also, Gala Rinpoche helped me with Days 11 and 12 in Australia, 1980–81, and Rilbur Rinpoche, one of Pabongka Rinpoche's few living disciples, provided a memoir of his guru: my appreciation to them both.

I also thank my many friends and colleagues in Dharamsala for their help, encouragement, and support: Losang Gyatso, Geshe Dhargyey's translator at the time, for suggesting I translate this book; Gyatsho Tshering and his staff at the Tibetan Library; all at Delek Hospital and Jean-Pierre Urolixes and Mervyn Stringer for their help after my road accident in 1983; David Stuart, who retrieved the draft translation of Days 9 and 10 from Jammu, where it finished up after the accident; Cathy Graham and Jeremy Russell, who offered valuable suggestions to improve the manuscript; my mother and late father, who have always helped and supported me; Alan Hanlay, Lisa Heath, and Michael Perrott; my late friends Keith Kevan and Andy Brennand; and my dear wife, Angela, who shared with me all the pain that this lengthy project brought and kept her patience and hope throughout; her encouragement and sacrifice were beyond measure.

Thanks to Eva van Dam and Robert Beer for their superb illustrations, Gareth Sparham, an old friend, and Trisha Donnelly for interviewing Rilbur Rinpoche, and those at Wisdom Publications who edited and produced the original edition: Nick Ribush, Robina Courtin, Tim McNeill, Sarah Thresher, Lydia Muellbauer, and Maurice Walshe.

Finally, many thanks to Chris Haskett, who spent three years checking my poor translation with the original under the supervision of John Dunne, and to David Kittelstrom for his guiding hand and editorial wisdom, making this new edition possible.

PABONGKA RINPOCHE

A MEMOIR BY RILBUR RINPOCHE

MY GURU, kind in three ways, who met face to face with Heruka, whose name I find difficult to utter, Lord Pabongka Vajradhara Dechen Nyingpo Pael Zangpo, was born north of Lhasa in 1878. His father was a minor official, but the family was not wealthy. Although the night was dark, a light shone in the room, and people outside the house had a vision of a protector on the roof.

Pabongka Rinpoche was an emanation of the great scholar Changkya Rolpai Dorje (1717–86), although initially it was thought that he was the reincarnation of a learned Khampa geshe from Sera Mae Monastery. Rinpoche entered the monastery at the age of seven, did the usual studies of a monk, earned his geshe degree, and spent two years at Gyuetoe Tantric College.

His root guru was Dagpo Lama Rinpoche Jampael Lhuendrub Gyatso, from Lhoka. He was definitely a bodhisattva, and Pabongka Rinpoche was his foremost disciple. He lived in a cave in Pasang, and his main practice was bodhichitta. His main deity was Avalokiteśhvara, and he would recite 50,000 *maṇis* [the mantra, *oṃ maṇi padme hūṃ*] every night. When Kyabje Pabongka first met Dagpo Rinpoche at a *tsog* offering ceremony in Lhasa, he cried from beginning to end out of reverence.

When Pabongka Rinpoche had finished his studies, he visited Dagpo Lama Rinpoche in his cave and was sent into a lamrim retreat nearby. Dagpo Lama Rinpoche would teach him a lamrim topic and then Pabongka Rinpoche would go away and meditate on it. Later he would return to explain what he'd understood: if he had gained some realization, Dagpo Lama Rinpoche would teach him some more, and Pabongka Rinpoche would go back and meditate on that. It went on like this for ten years (and if that's not amazing, what is!).

Pabongka Rinpoche's four main disciples were Kyabje Ling Rinpoche, Kyabje Trijang Rinpoche, Khangsar Rinpoche, and Tathag Rinpoche, who was a regent of Tibet. Tathag Rinpoche was the main teacher of His Holiness the Dalai Lama when he was a child and gave him his novice ordination.

I was born in Kham, in Eastern Tibet, and two of my early teachers were disciples of Pabongka Rinpoche, so I was brought up in an atmosphere of complete faith in Pabongka Rinpoche as the Buddha himself. One of these teachers had a picture of Pabongka Rinpoche that exuded small drops of nectar from between the eyebrows. I saw this with my own eyes, so you can imagine how much faith I had in Rinpoche when I finally came into his presence.

But I also had a personal reason for having great faith in him. I was the only son of an important family, and although the Thirteenth Dalai Lama had recognized me as an incarnate lama and Pabongka Rinpoche himself had said I should join Sera Monastery in Lhasa, my parents were not happy about this. However, my father died soon after this, and I was finally able to set out for Central Tibet. Can you imagine my excitement as I embarked on horseback on the two-month voyage? I was only fourteen, and becoming a monk really was the thing to do for a fellow my age. I felt that the opportunity to go to Lhasa to get ordained and live as a *rinpoche* as the Dalai Lama had said I should was all the wondrous work of Pabongka Rinpoche.

At the time of my arrival in Lhasa, Pabongka Rinpoche was living at Tashi Choeling, a cave above Sera Monastery. We made an appointment, and a few days later my mother, my *changdzoe* (the man in charge of my personal affairs), and I rode up on horseback. Although Rinpoche was expecting us that day, we had not arranged a time. Nevertheless, he had just had his own changdzoe prepare tea and sweet rice, which freshly awaited our arrival. This convinced me that Rinpoche was clairvoyant, a manifestation of the all-seeing Vajradhara himself.

After we had eaten, it was time to visit Rinpoche. I remember this as if it were today. A narrow staircase led up to Pabongka Rinpoche's tiny room, where he was sitting on his bed. He looked just like his pictures—short and fat! He said, "I knew you were coming—now we have met," and stroked the sides of my face. While I was sitting there, a new geshe from Sera came in to offer Rinpoche a special *tsampa* dish that is made only at the time of receiving the geshe degree. Rinpoche remarked how auspicious it was that this new geshe had come while I was there and had him fill my bowl just like his own. You can imagine what that did to my mind!

The room had almost nothing in it. The most amazing thing was a pure gold, two-inch statue of Dagpo Lama Rinpoche, Pabongka Rinpoche's root guru, surrounded by a circle of tiny offerings. Behind Rinpoche were five tangkas of Khaedrub Je's visions of Tsongkapa after he had passed away. The only other thing in the room was a place for a cup of tea. I could also see a small meditation room off to the side and kept peeking into it (I was only fourteen and extremely curious). Rinpoche told me to go inside and check it out. All it contained was a meditation box and a small altar. Rinpoche called out the names of the statues on the altar: from left to right there were Lama Tsongkapa, Heruka, Yamāntaka, Naeljorma, and Paelgon Dramze, an emanation of Mahākāla. Beneath the statues were offerings, set out right across the altar.

I was not yet a monk, so Rinpoche's long-time servant Jamyang, who had been given to Pabongka Rinpoche by Dagpo Lama Rinpoche and always stayed in Rinpoche's room, was sent to get a calendar to fix a date for my ordination, even though I had not asked for it. Rinpoche was giving me everything I had ever wanted, and I felt he was just too kind. When I left, I floated out on a cloud in a complete state of bliss!

Rinpoche's changdzoe was a very fierce-looking man, said to be the emanation of a protector. Once, when Rinpoche was away on a long tour, out of devotion the changdzoe demolished the old small building in which Rinpoche lived and constructed a large ornate residence rivaling the private quarters of the Dalai Lama. When Rinpoche returned he was not at all pleased and said, "I am only a minor hermit lama, and you should not have built something like this for me. I am not famous, and the essence of what I teach is renunciation of the worldly life. Therefore I am embarrassed by rooms like these."

I took lamrim teachings from Pabongka Rinpoche many times. The Chinese confiscated all my notes, but as a result of his teachings, I still carry something very special inside. Whenever he taught I would feel inspired to become a real yogi by retreating to a cave, covering myself with ashes, and meditating. As I got older I would feel this less and less, and now I don't think of it at all. But I really wanted to be a true yogi, just like him.

He gave many initiations such as Yamāntaka, Heruka, and Guhyasamāja. I myself took these from him. We would go to his residence for important secret initiations, and he would come down to the monastery to give more general teachings. Sometimes he would go on tour to various monasteries. Visiting Pabongka Rinpoche was what it must have been like to visit Lama Tsongkapa when he was alive.

When he taught he would sit for up to eight hours without moving. About two thousand people would come to his general discourses and initiations and fewer to special teachings, but when he gave bodhisattva vows, up to ten thousand people would show up. When he gave the Heruka initiation he would take on a special appearance. His eyes became very wide and piercing, and I could almost see him as Heruka, with one leg outstretched, the other bent. It would get so intense that I would start crying, as if the deity Heruka himself were right there. It was very powerful, very special.

To my mind he was the most important Tibetan lama of all. Everybody knows how great his four main disciples were—well, he was their teacher. He spent a great deal of time thinking about the practical meaning of the teachings and coming to an inner realization of them, and he had practiced and accomplished everything he had learned, right up to the completion stage. He didn't just spout words, he tried things out for himself. Also, he never got angry; any anger had been completely pacified by his bodhichitta. Many times there would be long lines of people waiting for blessings, but Rinpoche would ask each one individually how they were and tap them on the head. Sometimes he dispensed medicine. He was always gentle. All this made him very special.

I would say he had two main qualities: from the tantric point of view, his realization and ability to present Heruka, and from the sūtra point of view, his ability to teach lamrim.

Just before he passed away, he was invited to explain a short lamrim at his root guru's monastery of Dagpo Shidag Ling, in Lhoka. He had chosen the text called the *Quick Path,* by the Second Paṇchen Lama. This was the first lamrim that Dagpo Lama Rinpoche had taught him, and Pabongka Rinpoche had said that it would be the last he himself would teach. Whenever he visited his lama's monastery, Rinpoche would dismount as soon as it appeared in view and prostrate all the way to the door—which was not easy because of his build; when he left he would walk backward until it was out of sight. This time when he left the monastery, he made one prostration when it was almost out of sight and went to stay at a house nearby. Having manifested just a little discomfort in his stomach, Rinpoche retired for the night. He asked his attendants to leave while he did his prayers, which he chanted louder than usual. Then it sounded like he was giving a lamrim discourse. When he had finished and his attendants went into his room, they found he had passed away. Although Tathag Rinpoche was extremely upset, he told us what to do. We were all distraught. Pabongka Rinpoche's body was clothed in brocade and cremated in the traditional way. An incredible reliquary was constructed, but the Chinese demolished it. Nevertheless, I was able to retrieve some of Rinpoche's relics from it, and I gave them to Sera Mae Monastery. You can see them there now.

I have had some success as a scholar, and as a lama I am somebody, but these things are not important. The only thing that matters to me is that I was a disciple of Pabongka Rinpoche.

The Venerable Rilbur Rinpoche was born in Eastern Tibet in 1923. At the age of five he was recognized by the Thirteenth Dalai Lama as the sixth incarnation of Sera Mae Rilbur Rinpoche. He entered Sera Monastic University in Lhasa at fourteen and became a geshe at twenty-four. He meditated and taught Dharma until 1959, after which he suffered under intense Chinese oppression for twenty-one years. In 1980 he was allowed to perform some religious activities, and he helped build a new stūpa for Pabongka Rinpoche at Sera, the Chinese having destroyed the original. He then came to India and lived for several years at Namgyal Monastery, Dharamsala. Toward the end of his life, Rinpoche traveled several times to Western countries and lived for a period in the United States. He passed away at Sera Mae Monastery in Bylakuppe, South India, on January 15, 2006.

THE TEXT

A Profound, Completely Unmistaken Instruction for Conferring Liberation in the Palm of Your Hand, Pith of the Thoughts of the Unequalled King of the Dharma [Tsongkapa], the Written Record of a Concise Discourse on the Stages of the Path to Enlightenment, Pith of All Scripture, Essence of the Nectar of Instructions

rNam sgrol lag bcangs su gtod pa'i man ngag zab mo tshang la ma nor ba mtshungs med chos kyi rgyal po'i thugs bcud byang chub lam gyi rim pa'i nyams khrid kyi zin bris gsung rab kun gyi bcud bsdus gdams ngag bdud rtsi'i snying po

GURU ŚHĀKYAMUNI BUDDHA

INTRODUCTION BY TRIJANG RINPOCHE

Prasārīn paraṇa syakluṭaki yanta
Trayam guhyaṇaṭā tigolama eka
Sudhī vajradharottaraḥ muni akṣha
Prayachchha tashubhaṃ valāruga koṭa

O Lama Lozang Dragpa,
One with Śhākyamuni and Vajradhara,
O sum of every perfect refuge,
O maṇḍala guise complete
With three mysteries of enlightenment:
Rain upon us ten million goodnesses.
O my guru, my protector,
Who, through the Supreme Vehicle,
Vanquished the extreme of selfish peace,
Who, unattached to worldly comforts,
Upheld the three high trainings
And the teachings of the Victor,
Whose noble good works remained
Untarnished by the eight worldly concerns:
You were the very fountainhead of goodness.
Everything you said was medicine
To drive out hundreds of diseases;
Our childish minds were unfit vessels
For so vast an ocean of teachings,
So precious a source of qualities.
How sad if these teachings were forgotten!
Here I have recorded but a few.

Immeasurable, countless numbers of buddhas have come in the past. But unfortunate beings such as myself were not worthy enough to be direct disciples even of Śhākyamuni, the best of protectors, who stands out like a white lotus among the thousand great buddhas, the saviors of this fortunate eon. First we had to be forced into developing even a moment's wholesome thought; this took us to the optimum physical rebirth as a human. We have been taught this most unmistaken path, which will lead us to the level of omniscience, at which time we shall gain our freedom.

But, to be brief, I was saved time and time again from infinite numbers of different evils, and was brought closer to an infinity of magnificent things. My glorious and holy guru did this. His kindness is without equal. He was—and now I shall give his name in view of my purpose—Jetsun Jampa Taenzin Trinlae Gyatso Paelzangpo. Although people like me are immature, uncultured, and unregenerate, there was a time when I feasted on his oral instructions into the Mahāyāna [the Supreme or Great Vehicle] at Chuzang Hermitage, a solitary place that was blessed by the presence of great meditators.

He started the following informal teaching on the thirtieth, the new-moon day of the seventh month of the Iron-Bird Year [1921], and it lasted twenty-four days. People braved great hardships to get there from the three major monasteries in Lhasa, from the Central Province, from Tsang, Amdo, and Kham just to taste the nectar of his oral teachings, as the thirsty yearn for water. There were about thirty lamas and reincarnations of lamas, and many upholders of the three baskets of the teachings—in all a gathering of over seven hundred. The practical teaching he gave combined various traditions on the lamrim: the stages of the path to enlightenment. There were the two oral lineages related to the lamrim text *Mañjuśhrī's Own Words.* One of these lineages was quite detailed and had developed in the Central Province; another lineage of a briefer teaching flourished in the south of Tibet. He also included the concise teaching, the *Swift Path* lamrim; and in the part of the great-scope section that deals with the interchange of self and others, he taught the *Seven-Point Mind Training.*

Each part of the teaching was enriched by instructions taken from the confidential oral lineages. Because each section was illustrated by analogies, conclusive formal logic, amazing stories, and trustworthy quotations, the teaching could easily be understood by beginners, and yet was tailored for all levels of intelligence. It was beneficial for the mind because it was so inspiring. Sometimes we were moved to laughter, becoming wide awake and alive. Sometimes we were reduced to tears and cried helplessly. At other times we became afraid and were moved to feel, "I would gladly give up this life and devote myself solely to my practice." This feeling of renunciation was overwhelming.

These are some of the ways in which all of his discourses were so extraordinary. How could I possibly convey all this on paper! Yet what a pity if I were to forget all the key points contained in these inspiring instructions. This thought gave me the courage to write this book. As my precious guru later advised me, "Some of the people present could not follow the teaching, and I cannot teach them again. I'm afraid I do not trust all the notes people took during the classes. I therefore ask you to publish a book. Put in it anything you feel sure of."

In this book I have recorded my lama's teachings without any changes in the hope that this book, while no substitute for his speech, may still benefit my friends who wish to succeed in their practice.

Part One

THE PRELIMINARIES

KYABJE PABONGKA RINPOCHE

DAY 1

Kyabje Pabongka Rinpoche, a peerless king of the Dharma, spoke a little in order to set our motivations properly for the teaching to follow. He said:

So be it. The great Tsongkapa, the Dharma king of the three realms, has said:

> This opportune physical form
> Is worth more than a wish-granting gem.
> You only gain its like the once.
> So hard to get, so easily destroyed,
> It's like a lightning bolt in the sky.
>
> Contemplate this, and you will realize
> All worldly actions are but winnowed chaff,
> And night and day you must
> Extract some essence from your life.
> I, the yogi, practiced this way;
> You, wanting liberation, do the same!

In all our births from beginningless time till the present, there has not been any form of suffering we have not undergone here in saṃsāra, nor any form of happiness we have not experienced. But no matter how many bodies we have had, we have obtained nothing worthwhile from them. Now that we have gained this optimum human form, we should do something to derive some essence from it. So long as we do not examine this life, we will feel no joy whatsoever in finding such a supreme rebirth, and would probably be happier on finding some pennies; we will not feel at all sorry if we waste this optimum human rebirth; we would probably feel much more regret if we lost some money. But this physical form we have now is a hundred thousand times more valuable than any wish-granting jewel.

If you were to clean a wish-granting jewel by washing it three times, polishing it three times, and then offer it at the top of a victory banner, you would effortlessly obtain the good things of this life—food, clothes, and the like. You may obtain a hundred, a thousand, ten thousand, even a hundred thousand such gems, but they cannot do for you even the smallest thing that you can achieve by means of this rebirth, for they cannot be used to prevent you from taking your next rebirth in the lower realms. With your present physical form you can prevent yourself from ever going to the lower realms again. Moreover, if you want to achieve the physical rebirth of a Brahmā, an Indra, and so forth, you can achieve it through your present one. If you want to go to pure realms such as Abhīrati, Sukhāvatī, or Tuṣhita, you can do so by means of this present physical rebirth. And this is not all, for you can even achieve the states of liberation or omniscience through this present rebirth—unless you don't practice. Most important of all, through this physical rebirth you are able to achieve the state of Vajradhara [the unification of the illusory body and great bliss] within one short lifetime in this degenerate age; otherwise it would take three countless great eons to achieve. Thus, this rebirth is worth more than one thousand billion precious jewels.

If you meaninglessly squander this rebirth that you have managed to obtain, it would be an even greater pity than if you had wasted one thousand billion precious jewels. There is no greater loss; nothing could be blinder; no self-deception could be greater. Protector Śhāntideva said:

> No self-deception could be worse
> After gaining such a chance
> Than not cultivating virtue!
> Nothing could be blinder!

You must therefore try to extract essence from it now. If you don't, you are sure to die anyway, and you cannot know when that will happen.

We are now attending this Dharma teaching, but none of us will be left in a hundred years' time. In the past, Buddha, our Teacher, amassed the two collections [of merit and primal wisdom] over many eons, thus obtaining the vajra body. Yet even he, to the common appearance, went to nirvāṇa [beyond suffering]. After him, there came scholars, adepts, translators, and pandits to both India and Tibet, but they have all seemingly departed this life. Nothing is left of them but their names to say "There was this one and some other." In short, there is no one you can produce as an example of a person who death has spared. How could you alone live forever? You have no hope of being spared.

Therefore, not only are you sure to die, but also you cannot be certain when this will happen. You cannot even be sure that you will still be alive next year in the human realm, still wearing your three types of monk's robes.[1] By this time next year, you may have already been reborn as an animal covered in shaggy fur, with horns on your head. Or you may have been born as a hungry ghost, for example, having to live without being able to find any food or even a drop of water. Or you may have been reborn in the hells, having to experience the miseries of heat and cold, being roasted or on fire.

Your mental continuum does not cease after your death; it must take rebirth. There are only two migrations for rebirth—the upper and the lower realms. If you are born in the Hell Without Respite, you will have to stay there with your body indistinguishable from the hellfire. In the milder hells, such as the Hell of Continual Resurrection, you are killed and then revived hundreds of times each day: you continually suffer torments. How could we endure this if we cannot even bear to put our hand in a fire now? And we will suffer in these hells the same way that we would suffer from such heat in our present bodies. We might wonder, "Maybe the experience [suffering] is different, and easier?" but that is wrong.

If reborn as a hungry ghost you will not be able to find so much as a drop of water for years. If you find it hard to observe a fasting retreat now, how could you endure such a rebirth? And as for the animal rebirths, take the case of being a dog. Examine in detail the sort of places where they live, the way they have to go in search of food and the sort of food they eventually find. Do you think you could possibly bear living that sort of life? You may feel, "The lower realms are far away." But between you and the lower realms is only that you can still draw breath.

As long as we remain uncritical, we never suspect that we are going to the lower realms. We probably think that we more or less keep our vows, perform most of our daily recitations, and have not committed any serious sin, such as killing a person and running off with his horse. The trouble is we have not looked into things properly. We should think it over in detail; then we would see that we are not free to choose whether we go to the lower realms or not. This is determined by our karma. We have a mixture of virtuous and nonvirtuous karma in our mental streams. The stronger of these two will be triggered by craving and clinging when we die. When we look into which of these two is the stronger in our mental streams, we will see that it is nonvirtue. And the degree of strength is determined by the force of the *motive,* the *deed,* and the *final step.* Thus, although we might think we have only done small nonvirtues, their force is in fact enormous.

Let us take an example. Suppose you say one scornful word to your pupils, for instance. You are motivated by strong hostility and, as for the deed, you use the harshest words that will really wound them. And for the final step, you feel proud and have an inflated opinion of yourself. These three parts—motivation, deed, and final step—could not have been done better! Suppose you kill a louse. Your motive is strong hostility. You roll the louse between your fingers, and so on, torturing it a long while, then eventually you kill it. For the final step, you think "That was helpful" and become very smug. So the nonvirtue has become extremely powerful.

We might feel our virtue is very strong, but in fact it is extremely weak. The preparation, the motive, the main part of the deed, the final step, dedicating the virtue, etc.—all have to be done purely if the virtue is to be very strong. Contrast this with the virtue *we* perform. First, there is our motive. I think it is rare for us to be motivated by even the least of motives, a yearning for a better rebirth—let alone have the best of motives, bodhichitta [the mind that aspires to enlightenment], or the next best, renunciation. Right at the beginning, we usually aspire to achieve desires related to this life's trivia; any prayers we make to this end are in fact sinful. Then, for the main part of the deed, there is no pure joy or enthusiasm to it; when we recite even one rosary of *oṃ maṇi padme hūṃ,* for example, our minds cannot stay focused the whole time. Everything is either sleep or distraction! It is difficult to do things well for even the time it takes to recite the *Hundreds of Gods of Tuṣhita* once. And when it comes to making the final prayers and dedications, we slip back into directing them toward this life. So, although we might feel we have performed great virtues, in fact they are only feeble.

Sometimes we do not prepare properly; at other times we botch the motive or the final step; and there are times when we don't do any of them properly. Thus only the nonvirtuous karma in our mental streams is very strong; it is the only possible thing that will be activated when we die. And if this is what indeed happens, the place where we will go could only be the lower realms. That is why it is definite we shall be reborn in the lower realms. Now, we say that our lamas possess clairvoyance, and we ask them for dice divinations or prophecies on where we shall take rebirth. We feel relieved if they say, "You will get a good rebirth," and are afraid if the answer is, "It will be bad." But how can we have any confidence in such predictions? We do not need dice divinations, prophecies, or horoscopes to tell us where we will go in our next lives. Our compassionate Teacher has already given us predictions in the sūtra basket *[sūtra piṭaka]*. We have also received them from many pandits and adepts of both India and Tibet. For example, Ārya Nāgārjuna says in his *Precious Garland:*

> From nonvirtue comes all suffering
> And likewise all the lower realms.
> From virtue come all upper realms
> And all happy rebirths.

We cannot be certain—even by means of direct valid cognition—of such things as where we will go in our future rebirths. Nevertheless, our Teacher correctly perceived this extremely obscure object of valid cognition and taught on it without error. Thus we can be certain only by using the Buddha's valid scriptures for an inference based on trust.

So, if it is so definite that we shall be reborn in the lower realms, from this moment on we must look for some means to stop it from happening. If we really want to be free of the lower realms, we should seek some refuge to protect us. For example, a criminal sentenced to execution will seek the protection of an influential official in order to escape punishment. If we have become tainted by intolerably sinful karma through our misdeeds, we are in danger of being punished under [karmic] law and of going to the lower realms. We should seek the refuge of the Three Jewels [Buddha, Dharma, and Saṅgha], because only they can protect us from this fate. But we must not just *seek* this refuge; we must also modify our behavior.[2] If there were some way the buddhas could rid us of our sins and obscurations by, say, washing them away with water, or by leading us by the hand, they would have already done so, and we would now have no suffering. They do not do this. The Great One taught the Dharma; it is we who must modify our behavior according to the laws of cause and effect, and do so unmistakenly. It says in a sūtra:

> The sages do not wash sin away with water;
> They do not rid beings of suffering with their hands;
> They do not transfer realizations of suchness onto others.
> They liberate by teaching the truth of suchness.

Thus you should feel, "I shall seek refuge in the Three Jewels in order to be free of the lower realms, and I shall adopt the means to free me from these realms. I shall modify my behavior according to the laws of cause and effect." This is setting your motivation on the level of the lamrim shared with the small scope.

All the same, is it enough merely to be free of the lower realms? No, it is not. You will only achieve one or two physical rebirths in the upper realms before falling back to the lower realms when your evil karma catches up with you. This is not the ultimate answer, not something in which you can put your trust. We have in fact obtained many rebirths in the upper realms and afterward have fallen back into the lower realms. We are sure to fall back the same way yet again. In our past rebirths, we took the form of the powerful gods Brahmā and Indra and lived in celestial palaces. This happened many times, yet we left these rebirths and had to writhe on the red-hot iron surface of the hells. Again and again this happened. In the celestial realms, we enjoyed the nectar of the gods; then, when we left these rebirths, we had to drink molten iron in the hells. We amused ourselves in the company of many gods and goddesses, then had to live surrounded by terrifying guardians of hell. We were reborn as universal emperors and ruled over hundreds of thousands of subjects; and then we were born as the meanest serfs and slaves, such as donkey drivers and cowherds. Sometimes we were born as sun and moon gods, and our bodies gave off so much light that we illuminated the four continents.[3] Then we were born in the depths of the ocean between continents, where it was so dark we could not even see the movements of our own limbs. And so on. No matter what you achieve of this sort of worldly happiness, it is untrustworthy and has no worth.

We have already experienced so much suffering, but as long as we are not liberated from saṃsāra [cyclic existence], we must experience very much more. If all the filthy things—all the dung and dirt we have eaten in our past animal rebirths as dogs and pigs—were piled up in one place, the dung heap would be bigger than Meru, the king of mountains. Yet we will have to eat even more filth as long as we are still not liberated from saṃsāra. If all our heads cut off by past enemies were piled up, the top of the heap would be even higher than Brahmā's realm. Yet, if we do not put an end to our cyclic existence, we must lose even more heads. In our past hell rebirths, boiling-hot water was forced down our throats—more water than there is even in the great oceans—but we must drink even more, so long as we have not freed ourselves from saṃsāra. Thus we should be hugely depressed when we think about how in the future we will wander aimlessly, with no end to our cyclic existence.

Even the rebirths of gods and humans are nothing but suffering. The human rebirth has the sufferings of birth, old age, sickness, and death; it has the suffering of being separated from the things one holds dear, meeting with unpleasantness, and not finding the things one wants despite searching for them. The demigods also have sufferings, for they are maimed or wounded when they go to battle, and they suffer all the time from gnawing jealousy. When reborn as a god of the desire realm, one suffers because one displays the omens of death. The gods of the [two] higher realms do not have any manifest suffering. However, they are still, by nature, under the sway of the suffering that applies to all conditioned phenomena because they have not gained enough freedom to maintain their state. In the end they will fall, so they have not transcended suffering.

In short, as long as you are not free of saṃsāra for good, you have not transcended the nature of suffering. You therefore must definitely become liberated from it; and you must do so with your present rebirth.

We normally say, "We cannot do anything in this rebirth," and make prayers for our next rebirth. But it is possible to do it in this rebirth. We have gained the optimum human rebirth, and this is the most advantageous physical form to have for the practice of Dharma. We are free from adverse conditions—we have met with the Buddha's teachings, and so forth. We have all the right conditions, and so if we cannot achieve liberation now, when shall we ever achieve it?

Thus you should feel, "Now I definitely must liberate myself from saṃsāra, come what may. And liberation is achieved only by means of the precious three high trainings. I will therefore train myself in these three and gain my liberation from this great ocean of suffering." This is setting your motivation at the level of the lamrim shared with the medium scope.

But is even this sufficient? Again, it is not. If you achieve the state of a *śhrāvaka* [hearer] or *pratyekabuddha* [solitary realizer] arhat for your own sake, you have not even fulfilled your own needs and done virtually nothing for the sake of others. This is because you have not yet abandoned some of the things you ought, such as the obscurations to omniscience and the four causes of ignorance. It would be like having to bundle up everything twice to cross a river once: although you may have achieved all the steps up to arhatship in the path of the Hīnayāna [Lesser Vehicle], you must then develop bodhichitta and train in the tasks of a child of the victorious ones right from the basics, starting at the Mahāyāna path of accumulation. It would be like entering a monastery and working your way up from being a kitchen hand to the abbot; then, on entering another monastery, you have to go back to working in the kitchen again.

[Chandragomin] said in his *Letter to a Disciple:*

> They are kinsmen stranded in saṃsāra's ocean
> Who seem to have fallen into the abyss;
> When due to birth, death, and rebirth
> You don't recognize them and reject them,
> Freeing only yourself: there is no greater shame.

In other words, although we do not recognize each other as such, there is not one sentient being who has not been our mother. And just as we have taken countless rebirths, we have had countless mothers; no being has not been our mother. And each time they were our mother, the kindness they showed us was no different from the kindness shown by our mother in this life. Since they did nothing but lovingly care for us, there is not the slightest difference between our present mother's kindness and care toward us and that of every sentient being.

However, some may feel, "All sentient beings are not my mother. If they were, I would recognize them as my mother; instead, I do not!" But since it is quite possible that many do not recognize even their mother of this life, mere nonrecognition is not sufficient reason for someone not to be your mother. There are others who might feel, "Mothers of past lives belong to the past. It makes no sense to say they are still one's kind mothers." But the kindness and care that mothers showed you in the past, and the kindness and the care your present mother shows you, are not in the least bit different from each other, either in being your mother or in their kindness and care. The kindness is the same if you received some food or wealth from someone last year or this year. The time of the deed, past or future, does not alter the degree of kindness. Thus all sentient beings are nothing but kind mothers to you.

How could we ignore these kind mothers of ours, who have fallen into the middle of the ocean of saṃsāra, and doing only what pleases us, work only for our own liberation? It would be like children singing and dancing on the shore when one of their dearly beloved close relatives, such as their mother, was about to fall into the ocean's riptide. The rip is flowing out to the ocean, and she cries and calls out to them in terror, but they are completely oblivious to her. Is there anyone who is more shameful or contemptible? The currents in the oceans are said to be whirlpools, and it is a most horrifying thing when a boat, coracle, and so on, enters the maelstrom, for it is sure to sink. Just like in that example, though we presently do not seem to have any relationship with all sentient beings who have fallen into these ocean currents of saṃsāra, this is not so. All are our kind mothers, and we must repay their kindness. Giving food to the hungry, drink to the thirsty, wealth to the poor, etc., and satisfying their wants, would repay some of them their kindnesses; but this would really not be of much benefit. The best way to repay their kindness is to cause them to have every happiness and to be without every kind of suffering. There is no better way to repay their kindness.

With these thoughts you should come to think, "May these sentient beings have every form of happiness," which is the development of love. You also feel, "May they be without every suffering," which is the development of compassion. You develop altruism when you feel, "The responsibility for carrying out these two has fallen on me. I, and I alone, shall work for these ends."

Still, are you now able to do these? As for right now, forget about all beings—you cannot work for the sake of even one sentient being. Who then can? The bodhisattvas abiding on the pure levels[4] and the śhrāvakas or pratyekabuddhas can benefit sentient beings; but they can only do a little of what the buddhas are capable of doing. Thus a buddha, who is without equal in his deeds for the welfare of beings, is the only one. Each ray of light from the body of a buddha is able to mature and liberate immeasurable sentient beings. Buddhas emanate bodies that appear before each sentient being. These forms are tailored to the mental dispositions, sense faculties, wishes, and karmic tendencies of these beings. Buddhas can teach them the Dharma in their individual languages. These are some of the capabilities of buddhas.

If you wonder whether we can achieve the same level of buddhahood, the answer is, we can. The best of all physical rebirths to have for its attainment is the optimum rebirth. We have gained a very special type of physical rebirth: we were born from the womb of a human of the Southern Continent, and we have the six types of physical constituents. We are thus able to achieve in one lifetime the state of unification of Vajradhara, unless we do not apply ourselves. We have attained such a physical rebirth. The means to achieve buddhahood is the Dharma of the Supreme Vehicle; and the teachings of the second Victorious One [Je Tsongkapa] on this vehicle are completely unmistaken. His stainless teachings combine both the sūtras and the tantras. We have met with such teachings.

In short, we are free from any unfavorable conditions, except for cheating ourselves by not making effort. If now, when we have attained such an excellent foundation with all the favorable conditions, we cannot achieve buddhahood, it is certain that in the future we will not gain any better rebirth or Dharma. Some of us might claim, "Now is a degenerate time; our timing has been bad." But since beginningless cyclic existence we have never experienced a time with more potential benefit for us than now. We could have no better a time than this. We shall find such a situation only once. We must therefore work toward our buddhahood, come what may.

Thus, this should lead you to feel, "I shall do all I can to achieve my goal: peerless, full enlightenment for the sake of all sentient beings." This thought summons up bodhichitta, and it is how you set your motivation according to the great scope of the lamrim. You have developed bodhichitta if you genuinely experience this thought in an unforced manner.

You must practice in order to achieve this buddhahood, and you must know what to practice in order to succeed. Some people wanting to practice Dharma, but not knowing how to do so, may go to some isolated retreat and recite a few mantras, make a few prayers, or even manage to achieve a few of the [nine] mental states [leading to mental quiescence], but they will not know how to do anything else. You must study complete and error-free instructions that leave out nothing about the practice of Dharma in order to know these things. And the king of such instructions is the lamrim, the stages of the path to enlightenment. You must therefore develop the motivation: "I shall listen attentively to the lamrim and then put it into practice."

In general, it is vital to have one of these three motives at the beginning of any practice. Especially when you listen to a discourse on the lamrim, just any motive is not sufficient. You must at least listen in conjunction with a forced or contrived form of bodhichitta. For people who have already experienced the development of bodhichitta, it may be sufficient for them to think over a short formula such as "For the sake of all mother sentient beings..." However, this is not enough to transform the mind of a beginner. If you think over the lamrim, starting with the immense difficulty of gaining an optimum human rebirth, your mind will turn toward bodhichitta. This does not apply only to the lamrim. When we Gelugpas attend any teaching at all, be it an initiation, oral transmission, discourse, or whatever, we should go over the whole lamrim as a preliminary when we set our motivation. Even short prayers include all of the three scopes of the lamrim, with nothing left out.[5] My precious guru has said time and again that this is the supreme distinguishing feature of the teachings of the old Kadampas and of us new Kadampas. Those of you who will bear the responsibility of preserving these teachings must carry out your studies in this fashion. (However, when giving a long-life initiation, it is the practice not to speak about impermanence, [death], and so on, as this is an inauspicious gesture: one only speaks on the difficulty of obtaining this beneficial, optimum human rebirth.)

Some of the people attending this teaching of the Dharma might feel, "I am truly fortunate to be studying this, but I cannot put it into practice." Others attend because they are imitating others—"If you go, I'll come too." No one will attend this teaching in order to make a living out of performing rituals in people's homes; but this happens with other teachings like major initiations. When you attend other teachings—initiations for example—you may think you will receive the power to subdue evil spirits by reciting the mantra, and so forth; or you may think you will subdue sicknesses or spirits, achieve wealth, acquire power, etc. Others, no matter how many teachings they have received, treat Dharma as if it were, for example, capital to start a business; they then go to places like Mongolia to peddle the Dharma. Such people accumulate enormous, grave sins through the Dharma. The Buddha, our Teacher, discussed the means to achieve liberation and omniscience. To exploit such teachings for worldly ends is equal to forcing a king off his throne and making him sweep the floor. So, if you seem to have any of these above-mentioned bad motives, get rid of them; summon up some contrived bodhichitta and then listen. So much for the setting of your motivation.

Here follows the main body of the teaching to which you are actually going to listen.

Firstly, the Dharma you are going to practice should have been spoken by the Buddha and discussed and proven by the [Indian] pandits. Your practice must be one from which the great adepts derived their insights and realizations; otherwise, an instruction could be termed "profound" even if it were not something spoken by Buddha and were unknown to the other scholar-adepts. Meditate on such an instruction and you could be in danger of getting some result that no one else has ever achieved before—not even the buddhas! You therefore must examine the Dharma you are going to make your practice. As the master Sakya Paṇḍita says:

> With the pettiest business deal
> In horses, jewels, and so on,
> You question everything and examine all.
> I have seen how diligent you are
> With the petty actions of this life!
>
> The good or bad in all your future lives
> Comes from the holy Dharma,
> Yet you treat that Dharma like a dog eats food:
> You worship whatever comes along
> Without first checking whether it is good or evil.

When we buy a horse for example, we examine numerous things, get a divination beforehand, and question lots of other people. Take the example of an ordinary monk. Even when he buys a tea brick, he checks its color, weight, and shape many times over. He makes quite sure it has not been damaged by water, etc., and he asks other people's opinions. Yet if he is unlucky, it would only affect a few cups of tea.

You investigate such things as this thoroughly, even though they have only temporary value for you. But you do not seem to investigate at all the Dharma you are to practice, although this is the foundation of your eternal hopes for all your rebirths. You treat it like dog does food—whatever you chance upon is acceptable. How very wrong that is! If you go wrong here, you have ruined your eternal hopes. Thus, you must examine the Dharma you intend to practice before you engage in it.

If you examine our present Dharma, the lamrim, you will see it is the best of all. Even the extraordinary profundity of the secret tantras depends upon the lamrim; if you do not develop the three fundamentals of the path [renunciation, bodhichitta, and the correct view of emptiness] in your mindstream, you cannot be enlightened in one lifetime by means of the mantra path. I have heard of many supposedly profound teachings that derive from visions or from hidden texts, all of which are supposed to bestow such miraculous powers—but there is absolutely nothing in them to teach you the three fundamentals of the path, nor any instruction of outstanding value.

Now what we call the *lamrim* was not invented by Je Rinpoche [Lama Tsongkapa], or Atiśha, etc. Its lineage stems from the completely perfect Buddha himself and from him alone. But when you come to understand the teachings, beyond whether they have been given the name "lamrim" while others have not, you will see that all the scriptures are the lamrim. The precious set of the Perfection of Wisdom sūtras is supreme, outstanding, and most excellent among all the teachings of our Teacher. In these sūtras he taught directly the profound stages of the path [the wisdom of emptiness], which are the profound items of the eighty-four thousand bundles of the Dharma; he also covertly taught the extensive part of the lamrim in them [the methods of the buddhas]. This then is the source of the lineage. The extensive part was passed on to the Buddha's foremost disciple Maitreya, who in turn passed it on to Asaṅga. The profound part of the lamrim passed from Mañjuśhrī to Nāgārjuna. This is how the lamrim lineage split into two—the Profound and the Extensive.

In order to clarify the lamrim, Maitreya composed his *Five Treatises,* Asaṅga wrote the *Five Texts on the Levels,* Nāgārjuna his *Six Logic Treatises,* and so on. So the Profound and Extensive lamrim lineages came down separately to the great peerless Atiśha. He received the Extensive Lineage from Suvarṇadvīpa and the Profound from Vidyākokila; he combined the two into one stream. He also inherited the Lineage of Deeds Bestowing Great Blessing that Śhāntideva received from Mañjughoṣha, as well as the lineages of the secret tantras, and so on. Thus, the lineages he inherited carried the complete sūtras and tantras.

Atiśha composed his *Lamp on the Path to Enlightenment* in Tibet. This work combines the key points of the complete doctrine. Since that time, the convention of calling these teachings by the name *lamrim* developed. After that, the lineages concerning the profound view and the extensive tasks have been combined into one stream. But due to further expanding and condensing, this was split into three during the Kadampa period: the Classical, the Stages of the Path, and the Oral Instruction lineages. Later still, Je Tsongkapa received all three of these from Namkha Gyaeltsaen of Lhodrag, himself a great adept, and from Choekyab Zangpo, the abbot of Dragor. It has been a single lineage from that time on.

Great Je Rinpoche made petitions in his prayers [to the lineage holders of this tradition] below the Lion Rock at Radreng to the north of Lhasa; and there he started to write "Unlocking the Door of the Supreme Path." He had with him a statue of Atiśha that depicted Atiśha with his head bent over to one side. Whenever Je Rinpoche petitioned this statue, he received visions of all the gurus of the lamrim lineage, and they would discuss Dharma with him. In particular, he had visions of Atiśha, Dromtoenpa, Potowa, and Sharawa for a month. These latter three figures finally dissolved into Atiśha, who placed his hand at the crown of Je Rinpoche's head and said, "Perform deeds for the teaching and I shall help you." This means that it was he who requested Tsongkapa to write the *Great Stages of the Path*. Je Rinpoche completed it up to the end of the part dealing with mental quiescence. Venerable Mañjughoṣha requested him to complete the book. As a result, Je Rinpoche wrote the section on special insight. Thus, be aware that the book is a veritable treasure trove of blessings, even if we ignore everything else and only consider those who requested him to compose it. This is secretly taught in passages, such as the colophon, which begins "By the amazing good works of the victors and their children..." [see p. 724]

Later, he composed the *Stages of the Path* to summarize the essence of the matter treated in the *Great Stages of the Path*, leaving out the extra explanations. This work deals mainly with the whispered lineages and older explanation lineages; the two lamrims are said to complement each other with different key points from the oral instructions.

You may not know how to integrate these texts into your practice. Je Rinpoche later said:

> People will eventually find it almost impossible to understand how to put all these teachings into practice, so a condensed version of how to practice them should be made in the future.

Following this injunction, the [Third] Dalai Lama Soenam Gyatso wrote the *Essence of Refined Gold*. The great Fifth Dalai Lama wrote the *Mañjuśhrī's Own Words* lamrim as a commentary to this. The Paṇchen Lama Lozang Choekyi Gyaeltsaen wrote the *Easy Path*, and Lozang Yeshe [another Paṇchen incarnation] composed its commentary, the *Swift Path.* Je Rinpoche himself wrote three lamrims: the *Great, Medium,* and *Small* (also known as *Songs from Experience*). And, in addition to the above four concise teachings by the Dalai Lamas and Paṇchen Lamas, Ngagwang Dragpa of Dagpo wrote the *Essence of Eloquence.* These are the eight most famous teachings on the lamrim.

You must receive the lineage discourses for these root texts and commentaries separately: these do not relate as root texts and commentaries. In particular, there are two lineages of discourses on *Mañjuśhrī's Own Words,* one more detailed than the other. One of these was maintained in the Central Province, while the other was upheld in the south; this resulted in the two splitting off from each other. You must also receive the lineage discourses for both of these separately. Chancellor Tapugpa and his followers later assessed the lineages of this text. He claimed that if he had read this text earlier, he would not have had so many problems with lamrim meditation topics. And it is as he says: the concise teaching of the *Swift Path* and the two lines of *Mañjuśhrī's Own Words* go together to make something particularly profound that just one text would not.

When our Teacher Buddha taught, there was no difference between the two lineages—one for the oral transmission and one for the oral discourse. Only later, when his teachings were no longer fully comprehensible, were those discourses given separately. The discourses that painstakingly give a detailed and elaborate discussion of the individual words in a text have been called *formal discourses.* The *concise discourse* refers to oral teachings that do not elaborate much on the words of the text but instead expose the heart of the instruction, much as skillful doctors dissect a fresh corpse in front of their students. The way they point out the five solid organs, the six hollow organs, etc., would give a vivid introduction. In the *practical discourse,* the lama speaks from his own experience, according to what the students' minds can manage. The *experiential teaching* is as follows. The disciples stay together around a retreat house. They are taught a set of visualizations, which they then begin to meditate on. They are not taught the next topic until they have gained some meditative experience on those practices. When they gain some experience, they are taught the next one. These discourses come down to us in lineages blessed by insight. They are most beneficial for taming the mindstream.

The teaching I shall now offer is a practical discourse. A few of those present are unfortunate enough only to have the time to attend this sort of teaching once or twice. They are interested in these teachings, although they must later go their separate ways. For their sakes I shall be combining the *Swift Path* and the brief and detailed lineages of *Mañjuśhrī's Own Words.* Later on, when we get to that part, I shall give the seven-point mind training on the interchange of self and others.

I have no reservations about giving this teaching. It will create root merits for the two departed aristocrats in whose memory this teaching is being given. And when I teach the lamrim, I do not have to weigh the benefits or dangers to guru or disciple, something I have to do when I give other teachings, such as initiations. A lamrim teaching can only be most beneficial.

All of you, practice what you can; and you must pray on behalf of these two departed noblemen.

Kyabje Pabongka Rinpoche gave a short oral transmission of the opening lines of these lamrim texts. Then we were free to go.

DAY 2

Lama Pabongka Rinpoche began:

Great Tsongkapa [in his introduction to the *Three Fundamentals of the Path*] wrote:

> I shall explain, as best I can,
> The import of the essence of all the victors' scriptures,
> The path praised by holy victors and their children—
> The gateway for the fortunates wanting liberation.

This teaching is the quintessence of all the scriptures of the Victorious One. In the small scope section, you become moved to renounce the lower realms and in the medium scope, you are moved to renounce all saṃsāra, and so on. But you will not achieve these unless you depend on the lamrim. Precious bodhichitta is the path praised by the holy victorious ones and their children. The gateway for people who want liberation is the [correct] view [of emptiness] that is free of the [two] extremes [of substantialism and nihilism]. Yet you will not achieve these unless you depend on the lamrim system of teachings. Therefore, in order to gain buddhahood, you must develop these three fundamentals of the path in your mindstream. You must depend on the lamrim to generate these three in your mindstream. So, from the very start, adopt this for your motive: "I shall gain buddhahood for the sake of all sentient beings—and for that reason I shall practice, after taking this practical teaching on the three different scopes of the lamrim." Bring all your motives and actions in line with such thoughts and only then listen.

And what is the Dharma you are going to hear? It is the Dharma of the Supreme Vehicle, the system that leads the fortunate to the level of buddhahood. It is the traditional path of the two great champions, Nāgārjuna and Asaṅga. It is the essence of the thoughts of peerless Atiśha and the great Tsongkapa, the Dharma king of the three realms. This is how the instruction is profound. It contains every single key point of the essence of the eighty-four thousand bundles of scripture, and organizes in their proper sequence the practices leading to an individual being's enlightenment.

The practical discourses on the stages of the path to enlightenment can be brought under the one basic heading: "The Actual Teachings." But more headings have been introduced in order to fix the nature of the lamrim, its various lists, and the sequence of this teaching. You must familiarize yourself with these headings so as to be sure which of them come under a particular topic of meditation, how they are explained, the quotations cited in them, the lineage of their oral teachings, and the instructions they contain. Otherwise, if you receive an off-the-cuff teaching, mixed together randomly without any headings, it would be hard to make the meditations beneficial for your mindstream. It would be like trying to use tea, butter, salt, soda, etc., all mixed together instead of from separate jars. Though there are many different sets of headings—some for the brief lamrims, and some for the longer versions—you should follow the headings of the particular teachings you have received.

Now my teacher's own practical method consists of a series of topics that are based primarily on the *Swift Path* and adorned with many oral instructions. It had never before been written down, but I was most careful when he gave them in public, and I also received them in private. I have taken great care to collect them and commit them to paper. They are neither too short nor too long, and their manner of producing meditative experiences is exceptional and has unique points. This is how I shall present these to the assembly.

The scholars of Śhrī Nālandā Monastery used to say that it was important to teach the three purities before giving a teaching: the purity of the master's oral teachings, the purity of the mindstream of the disciple, and the purity of the Dharma being presented. The scholars of Vikramaśhīla in their introductions used to discuss the greatness of the author, the greatness of the Dharma, and the way to explain and listen to that teaching. I shall follow this latter tradition.

The discourse on the stages of the path to enlightenment has four major parts: (1) the greatness of the authors, given in order to show that the teaching has an immaculate source; (2) the greatness of the Dharma, given to increase one's faith in the instruction; (3) the right way to teach and listen to this Dharma with these two greatnesses; (4) the sequence in which the disciples are to be taught the actual instructions. These four headings are found in [Tsongkapa's] *Great Stages of the Path.* No matter which lamrim is being presented—the *Easy Path,* the *Swift Path,* and so forth—and no matter how much detail it is being given in, the oral tradition says you must start with these headings, otherwise people will not develop enough conviction.

THE GREATNESS OF THE AUTHORS, GIVEN TO SHOW THE TEACHING HAS AN IMMACULATE SOURCE (1)

As I said yesterday, according to the tradition of Indian scholars, the Dharma you are to practice must be one taught by Buddha, proven by the pandits, and utilized in the meditations of great and powerful adepts to produce realizations and insights in their mindstreams.

On our part, when we don't have faith, wisdom, or effort, or when we practice a specious Dharma, we will get absolutely no results at all. We have seen for ourselves many people who possess both wisdom and perseverance wasting their time on such things. Further, no matter how profound a teaching derived from visions and so forth is said to be, the deity sādhanas [methods for accomplishment] or the petty teachings on how to achieve any resultant miraculous powers won't even make the difference that comes from an acquaintance with the Three Jewels, let alone giving any insight into the three fundamentals of the path.

To trace a river back to its source, you need to go right back to the snow line. So too must you trace a Dharma back to the Buddha, our Teacher. If I had but the time and knew enough to discuss this in detail, I would have to take the Buddha as my starting point and give the biographies of all the lineage gurus, telling how they made use of this very path to attain their high state. But I do not have enough time for such an extremely lengthy discussion. I shall only tell you a little of this.

Pabongka Dorje Chang then told us a little of how there came to be two lineages from the Buddha down to Atiśha, and how Atiśha combined the two into one stream. He continued:

Atiśha wrote the *Lamp on the Path to Enlightenment* in Tibet; the term *lamrim* came later. The root text for the subject matter in all teachings such as the lamrim, the supreme path, the graded teachings, and so on, is his masterpiece, the *Lamp on the Path.* Thus Atiśha becomes the virtual author of them all. Even great Je Tsongkapa wrote, "The author of this is really Atiśha." So I really ought to give you a detailed life history of Atiśha, but I have time only for a short version.

This has three headings: (1) how he was born to one of the highest families; (2) how he attained his good qualities in that very rebirth; (3) the things he did to further the doctrine after gaining these qualities.

HOW ATIŚHA WAS BORN TO ONE OF THE HIGHEST FAMILIES (2)

Atiśha was born in the celebrated land of eastern India known as Bengal, in a large city in and around which there were one hundred thousand households, and he had thirty-five thousand servants.[6] His father's palace was called the Palace of Golden Victory Banners. It had thirteen golden pagodas, and twenty-five thousand golden victory banners. The family was extremely wealthy and powerful. His father was King Kalyāṇaśhrī; his mother was called Prabhāvatī. At his birth there were many miraculous signs.

HOW HE ATTAINED HIS GOOD QUALITIES IN THAT VERY REBIRTH (3)

When the young prince was only eighteen months old, his parents visited a nearby temple at Vikramapura.[7] All the people of the city lined the streets to see the young prince. He saw the great crowds and asked his parents, "Who are they?"

They replied, "These are your subjects."

The child looked on the people with compassion and said in verse:

> If only they were like me: wealthy parents,
> Dominion and dazzling merits,
> Heir to a king, a powerful prince.
> May all be sustained by holy Dharma!

This astonished everybody.

In the temple, everyone else, including his mother and father, prayed for illness-free long lives, great wealth, for their not falling to the lower realms, for their being reborn in the upper realms, and so on. The prince instead prayed:

> I have gained the optimum human rebirth,
> With faultless sense have I beheld the Three Jewels;
> May I always respectfully touch the Three Jewels to the crown
> of my head.
> From today may they be my refuge.
>
> May I never be bound by household duties;
> May I be endowed with Dharma in the midst of the Saṅgha.
> Without any pride, may I make offerings to the Three Jewels;
> May I look on all beings with compassion.

Hardly eighteen months old, the prince was already talking about refuge and the development of bodhichitta. He is already the object of our faith at this point in his life story.

The *Book of the Kadampas* tells us of his early development:

> When the prince reached three years old,
> He was skilled at astrology and grammar.
> When the prince reached six years old,
> He could distinguish between Buddhism and non-Buddhism.

Knowing how to distinguish between Buddhism and non-Buddhism is actually extremely difficult. Perhaps the following will give you some idea. Atiśha once said:

> In India only three people knew how to distinguish between Buddhism and non-Buddhism: Nāropa, Śhāntipa, and myself. Nāropa is dead, and I have gone to Tibet. When has India been in a worse position?

The very fact that Atiśha could do this at age six seems to me to be a sign that he was most learned even then.

When he was eleven, many princesses who were suitable to be his concubines employed various arts of seduction before the prince, such as singing and dancing; but these inspired renunciation and revulsion in him.

In particular, one girl who had a dark complexion and was an emanation of Tārā, pleaded with him:

> Your grace! Do not be attached!
> Fortunate one, do not be attached!
> If a hero such as you were caught
> In the quagmire of desire,
> Like an elephant trapped in a muddy bog,
> May not those clothed in ethics also sink?

Let us consider at length what she was saying. She was asking him not to be attached, firstly, to the things of this life and, secondly, to those of saṃsāra in general. The illustration she gave of the trapped elephant has this meaning: an elephant has a huge body and is therefore harder than other animals to pull out of a bog. She was comparing this image with her statement, "If a hero such as you were caught..." If commoners commit some misdeeds, it only causes harm to themselves and cannot harm the spread of the teachings. But if great lamas or the reincarnations of lamas act waywardly, it weakens the teachings in their areas. If these people act in the right way, it furthers the teachings there. Also, it seems to me to be saying it is most important that great people such as yourselves should be learned, ethical, and kind, and that you should uphold the pure Gelugpa traditions.

The prince replied that her plea had pleased him very much.

Then, without delay, the prince went out disguised as a soldier with one hundred and thirty armed cavalrymen. The prince skillfully pretended to explore the rocky mountains in the nearby countryside. His real purpose was to look for a guru. He met the Brahman Jitāri who lived on one of these mountains. Jitāri gave the prince the refuge and bodhisattva vows, and told him of Bodhibhadra of Nālandā, with whom Atiśha had karmic links from the beginningless past, and told him to go there. The prince saw this guru and made him a precious offering. This pleased Bodhibhadra. The guru entered meditative absorption and blessed the prince's three doors [body, speech, and mind]. He also gave the prince many instructions concerning the development of bodhichitta and then sent Atiśha to Guru Vidyākokila, who also gave him instructions on developing bodhichitta. Vidyākokila sent Atiśha to another guru from Atiśha's past, Avadhūtipa [Vidyākokila the younger].

He met Avadhūtipa, who told him, "Go back to your father's kingdom today. Look into the drawbacks of a layman's way of life!"

And so he returned home, much to the delight of his parents. "Where have you been, Chandragarbha?" they asked. "Are you weary? Are you sad? How good it is you've returned."

He replied:

> I have been in search of a guru,
> the sage's place of refuge.
> I have been to mountain caves and empty places in my search.
> No matter where I went,
> I saw the drawbacks of saṃsāra.
> Whoever I befriended
> told me of the drawbacks of saṃsāra.
> No matter what I do, dissatisfied am I—
> Set me free, and I shall turn to the Dharma!

His parents told him that if saṃsāra made him so unhappy, he should take up his royal duties. Then he should make offerings to the Three Jewels, make donations to the poor, build temples, invite the Saṅgha, and so on. Then he would be completely happy.

"I have seen much of saṃsāra," he replied. "I am not even minutely attached to the trappings of royal life. A golden palace is no different from a prison. Queens are no different from the daughters of Māra [evil forces]. The three sweet substances are no different from dog-meat, pus, and blood. There is not the slightest difference between the beauty of wearing silks and jewels and donning a filthy blanket in a cemetery. I shall go into the forest to meditate. Today give me a little meat, milk, honey, and sugarcane; I will go to venerable Avadhūtipa." This was the gist of the songs sung to his parents. His mother and father gave him permission to do as he wished, and he set out for the forest with one thousand horsemen.

He became a follower of Avadhūtipa, who initiated him into the development of bodhichitta. "Go to the temple of Kṛiṣhṇagiri [the Black Mountain]," said Avadhūtipa, "where Śhrī Rāhulagupta lives. He, too, was once your guru."

Guru Rāhula happened to be giving a tantric teaching when he saw the prince coming and, although he knew that Atiśha had come in quest of Dharma, he hurled a bolt of lightning at the prince to test him. Then

ATIŚHA AND HORSEMEN LEAVING THE PALACE

Rāhula went to the top of the mountain, where there was a black tīrṭhika stūpa. His retinue of yogis asked the guru who this person was.

Rāhula replied, "For 552 rebirths he has been nothing but scholarly pandits. At present he is heir to the Bengali Dharma king, Kalyāṇaśhrī. He is unattached to the royal life and wishes to take up ascetic practices."

Everyone was astonished. They stood up and welcomed him.

As soon as he saw the guru, Atiśha said:

> Holy guru, hear me!
> I have left my home and wish to achieve liberation
> But have been born to a famous family
> And am in danger of being bound to Bengal.
> I have devoted myself
> To Jitāri, Bodhibhadra,
> Vidyākokila and Avadhūtipa—
> Gurus with psychic powers;
> Yet, even now, I am not free of my royal obligations.
> I have now been sent to you, O guru;
> Initiate me into the Mahāyāna and the development of bodhichitta.
> May I be free of these bonds!

The guru responded by happily giving the initiation of Hevajra and all the instructions to the prince alone for thirteen days. He was given the secret name Jñānaguhyavajra.

Rāhula then addressed eight terrifying and naked yogis and yoginīs: "Follow him back to Bengal. Change the mind of the king, his father. When he is released from royal duties, take him back to his guru, Avadhūtipa."

The prince now dressed himself as Heruka, and when he approached the palace grounds, everyone who saw him recognized him and became afraid. He wandered aimlessly for three months, behaving like a madman. The yogis and yoginīs ran and jumped about. Everyone saw that he was set on abandoning his kingdom, and they could not hold back their tears.

His father was the most affected, and said:

> Alas my son! At your most excellent birth
> I saw wondrous signs, and thought you would pursue your
> royal duties.

My faculties revived with this happy thought.
What then has your forest retreat done to your mind?

The prince replied:

What say you? If I pursued duties royal
I could, father, be with you for this momentary life,
But father wouldn't know the son in all rebirths to come.
How very wrong when no benefit's to be had.

If I forego the great demands of royal life
And practice the sure path to liberation and enlightenment,
We shall be together happily in all our future lives.
Therefore, grant me this opportunity!

His mother said:

What's the use when this child is so determined!
Karma is the foremost thing that throws us to all our births.
O holy one, practice the Dharma you think best;
Make prayers that we will be together always in all my future lives.

And she gave him permission.

The prince, yogis, and yoginīs left at first light for the forest hermitage of Guru Avadhūtipa, where he studied the Dharma of the Madhyamaka school. Atiśha was taught the subtleties of the law of cause and effect, and from the age of twenty-one to twenty-nine emulated Avadhūtipa. In short, he contemplated and meditated on everything he studied. The *Blue Compendium* says: "He followed Avadhūtipa for seven years."

Atiśha could have been a king whose splendor would have equaled the Chinese emperor Li Shih-min. One hundred thousand households were tenants of the king's palace with its victory banners, twenty-five thousand bathing pools, seven hundred and twenty pleasure groves, and fifty-six thousand palm trees. He could have had three million, five hundred thousand subjects.[8] The palace was surrounded by seven walls interconnected by three hundred and sixty-three bridges. It had twenty-five thousand golden victory banners, and the central palace had thirteen pagodas. But great Atiśha gave himself up to the Dharma and rid himself of these unmatched trappings of princely power as one spits in the dust. Our Teacher, the Buddha, did the same: although he held the power of a universal emperor in the palm of his hand, he forsook it to become ordained. Thus, you must avidly read their biographies. If someone were now to say, "Give up your vows and you will be appointed governor of a district," we would do it without hesitation; that just shows the extent of our resolve.

It is hard for us even to give up the things in our poky little rooms, let alone the power of a prince. Contrast this with great Atiśha, who gave up his royal position, treating it like spittle left in the dust, and who for seven years depended mainly on Avadhūtipa. He also studied the Vajrayāna under many other gurus who too were endowed with psychic powers. He became a scholar in all the classics and in every instruction. Once the thought came to him, "I am well versed in the secret tantras." But he lost his pride when some ḍākinīs showed him in a dream many volumes on tantra he had never seen before. When he thought, "I shall gain the supreme psychic powers of the mahāmudrā [the great seal] in this life by engaging in tantric behavior" [that is, taking on a consort], Guru Rāhulagupta came to him by miraculously passing through a wall.

"What!" said the guru. "Where are you going, forgetting sentient beings? Get ordained! It will benefit the teachings and many sentient beings."

Then Śhrī Heruka appeared in space before Atiśha and made a similar appeal. Our Teacher Śhākyamuni, the Master of Sages, and Lord Maitreya, also in Atiśha's dreams, asked him to get ordained. He took his full ordination from Śhīlarākṣha, an abbot of the Mahāsaṅgika subsect, who had achieved the patience stage of the path of preparation.[9] Atiśha was ordained at the age of twenty-nine.

Atiśha depended on one hundred and fifty-seven gurus; he studied all the sciences, sūtras, and tantras along with their oral instructions. He made a particular study of all the key points of the four divisions of the *Transmission of the Vinaya* under Guru Dharmarakṣhita, as well as a huge text that covers in some eight hundred cantos the seven divisions of the Abhidharma [metaphysics] called the *Great Discussion of the Particulars.* He listened to this teaching for twelve years and studied it thoroughly. Because he knew all the subtle and unconfused differences of the practices of the eighteen subschools [of the Vaibhāṣhika sect] on such topics as taking alms or what water is fit to drink, he became the crowning jewel of all eighteen of these Indian subschools.

But although he received and practiced all the Dharma on sūtra and tantra to be found in India at that time, he continued to wonder which path was the swiftest to enlightenment. Rāhulagupta, who was living in a cave on Mount Kṛiṣhṇagiri, knew this through his clairvoyance. He went to Atiśha and said, "What good is it merely to have the visions of tutelary deities, to manifest many sets of deities in their maṇḍalas, to achieve many of the common psychic powers, or to have single-pointed concentration as firm as a mountain chain? Train your mind with love and bodhichitta! Thousand-armed Avalokiteśhvara is the deity of compassion. Take him as your tutelary deity and pledge yourself to work for the sake of sentient beings till saṃsāra is emptied."

One day, Atiśha was walking round the vajra seat of enlightenment at Bodhgaya. While on the circumambulation path, it seemed he witnessed a conversation between two statues. Another time, two girls who had transcended the human body were having, it seemed, a conversation in the southern sky over Bodhgaya.

"In what Dharma should someone who desires swift and complete enlightenment train?" asked one girl.

The other replied, "Train in bodhichitta!"

Then one told the other of a noble method for training in that mind.

He stopped circumambulating in order to listen and took it to heart like one vessel receiving all the contents of another.

One time, he was standing by the stone fence that Āchārya Nāgārjuna had built. There was an old woman and a girl. "Anyone who desires complete enlightenment quickly," said the woman to the girl, "should train in bodhichitta."

A statue of the Buddha under a balcony of the Great Temple at Bodhgaya once spoke to Atiśha while he was circumambulating. "O mendicant!" it said. "If you wish to achieve complete and perfect enlightenment soon, train yourself with love, compassion, and bodhichitta."

Once, while he made a circuit round a small stone-walled cell, an ivory statue of Buddha Śhākyamuni said to him, "O yogi! Train in bodhichitta if you want true and complete enlightenment soon!"

Thus Atiśha developed more bodhichitta than he had ever done before, and in order to fully increase and develop the bodhichitta he already possessed, he wondered, "Who holds the complete set of instructions on this?" He made enquiries and discovered that the great Suvarṇadvīpa Guru was famous for being a master of bodhichitta. Atiśha made plans to go to

Suvarṇadvīpa [in Indonesia] in order to receive the complete instructions on bodhichitta at the feet of the great Suvarṇadvīpa Guru. He traveled the ocean for thirteen months in a boat with some traders who were going there on business and knew the way. Kāmadeva, the powerful demon-god of lust, could not bear to see the Buddha's teachings spread and, to hinder Atiśha's bodhichitta, made the boat turn around by blowing up a head wind. Then he blocked the boat's passage with an enormous sea monster the size of a mountain, hurled lightning bolts from the sky, and so on. This caused much havoc, and Pandit Kṣhitigarbha fervently implored Atiśha to use his wrathful powers. Atiśha entered into the samādhi of Red Yamāntaka and subdued the demon hordes. Gradually his party made its way to Indonesia.

Atiśha had already become a great scholar and adept. As we have said, when only eighteen months old he had without any prompting spoken words that proved he was already conversant with bodhichitta. And yet he willingly underwent these hardships [to reach Indonesia], which must convince us that nothing is more fundamental in the Mahāyāna than precious bodhichitta.

Atiśha spent thirteen months on this journey, yet he never took off his robes, the sign of ordination. He did not travel as we do, changing clothes outside of the monastery. When monks nowadays go on pilgrimage—supposedly for the sake of benefit of the teachings—they put on lay clothes the moment they cross the bounds of the monastery. Some of them even carry long spears. I think strangers must feel cowed and afraid of them and wonder, "Are these fellows cutthroats?" We must in the future set an example by not taking off our robes—the sign that we are ordained. This will benefit the teachings. Omniscient Kaedrub Rinpoche said:

> The bodies of the ordained are made beautiful
> By the two saffron robes.
> When the ordained adopt the signs of lay people,
> This kind of behavior will ruin the teachings.

Some might claim, "One must be ripe on the inside," and not preserve the externals at all. This generally sets a bad example for the teachings. All the Saṅgha's external actions must be done in a calm and disciplined manner. Shāriputra was led to the truth [of the path of seeing] just by Ārya Aśhvajit's behavior.

To return to the story, Atiśha reached Indonesia. They landed at the tip of the island and saw some meditators who were staying there, disciples of the great Suvarṇadvīpa. Atiśha and all his own disciples rested a fortnight and asked the meditators for the story of Suvarṇadvīpa Guru's life. If we had been there, we would have gone as quickly as possible into his presence, but Atiśha did not. Instead, he examined the life of the guru. He was setting us an example: we must properly investigate a guru first.

A few of the meditators hurried on ahead to Suvarṇadvīpa Guru and told him, "The great scholar Dīpaṃkara Śhrījñāna, the foremost scholar throughout eastern and western India, along with one hundred and twenty-five disciples, has traveled for thirteen months on the ocean, enduring great hardships. They have come to receive from you, O guru, the fundamental mother [the Perfection of Wisdom sūtras] that gave birth to all victorious ones of the three times. They have also come for the Mahāyāna practice of training the mind to develop the aspiration and engagement forms of bodhichitta."

"How marvelous that such a great scholar has come to our land," said Suvarṇadvīpa. "We must welcome him."

As great Atiśha approached Suvarṇadvīpa Guru's palace, he and his party saw a procession in the distance coming to welcome them. It was led by Suvarṇadvīpa Guru himself. There were five hundred and thirty-five monks behind him. They looked like arhats. They wore the three robes of the proper color denoting a monk, carried the prescribed water vessels, and held beautiful iron staffs. Sixty-two novices attended them. In all, there were five hundred and ninety-seven ordained people. It was awesome to behold. As soon as Atiśha saw this imposing procession coming to receive him, [with Suvarṇadvīpa looking] so like the Buddha in his time, surrounded by arhats, he rejoiced to the depths of his heart.

Then Atiśha, followed by Kṣhitigarbha, the other pandits well versed in the five sciences, and the monks learned in the three baskets set off for Suvarṇadvīpa Guru's residence. They wore the prescribed sandals of a monk, and each wore three robes beautifully dyed with the Kashmiri saffron so highly prized by the Mahāsaṃgika school. So that other people could make them the very auspicious gesture of giving alms, they all carried iron begging bowls in good repair. They had with them all the prescribed utensils, such as the copper water-container having the capacity of one drona measure of the country of Magadha, and the iron staff that the Lord of our teachings praised so highly. They all wore the pandit's hat with blunt tips—blunt to denote a lack of pride. All held ceremonial white fly-whisks. The hundred and twenty-five followed Atiśha in single file, maintaining the prescribed distance from each other, neither too close nor too far—a line [as perfect] as the five-colored arc of the rainbow. When they arrived where Suvarṇadvīpa Guru was staying, everything was so magnificent that the virtuous gods were much pleased and let fall a rain of flowers in respect. All the people of the island wondered at the actions of these two gurus and gained faith. Atiśha gave the guru a completely transparent vase. One could see that it was full of gold, silver, pearls, corals, and lapis. This auspicious gesture foretold that he would receive the complete instructions into the bodhichitta trainings, just as one pot receives the full contents of another.

They returned to the guru's room in the Palace of the Silver Parasol. As an even greater gesture of auspiciousness, Suvarṇadvīpa Guru taught them [Maitreya's] *Ornament to Realization* along with the accompanying oral instructions for fifteen sessions as his first teaching. The master immediately took to Atiśha, and they slept with their pillows side by side. And so began twelve years in which Atiśha and his disciples received the complete instructions, without any omissions, on all the hidden meanings to the Perfection of Wisdom sūtras—the "holy mother"—from the lineage Maitreya gave to Asaṅga. They also received exclusive instructions on training the mind in bodhichitta by means of the exchange of self and others; the lineage for this was given by Mañjuśhrī to Śhāntideva. They studied, contemplated, and meditated upon these instructions most thoroughly. By means of this exchange of self and others, they developed at the feet of this guru genuine bodhichitta in their minds.

The guru authorized Atiśha as a master of the doctrine and predicted he would make disciples by going to Tibet:

> Your grace, do not stay here.
> Go to the north.
> Go north, to the Land of Snows.

THE THINGS HE DID TO FURTHER THE DOCTRINE AFTER GAINING THESE QUALITIES (4)

This has two parts: (1) how he did this in India; (2) how he did this in Tibet.

HOW HE DID THIS IN INDIA (5)

When Atiśha returned to Magadha, he lived in Bodhgaya and three times defeated in debate the upholders of the evil tīrṭhika religions, converting them to Buddhism. He upheld the teachings in other ways, too. King Mahāpāla appointed him to the temple of Vikramaśhīla Monastery. Although Atiśha followed mainly the traditions of the Mahāsaṃgika school, he was also well versed in the traditions of all the other schools; and because he showed absolutely no sectarianism, he became the crowning jewel of all the Saṅgha in Magadha as well as across India. He was the acknowledged master of the whole teachings of sūtra and tantra to be found in the three baskets and four classes of tantra. And as for the teachings themselves, it was as if the Victorious One himself had returned.

HOW HE DID THIS IN TIBET (6)

The teachings first promulgated in Tibet had, by this time, died out. The later dissemination of the teachings was gradually gaining momentum. But some people concentrated on the vinaya and disregarded tantra; others did just the opposite. Sūtra and tantra had become as opposite as hot and cold. Many well-known pandits came to Tibet from India, lured by the prospect of gold. They deceived the people of Tibet with many evil mantras and tantric sex, and it had become most difficult for the pure teachings of the Victorious One to spread. The Tibetan king, Lhalama Yeshe Oe, was not happy about this, and in order to promulgate pure teachings he sent twenty-one bright Tibetan students to India to bring back pandits who would be more beneficial to Tibet. All but two of them died; the senior translator Rinchen Zangpo and the junior translator Legdaen Sherab both became steeped in Dharma but still were unable to bring Atiśha back with them. When they returned to Tibet, they had an audience with the king on how to harmonize the sūtras and tantras with the practices and beliefs of all the Indian scholars.

"There is no other pandit who can benefit Tibet," they said. "In Vikramaśhīla, there lives a monk who left behind royal birth for monastic life. His name is Dīpaṃkara Śhrījñāna. If you invite him, it is certain to benefit Tibet." They said that all the other pandits agreed on this.

Their speech settled the king's doubts but, more importantly, he developed strong and unconquerable faith in Atiśha merely through hearing his name. He sent Gyatsoen Senge, together with eight others, to bring Atiśha back. They took with them much gold—but failed. The Dharma king himself went in search of more gold to help bring the pandit back.

The khan of Garlog knew that the king was acting to further the doctrine, so he captured Yeshe Oe and threatened him with death if he did not abandon his teachings. The king was thrown into prison. His paternal nephew Jangchub Oe went there in an attempt to free his uncle, only to be told by the khan of Garlog, "You can either abandon your plans to bring the pandit and become my vassals, or you can bring me the king's weight in gold. Either way, I shall set him free." Jangchub Oe promised to hand over the gold. He offered the khan the two hundred ounces in gold he had with him, but the khan would have none of it. Eventually he brought the khan the weight of the king's body in gold, but minus the head. The Garlog khan was not interested. "I want the head and all," he said. Jangchub Oe did not have the means for any more gold. Instead he went to the gate of Yeshe Oe's prison. "Uncle," he cried, "You have been most kind. You are a victim of your past actions. If I wage war against this man to defeat him, very many warlike people will perish, and I fear they will be reborn in the lower realms. I was told by this fellow not to invite the pandit but instead become his vassal. But if we abandon the Dharma, we will have given in to this sinful king. I think it is better for you to remain true to the Dharma. He told me he wanted your weight in gold. I have been searching for gold, but have only found enough to equal your body without the head. This did not satisfy him, and now I shall go to find the rest. I shall return with the ransom. Until then, you must think on your past karma, petition the Three Jewels, and above all take courage and create merit."

His uncle laughed and said, "I thought you were just a spoiled child who gorged on rich food, unable to brave any difficulties or display any courage. Now I feel you can uphold the traditions of our forefathers when I die. You have acted well. This makes me content. I thought it would be wrong for me to die without having established a faultless rule of Dharma in Tibet. I am old, and if I were not to die now, I would live only another ten years. If I give away so much gold just for that, it would shame the Three Jewels! In my past lives in beginningless saṃsāra, I have not once died for the Dharma. Do not, then, give this khan so much as a speck of gold; how excellent for me to die for the Dharma. If it was such a mighty task to find the gold for just me, where could we find gold for my head? Take all the gold to India, and do all you can to bring Pandit Atiśha back.

"If he will see you, give him my message: 'I gave up my life to the Garlog khan for both the Buddha's teachings and your own. Look after me with your compassion for the rest of my lives. My foremost thought was for you to come to Tibet. I did this so that the Buddha's teachings could spread in Tibet. You therefore, should do only as I ask. Bless me so that we definitely meet in my future lives.' Nephew, forget about me; think of the Buddha's teachings!"

The uncle was in a weak state, and the sound of his voice was most piteous. Yet Jangchub Oe could well believe that his uncle had the courage to think only about the sentient beings of Tibet, of the Buddha's teachings, and of Atiśha. He forced himself to leave his uncle. Prince Jangchub Oe's courage greatly increased, and he acted to fulfill his uncle's wishes completely.

In Tibet, there were many people passing off numerous crude religions as tantra. Some of these were the Red Āchārya, the infamous Blue-Skirt Pandit, and the Eighteen Mendicants of Artso. In order to defeat these people skillfully, King Jangchub Oe prayed to the Three Jewels for guidance as to which of his subjects would be the right person to bring Atiśha. All the dice divinations and astrological calculations suggested Nagtso the translator. Nagtso happened to be living in the Gilded Temple at Gungtang. The king summoned him to Ngari but feared the translator would not promise to go to India. King Jangchub Oe therefore had Nagtso sit on his very own royal throne to show his respect, and praised his scholarship, ethics, and kindheartedness.

"You must plead with Atiśha," said the king. "Tell him, 'My forefathers, and the past kings and ministers of state, established the Buddha's teachings here. It became the custom, flourished, and spread. Now the Buddha's teachings are in a sorry state. A race of demons has taken over. All the scholars have passed away. Both I and my uncle are most saddened by this and have sent much gold and many men to India, but after such a great expenditure of both wealth and men, we still have not brought Atiśha back. Our king could not bear this and went in search of gold. An evil khan imprisoned him. His Majesty gave his life. When we ignorant sentient beings of the remote land of Tibet have shown such courage, how could you be considered compassionate and an object of refuge for sentient beings?'

"I have fourteen hundred ounces of gold. Take them and place them in this guru's hands. Tell him, 'Our Tibet is like the city of hungry ghosts. Finding gold in our country is like looking for a single louse on a sheep, it is so hard to find. The gold you see here is the entire wealth of the people of Tibet. But if you, O protector, do not go to Tibet, it would show how little compassion you holy beings have. We would then never do anything to better ourselves.' Nagtso, you uphold the vinaya. Tell Atiśha our story in person. If he still refuses, explain the situation until he completely understands it."

The king was crying so much that there were tears on his lap and on the table in front of him. Nagtso the translator, whose real name was Tsultrim Gyaelwa, had not done much traveling before and was not at all keen to go off to distant places, but he could not bring himself to say yes or no. We have a proverb: "The one who sees a person crying will begin to cry himself." He knew full well that what the king was saying was quite true although he had never met Yeshe Oe before. He was aware that the uncle and his nephew had spent much in wealth and men, and that the two of them had suffered greatly, for the sake of Tibet, so that we could be happy. The power of the words of the king, a man of high rank, had deeply moved Nagtso. He was speechless, his body was shaking, and his face was covered in tears; he was unable to look at the king's face. The king was asking him to risk both life and limb, but Nagtso was not attached to any of this life's happiness, and so he said he would go.

The king's seven ministers carried the fourteen hundred ounces of gold as they saw him off on the road to India. The king accompanied him for a great distance. "Monk, you are doing this on my behalf," said the king. "You are risking life and limb, and with great perseverance are now traveling to places that will create much hardship for you. When you return, I will repay your kindness." The king went back a little way; then he said, "Petition the Great Compassionate One [Avalokiteśhvara] while you are journeying."

When Nagtso the translator and his party reached the kingdom of Nepal, they met a tall man who said, "I think you are going to faraway places on a great mission. You will succeed in your mission if you repeat this while you travel: "Homage to the Three Jewels! May the holy Dharma, the source of the buddhas of the three times, spread in the Land of Snows!" Say this as you go. Then there will be no misfortune." They asked him who he was. "Eventually you will come to know who I am," he said.

There were also many other emanations of Dromtoenpa [soon to be Atiśha's chief disciple]. These removed the many dangers that threatened Nagtso and his party on the road.

At last they arrived at the gate of Vikramaśhīla. There was a parapet over the gate, and Gyatsoen Senge, because he could understand Tibetan, called down to them from a cleft in the parapet. "Tibetan sirs, where have you come from?"

"We have come from Upper Ngari," they answered.

"There is a young boy, a gatekeeper. Leave all your things with him. Have a good night's sleep in some shelter. The gate will be opened just after first light."

They gave their gold to the youthful gatekeeper, who put it in an inner room. "Trust me as you would your best friend," he said. "Don't worry. Sleep well." They thought that the small child, saying such things, could not be an ordinary person. This set their minds at rest.

Next morning, as soon as the gate was opened, a young child appeared. He wore a pointed hat and was dressed like a Tibetan nomad—complete with two layers of woolen clothes and carrying a small wooden bowl. "Where have you Tibetans come from?" the child asked. "You seem to be none the worse for your journey."

Nagtso's party found it heartening to run into someone so fluently speaking the nomad dialect. "We have come from Upper Ngari," they said. "We have had a smooth journey. What brings you here? Where are you going?"

"I'm also Tibetan," replied the child. "We're going to Tibet. We Tibetans have very loose tongues. We are too naïve. We don't know how to keep a secret. Important things must be done in secret. Gyatsoen Senge is staying in the Tibetan quarters. Ask around and you'll find it." And with that he was gone in an instant.

They entered a long narrow lane, followed it, and came upon an old holy man with a bamboo walking stick. "Where have you come from?" he asked. "What was so important to make you come?"

"We have come from Upper Ngari," they replied. "We have come to bring back the illustrious Atiśha. Where is Gyatsoen Senge's house?"

The old holy man leaned on his stick and rolled his eyes. "The child you met this morning spoke the truth. Tibetans can't keep their mouths shut! Even a Tibetan mute would tell all their deepest secrets to people lurking in alleys. How can you possibly hope to accomplish anything this way! It's a good thing you told me. But speak of this to no one but Atiśha. I will show you Gyatsoen Senge's door."

The old man made his way slowly, and yet Nagtso could not keep up with him. Nagtso found him waiting on the threshold of the Tibetan quarters.

"Great matters must be done slowly," said the old man. "Make haste slowly. What you want lies far away, and you must climb a mountain step by step. This is his house."

Nagtso went inside and made an offering of gold to Gyatsoen Senge the translator. Gyatsoen saw him and asked, "Where have you come from?"

He told his story in detail.

"It appears that you were once my disciple," Gyatsoen said, "and yet I do not recognize you. Tell no one you have come to invite Atiśha. Say you have come to learn. There is an elder called Ratnākaraśhānti. He is very powerful here and is Atiśha's master. He must not suspect what you intend to do. We shall now make him an offering of an ounce of gold. Tell him, "We have come from Tibet. We have failed to invite any pandits. I have now come to study and to ask you to assign to us a pandit." That is how to present your request. After that, be in no hurry and don't let things worry you—just relax. When the time is right, we shall skillfully invite Atiśha to come here."

Nagtso and Gyatsoen Senge went to see the elder, Ratnākaraśhānti, and presented him with the ounce of gold. Nagtso spoke with him for some time, giving the agreed-on story.

The elder then said, "That is wonderful! The other pandits cannot subdue sentient beings. This is no exaggeration. The Buddha's teachings may have originated in India, but without Atiśha, the merit of sentient beings here will decline." He also said many other things.

For some time it was very difficult for them to see Atiśha. Just the same, emanations of Avalokiteśhvara had provided many auspicious opportunities for Atiśha to travel to Tibet. Then, a day came when there were no other Indian pandits or kings around to suspect what was happening; Gyatsoen Senge told Nagtso to come, and took him to Atiśha's room. They offered Atiśha a world maṇḍala one cubit high, surmounted by a gold piece, which was itself surrounded by small pieces of gold.

Translator Gyatsoen Senge spoke for both of them. He told how the king of Tibet was a bodhisattva, and how the Dharma had spread under the three Dharmarājas [Songtsaen Gampo, Trisong Detsaen, and Raelpa Chaen]. He told how King Langdarma had persecuted the teachings, and how the great lama Gompa Rabsael had managed to preserve the Saṅgha and increase its numbers. He spoke of the sacrifice the king's uncle had made to bring Atiśha to Tibet. He gave Jangchub Oe's message, and described the sort of perverted Dharma prevalent in Tibet.

"The bodhisattva king of Tibet," Gyatsoen said, "has sent this monk to invite you, O protector. Don't just talk of 'going next year.' Look compassionately on Tibet!"

"The Tibetan king is a bodhisattva," said Atiśha. "The three Dharmarājas were the emanations of bodhisattvas. Gompa Rabsael was an emanation of a bodhisattva, otherwise how could he have rekindled the embers of the teachings. The kings of Tibet are bodhisattvas. It would not be right to disobey the orders of a bodhisattva. I feel ashamed before this king. He has spent much wealth and many men. You Tibetans are in a piteous state, but I am responsible for the many keys [of the temples of the monastery]. I am now old. I have many offices to perform. I cannot hope to return from Tibet. Still, I shall investigate this matter. Keep your gold for the time being." Then he sent them away.

Atiśha then investigated whether it would benefit the Buddha's teachings if, out of his love for his potential Tibetan disciples, he went to Tibet. He also checked whether it would be a hindrance to his own lifespan. Avalokiteśhvara, Ārya Tārā, and so forth, told him that it would prove most beneficial to sentient beings and the teachings if he went. Moreover, there would be much benefit resulting from a lay vow holder *(upāsaka)*. But if he did go, his life would be shortened. Atiśha asked by how much. They told him he would live to ninety-two if he did not go, and if he did go he would not reach seventy-three, meaning that his life would be shortened by almost twenty years. At this point, Atiśha thought of all the benefits of his going to Tibet—and if it meant a shorter life, then so be it. He had developed such strength of purpose that he did not care for his own life at all.

However, Atiśha did not want to go to Tibet immediately, because the Indian Saṅgha and their benefactors would say that India, the very fountainhead of the teachings, would go into decline. In order to prevent such talk, Atiśha employed his skillful means: instead of telling people he was going to Tibet, he said he was to go on an extensive tour to make offerings at Bodhgaya and other great places of pilgrimage, traveling back and forth. Dromtoenpa, being in the true sense a Dharmarāja, skillfully manifested in the forms of traders, and without anyone suspecting it, they took back to Tibet many holy statues of Mañjuvajra [a form of Guhyasamāja], etc.—the symbols of the bodies of the buddhas—as well as many scriptures—the symbols of the Enlightened One's speech. Atiśha asked the elder [Ratnākara

Śhānti] if he would be permitted to go to Nepal and Tibet. There were many exceptional stūpas and places of pilgrimage there, and he would be gone only as long as it would take to see them. The elder observed that Atiśha seemed rather keen to go and that the Tibetans had been most determined to take him, so he allowed him to go for a short while; Nagtso the translator had to promise to bring him back within three years.

Thus Atiśha and his disciples left India for the kingdom of Nepal. The Tibetan king came with about three hundred horsemen and gave a lavish welcome. We are told how the local people would instantly develop faith at the mere sight of him, and how their mindstreams became subdued.

Pabongka Dorje Chang also spoke in detail on the meeting between Atiśha and the great translator Rinchen Zangpo.

King Jangchub Oe made this supplication to Atiśha, telling how in the past the three Dharmarājas had endured hundreds of difficulties to establish the Buddha's teachings here in the northern Land of Snows. But Langdarma had persecuted the teachings. Jangchub Oe's own forebears, the Dharmarājas of Ngari, had reestablished the Buddha's teachings in Tibet without regard for their own lives. But now some people had taken to the tantras and ignored the vinaya. Others swore by the vinaya and ignored the tantras. The sūtras and tantras were held to be as opposite as hot and cold. People carried out their own fanciful practices, and, more to the point, Āchārya Red Skirt and Āchārya Blue Skirt taught doctrines of liberation through intercourse to the matted-haired and topknotted practitioners of the old tantras. The teachings had declined so much they were like meaningless babble. He went on in much detail and his eyes filled with tears.

"Compassionate Atiśha," he said, "for now, do not teach the profoundest and most amazing of Dharmas to your uncivilized disciples of Tibet. I ask you to teach instead the Dharma of the law of cause and effect. Also, may it please the protector to compassionately teach some error-free yet easy-to-practice Dharma, one that you yourself practice, one that includes the whole path, would be beneficial to Tibetans in general, and encompasses all the intent of the Victorious One's scriptures—the sūtras, tantras, and commentaries.

"Further, must one have the pratimokṣha vows[10] in order to be a candidate for the vows in the involvement form of bodhichitta? Can one be enlightened without the combination of method and wisdom? Is one permitted to teach tantra to one who has not obtained the initiation? Is one permitted to confer the actual wisdom initiation [where one gives the disciples a real consort] to vowed celibates? Is one permitted to perform the practices of the secret tantric path without having already obtained the vajra master initiation?"

These were but some of the questions he asked.

Atiśha was highly pleased by this, and so composed the *Lamp on the Path to Enlightenment.* In only three folios this elucidates all the thinking of the sūtras and tantras. It begins:

> Most respectful homage to all holy victors of the three times,
> To their Dharma, and to the Saṅgha.
> Requested by my noble disciple Jangchub Oe,
> I shall light the *Lamp on the Path to Enlightenment.*

Atiśha did not say "my noble disciple Jangchub Oe" because he had received many offerings from him; rather it was because he was delighted with the way Jangchub Oe had asked about Dharma. My own precious guru told me, "Atiśha would not have been at all pleased if he had asked, "Please give me a major empowerment or a minor initiation."

The *Lamp on the Path* includes the answers to Jangchub Oe's questions. Soon after its appearance, the crude and perverse teachings in Tibet disappeared from whence they came.

Atiśha furthered the doctrine in the Upper Ngari area, but when the three years were nearly over, and because of his promise to the elder, Nagtso the translator said, "We must now return to India."

Atiśha appeared to consent, and so they went to Puhreng. But previously Tārā had told Atiśha repeatedly, "It would be most beneficial for the teachings if you took on a great upāsaka in Tibet." Now she was repeatedly telling him, "The upāsaka will soon be here," so Atiśha was constantly on the lookout for him.

"My upāsaka hasn't come," he said. "How could Tārā lie!"

One day Dromtoenpa turned up while Atiśha was visiting a benefactor. Drom went to Atiśha's room and was told that Atiśha had gone to see his sponsor but would now be on his way back. "I can't wait another moment," said Drom Rinpoche, the sooner I meet my Mahāyāna spiritual guide the better. I'm going to where he is." He left and met Atiśha in an alley. Drom Rinpoche made full-length prostrations and went up to

Atiśha, who put his hand on Drom's head while saying many auspicious things in Sanskrit.

Atiśha, while with his sponsor, had said, "I need a portion of food for my upāsaka," so he was carrying food with him. Atiśha was a strict vegetarian, and the meal he had been given that day consisted of barley dough steeped in ghee. Drom ate the barley dough but saved the clarified butter, making a large butterlamp big enough to burn all night. He placed it by Atiśha's pillow, and he is said to have placed similar butterlamps by his teacher's pillow every day without fail for the rest of Atiśha's life. That night, Atiśha gave Drom Rinpoche a major initiation and adopted him as his spiritual son.

They set out from Puhreng and went to Kyirong in the Mangyul district, planning to pass through Nepal en route to India, but the way was blocked because a war had broken out. They could not go any further. At this point, Drom urged Atiśha to go back to Tibet, while Nagtso pleaded with him to travel on to India; the translator was frustrated because he could not travel back to India.

Atiśha said to him, "You should not worry so much. You have not done anything wrong, for you are unable to carry out your promise.

This made the translator very happy. "Very well," he said. "Let us return to Tibet."

So, Atiśha decided to return to Tibet. He could not go on to India because the road was blocked at the time as a result of the Tibetans' collective merit.

Because Atiśha could not proceed, they sent a messenger to India saying, "Atiśha cannot travel back through Nepal because of the fighting on the way, so he cannot return as the elder had ordered. This means that we have to return to Tibet for a while. Could you invite Atiśha back when the trouble dies down? Because it would be most helpful for sentient beings, could you allow Atiśha to remain in Tibet? While he is there he will write more treatises like the one enclosed." They sent Atiśha's signed copy of the *Lamp on the Path* along with much gold.

At that time, India was not like our [present-day] Tibet. The year's new books were submitted to an assembly of pandits, and each of the folios was passed along the lines of judges so that they could assess them. Books error-free in both grammar and content were presented to the king, and the author was rewarded. These works were granted general publication. The treatises with faulty content—despite being faultlessly written in verse—were tied to a dog's tail. The dog was led through the alleys of the town, and thus both the author and the book were ridiculed. The king would be asked to forbid this treatise being published. Such was the custom concerning publication. Great Atiśha's composition really did not need to be subjected to such a test. All the same, it was submitted to the rows of pandits. They were most impressed, because the *Lamp on the Path*, only three folios long, taught in brief the whole subject matter of all sūtra and tantra, and if one were to depend on this work, one would come to consider all scriptures as instructions for oneself.

In their delight they unanimously declared, "Not only was Atiśha's going to Tibet an excellent thing for Tibetans, it also proved to be the best thing for us Indians. Atiśha would not have taught such a thing if he had remained in India, because Indians are wiser and have more perseverance. He knows that Tibetans are stupid and short of perseverance, and so he wrote this terse and most meaningful treatise." They were lavish in their praise of Atiśha's sojourn in Tibet.

Ratnākaraśhānti the elder wrote to them: "This is the way the pandits praised him, and Atiśha himself would like to stay in Tibet. I therefore give him my permission to stay in Tibet as it will be so beneficial for beings. I only ask that he write and send us his own commentary to this work as a substitute for his not being here." (However, the work found in the present editions of the translated commentaries purporting to be Atiśha's own commentary [to the *Lamp on the Path*] is said to be corrupt.)

Nagtso was extremely happy. "I had shouldered a mountain of responsibility imposed on me by the elder. Today I have had it lifted from me."

Not long before Atiśha was to go to the Central Province, Drom Rinpoche wrote to the important people there, saying, "How hard I worked toward inviting Atiśha to come to the Central Province! When you receive my next letter, set out immediately to welcome him." Later he wrote, "May teachers of the Central Province, such as Kawa Śhākya Wangchug, etc., immediately set out to welcome him." Drom had singled out this Kawa as the most important teacher of Tibet.

At the start of this journey, a person called Kutoenpa exclaimed, "Where's my name?" He was told, "You were included among the etceteras."

"I'm not a man who deserves to be relegated to the etceteras!" he said, and tried to be at the head of the procession. Then all of them jostled for a leading position.

Tibetan teachers of this period used to wear broad-brimmed hats, brocade cloaks, and so on—a costume to denote high lamas. As soon as Atiśha saw these people coming in the distance he said, "A lot of Tibetan devils have turned up!" and covered his head with his shawl. The high lamas then dismounted, put on the three types of robes, and approached. Even Atiśha was pleased, and received them.

He eventually reached the Central Province and did much there to turn the wheel of Dharma. He proved to be a great force behind the teachings and [benefited countless] sentient beings. He spent three years in Upper Ngari, nine years in Nyetang, and five in the Central and Tsang Provinces and elsewhere—a total of seventeen years in Tibet. Works like the *History of the Kadampas* say he was there for only thirteen years, but our tradition of seventeen years was begun by great Tsongkapa. As he said:

> Nagtso devoted himself to him for two years in India and seventeen years in Tibet. Thus he served him for nineteen years.

The essential reason why the great Jangchub Oe tried so hard to bring Atiśha to Tibet was for him to teach the Dharma, and the most important of his teachings was the *Lamp on the Path.* When Atiśha was about to leave for Tibet, Tārā and one of his gurus, Halakṛiṣhṇa, predicted:

> If you go to Tibet, the children will be richer than the parent. The grandchildren will be richer than the children. The great-grandchildren will be richer than the grandchildren. The great-great-grandchildren will be richer than the great-grandchildren. Then it will become less rigorous.

Here, the father is Atiśha himself. The children are Dromtoenpa, Legpai Sherab, etc. The grandchildren are the three Kadampa Brothers [Potowa, Puchungwa, Chaen Ngawa]. The greatgrandchildren are Langri Tangpa, Geshe Sharawa, and so forth. The great-great grandchildren are Sangyae Oentoen, Sangyae Gompa, and others of that generation. The meaning of "will be richer" is that the teaching will spread by being passed down from generation to generation. Then the teachings on the stages of the path would be overshadowed by certain useless tantras and minor initiations, and so the teachings were to become somewhat less rigorous. Atiśha revived teaching traditions that had died out and spread other rare traditions. He purged them of any wrong ideas diluting and staining them; and so he made the precious teachings spotless.

This teaching of the stages of the path to enlightenment was given to Drom. Drom asked, "Why have you given the others instructions on tantras and the lamrim solely to me?"

"I have found no one else besides you to entrust it to," Atiśha replied.

He gave the teaching to Drom in private. Drom gave it in public, and from this came three lineages. The Kadampa Classical Tradition was the lineage handed down from Potowa to Sharawa. It dealt with the stages of the path to enlightenment through the medium of the great classics. The Kadampa Lamrim Tradition was a lineage passed down from Gonpawa Wangchug Gyaeltsaen to Neuzurpa. This was a briefer treatment of the lamrim, giving the stages of the path in their order. The Kadampa Tradition of Oral Instruction came down from Geshe Chaen Ngawa to Jayulwa. This treatment was according to the instructions of the gurus on such teachings as the essence of the twelve interdependent links.

These teachings still exist but no longer under these names. The traditional interpretation stemming from Ngagwang Norbu, an occupant of the Gandaen throne, says that the most academically inclined should practice the lamrim according to the five major topics of debate.[11] This is in the Classical Tradition. People who cannot practice this way, but have keen perception and perseverance, should study and contemplate the greater and shorter lamrims [of Tsongkapa]. This practice is in the Kadampa Lamrim Tradition. The people who cannot practice these should work according to some brief instruction, for example, the *Easy Path* or the *Swift Path.* They would be following all the sections in the stages of the path. This would be the Kadampa Tradition of Oral Instruction. My own precious guru, my supreme refuge, gave me this traditional interpretation.

As I have already told you, great Je Tsongkapa took these three Kadampa lineages and combined them into one stream. I have also told you how great Tsongkapa came to write the great, medium, and small lamrims. Mañjuśhrī appeared to Je Rinpoche all the time, and they had a guru-disciple relationship. Mañjuśhrī gave Tsongkapa an infinite amount of profound Dharma on sūtra and tantra. This can be found in Je Rinpoche's biography. One might therefore claim that Je Rinpoche received the lamrim from Mañjuśhrī, but Je Rinpoche himself concentrated on tracing the lineage back to our Teacher Śhākyamuni. He never said it came from any vision, or any more recent lineage, and so on. This is one of the wonders of his biography.

When Je Rinpoche was writing the *Great Stages of the Path* and had reached the section on special insight, Mañjuśhrī joked with him:

"Doesn't all this come under my teaching of the Three Fundamentals of the Path?"

Tsongkapa answered that he had written the book [the *Great Stages*] in the following way. He had taken the Three Fundamentals taught by Mañjuśhrī as the lifeblood of the path and had used the discussion points in the *Lamp on the Path* as his root. He had fleshed it out with many other Kadampa instructions. But Tsongkapa thought that even if he did write the special insight section of his *Great Stages,* it would not be of much help to sentient beings. Tsongkapa, because of such thinking, would not compose it, but Mañjuśhrī said, "Write about special insight: it would be of middling benefit to sentient beings."

There are many such inconceivable and mystic biographical details about him. At this point in the teaching I should give Je Rinpoche's biography in detail, but we do not have time for this. You should make a detailed study of his written biographies.

This teaching of Je Tsongkapa's includes all and every teaching of Atiśha. It also has peerless instructions of exceptional profundity, through which one can achieve the unification of the no-more-learner within one short lifetime even in these degenerate times. Je Rinpoche's lamrim writings contain many particularly profound things not found even in the lamrims of the Kadampas of the past. One will come to know this after reading them in detail.

Now there are many traditional lineages that come from Je Rinpoche concerning the lamrim. The most famous of these principal lineages are the eight oral traditions associated with the eight great teachings. We did this yesterday. Both the *Essence of Refined Gold* and *Mañjuśhrī's Own Words* are said to be composed strictly according to the sūtras. The *Easy Path* and the *Swift Path* are said to be related to the tantras.

Here is a little on how the Southern Lineage of *Mañjuśhrī's Own Words* was passed on. This is the shorter of the two types of teachings on this text. The Fifth Dalai Lama indicated a shorter teaching by marking certain passages in the text. He also gave a set of instructions on the refuge visualization, the merit-field visualizations, and visualizations concerning the bathhouse, etc., different from those of the lineages of the Central Province. The Dalai Lama gave the Southern Lineage to Lama Purchog Ngagwang Jampa Rinpoche of Epa, who in turn gave it to Lozang Kaetsuen, the monastic official responsible for running the Dalai

MAÑJUŚHRĪ APPEARS TO JE RINPOCHE

Lama's quarters. Lozang Kaetsuen's biography has one extraordinary detail. He was exceptionally intelligent and devised many variations on the teaching—some in more detail, some in less. In order to dispel his confusion, he knew he would have to ask the lord of this Dharma, the Fifth Dalai Lama himself. He had an audience and received the whole teaching in an hour or two. The Dalai Lama made him abbot of the Potala. Lozang Kaetsuen spent the last part of his life practicing in a solitary place called the Lamrim Choeding, where he reached a high degree of attainment.

Lozang Kaetsuen gave the teaching to Puentsog Gyatso, that great adept from Yerpa, who completed the whole experiential teaching [see Day 1, p. 23] in three months. Puentsog Gyatso developed an extraordinary realization into mental quiescence and special insight, and nurtured many disciples in Yerpa through experiential teaching. He developed his powers by means of the practice of the Heruka body maṇḍala, and most of the lamas of the Southern Lineage are said to have followed this pattern.

Puentsog Gyatso gave the lineage to Lama Kachoe Taendar of Epa, who in turn gave it to Abbot Genduen Jamyang. Genduen Jamyang wrote a separate work on the Southern Lineage, because he feared that some errors had been perpetuated as to which passages in *Mañjuśhrī's Own Words* had actually been marked by the Fifth Dalai Lama for the Southern Lineage's benefit. Genduen Jamyang's book circulated only in handwritten copies until Kyabje Drubkang Geleg Gyatso had it made into woodblocks.

Genduen Jamyang passed the lineage on to Je Ngagwang Tutob. He in turn gave it to Taenpa Gyatso, abbot of Dagpo College. While Taenpa Gyatso was completing his studies, he was rostered for various menial chores, and is said to have attained the view of the middle way [the correct view of emptiness] when chopping wood. He in turn gave the lamrim teachings to Seto Lama Kaeldaen. Seto Lama's biography has this amazing fact: He was completely unattached to any offerings he received, no matter what they were—money, ceremonial scarves, woollen clothing, and the like. He did not give them away either. He just threw them into a nearby cave. Several generations later, the coins and rotted wool could be found there. He had not even given them away because he thought there was a danger this would later increase his arrogance.

Then Seto Lama gave the teaching to Je Lozang Choepel, who gave it to Geshe Tubtaen Rabgyae. Whenever Tubtaen Rabgyae did his meditations, he would chant the lamrim petition prayers and then fall silent. Other people thought he was asleep when they came to see him; in fact they were witnessing him in single-pointed meditation. He gave the lineage to a monk named Jangchub Togme.

This man was only a simple monk from Bangchoe Monastery—neither geshe nor lama nor anything else. He lived in Drangri Hermitage. Every day, after offering ritual cakes on the small grass patch there, he would practice the lamrim single-pointedly. He developed such love and compassion in his mindstream that he was always sad. Every day the boys who tended the herds and flocks used to amuse themselves by secretly watching him. To them he appeared to be just an old man crying to himself.

At this time, the Southern Lineage of *Mañjuśhrī's Own Words* was in danger of dying out because the lineage of the discourse had been given only to this monk. A retired abbot of Dagpo College, Lozang Jinpa by name—who, incidentally, ordained my own precious guru—made an exhaustive search for other people with the Southern Lineage discourse, but discovered that only this monk had actually received it. Lozang Jinpa doubted that he was capable of giving a practical discourse, but feared if he did not ask him for any discourse at all, the lineage would be broken.

He went to see the monk one day and said, "There is no one else who holds the discourse lineage for the Southern Lineage of *Mañjuśhrī's Own Words.* What a great pity if this lineage were broken! Would you give it to me just for the sake of the line? I could then give a more elaborate discourse back to you, but this time embellished with scriptural references and logical proofs."

"How could someone like me give this?" asked the monk.

He kept on claiming to be incapable of doing it, but when he finally gave the discourse, he threw in many profound instructions that were solely the result of his personal experiences. Je Lozang Jinpa was astonished by it.

"To my shame I told him I would offer the lineage back to him." Lozang said in praise. "He is a great Kadampa geshe of the Oral Instruction Tradition!"

Lozang Jinpa himself had achieved extraordinary single-pointed concentration into mental quiescence and special insight. He, too, developed these through the practice of the Heruka body maṇḍala. He lived in Bangrim Choede Monastery of Lower Dagpo. Je Kaelzang Taenzin was a younger brother of his who later went to live in Lhading Hermitage in Upper Dagpo. He often said that Je Lozang Jinpa should visit Lhading, but he was always unable to get away. Later, while in meditative absorption, he saw every detail of the hermitage clearly, both inside and out.

"I had a look at your hermitage and saw everything," he told Kaelzang Taenzin when he visited Lozang one day. He even told Kaelzang of such details as the juniper trees to the right and left of the house. "And there is a big white thing that kept on moving on one of the balconies of the house. What is it?" he asked. It was a curtain being moved by the wind. Lozang Jinpa had seen it in his meditative absorption.

Lozang Jinpa gave the lineage to his brother Kaelzang Taenzin. Kaelzang later became a great adept through both sūtra and tantra. When he gave teachings, white rays of light would issue from both his eyes and encircle the audience of disciples. At the end of the teaching, the rays would dissolve back into his eyes. People saw this many times. Many people were amazed to see him giving teachings while at the same time walking on the circumambulation path. And so on. He had visions of the whole merit field of the *Guru Pūjā* practice. When he died, the top of his skull had a miraculous drawing of the *Guru Pūjā* merit field on it. It is still at Lhading Hermitage.

He gave the teaching to the powerful adept Kaelzang Kaedrub, who also achieved his clairvoyant powers through the Chakrasaṃvara practices. My own precious guru, my refuge and protector, heard the teachings from him.

That was a brief discussion on how the Southern Lineage of *Mañjuśhrī's Own Words* was passed down. You ought to know this in more detail. Refer to the standard biographies.

Now for the Central Province Lineage of *Mañjuśhrī's Own Words.* The all-seeing great Fifth Dalai Lama gave it to Jinpa Gyatso, an occupant of the Gandaen throne. Eventually the lineage came down to Lozang Lhuendrub, another successor to the Gandaen throne. Je Lozang Jinpa received it from him.

The concise discourses for the *Swift Path* have the following history. The all-seeing Paṇchen Lama Lozang Yeshe dictated the text, but no one ever asked him for the lineage discourse. The Paṇchen Lama became partially blind in his old age, and when someone wanted an oral transmission of a few important pages of text they had to have the pages rewritten in very large letters. The great adept Lozang Namgyael was visiting Jadrael Hermitage at the time. He read the *Swift Path* and thought that posterity would be all the poorer if he did not obtain the lineage of its discourse. He bundled up his possessions and went to Tashi Lhuenpo. He told the

Paṇchen Lama's steward he wanted the transmission of the Paṇchen Lama's *Collected Works* in general; he was especially keen, however, to get the discourse of the *Swift Path.*

Now, Lozang Namgyael was only an ordinary monk, yet he was asking for so much, and the Paṇchen Lama's eyesight was weak. The steward was taken aback and scolded Lozang Namgyael roundly; Lozang returned home but could not endure the situation. He made the request three times more, but the steward did absolutely nothing about it. In desperation, Lozang Namgyael returned, and insisted that the caretaker not be so self-cherishing, saying, "Listen, I'm not asking you to give me the teaching! Take my request to the Paṇchen Lama!" The steward lost his temper and told the Paṇchen Lama while still in a rage. The Paṇchen Lama, however, was only too happy to give Lozang Namgyael the transmissions, and throughout the whole teaching, he had no problems at all with his eyesight and so on.

My own precious guru told me this story many times. Nevertheless, Lozang Namgyael is not officially listed as one of our lineage gurus. It is supposed to have come down through Purchog Ngagwang Jampa as is made clear in the preparatory rite recitation entitled *An Ornament for the Throats of the Fortunate* [see Day 6, p. 208; and pp. 695 and 718].

So, now I have given in brief a rough outline of the greatness of the authors, although I have not mentioned all the lamas and their disciples. If I were to do so in detail, I would follow the two volumes of biographies on the lineage gurus written by [Yeshe Gyaeltsaen], a tutor to His Holiness the Dalai Lama. At least, that is what my own precious guru said. I have not the time to do this now, but if you ever obtain a copy of the book, read it all the time, and at the end of each life story, make prayers such as:

> O guru, may my body be exactly like yours,
> May my retinue, life, and surroundings
> Become the same as yours;
> May even my very name be your supreme name.

We should also meditate on the (limb of) rejoicing [see Day 6, page 190].

DAY 3

As Lord Śhāntideva said:

> I have obtained the optimum human rebirth, so hard to achieve,
> Which can achieve a person's aims.
> If I derive no benefit from it now,
> How would such an endowment happen again?

In other words, now that we have obtained the optimum physical rebirth, we should not be attached merely to the happiness of this life. Neither should we deceive ourselves and be immersed in subduing our enemies, protecting our dear ones, and so on: even the animals are capable of doing these things. If we do not practice the Dharma—something that is sure to benefit our future rebirths and that sets us apart from the animals—it will be difficult for us to gain such a rebirth in future. Now that we have obtained such a thing this once, we must take it seriously.

Benefit in your future lives depends on your practicing this very Dharma—the stages of the path to enlightenment. So you should make bodhichitta your motive and think, "I shall achieve buddhahood for the sake of all motherly sentient beings. I shall therefore listen to these profound instructions on the stages of the path to enlightenment and put them properly into practice." Only then should you listen.

What is the Dharma you are about to hear? It is Mahāyāna Dharma, Dharma that leads the fortunate to the level of buddhahood...

And Kyabje Pabongka Rinpoche continued in the same vein as yesterday. Then he reviewed the four headings that he had mentioned, which come under the one general heading, "The Discourse on the Stages of the Path to Enlightenment."

Although we had covered the first of these four headings yesterday, he now reminded us how this teaching was handed down from our Teacher the Buddha. He also briefly reviewed how, much later, there came to be many variations on the teaching, such as the lamrim, the stages of the teachings, and so on. All these, however, took the Lamp on the Path *as their root text. This is dealt with in great detail in the biographies of the lineage gurus of the lamrim.*

After this brief résumé, he continued:

Today, I shall teach the second of these headings.

THE GREATNESS OF THE DHARMA, GIVEN TO INCREASE ONE'S RESPECT FOR THE INSTRUCTION (7)

The lamrim has four greatnesses and three features that distinguish it from the other classical teachings. The four greatnesses are as follows: (1) the greatness of allowing you to realize that all the teachings are without contradiction; (2) the greatness of allowing all the scriptures to present themselves to you as instructions; (3) the greatness of allowing you to easily discover the true thinking of the Victorious One; (4) the greatness of allowing you to save yourself from the worst misdeeds.

THE GREATNESS OF ALLOWING YOU TO REALIZE THAT ALL THE TEACHINGS ARE WITHOUT CONTRADICTION (8)

"The teachings" here refers to the scriptures of the Victorious One. As [Bhāvaviveka's] commentary, the *Lamp of Wisdom,* says:

> "Teachings" means the following: the scriptures of the Bhagavān that teach without distortion the things gods and humans wishing to gain the nectarlike state should know, the things they should abandon, the things they should make manifest, and the things they should meditate upon.

"Realizing that all the teachings are without contradiction" means that one person should understand them as practices in order to be enlightened.

"To be without contradiction" means "to be harmonious." The Mahāyāna, Hīnayāna, Vinaya, and tantras, etc., seem to contradict each other from a literal point of view, but they are all nothing but the main practice to take us to enlightenment or a branch of its attainment. They are, therefore, without contradiction. Suppose you have come down with a high fever. Initially your doctor will forbid you meat, alcohol, and so on. He tells you "These could prove fatal for you if you do not give them up." But later, when the fever has passed its crisis and there is now an excess of the wind humor,[12] the doctor will instruct you to take meat, alcohol, etc. Now, only one person is being told these things, and there is only one person saying them. The two statements—the earlier one forbidding the meat and alcohol and the later one allowing them—seem to be inconsistent, but this is not so. Both of them were meant to cure the one patient.

You may similarly feel, "The Hīnayāna, Mahāyāna, the sūtras, tantras, etc., were tailored for particular disciples, so all of these teachings are not mandatory in the one person's practice in order to become enlightened." Again, this is not so. The one speaker was telling the one person about the practices to enlightenment. When that person was at the level of the small and medium scopes, the Buddha first explained the Hīnayāna basket of teachings. That person was to meditate on things like impermanence and suffering. After some improvement, the person was now at the level of the great scope, so the Mahāyāna basket was explained. He now received explanations into bodhichitta, the six perfections, and so on. And when that person became a suitable vessel for the tantras, the Buddha explained the Vajrayāna: the two stages [of the highest yoga tantras] and the tantric practices. All these practices are harmonious for a person such as yourself to follow in order to be enlightened. Hence any one of the Victorious One's scriptures belongs to either the mainstream of the path or one of its branches; not one of these scriptures is superfluous in a person's practice leading to enlightenment.

The main concern of a bodhisattva is to work for the sake of sentient beings. Thus, bodhisattvas must teach the three paths that will lead the three types of disciples [the śhrāvaka, pratyekabuddha, and bodhisattva] to their particular form of liberation, but unless bodhisattvas know these paths themselves they cannot teach them to others. [Dharmakīrti] says in his *Commentary on Valid Cognition:* "The means to these ends are obscure; it is difficult to explain them." The way leading to an understanding of the paths belonging to the three vehicles is something bodhisattvas should develop in their mindstreams in order to be sure of the different routes to achieve benefit for others. It says in a sūtra:

> O Subhūti, the bodhisattvas develop in all the paths, be it the path of the śhrāvaka, the path of the pratyekabuddha, or the path of the bodhisattva. They understand all the paths.

In [Maitreya's] *Ornament to Realization* we find:

> Those who work for the sake of beings benefit the world by knowing the paths.

Another point: the goal is buddhahood, and this is a state possessing all good qualities, all faults having been eliminated. In order to achieve this state, the Mahāyāna path must be one that eliminates all of a person's faults, and must bring every kind of good quality into effect. Since there is not a single scripture that does not eliminate some type of fault or cause some type of good quality to be developed, surely all the scriptures are to be included among the divisions of the Mahāyāna.

Let us examine this question of scriptural consistency in more detail. There are two ways: how you should understand that all the transmitted teachings—that is, the presentations of the subject matter—are consistent; and how you should understand that the realized teachings—that is, the subject matter itself—are consistent.

As already explained, the three baskets, the four classes of tantra, and so forth, and the scriptures and their commentaries, constitute a harmonious practice to take one person to his or her enlightenment; so there is utterly no contradiction between them whatsoever. This is how all transmitted teachings are to be understood as being without contradiction.

The subject matter of these teachings can be included in the various paths of the three scopes. The small scope covers the causes to achieve the high rebirth states of the gods and humans: the ethics of abandoning the ten non-virtues, etc. The medium scope includes the practices that will cause one to gain the definite excellence of liberation—such practices as abandoning [the first two of the] four truths, engaging in [the last two of these truths], and the practice of the three high trainings. The great scope contains the practices that bring about the definite excellence of omniscience—such practices as the development of bodhichitta, the six perfections, etc. Hence, all this subject matter forms a harmonious practice that will take a person to enlightenment and should be understood as being completely without contradiction. Such is how to understand that all realized teachings are without contradiction.

Dromtoenpa, one of the kings of the Dharma, said: "My lama knows how to take all the teachings as a four-cornered path." This is the root of the explanations (given above), which has been interpreted in many ways. The four sides are the three scopes, with the tantras making the fourth. Or, no matter how you throw a die, a four-sided face will always come up; similarly, each meditation topic includes the whole path within it.

One could follow these interpretations, but my own precious guru, my refuge and protector, told me: just as when one moves one corner of a square mat one moves the whole mat, similarly, Atiśha understood all the subject matter of the scriptures and commentaries as boiling down to a practice to enlighten a single person. This is a most important point.

THE GREATNESS OF ALLOWING ALL THE SCRIPTURES TO PRESENT THEMSELVES TO YOU AS INSTRUCTIONS (9)

If you have not met with anything like the stages of the path to enlightenment, all the scriptures will not present themselves to you as instructions. But the supreme instructions are the Victorious One's scriptures and the great classics that comment on these scriptures. There has never in this world been a better teacher than Śhākyamuni Buddha, the Bhagavān, the transcendent, fully accomplished destroyer of all defilements. His scriptures are the best instruction of all. [Maitreya's] *Sublime Continuum of the Great Vehicle* says:

> There is no scholar in this world surpassing the Victorious One!
> With omniscience he knows all things as they are and suchness supreme; the others do not.
> So do not tamper with anything the Sage put in his own sūtras,
> For that would destroy Śhākyamuni's system and would harm the holy Dharma.

These days, no one suspects the scriptures of the Victorious One—for example the precious *Translated Word of Buddha*—are something to be put into practice, only something meant to be recited in ceremonies. People *do* study the classics of the two champions [Nāgārjuna and Asaṅga] that comment on these scriptures—but only so that they can quote them while debating. Even the most learned of scholars, when about to embark on some meditative practice, do not know how to integrate into their practice what they have determined through their lifelong study and contemplation. So they go to some know-nothings who have the reputation of being great meditators, learn some sādhanas or how to observe the conscious workings of the mind; then they slavishly meditate on these things. Great Tsongkapa had this to say:

> They have studied much, yet are poor in Dharma;
> Blame it on their not taking the scriptures as instructions.

That is, it is damaging not to take the scriptures as being instructions.

For example, there was a geshe at our monastery who visited his homeland in Kham. He asked a Nyingma lama for practical instruction and then meditated on the lama's small instruction. Because of this the local people decided that Gelug Dharma is definitely only for debate, never something to be practiced, so everyone ignored the Gelug teachings. This stuff pulls the legs out from under the teachings; personally, I find this most depressing.

You must put into practice anything whose meaning you have determined through study or contemplation; and the meaning of whatever you practice should have been ascertained through study and contemplation. If you ascertain one thing through study and contemplation and then practice something else, it is like pointing out a racetrack to someone and then using another piece of land for your horse race. The *Great Stages of the Path* uses these very words. Perhaps they require some explanation. You are about to hold a horse race and point out a particular valley, saying, "This is going to be the racetrack tomorrow." Yet on the actual day of the race, you hold it somewhere else.

So if you are unable to take the scriptures as instructions, the fault is that you have not understood the stages of the path to enlightenment. But with this comprehension comes the knowledge that all classics—the Victorious One's scriptures, for example—are included within the lamrim framework, and you know how to put the lot into practice.

Ngawang Chogdaen once occupied the Gandaen throne. After he completed his monastic training, he received many instructions from Jamyang Shaypa—for example [Tsongkapa's] *Three Fundamentals of the Path.* He was introduced to the way to meditate on the thoughts contained in the entire body of the Buddha's word—the sūtras and tantras—as a coherent whole. He later said he had come to understand that during his studies of the vast field of the classics, he had in fact been studying the *Great Stages of the Path.* This showed that the scriptures were, for him, instructions.

When that great adept Lozang Namgyael was giving the oral transmission of the *Eight-Thousand-Verse Perfection of Wisdom Sūtra,* he remarked from time to time, "Ah, if only I were not so old—this is something I should meditate on!"

When you understand the lamrim, all your debating practice in the monastery courtyard would also come under the lamrim; you would take this debate as a meditation instruction. Suppose you were debating the development of bodhichitta: you would instantly draw comparisons with the section of the great scope that deals with training the mind for bodhichitta. Or you would compare a debate on the twelve interdependent links with the medium scope. Or, in a debate on the dhyāna-concentration states of the form realm and the levels of the formless realm, you would readily compare these with the mental quiescence section of the lamrim. Even when you go to recite some Dharma ritual, you would be able to integrate it into the lamrim, no matter from which scripture the recitation was taken.

You would even readily see how any discarded scrap of paper in a wayside shrine you chance on becomes a topic of meditation within your practice. Once, when I was very young, I saw a discarded page in a wayside shrine on the path around a monastery. The page was one of the songs by the Seventh Dalai Lama, Kaelzang Gyatso:

> The young bee in the rhododendron
> Flies from brightly colored flower to flower.
> See how quickly he moves from one to the next.
> Now my song explains this image:
> Many people in these degenerate times
> Have impure minds and wallow in trivia.
> Look! Friends one moment, enemies the next;
> I have not found a constant friend.

I readily associated what I found at the shrine with the section in the medium scope dealing with saṃsāra's bane of uncertainty. So, having a single letter taken from all the (Buddha's) word *(ka)* and the commentaries appear as personal instructions *(dam)* not to be ignored is known as "Kadam."

Je Rinpoche asked Rinchen Pel, a great scholar, for the meaning of the word *Kadam* [literally "scripture-instruction"]. Rinchen Pel's reply was, "To have even a single letter *n* from of the word of the Victorious One appear to you as an instruction not to be ignored." This pleased Je Rinpoche so much that he said in praise while giving a public teaching, "Today a scholar has extended my thinking. It is as he said."

Therefore, all scriptures—even that discarded page in the wayside shrine—can be completely integrated as instruction taking a person to enlightenment. Moreover, these can be completely integrated as instruction taking you yourself to enlightenment. Once you understand that it is as if Buddha and the other authors had given all these scriptures especially for you, you will develop the utmost respect for all of them.

As one yogi, Jangchub Rinchen, said: "We are not told we will find instruction for gaining certain enlightenment in some palm-sized anthology of spells—we should look upon all scripture as instruction." We must think this way; these words strike at the very root. So, taking all the scriptures as instructions has much point to it.

You might wonder, "Is it really enough to study just the lamrim?" The meaning of the scriptures and their commentaries is contained within the lamrim—right from the section on relying on a spiritual guide to the mental quiescence section. A particular lamrim may have an elaborate set of headings, and another set may be brief. Some of these headings require analytic meditation, while others demand fixation meditation. When you have mastered the framework of these headings, you will know which type of meditation to apply to each heading. With this understanding, you will readily associate any scripture you come across with your own practice of a particular lamrim meditation topic—this shows you are taking the scriptures as instructions.

Here is an easy analogy that my precious lama used to give. Suppose a person who has no store of rice, wheat, beans, and so on, happens to find a handful of rice, say. He will not know what to do with it and will undoubtedly just throw it away. So if you have not grasped the full structure of the path and you see some scriptural text, because you don't know where that scripture applies, you will not know how to put it into practice. If you happen to have just one pound[13] each of rice, wheat, and beans, and you acquire another handful of rice, you can add that rice to what you have already. If you have a complete grasp of the framework of lamrim meditation topics, you will readily apply any scripture at all to a particular [lamrim heading].

Rinpoche then spoke in some detail on how a lamrim text that has the full lamrim framework can lead one through the path, no matter how brief the text. He compared this with two rooms, one of a government official and the other of a simple monk: both contain enough furniture to serve their purposes.

Also note: there is a difference between the realization that a scripture is consistent and that of taking all scriptures as instructions. Having the first does not necessarily mean you have the second. But if you have the second, you necessarily have the first.

THE GREATNESS OF ALLOWING YOU TO EASILY DISCOVER THE TRUE THINKING OF THE VICTORIOUS ONE (10)

The words of the Victorious One and their commentaries are, as I have already said, the best of instructions. Yet you cannot discover the ultimate thoughts of the Victorious One merely by referring to these great classics without any instruction from your guru on the stages of the path to enlightenment, despite the fact that the Victorious One's ultimate thoughts are in these classics. To discover these thoughts [from the classics alone], you would have to grapple with these texts for a long time. By depending on the lamrim, you easily discover them without such a struggle.

Perhaps you are wondering, "What are these thoughts of the Victorious One?" My own precious guru, my refuge and protector, told me that in general they are taken to be the three scopes; but even more importantly, they must be taken as the three fundamentals of the path. This is surely correct. The great Tsongkapa clarified the Victorious One's ultimate thoughts on the correct view. In the *Three Fundamentals of the Path,* Tsongkapa said:

> Appearances, mutually interdependent,
> And emptiness, being without assertions:
> So long as you think these two seem separate from each other,
> You have not yet realized the thought of the Sage.

This is actually saying that you have not realized the thought of the Victorious One unless you have realized the correct view—implying that it is the strength of your realization of that view that enables you to discover the thought of the Victorious One. In the same poem, Tsongkapa says: "...the import of the essence of all the Victor's scriptures." This refers to the fundamental of renunciation. He goes on to say: "...the path praised by holy victors and their children..." This refers to the fundamental of bodhichitta. Lastly he says: "...the gateway for the fortunates wanting liberation." This refers to the correct view. Thus, by implication, you still need the other two fundamentals—renunciation and bodhichitta. So, when you depend on the lamrim, you will easily discover that the subject matter of the great classics aims at developing these three fundamentals in your mindstream. With such a discovery, the view arises in your mind effortlessly, and you will have then easily discovered the thoughts of the Victorious One.

Suppose the great classics were an ocean. The thoughts of the Victorious One—the three fundamentals of the path, for example—would be the jewels within that ocean; the lamrim is like the boat; the guru who teaches the lamrim is like the captain. Although the ocean contains these jewels, if you searched for them without the boat, you would only lose your life. Similarly, if you do not make use of the lamrim, it will be difficult for you to discover the thoughts of the Victorious One even though you consult these great classics. Depend on a guru, the skillful captain, get on board the boat, the lamrim, and you will easily find the jewel in the great ocean of the classics: the ultimate thought of the Victor.

THE GREATNESS OF ALLOWING YOU TO SAVE YOURSELF FROM THE WORST MISDEED (11)

Here, the *Great Stages of the Path* and other texts explicitly instruct that you not do anything that will give you the karma, and the resulting obscurations, that goes with abandoning the Dharma. But if you have not taken the first three of these four greatnesses to heart, you will make petty distinctions that cause you to respect one part of the Dharma more than others—distinctions such as Mahāyāna versus Hīnayāna, or theoretical Dharma versus practical Dharma—and abandon part of the Dharma, producing a continual stream of the direst type of karma. The obscurations that result are extremely heavy. The *Sūtra Weaving Everything Together* says:

> Mañjuśhrī, the obscurations that result from the karma of abandoning the holy Dharma are subtle. Mañjuśhrī, one abandons the Dharma when one considers some of the Tathāgata's scriptures to be good, some to be bad. Whoever abandons the Dharma also disparages the Tathāgata as a result; he also speaks badly of

> the Saṅgha. One abandons the Dharma when one claims "this [scripture] is correct" and "this one is incorrect." One abandons the Dharma by claiming "this was taught for bodhisattvas" or "this was taught for śhrāvakas." One abandons the Dharma by claiming "this was taught for pratyekabuddhas." One abandons the Dharma by claiming "this is not one of the things a bodhisattva should train in."

The bane of abandoning the Dharma is an extremely heavy one for, as the *King of Single-Pointed Concentration Sūtra* says:

> Abandoning the sūtra basket
> Is a far heavier sin
> Than destroying all the stūpas
> In this Southern Continent.
>
> Abandoning the sūtra basket
> Is a far heavier sin
> Than killing as many arhats
> As there are grains of sand at the bottom of the Ganges.

If you are convinced about the first three of these greatnesses, you will not ignore any of the Victor's teachings; you will pay the same respect to all of them, as things to be put into practice. You would save yourself from holding some of the Dharma to be good and some bad—the biggest contributing factor to abandoning the Dharma. Also, if you think over the ways to devote yourself properly to your spiritual guide, you will rid yourself of any karmic obscurations you may have in relation to him or her. And when you become convinced about, for example, the truth of the optimum human rebirth or impermanence, you will automatically cease doing misdeeds related to clinging to this life. You will stop your misdeeds associated with self-cherishing when you pursue the meditation topic on the development of bodhichitta. You then train in the meditation topic of selflessness until the topic of self-grasping. They are produced sequentially in your mindstream, one after another. You automatically stop all your most wayward behaviors as a result of realizing the lamrim meditation topic that is each behavior's opposite.

Let me give you an illustration to explain how these first three greatnesses promote your development. A painter of a deity image needs his materials to make his tangka. The painter needs to gather together a canvas, paints, brushes, etc. He knows he needs to have all the tools and materials to facilitate his painting and have none of the conditions that will hinder him. This knowledge is analogous to the realization that all scripture is noncontradictory. Such knowledge of tangka painting through the use of these tools is like taking all the scriptures that come up as personal instruction. And making a good job of the painting, once you know that, is similar to discovering with ease the thoughts of the Victorious One.

These four greatnesses are conventionally taken in two ways: the four greatnesses of the presentation—that is, the actual words used—and the four greatnesses of the subject matter—that is, the meaning of these words. The treatises themselves have the four associated with presentation. However, it is said to be more important that the person comes to have the four associated with the subject matter.

This concludes the four greatnesses. The lamrim has, in addition to these four, three further features: (1) the lamrim is complete because it contains all the subject matter of sūtra and tantra; (2) it is easy to put into practice because it emphasizes the steps in taming the mind; (3) it is superior to other traditions because it is enhanced with instructions from two gurus who were schooled in the traditions of the Two Great Champions.

THE LAMRIM IS COMPLETE BECAUSE IT CONTAINS ALL THE SUBJECT MATTER OF SŪTRA AND TANTRA (12)

While it is impossible for the lamrim to include all the actual words of the scriptures and commentaries, it does contain and teach their key meanings completely, teaching these in a condensed form. The whole meaning of these scriptures and commentaries comes under the three scopes of the lamrim. With [all] this condensed into this small lamrim, I am teaching a condensation of the entire subject matter of the scriptures. Great Tsongkapa said the following in a letter to Lama Umapa:

> This instruction from Dīpaṃkara Shrījñāna—the stages of the path to enlightenment—seems to incorporate and teach within the stages of the path all the instructions of the scriptures and their commentaries. If taught and practiced by those who know how to teach and practice it, it seems to arrange in sequence not

> only the large and small instructions, but also encapsulates the whole of the scriptures. Thus I do not teach a long list of different types of discourses.

The teachings of the other schools may have the convention of various lists of teachings: the four great teachings on the preliminary practices such as taking refuge and the like, teachings on the main practices, etc., etc. Even so, the original Kadampas and we neo-Kadampas traditionally dispense with these many long lists, for everything is already in the lamrim. The *Lamp on the Path* teaches the synthesis of the entire subject matter of the scriptures within the space of three folios. All the other lamrim texts similarly compress all this material, because they take the *Lamp on the Path* as their root text. Thus, the great Tsongkapa said:

> It condenses the essence of all scripture.
> By teaching and studying this system for a session,
> One gains the benefit of discussing and studying all holy Dharma.
> Contemplate its meaning, for that is certain to be powerful.

In other words, the study, contemplation, teaching, and receiving of a teaching on the lamrim are study, contemplation, and learning about the full meanings of the scriptures and their commentaries. When you perform even a single sequence of retrospection meditations on the lamrim, you are practicing the meaning of the scriptures and commentaries. That great Kadampa figure, Geshe Toelungpa, said:

> When I teach you the stages of the path to enlightenment, you gain a conceptual understanding of all the world's books and volumes. All these books feel, "That grey-haired old monk has plucked out all our hearts!" and shudder at the thought.

How true, because if a discourse on the lamrim has gone well, the essence of all the world's books has been discussed in that discourse. Thus, on the one hand, the lamrim includes the meaning of all the scriptures within it, while on the other, it is like a key opening a hundred doors of scripture. There could be no better summary of the Dharma. So, that is why Geshe Toelungpa said on the subject of teaching the lamrim, "I have butchered the great yak of the Dharma."

People who think at a lower level may not understand the more elaborate lamrim texts; they can still depend on a short text—for example one of the concise teachings—that has the full lamrim framework. This concise teaching is still able to lead them along the path. But if the text leaves out even one of the topics of meditation, it cannot lead anybody along the path.

Take the medicine for fever called camphor twenty-five.[14] You do not need to go out and obtain a bulky package of each of its twenty-five ingredients and then take them individually; as long as the medicine has been compounded properly with all twenty-five, it will bring down the fever. But if one of the ingredients is missing, the remaining medicine will not rid you of the fever, no matter how much of it you take.

Now that you have been fortunate enough to meet with this king of all instructions, you ought to focus on it.

IT IS EASY TO PUT INTO PRACTICE BECAUSE IT EMPHASIZES THE STEPS FOR TAMING THE MIND (13)

We have undergone the many varied sufferings of saṃsāra, and we have gained the highest bliss saṃsāra has to offer. Our own minds were responsible for all these things. Nothing is said to be better than the lamrim for taming the mind; the lamrim places great emphasis on the means for achieving this. The lamrim is therefore easy to put into practice.

IT IS SUPERIOR TO THE OTHER TRADITIONS BECAUSE IT CONTAINS INSTRUCTIONS FROM TWO GURUS WHO WERE SCHOOLED IN THE TRADITIONS OF THE TWO GREAT CHAMPIONS (14)

The guru skilled in Nāgārjuna's school was Vidyākokila, and in Asaṅga's school, Suvarṇadvīpa Guru. This teaching is enriched by their instructions and is therefore superior to all other traditions. As great Je Tsongkapa said:

> The stages of the path to enlightenment
> Stem from Nāgārjuna and Asaṅga—
> The crest jewels of the world's scholars,
> The pennant of whose fame is raised before all beings.

Not even [Maitreya's] *Ornament to Realization* has these three features. Even the king of tantras, Śhrī Guhyasamāja, does not have them. These two texts do not contain all the subject matter of sūtra and tantra, nor do they emphasize the taming of the mind.

Now that you are fortunate enough to study, contemplate, and meditate on such an exalted path as this lamrim, exceptional due to these three greatnesses and distinctive features, you should not be satisfied with some incomplete or specious instruction. It is vital for you to put the utmost effort into this path.

This completes the second major heading: "The Greatness of the Dharma."

HOW TO TEACH AND LISTEN TO THE DHARMA THAT HAS THESE TWO GREATNESSES (15)

This is a most important heading. Ngagwang Dragpa, a great meditator from Dagpo, said:

> The best preliminary instruction
> Is on the right way to teach and listen.
> Cherish it...

In other words, this heading will determine whether the following teachings will challenge your mindstream into following the path or not. It will be difficult for you to translate my teaching into contemplation and meditation if you get this heading wrong, just as you would be wrong about all the dates until the fifteenth [the day of the full moon] if you took the wrong day to be the first of the lunar month [the day of the new moon].

There are three headings at this point: (1) the way to listen to the Dharma; (2) the way to teach the Dharma; (3) what things the disciples and teacher should do together at the end.

THE WAY TO LISTEN TO THE DHARMA (16)

Here there are three subheadings: (1) contemplating the benefits of studying the Dharma; (2) how to show respect for the Dharma and its teacher; (3) the actual way to listen to the Dharma.

JANGCHUB OE OFFERS RANSOM TO THE KHAN OF GARLOG (SEE P. 41)

CONTEMPLATING THE BENEFITS OF STUDYING THE DHARMA (17)

It is vital to contemplate first the benefits of studying the Dharma, because only then will you develop the strong desire to study it. If the contemplation is done properly, you will be extremely happy to embark on such a study; you therefore must contemplate such benefits. In the *Sayings of the Buddha* we find:

> Owing to your study, you understand Dharma;
> Owing to your study, you stop sinning;
> Owing to your study, you abandon the meaningless;
> Owing to your study, you achieve nirvāṇa.

In other words, by virtue of your study, you will know all the key points for modifying your behavior. You will understand the meaning of the vinaya basket and, as a result, will stop sinning by following the high training of ethics. You will understand the meaning of the sūtra basket, and as a result you will come to abandon such meaningless things as distractions by following the high training in single-pointed concentration. And you will understand the meaning of the Abhidharma basket, and so come to abandon delusions by means of the high training in wisdom. Hence your study will enable you to reach nirvāṇa.

In the *Jātaka Tales,* it is said:

> Study is the lamp to dispel the darkness of benightedness.
> It is the best of possessions—thieves cannot rob you of it.
> It is a weapon to defeat your enemy—your blindness to all things.
> It is your best friend who instructs you in the means;
> It is a relative who will not desert you, though you be poor.
> It is a medicine against sorrow that does you no harm.
> It is the best army, which defeats great legions of misdeeds.
> It is also the best of treasures, of fame, and of glory.
> You could have no better gift when meeting the most high.
> It pleases the scholars in any gathering.

Study is like a lamp to dispel the darkness of benighted ignorance. My own precious guru told me that if you know only one letter of the alphabet, like the letter A, you have to rid yourself of your darkness concerning it. You will have added to your stock of wisdom. So, when you know the other letters, you have dispelled your ignorance about them, too, and added even more to your wisdom. Without any study, we would not be able to recognize the letter A, even if it were as large as a donkey's head; we would just [be stubborn and] act stiff-necked. Just think about the people in your family who know nothing at all and you will understand my point.

The amount of ignorance you manage to rid yourself of similarly depends on how much study you have done. The light of your wisdom has grown proportionally. In the *Sayings of the Buddha* we find:

> As in a well-curtained house
> Whose inside's sunk in darkness,
> Though there be shapes therein to see,
> The sighted do not see thereby;
>
> So a man of good family
> May be discerning;
> But until he studies, he will not know
> Sinful things from virtuous.
>
> As the sighted with a lamp
> See visual forms, so too,
> Through study, one comes to know
> Virtuous things from sinful.

In other words, you cannot see anything in a completely dark place of study, you will know nothing of the points required for modifying your behavior. If you light a lamp in the darkened room, you will be able to see all the things inside it vividly with your existing eyes; thus by reliance on the lamp of study, you can come to understand all phenomena with the eye of wisdom.

[Asaṅga's] *Bodhisattva Levels* talks in some detail about these benefits, and on how one should listen to teachings with five attitudes. The first attitude is to regard the teaching as an eye, by means of which you develop more and more wisdom. Then you should regard the teaching as illumination, through which your given wisdom-eye sees things as they seem to be and as they really exist. You should regard it as something precious that occurs but rarely in the world. Regard the teaching as something most beneficial, for through it you will obtain the fruit enjoyed by great bodhisattvas. Lastly, henceforth you should regard the teaching as something completely sanctioned, because it will enable you to achieve the bliss of mental quiescence and special insight.

Your studies are also the supreme possession that thieves and so forth cannot take from you. Thieves can carry off your worldly goods, enemies may confiscate them, and so on, but it is impossible to lose to thieves the seven jewels of the āryas—that is, your studies, etc.—nor the three good qualities of scholarship, ethics, and kindheartedness. When it comes to transportation, they are not like your worldly goods, which give you many hassles, for example, when you go back to your birthplace—deciding which of your possessions to take with you on the journey. Your studies are not like this: you can even take them with you when you die. So they say it is most important that we simple monks should not long for fancy tea churns decorated with brass hoops, or for copper pots, and so on; we should long for the seven jewels of the āryas.

Study is like a weapon to overcome your enemy, your blindness. Through study, you will root out all your enemy delusions. Study is also your best friend, who will give you unmistaken advice. When you are about to begin some action, your former studies will advise you whether it is right or not; if right, how to do it; if wrong, how to prevent it; its benefits and drawbacks; etc. My own precious guru told me, "While King Lhalama Yeshe Oe was alone in prison, he became more and more determined. This was because of the advice he received from his companion—his former studies."

Study is a friend who will never forsake you in hard times. Ordinary relatives act friendly when you are well off; when times are bad, they pretend not to recognize you. But study is the best of relatives, for it will be particularly helpful to you when times are bad and you undergo suffering, illness, death, etc.

Before great Tsechogling Rinpoche became tutor to one of the Dalai Lamas, there was a time when he looked like a penniless hermit. He met an uncle of his on the road, who was going off to do some trading. Tsechogling Rinpoche said something to him, but the uncle spoke as if he did not recognize Rinpoche. After Rinpoche became the Dalai Lama's tutor and occupied one of the highest positions of authority, the uncle went to see him and told Rinpoche that he was his uncle.

Once there was a man who started out poor. Not one person claimed to be his relative. Then he made a little money from trading, and many people later came and claimed kinship with him. He summoned them to have lunch with him. He placed piles of money at the head of the table; then he recited the following verse while he prostrated himself before the money: "A man who was not my uncle became my uncle. O lovely piles of money, I pay homage to you!" In other words, you cannot trust even your ordinary friends and relatives.

If we must seek out friends and relatives, better to seek study, contemplation, and meditation.

By the way, in *Ketsang's* lamrim, the last line of the above verse reads, "O my meal ticket, I pay homage to you!" But the version I gave is exactly how my own precious guru used to tell this story, and so I have given it to you unedited.

Study is also a medicine for the sickness of delusion and an army to destroy the legion of nonvirtue. It is also the best fame, glory, and the greatest of treasures; the best gift to present to holy beings; the best way to gain the respect of the assembly of scholars.

The *Jātaka Tales* also tells us:

> Whoever has studied will develop faith;
> He will be steadfast and will delight in the excellent;
> He will develop wisdom and have no benighted ignorance.
> It is right even to sell one's flesh to obtain it.

In other words, study has infinite good qualities. You will develop faith in the good qualities of the Three Jewels through your study; you will then work hard at making offerings to the buddhas, and so forth. Also, because of your belief in the certainty of karma, you will be happy to modify your behavior, and so on. You will come to understand the faults of the first two of the four truths [suffering and the origin of suffering], and the good qualities of the last two [cessation and the path]. Thus you will be steadfast in working toward your final goal [buddhahood].

We are told, "It is right if needs be to cut off your flesh and sell it for the sake of your studies." But now that you can study in comfort, without having to mutilate your body, you ought to study with enthusiasm. The above verse was given to the bodhisattva, [Prince] Chandra [Vyiligalita, one of Śhākyamuni's former lives], after he had offered one thousand gold coins for each line in the verse.

The depth of your studies determines how many times you have to contemplate. This number determines how soon you will develop insight through your meditations; and in turn, you will come to have wisdom.

Young people ought to study the five standard debate subjects when they enter one of the big monasteries. There is a huge difference between those who have studied and those who have not—even in the things they recognize to be the Three Jewels. Even if a teacher is little read, his disciples shouldn't follow after him. If he makes them study, in his next life he, too, will develop as much wisdom as they will in this. The old, the dull-witted, and so on, may want to study the great classics, but death will come and interrupt their studies before they have rid themselves of their misconceptions. Such people are, therefore, incapable of completing a great amount of study. But if they study and contemplate something like the lamrim, they gain some understanding of the whole path. Tsongkapa once told the Paṇchen Lama Lozang Choekyi Gyaeltsaen in a dream:

> In order to benefit yourself and others,
> Never be satisfied with your studies.
> Observe bodhisattvas on the third level:
> They are dissatisfied with their amount of study.

You should do as he says.

No matter on how low a level people think, how could they not know how to study—or have enough time to devote to studying—a concise discourse on the lamrim, for example? How could they claim, "We are not bookish types?" and live with having wasted their share of the Dharma? Why even horses, cows, and sheep carry their own share, each according to their capacity. You must, then, study at your own intellectual level. But whatever text you study, be it brief or elaborate, be sure it is one containing the whole range of meditation topics, starting with depending on your spiritual guide and ending in the unification of the no-more-learner. If a text does not have the full range of meditation topics, even though you may come to know some topics most extensively, this would not compensate you for the incomplete set of meditation topics. It is like the contents of a room: having a hundred carpets but no clothes to wear; or like having a hundred outfits and no carpets. If the text is complete, it can lead you along the path, regardless of the amount of detail it has to offer—in the same way that the huge room of a minister of state and a monk's cell both serve their own purposes.

HOW TO SHOW RESPECT FOR THE DHARMA AND ITS TEACHER (18)

The *Sūtra for Kṣhitigarbha* says:

> Listen to Dharma with singular faith and respect.
> Do not mock it nor disparage it.
> Make offerings to the teachers of the Dharma;
> Develop the attitude that they are Buddha's equal.

You must pay the same respect to the teachers of the Dharma when you listen to their teachings as you would to our Teacher Buddha.

[Asaṅga's] *Bodhisattva Levels* says that you must listen quite free of delusions, the mind undistracted by the five things [explained below]. You should also be free of pride. There is further mention of six things that should be present while you listen: (1) the right time; (2) deference; (3) respect; (4) a lack of anger; (5) [the intention] to put the teaching into practice later; (6) an absence of arguing with the teaching.

Let us take the first of these: the right time. The guru must give a teaching if he feels happy to do so, if he has no other pressing duties, etc. So you would not request or listen to his teaching whenever it suits you, as this would be most presumptuous and selfish. Geshe Potowa was once staying in Kakang Monastery in the uplands of the Central Province editing many scriptural texts, which was a headache. A man came to him and requested teachings. Geshe Potowa stood up and, adopting a rather angry manner, drove the man away. The man beat a hasty retreat, which only goes to show you should be skilled in your timing.

One shows deference through prostrations and rising in the teacher's presence. Paying respect includes washing his hands and feet. "A lack of anger" is not getting upset if you have to do a chore on his behalf. "Arguing with" means being haughty. It could also mean holding some of the Dharma and its teacher in contempt—an action related to your delusions.

One should also not dwell on five things: his degenerate ethics, his low caste, his poor clothes, his poor way of speaking or bad usage of words, and his use of unpleasant language. One must give up any idea of seeing these five things as faults.

THE ACTUAL WAY TO LISTEN TO THE DHARMA (19)

This has two parts: (1) abandoning the three types of faults hindering one from becoming a worthy vessel, and (2) cultivating the six helpful attitudes.

ABANDONING THE THREE TYPES OF FAULTS HINDERING ONE FROM BECOMING A WORTHY VESSEL (20)

These three are as follows: (1) the fault of being like an upturned vessel, (2) the fault of being like a stained vessel, (3) the fault of being like a leaky vessel.

THE FAULT OF BEING LIKE AN UPTURNED VESSEL (21)

If a vessel is upturned, no matter how much nourishing liquid is poured over it, none of the nourishment will go inside. Your body may be sitting among the audience of a teaching, but you will understand nothing if your mind is distracted and your ears are not taking in what is being said. This is no different from not going to the teaching at all. You must listen like a deer—an animal much attached to sound. You must give the teaching your full attention. "Giving it your full attention" does not mean listening to Dharma with only half of your attention while the other half of your mind is distracted. It means you focus entirely on everything. Be like deer: because of their attachment to sound, when they listen [to a flute being played], they don't even know a hunter is shooting his arrows.

THE FAULT OF BEING LIKE A STAINED VESSEL (22)

A vessel may not be upturned, but if it contains poison, impurities, and so on, then even a wholesome liquid poured into it will not be fit for use. Your ears may be taking everything in, but you may be motivated by thoughts of furthering your studies, or by thoughts of repeating what you hear to other people, and so on. Compared to these motivations, being motivated by, for example, a yearning for the peace [of liberation] merely for yourself is an improvement, but even this is still said to be a fault and to resemble a stained vessel. You must therefore listen with at least contrived bodhichitta as your motive.

THE FAULT OF BEING LIKE A LEAKY VESSEL (23)

A vessel may be neither upturned nor stained, but if the bottom leaks it will not retain any liquid, regardless of how much has been poured into it. Your ears may be taking in everything and your motivation may be faultless, but unless you listen carefully, you will immediately forget everything. It is very difficult to take measures to prevent ourselves from forgetting a teaching, so we must use something as a reminder—a book or a set of headings, for example. We must continually go over the material by thinking, "What was taught at this particular point?" It is especially important to get together with your colleagues between teaching sessions and review what was said.

As to abandoning these faults of the vessel, in one of his sūtras the Bhagavān stressed, "Listen well, listen the best way, and retain it in the mind." "Listen well" refers to abandoning the fault of the filthy vessel; "listen the best way" refers to abandoning the fault of the upturned vessel; and "retain it in the mind" means abandoning the fault of the container with the leaky bottom.

This, then, is how you should listen.

CULTIVATING THE SIX HELPFUL ATTITUDES (24)

These are: (1) the attitude that you are like a patient, (2) the attitude that the holy Dharma is medicine, (3) the attitude that your spiritual guide is like a skillful doctor, (4) the attitude that diligent practice will cure the illness, (5) the attitude that the tathāgatas are holy beings, (6) the attitude that the Dharma should be preserved for a long time.

[DEVELOPING] THE ATTITUDE THAT YOU ARE LIKE A PATIENT (25)

This is a vital attitude to have; if it is present, the others will follow naturally. It might seem perverse to meditate on being patients when we are not ill, but the point of this is that we are seriously ill with the disease of delusion. As Geshe Kamaba pointed out, it might be perverse for a person who is not ill to meditate this way; but we have in fact contracted the grave and chronic illness of the three poisons [attachment, hatred, and ignorance] though we do not know it.

We might be wondering, "How could I be sick and not know about it?"

Yet when you have a high fever, you may be delirious, sing songs and so forth, and not feel sick. We have been most seriously ill with delusions for such a long time that we are not aware of it.

Again you might wonder, "If I have a disease, shouldn't I have aches and pains? But I haven't." But time and time again you get the acute aches and pains that result from the three poisons. You may wonder, "What are they?" Suppose you go to the market, and see some attractive item but cannot afford it. When you return home, you are most upset and wonder how you can get it. This is the pain of attachment. When you see, hear, or recall something unpleasant—a stinging remark, for example—you feel unbearable anguish. This is an example of the pain of hostility. Examine this part in detail, and go into pride, jealousy, and so forth. Delusions are serious, painful, intolerable, chronic diseases.

Hence you have contracted many diseases—the diseases of attachment, hostility, jealousy, and so forth. You take great care not to contract even one ordinary disease, but why doesn't suffering from the many varieties of delusions worry you at all? Śhāntideva says in *Engaging in the Deeds of Bodhisattvas:*

> If you must obey your doctor's orders
> When you have a normal disease,
> What need be said about the disease you have always had
> A hundred times worse, such as attachment?

We are most afraid if we are sick and the illness has already lasted a month or two. But we have suffered under the disease of delusion in beginningless saṃsāra until the present, and still it is impossible for us to recover from this disease until we manage to achieve liberation from cyclic existence. As Geshe Potowa said, "The patient who will never get well, the traveler who will never reach his destination..." This is the perfect description of ourselves.

DEVELOPING THE ATTITUDE THAT THE HOLY DHARMA IS MEDICINE (26)

When patients realize they are ill, they need to look for the right medicine. The only medicine that will pacify the disease of delusion is the holy Dharma; this is the medicine you must seek.

DEVELOPING THE ATTITUDE THAT YOUR SPIRITUAL GUIDE IS LIKE A SKILLFUL DOCTOR (27)

When you are sick but have no doctor and instead just take some medicine, you may mistake your condition—is it a "hot" or "cold" disease, for instance—and the stage the illness has reached. The medicine you take may not help and could even endanger your life. You most assuredly need to depend on a skillful doctor. You might not rely on a spiritual guide and instead feel, "It is enough to practice Dharma from books." But you will not develop any realization or insights from your recitations, meditations, and so on. Your mindstream would become more and more set in its ways. Thus, when you decide you should practice the Dharma, you must seriously rely on a spiritual guide as you would rely on a skillful doctor. As a patient you are very happy when you find a doctor. You will listen to whatever he tells you, and out of respect, you will treat the doctor with reverence. You should do the same when you find a spiritual guide. As it says in the *Summary of Precious Good Qualities:*

> Thus, the wise who strongly wish to seek
> Holy enlightenment should completely subjugate their pride.
> Just as patients in order to be cured depend on doctors,
> So should the seeker depend steadfastly on a spiritual guide.

DEVELOPING THE ATTITUDE THAT DILIGENT PRACTICE WILL CURE THE ILLNESS (28)

The medicine is the thing that helps the patient's illness, but perhaps the patient doesn't follow the doctor's advice and instead just leaves the prescribed medicine by his bedside. When the patient does not do what the doctor says, and does all the things he says not to do, and never gets better, you cannot blame the doctor and you cannot blame the medicine, because the patient brought it on himself.

The spiritual guide is like a skillful doctor, but if you listen to many oral instructions, which are like a medicine to pacify the disease of delusion, and do not put them into practice, they will not benefit your mindstream, no matter how profound or extensive they may be. You should not blame the guru; you should not blame the Dharma. It is the very student not putting the Dharma into practice who is at fault. As it is said in the *King of Single-Pointed Concentration Sūtra:*

> After constant searching, the patient finds
> A skilled and intelligent doctor,
> Who, eyeing him with much compassion,
> Tells him, "Take this medicine," which he dispenses.
>
> Yet the patient does not take this most wholesome
> And precious medicine, the potential cure.
> Do not blame the doctor; the medicine's not at fault.
> Rather, the patient himself is to blame.
>
> So too with people ordained into this doctrine:
> They may know full well about
> The [ten] forces, the dhyāna concentrations, the [ten] powers—
> But make no true effort to meditate.
> How could nirvāṇa come without the right effort?

And:

> I have taught you most wholesome Dharma.
> If you do not practice what you've heard,
> You are like the patient who left the medicine
> In its pouch, thinking, "This cannot cure my disease."

[Śhāntideva] says in *Engaging in the Deeds of Bodhisattvas:*

> Physically make use of these:
> Mere words accomplish nothing.
> Will the sick be helped
> Just by their reading the prescription?

So it is not enough that you possess the medicine; in order to be cured you must properly administer it and follow the doctor's orders. You must apply your knowledge of the meaning of the oral instructions on pacifying this disease of delusion by putting these instructions into practice, applying them to your mental stream. In [Tsongkapa's] *Great Stages of the Path* we find:

> One is made to understand through study, yet it is most vital to

> put the meaning of the studies into one's every practice according to one's ability.

The *Plea for Altruism Sūtra* has this to say about people whose habit has been to acquire a long list of received teachings and initiations but put nothing into practice:

> The bark of sugarcane has no juice;
> The delightful taste is inside.
> People who chew the bark cannot
> Discover the flavor of sugarcane.
> Now the bark is like mere talk;
> The taste is thinking about the meaning.

In other words, these people are like those who crave sugarcane but are more attached to the taste of its bark—and that is all they will eat of the cane.

> Like people who go to watch a play
> And sing the praises of other heroes,
> They have lost track of the important,
> Such are the dangers of being overfond of talk.

They are said to be like people who imitate the actors in a play. You should not be lazy by merely studying; you must strive to put your studies into practice. If you do not do this, the Dharma has made you intractable, and nothing could be worse. "Too much study and too little meditation is cause to become unyielding toward the Dharma"; so it is said. In the early stages, your studies seem to be only a little benefit to your mind. But your studies will have even less impact on you if you do not take them any further through frequent reflection and meditation. Eventually you will be sick of the teachings. Later, there will be even less impact when you study further, and subsequently even less still. Eventually, no matter how profound an instruction you study, you will think such things as, "Done that!"and your studies will be of no benefit at all to your mental stream. You have become unyielding to the Dharma, and as Āchārya Vararuchi says in his *One Hundred Verses:*

The monk who's been disrobed,
The woman who's left three husbands,
The jackal who's escaped a trap—
Know these three as crafty types!
The Kadampas of old used to say:
Dharma will subdue the sinful
But not those unyielding to the Dharma.
Oil will soften up a tough old hide
But not the skin used to carry butter.

In other words, this is the worst thing that could happen. If people who have become unyielding to other teachings are taught the lamrim, they can be subdued; but if they are unyielding to the lamrim, they are quite impossible to subdue. You should therefore be wary of this point.

Study anything you are going to practice, and relate whatever you study to your own mindstream. Dromtoenpa, that king of Dharma, said the following on the need to combine study, contemplation, and meditation:

When I study, I increase my contemplation and meditation.
When I contemplate, I increase my study and meditation.
When I meditate, I increase my study and contemplation.
I know how to gather them as the one foundation,
And take the Dharma as my path
I am a Kadampa and don't do things in parts.
People who wear blinkers are deceived;
Those who well understand the excellent are Kadampas.

If lepers with deformed hands and feet take medicine only once or twice, their condition will not change; they need to take a powerful medicine over a long period. We have been suffering from the virulent, chronic illness of delusion since beginningless time, and it is not sufficient that we put the meaning of an instruction into practice only once or twice. We have to work at it seriously—as constantly as a river flows. Āchārya Chandragomin said:

But the mind has long been blinded,
And this disease has long been festering;
What could a leper, with mutilated feet and hands,
Derive from taking his medicine only a few times?

One should put everything into immediate practice, just like Geshe Chaen Ngawa. He was reading a section of the vinaya that discussed leather and hides; he saw that it forbade someone ordained from handling animal hides. He happened to be sitting on a hide at the time. He immediately threw it out. On reading further he found an exception to this rule for remote countries and that the ordained there were permitted to handle hides. He retrieved the hide and spread it on his seat again.

DEVELOPING THE ATTITUDE THAT TATHĀGATAS ARE HOLY BEINGS (29)

The first person to teach the Dharma was our Teacher the Buddha, and he himself made manifest the path and its results. He taught it to others properly, and the points he taught on the subject of modifying one's behavior were without the slightest error. Thus he is an authority. One must therefore feel, "How could his teachings on the Dharma be mistaken?" when one recalls these facts about Buddha. In one tradition, one can conjoin this with the attitude that a holy being is a tathāgata. One should then feel, "This holy being—my guru—is an emanation of the tathāgata Śhākyamuni."

DEVELOPING THE ATTITUDE THAT THIS TRADITION SHOULD BE PRESERVED FOR A LONG TIME (30)

Through listening to such Dharma as this, one comes to think, "How wonderful it would be if the teachings of the Victorious One were preserved in this world for a long time!"

The first five attitudes are examples of recalling the Tathāgata's kindness. [This] sixth attitude is a meditation on repaying Buddha's kindness.

When listening to the Dharma, these are crucial. The reason for attending teachings is to bring some pressure to bear on your mindstream, otherwise your mind will only stay the way it is. And if you have experienced no change after listening to a teaching, then there has been absolutely no benefit for your mindstream, even though the instruction may have been particularly profound and you listened closely. An illustration: you need to look into a mirror in order to see whether your face is dirty; then you can remove any dirt that may be there. You examine your own mindstream and behavior in the mirror of the Dharma: you listen to Dharma to tell whether your mind has any flaws. If you find any, you should be distressed and think, "Has my mind come to this!" You will then want to do all you can to rid yourself of the faults. The *Jātaka Tales* tell us:

> When I see the form of my evil deeds
> Clearly in the mirror of the Dharma,
> My mind is horribly tormented;
> I shall now turn to the Dharma.

Sudāsaputra—also known as Prince Kalmāṣhapada—said this to Prince Chandra. His story serves as an example to us all.

When the Blessed Buddha was still a learner treading the path, he was reborn as [the bodhisattva] Prince Chandra. There was a man called Sudāsaputra, who used to kill people and eat his victims.

One day the prince went into a grove, and an eloquent Brahman came to him. While the prince was receiving a Dharma teaching from this eloquent Brahman, suddenly they heard a great noise. People were sent to see what was happening. They found that Sudāsaputra was coming.

The prince's bodyguards said, "Sudāsaputra Kalmāṣhapada eats people. He is a man to be feared; our army, its many horses, elephants, and chariots have scattered and fled. What are we to do? The time has come to parley with him."

This idea pleased the prince and, deaf to the pleas of his wives and entourage, he went to where the great clamor was coming from. The prince saw Sudāsaputra pursuing the king's army in a rage, his sword and shield held high. But the prince fearlessly and without hesitation said, "I am Prince Chandra. I am here; come here to me."

Suddsaputra turned around and made for the prince, saying as he ran, "It's you I want." He flung the prince over his shoulder and ran off with him to his lair. This terrifying place was full of human skeletons; the floor was red, and the whole place resounded with the gruesome calls of ferocious flesh-eaters such as jackals, vultures, and ravens. The lair was black with the smoke of roasted corpses. Sudāsaputra put the prince down in this horrifying place and rested—but with his eyes fixed on the handsome body of the prince.

The prince thought to himself, "I had no chance to make an offering to that eloquent Brahman in the grove for the Dharma I received." This thought made him cry.

"Cease! Enough!" Sudāsaputra said. "You, Prince Chandra, are famed for your steadfastness. How strange you should be crying now that I've captured you. They say, "Steadfastness is useless when you undergo pain. Studies don't help when you suffer. Everyone cringes when struck." You know, I think this is true. Tell me honestly: are you afraid I am going to kill you? Are you afraid you will be parted from your friends, relations, wives, children, and parents? Tell the truth, whatever it may be: why are you crying?"

"I was receiving the Dharma from a Brahman," the prince replied, "but I was unable to make him an offering. Let me go to him and give him something, and I will definitely return to you."

"That cannot be true, no matter what you say," said Sudāsaputra. "After once being saved from the jaws of the Lord of Death, who would return to his presence?"

"Have I not given my word and promised to return? I am he known as Prince Chandra, and I value the truth as much as my own life."

"I do not trust what you say; however I am willing to test you," he said. "Go back, and we shall see if you really value the truth. Go back, complete your business with the Brahman—whatever it is—then return quickly. I will get the fire ready to roast you, and I will wait for you."

The prince returned to his home and gave the Brahman four thousand ounces in gold as payment for the four verses the Brahman had taught. The prince's father tried various means to stop him, but to no avail. The prince returned to the lair of Sudāsaputra, who was astonished to see him in the distance. The prince told him, "You may now eat me."

"I know the time to eat you," Sudāsaputra replied. "The fire is now smoking. If I roast flesh when the fire is smoking, it will stink of smoke and the taste will be ruined. In the meantime, teach me what you heard from the Brahman, which you claim is so important."

"The Brahman's eloquent words told how to distinguish between non-Dharma and Dharma. Your evil ways are worse than the man-eating rakṣhas. What good could study possibly do you?"

Sudāsaputra could not bear this remark. "Stop! Enough! You kings kill deer with your weapons. That goes against the Dharma!"

"Kings who kill deer contravene the Dharma," replied Prince Chandra, "but eating human flesh is worse. Humans are higher than deer. And if it is wrong to eat the flesh of someone who died a natural death, how could killing people to eat them be right?"

Sudāsaputra then said, "You haven't learned much from the scriptures if you came back to me!"

"I returned in order to keep my word, and so I have learned much from the scriptures."

"The other men were afraid when I had them in my clutches. But you have proved to be a steadfast hero: you have not lost your composure. You seem unafraid to die."

"Those men were full of remorse because they had sinned," said the prince. "But there is no sin I can recall ever having done. I am therefore unafraid. I offer myself to you—you may eat me."

Sudāsaputra had by now developed faith in the prince. His eyes were full of tears, and the hairs on his body were standing on end. He looked at the prince in awe and told him about his sinful nature. "Deliberately sinning against a person like you," Sudāsaputra said, "would be like drinking strong poison. Teach me, I beg you, what the Brahman so eloquently taught you." He also said at this point the verse we had above:

> When I see the form of my evil deeds
> Clearly in the mirror of the Dharma,
> My mind is terribly tormented;
> I shall now turn to the Dharma.

Prince Chandra saw that he had become a suitable vessel for the Dharma and said:

> Drink the nectar of these words
> While sitting on a low seat,
> While wonderfully subdued in manner,
> Your eyes bright with joy.
>
> Develop respect; listen single-pointedly.
> The mind most clear and undefiled,
> Listen to these words as a patient heeds his doctor;
> In reverence, listen to the Dharma.

Sudāsaputra laid out his upper garment on a flat stone and invited Prince Chandra to sit on it. Sudāsaputra sat in front of the prince and, while gazing at his face, said: "O noble one, now teach."

Prince Chandra then began:

Meeting the holy saints just once
Is enough to grant whatever you desire.
You need not know him well;
It still will make you steadfast.

And so on. He subdued Sudāsaputra's mind with the Dharma teaching. Sudāsaputra, to return this kindness, presented Chandra with the ninety-nine princes he had been holding prisoner in order to eat them; he vowed from then on to uphold right behavior and to give up killing sentient beings and eating human flesh.

So, when you listen to the Dharma, probe your own mind all the while. If you do, your mindstream will be subdued—even if it is as wild as Sudāsaputra's. But if your mind and the Dharma both go their separate ways while you listen, you will derive no benefit, no matter how good the lama, no matter how penetrating the instruction.

While listening to Dharma some people wonder, "What is he going to say that I don't already know or haven't already studied?" Listening like this will not benefit you at all.

Others only pay attention to the interesting anecdotes and do not take profound points of the instruction seriously. Here is an illustration. When Kaelzang Gyatso, the Seventh Dalai Lama, was giving a teaching on lamrim, a man was heard to remark, "Today was really informative! The Dalai Lama told us that Lhuendrub Fortress in Paenpo District was also known as Mayi Cha Palace." We mustn't be like such people.

Still others listen as if to check on the lama, whether his teachings conform with the texts or not. Lama Tsechogling Rinpoche, a tutor to one of the Dalai Lamas, has said, "These days disciples seem to be checking the lama's accuracy." Listening to a teaching like this will never benefit you. It is most important to bring pressure on your mindstream while you listen. When lamas teach the lamrim, their main concern is not the correction of verbal faults; they are teaching mainly as a means to subdue the mental streams of their disciples.

Disciples at a teaching should not listen in the above ways. Anything the lama says should challenge your own mindstream. You should listen primarily to subdue your mindstream. If you do so, the first buds of your realizations develop during that Dharma teaching. This is something that will not happen when a lama visits your room and you give him a bowl of tea—even if he is a lama who gives teachings from a high throne. Even when you study on your own, your studies will not have the same impact on your mind as listening to a teaching.

Whatever Geshe Potowa taught benefited people's minds—even his anecdotes about birds. There was also a great scholar called Geshe Choekyi Oezer; but his instructions were not beneficial for the mind, no matter how profound or extensive they were. Some people mentioned this to Potowa, and Potowa said, "All his teachings are rather eloquent, but there is a difference between the way we teach." Potowa was asked to explain further. "He teaches in order to communicate facts, while all my Dharma targets the internal. That is the difference in our teaching."

Geshe Choekyi Oezer heard of this remark and went to receive teachings from Geshe Potowa. The teachings proved to be most beneficial, even though there was nothing in the teaching he did not already know. Geshe Choekyi later commented, "I understood things I had never understood before." We should be like this.

We should do as Geshe Dromtoenpa said:

> I will explain what is meant by "Mahāyāna gurus." They give people infinite understanding. They teach any practice that will be helpful after the teachings. And they teach anything that will be of direct benefit.

The phrase "after the teachings" has been interpreted in various ways. According to my own precious guru's oral tradition, it means that no matter how much Dharma you teach, it must be as beneficial as possible for the disciple's mindstream after the teaching is over.

This particular set of headings contains the instructions on how to teach and listen to teachings on the path. As I have already told you, a mistake at this point could be disastrous, just as they say that if you get the date wrong on the first day of the lunar month, you'll be wrong until the fifteenth [the full moon]. No matter how profound or extensive are the Dharma teachings you receive, like a god turned into a devil, the Dharma will only bolster your delusions. I think this is all too common. You must take this most seriously.

THE WAY TO TEACH THE DHARMA (31)

This has four parts: (1) thinking about the benefits of teaching the Dharma, (2) being respectful to the Dharma and its teacher, (3) what to think and do while teaching, (4) the difference between the people you should teach and those you should not.

THINKING ABOUT THE BENEFITS OF TEACHING THE DHARMA (32)

It is vital that the person teaching the Dharma does not turn the act of giving Dharma to others into something motivated by delusion. [Vasubandhu] says in *A Treasury of Metaphysics:*

> The act of giving others Dharma should not be a deluded one.
> Teach the pure sūtras, and so forth, properly.

If you hope, "I wonder if I'll get any offerings"; or "I wonder if I will be famous, and so on, because I'll have many disciples"; or "I wonder if I will gain a reputation of being a scholar, and so on"—then your teachings, instead of benefiting, will be most harmful. Your merits will even decline. You must at least teach compassionately for the benefit of your disciples, even disregarding any karmic effects you are supposed to receive from the act of teaching, and hope, "Maybe this will benefit them." As Chuzang Lama Rinpoche Yeshe Gyatso said:

> I overheard him giving teachings and initiations: he does these well.
> But I was deeply saddened when he eagerly took pledges for donations.

In other words, this must not happen: a teaching is most beneficial when the teacher cares nothing for material offerings.

The *Plea for Altruism Sūtra* mentions twenty benefits:

> Maitreya, any act of giving Dharma, made without any desire to receive material offerings or to be respected as a result, has twenty benefits. What are these twenty? They are: one will have a good memory, one will have discernment, one will become intelligent, one will be steadfast, one will have wisdom, one will gain full realization into supramundane wisdom, one's attachment will lessen, one's hostility will lessen, one's benighted

> ignorance will lessen, the demons will not get the better of one, the bhagavān buddhas will pay heed to one, nonhumans will protect one, the gods will lend one their brilliance, foes will not get the better of one, one will not be parted from dear ones, one's words will carry weight, one will gain fearlessness, one's mind will be more at ease, scholars will praise one, one's act of giving the Dharma will become worthy of remembrance.

The first of these, having a good memory, means one will not forget the Dharma. Having discernment refers to one's conviction gained from meditation on ultimate [truth]. Having intelligence refers to conviction gained from the more usual contemplations. Steadfastness means that one cannot be swayed. Having wisdom refers to the mundane wisdoms acquired during the paths of accumulation and preparation; supramundane wisdom means the wisdom acquired during the paths of seeing and meditation.

Six of these twenty benefits are results that correspond to the initial cause. Four of the benefits result from states of separation. Nine benefits are environmental results, and there is one karmic maturation result [see Day 13, pp. 406ff.].

Pabongka Dorje Chang actually spoke on this subject in more detail than is recorded here.

Other benefits are mentioned in the *Sūtra Requested by Ugra,* where we are told that an ordained person acquires more merit through the act of giving even one verse of Dharma than a lay person can receive through immeasurable acts of material generosity.

You should bear these benefits in mind. You should teach, feeling that your own happiness will result from doing so. These are not merely benefits that follow from teaching the Dharma from a high meditation throne. Teachers who take their pupils through their textbooks also receive such benefits. Also when, for example, you recite a Dharma text, you should imagine you are teaching it to a multitude of gods, nāgas, nonhumans, and so forth, who surround you. You will receive the same benefits if you do this. Do the same thing when you memorize a text. You receive these benefits from your conversations with other people if you teach them the key points of modifying one's behavior. But note: whether you are a person's guru or not also makes a difference.

BEING RESPECTFUL TO THE DHARMA AND ITS TEACHER (33)

Ngagwang Dragpa of Dagpo said: "Buddha, our Teacher, set up his own throne when he taught the 'holy mother.'" That is, when the Bhagavān taught the perfection of wisdom sūtras, he made a teaching throne for himself with his own hands—hands that bore the marks and signs of a buddha and were as beautiful as the outstretched bough of a golden tree. When Dharma commands this respect even from buddhas, one should teach it with great reverence indeed.

When the first Buddhist convocation was held, Ānanda and the other speakers were seated on a pile of five hundred saffron shawls provided by other arhats. This was done out of respect for the greatness of the Dharma being taught. (Here, I should add that the three robes of a monk were the dress adopted by the Buddha, yet many monks nowadays use their shawls to wipe things, or as cushions. It is utterly wrong to do this.)

The Dharma must be respected because of its greatness. You must recall our Teacher's good qualities and his kindness, and develop respect.

WHAT TO THINK AND DO WHILE TEACHING (34)

WHAT TO THINK (35)

Ngagwang Dragpa of Dagpo said:

> Abandon niggardliness, singing your own praises, and drowsiness while teaching,
> Discussing others' faults, postponing teachings, and jealousy.
> Have love for your followers, and teach while keeping the five attitudes.
> Think that the virtues of teaching properly are the provisions for your happiness.

That is, don't hold back with the key points of the instruction, for that would be a form of miserliness with the teachings. During your Dharma teaching, you should not sing your own praises by saying, "In the past I even did this, that, and the other." You should not become drowsy while teaching. You should not discuss other people's faults with attachment or hostility as your motive. You should not be lazy and postpone a teaching because you do not want to give it. And you should give up jealousy that arises because you suspect other people are higher than you.

You must have strong love and compassion for your listeners; you must also hold five attitudes. These five are the same as the above six attitudes, but omit the attitude that your diligent practice of the Dharma will cure you. In other words these five attitudes are: they are patients, the Dharma is the medicine, you are the doctor, and so forth. You should then feel that "the virtues that result from teaching properly are the provisions for my happiness."

The reason one of the six was omitted is that it applies more to the disciples than to the teacher.

WHAT TO DO WHILE TEACHING (36)

You should wash yourself beforehand; your appearance should be neat, and your clothes new. Sit on a high teaching throne. Your manner should be cheerful. Teach by means of analogies, quotations, and formal logic so that the meaning will be made clear.

All the same, I am very embarrassed and rather unhappy to be sitting on this high throne when high incarnate lamas are sitting below me. However, I must sit here out of respect for the greatness of the Dharma. In fact, it is wonderful that this custom has not died out in the Central and Tsang provinces. If this custom were no longer followed, and the lama sat on a low throne while teaching, people would think it odd when he tells them, "I received this lineage from several great lamas," as one story tells.

"Your manner should be cheerful" means you ought to smile at your disciples when you teach. Longdoel Lama Rinpoche on the other hand used to scold his disciples and threaten them with the rod in his hand when he taught.

If you confuse the order of the headings, your teachings will be as messy as a crow's nest. If you omit the difficult points and teach only the easy material, your teachings will be like gruel made for an old person. Teachers who do not properly understand the inner meaning of the teaching and have to resort to guesswork are like blind people depending on their canes. This is wrong.

My own precious guru, my supreme refuge, told me the following. When you are about to teach the Dharma you should set your motivation properly while walking from your room to the teaching. Imagine that the root lineage gurus of the particular Dharma you will teach are seated on your throne, one guru on top of another. Prostrate yourself three times to the throne. The gurus merge into each other, one by one; all of them finally merge into your own root guru. As you mount the throne your own guru merges into you. Then as you sit, you should snap your fingers and recite a verse on impermanence, such as,

> Like a phantom, a star, or flickering butterlamps,
> Happiness is an illusion, and lasts like a bubble,
> A dream, a lightning flash, or a day.
> All conditioned phenomena are like this.

You should feel, "This is only for a few minutes; it is only something impermanent." Suppress any inflated opinion you may have of yourself; otherwise, as my lama told me, you might develop pride when you sit on the high throne and feel, "Now I am someone important!"

They say you should recite mantras to defeat the demons, but traditionally we recite the *Heart Sūtra* and a prayer to block [hindrances marked by three] handclaps. Then perform the six preparatory rites using the slow chants and melodies, the practice of Je Drubkang Geleg Gyatso. In fact, when he gave a lamrim teaching, he adopted very slow tempos for these rites. Some people criticized the long duration of the teachings and requested him to shorten the preparatory rites, because it was dragging out the discourse. "What are you saying?" he replied. "The entire success or failure of the main part depends on the preparatory rites." He did not shorten them.

As I have already mentioned, you could develop the first buds of realizations into the lamrim during this teaching. Such should be your hope. Their development depends on your building up your accumulations [of merit and primal wisdom], purifying your obscurations, making petitions in prayer, and so forth. This is the thinking behind the preparatories, so you should not be impatient the whole time—your eyes wandering, your mouth automatically reciting formulas—while you perform them. It is vital to take seriously accumulating merit, self-purification, and petitionings, for they are crucial for developing, in this very assembly, some insight into the meditation topics while you attend the teachings.

After offering a world maṇḍala [see Day 5, pp. 178ff.], touch your copy of the text to your head [out of respect and as a blessing], and again set your motivation. Pray that what you are about to do will benefit your listeners' mindstreams. Drubkang Geleg Gyatso's practice was to make these prayers not only when he put the book to his head, but also when he put on his hat.

Now most of you know that when a teaching is about to be given there has to be a slight change to the verse of refuge. [This verse normally runs:]

> Until enlightenment, I take refuge
> In the Buddha, the Dharma, and the Supreme Assembly.
> With the merit I earn through generosity, and so on,
> May I gain buddhahood for the sake of all beings.

The lama says: "With the merit I earn through the act of giving Dharma ..." while the disciples say: "With the merit I earn through listening to the Dharma..."

Another thing I should mention is the tradition of reviewing the part of the lamrim text to be taught that day. It is supposed to be best if the person giving the teaching does the review every day, or at least every one, two, or three days, whatever is possible, and then the job can be taken over by the chief disciple. If even this much is impractical, one definitely should say "Such is tradition."

You should make the gesture of teaching Dharma while reciting [the verse], "Gods and spirits." As you teach you should imagine that gods like Indra, the nāgas, and other spirits have come to listen. Apparently, the gods cannot endure sitting on the ground. So the guru should imagine giving them permission to remain in the air and listen. People who have shouldered the responsibility of preserving the doctrine should take these traditions to heart.

THE DIFFERENCE BETWEEN THE PEOPLE YOU SHOULD TEACH AND THOSE YOU SHOULD NOT (37)

In general, as it says in the *Transmission of the Vinaya:* "When not requested, do not do." In other words, it is not suitable to teach something you have not been requested to teach. Also, even when requested, you should not immediately agree to teach. You should say, out of modesty, "I do not understand this subject properly, so I cannot teach it," or, "How could I teach this to such great people as yourselves?" You should put to the test people's desire to have the teaching, and only when you are sure they are fit vessels to receive it should you teach. The *King of Single-Pointed Concentration Sūtra* says:

> At first tell them
> These words: "I am not well studied."
> Then, if you be knowledgeable and skilled,
> Tell them: "How could I discuss this
> Before such great ones as yourselves."
> You are to speak like this.

However, you are obliged to teach certain people something that has not been requested if there is some pressing reason to do so. As the same text says:

> If you know of a suitable vessel,
> Teach although not requested.

It is said you should also follow the twenty-six rules laid down in the vinaya: you should not teach to people who are seated while you yourself are still standing; or to people reclining [on the floor] while you are sitting; or teach from a lower seat to people who occupy a higher, [and so on].

Here, we come to the third major heading.

WHAT THINGS THE DISCIPLES AND TEACHER SHOULD DO TOGETHER AT THE END (38)

After offering a thanksgiving maṇḍala, the teacher and the audience should dedicate the root merits they have acquired in the course of the teaching to the causes of furthering the teachings and to their own complete enlightenment, by reciting the *Lamrim Prayer* [from the colophon of Tsongkapa's *Great Stages of the Path;* see p. 696]. Everyone should not rush out together after the teaching period is over. The practice is that people should file out one by one, as if they cannot bear to part with the guru and his teachings.

PART TWO

THE PREPARATORY RITES

DAY 4

Pabongka Dorje Chang began the day's teaching with:

> As the glorious Chandrakīrti said:
> Any time you have freedom and your state is favorable,
> If you do not take their advantage
> And lose your freedom by falling to the lower realms,
> Who will then raise you up again?

In other words, we are now free of the unfortunate rebirth states because we have received the optimum human rebirth; we are free to practice the Dharma. But if we do not take advantage of our situation and achieve our eternal hope, we will only fall again into the abyss of the lower realms, where we will be overpowered by suffering, and not be fortunate enough even to hear the word Dharma. If we descend to such a state, who will even try to lift us out? Thus, while we are still free, we must try to achieve our eternal hope, come what may. We could fulfill this hope by means of the lamrim. We should therefore feel, "I shall achieve buddhahood for the sake of all sentient beings; so I will listen to, and put into practice, this discourse on the stages of the path to enlightenment."

Only after setting your motivation in this way should you listen to this teaching. And what is the teaching you will be listening to? It is Dharma in the tradition of the Supreme Vehicle, Dharma that leads the fortunate to the level of the buddhas.

After this introduction, Pabongka Rinpoche reminded us of the headings we had already covered up to this point in the discourse. He also briefly revised yesterday's material. He then began the day's discourse proper:

THE SEQUENCE IN WHICH THE DISCIPLES ARE TO BE TAUGHT THE ACTUAL INSTRUCTIONS (39)

This is subheaded: (1) the root of the path, devotion to a spiritual guide; and (2) the stages on how to train the mind after you have begun to rely on him.

These headings were drawn from great Tsongkapa's writings. They teach one of the points most crucial to our practice. The words "the root of the path" tell us the following. All of a tree's leaves, fruit, and so on depend on its roots. All insights and realizations—from the difficulty of gaining the optimum human rebirth to the unification of the no-more-learner—similarly derive exclusively from one's devotion to a spiritual guide. The conjunction "after" in "how to train the mind after you have begun to rely on him" tells us which action should come first. It tells us that all realizations up to the unification come from proper devotion to our spiritual guide. Thus it is vital to devote ourselves properly to a spiritual guide at the outset.

The first three major headings we have already covered are also found in the *Great Stages of the Path.* The headings that follow are different; they are drawn instead from the concise discourses.

THE ROOT OF THE PATH: DEVOTION TO A SPIRITUAL GUIDE (40)

This has two main sections: (1) what to do in your meditation sessions, and (2) what to do between meditation sessions.

A most important point is being made by having these two headings, one heading for the meditation sessions and one for the times between sessions. The whole of a person's daily routine can be broken up into full-day periods, and each can be divided into what happens during meditation sessions and what happens outside these sessions. Thus any action of your body, speech, and mind occurs either during the meditation session or between sessions. If you make both of these periods meaningful, the whole day becomes meaningful. Extend this over a period of months, years, and so on, and your whole life becomes meaningful. This is crucial.

WHAT TO DO IN YOUR MEDITATION SESSIONS (41)

This heading has three steps: (1) the preparatory rites, (2) how to pursue the main part of the session, (3) what to do at the end of the session.

It is wrong to pay scant attention to the preparations. If you want to make a good cup of tea, for example, you must take it seriously from when you buy the tea. Similarly, if you want to develop religious experiences during the main part of the meditation session, you must accumulate the causes by diligently carrying out the preparatory rites.

THE PREPARATORY RITES (42)

There are six of these: (1) cleaning your room and arranging the symbols of enlightened body, speech, and mind; (2) obtaining offerings without deceit and arranging them beautifully; (3) adopting the seven-featured sitting position of Vairochana on a comfortable seat, after which you take refuge, develop bodhichitta, and so on, while "in an especially virtuous frame of mind"; (4) petitioning the merit field; (5) offering the seven-limbed prayer and a world maṇḍala—practices that contain all the key points of accumulation and self-purification; (6) further petitions, which follow the oral instructions, made in order to be sure your mental stream is sufficiently imbued [by your meditations].

CLEANING YOUR ROOM AND ARRANGING THE SYMBOLS OF ENLIGHTENED BODY, SPEECH, AND MIND (43)

Suvarṇadvīpa Guru, according to his biography, used to clean out his own room. The source of this practice is a sūtra that says: "The bodhisattvas sit cross-legged in clean surroundings."

The reason why you must clean your room is as follows. If you invite your guru or some official to your home, you would give your room a good sweep, wouldn't you! Similarly, when you invite your guru, the victorious ones, and their children into your room [in the course of your meditations], you should clean it out of respect for them.

There is no benefit at all if you do this with the same motives as the lay cleaning staff of the Potala, Sera, or Drepung, for example, because they do their job for the sake of their own happiness or to impress others. Instead, you should feel you are doing this out of reverence and respect for the merit field, whom you will be inviting into your room as a prelude to pursuing a particular meditation topic that you were taught in the lamrim; you will be doing this meditation in order to achieve buddhahood for the sake of all sentient beings. It is most beneficial to think this way.

One sūtra tells of five benefits: One's mind will become clear, other people's minds will become clear, it pleases the gods, one collects the karma to be beautiful, and one will be reborn in the celestial realms when one leaves this body. My own precious guru told me that the gods who uphold virtue are constantly visiting the human realms and protecting people who practice Dharma properly. But not cleaning your room discourages them, and they cannot offer their protection, because they avoid unclean things, and would be unable to surround you. And cleaning your room pleases your guru, the buddhas, and so on, not just the gods who uphold virtue.

You will collect the karma to be beautiful. This does not merely refer to having physical beauty; it will also cause you to have pure ethics. Pure ethics may not make the body handsome, but it is something most beautiful to the perception of the buddhas and their children. As great Tsongkapa said:

> The discerning are clothed in modesty:
> This is ethics—not fine satins.
> Eloquence adorns their throats—not a necklace.
> Their guru is their crown jewel—not some gem.

We are told we will be born in the celestial realms, but we should take this to mean, above all, the buddhafields.

Ārya Chūḍapanthaka achieved arhatship through cleaning a room. I shall briefly tell you his story.

In the city of Śhrāvastī there was once a Brahman. All his sons had died at birth. One of the old women of the neighborhood told him, "If ever you have another son, call me." The Brahman did have a son and so summoned the old woman. She told him to wash the baby, swaddle it in white, fill its mouth with butter, and give it to a girl to look after. The Brahman was instructed to tell the girl to take the baby to a certain crossroads where four highways met. She was to pay her respects to any holy men or Brahmans who happened by and say to them, "This baby pays homage at the feet of you noble ones." If the baby lived, she should return with it at sunset; if it died, she should abandon it.

The girl was conscientious and spent the day at the great crossroads. First some tīrṭhika priests passed by, and the girl followed the old woman's orders. The priests said, "May this child survive a long while, may its life be long, and may its parents' wishes be fulfilled."

Later, some monks passed by, and they said much the same. The girl then took the child on the road to the Jetavana Grove. She met the Buddha on his alms round. She did as before, and the Buddha said the same as the others, adding: "May its parents have all their Dharmic wishes fulfilled."

Come sunset, the girl saw that the baby still lived, so she took it back home. It was given the name Mahāpanthaka ["Great Road"] because it had been taken to the highway. Mahāpanthaka grew up and became a scholar in all branches of Vedic lore. He taught the esoteric teachings to one hundred Brahman boys.

The Brahman had another son, and so again he summoned the old woman. The same course was taken, but this time they entrusted the baby to a lazy girl who only took him to a small lane. No holy men or Brahmans came by. The Buddha, who constantly looks upon all beings throughout the six periods of day and night, could tell that no one was going to use the lane, so he went there himself. The girl prayed to him, and he responded with the same words as before. Later, she saw the child was still alive and carried him home. He was named Chūḍapanthaka ["Small Road"]. When he grew older, he tried to learn to read. He had to learn words like *siddhaṃ*, but when he could read the syllable *sid* he would forget the *dhaṃ*. By the time he had remastered *dhaṃ*, he had forgotten the *sid*. Chūḍa's teacher told his father, the Brahman, "I must teach many other Brahman boys to read. I cannot teach him."

Chūḍapanthaka was sent to a professional reciter of the Vedas and made to read these. First he had to study the word *oṃ bhū*. By the time he mastered the *oṃ* he had already forgotten the *bhū*. On mastering the *bhū*, he had already forgotten the *oṃ*. It drove his teacher to despair. The teacher told the boy's father, "Your other child Mahāpanthaka understands with only a minimum of instruction, but I cannot teach *him*—I have other boys to teach."

So the name Chūḍapanthaka came to mean "dull," "dullest of the dull," "small," and "smallest of the small."

The parents of the two Panthakas later died. Mahāpanthaka became a Buddhist and a monk. He became a scholar in the three baskets and an arhat. Chūḍapanthaka's inheritance ran out, and so he went to his elder brother. Mahāpanthaka examined his brother to see if he had any potential for the Dharma. Mahā discovered that he did, but that it depended on Mahāpanthaka himself, so he ordained Chūḍa.

Chūḍa then spent the next three months trying to learn this verse:

> Do not let your body, speech, or mind sin.
> Be free of the desire that afflicts all the worldly.
> Have remembrance, be vigilant:
> Avoid anything harmful, any suffering.

The local cowherds overheard the verse, and even they learned it—but Chūḍa failed.

Ārya Mahāpanthaka had at one time thought to himself, "How can I tame Chūḍa? Shall I praise him or insult him?" He saw that insulting him would tame Chūḍa, so he upbraided Chūḍa, grabbed him by the collar, and drove him out of the Jetavana Grove.

Mahā said: "You are dull, the dullest of the dull—why did I ever ordain you? Stay here."

Chūḍa thought to himself, "Now I am no longer even an ascetic. I am not even a Brahman," and he wept.

The Buddha, our Teacher, went to him, urged by great compassion. "Panthaka, why are you crying?" asked Buddha.

"My abbot has insulted me."

The Buddha said:

> Some things are praised by churls;
> Some things are disparaged by scholars.
> Better to be disparaged by a scholar
> Than to be praised by a churl.

"My son, your abbot did not endure many hardships for three countless eons to complete the six perfections. He did not compose your verse for you—I did. Cannot the Tathāgata teach you to read?"

"O monk," said Chūḍapanthaka, "I am the dullest of the dull, the very smallest of the small. How could I ever learn to read?"

Buddha, our Teacher, replied:

> The churl who knows he's a churl
> Is truly a scholar.
> The churl who's proud of his scholarship
> Is the most churlish of all.

The Buddha gave Panthaka these words to memorize: "Abandon dirt, abandon stains." But again, this proved too much for Chūḍapanthaka. The Bhagavān Buddha then thought, "I shall purify him of his karma."

"Panthaka, can you polish the sandals of the monks?" asked Buddha.

Chūḍa replied, "Yes, O monk, I can."

"Then humbly polish the monks' sandals and shoes," said the Buddha. "And monks, you must let him do this so that he can purify his karma. Afterward, recite these words and afterward teach him." They did according to his instructions.

Then, when Chūḍa had learned this second recitation, the Buddha told him, "You no longer have to polish their sandals. Do the second recitation while you sweep out the temple."

Now that Chūḍa had been given the job of sweeping the temple, he developed perseverance while he swept. But when he had finished sweeping the right side of the temple, the left side had become filthy, and by the time he had finished sweeping the left side, the right was filthy again. This happened through the power of the Buddha. All the same, Panthaka persisted, and his karma and obscurations were purified. Then the thought came to him, "When the Teacher said, 'Abandon dirt, abandon stains,' did he mean internal or external dirt?" Then into his mind came three verses he had never heard before:

> Here "dirt" is attachment, not dirt.
> "Dirt" is a name for attachment, not dirt.
> Scholars reject this kind of dirt.
> They scrupulously follow the Sugata's teachings.
>
> Here "dirt" is hostility, not dirt.
> "Dirt" is a name for hostility, not dirt.
> Scholars reject this kind of dirt.
> They scrupulously follow the Sugata's teachings.
>
> Here "dirt" is benighted ignorance, not dirt...

And so on. He tried to fathom these verses, and through his meditations he achieved arhatship.

By the way, this is how the verses appear in the sūtra. Texts on the preparatory rites, and the oral tradition of the gurus, give this version of the verses:

CHŪḌA SWEEPING

"Dirt" is not the dirt on the ground:
It is the dirt of attachment.

This is easier to understand in terms of practice. But still, it is better to revert to the original version.

The Buddha then announced Panthaka's good qualities to everyone by saying, "Ānanda, go tell Panthaka, 'You are to teach the nuns Dharma.' Also, tell the nuns, 'Your teacher is now Panthaka.'" They did according to his instructions.

Panthaka understood that the Buddha was announcing his own good qualities, so he promised to do as ordered.

The nuns were stunned by the news and said, "See how we women are being made fun of! He couldn't even learn a single verse in three months. How could he teach us upholders of the three baskets?"

Later some of them said, "We'll do something so that we will not have to put up with such ignoramuses." Twelve of the nuns got together. Some of them built an extremely tall teaching throne—but one without any stairs. Others went to the great city of Śhrāvastī and announced to its inhabitants, "Tomorrow our teacher is visiting us. He is one of the greatest of the śhrāvakas. People who have heard the Dharma but are yet to see the truth [that is, gain the path of seeing] must come and listen to him, or they will have to wander a long while in saṃsāra."

Hundreds of thousands of people turned up for the teaching. Some came to be entertained, others came in hope of collecting root virtues. That day Panthaka went out to beg for alms. Then he led the rest of the monks, after they had risen from their meditative absorption, to the monsoon retreat house of the nuns where he was to teach the Dharma. As he approached the throne, he saw it was much too high. He thought, "Either they have much faith in me or they are putting me to the test." He entered meditative absorption for a short while and came to know it was to test him. He stretched out his arm as an elephant puts out its trunk and pushed the throne down. Some people saw this happen; others did not. He sat on the throne and re-entered meditative absorption. Panthaka disappeared from the seat, rose into the sky, and produced the four types of miraculous emanations in each of the four cardinal points of the compass. These merged back into him, and now his throne was supported by lions.

"Sisters," he began, "I took three months to learn a single verse. I shall now, for the next seven days and nights, explain its meaning. The Bhagavān said, 'Do not let your body, speech, or mind sin.' He was teaching us to abandon the ten nonvirtues. When he said, 'All the worldly,' he was referring to the five aggregates. The word 'afflicts' refers to the attachment, hostility, and benighted ignorance that afflicts these aggregates..."

He taught only the meaning of the first half of this verse in detail, yet twelve thousand beings still came to see [ultimate] truth. Others manifested one of the four types of results [by becoming a stream-enterer, once-returner, never-returner, or arhat]. Some people became śhrāvakas, others pratyekabuddhas, and still others entered the Mahāyāna; each of these people developed the wish to gain their particular type of enlightenment [as a Hīnayāna or Mahāyāna arhat]. Most of the audience developed faith in the Three Jewels.

When Panthaka later returned to the Jetavana Grove, Buddha the Teacher declared, "Among my śhrāvakas, Panthaka is the most skilled at converting people."

Thus it is wrong to feel, "Meditation is of most value; actions like sweeping are of little worth." Even the householder Anāthapiṇḍika [the man who donated the Jetavana Grove to the Saṅgha] used to turn up every day to sweep out the grove. One day he was too busy to come, and as there was no one else to sweep the place, the Buddha himself—as the sūtras relate—swept the grove with his own golden bough-like hands.

My own precious guru used to tell me that the various reincarnations of the omniscient Dalai Lama used to practice the preparatory rites. They used to wear down their brooms from so much sweeping that there were no bristles left—the brooms looked like donkey tails. Many of these have been preserved with yellow sashes tied to the handles [to show they were once a Dalai Lama's property]. This is a very important biographical detail. So beginners like ourselves should take this sort of thing seriously.

It is best to sweep your room before each meditation session, whether the room needs it or not. At the very least, you should sweep your room every day. In any case, your motive should be the one I outlined above. You should imagine you are sweeping out the filth obscuring other beings' and your own mindstreams. Imagine that—among perfecting, ripening, and purifying—your broom strokes are causes for purifying the buddhafield. You should recite something while you sweep, just as Chūḍapanthaka did in the story. You could say, "Abandon dirt, abandon stains," or even better:

> Here "dirt" is attachment, not dirt.
> "Dirt" is a name for attachment, not dirt.
> Scholars reject this kind of dirt.
> They scrupulously follow the Sugata's teachings.

Repeat the verse, substituting "hostility" and "benighted ignorance" for "attachment." When you are emphasizing the practices related to your devotion to a spiritual guide, the verse becomes: "Here 'dirt' is lack of faith, not dirt..." In fact you can make the symbolic dirt represent anything—even dualistic grasping. You should be able to understand how to modify the recitation to conform with any particular practice you are concentrating on at the time.

If you are too old or sick to do the sweeping yourself, get one of your pupils to do it; meanwhile, you should recite the verses and do the visualizations.

The depth of your motivation will also make a huge difference in the benefit you gain with each stroke of the broom.

You should put four stones outside your room and imagine they are the four mahārājas.[15] Or you could visualize one stone to be all four mahārājas. You could even visualize the one stone to be Vaiśhravaṇa alone. They say there is much point in doing these visualizations, because you will not receive any hindrance and your ethics will be pure. It might not be convenient to put stones outside your room if you live in a large monastery, and so on. It is then quite all right to visualize the outer walls of the building as the mahārājas; this particular oral tradition stems from Jamgoen Rinpoche.

Let us now turn to the arrangement of the symbols of the enlightened body, speech, and mind. The guru, meditation deities, etc., must follow the same order or precedence as in the merit-field visualization [see Day 5]. However, you can depart a little from this order if the objects would otherwise not fit on the altar. Some people think it more effective to pray to the Dharma protectors, spirit kings, spirits of power, and the like; they give them a more prominent position than their Buddha statue. I have seen this many times. It is a sign that these people have not taken proper refuge: the act of taking refuge is not within their mindstreams. Some people give pride of place to any statue made of gold, silver, or bronze; they put the clay figures at the end of the row. This is a sign they only regard these figures as pieces of property. It is also not right to arrange your religious paintings according to their age. Some people even hang their paintings on the curtains they use as doors. How could that be right! There are people who sleep with their feet pointing at the figures of buddhas and bodhisattvas. This is being most disrespectful—a clear sign they have not taken refuge at all. Others treat old and shabby statues, paintings, and so forth, like dirt and leave them in some wayside shrine. This is said to be like taking your merits out of your house. You must regard these statues and the like as if they really were that particular buddha or bodhisattva.

You might not have many of these symbols of enlightened body, speech, and mind, but to symbolize the enlightened body, you definitely must have a figure of our Teacher, the Buddha, so as to be reminded of him, as well as a figure of Je Rinpoche to remind you of your guru. A short sūtra or a copy of the lamrim could serve as the symbol for enlightened speech. A *tsatsa* [a small clay cone in the form of a stūpa] will do—at a pinch—to symbolize the enlightened mind. If you have a vajra and bell, they should stand as the symbol for the enlightened mind. Some people seem to regard vajras and bells as only symbolic implements wielded by deities; in fact these represent the enlightened mind. It is a grave misdeed to undervalue your vajra and bell as not being symbols of the enlightened mind.

After the first day, you don't have to set up your altar every day thereafter, but you must regard the figures on your altar as real when you look at them in order to fulfill this heading.

It is wrong to feel, "I already know the figures in my room—what is there to look at?" Every time you see them in the course of the day, you are instilled with exceptionally strong instincts. We are told it is sixteen times more beneficial to look at a representation of a buddha than to look at the real thing. As it says in the *White Lotus Sūtra:*

> If one looks at the Sugata's form depicted on a wall
> [Even] while in an angry frame of mind,
> One will eventually come to see ten million buddhas.

Actually the sūtra says "If one makes offering [to the Sugata's form]..."; the version I quoted is according to the oral tradition. If we are taught that it is so beneficial to look at a buddha figure when angry, think of the benefit we get while looking at them with faith! Ārya Shāriputra was one of the two major disciples of the Buddha and was constantly at his side. This is said to be the result of an action he did in a past life: he looked at a drawing of a buddha and was filled with a sense of wonder.

Ārya Shāriputra was a messenger in that past life. One night at dusk he saw a temple and went inside to stay. He lit a very bright oil lamp and started to repair his boots. When it was time for him to go to sleep, he saw the mural of a tathāgata on the wall opposite him, and thought to himself, "This is such an amazing being! Why not meet him in person!" He made silent prayers, and they say he became a major disciple of Buddha as a result.

We now see buddhas made of clay, brass, and so on, but when we gain the single-pointed concentration called "the stream of Dharma," we will see supreme nirmāṇakāyas, [emanation bodies]. And when we reach the first [of the ten] bodhisattva levels, we will meet the saṃbhogakāyas [enjoyment bodies] in person. This is why it is so important to hold the attitude that Buddha statues are real buddhas.

OBTAINING OFFERINGS WITHOUT DECEIT AND ARRANGING THEM BEAUTIFULLY (44)

Here, "without deceit" refers to an absence of two things: deceit with respect to the object being offered, and deceitful motives.

"Deceit with respect to the object being offered" means that some faulty action was committed while one obtained the thing to be offered. That is, either an ordained person obtained the thing by means of the five wrong livelihoods, or a lay person obtained it through taking life, dealing out short measures, shortchanging, or some other evil means.

It is better not to offer [at all] than to offer such things. The Sanskrit for "offering" is *pūjā,* which has the connotation of "to please." So the offering you make must be pleasing to the victorious ones and their children. How could they be pleased if you offered these sorts of things? All the same, if you have already obtained offerings in these above ways, it is good to offer them as a means to purify the sin that naturally followed the act of acquiring these goods.

The five wrong livelihoods are: flattery, hinting, giving in order to receive, exerting pressure on others, and being on one's best behavior.

"Flattery" is as follows. You compliment your benefactor, for example, in the hope that you will get something in return. If they actually give you something, the act of flattery has become a wrong livelihood. However, if you compliment someone sincerely, and without the above motive, it is not a wrong livelihood, even if they give you something.

"Hinting" is telling your benefactor things like, "I have tea and butter at the moment but not a great deal of grain," in the hope of receiving a gift. Or you might say, "That barley flour you gave me last year was a big help." In other words, you are hinting that you want grain or barley flour. However, if you say these things in all honesty without any motive of receiving a gift, it is not "hinting."

"Giving in order to receive" is giving some trifle in order to receive something better. For example, you might take a ceremonial scarf or a brick of tea to your benefactor, or anyone else for that matter, so that they will reward you or make an offering to your monastery on your behalf. In other words you have gone to the expense of the gift as a means of getting something better in return. We call this "baiting the hook" nowadays and commit this wrong livelihood intentionally. But if you make a present to your benefactor sincerely and without this motive, it is not a wrong livelihood—even if they reward you.

"Exerting pressure on others" means pestering someone for something they do not want to give you, or getting someone to give you something they were going to give someone else. Or you could indirectly ask for a gift by saying, "My benefactor so-and-so gave me some tea and butter, which was a big help." But if you say these things out of sincerity, without any motive of receiving gifts as a result, it is not the wrong livelihood of "exerting pressure."

"Being on one's best behavior" means doing whatever you like in the privacy of your own room but acting like a good monk who observes all the rules in front of your benefactors in the hope they will give you something because of your disciplined behavior. But my own precious lama, my refuge and protector, told me that if you do not have these motives, and instead feel, "It wouldn't be right to upset this lay person," and behave like a good monk—in contrast to the way you behave at home—you are not "being on your best behavior."

Another point: should ordained people, such as ourselves, break the restrictions pertaining to the three types of vows we have taken and obtain materials through selling things, there will be heavier consequences than benefit if we use these materials in an offering.

"Deceitful motives" means making offerings out of a desire for fame or to impress others. In other words, one's actions are tainted with bad motives. As Drogoen Rinpoche says:

> Even the offerings you make to the Three Jewels
> Are done only to be seen by others.

In other words, every offering we make is done out of a desire for fame, self-advancement, and so on. We slip back into the eight worldly concerns [see Day 10, p. 296]. Those who are a bit better make offerings with the motive of simply wanting a long life or merely to be free of illness. Even when we are giving offerings to the Saṅgha out of our deep respect, we mainly wish that people will not say we did it in the hope of receiving merit.

If someone were expected in your house today, you would sweep it out more conscientiously and put out more offerings on your altar than usual. You would also offer a butterlamp and fill the house with sweet-smelling incense. Investigate carefully your motivation and for whose benefit this respect is being paid. It is very difficult to tell whether the offering will benefit or harm you. Geshe Baen Gung-gyael was told one day that a benefactor was coming to see him. Geshe Baen set up the best offering to the Three Jewels he could manage. He sat down on his meditation mat and examined his motives. He saw that he had made the offering to impress his benefactor. He sprang off his mat and threw ash all over the offering, saying, "O monk! Sit down and don't try to fool yourself!" He left his offerings covered with piles of ash.

Padampa Sangyae heard about this while at Langkor in Upper Dingri and said in praise that, of all the offerings made in Tibet, Baen Gung-gyael's was the noblest. People asked Padampa Sangyae why this was so. Padampa replied that the geshe had managed to stuff ash into the mouth of the eight worldly concerns. Padampa was extremely happy and was, of course, not praising the offering Geshe Baen had originally set up. He was praising the act of covering it with dust!

So it is most important to make an offering in conjunction with bodhichitta. Let alone being motivatated by the eight worldly concerns of this life, do not even be motivated for the sake of a high rebirth, of definite excellence [of liberation], and so on.

We are told to "arrange them beautifully." Some people might claim, "I don't want to impress people," and arrange the composition of their offerings any old way. You should not do this: you must take pains over the composition of the arrangement and make it as beautiful as possible. It is said that making a beautiful arrangement on your altar will act as a cause for the marks and signs of a buddha when you are enlightened.

You must put the offerings out yourself, with your own hands; if you make your pupils or servants arrange the offerings you will not receive any of the merits. When Atiśha was extremely ill, he would offer water bowls even though his legs were unsteady. People would tell him, "O Atiśha, that's too much for you. We will put them out for you."

Atiśha's reply was, "So when I eat shouldn't you be telling me, 'O Atiśha, that's too difficult,' and eat my portion of food for me?"

When the great Dharmarājas of ancient India practiced great acts of generosity, they would not delegate some minister or other official to distribute the gifts. Instead, the rāja would erect a pavilion and then sit inside it surrounded by piles of jewels for distribution, which he himself would personally hand out. This was called the "extraordinary practice of generosity." So it is most important that we put out an offering with our own hands.

You should also offer the first portion of your food—but only the best portions; you should not offer the withered parts of your vegetables or, if you are rich, the moldy parts of your *tue* [a Tibetan sweet].

We tend to save the best butter and barley flour for ourselves and set aside the worst parts, saying, "That's only for the offerings!" Isn't that like sweeping away our merits? All the same, butterlamps are an offering of light, not of melted butter, so they say it is quite all right to offer slightly rancid butter.

There is no need to feel intimidated by all this if you are a poor renunciate, thinking "I have no money, so I do not have the means to put toward offerings." If your faith is strong enough, then you do not want for things to offer. As great Atiśha said:

> The water in Tibet has eight properties, and so one need only offer water bowls in Tibet. If there were any of these wildflowers in India, we would pay gold for them.

So you may have nothing else to offer, but you still can have great force behind your accumulation of merit if you offer only water bowls.

Now I shall discuss these eight properties of our water. I will follow my own precious guru's explanation of the [karmic] benefits you gain from each of these eight properties. In Chim Jampaelyang's *Commentary to Vasubandhu's "Treasury of Metaphysics"* we are told these eight are:

Cool, delicious, light, and soft,
Clear, odorless, easy on the throat,
And kind to the stomach is the water
With the eight properties.

The eight corresponding [karmic] benefits are said to be the following. Your ethics will be pure because the water you offer is cool. Because it is also delicious, you will come to enjoy most delicious food. The lightness of the water means your mind and body will become fit [and pliable]. The water's softness results in a gentle mindstream. A clear mind results from the water's clearness; its odorlessness will purify you of [karmic] obscurations. And because the water does not hurt the stomach, your body will be free of illness. Its being easy on the throat means you will come to have pleasant speech.

When Drubkang Geleg Gyatso first moved into a retreat house belonging to Sera Je College, he had very few belongings and provisions. He did not even have a set of bowls for his water offering. In order to make this offering, he had to give his own eating bowl a good wash and then pour his water offering into it. If he wanted to drink tea, he would first ask the precious Three Jewels for leave to borrow the bowl. He would then use it, and when he had finished his tea, he would rewash the bowl and make another water offering.

You can mentally offer anything at all. It could be summer flowers, fruit, clear and cool water, and so forth. My own precious guru told me, "You could also consecrate the offerings by reciting the dhāraṇī for the Cloud of Offerings [see Day 5, p. 155], offer them, and then finally dedicate the virtue and so on. Refer to Tridagpo Tsepel's biography on the practice." In any case, your faith is the main factor—not the things you offer.

Now some may think, therefore, it is enough to offer water, flowers, and such, which may lead them to wonder whether they could reserve the really valuable things for their own use. Such thoughts could make you take rebirth as a hungry ghost. You should offer the best of whatever you have.

Some ordinary monks who have given up all worldly work might feel, "It is fitting that I don't have the makings for material offerings. We are told that the ordained should concentrate on offering what they have accomplished through their [meditation] practices. It is enough if I make only this sort of offering." But if this thought leads you never to make any material offerings at all, in rebirth after rebirth you will not have even small things to make offerings with!

If all you have for offerings are finger-sized ritual cakes and half a stick of incense, do not underestimate their worth: you will increase your merits if you offer them. Later this merit will bring you materials to make much grander offerings. This is illustrated by Geshe Puchungwa's life story. As Geshe Puchungwa himself said:

> At first I only burned gentian for incense; I offered so much, it made my eyes water. Later I had sweet-smelling incense made out of four ingredients. These days, I offer the fragrance of myrobalan, duraka, and so on.

In fact he once offered twenty-two gold coins' worth of incense. Still, some might claim, "Geshe Puchungwa was a realized being who devoted himself entirely to meditation. Do not hope for enlightenment from such external actions." Such a claim shows they have very little acquaintance with the Dharma. You should think about the fact that bodhisattvas who have reached one of the ten levels make offerings to the victorious ones for eons, by means of hundreds of thousands of emanated bodies, each with hundreds or even thousands of arms. Surely you with your single body ought to strive to make as many offerings as you can.

Now, a little on the tradition of making offerings. Let us take offering water bowls as our example. You should give the bowls a good wipe. You must lay the bowls out in a straight line. They should not be too far apart, for that may result in your becoming separated from your guru. If they touch each other, you may become dull-witted. And if you put the bowls down noisily, you may become mad, and so on. Avoid doing these sorts of things. If you lay out the bowls while they are still empty, your merits will decline. Instead you should hold the stack of bowls in your hand and pour a little water into the top bowl. Consecrate this with the three syllables *oṃ, āḥ, hūṃ.* Pour most of the water from this bowl into the next, leaving a little behind. Put the first bowl on the altar and continue this process. In that way, you will not be putting empty bowls on your altar. When you fill the bowls on the altar, do not do disrespectful things like holding the water jug in only one hand. You must act as if you were pouring tea for a mahārāja.

"Like barley" means this: a barley grain is thick in the middle and thin at both ends; this is how you should pour the water [that is, a little at first, then a lot, and then taper off]. If you spill water over the rim of the bowls, it may result in your ethics becoming loose, but if the bowls are insufficiently filled, your standard of living might decline. The water surface should be below the level of the rim of the bowls by about the thickness of a grain of barley.

Butterlamps are [an offering of] light, so they should give off much light. It is said they should burn for as long as possible, because it is an auspicious gesture for having a long life. Extrapolate these ways of offering for other offerings, like flowers.

The sūtras say that each offering you make has ten advantages.

ADOPTING THE EIGHT-FEATURED SITTING POSTURE—OR WHATEVER POSTURE IS CONVENIENT FOR YOU—ON A COMFORTABLE SEAT, AND THEN TAKING REFUGE, DEVELOPING BODHICHITTA, AND SO ON, IN AN ESPECIALLY VIRTUOUS FRAME OF MIND, MAKING SURE THAT THESE PRACTICES PROPERLY SUFFUSE YOUR MINDSTREAM (45)

The rear of your meditation cushion should be slightly raised and the front slightly lower. This has a profound tantric significance; it will also prevent pain in your buttocks and other problems while you sit in meditation for long periods.

You should draw a clockwise swastika under the mat in white chalk powder. The swastika stands for the vajra cross and reminds you of that part of Buddha's life story when he sat on the vajra throne [at Bodhgaya]. It also symbolizes that your practice will become firm. However, it is not proper to sit on a real vajra cross as this is one of the symbolic implements held by tutelary deities. Place dūrva grass [a long grass with many segments] and kuśha grass at the front tip of the swastika. Again the source of this practice is the Buddha's life story; the Buddha attained enlightenment on a seat of grass. The dūrva grass increases your lifespan. It is said: "Dūrva increases the life-span..." That is, your life is lengthened by sitting on it. Also we are told: "Kuśha is clean and virtuous." In other words, kuśha is a substance that eliminates pollution and uncleanliness. When Indian Brahmans received a caste pollution, they would spend a night in a patch of kuśha grass. Spread kuśha under your cushion to eliminate such things.

The "eight-featured sitting posture" mentioned in the above heading refers to the seven-featured Vairochana posture; the extra feature is the act of counting your breath. Gyaelwa Ensapa said:

> The legs, the hands, and spine make three,
> Brought to four by teeth, lips, and tongue.
> The head, eyes, shoulders, and breath are four.
> These are the eight practices of Vairochana.

The legs are in the vajra [or "full-lotus"] position. It is also permissible to sit in a half lotus or merely cross-legged in the "bodhisattva posture." However, the vajra position is mandatory for the tantric completion-stage meditations.

Place your two hands in the gesture of meditative absorption. The right hand lies in the left. The tips of the two thumbs touch at about navel level. Your [lower] back should be straight, with the vertebrae as straight as a stack of coins. We are told that the energy-wind channels are straightened when the body is straight, straightening the energy winds flowing through them, making the mind more amenable.

The teeth and lips should not be too clenched or too loose, so it is best to leave them in their natural position. Place the tip of your tongue on your palate, so that your mouth does not dry out. Also, when you enter deep meditative absorption, it will prevent your saliva from running out of your mouth, and so on.

Your head should be bent slightly forward, exerting a slight pressure on your adam's apple. We are told "the eyes should be focused on the tip of one's nose," but you really need only focus your eyes so that you can see both sides of your nose. The point of doing this is that it makes it easier for you to cut short mental dullness or excitement [see Day 21, pp. 604ff.] Some people shut their eyes tight when they visualize. This is incorrect. Other sects advise us to direct the eyes upward, and so on, in imitation of people who have the best sense faculties, whose perception is the perception of dharmakāya [truth body]. However, this is foreign to our own tradition.

The shoulders should be level, not one higher than the other.

These are the seven features of Vairochana's posture. They have the profoundest significance for the completion stage, but this is not the place to discuss it. This sitting posture is of crucial importance; as Marpa of Lhodrag tells us: "The sum of all Tibetan meditations is no match for the way I, Marpa the translator, sit." The posture is said to be attributed to

Vairochana Buddha because he is the purified aspect of the form aggregate in the shape of a deity.

The eighth feature is the act of counting your breath. When the primary mind is nonvirtuous, its accompanying secondary mental factors are nonvirtuous as well. In this situation, it is difficult to summon up an extremely virtuous frame of mind. For example, you may mechanically go through the motions of developing bodhichitta while you are extremely angry and recite, "For the sake of all sentient beings, who were my mothers…," but you will not summon up a virtuous mental direction while the primary mind is unvirtuous and its accompanying mental factors have become unvirtuous. You should instead change your mental state into a neutral one. Then it will be easier to change to a virtuous mental state. For example, suppose a piece of cotton is white but with black stains. Such a cloth is difficult to dye another color. But if you give the cotton material a good wash in water, it then becomes completely white and is much easier to dye red, yellow, or whatever color you like.

The so-called neutral state of mind is neither virtuous nor nonvirtuous. It is like the white piece of cotton without the stains. You might then wonder, "What is the technique of counting the breath to change one's mental state into a neutral one?" You direct your mind inward and examine your motivation. If you find you are under the power of attachment, hostility, and so forth, you should breathe in and out in a more relaxed fashion. Do not let your breath pass noisily through your nostrils. It should be neither too strong nor too uneven. As you breathe out, think, "I am breathing out." Then as you breathe in, think, "I am breathing in." Then think, "That is the first time." Then do this a second time. Continue to number seven, eleven, fifteen, twenty-one, or whatever, but do not use your rosary to keep count. Do not get distracted from your counting. Ordinary beings cannot retain two things in the mind at once, and this is why the attachment and so on will subside, and the mind will change into a neutral state.

They say you should do the following visualization. When you breathe out, imagine that your delusions take the form of black rays situated within your outgoing breath. When you breathe in, imagine the blessings of the victorious ones and their children within the incoming breath, this time in the form of white rays of light. However, this is not mandatory; it is merely an enhancement.

Once the mind has become neutral, it is easier to summon up a virtuous mental state. My own precious lama gave me this illustration. Suppose it is the dead of winter and there is only one cushion on the floor—yours—but someone is already sitting on it. If you just say, "Get up!" he will refuse no matter how forcefully you order him, so instead, go off a little distance and say, "What a great to-do is going on over there!" Pretend you are going off to have a look. He will get up to have a look himself. You can now sit down on your cushion if you are fast enough! Similarly, it is difficult to stop having attachment while in a nonvirtuous mental state, no matter how hard you try. If you fix your mind on the motions of your breath, it redirects the mind and pacifies delusion. It is then easier to summon up a virtuous mental state. But bear in mind that if it is easy to summon up a virtuous mental state, and your mind and its accompanying mental factors happen not to be nonvirtuous, it won't be absolutely necessary to count your breath. That is the point of saying there are either seven or eight features.

You may not have to count your breath, but you must nevertheless summon up a virtuous mental state at the beginning of your meditation session. When you commence any virtuous practice, it is vital to set your motivation correctly at the start. Great Tsongkapa wrote his *Questions on the Whitest Altruism of All,* in which he indicates a number of things to the meditation masters of Tibet. One of the questions was: "What is as important at the start of a meditation as the words 'In Sanskrit' [are at the beginning of a text]?"[16] The Paṇchen Lama Lozang Choekyi Gyaeltsaen answered this and the other questions in his text the *Melodious Laughter of Lozang—Answers to "Questions on the Whitest Altruism of All."* He said:

> Before any meditation [one should]
> Examine one's mental stream properly, just as the words
> "In Sanskrit" should appear at the start of a text.
> This is what you meant, O peerless guru.

In other words, it is crucial to set your motivation at the beginning of any meditation. In a sūtra we find:

> The condition for all Dharma
> Lies at root in your aspiration.

Āchārya Nāgārjuna said:

> Nonvirtue is produced from
> Attachment, hostility, and ignorance.
> Virtue is produced from
> An absence of attachment, hostility, and benighted ignorance.

Great Atiśha said:

> If the root is poisonous, the branches and leaves will also be poisonous. If the root is medicinal, the branches and leaves are also medicinal. Similarly, if the root is attachment, hostility, or benighted ignorance, whatever one does will be nonvirtuous.

In other words, if you are motivated by delusion, any study, contemplation, or meditation you do will only ripen into a most undesirable karmic result. But if you are motivated by noble thoughts, even if you commit some nonvirtuous action such as killing, it will be a great impetus to the completion of your accumulation [of merit and primal wisdom].

While our Teacher, the Buddha, was still on the learner's path, in one of his rebirths he was a brave ship's captain called Mahāsattva. He went to sea with five hundred traders on an expedition to find jewels. There was also a villain named Kālaśhakti on board, and on the way back he planned to kill the five hundred traders. The captain, because of his great compassion, killed the black-hearted one, not only to immediately save the lives of the traders, but also to save Kālaśhakti from the lower realms in the end. This act is said to have accumulated [the merit] of over forty thousand great eons. Though it is impossible for the result of an act of killing to be the completion of one's merit collection, his strong great compassion gave great impetus to his accumulation.

Motivation determines everything: virtue, nonvirtue, the ripening of karma into either desirable or undesirable effects, the relative strength of one's karma, and so on. Once, in India, there were a Brahman and a beggar of the Kṣhatriya [royal or military] caste. The Brahman went out to beg at the wrong time of day; no one gave him anything because the Saṅgha would not give food to others until they themselves had eaten. The Kṣhatriya was more skillful in his timing: he went to beg when the leftovers were about to be thrown away. As a result he received a huge amount of food.

"Didn't you get anything at all?" he asked the Brahman.

The Brahman lost his temper and said, "If I had the chance, I would cut off the heads of all of Śhākyamuni's holy men and leave them to rot on the ground."

The Kṣhatriya had developed faith [in the Saṅgha] because he had received so much food. "If I had the means," he said, "I would like to give Buddha and his Saṅgha food that tastes a hundred different ways every day."

They had been walking while they talked to each other, and by now they had reached the city of Śhrāvastī. They took a nap in front of a tree. A runaway cart passed by them, and its wheels cut off the Brahman's head.

About the same time, a merchant died in Śhrāvastī. He had had no son, and all the free men of Śhrāvastī met to decide who had the greatest merits, for that person would be made the merchant's heir. They found the Kṣhatriya asleep; he was always in the tree's shadow even though the other trees' shadows had since moved. They made him head of the merchants. The Kṣhatriya was as good as his word and made donations to Buddha and the Saṅgha. He listened to the Dharma and came to see the truth. As it says in that particular sūtra:

> The mind takes precedence over other things.
> The mind works quickly; it is paramount.
> However poisoned is the mind,
> Anything one says or does will follow suit,
> And will beget suffering—
> Like the head severed by the wheel.
> However pure is the mind,
> Anything one says or does will follow suit,
> And will beget happiness—
> Like he followed by the shadow.

In other words, such tangible karmic results follow from one's motivation—be it good or evil.

Still, you should not have a good motivation only at the start of some virtuous practice; it is crucial to have good motives all the time.

These days we usually ask people about their health, saying "Are you well?" but Atiśha used to ask, "Have you a kind heart?" As Tsongkapa said:

> Black or white karma
> Comes from good or evil motives.

If the motive is good,
So too will be the path and its level.
If the motive is bad
Then low will be the path and its level.
Everything depends on one's motives.

The difference in our motivation makes an enormous difference to the sort of virtuous karmic results we will receive, and to the measure of strength of these results. Suppose four people are reciting together the Praise of the Twenty-One Tārās. One has bodhichitta as a motive. Another is motivated by renunciation. The third yearns for a better rebirth. The last only aspires to the concerns of this life: long life, good health, and so on. Although all four recite the same amount of words, there is a great difference in the sort of karmic results they will obtain. The first person's recitation was done in conjunction with the development of bodhichitta; the recitation will therefore act as cause for complete enlightenment. It is also a deed of a child of the victorious ones, and is Mahāyāna Dharma. This does not apply to the other three.

The second person's recitation was done in conjunction with renunciation. It will therefore act as cause for liberation and will be an antidote against saṃsāra. It is Dharma from the medium scope. The remaining two people's recitations will not even contribute to their liberation: the recitations would come only under the truth of the origin of sufferings.

Though the third's recitation contributes to neither omniscience nor liberation, it is a means to prevent him from being reborn in the lower realms. It is Dharma from the small scope.

The fourth's recitation belonged only to this life and so was not even Dharma. And it would even be difficult for it to have any of the the hoped-for effect on his life. As Atiśha said:

> Ask me what the results are of actions done desirous of the happiness, fame, and respect of this life and I will tell you: they are only the results of this life. Ask me what will happen in your next lives and I will tell you: you will be a hell being, a hungry ghost, or an animal.

So, when even those of us of the great monasteries attend ceremonies or debating practice, if we do these in conjunction with a bodhichitta motivation, then even our very footsteps will be deeds of a child of the victorious ones, worth more than a hundred thousand gold coins. But if we make any donation of alms, tea, soup, or whatever in order to ingratiate ourselves with the monastic hierarchy, the donation will only fit Atiśha's description.

The meditator's motivation also determines whether the meditations will have any point. Atiśha said:

> [A practitioner might say that] his meditation is on his precious guru. But if you meditate out of a desire to receive tea, bolts of silk, and so on, however much you may meditate, your meditations are sinful. If you meditate with even the slightest thought of putting an end to the ocean of rebirth, or sowing the seed of highest liberation, the merit you receive overflows the bounds of space itself.

Thus, in your study, contemplation, and meditation, your practice of sādhanas, your generosity with offerings, praise, and gifts, and so on, if you do not adopt the right motives to practice virtue—be it large or small—the entire practice will amount to nothing. You must therefore be serious about adopting the right motives at the outset. Further, as this is Mahāyāna Dharma, mere virtuous intentions are not sufficient; you must do your practices while holding a very special type of virtuous mental state—bodhichitta.

If your bodhichitta is unforced, it will develop of its own accord, and you will not have to do the following. If your bodhichitta is of the forced variety, you must consciously activate it. Your mind will not change its course if, without any further preparation, you merely recite, "For the sake of all sentient beings…" Instead, you should begin with something like, "I have obtained the optimum human rebirth…" and end with, "…I shall obtain full enlightenment for the sake of all sentient beings. So, I shall meditate upon this discourse on the stages of the path to enlightenment." I dealt with this a few days ago. In other words, you should work your way in an orderly fashion from the subject of the difficulty of obtaining the optimum human rebirth to the section on the development of bodhichitta. Your mind will then be transformed.

The saints of the past gave various teachings—some brief, some detailed—on how to set one's motivation. Some of them claimed that if we have not been able to effect any mental transformation through some thought process, it is sufficient to set our motivation by means of certain recitations. But it is the mind that sets our motivation, not the mouth. So one must transform one's mind by suffusing it with the meaning of the piece being recited.

So, while in this especially virtuous mental state, you should now take refuge and generate bodhichitta. But take care: I am combining three lamrim texts in this discourse, and you must not get confused, for each text has its own version of the preparatory rites, the refuge visualization, and the merit field. It is current practice to use the preparatory rites according to the Southern Lineage version in assemblies because of its convenience. However, you ought to use the *Swift Path* version in your daily recitation.

To take refuge, you first have to evoke the refuge visualization. The *Swift Path* version of this visualization goes as follows. Visualize in the space in front of you a huge and precious throne supported by eight huge lions. If you situate the throne too high, your mind will become too excited; if it is too low, you will become too dull. Ideally the throne should be level with the gap between your eyebrows. Five small thrones sit on this huge throne: one in the center, the others around it in the four cardinal directions.

The central throne is slightly higher than the other four. Generate the visualization of the lama on this central throne; by nature he is your root guru who teaches you the Dharma, but he appears as Śhākyamuni Buddha, our Teacher. The details of this visualization of the Buddha should conform with the text you are reciting. You must feel he is your guru by nature, because in dependence upon your guru you will develop all realizations—the results of following the path. Your guru takes the aspect of Śhākyamuni because Śhākyamuni is the lord of the teachings, the very source of the Dharma. His right hand adopts the earth-touching mudrā, signifying the defeat of Kāmadeva, the demon of lust. The nectars in Śhākyamuni's begging bowl are: the all-curing nectar symbolizing the defeat of the demon of the [five] aggregates; the nectar of immortality symbolizing the defeat of the demonic Lord of Death [Yama]; and the nectar of uncontaminated primal wisdom symbolizing the defeat of demonic delusions. You must think that this means Buddha has defeated these four demons that once plagued him and that we too shall soon vanquish our own four demons.

At Buddha's heart is Vajradhara; this is the wisdom being. At Vajradhara's heart is a blue syllable *hūṃ;* this is the concentration being. This visualization is related to tantra. You must visualize these three beings, one inside the other.

You may be wondering, "Many people have taught me the lamrim. Which of these should I be visualizing as this central figure?" Adopt as your main guru the one who has been most beneficial for your mindstream.

Maitreya sits on the smaller throne to the Buddha's right. Maitreya's smaller throne is surrounded the gurus of the Lineage of Extensive Deeds. Mañjuśhrī sits on the smaller throne to Buddha's left. As before, he too is surrounded by the lamas of the Lineage of the Profound View. Vajradhara sits on the throne behind Buddha; Vajradhara is surrounded, as in the foregoing, by the gurus of the Lineage of Consecrated Practices.

On the throne in front of Buddha sits your root guru, this time in his normal aspect. You do not visualize his physical faults; for example, he may be blind in real life. His right hand is in the gesture of teaching Dharma, his left in the gesture of meditative absorption. A life-giving initiation vase, full of the nectar of immortality, sits on the palm of his left hand. The two gestures indicate that he is a buddha, for he can teach Dharma while absorbed in meditation on profound emptiness. The teaching-Dharma gesture also encourages his disciples to study; the meditative-absorption gesture encourages them to put their studies into practice. Great Tsongkapa said:

> The main obstacles for the fortunate in their practice of the path
>   to liberation
> Are delusion, which defeats the mind, and Yama, who defeats
>   the body.

In other words, the prime hindrances to Dharma practice are delusions, for these conquer the mind, and the Lord of Death, for he conquers the body. As a countermeasure to them, your guru makes the teaching-Dharma gesture to signify the defeat of delusion by his teaching the Dharma. The life-giving vase and the nectar of immortality signify the defeat of the Lord of Death. There are many other profound points here to do with your achievement of the four types of miraculous powers—the powers of peace, increase, influence, and wrath—which derive from this.

He is surrounded by gurus from whom you have received Dharma teachings, starting with the person who taught you to read. If somebody asks us the number of our gurus, we have no idea and have to count them on our rosary. But we can immediately say how much money we have in our purse! This shows we do not seriously regard the guru as the root of the path.

In this visualization, your gurus who are still alive sit on cushions. Those who have already died sit on lotuses and moon discs.

We shall be using the term *the five sets of gurus* because the gurus in this visualization sit in five groups. The other figures of the merit field—from tutelary deities to Dharma protectors—surround these gurus.[17] These other figures are on the largest throne [that supports the smaller thrones]. In my own precious guru's oral tradition, the meditation deities are positioned around the five sets of gurus. This follows Tutor Tsechogling Rinpoche's practice. The deities of the innermost circle are of the highest yoga tantra. They are surrounded by the yoga tantra deities. Then come those of the charyā [performance] tantra and, finally, the kriyā [action] tantra. So there are four concentric rings of deities. Chuzang Lama Yeshe Gyatso put the four types of deities in the four cardinal directions: highest yoga tantra in front, yoga tantra to the central Buddha's right, and so on. Owing to this arrangement, in drawings of Chuzang's version of the merit-field visualization, only the highest yoga tantra deities are visible.

In any case, the meditation deities are surrounded by the buddhas taking their supreme nirmāṇakāya form. Prominent in this group are the thousand buddhas of this fortunate eon, the eight tathāgatas [Sunāman, Ratna, etc. (see p. 707)], the thirty-five buddhas of confession, and so on. The point of doing this is as follows. There are, in general, infinite numbers of buddhas; however, we have the strongest relationship with the buddhas of this fortunate eon. We are told that prayers to the other seven tathāgatas made during the reign of teachings of Śhākyamuni Buddha will succeed. The thirty-five buddhas of confession have great powers to purify sins and broken vows [see Day 6, p. 189].

The buddhas are in turn surrounded by the bodhisattvas, such as the eight closest children [of Śhākyamuni Buddha: Mañjuśhrī, Vajrapāṇi, etc. (see pp. 707–8)] and so on. They take the form of divine princes.

The bodhisattvas are surrounded by pratyekabuddhas such as the twelve pratyekabuddhas. They are surrounded by the śhrāvakas—the sixteen elders of the arhats [Aṅgaja, Ajita, etc. (see p. 708)], and so on. All these take the form of monks. They display the good qualities of purity and hold begging bowls, iron staffs, and palm-leaf books in their hands. Śhrāvakas can be distinguished from the pratyekabuddhas by the slightly smaller protrusion on the crown of their heads. In fact, this group displays marks similar to the marks and signs [of buddhas].

The śhrāvakas are surrounded by ḍākas and ḍākinīs such as Khaṇḍakapāla and Prachaṇḍāli. They take the form described in the Heruka tantra.

The ḍākas and ḍākinīs are surrounded by the supramundane Dharma protectors—principally the lords of the Dharma of the three scopes [Six-armed Mahākāla, Vaiśhravaṇa, and Kāmayama].

There are two oral traditions concerning the four mahārājas of the four cardinal points of the compass. One tradition places them on the main throne; the other tradition has them standing on cloud cushions below this throne. The reasons for this are as follows. The first tradition regards these four mahārājas to be supramundane figures; the second gives them only mundane status.

It is wrong to include petty mundane figures like spirit kings in this visualization. Once Lama Tsechogling Rinpoche, a tutor to one of the Dalai Lamas, was shown a painting of this merit field. The artist had drawn a spirit king among the protectors. Rinpoche pointed a finger at it and said, "If only he had painted a wish-granting jewel there instead!"

Visualize loose-leaf[18] books on the Dharma in front of each of the figures in this refuge visualization. The books are by nature the jewel of the realized Dharma, but take the form of books—that is, the transmitted Dharma. The books are wrapped in watered silks with brocade bookmarks. Visualize that these books are teaching you Dharma [by speaking the words they contain].

There are many versions of the refuge visualization. One tradition has all Three Jewels embodied in the one figure [the guru]; other versions have various figures standing on different horizontal levels. However, the above description has all the necessary symbolism that relates to the Three Jewels. But note: this visualization is not two-dimensional like a painting. Nor are the figures solid like clay statues: they are rainbow bodies, whose nature is clear, bright light. They are there in person, and radiate brilliant light. In the *Transmission of the Vinaya* we find three similes in praise of the enlightened body:

> It is like a flame in the shape of a body. It is as if filled with tongues of flame. It is like a golden vessel with an oil lamp placed inside.

The figures are also debating the Dharma among themselves. In fact there is a great deal of activity going on: some of them are arriving while others leave to perform various tasks. There is much coming and going, rather like people on royal business going back and forth through the gates of a king's palace. The figures—from Śhākaymuni Buddha to the mahārājas—are sending out emanations for the sake of sentient beings, while other emanations are returning into them. Each pore of these figures is also a buddhafield. And so on. The visualization must be as detailed as you can manage.

You should also think that the figures in this merit field are extremely pleased with you. As Drubkang Geleg Gyatso says, you don't usually do the things the victorious ones and their children tell you to do; instead you do the things they tell you not to. So they have no occasion to be pleased with you. But now you are doing a little to please them. Suppose a mother has a son who continually does only bad things. If he does something good for once, it pleases his mother more than anything else could. We also continually do only the wrong things. But here we are, attempting to meditate on the lamrim. This pleases the victorious ones and their children more than anything else could.

At this point, you summon up the reasons for taking refuge. You do this by means of the following recitation [from Jampael Lhuendrub's *Ornament for the Throats of the Fortunate*]:

> Since beginningless time, I and all sentient beings, who have been my mothers, have been born into saṃsāra and for a long while, up until now, have experienced the very many different sufferings of saṃsāra in general, and those of the three lower realms in particular. Even now, it is hard to understand the extent and depth of that suffering. But I have gained something special that is difficult to achieve, and once achieved is most beneficial: the optimum human rebirth. It is difficult to meet with the precious teachings of the Buddha. Now that I have met with these teachings, if I do not achieve pure and complete buddhahood, the best form of liberation from all the sufferings of saṃsāra, I must again experience the whole range of sufferings that saṃsāra in general involves and, more importantly, the sufferings of the three lower realms. The power to protect me from these sufferings resides in the guru and the Three Jewels.

> So, for the sake of all sentient beings, my former mothers, I shall achieve complete buddhahood. I therefore take refuge in the guru and the Three Jewels.

The outcome of your summoning up the causes for taking refuge will be that you take refuge properly. These causes are fear and faith. The fear is from remembering the general and specific sufferings of saṃsāra. The faith is the belief that the Three Jewels can protect you from these sufferings. And in order to take the uncommon refuge, the Mahāyāna type, you need an additional cause on top of these: love and compassion for the other beings tormented by these sufferings. I shall be dealing with this subject—the causes of taking refuge—in greater detail in the main part of the discourse.

You visualize that you are surrounded by all sentient beings, symbolized by your mother and father. They sit together and are undergoing the suffering of their various types of rebirth; however, you visualize them in the form of human beings—in other words, as beings capable of speech and comprehension and who are bewildered. When you lead them in the recitation of the refuge formula, you must think that all sentient beings are taking refuge along with you.

They say that when you recite the fourfold refuge formula in public ceremonies, you should repeat it in sequence, that is:

> I take refuge in the guru.
> I take refuge in the Buddha.
> I take refuge in the Dharma.
> I take refuge in the Saṅgha.
>
> I take refuge in the guru…

and so forth. But when you are taking refuge during your meditations, you should repeat each part of the formula a number of times on its own, so that the refuge visualization will appear more easily.

So when you are repeating "I take refuge in the guru," you focus your attention on the five sets of gurus and take refuge while the purifying nectars descend from them. Suppose you are going to recite one rosary's worth of this part of the formula. For the first fifty repetitions you must visualize that the nectars purify you of non-Dharmic qualities; during the last fifty repetitions you visualize that your Dharmic qualities increase. Thus, for the first half of the recitation, you imagine that the five types of colored nectars, together with lights of the five colors [white, red, blue, yellow, and green], descend from the gurus. The white nectar predominates. They enter your own body and mind and all the bodies and minds of the others; the nectars purify all the sins and obscurations that you and they have accumulated since beginningless time. This applies especially to actions such as endangering your guru's body, disobeying his orders, disturbing his mental peace, disparaging him, and not having faith in him—in short, all the sins and obscurations you have acquired in relation to your guru. These all ooze from your body in the form of smoky and coal-black sludge, and you feel you have been completely purified.

The second half of the recitation goes as follows. The Dharmic things to be increased are, by nature, the good qualities of the gurus' body, speech, and mind, but they take the form of the five types of colored nectars and lights. This time the yellow nectar predominates. They descend [from the gurus]. Think that you and all other sentient beings generally receive an increase of lifespan, merits, and the good qualities of the transmitted and realized teachings. In particular, you and these beings receive the blessings of your gurus' body, speech, and mind.

You do much the same when you repeat, "I take refuge in the Buddha." According to the tantras, "Buddha" means the tutelary deities of the four classes of tantra; the sūtric buddhas are the supreme nirmāṇakāya forms. Purifying nectars descend from both types of buddhas.

The sort of sins one collects in relation to buddhas are: with evil motives extracting blood from the body of a tathāgata, making judgments on the quality of Buddha images, pawning images, regarding images as merchandise to be bought and sold, maliciously destroying the symbols of the enlightened mind [that is, stūpas], and so forth.

An example of the first type of sin—drawing blood from a buddha—is Devadatta [Buddha's jealous cousin], who used a giant catapult to hurl rocks at Buddha [see Day 12, p. 357]. This act made the Buddha bleed. We have not committed this particular sin, but we have committed the rest.

When you examine [Buddha] images for faults in the workmanship, you are judging their quality. Once Mahāyogi showed Atiśha a Mañjuśhrī statue. He asked Atiśha if it was any good, and was it worth buying with the four golden *sho* [a coin] that Rongpa Gargewa had given him. Atiśha

“O MONK! DON’T TRY TO FOOL YOURSELF!” (SEE P. 117)

replied, "A statue of Mañjuśhrī could never be bad. But the artist was only mediocre." In other words, only speak about the quality of the artist, for it is not right to point out the faults in the image itself. Pawning images and making money out of them are very common sights. You must avoid doing such things at all costs.

In the second half, the part where you increase your good qualities, imagine that the ten powers, the four fearlessnesses, and the eighteen unique qualities, take the form of descending nectar. The rest is the same as above.

Then you recite, "I take refuge in the Dharma." The purifying nectars descend from the books in the visualization. This nectar is by nature the realized Dharma.

The sins we accumulate in relation to Dharma are: abandoning holy Dharma, selling scriptures, not showing scriptures enough respect, profiting from the sale of a book, consuming the profit from a book, etc. We are very much in danger of committing these sins, and they have extremely heavy consequences.

Abandoning Dharma is, in the final analysis, disparaging the Hīnayāna because of the Mahāyāna; favoring the Hīnayāna on account of the Mahāyāna; playing off sūtra against tantra; playing off the four classes of the tantras against each other; favoring one of the Tibetan schools—the Sakya, Gelug, Kagyu, or Nyingma—and disparaging the rest; and so on. In other words, we abandon Dharma any time we favor our own tenets and disparage the rest. We also abandon Dharma when we step over texts or writing, throw any writing away, and so forth. Some people even do things like sitting on writing. They deliberately accumulate evil karma by doing so. Abandoning the Dharma is an extremely heavy misdeed, as we are told in the *King of Single-Pointed Concentration Sūtra* and other sūtras. But I have already covered this in greater detail [see Day 3, p. 68].

Selling scriptures means buying and selling them with the attitude that they are material goods.

"You do not treat scriptures with enough respect" if you put them on the floor without their wrapping cloth; if you pick your teeth and use the plaque to stick colored pieces of paper to the pages,[19] lick your fingers to turn a page, or put things on top or among Dharma books. These, too, are extremely heavy misdeeds. When Atiśha was in Ngari, he and a tantrist, who rejected his teachings, saw a scribe use his finger to pick his teeth and then stick a colored patch on the page of a Dharma book. Atiśha could not bear to see it. He turned to the tantrist and said, "Oh how wrong, how wrong!" They say this stirred the tantrist's faith in Atiśha—so much so that he then took teachings from him. People like ourselves, who are always handling books, should be particularly careful: we always run the risk of committing these misdeeds all at once.

If you use a thing bought with the proceeds gained from selling a book, you have "consumed the profit." This also has heavy consequences. The fifth of the seven Shangpa Rinpoches, Woentoen Kyergangpa, was a great adept in the Avalokiteśhvara tantra. His benefactor, a layman, ran short of money and sold a set of the *One Hundred Thousand Verse Perfection of Wisdom Sūtra.* The benefactor invited Kyergangpa and three other monks to his home, thinking that doing this would expiate his sin. He served the food bought with the money he had made on the sale of the books. That night Kyergangpa fell seriously ill. Kyergangpa could see, while in single-pointed meditation, a white letter A moving swiftly back and forth throughout his body. This caused him fierce pain. He made petitions to his tutelary deities, and Avalokiteśhvara came to him.

"You and the others," Avalokiteśhvara said, "have consumed the profit from the sale of a scripture. This is most evil. You have few sins and obscurations, and so the karma of this deed has ripened on you in this life. The others can only go to the hells. You should commission a copy of the *One Hundred Thousand Verse Perfection of Wisdom Sūtra* in gold ink to expiate the sin. You must also carry out many practices such as offering special ritual cakes."[20] Kyergangpa did as he was instructed, and the sickness went away.

When you come to do the increase visualization, you imagine that the Dharma—the truth of cessation, the truth of the path, and so forth—descend in the form of nectar.

Next, you repeat, "I take refuge in the Saṅgha." According to the sūtras, śhrāvakas, pratyekabuddhas, and bodhisattvas make up the Saṅgha. The tantric Saṅgha is the ḍākas, ḍākinīs, and Dharma protectors. Purifying nectars descend from these figures.

The sins and obscurations you accumulate in relation to the Saṅgha are: creating schisms in the Saṅgha, stealing their offerings, criticizing them, and breaking a commitment to offer ritual cakes to the Dharma protectors. You may try through the four powers to expiate any sins and obscurations committed in relation to the Saṅgha, but you will be unable to purify them enough never to experience any ripening effect of the karma. Refer to the story of the teacher Supuṣhpa Chandra.[21] These sins are far more grave than those related to either the Buddha or Dharma. In our country the Saṅgha is numerous and we must mix freely with the Saṅgha; we are, therefore, in danger [of committing this type of sin], so we must be careful.

Strictly speaking, one can only cause a schism during the Buddha's lifetime, so this cannot happen at present. However, very much friction occurs among the Saṅgha, and this resembles a schism.

The Ārya Saṅgha consists of people who directly perceive emptiness. Its members may be either lay people, monks, or nuns. Four ordinary beings [who have not perceived emptiness this way] are deemed to be Saṅgha if their [pratimokṣha] vows are still pure. But whether the members of the Saṅgha are ordinary beings or not, they could divide into two groups of at least four members each over some disagreement because someone indulges in divisive talk that causes friction between the two groups. Everyone involved—not merely the person causing the dissension—will go hand in hand to the lower realms.

There was once a Kadampa geshe named Saelshe who caused dissension among the Saṅgha. Later, after the geshe's death, Geshe Dromtoenpa remarked, "If my disciple Saelshe had died three years earlier, he would have died as an upholder of the three baskets, but he died three years too late. His monastery Toepur," said Drom, "was his undoing." And according to the oral tradition of the lamrim teachers, Saelshe is still in hell. The place where the schism was committed is also said to be scorched by the sin: other people will not be able to develop realizations at that place, even if they practice there for twelve years.

Hostility or attachment can divide the Saṅgha into cliques whose members think in terms of "us" and "them" and "if only there were more people on our side." I think this is the main cause of friction. If the members of the Saṅgha do not get on, reading, study, or contemplation cannot flourish—nor yet the dhyāna-concentration states that they could use to abandon [manifest] delusion. The worst damage such friction can cause is bringing the teachings into decline. One sūtra says:

> A harmonious Saṅgha is happy;
> The asceticism of those in harmony is easy.

This quotation tells us, in other words, that the main thing members of the Saṅgha must do is get along.

"Stealing offerings made to the Saṅgha" is misappropriating the Saṅgha's funds, not turning over to the Saṅgha taxes levied in its name, a Saṅgha member's keeping and using something meant for the Saṅgha's general use, etc. The administrators of monasteries are most vulnerable to these things. Some monks whose job is to liaise with a monastery's benefactors act as though they have more concern for the benefactor, and so might tell him, "We don't need all of these." This is an act of depriving the Saṅgha. Depriving the Saṅgha of even a slice of butter is stealing from the mouths of the general community; it is a cause for being born in the Hell Without Respite. Other forms of embezzling from the Saṅgha result in rebirth in the surrounding hells.

This is illustrated by the story of Ārya Saṅgharakṣhita. While returning from a visit to the nāga regions, he saw some beings in an occasional hell by the ocean shore. These hell beings took many shapes and forms: some looked like rope, some like clay pots, others like brooms, pestles, pillars, walls, and even a water pipe. They were all wailing and making heart-rending moans. Saṅgharakṣhita later asked the Buddha, "What was the karma that ripened into such results?"

The Buddha told him the following. The hell creatures who were like ropes and brooms were once people who withheld ropes and brooms from the Saṅgha when the teachings of Kāśhyapa Buddha [the previous Buddha] were still in existence. The ropes and brooms were meant for the Saṅgha's general use, but these people set them aside for their own personal use.

The creature who looked like a clay pot was once a lay helper of the Saṅgha. He was boiling up some medicine in a clay pot, and some monks made unpleasant remarks to him. He lost his temper and broke the pot. This was the result of that action.

The pestle creature was once a monk. He ordered a novice, one scheduled for debate, to grind him some roasted grain. The novice was busy and said he would do it in a little while. The monk lost his temper and said, "If I could get hold of a pestle, I would pound you and never mind about the roasted grain!" He was reborn in the shape of a pestle as a result of these insulting words.

The beings looking like walls and pillars were once people who had done inappropriate things with their saliva and mucus in temples of the Saṅgha.

The creature who looked like a water pipe had a tiny waist. This was the ripening effect of the following karma. He used to be a contractor who starved the Saṅgha by not distributing supplies meant for the summer until the following autumn.

Thus, if you take something belonging to the Saṅgha without permission, even so much as a stick from the Saṅgha's woodpile, you are sure to be reborn in an occasional hell.

"Criticizing the Saṅgha" means abusing its members with harsh words, calling them bad names, and so on, either to their faces or behind their backs. A Brahman called Mānavakapila insulted members of Kāśhyapa Buddha's Saṅgha. He was reborn as a type of sea monster. Here is a brief version of his story.

In India there were once five hundred fishermen who used to cast their nets in the Gaṇḍaka river to catch fish, turtles, and so on. One day, a sea monster got caught in one of the nets. Its body was enormous. The five hundred fishermen were unable to land the monster while it drifted into the current. They asked cowherds, grass-cutters, harvest workers, and passersby for help. Hundreds of thousands of people lent a hand, and the thing was dragged ashore. They saw that it had eighteen heads and thirty-six eyes. Many hundreds of thousands of people gathered to watch the spectacle. Among the crowd were six tīrṭhika teachers and other such people. Buddha, who can perceive anything, regardless of when it happens, went there to make a pronouncement concerning the laws of cause and effect. He was accompanied by many monks of his Saṅgha.

Scoffers said, "This holy man Gautama claims to be above such vulgar spectacles. Yet here he comes!"

People who believed in him said, "The Buddha is above such things. The Buddha will take this opportunity to teach some wonderful Dharma to the people here."

A throne was set up, and Buddha sat on it, surrounded by his retinue. He blessed the monster so that it could recall its past lives and understand human speech. Buddha then said to it, "You are Mānavakapila, are you not?"

"Yes," it said, "I am Kapila."

"Are you undergoing a ripening of some misdeed of body, speech, and mind?"

"I am."

"Who misguided you?"

"My mother."

"Where was she reborn?"

"In hell."

"How were you reborn?"

"As an animal."

"When you die, where will you be reborn?"

"I will be born in hell." And at that, the creature began to cry.

The Buddha's retinue was completely astonished. At their insistence Ānanda asked who this creature was that could remember its past lives and speak in a human tongue. Buddha then recited its story:

"Once, in the time of Kāśhyapa Buddha, during the reign of King Kṛikin, some Brahmans came from another country and challenged people to debate. A Brahman called Kapilaśhānti defeated the other philosophers in debate, and the king gave him the deed to the mountain where the debate was held. The Brahman's son had long blond hair, and was therefore named Mānavakapila [Blond-haired Brahman]. This son studied the art of writing and so on, and became a scholar who could also defeat others in debate.

"His father died and his mother feared that other people might take from him the prizes he had won in debates. She asked her son, 'Can you defeat all philosophers in debate?'

"'I can defeat anyone—except Kāśhyapa's holy men,' he replied.

"'Go and defeat even them,' she said.

"Out of respect for his mother, he went out to debate with them. He met a monk who asked him what a certain verse meant. He could not come up with an answer; he developed faith in the Saṅgha and returned home.

"'Did you defeat the holy men?' asked his mother.

"'Mother, if there had been any witnesses, today I would have been defeated.'

"'Son, in that case read Buddha's scriptures.'

"'They are kept from lay people.'

"'Then become ordained. After you become a scholar, give up your monkhood.'

"She was so insistent that he took ordination and became a scholar of the three baskets.

"Again his mother asked, 'Did you defeat these holy men?'

"'Mother, I have only received the transmission of the teachings. They have both the transmissions and realization into the teachings. I cannot defeat them.'

"'Son, no matter how much Dharma you've been taught, in debate, use insulting words against them. They are fearful of committing any misdeed and will not say anything at all in retaliation. People will think that you have won the debate.'

"Kapila did as she instructed. When he debated with the monks, he lost his temper and said, 'Elephant-head! How could you know what is Dharma and what is not!' He also called them, 'Horse-head,' 'Camel-head,' 'Donkey-head,' 'Bull-head,' 'Monkey-head,' 'Lion-head,' 'Tiger-head,' and so on. He used eighteen different insults against them. As a result of this misdeed, he was reborn as a type of sea monster with eighteen heads."

Such was Buddha's pronouncement.

It is also wrong to disparage the ordinary members of the Saṅgha. People may say, for example, "Those depraved monks," but, as I have already mentioned, there is no difference between four ordinary beings who are monks and the Ārya Saṅgha. Would there be any difference in saying these things to Maitreya or Mañjuśhrī?

We treat members of the Saṅgha of our own social class far too offhandedly. We might say, "I take refuge in the Saṅgha," but we act differently. As my own precious lama said, when ordained ones sit among the rows [of Saṅgha in the temple], they should all regard one another, the monks on their left and right, as their refuge. But this is not what they in fact do; instead they pick faults with each other. They think to themselves: "So-and-so, the old monk in the middle of that row, is very stingy. Such-and-such, the monk behind him, is even worse—such a foul temper!" and so on. They think every member of the Saṅgha has this or that fault, and taking a cynical turn in their mindstreams, then conclude, "None of them are better than me!" But the formula "I take refuge in the Saṅgha" applies to the whole Saṅgha to be found in the ten directions. Perhaps you ought to compose your very own refuge formula. Might I suggest: "I take refuge in the Saṅgha—except for this person, that person…" Lama Koenchog Yaenlag said:

> Whenever you see your true friends, the Ārya Saṅgha,
> Remember they are true friends to help you on your way.

In other words, whenever you meet members of the ordinary Saṅgha or the Ārya Saṅgha, you must regard them as your refuge, as people who help you leave a place of danger.

In the second half of the visualization, you again imagine that your Dharmic qualities increase. Imagine the nectar descending. The nectar is really the six perfections, which are the tasks of the bodhisattvas; the twelve pure qualities of śhrāvakas and pratyekabuddhas; the three high trainings; the primal wisdom into bliss and emptiness held by ḍākas and ḍākinīs; the four types of good works carried out by Dharma protectors; and so on. These take the shape of nectar.

When you recite the refuge formula many times, you visualize the descent of the purifying nectars in three ways: the introduction, the long section, and the last section.

For the introduction you repeat "I take refuge in the guru" while nectars descend from all five groups simultaneously. During the long section, nectars descend from each of the five groups of gurus in turn. Then, in the last section, nectars again descend from all the gurus. Suppose you allot one rosary for each step; the whole process would take seven rosaries to complete.

You do exactly the same with the other three parts of the refuge formula. Buddhas fall into the following five groups: deities of the four classes of tantra, and the sūtric buddhas. The five groups of Dharma are Dharma of the śhrāvakas; Dharma of the pratyekabuddhas; the common [sūtric] Mahāyāna Dharma; the lower kriyā, charyā, and yoga tantras; and the higher highest yoga tantra. The five groups of Saṅgha are bodhisattvas; śhrāvakas; pratyekabuddhas; ḍākas and ḍākinīs; and Dharma protectors.

Though the texts are not clear on this, there is also a practice to recite "I take refuge in the guru, meditation deities, and the Three Jewels," accompanying this with the visualization of descending purification nectars. We are told the visualization of descending purification nectars is a tantric tradition; the descent of purifying light rays is sūtric. The purifying nectars can descend in three ways. They can come to you within a tube of light; they can wind down around rays of light; or they can descend in a heavy rain.

Next you recite [from Jampael Lhuendrub's *Ornament for the Throats of the Fortunate*]:

> Until enlightenment, I take refuge
> In Buddha, Dharma, and the Supreme Assembly.
> With the merit I earn through generosity and so on,
> May I gain buddhahood for the sake of all beings.

Take refuge in the first part, and develop your bodhichitta further when you say, "With the merit I earn through generosity and so on." Think to yourself, "By virtue of my root merits, which I acquired through practicing generosity, maintaining my ethics, practicing patience, and so on, may I gain buddhahood for the sake of all sentient beings." I do not have to give any further details on this now, for I shall discuss in detail later how to internalize this topic [see Day 12, pp. 353ff.]. Taking refuge is like becoming a king's subject; developing bodhichitta is like offering him tribute.

At this point, you must visualize taking the results of your development of bodhichitta as a part of the path. You do this as follows. Out of Guru Śhākyamuni emerges a duplicate image of himself that dissolves into you. You become Śhākyamuni by nature—that is, a buddha. Countless Śhākyamunis emanate from you and dissolve into sentient beings who also become Śhākyamuni by nature; they too are now buddhas. Rejoice and feel, "When I developed bodhichitta, I thought to myself. 'I will lead all sentient beings to the state of buddhahood.' Now I have achieved my aim."

This visualization simulates the results of developing bodhichitta: that you have been completely successful in the tantras and their maṇḍalas. Performing this visualization has corresponding benefits, and it also contains all the distinctive profound key points to be found in teachings like *Shaking the Depths of Saṃsāra,* or *Purification of the Six Types of Sentient Beings and Their Abodes.*

Next you meditate on the four immeasurables. Think as follows: "But I am actually unable to take all sentient beings to such a state—I can only do this in my visualizations. What is to blame for this? My feelings of attachment for beings on my side, and feelings of hostility for those on the other side." [Then think over these words from Jampael Lhuendrub's *Ornament for the Throats of the Fortunate* as you recite them]:

> How welcome it would be if all sentient beings remained in a state of equanimity: free of feelings of intimacy or distance, attachment or hostility. May they come to this state! I will bring them to this state. May I be blessed by my gurus and deities to have the power to do this!
>
> How welcome it would be if all sentient beings possessed happiness and its causes. May they come to have them! I will make them have them. May I be blessed by my gurus and deities to have the power to do this!

> How welcome it would be if all sentient beings were free of suffering and its causes. May they come to be free of them! I will make them free of them. May I be blessed by my gurus and deities to have the power to do this!
>
> How welcome it would be if all sentient beings were never separated from the holy bliss of high rebirth and liberation. May they come to have these! I will make them have these. May I be blessed by my gurus and deities to have the power to do this!

With these you initiate the internalization process for the four immeasurables [immeasurable equanimity, love, compassion, and joy]—you do not do this for only the four immeasurables, one after another; the above wording of the recitation contains four additional immeasurables within each individual immeasurable. Each time you think "How welcome it would be if..." this is the immeasurable aspiration of each. The thought "May they come to have these" is the immeasurable prayer of each. Thinking "I will make them..." or "I will bring them..." is the immeasurable altruism of each. Finally, the thought "May I be blessed by my gurus and deities to have the power to do this" is the immeasurable petition of each. This is the traditional oral explanation.

More to the point, the formula "...all sentient beings, who have been my mothers..." applies only to the development of bodhichitta. Thus this wording is not used in the above recitation for the reason that this instruction on the four immeasurables is not meant to be used for the initial development of bodhichitta; instead it is an oral instruction given to increase one's ability to develop bodhichitta.

Some more points on the development of equanimity: You could increase your bodhichitta by thinking, like a child whose parents quarrel, "I shall achieve buddhahood in order to place all sentient beings in a state of equanimity, free from attachment and hostility." Or you could think, "I shall achieve buddhahood in order to lead all sentient beings to happiness—beginning with the happiness that would result from my cooling the hot hells, and ending with the bliss of complete enlightenment." Or you could think, "I shall achieve buddhahood in order to free them from suffering—from the sufferings of the hells to the subtlest obscurations preventing their enlightenment." Each of these above three ways of developing equamimity contains the whole path of the three scopes within it.

You might then wonder, "In that case, why does the development of bodhichitta and so on come at this point, before training one's mind in the small scope section of the path?" But even when you train in the small and medium scope sections of the path, you follow these trainings in order to develop your bodhichitta—although this may not be obvious. You have to appreciate this fact right from the start. Here are a couple of illustrations. If you want to go to the top of a pass, you must first have the thought of wanting to go there, and so make your way on foot through the approach to the pass. Or, when you draw the figure of a deity, you must first make sure the proportions of the figure are going to come out correctly, by drawing a grid, etc.

There are two kinds of rapidity. The first type is the attainment of enlightenment in one lifetime by making more rapid progress than one could by using the Perfection Vehicle [Pāramitāyāna]. The second is even more rapid than the first: being enlightened in the short lifetime available to someone in these degenerate times. The first type is achieved by means of the lower classes of tantra; the second is the exceptional speed of the highest of the four classes of tantra.

There is another version of these two types of rapid progress. The first type is achieving enlightenment in the short lifetime available in these degenerate times by means of the highest class of tantras. This is a feature that the Sakya, Gelug, and Nyingma schools hold in common. The second type, which is supposed to be even swifter, is achieved by regarding the guru yoga practices, according to the confidential oral instructions of the Gelug school, as the lifeblood of the path. If you practice a combination of the Guhyasamāja, Heruka, and Yamāntaka tantras, you may achieve enlightenment in only twelve human years. Whatever could go wrong is from the side of the practitioner. Before these confidential lineages evolved —they stem from the great Tsongkapa—there were people who were capable of carrying out great austerities—people like Milarepa, Gyalwa Goetsang, and so forth, who needed only three years to reach enlightenment. This interpretation is the oral tradition coming down from Chancellor Tapugpa. His reasoning was that many of the Gelugpa masters of the past, such as Ensapa and his disciples, seem to have reached buddhahood in one lifetime without such heroic efforts. They followed the *Swift Path* tradition on how to take refuge and develop bodhichitta.

The Central Province Lineage of *Mañjuśhrī's Own Words* does not give the same merit-field visualization, to be used as one's object of refuge, as the tradition I have just described. This is also the case with the Southern Lineage: this tradition discusses a quite different merit-field visualization as one's object of refuge. It is in fact a completely different confidential oral tradition.

The Southern Lineage visualization is as follows. You visualize in front of you many lotuses growing out of the ground. They grow in the midst of beautiful clouds and rainbows, so only the tops of the flowers are visible. The central flower is the largest, and on it sits Śhākyamuni. To his right and left sit Maitreya and Mañjuśhrī respectively—each on his own lotus flower. Their shoulders are level with Buddha's. Behind Maitreya and Mañjuśhrī sit gurus belonging to the Lineage of Extensive Deeds and the Lineage of Profound View respectively. These gurus form two lines; they sit one behind the other, the first of each sitting behind either Maitreya or Mañjuśhrī. The lines of gurus curl round in a spiral, thus surrounding Śhākyamuni. The last gurus of these lineages sit beside each other. You must visualize that each guru sits on his own lotus flower. In front of Śhākyamuni, but at a slightly lower level, sit your own gurus—the gurus from whom you have actually received teachings. You do not have to visualize the Lineage of Consecrated Practices.

The buddhas sit high in space among clouds and rainbows; they fan out to the right and left of the gurus. Below the buddhas sit the bodhisattvas, śhrāvakas, and pratyekabuddhas; the Dharma protectors are below them.

Below your own gurus are three multicolored lotus flowers. On the central flower stands [Six-handed] Mahākāla upon a sun disc. He is in his Kurukullejñāna form. He is lord of the Dharma of the great scope. To his right stands Vaiśhravaṇa, on the lotus flower and moon disc. He is lord of the Dharma of the medium scope. To Mahākāla's left stands Kamayama on a sun-disc and lotus flower. He is lord of the Dharma of the small scope.

The reasons for taking them as the lords of the Dharma of the three scopes are these. The Kurukullejñāna form of Mahākāla is really Avalokiteśhvara, the embodiment of the compassion of all the victorious ones arising in the form of a protector deity. The point being made here is that one will sooner develop love and compassion while following the great scope if one relies on this protector. In the medium scope, one must practice mainly the three high trainings—with the greatest emphasis on the training of ethics. The mahārāja Vaiśhravaṇa promised before Buddha to principally guard the vinaya part of the three baskets, as well as the high training of ethics from among the three high trainings. If one relies on this particular Dharma protector, one will develop these parts of the path in one's mental stream. Dharmarāja Yama represents the impermanence of all rebirths; he also classifies people according to the laws of cause and effect and according to what sins or virtues people have done. If one relies on this Dharma protector, one will easily develop realization into the small scope—that is, into impermanence, cause and effect, and so on.

That is how you should relate to these Dharma protectors as they lead you on through the path. There are an infinite number of secret and profound points on how the gurus, meditation deities, and so forth hasten you on through the path, taking you very soon to your enlightenment. Mañjuśhrī taught these points to great Tsongkapa, but this is not the time to discuss them.

Other Dharma protectors stand to the right and left of the three lords of the three scopes. The three lords should also be placed so that their lotus bases stand at different levels [with Mahākāla highest].

The procedures for internalizing the taking of refuge and the rest are the same as above, and there will be more below.

This particular lineage then adds a passage entitled "Petitions to the Refuge." This passage runs, "Guru and precious Three Jewels, I take refuge in you and pay you homage. Please bless my mindstream." It is based on great Sakya Rinpoche's oral instructions.

DAY 5

Pabongka Dorje Chang gave a short talk on how we should set our motivations. He quoted this verse from Nāgārjuna:

> It is stupid to discard disgusting filth
> Into a golden, jeweled container;
> It is even more stupid for a person
> To sin after being born a human.

You should listen to this teaching only after setting your motives properly and adopting the right manner. The Dharma you are about to hear is Dharma that will take the fortunate to the level of the buddhas...

Then Rinpoche referred back to the headings he had already covered:

The fourth major heading of the lamrim is: "The Sequence in Which the Disciples Are to Be Taught the Actual Instructions." This heading has two subdivisions; the first of these tells how to devote yourself properly to a spiritual guide. There are six preparatory rites that have to be followed in this particular practice. I have been teaching the six preparatory rites in a concise discourse version, that is, the *Swift Path.* Yesterday, I covered the first three of these rites. The fourth is as follows.

PETITIONING THE MERIT FIELD (46)

As great Tsongkapa said, when our mind is very feeble—that is, when we study but cannot retain the words, contemplate but do not understand, and meditate but nothing develops in our mindstream—we are instructed to rely on the power of the merit field.

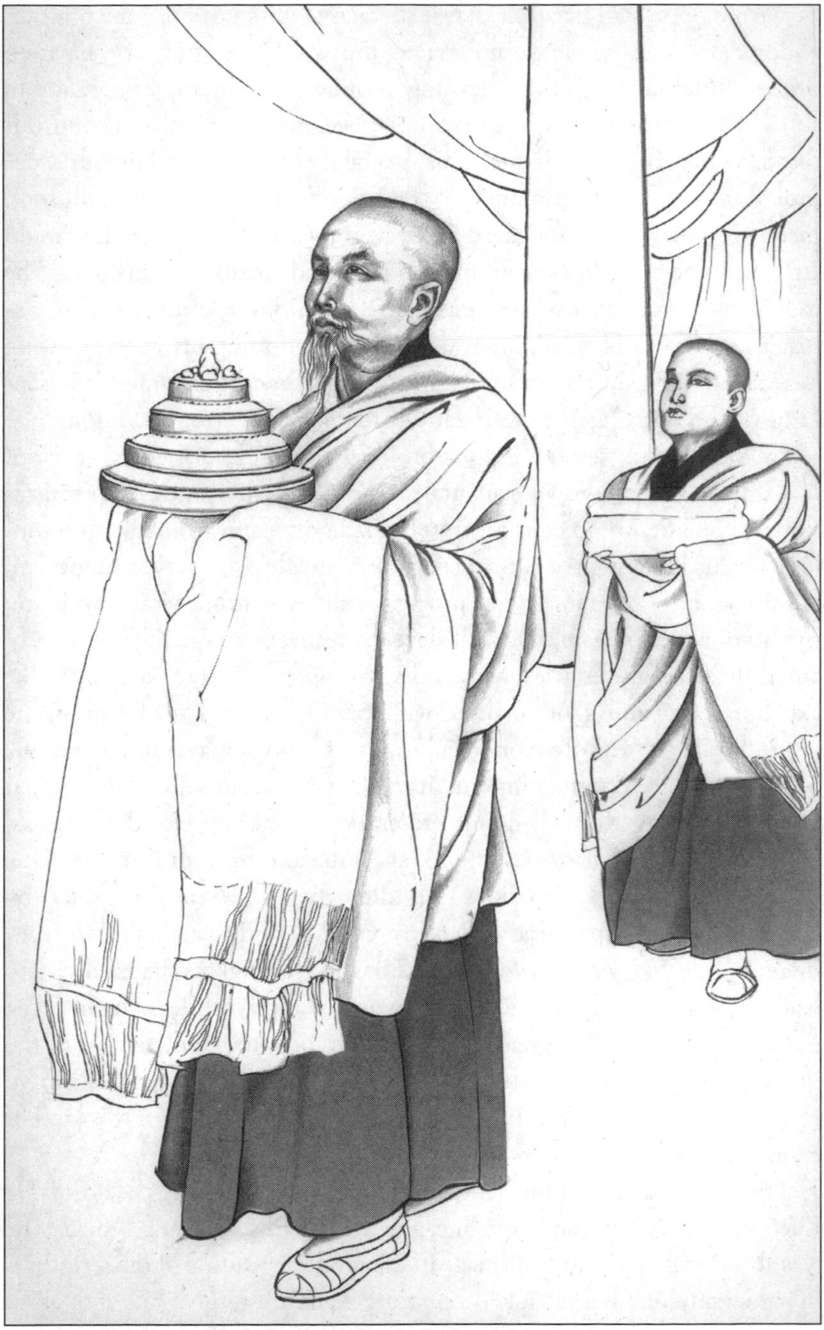

REQUESTING ATIŚHA TO COME TO TIBET (SEE P. 45)

We are oppressed by a thick layer of karmic obscurations; our position is desperate because we do not retain the words we study, we have no proper understanding of the meaning, despite our contemplations, and in spite of our meditations, we have not developed any realization in our mindstreams. But if we petition this special merit field, build up our accumulations [of merit], and purify ourselves of obscurations, we will soon make progress. Great Tsongkapa asked Mañjuśhrī what method he should strive in to develop quick realization in his mindstream. Mañjuśhrī said he must concentrate on a combination of three things: regarding his guru as inseparable from his meditation deity and petitioning his guru; working hard at building up his accumulation [of merit] and purifying his obscurations; and pursuing the visualizations that are cause [for liberation].

So, building up your accumulation [of merit] and purifying yourself of obscurations will ripen your mental stream. You will not develop realizations if you attempt to continue internalizing the lamrim meditation topics without invoking the blessings of the merit field by petitioning them; despite your perseverance, your progress will be painfully slow. But if you ripen your mindstream, you will develop realizations quickly in spite of any difficulties or obstacles, your faults will ripen quickly and easily—like expelling pus. Your good qualities will also ripen, like fruit fallen on the ground by itself, ready for you to enjoy. Great Tsongkapa set us an example by energetically accumulating [merit] and carrying out self-purification at Oelga Choelung through doing prostrations, offering world maṇḍalas, and so on. He then had a vision of Nāgārjuna and his four disciples. One of these disciples in the vision—Buddhapālita—blessed Tsongkapa [by placing on Tsongkapa's head] a Sanskrit copy of Buddhapālita's own commentary, the *Pursuit of Buddhahood.* That day Tsongkapa had a desire to read this commentary, and to common appearances, while going over the eighteenth chapter, he developed realization into the stainless view of the Prāsaṅgikas. He had read this commentary many times before, but to common appearances, this time his mental stream was ripe for this kind of realization.

There are many such incidents in the life stories of other past saints. Je Kaelzang Taenzin is one of the lineage gurus of this Dharma. One day he was about to go to Drungpa village in Dagpo for a reading of the scriptures in somebody's house. He asked Kaelzang Kaedrub to give him a book to take to read; he was given a copy of *Much-Loved Kadampa Anthology,* which contained a vajra song based on the mind-training practice. As soon as Kaelzang Taenzin read it, he developed genuine bodhichitta in his mindstream. The next day, while he was petitioning the merit field during his preparatory rites, he came to the section that invokes the names of the authors of the lamrim. This passage begins: "You virtuous ones, who lovingly care for all sentient beings." At that moment, when he invoked the names of these authors, they say he felt a vivid burning sensation in his forehead.

Thus, when one's mindstream is ripe enough, one will suddenly develop realizations with ease from even the most trivial circumstance. As Doelpa Ripoche has said:

> While you accumulate your collections [of merit] and purify yourself of obscurations, think that you are conscientiously petitioning your gurus and deities. Even though you think these things will never happen, not in a hundred years, they will happen. This is so for all conditioned phenomena: they do not remain static.

And the saints of the past traditionally gave this oral instruction: "You are like a seed without moisture when you do not build up a stock of merit." Thus accumulation, self-purification, and petitioning the merit field are crucial. People in the great monasteries do not merely debate all the time: they also do lots of chanting during their assemblies, debating practice, daily recitations, and so on. One must take these things seriously; their point is accumulation and self-purification.

Whom do you petition in order to accumulate merit and to purify yourself? You petition the merit field. Meditation on the merit field is therefore vital and has been made into a separate heading. The term *merit field* means that this visualization is a fertile field for building up your stock of merit. People value an ordinary field that produces good crops; the merit field gives great force to your accumulation, self-purification, and petitioning. You must therefore take seriously the visualizing of this field of merit. An ordinary field will only produce a few bushels. The merit field will produce results of immeasurable energy from tiny seeds. Ordinary fields can only be planted at certain times of the year. The merit field is always ready for planting in any season with the seeds of health and happiness. What a pity if you let this field lie fallow and fail to sow any seeds of merit in it. As Great Tsongkapa says:

> There is a sūtra that says: "This holy field—the source of all your future welfare and happiness—is always ready for planting with the seeds of welfare and happiness at all times, in any season. May you therefore turn up this field with the plough of faith." What a great pity if one does nothing with this field!

Also:

> We don't give the merit field, the supreme field, the same respect we give ordinary fields. We do not act in the right way.

Thus, if petitioning the merit field is so crucial, you may now be wondering, "How should I go about doing this?" So I shall explain this process, beginning with the *Swift Path* version of the merit field, because each lamrim text has its own version of the preparatory rites.

At this point you may be wondering, "Before I can begin the visualization of the merit field, I should dissolve the refuge visualization. How should I do this, since the text books are not clear on it?" There are in fact three different instructions on the dissolution of the refuge visualization; they are not discussed explicitly so as to give you some leeway. These instructions are: the refuge visualization turns into yellow light, which dissolves into the space between your eyebrows; or you imagine the visualization becomes sealed into unfocused emptiness; or the whole refuge visualization rises into space, and after you have visualized the merit field below it, you merge the refuge visualization into the merit field when the time comes for the wisdom beings to enter the merit field. These three instructions are left vague as you have to receive them orally and in person.

The first step to visualizing the merit field is the consecration of the earth's surface. You recite [from Jampael Lhuendrub's *Ornament for the Throats of the Fortunate*]:

> May the ground everywhere
> Have no pebbles and so forth,
> Be flat as the palm of one's hand,
> Have the nature of lapis lazuli,
> Yet remain soft.

You must not think all the following takes place within the confines of your room. You visualize that the ground surface is vast—as if you are in the middle of a vast plain. This surface is flat, and either made of gold inlaid with designs in lapis lazuli, or of lapis inlaid with designs in gold. The surface yields when touched and recovers its shape when there is no pressure. Its very touch is blissful. The surface is dotted with precious trees, and various magical birds sit in the trees and sing of the Dharma. There are pools of water whose bottoms are covered with gold dust. The whole plain is surrounded by mountains of jewels, and so on. Visualize in accordance with the *Sūtra on the Layout of the Pure Fields.* The pebbles also include rough stones and clay shards: people in India used to throw away old containers, and the country was littered with clay fragments. The surface is free of faults such as fissures or gullies.

The offerings must then be consecrated. You may in reality only have put out a set of seven water bowls and lit a stick of incense, but if you think in your meditations that the whole earth and sky are filled with a great profusion of offerings—like Ārya Samantabhadra's[22]—you will accumulate the merit that goes with such an offering. As the *Avataṃsaka Sūtra* says: "Most of the offerings are offerings of canopies..." In other words, the sorts of thing you offer are: parasols, canopies, and victory banners. You also should include flowers, incense, butterlamps, perfume, food, etc. The offerings that are hard to come by, the food, for example, should be visualized with a surrounding network of light rays. It is useful to recite the spell (dhāraṇī) for a profusion of offerings, or the offering mantra:

> *Oṃ namo bhagavate, vajra sāra pramardane tathāgatāya, arhate samyaksaṃ buddhāya, tadyathā, oṃ vajre vajre, mahā vajre, mahā tejra vajre, mahā vidyā vajre, mahā bodhichitta vajre, mahā bodhi maṇḍopa saṃkramaṇa vajre, sarva karmāvaraṇa viśhodhana vajre svāhā.*

They say that if you recite these mantras, a great rain of offerings will fall around the victorious ones and their children, even though you may have only laid out the barest minimum of real offerings.

Then you invoke the power of truth [from Jampael Lhuendrub's *Ornament for the Throats of the Fortunate*]:

> By the truth of the Three Jewels; by the great might of the blessings of all the buddhas and bodhisattvas, along with their might

> from completing the two accumulations; by the power of the purity and inconceivability of the dharmadhātu [sphere of truth], may everything become suchness.

When you say, "…may everything become suchness," your visualization turns into suchness—no matter how large or small you imagine your visualization to be.

Now to the actual process of visualizing the merit field. According to the *Swift Path,* there are two ways of visualizing the merit field. One of them follows the concise discourses; the other follows the *Guru Pūjā*—an extraordinary piece of instruction taken from the *Miraculous Book of the Gelugpas.* This practice was the yoga of Gyaelwa Ensapa and Choekyi Dorje, another great adept. They achieved the unification in only one lifetime by depending on this visualization of commitment, wisdom, and concentration beings, one inside the other.

At this point recite [from Jampael Lhuendrub's *Ornament for the Throats of the Fortunate*]:

> In space, the broad road used by the gods, seen as bliss and void combined,
> At the center of overlapping banks of cloud of Samantabhadra's offerings,
> Stands a wish-granting tree bedecked with leaves, flowers, and fruit.
> At its summit is a precious throne ablaze with five colors of light;
> On this rests a huge lotus with sun and moon discs.
> On these sits my root guru who is thrice kind to me.
> He is by nature all buddhas; in aspect, a saffron-robed monk,
> With one face, two hands, and a radiant smile.
> His right hand makes the Dharma-teaching mudrā;
> The left, the gesture of meditative absorption
> While holding a nectar-filled begging bowl.
> He wears the three bright-saffron Dharma robes;
> On his head is a yellow pandit's hat.
> At his heart are Śhākyamuni and blue Vajradhara
> Of one face, two hands, holding bell and vajra.
> Vajradhara sits in union with Dhatvīśhvarī;
> They experience bliss and void combined;
> They wear precious ornaments and robes of celestial silks.

At this point your mind apprehends the primal wisdom of inseparable bliss and emptiness; the appearance of this wisdom is made to take the form of space—"the road used by the gods." Within this space, you form the merit-field visualization. The reason you do this first step is in order to see everything as the interplay of bliss and emptiness. Here I could discuss many profound things about the way you convince yourself about the bliss and emptiness associated with the meaning of the mantra *evaṃ* [suchness] and how then, within this apprehension, you appear as a deity. There are many people in the audience here, however, who have not been initiated [into the highest tantras], so this is not the time to discuss these things, and this much will have to do. In any case, you must visualize the offerings of Samantabhadra on billowing banks of clouds.

In the center of the precious ground surface is a lake of milk, in which stands a wish-granting tree. This tree is made of seven precious substances: golden roots, a silver trunk, lapis lazuli branches, crystal leaves, red pearls for flowers, jade petals, and diamond fruit. All the parts of the tree—the roots for instance—come in multiples of seven. The tree fulfills your every need and desire, exactly as you would wish, just as the wish-granting gem does. The rustle of its leaves, and so on, tells of the four seals of the Dharma, that is, impermanence, selflessness, [suffering, and nirvāṇa].[23] A precious throne stands at the center of the tree on a huge flower; this throne is supported by eight lions who have the following significance. The great bodhisattvas take the form of lions and support this throne to show their respect, and so on; and just as the lion dominates all other wild animals, the buddhas dominate all the worldly gods and demons and tirṭhikas. There are eight lions to symbolize the eight riches, and they are grouped into four pairs to denote the four fearlessnesses.

Above this throne are eleven lotus bases. The higher the lotus base, the greater the distance between levels. The topmost base has four petals. A sun disc, made of costly fire crystal, sits on the anther of the lotus. A moon disc made of water crystal sits on the sun disc. These two discs are like two horizontal drum skins (note that these drums do not have handles).

The lotus symbolizes renunciation. A lotus grows in the mud yet remains unsullied by it. Renunciation is similarly unsullied by the faults of saṃsāra. The sun ripens the unripe; the sun disc thus symbolizes the ripening effect of ultimate bodhichitta [the wisdom understanding emptiness, see Day 22, pp. 620 ff.] has on one's mindstream. The moon's white rays provide relief from heat. The moon disc symbolizes relative bodhichitta [the mind aspiring to enlightenment]—something by nature white that provides relief from feelings of hostility. The lotus bases are therefore made up of these three components to symbolize that the figures standing on them are masters of the three fundamentals of the path. The lotus also symbolizes the small and medium scopes; the sun and moon discs symbolize the great scope.

Next you must visualize the main figure on this lotus base. Who is the main figure of the *Guru Pūjā* merit field? Some say he is Je Rinpoche; others say he is your root guru; some even call him the "Guru Pūjā Je Lama." But he is called Lama Lozang Tubwang Dorje Chang. He is called "Lama" because he is your own lama; "Lozang" because he is Tsongkapa [whose ordination name was Lozang Dragpa]; "Tubwang" because he is our Teacher Śhākyamuni; and "Dorje Chang" because he is Buddha Vajradhara. So he is four things, yet the four are an inseparable entity. This is the principal figure of the merit-field visualization. Does that mean we must think that four different mindstreams are combined together into one? This is not what in fact happens: how could we make four different mindstreams into one! The four have been one entity right from the start. We may take them to be separate mindstreams, but there are proofs using logic and scriptural authority that should convince you that these four are in fact one.

The four are the one entity. But for us, Vajradhara is blue, holds a vajra and bell, and wears the costume of the saṃbhogakāya; Śhākyamuni has a shaven head, wears nothing on his feet, and maintains the aspect of the nirmāṇakāya. Thus, while we never associate the two together, this is not how things are. Buddha displayed his supreme nirmāṇakāya form whenever he taught the vinaya or sūtras. When he taught tantras, he displayed his Vajradhara form. Moreover, when he taught the Guhyasamāja tantra, he appeared as Vajradhara with three faces and six hands. He appeared as four-faced Heruka with twelve hands while teaching the Heruka tantra. And so on. He appeared in infinite numbers of different forms to suit a particular sūtra or tantra, yet in reality was still Śhākyamuni. Thus Vajradhara and Śhākyamuni are one entity: they are not separate mindstreams. When Śhākyamuni had no more direct disciples, he went into nirvāṇa. But even after this, he appeared many times in India as pandits and adepts, and taught the Dharma while in these forms. During the first dissemination of the teachings in Tibet, he appeared as Śhāntarakṣhita, Padmasaṃbhava, etc., and taught the Dharma. In the second dissermination in Tibet, he manifested as many scholar-adepts in order to teach the

Dharma: Atiśha, Je Tsongkapa, and so on. So Je Lozang Dragpa, too, is Śhākyamuni by nature.

Buddha said that Śhākyamuni-Vajradhara in the future would take the form of gurus when the five degenerations prevail. So you may be wondering, "Who then is the emanation of Śhākyamuni-Vajradhara that is supposed to be working now for my sake?" Look no further than your guru. The *Śhrīkhasama Tantra* says:

> All these beings are the embodiment of the five dhyāni buddhas,
> Appearing like actors, or a faithful portrait.
> That known as "great bliss" is but one—
> The one experience in varied guises.

You can take this quotation in many ways. It could apply to the isolation of the body level of the completion stage; or you could apply it to the way you should devote yourself to your spiritual guide, as follows:

Suppose a leading dancer [in a monastic ritual] puts on the Black Hat costume and then makes his entrance. People will say, "Here comes the Black Hat," yet it is only the dancer. Then he goes off and puts on the Dharmarāja mask [becoming the Dharma protector, Yama], and when he re-enters, people will say, "That's Dharmarāja." But it's really only the lead dancer himself. Though we designate him with different names when he dons each different costume, he is still just the lead dancer. The Victorious One, Vajradhara, similarly appears in the aspect of Śhākyamuni, Je Tsongkapa, or your own guru. Their different aspects aside, they are one entity.

You should visualize the main figure of the merit field with like conviction. This figure has been given the name Lama Lozang Tubwang Dorje Chang, but he is even more. As it says: "He is by nature all buddhas." You must become convinced that the guru is an entity that includes all the buddhas' primal wisdom embodied in the one physical form. I will discuss this in some detail in the section on devotion to a spiritual guide.

Without a proper understanding of these things, your meditations on the guru yogas, no matter how profound, will only be a pale reflection. We find in the *Great Stages of the Path:*

> One should understand the foregoing to be the famous instruction called "guru yoga." But nothing will come of it if one meditates on it only a few times.

[The recitation refers to] three types of kindness. According to the sūtric tradition these are: giving vows, transmissions, and discourses. In the tantric tradition they are: giving major initiations, explaining the tantras, and giving instructions. We say "thrice kind" because one receives all three from the one guru.

Externally, the main figure takes the form of the victorious one, great Tsongkapa—a monk clad in saffron robes. They say this particular saffron of the robes he wears is approximately the color of the ruddy duck. His right hand makes the teaching-Dharma gesture; his left holds a begging bowl full of nectar while making the meditative-absorption gesture. The thumb and forefinger of both hands hold the stems of blue lotuses [or utpala]. Their petals are level with his shoulders. The sword of wisdom, its tip lightly aflame, stands on the fully blossomed flower to his right. A copy of the *Eight-Thousand-Verse Perfection of Wisdom Sūtra* sits on the lotus to his left; this book speaks its contents. You could also imagine the text is the one you are specializing on in your study, contemplation, and meditation.

The three robes he wears are saffron colored. There are actually three types of saffron color: yellow, reddish-yellow, and red. These colors correspond with his ceremonial shawl, sleeveless upper garment, and lower garment. He wears a yellow pandit's hat; its sharp peak stands upright. All these different colors imply many things, but it would take too long to discuss them here. You will find these details in discourses on the *Hundreds of Gods of Tuṣhita* and the *Guru Pūjā* practices.

Visualize Śhākyamuni sitting at Tsongkapa's heart. Vajradhara sits at Śhākyamuni's heart. At Vajradhara's heart sits the concentration being—a blue syllable *hūṃ*. These figures are not separate beings sitting one inside the other, like a set of containers. Śhākyamuni is placed at Tsongkapa's heart in order to show that the guru externally seems to take the form of a monk but internally he is Śhākyamuni. And Vajradhara sits at Śhākyamuni's heart to show that the guru is secretly Vajradhara. We speak of "the three beings sitting one within the other," so you might be tempted to think these above three figures will suffice. However, the first two are both commitment beings; victor Vajradhara is the wisdom being. Thus it is necessary to put a blue *hūṃ* at his heart to serve as the concentration being. This meditation on the three beings is one of the profoundest keys of tantra, and I dare not discuss it here.

The recitation [from *An Ornament for the Throats of the Fortunate*] continues:

My guru has the marks and signs
And blazes forth thousands of light rays;
A five-colored rainbow encircles him.
He sits in vajra posture; his pure aggregates
Are the five dhyāni buddhas;
His four constituents, the four consorts;
His senses, veins, muscles, and joints
Are actually bodhisattvas; his skin pores
Are twenty-one thousand arhats;
His limbs—powerful wrathful ones.
The light rays from his body are direction protectors.
Indra, Brahmā, and other gods
Throw themselves at his feet. Around him sit:
My own lamas, a profusion of tutelary gods,
Their maṇḍalas, their attendant gods,
The buddhas and bodhisattvas,
Ḍākas, and the protectors of the teachings.
All their three doors are marked by the three vajras.
Hooked rays of light spread out from their *hūṃ* letters,
Bringing back wisdom beings from their natural abodes,
Who indistinguishably merge and stabilize.

The guru sits in the vajra position. You meditate that his [five] aggregates [see Day 22, pp. 632ff.] are the five dhyāni buddhas, and so on. This meditation is taken from the root tantra of the Guhyasamāja body maṇḍala. I shall discuss this only briefly. This instruction is treated in detail in the *Vajra Garland*, the explanatory tantra [for Guhyasamāja]. The detailed method of generation is the body maṇḍala of three-faced, six-handed Guhyasamāja. If you cannot manage this, visualize according to the one-faced, two-handed version discussed in the yoga tantras. The guru's [symbolic] form aggregate extends from the tip of his crown protrusion to his hairline; this aggregate is Vairochana Buddha by nature. The guru's recognition aggregate extends from his hairline to his throat; this aggregate is Amitābha Buddha by nature. And so on, [as described in the Guhyasamāja tantra].

So, the five dhyāni buddhas, symbols of the five aggregates, sit one on top of the other. Each of their crown protrusions touches the lotus base of the dhyāni buddha above it. Generate this visualization in the center of the guru's body—like the heartwood of a tree. His four physical constituents are represented by the four consorts who embrace these buddhas. The eight bodhisattvas—Kṣhitigarbha and so on—represent his veins, muscles, and joints, as well as his six senses: his eyes, etc. His veins and muscles are by nature Maitreya, who sits on his crown protrusion. Samantabhadra sits on his eight major joints. The recitation does not explicitly mention the five vajra consorts—Vajrarūpa, etc.—but, as in the Guhyasamāja body maṇḍala, they are in sexual union with some of these male bodhisattvas.

The text says "his skin pores are...arhats." These arhats are not śhrāvakas and pratyekabuddhas: they are Mahāyāna arhats, that is, ārya buddhas. In fact, each of the main figure's pores is a buddhafield. Think that in these fields, infinite numbers of buddhas are performing the twelve deeds: some of them are subduing Māra, others are turning the wheel of Dharma, and so on. This is the meaning of the expression "all buddhafields appear in a buddha's body" [see Day 12, p. 360]. One of the Avalokiteśhvara tantras tells us the name of each buddhafield in these pores, as well as the name of the tathāgata who resides there. You should apply this information to all buddha figures. Most of the texts give the number twenty-one thousand, but the actual number is not so fixed.

Visualize the ten wrathful deities on, and of the same nature as, the ten segments of his limbs—for example, Yamāntaka on his right hand.

There are now five deities at the central figure's heart. The way these are placed is as follows. The biggest is Akṣhobhya [the dhyāni buddha]. Śhākyamuni sits at his heart. Vajradhara is at Śhākyamuni's heart. Māmakī sits in front of Akṣhobhya, in sexual union with him. Mañjuśhrī [one of the eight bodhisattvas] sits behind Akṣhobhya, facing forward.

The body of the main figure emits rays of light, with various emanations at the tips of these rays—emanations such as the direction protectors, and so on. Think that spirits such as yakṣhas and guhyakas [i.e., Indra and Brahmā] lie prostrate beneath the main figure's legs.

Although you might not be visualizing all this very clearly, it is still vital to reach the conviction that your guru's aggregates, physical constituents, senses, etc., are really the five dhyāni buddhas, the tathagatas in union with their consorts, peaceful and wrathful deities, and so forth.

So much for the way you visualize the main figure. Here is how you visualize his retinue. Light rays come out of the main figure's heart. Some go to the right and broaden—upon them sit [the lamas of] the Lineage of Extensive Deeds; others go to the left and broaden, for [the lamas of] the

Lineage of the Profound View. Some rays go out front, for the gurus who have taught you the Dharma in person; other rays go behind—[the lamas of] the Lineage of Consecrated Practices sit on these, but on a slightly higher level than the other groups.

Now, there are many profound points I could make on the way you arrange the members of the Lineage of Consecrated Practices. The most famous members of this lineage are Vajradhara, Tilopa, Nāropa, Ḍoṃbhīpa, Atiśha, and so on. But, as Drubkang Geleg Gyatso pointed out, in the Profound Extensive Lineage itself, there is an undegenerated, continuous stream of blessings from one lama to the next. One therefore need not visualize another lineage. Kardo Lozang Gomchung on the other hand claimed that the Consecrated Practices Lineage consisted of members of the Guhyasamāja, Heruka, and Yamāntaka lineages. Je Ngagwang Jampa and Lama Yongdzin Rinpoche claim it is composed mainly of two lineages: the Sixteen Droplets of the Kadampas tantra and the Gelug Confidential Lineage.

A profound instruction that I received from my own precious guru gives a way to combine these different versions into one. I shall now give to you the whispered lineage, which I heard from his very mouth, and withhold nothing. Visualize a vertical row of figures in this group behind the main figure. All the figures in this row—except for Vajradhara [the topmost figure]—take the shape of Mañjuśhrī, beginning with Mañjuśhrī himself and going down to your own guru. To this vertical line's right are the gurus of the Guhyasamāja and Yamāntaka tantras. Each of these two lineages forms its own vertical line. To the Mañjuśhrī figures' left are the lineages of the Heruka tantra and Sixteen Drops tantra. Again, each of these forms its own vertical line. Je Sherab Gyatso in his writings described a similar arrangement. There are other instructions, but for further details you will have to consult the *Book of the Kadampas,* Kachen Namkha Dorje's works on the *Guru Pūjā,* Tutor Tsechogling's recorded discourses on the *Guru Pūjā,* the biographies of the lineage gurus of that practice, and the abovementioned writings of Sherab Gyatso.

There is also a very special oral instruction on how to arrange the gurus of the old and neo-Kadampa schools [see Day 6, p. 207]. So much for the visualization of the gurus.

Next, the lotus base on the first level has four petals. Place the thirty-two deities of the Akṣhobhya vajra system of the Guhyasamāja group on the front petal; the thirteen deities of the Yamāntaka tantra stand on the petal to Guhyasamāja's right; the sixty-two deities of Luipa's version of the Heruka tantra are on the petal to Guhyasamāja's left. The nine deities of the Kāpālin version of Hevajra stand on the rear petal.

According to another tradition, you visualize Guhyasamāja—the king of father tantras—on the petal to the main figure's right. Then Chakrasaṃvara—the king of mother tantras—stands to the main figure's left. Deities of Yamāntaka—the tantra that has all the key points of both mother and father tantras—stand on the middle petal in front of the main figure.

In any case, if you can manage it you should visualize the whole maṇḍala of each tantra along with their resident deities. If this is too much for you, visualize the principal deities and their complete retinues [without their maṇḍalas]. And if you cannot do this, it is enough to simply visualize the principal deities.

On the second level down, visualize the other highest yoga tantra deities, with Kālachakra to the forefront. The yoga tantra deities belong to the third level. The charyā tantra deities stand on the fourth level. The kriyā tantra deities on the fifth. On the sixth, we have the buddhas, taking their supreme nirmāṇakaya forms. On the seventh, the bodhisattvas. On the eighth, pratyekabuddhas. The ninth has the śhrāvakas. The tenth, ḍākas and ḍākinīs. And on the eleventh, visualize the Dharma protectors.

Syllable letters—by nature the three vajras [enlightened body, speech, and mind]—are visible on three points of the bodies of the merit-field figures: that is, a white *oṃ*, the nature of the vajra body and Vairochana Buddha, on the crown of their heads, [a red *āḥ* (vajra speech and Amitābha Buddha) on their throats, and a blue *hūṃ* (vajra mind and Akṣhobhya Buddha) at their hearts]. Although the recitation texts do not explicitly say so, we are told a yellow *svā* should be visible at their navels: it is Ratnasaṃbhava Buddha by nature. A green *hā* should also sit at each figure's private parts: its nature is Amoghasiddhi Buddha. The three vajras are exclusive to buddhas. Thus you should regard all the merit field to be buddhas by nature—even the śhrāvakas, pratyekabuddhas, and so on, who, except for just showing themselves in this aspect here, are nothing but buddhas in nature. Also understand them to be nothing but emanations of your guru. There is even an instruction to make each figure out of commitment, wisdom, and concentration beings.

We are also told to develop three more attitudes toward the merit field: on the appearance side, we visualize it well; from the devotion side, we believe "this one and that one are the actual so and so"; and from the faith side, we believe it is a marvelous thing to which to make offerings.

When you have completed this visualizing process, invite the wisdom beings. Actually, they do not need to be invited: they will come before you if you just imagine them. One sūtra says: "The sages will come in front of anyone whose visualization is made paramount."

In debating we hear the assertion that "there is no place unperceived by the valid cognitions of buddhas." We must put such assertions to good use. We can readily compare this with a point made in tantra: for beings who have achieved the bliss of the unification, the enlightened mind and body have become the same entity. Any place pervaded by their omniscience is also pervaded by the enlightened body.

> In but one moment, their omniscience
> Pervades the maṇḍala of all knowables...
> Wherever their primal wisdom pervades
> So, too, do their bodies.

That is: even in the place in front of us, because the wisdom of all the buddhas pervades that place, so too do their bodies pervade it as well. If we merely try to visualize the deities of the merit field, the deities will take their place in front of us—only we cannot see them because of our karma and [resulting] obscurations. This is illustrated by the stories telling how Asaṅga achieved visions of Maitreya, or how Chandragomin did this with Avalokiteśhvara.[24] So, the sages come before us as effortlessly as the moon's reflection appears on the surface of water in a pot. As soon as we begin to visualize the merit field, the buddhas come to us, but we do not see them. Similarly, we do not see, for example, the nāgas and spirits living in waterholes and wayside shrines.

Still, whether you receive any blessing or merit [from the presence of the buddhas] depends on whether you have the attitude that they are there in person. You therefore invite them to come so as to allay fears that these refuge beings before you might not actually be there; you also invite them to stabilize your conviction about the visualization.

Then you recite [from *An Ornament for the Throats of the Fortunate*]:

The protectors of each and every sentient being,
Gods who conquer mighty Māra and his hordes,
You who perfectly know all things—
O bhagavān buddhas and your train, please come here.

Jāḥ hūṃ baṃ hoḥ:
You become inseparable from the commitment beings.

As you recite these words, think: "The members of the merit field have the three qualities of omniscience, love, and ability. So, as in the story of Magadhabhadrī, all of them are coming in a magical, infinite procession.[25] At the same time, light radiates from the seed syllables at the hearts of the beings in the merit field. This light strikes the hearts of all the buddhas in the ten directions, and complete merit fields are drawn out of the heart of each buddha. All these merit fields merge into the one field that stands above your original visualization. This field then radiates many full sets of wisdom beings again, and these full sets dissolve into each member of your merit field. You now visualize that each member of your merit field now by nature completely embodies your place of refuge.

If we do this visualization, we won't make value judgments about the merit field; the visualization is also an auspicious gesture for the future, when we will actually travel the path and enjoy its fruits.

By the way, this is a tantric tradition, so one attracts the wisdom beings, they come, they are bound to the commitment beings, and then one delights them [with offerings].

That done, we then bathe the figures. The merit field is unsullied by sin, karmic obscuration, dirt, and so on, and has nothing to be purified, but as once was said: "Dharmakāya has no stain; but just to serve you and pay my respects…" In other words, we shall do this practice to purify *ourselves* of karma, obscurations, etc.

There are a number of ways to visualize the bathhouse, but as this particular practice relates to highest yoga tantra, the bathhouse has four sides, four doors, and ornamental facades [like the celestial palaces at the heart of a tantric maṇḍala]. The house has only one story; its pagoda is supported by four pillars made of precious substances. Inside the building, the underside of the pagoda is decorated with a canopy of pearls. A bathing pool is in the center of the building. The bottom of the pool is of crystal covered with a layer of gold dust, the center raised slightly higher than its edges—

like a turtle's shell. The remaining architectural details conform to the usual descriptions in the highest yoga tantras. There are the required number of wooden platforms or thrones to accommodate the members of the merit field; walkways lead to these thrones or platforms from three sides, and each walkway has four steps. A low wall made of a precious substance surrounds the building; there is a jeweled niche in this wall to hold the merit field's soon-to-be discarded clothes. Visualize the new clothes you will offer the merit field, the ewers [in the bathhouse], and so on.

If you have implements for the bath ritual, use the bowl to represent the bathing pool. Pour a little water from your initiation vase into the bowl. Draw two horizontal lines on your ritual mirror with water from the vase [use the peacock-feather vase ornament as the writing instrument]; then make two vertical lines to form nine spaces in a square array. Draw dots with more water from the vase: one in the center square and one each in the four cardinal directions [leaving the corner squares blank]. The square array represents the bathhouse; the five dots, the five dhyāni buddha families.

Next recite:

Here is a perfumed bathhouse,
With clear and brilliant crystal floor,
With radiant, exquisite pillars made of precious substances,
Adorned with a canopy of dazzling pearls.

Just after [Buddha's] birth,
The gods washed his body;
So I also wash with celestial waters
The bodies of the sugatas.
Oṃ sarva tathāgata abhiṣhekata samaya śhrīye āḥ hūṃ

Body born of ten million virtues and excellences,
Speech that fulfills the hopes of infinite beings,
Mind that sees all knowables as they are:
I wash the body of Śhākyamuni-Vajradhara.
Oṃ sarva tathāgata abhiṣhekata samaya śhrīye āḥ hūṃ

I wash the bodies of the Lineage of Extensive Deeds.
I wash the bodies of the Lineage of Profound View.

I wash the bodies of the Lineage of Consecrated Practices.
I wash the bodies of the gurus of my lineage.
Oṃ sarva tathāgata abhiṣhekata samaya śhrīye āḥ hūṃ

I wash the bodies of the buddhas, our teachers.
I wash the body of holy Dharma, our protector.
I wash the bodies of the Saṅgha, our saviors.
I wash the bodies of the Three Jewels, our refuge.
Oṃ sarva tathāgata abhiṣhekata samaya śhrīye āḥ hūṃ

At the start of this passage, you either visualize that the merit-field beings fly down to the bathhouse, or you visualize stairways that they use to come down. In any case, you say the mantra *oṃ sarva tathāgata…* and emanate three offering goddesses in front of each member of the merit field. One goddess washes the body, one anoints the body, and one provides new clothes. While the figures are being washed, you visualize that the first goddess takes water from the pool and offers it to her member of the merit field; the minds of the merit-field beings develop great bliss while this is happening.

After the bathing, their bodies are wiped to the mantra:

I wipe their bodies with peerless cloth—
Clean and steeped in choice perfume.
Oṃ hūṃ trāṃ hrīḥ āḥ kāya viśhodhanaye svāhā

The practice conforms with the traditional consecration ceremonies. The second set of goddesses dry the merit-field beings by wiping five points on their bodies: forehead, throat, heart, and both shoulders—for all the water on their bodies has settled on these points. They do not need to be wiped from head to foot as we do when we bathe.

They are then anointed. Recite:

I anoint the dazzling bodies of the sages—
As dazzling as burnished, refined gold—
With the choicest fragrances
The billion worlds have to offer.

The lotion is a golden color, exquisitely perfumed, and not at all greasy.

Then you imagine that the third set of goddesses gives them new clothes. Recite:

> Out of my unceasing faith, I offer
> Celestial robes—soft, light, diaphanous—
> to you who have achieved the indestructible vajra body.
> May I, too, gain the vajra body.

Each figure receives the appropriate costume: the garments of a peaceful deity or of a wrathful deity. Imagine that Dromtoenpa receives a blue coat lined with lynx fur on the inside; he also receives a belt that is wound six times round his waist. His clothes symbolize that the path of the three scopes is covered by the six perfections. Doing this is a most auspicious gesture.

Then the goddesses give the merit field their appropriate ornaments and implements. Recite:

> Because the victors are naturally adorned with the marks and signs,
> They have no need of other ornaments;
> But I offer the best of jewels and ornaments
> So that all beings may obtain a body with these self-same marks.

The figures then go up to resume their places while you recite:

> Because you bhagavāns love
> All beings and myself, I ask you to remain
> Through your magiç powers
> As long as I still make offerings to you.

The old clothes [left on the jeweled niches by the deities before they entered the bathhouse] turn into light, which dissolves into you between your eyebrows. Alternatively, you may imagine that a representative from each of the six types of rebirth comes forward to receive his share of these relics. Six gutters come out of the bathing pool. These gutters take the bathwater to the six realms; feel that this water has removed all suffering from all other beings. Also—as human beings are so insatiable—visualize that the water turns into goods to supply every imaginable human need. Then think that the bathhouse, etc., dissolve into unfocussed emptiness.

OFFERING THE SEVEN-LIMBED PRAYER AND A WORLD MAṆḌALA—PRACTICES THAT CONTAIN ALL THE KEY POINTS FOR ACCUMULATING MERIT AND SELF-PURIFICATION (47)

Geshe Doelpa said:

> While you accumulate your collections [of merit] and purify yourself of obscurations, if you think that you are conscientiously petitioning your gurus and deities, even though you think these things will never happen—not in a hundred years—they will happen. This is so for all conditioned phenomena: they do not remain static. At some point you will develop them.

That is, it is vital to build up your stock [of merit] and purify [your obscurations]. The practices of the seven-limbed prayer and offering the world maṇḍala contain all the key points of this building process; these practices are crucial throughout your whole practice.

Some people might treat these practices off-handedly, thinking: "They are for people who cannot practice vast amounts of virtue," or "They are only an introductory practice that is superfluous to the main practices." This is not the case: there is no better way in either sūtra or tantra to purify oneself than building up a [merit] accumulation and purifying one's obscurations by making the seven-limbed prayer to the supreme merit field—that is, one's guru, the victorious ones, and their children. The seven-limbed prayer is even important in tantric contexts. All four classes of tantra fully discuss the seven limbs; and it is said that even in the generation stages of the highest yoga tantras, one should build up one's accumulations and purify one's obscurations by making the seven-limbed prayer to the merit field, that is, through homage, offering, and so on. Great Tsongkapa—the very embodiment of Mañjuśhrī—carried out the practices of accumulation and self-purification at Oelga, developing extraordinary insights and experiences as a result. This is an example of realizations developing quickly when the practitioner's mental stream has been sufficiently ripened. Even the bodhisattvas on the [ten] great stages work mainly toward accumulation and self-purification. Bodhisattvas on the first stage emanate hundreds of bodies; these bodies go to hundreds of buddhafields and make offerings. And bodhisattvas on the second stage onward emanate more and more bodies, making more numerous and extensive offerings until they reach buddhahood. So it is plain that we should also make offerings.

Kyabje Pabongka Rinpoche discussed this in more detail.

Thus the seven-limbed practices greatly distill both sūtric and tantric accumulation and self-purification. Some illustrations: your faults will ripen like a ready-to-burst boil, and your good qualities will mature like fruit ripe for the picking. Past saints have instructed us: "You are like a dry seed if you do not build up your accumulations." In other words, while you must continue to pursue the lamrim meditation topics, you must definitely also work hard at accumulation and self-purification by means of the seven-limbed prayer. They say you will get nothing out of the path if you only practice the portions that seem plausible to you.

I can illustrate the name "seven-limbed" as follows. Suppose something is constructed out of seven mechanical parts: a cart, say, will not go if one of them is missing. So too, if one of the seven limbs is missing, one's accumulation and self-purification will not proceed properly.

I shall now discuss the seven limbs.

THE FIRST LIMB: HOMAGE (48)

There are three types of homage: prostration of the body, verbal homage, and mental homage. [The following seven-limbed prayer is taken from the *Royal Prayer of Noble Deeds*]:[26]

> To all the tathāgatas of the three times—those lions among humans—
> To be found in the ten directions of the universe,
> I pay homage to each and every one of you
> With cleansed body, speech, and mind.
>
> With this powerful prayer of noble deeds,
> I prostrate before all the victors,
> Imagining I have as many bodies
> As there are atoms in the world.

According to the written teachings on this prayer, each body you emanate should have infinite numbers of heads. If this does not appear to you easily, it is enough to imagine all the bodies you have been born into since beginningless time—but in human form.

The prayer continues:

> On each atom there are as many buddhas
> As [the universe] has atoms, and those buddhas
> Sit among bodhisattvas. So too do I believe
> That all victors fill the expanse of all phenomena.

This verse means that every Buddha in existence can sit upon a single, tiny atom. Suppose one hundred people look simultaneously at one barley grain: that one grain occupies the eye consciousness of one hundred people. The primal wisdom of all buddhas can similarly be occupied with a single atom. A buddha's physical body is also found on any atom engaging that buddha's primal wisdom. This is a property of the unification and is because their mind and energy winds are always found together.

The prayer continues:

> I sing of the qualities of all the victors
> With an inexhaustible ocean of praise,
> With a great ocean of every melodious sound.
> And thus I praise all sugatas.

Even raising a single finger to the merit field in respect is paying homage with the body. There is a list of different ways to pay physical homage. Touching your four limbs and head to the ground is called the *semi-prostration.* The *full prostration* is laying your whole body on the ground. The full prostration was first mentioned in the *Laying Out of Stalks Sūtra,* where it says:

Look at the prostrations of Subhadra, who lays his whole body on the ground like a fallen tree.

The benefits of prostrating are these. The *Sūtra for Classifying Karma* mentions ten benefits—one will have a handsome body, a golden complexion, and so on. Other sūtras say that one acquires the merit to become a thousand world emperors for each atom in the ground covered by one's body. The full prostration was discussed in the tantras; it was how Pandit Nāropa used to do his prostrations. Purchog Ngagwang Jampa is supposed to have said, "If you believe in the benefits of making prostrations, you will feel, "If only my body, hands, and feet were longer."

[Before you prostrate, you join your hands together.] The tīrṭhikas traditionally press their palms together, but we do not follow this practice: we place our thumbs inside our cupped hands so that our hands are not empty. The shape of our hands then resembles the [wish-granting] gem.

You then place your cupped hands on your head: this imparts the potential to achieve the crown protrusion. Then place your hands on the space between your eyebrows. This imparts the potential to achieve the *urṇa*—the curled hair on the forehead. Then place your hands at your throat to impart the potential to achieve the enlightened speech, a voice with sixty melodious nuances. Then place your hands at your heart to impart the potential to gain the enlightened mind. All these actions both collect merit and purify: they purify the karma and obscurations of your body, speech, and mind.

If you cup your hands when you go down or get off the floor, they say it will cause you to be reborn with round animal hooves. You therefore should keep your fingers straight, close together and spread flat on the ground. Do not make a fist. These actions will help you achieve webs of light between your fingers and toes [one of the marks of a buddha]. Place your hands and forehead on the ground. Note that a relationship exists between how you get off the floor and how soon you will transcend saṃsāra—so you must get up as quickly as a scurrying fox. Also, if you do not get up soon enough and remain sleepily on the ground, you may be reborn as one of the animal species that go about on their bellies—a reptile for example. So do not give in to the temptation to have a rest on the floor; do not leave your head at rest [on the ground]. If you do not completely straighten your body between prostrations [after you get up] and instead leave your posture hunched over, you will be reborn hunched, like an animal. So straighten your body properly. You should not do hasty prostrations to get to some large number; you should do each of them properly so as to build up your merit accumulation. Je Rinpoche advised us not to focus on the number of prostrations—doing a hundred thousand as a preliminary practice, and so on; go instead for quality, even if that means not doing as big a number.

Some might claim "I am going to do my preliminary retreat,"[27] and then take shortcuts when they do the hundred thousand prostrations. This is wrong. You must build up your accumulations and purify your obscurations

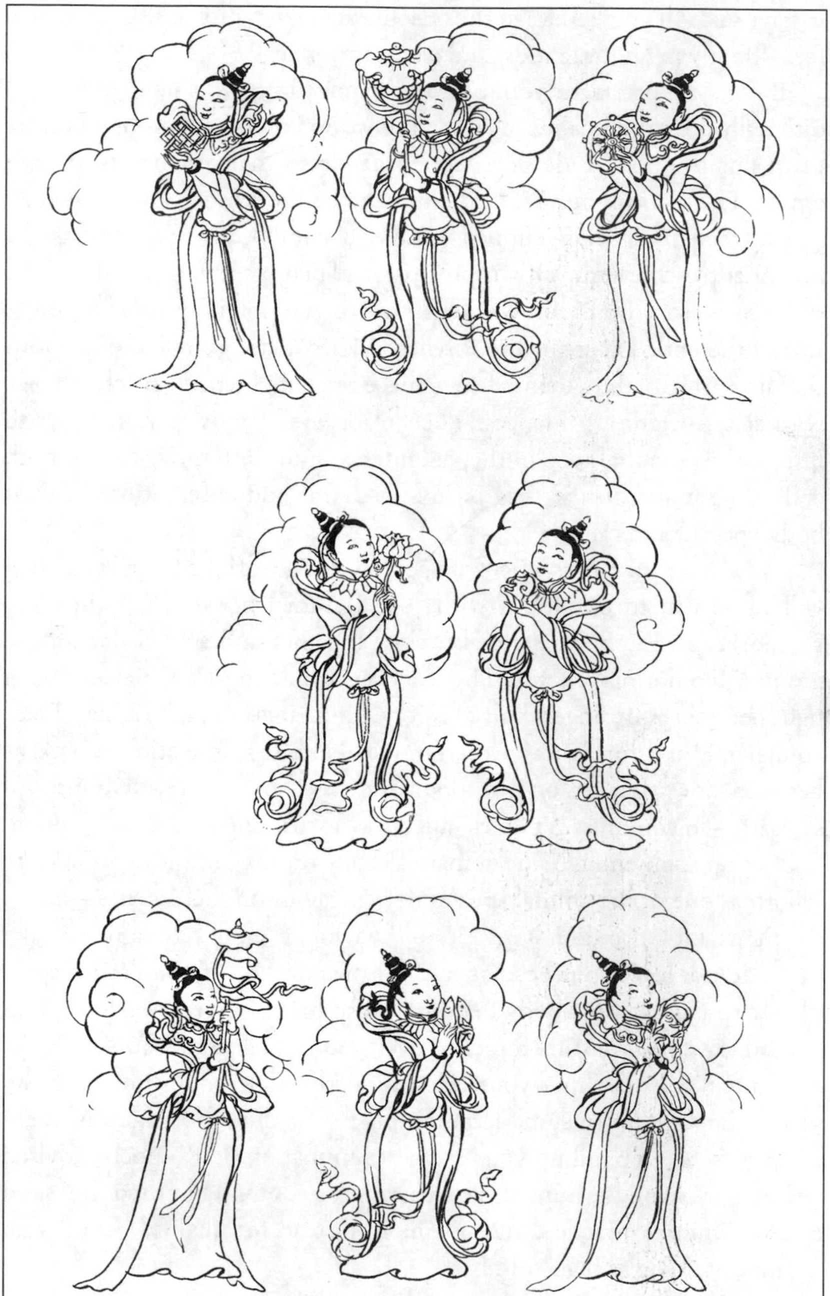

THE EIGHT OFFERING GODDESSES (SEE P. 174)

right up until you reach enlightenment. Beginners like ourselves must work hard at accumulation and purification all our lives. Accumulation and self-purification are much more important than meditation: you will not achieve anything at all if you claim "I have finished my preliminary retreat" and take things easy thereafter.

If your prostrations are already building up your stock of merit and already purifying your obscurations, you should not worry or overexert yourself if you have not yet completed a hundred thousand prostrations. This is illustrated by a story. There were four people in retreat together. One of them had not completed the [set] number [of repetitions of the refuge formula], and the other three asked him what number he had reached. He said, "Has your only goal been the number?" Ideally you ought to complete a large number of prostrations done properly; keeping count of your prostrations is for the virtue of rejoicing [in your virtuous accomplishments].

You can usually pay homage when you go about your daily routine. When you are walking along a road and happen to see, for example, the symbols of enlightened body, speech, and mind, you should respectfully join your hands together; even this becomes prostrating. They say that if you really know how to practice, you can convert every motion of your body into Dharma.

THE SECOND LIMB: OFFERING (49)

The *Royal Prayer of Noble Deeds* continues:

> I offer the victorious ones exquisite flowers,
> Choice garlands, the clash of cymbals,
> The best of lotions, of parasols,
> Of oil lamps and choice incense.
>
> I offer the victorious ones
> Exquisite robes, the best of fragrances,
> Mounds of incense powders high as Meru—
> A sublime array of matchless things.
>
> All this peerless, expansive offering
> I imagine for all the victors. To all the victors

> I pay this homage, making this offering
> By the power of my faith in noble deeds.

We think it a great shame if we leave a productive field unplanted for a year; yet this is no great pity. It is a hundred or even a thousand times more unfortunate if we do not accumulate merit through the merit field. Although any root virtues we accumulate would not be Dharmic if done without at least a yearning for a better rebirth, the end result is always the same with the merit field. If you accumulate merit by paying the merit field homage, making it offerings, and so on, that merit will definitely be a cause for you to gain buddhahood—even though your motive might not even be a wish for a better rebirth. Even if you make offerings to the buddhas with evil motives, this action will contribute to your enlightenment. The results you obtain are special due to the power of the merit field. An illustration: even if you do not plant seed properly in a fertile field, you are still certain to get results.

In the above verses, the lotion referred to is a liquid made by boiling down various fragrant ingredients, such as incense. The "exquisite flowers" and so on may not be supreme offerings, but the phrase "A sublime array..." must refer to all the offerings mentioned above it. The "incense" should only be of one type—sandalwood for example. The "incense powders" are of sandalwood, etc. "Mounds" refers to heaps of incense powders. "Mounds of incense powders," however, has another interpretation. "Incense powders" of course means fragrant powders; "mound" may be a cloth sachet, say, that holds these incense powders. The sachets are attached to canopies and release fragrance when blown by the wind. This *Prayer of Noble Deeds* mentions seven kinds of offerings—exquisite flowers, and so on.

Supreme offerings are the most sublime emanations of buddhas and bodhisattvas, which they produce through their bodhichitta and prayers. Though we cannot make this kind of offering, there are things we can offer. The *Sūtra Requested by Sāgaramati* mentions two: upholding the Dharma, and developing the wish for supreme enlightenment. The *White Lotus of Compassion Sūtra* mentions a third—utilizing one's studies by putting them into practice. Our gurus instruct us to make a fourth type of supreme offering: one's root virtue transformed into offering materials.

The supreme offering of "upholding the Dharma" ranges from upholding the transmitted and realized teachings to just memorizing a single syllable from a mantric spell. "Putting one's studies into practice" means practicing the meaning of anything we have studied or memorized. We should follow the example of Geshe Chaen Ngawa reading the book on the vinaya and throwing out his leather hide [see p. 87]. They say that if we keep waiting for an auspicious alignment of the planets and such to begin our practice, we will die first. Even putting into practice what you know about cleaning your house is an offering of your practice. People who are immersing themselves in the classics should do nothing else but put the meaning of their studies into practice; as Butoen Rinpoche said:

> They want to win and humiliate others;
> They act deceitfully, swear, and fume;
> Speak all manner of drivel, infuriate others:
> This kind of debating takes them to hell!

That is, one should not act like this.

Another word about offering your root virtues transformed into offering materials: you imagine virtue you have gained from study and so on as physical offering materials—as in these quotations: "In the midst of an ocean whose waters are pure ethics..." "Compile your study into an offering ocean." And in the *Guru Pūjā* we find: "Beside a wish-granting lake are my offerings, both real and imagined..." This is an offering of your root merits, imagined in the form of a pleasure garden.

"Developing the wish for supreme enlightenment" means developing bodhichitta and offering it to the victorious ones and their children to please them.

These four things are the sort of supreme offerings we can make. There can be no better offering than these four. Those of us who are ordained must principally offer the things we practice; then, when we are poor, we will not practice wrong livelihoods. Even if we do have money, ordained people must work hardest at offering our practice. Drolungpa says in his *Stages of the Teachings:*

> There are ten types of offering of accomplishment;
> Statues and stūpas, both real and imagined,
> The things one has done oneself or has others do,
> One's service, and one's own lack of delusion.

So he claims we must also make these offerings.

You offer a world maṇḍala at this point. *Mañjuśhrī's Own Words* differs from the *Swift Path* and the *Easy Path* lamrims. According to these last two texts, you make your offerings first, then offer the world maṇḍala. *Mañjuśhrī's Own Words* says we should offer the world maṇḍala first; this follows the practice of making a first offering to the guru, and so on.

Maṇḍala in Tibetan is *kyil kor* [circling the center]. *Kyil* or "center" implies "essence"; *kor* or "circling" implies "extracting." Thus the word *maṇḍala* means "to extract the essence." This has great significance.

[The maṇḍala is usually circular.] Its shape, however, should conform with your karmic propensities—so square maṇḍalas and the like are acceptable.

Some people claim, "External offerings are not as important as inward meditative absorption," but, in the tantric context, we find that [Aśhvaghoṣha's] *Fifty Verses on the Guru* says:

> Honor your guru, your teacher,
> With maṇḍalas, flowers, and folded hands.

One day Dromtoenpa visited the great yogi Goenpawa. Goenpawa was spending his whole time in single-pointed meditation, and his maṇḍala set lay neglected, covered in dust. Drom asked him why he was not offering maṇḍalas. Goenpawa told Drom he was contemplating internal things for the time being, and had become too engrossed. "What do you mean?" Drom said in reproof. "Atisha was a much better meditator than you, yet he made maṇḍala offerings every day at the three times." After this, the yogin Goenpawa put much more effort into making maṇḍala offerings and, as a result, developed realization.

If you are wealthy, you should have a maṇḍala set made of gold, silver, copper, or the like. Otherwise stone, slate, ceramic, or wooden maṇḍalas will do. Je Rinpoche used a stone maṇḍala during his retreat at Oelga. The contents of a maṇḍala could be jewels, grains, and medicines. Or pebbles, sand, and so on, will do. If you are rich, you will build up a huge merit collection by offering the best. The maṇḍala base should be as big as possible and at least no smaller than your own food bowl. You must offer a maṇḍala at least once a year, or once a month.

Put a drop of perfume on your fingertips. You then either put your thumb in the center [on top of the base] and move your fingers round the rim, or you put your fingers on the center and move your thumb round the rim. Make the offering as follows. Hold the maṇḍala base in your left hand with a little grain [in the palm]. Rub the base many times [clockwise] with your right forearm. Imagine you are wiping away your sins and obscurations. Then, rub the base three times in the opposite direction: imagine your lifespan, body, speech, and mind are thereby blessed.

Here are the various traditional ways to fill the maṇḍala. You take east on the maṇḍala base to be either the side facing the merit field—the beings to whom you make the offering—or the side facing you. During an offering maṇḍala, take east to be the side of the maṇḍala base facing the beings to whom you make the offering. Make east the side facing you during a maṇḍala of request. It is best here to adopt the second convention, because you are requesting the merit field to bestow their blessings unto you.

The thirty-seven-heap version of the maṇḍala belongs to Sakya Drogoen Choepag's tradition. These thirty-seven heaps represent: Mount Meru (1); the [four] continents (4); the [eight] minor continents (8); the precious mountain (1); three miscellenia: [wish-granting trees (1); wish-granting cows (1); the unploughed wild crops (1)]; the seven signs of regal power—the precious wheel, etc. (7); the treasure vase (1); the eight goddesses, such as She Who Is Charming (8); sun (1); moon (1); parasol (1); and victory banner (1).

Je Rinpoche followed the tradition of twenty-three heaps. The difference between this and the twenty-five-heap maṇḍala is: you do not make two heaps for the most powerful golden base and the iron mountain chain.

The layout of the visualized Mount Meru and four continents in the maṇḍala follows [Vasubandhu's] *Treasury of Metaphysics.* There is an even more elaborate practice that follows that book. You must have at least an approximate understanding.

Kyabje Pabongka then explained this briefly:

The oceans and Mount Meru are surrounded by a circle of iron mountains. At their center stands Mount Meru, which is made out of four kinds of precious substances. The eastern continent is white; the southern, blue; the western, red; and the northern, gold.

Imagine there are vast quantities of precious mountains and the like, on each particular continent. These precious mountains, wish-granting trees, etc., are resources of each particular continent, and so you must pile some maṇḍala contents on each of them. The wish-granting cow is by nature precious; its urine and droppings are golden. The unploughed wild crop is a huskless rice, and so on. If harvested in the morning, it has grown again by evening; if harvested in the evening, it has grown again by morning. In the twenty-five-heap maṇḍala offering, you do not make separate heaps for each of these four things—they are implicitly included within the offering of the four continents.

The seven precious symbols of regal power are mentioned in the verse: "Made of gold from the Jambuna Ocean..." These seven things [plus the treasure vase] float in space, occupying the cardinal and subdirections between the continents and Mount Meru.

The heaps representing the eight goddesses—the goddess of beauty, etc.—belong to the above thirty-seven-heap offering, although the goddesses themselves are supposed to be standing on the ledges around Mount Meru [in the visualization]. But in the twenty-five-heap version you do not make any heaps to represent these goddesses, for you have already offered one to represent Mount Meru itself.

The heap to represent the sun goes to the left of Mount Meru; that of the moon goes to the right of the mountain; that of the precious parasol behind Mount Meru; the victory banner goes in front of the mountain and toward you—it is auspicious to do this. Alternatively, you could put the sun's in the west, the moon's in the east, the parasol's in the north, and victory banner's in the south. This is also auspicious.

Offer all the myriad cherished riches of gods and humans while making a heap in the center.

Do not visualize the maṇḍala to be bigger than it already is, yet visualize the four continents, the celestial realms and all, in such a way that they do not get smaller either. Tutor Tsechogling gave a helpful illustration while he was staying at Tashi Lhuenpo: You can see all of a person's face "in a bubble on the surface of a bowl of tea." It is also like seeing a small face in a [curved] mirror, or a mountain through the eye of a needle.

You should gradually work up to visualizing the billion universes in three stages—multiply your visualization a thousandfold each time. In other words, begin with a group of one thousand worlds, then have a thousand groups of one thousand worlds each, then a thousand of these latter groups.

In my opinion, the verse "I offer this base, anointed with perfume..." was the one used by Sadāprarudita when he made offerings to Dharmodgata [see Day 7, p. 220], but this must be looked into. There are two versions to this verse. One says "All visualized *for* the buddhafield..."; the other has "All visualized into a buddhafield." The "for" means that the visualization is performed "for the buddhas in the merit field," which may be acceptable, but has the flaw of offering them the impure world of Mount Meru and the four continents. Thus "into a buddhafield..." means that Mount Meru, the four continents and all, are an impure world for only the first moment [of the visualization]; in the second moment they are all transmuted into a pure field. These two visualizations have their own corresponding benefits.

Dagpo Rinpoche says in his *Verses on the Maṇḍala:* "Brahmā and Indra and the vow holder are the offering assistants..." That is, he is saying you should imagine Brahmā assists you [to make the maṇḍala offering] if you hold monks' and nuns' vows. If you do not have these vows, you must have a fully ordained monk and Brahmā helping you. But Mount Meru and the four continents were formed out of sentient beings' collective karma; you therefore do not need the help of Brahmā and Indra to make the offering: the complete world system of Mount Meru and continents are an environmental result of your own share of that collective karma.

Visualize one billion sets of Mount Meru and the four continents—if you can manage this visualization. If not, it is enough to visualize just one complete world system. If you offer the maṇḍala properly, you gain the benefits of actually offering the four continents, Mount Meru, and so on. For example, when Dharmarāja Aśhoka was a child in a former rebirth, he put dirt into Buddha Vipaśhyin's begging bowl, imagining this dirt was gold. Yet he received the same benefits as offering real gold, and as a result, in his later rebirth as Aśhoka, he built ten million stūpas in a single evening. Thus there is nothing better than offering a world maṇḍala to accumulate merit—it completes your accumulations, it is convenient and straightforward to do, and so on. So this round copper base is a vital thing to have!

At the end of the maṇḍala offering, you either tilt the base toward you or away from you when you pour the contents back into their cloth container. If you wish to receive more blessings, pour the contents toward you; pour it away from you when you seek to ward off interferences.

Emphasize doing the visualization properly rather than making a large number of maṇḍala offerings. If ever you want to accumulate a large number of anything, it is enough to do this offering section of the preparatory rites many times. Recite the verse "I offer this base, anointed with perfume..." along with "Until enlightenment, I take refuge in Buddha, Dharma, and the Supreme Assembly..."; then make the seven-heap offering: one for Mount Meru, four for the continents, and one each for the sun and moon.

Bhikṣhuṇī Lakṣhmī had her visions of Ārya Avalokiteśhvara after she had made a number of maṇḍala offerings; Je Tsongkapa strenuously made maṇḍala offerings, and so on, while at Oelga Choelung—and as a result developed the correct view. Thus everyone should make an effort at doing this practice.

DAY 6

Āchārya Chandragomin said:

> If a calf is attracted
> To some grass and dry leaves at the lip of a deep well,
> He may not manage to reach them, but instead fall into the abyss.
> He who desires the pleasures of worldly life is just like this.

In other words, when an elephant goes to the edge of a terrifying cliff because of his attachment for the grass growing at the edge, he may fall over. Similarly, when we are attached to the happiness of this life alone, we commit various nonvirtues, and eventually, when we fall down the cliff to the lower realms, it will be hard for us ever to be free of them. We must therefore achieve our eternal hope. There is no better way of doing this than by properly following the stages of the path to enlightenment. We must set our motivation by thinking: "I shall achieve buddhahood for the sake of all sentient beings. So I shall listen to this lamrim discourse and put it into practice."

Then Kyabje Pabongka reviewed the headings he had already covered.

The meditation session is divided into three sections: the preliminary rites, the main part, and the conclusion. There are six preparatory rites; the fifth of these rites is offering the seven-limbed prayer and the world maṇḍala. I have finished discussing the second of the seven limbs.

THE THIRD LIMB: CONFESSION OF SINS (50)

We do not develop in our mindstreams any new realizations we have not already developed, and those we have already developed are degenerating. Our sins and obscurations are responsible for this. Further, our sins will be responsible for all the unfortunate things in this and our next life. If we do not want these things to happen, we must expiate our sins.

Through confession, we can purify infinite amounts of karma—even the [five] heinous crimes or great sins whose results we would normally have to undergo. The Vaibhāṣhika system of tenets claims that one cannot purify such things, but the Prāsaṅgikas claim that one can. In [Nāgārjuna's] *Letter* we find:

> Whoever was once reckless
> May later become scrupulous;
> They are then as comely as the cloudless moon,
> Just like Nanda, Aṅgulimālā, Ajātaśhatru and Śhaṃkara.

Also it has been said: "The heavy sins of the skillful are very slight; the slightest sin of the fool is heavy." In other words, the determining factor is whether one is skilled or not at expiating one's sins. Brahman Śhaṃkara had killed his own mother; Aṅgulimālā killed nine hundred and ninety-nine people; Ajātaśhatru executed his own father. Yet after they had committed these heinous crimes, they were able to see the truth [that is, enter the path of seeing] because of their fervent confessions.

With the strongest form of confession, you purify the sin to its very roots; the medium form lightens the sin; and at the very least you prevent the sin from increasing in strength. But if you do not confess the sin at all, the sin doubles every day, and small sins become large. For example, killing a louse is a light sin, but if you do not expiate it, after fifteen days the sin is 16,384 times stronger. It has become about the same as killing a human being.

We do not want to confess our sins; our lack of belief in the laws of cause and effect is at fault and means that we are not afraid of our sins. If we had that belief, we would avoid committing even the smallest sin. For example, whenever Atiśha committed the slightest misdeed while he was traveling, he would halt the caravan and rigorously expiate it. We could do this too, yet we normally think we have no great sins to confess—that is only because we have not thought through how we commit sins. If we were to think about it deeply enough, we would come to know just how many sins we have committed with our mind and speech—harmful intent, idle gossip, insults, and so on—since we got up today. We may be ordained, for example, yet, leaving aside any major vows we may have broken, we not only break our other vows with the frequency of raindrops in a cloudburst but also say that this does no harm. Yet not putting the lower garment of our robes on straight, for example, is all that is needed to break a major tantric vow.[28] We also break the major bodhisattva vows as frequently as raindrops fall. Breaking a minor bodhisattva vow is one hundred thousand times more serious than breaking the major pratimokṣha vow of a monk. Breaking a major bodhisattva vow is one hundred thousand times more serious than breaking a minor bodhisattva vow; breaking a secondary tantric vow is one hundred thousand times more serious; and breaking a root tantric vow, one hundred thousand times more serious still. So if we count up the misdeeds we have done since, say, we got up this morning, we will see we have many full sets of causes for rebirth in all the lower realms. Every day we are burdened with many misdeeds—the ten nonvirtues, transgressions of the three vows, etc. We are told that the greatest of these will get us rebirth in the hells; the medium, rebirths as hungry ghosts; and the least, rebirths as animals. A "great sin" need not be killing a person and stealing their horse; it could even be calling your pupil a mangy old dog in a great fit of anger. Such things as criticizing karmically potent beings also become greater sins because of the object [of the criticism]. So just today we have acquired a complete set of causes to take us to the three lower realms.

You may then be wondering, "If that's the case, what can be done?" It is not helpful merely to stay frightened by this; you must—by doing hundreds of thousands of prostrations, recitations of the hundred-syllable mantra, and so on—expiate and purify all the sins you have committed since the beginning of saṃsāra. Unless you receive the signs that these sins have been purified, you must do these practices until your death. These signs were mentioned in the *Dhāraṇī of Chundā,* and you should refer to the *Great Stages of the Path* and so on. So you should perform the Vajrasattva meditation and recite his hundred-syllable mantra twenty-one times before going to bed at night. You should also strenuously perform full prostrations while reciting the *Confession of Transgressions Sūtra.* In the evening, confess the vows you broke during the day; in the morning, confess the vows you broke last night. Don't leave a broken vow untended for a whole day. Even if you do not do many other practices, working hard at this one will be more than enough.

Your sins are the source of all suffering in this and future lives, and if you can expiate them, you will rid yourself of suffering and develop realization and insights. For example, when you are sick in this rebirth, the thing causing you to undergo the illness is some nonvirtue you have already accumulated, so getting rituals and so on performed on your behalf may not help, because the results of these rituals will ripen independently of the illness. But do not have the wrong view that such rituals are of no benefit. Suppose some peas are already growing in a field, and you sow barley there to stop the peas from growing any further: this would have about the same effect as the rituals. If a sin has already borne fruit, you can do nothing about it. You should therefore confess your sins *before* you experience their results; this is like destroying the seeds. If you expiate small sins, they will be totally purified; greater sins will be weakened. If you confess your great sins and the sins whose results you were otherwise certain to experience in the lower realms, the outcome will be their ripening in this life as serious illness and so on. Though sins generally have no good qualities at all, they do have the property that they can be purified. In fact, there is no sin that cannot be purified through confession. The extent to which a sin will be purified is determined by the power of your intention and actions to expiate it. So you must have strong regret, exercise strong restraint, and so on.

Some Dharma practitioners in this life suffer from many undesirable things, but this is best because it means that evil karma, whose results these practitioners would otherwise have experienced in future rebirths, has ripened on them in this life. These practitioners may suffer a drop in their living standards for example, but this means some karma that would have resulted in their taking rebirth as hungry ghosts has ripened on them in this life. Some sinners seem to have all the luck, have long lives, and so on. This is the result of some remnants of virtuous acts in their past lives that happen to have ripened on them during this life; later they will descend to states where they will be tormented and have only suffering. An example of a practitioner suffering is Dromtoenpa—a true being of Dharma—who appeared to have contracted leprosy late in life. So do not hold wrong views; meditate on joy even when you get sick and so forth. You suffer an enormous loss if you destroy some of your virtue by anger; you also profit greatly from any sins you expiate.

In order to expiate a sin, you must have a full set of the four opponent powers.

The *power of the basis* is recognizing exactly to whom you will make confession. However, in our tradition it means that, because you accumulate a sin in relation to a particular basis, the purification of that sin relies on that same basis, just as when you fall on the ground you rely on the ground to get up again. So, as you commit sins in relation to either buddhas or sentient beings, the power of the basis is taking refuge [in the buddhas and so on] and developing bodhichitta [toward sentient beings]. I have already explained both of these.

The *power of repudiation* is regret; if you have this, you will also refrain [from committing the sin again]. You must know about the laws of cause and effect for this to happen with any force. Suppose three people have eaten poisoned food. One of them dies, one is taken ill, and one suffers no ill effects. This last person will have great remorse, try any means to get the poison out of his system, and decide never to eat that food again. Sentient beings have all accumulated the same sins, which resemble the poison. Some of them have already taken rebirth in the lower realms. Others are forever suffering from the serious and chronic diseases of the three poisons—this resembles the second person's falling sick. They, too, are going to fall to the three lower realms. We are no different—we have already committed the same karmic actions, so we should feel regret and refrain from committing them ever again.

The *power of refraining* from recommiting misdeeds is restraint. You must do this properly: your resolution must be extremely firm. And you should not remain apathetic after studying the benefits of confessing sins. You exercise restraint in the following way. The actions you are in danger of doing, such as using harsh language, also threaten to give the lie to your promise never to do such things again. If you do not exercise restraint, the four powers are not complete. Abandon to the very root the things you can abandon to their very root. There are still some things you can abandon for only a year; others you can abandon for only a month. But if you decide every day to abandon these things, you will then abandon things you can abandon for only a day. The point of training yourself this way is so that you can break the continuity of doing these things. This is a particularly skillful means, a most practical instruction from my own precious guru.

There are said to be six main types of *power of applying an antidote;* these are the actual means to purify the actions that caused you regret. So this power is any action done in relation to the names of the tathāgatas, to any mantra, to any sūtra, meditating on emptiness, making offerings, and anything done in relation to images. You may not actually say, "I admit these, I confess these" [words from the *Confession of Transgressions*], but if you do some virtuous acts—even reciting a number of *oṃ maṇi padme hūṃ* mantras—in order to purify some sin, this action then becomes the application of an antidote. If we ordinary monks and nuns think that we are enduring, as an act of purification, all the hardships of heat and cold that we undergo in order to attend our classes, these acts also become examples of this particular power.

You must make use of all four powers. The easiest of the six types of power of applying all antidotes is the actions done in relation to the names [of buddhas]; it was the practice of past saints to make prostrations while reciting the *Confession of Transgressions* [also known as the *Sūtra of the Three Noble Heaps*]. This recitation contains all four powers and is so beneficial. Great Je Rinpoche, whose good works were as extensive as space itself, used it to build up his accumulations and perform self-purification. So it was great Je Rinpoche's practice to perform his confession while prostrating and reciting the *Sūtra of the Three Noble Heaps.* Even great adepts like Namkha Gyaeltsaen of Lhodrag purified their obscurations this way. All later scholar-adepts did this practice, and the great adept Lozang Namgyael said it was the noblest. When you have purified your sins, your mind is at ease—like someone who has stopped the interest on a huge loan.

People doing a large number of prostrations should set their thoughts properly while they do the limb of homage; but all they need do [physically] at that particular part of the seven-limbed prayer is fold their hands together, for it is better to incorporate the act of doing a large number of prostrations into the limb of confession.

You do this practice as follows. First, you recite three times the mantra to multiply virtue:

> *Oṃ sambhara sambhara vimanasara mahājapa hūṃ. Oṃ smara smara vimanaskara mahājapa hūṃ.*

You then recite the *Confession of Transgressions* [see pp. 711–13].

Although the deities in this sūtra are already members of the merit field, do the following visualization to give them special prominence. Thirty-four light rays radiate from your guru's heart. Ten light rays go upward, ten go down. Seven go to your guru's right, and another seven to his left. There are thirty-four precious thrones, each resting on one of these rays. The thrones are supported by elephants and decorated with pearls. The elephant is the strongest animal, so the thrones have elephants supporting them as an auspicious symbol that these buddhas have the greatest power to purify sin. All thirty-five deities have many different body colors and display many different symbolic implements in their hands, but for ease of visualization, divide them into five groups of seven each, with each group having the same body color and implements as one of the five dhyāni buddhas. The first group of seven takes the form of Akṣhobhya; the next, Vairochana; then Ratnasaṃbhava; Amitābha; and Amoghasiddha. There are two exceptions to this scheme. Śhākyamuni Buddha actually belongs to the first group of seven, but the Śhākyamuni figure at the guru's heart will suffice. King of the Powerful Nāgas [Nāgeśhvararāja] is white above the neck; the rest of him is blue. He makes the subduing-the-nāgas gesture: middle fingers held upright out of closed fists and touching together. All these figures should be somewhat in front of the merit field.

There are three oral instructions on how to recite this sūtra. One is to recite the whole sūtra from start to finish the required number of times. Or you could recite only the first section, starting with our Teacher Buddha Śhākyamuni and ending with Buddha, King of the Lord of Mountains [Śhailendrarāja], the required number of times; in this system you only repeat the names a number of times and the second part of the sūtra [only once]. Or suppose you are going to recite the sūtra twenty-five times in the one meditation session; you then recite the name of each tathāgata twenty-five times individually. This third instruction makes it easy to direct yourself to each buddha and receive their individual help. As in the second system, after you have finished reciting the names, you need only go through the rest of the sūtra once.

Reciting the names of each tathāgata holds many benefits. Refer to the relevant commentaries such as the *ṭīka* to ascertain these.[29] If you add the names of the seven Medicine Buddhas to the other thirty-five, we are told that any prayers made during these degenerate times, while there are still Buddhist teachings, will be fulfilled [see Day 4, p. 131]. We should be yearning for immediate benefits and blessings, so make further prostrations while reciting the names of these seven buddhas.

All of the repetitions of the word *tathāgata* in our version of the *Confession of Transgressions* do not appear in the original sūtra, but it would not be right to recite the names of these buddhas without an epithet. You must therefore add the title "tathāgata" before each of the names, as was Je Rinpoche's custom.

You should then recite the *General Confession,* or the like [see pp. 713–14]. This text says "attachment, hostility…" as in the classical treatises; their causes are the three poisons. The three doors are body, speech, and mind, and their nature would then be nonvirtuous.

When the *Confession of Transgressions* says, "I confess each and every sin," it means this is a way to confess transgressions of each of the three types of vows. The point is to bring to our attention the sins we are forever committing so that we will take their expiation seriously.

The *Royal Prayer of Noble Deeds* says:

> Under the power of attachment, hostility, and benighted ignorance,
> I have sinned with my body, speech, and mind.
> I confess all these individually.

THE FOURTH LIMB: REJOICING (51)

Rejoicing is a bodhisattva's practice, so it is difficult for us to do it even a little in our thoughts. But if we do this well, there is no better way to build up our accumulations. Once Sūrata the beggar rejoiced at the donations King Prasenajit made to the Buddha and his śhrāvakas; the beggar received more benefit than the king. As Je Tsongkapa says:

> To give great impetus to your accumulation from the
>   merest effort,
> They say: best to rejoice over virtue.

In other words, there is no need to wear out your body and voice, for you can collect an immeasurable stock of merit by rejoicing while at ease.

King Prasenajit once asked the Buddha for teachings on some Dharma that would be convenient for him to practice while he pursued his royal duties. He was told to practice three things: to rejoice, develop his bodhichitta, and dedicate his virtue. But one's rejoicing must be without any jealous thoughts or competitiveness. If someone we dislike does something virtuous, we say out of jealousy, "They're only doing it for form's sake—it is of no benefit at all." We should not do this. If we ordinary monks, for example, rejoice properly when our roommate performs a hundredfold offering ceremony, we are sure to receive some benefit. If his level [of realization or ordination] is lower than ours, we will receive twice the benefit that he did; if he is our equal, we get the same benefit; even if he is higher, we are still certain to get half. What could be more profitable? And if we rejoice in the deeds of past buddhas, bodhisattvas, and so on, we will receive a tenth of the benefits they gained because their mindstreams are so much higher than ours. If we labor at virtuous practices for the whole of our human lifespan, we would only achieve a fraction of the root virtues performed in a single day by a bodhisattva on the first level, while the root virtues of a buddha would be quite beyond us. But if we rejoice over the root virtues of these bodhisattvas, we will get half as many as they have. This one mental technique is a most effective way to build a huge collection [of merit]. The Dharma is flourishing here in the Central Province, and many people make prostrations, offerings, circumambulations, serve [teachers], practice meditation, study, and so on. If we rejoice over all these, we will receive a huge amount of root virtues.

The *Royal Prayer of Noble Deeds* says:

> I rejoice over all merits of the victors
> Of the ten directions, of their children,
> The pratyekabuddhas, still-learners,
> And no-more-learners, and every other being.

At this point, the gurus would treat this subject in the following order: rejoicing over such deeds as when the [soon-to-be] buddhas developed bodhichitta for the first time; then rejoicing over the deeds of past scholars and adepts in India and Tibet; and rejoicing over even your roommates' recitations. However, there are two ways to meditate on this limb: (1) rejoicing over your own virtue; (2) rejoicing over the virtue of others.

REJOICING OVER YOUR OWN VIRTUE (52)

This has two subheadings: (1) rejoicing over the virtue done in your past lives that you can discern by means of inferential valid cognition; (2) rejoicing over your virtues from this life that you can discern by means of direct valid cognition.

REJOICING OVER YOUR PAST LIVES' VIRTUE, WHICH YOU CAN DISCERN BY MEANS OF INFERENTIAL VALID COGNITION (53)

You have received a good physical rebirth in this life. Look at the favorable conditions you have inherited for Dharma practice and think, over and over again, "In my rebirths before this one I must have upheld my ethics, practiced generosity, patience, etc., and done these extremely well." Because you were unmistaken in a previous life about how to do something meaningful for yourself, your present life is this magnificent, optimum human rebirth of yours. So now, O monk, you know just what rebirth your next one will be like. Some saints in the past said:

> Your precious past life
> Gave you your present precious human body.
> So, current precious monk,
> Don't throw your future over the precipice!

If we examine our present mode of behavior, we can see where we will be reborn in our future lives. We need not ask people with clairvoyant powers to perform divinations, and so on.

REJOICING OVER YOUR PRESENT LIFE'S VIRTUES, WHICH YOU CAN DISCERN BY MEANS OF DIRECT VALID COGNITION (54)

Recall all the virtue you have personally performed: any recitations; any generosity; any service you have performed; any of your study, contemplation, or listening; the rigors you have endured at any public ceremonies or debating practice; and how you have upheld your ethics. Then, without the feeling of arrogance, rejoice over these things; your root virtues will lessen if you feel proud. This is the sort of calculation you should be doing.

We quite often calculate our finances, etc., but no matter how much we increase our holdings, we only receive a minuscule part of this life's happiness. If we increase our virtues, we will receive [everything] from good physical rebirths as gods or humans to our enlightenment. Our sins will take us to places like the Vajra Hell many leagues under the ground; that is the calculation for us to make!

Kyabje Pabongka Rinpoche then told a story about Geshe Baen Gung-gyael, who used to calculate the virtue or sin [he did each day; see Day 13, p. 419].

These are the sort of calculations we should be making from now on. We will be helpless when the big reckoning [of our sins and virtues] is made for us in the presence of Yama.

REJOICING OVER THE VIRTUE OF OTHERS (55)

This means rejoicing over the virtue of your enemies, friends, and strangers; or over the virtue of persons in the five types of rebirth; or over the deeds of past saints when you read their life stories. With this form of rejoicing, you develop merit afresh; when you rejoice over your own virtue, you increase old merit. As Gungtang Rinpoche says:

> How to perform great virtue while relaxing:
> Rejoice! Meditate on that!

We live in Tibet, a land with the Dharma; so it is enough if we make it our practice to rejoice while we walk, sit, or rest. But our rejoicing must be that of a bodhisattva—done with a yearning to benefit others. Suppose everyone within a particular family is completely dependent on the father for their standard of living. Nothing else would make the father happier than if the eldest son could manage to support himself. So this is the slight difference between the practice in general and this specific [bodhisattva] form.

THE FIFTH LIMB: REQUESTING THE WHEEL OF DHARMA TO BE TURNED (56)

Originally, our Teacher the Buddha did not turn the wheel of Dharma for seven weeks [after his enlightenment], but as it is said:

> They [the five disciples]
> Had faith in Brahmā,
> Who requested [Buddha];
> And so the wheel was turned.

In other words, the god Brahmā requested Buddha to teach, so Buddha turned the wheel of Dharma for the first time, teaching the four truths to the first five disciples. Buddha listed the four truths three times; he therefore talked about twelve aspects. This was turning the wheel of the transmitted Dharma. Then Ājñatakauṇḍinya became the first of these five to achieve arhatship, and the other four became stream-enterers. So the disciples managed to achieve the turning of the wheel of realized Dharma in their own mindstreams; this attainment depended on the transmitted wheel of Dharma being turned. This in turn depended necessarily on the request for the turning of the transmitted wheel of Dharma. That is why requesting this wheel to be turned is one of the seven limbs. As [Vasubandhu] says in his *Treasury of Metaphysics:*

> [First the turning of] the Dharma's wheel,
> [Then follows] the path of seeing…

Kyabje Pabongka Rinpoche then explained this passage at some length.

When you request the turning of the wheel of Dharma, and if you have a maṇḍala set, arrange nine handfuls on the base and visualize all this as a thousand-spoked golden wheel while making the request. You could even visualize yourself as the great Brahmā. Then emanate numberless replicas of yourself, which go out to the buddhas in the ten directions. If this is beyond you, you could emanate a replica of yourself for each member of the merit field. And if even this proves too much, just imagine that one of you offers a wheel to them.

The *Royal Prayer of Noble Deeds* continues:

> O lamps to worlds in the ten directions,
> You who achieved nonattachment
> And the level of enlightened buddhas,
> I beseech you, O protectors:
> Turn the supreme wheel!

THE SIXTH LIMB: PETITIONING THE MERIT FIELD NOT TO ENTER NIRVĀṆA (57)

One sūtra says: "The buddhas never go into nirvāṇa…" In other words, the buddhas in general do not go into nirvāṇa, nor does the Dharma disappear, but to common appearances the supreme nirmāṇakāya enters nirvāṇa. One therefore must request Buddha, the Teacher, not to go to nirvāṇa. It is a grievous fault not to do this. When the Buddha was about to enter nirvāṇa, he said to Ānanda, "The tathāgatas have become much accustomed to cultivating the four fearlessnesses and four miraculous legs. Buddhas have achieved a vajra-like body, so they can live for an eon or more if they so wish." Ānanda, however, did not catch the Buddha's meaning, because he was influenced by a demon. Ānanda therefore did not make this request to our Teacher: as a result Buddha, to common appearances, went into nirvāṇa in his eightieth year. So it is vital to make this request before it is too late. Here, you should put five handfuls on your maṇḍala base and imagine it to be a vajra throne. You could imagine you offer a vajra throne for each member of the merit field, or if you cannot manage this, only one vajra throne that dissolves into the merit field's throne.

The *Royal Prayer of Noble Deeds* says:

> To those who, to common appearance,
> Intend to go to their nirvāṇa,
> With folded hands I plead:
> Stay for as many eons
> As there are atoms in this world
> To help and bring happiness to all beings.

While you perform the limb of petitioning and the limb of requesting, you should imagine the members of the merit field accepting both requests.

THE SEVENTH LIMB: THE DEDICATION (58)

It is vital then to dedicate one's merit. The Kadampas in their mind-training texts say:

> The two things to do:
> One at the start, one at the end.

This refers to setting one's motivation [at the beginning] and dedicating [merit at the end]. Dedications are necessarily a form of prayer, but for a prayer to be a dedication, there must be something to be given in dedication.

There are six points to be made here: (1) What is being dedicated? Your root virtues. (2) Why do you dedicate them? So that they will not run out. (3) To what end do you dedicate them? To your supreme enlightenment. (4) For whose sake do you dedicate them? For the sake of all sentient beings. (5) How do you dedicate them? As it says in the *Ornament to Realization:* "Through method and right perception." In other words, you perform the dedication with the sort of thinking that combines method and wisdom by having, for instance, right perception of the three components of the act of dedication [that is, that the thing being dedicated, the end to which it is dedicated, and the beings for whose sake this is being done all lack inherent existence]. This prevents you from clinging to the thing being dedicated as if it were established as true. (6) The nature of the dedication: it is done in conjunction with a wish that your root virtues may not disappear; do it together with the wish that those virtues held will change into the cause for your complete enlightenment.

This type of prayer has great power. For example, we at present do not lack for the Dharma by virtue of the prayers made by our Teacher the Buddha. Shāriputra became wisest of the wise; this was through the power of his dedications, prayers, and the like. Our virtue is like the horse; our prayers, the bridle. Also, the raw materials, gold and silver for example, can be fashioned into either a statue of a deity or a common container—it all depends on the craftsman. The results of our virtue will similarly be either high or low, depending on our prayers and dedications. There was once a man who had powerful root virtues, which would act as causes for him to be reborn as a Brahman six times. But at the point of death he saw a particularly handsome elephant and developed craving, and as a result was reborn as Airāvaṇa, the elephant that serves as Indra's mount.

Ever since I was a little child, I have always recited this prayer:

> In any place the precious teachings have not reached,
> Or where they have since declined,
> May I, moved by great compassion,
> Shed light upon these beneficial treasures.

As a result, I am now forever giving teachings incessantly! I'm sorry I didn't pray instead to practice single-pointedly on a deserted mountainside.

In your prayers, do not dedicate your virtue to having happiness in this life.

If you do not dedicate [virtue], it could be destroyed when you get angry. From *Engaging in the Deeds of Bodhisattvas:*

> No matter how many excellent deeds
> You may have performed for a thousand eons,
> Such as generosity or making offerings to tathāgatas,
> They all perish in one fit of anger.

That is, anger destroys root virtues collected over one thousand eons. Chandrakīrti's *Engaging in the Middle Way* says:

> Whenever you get angry at the buddhas' children,
> A hundred eons' virtue from giving
> And from ethics are destroyed in an instant.
> So there is no worse sin than losing patience.

Here we are told that anger destroys root virtues collected over a hundred eons. We destroy either one thousand or one hundred eons worth of root virtues, depending on the level of realization of the one getting angry and the subject of the anger. If non-bodhisattvas get angry at bodhisattvas, they are said to destroy root virtues collected over one thousand eons. If higher bodhisattvas get angry at a lesser bodhisattva they destroy one hundred eons of root virtues.

The means to prevent one's root virtues from being destroyed by anger is discussed in the *Sūtra Requested by Sāgaramati:*

> Just as a drop of water poured into a great ocean
> Will not disappear until the ocean runs dry,
> So too will virtue dedicated to perfect enlightenment
> Not disappear before enlightenment is gained.

Our root virtues are like the drop; the root virtues of the victorious ones and their children are like the ocean. We mix our root virtues with theirs when we dedicate them, and so these virtues will not have disappeared by the time we gain enlightenment.

Kyabje Pabongka Rinpoche gave the analogy of the two messengers who mixed their different grades of barley flour together.[30]

The above quotation is not in the well-known current version of that sūtra, but Buddha taught so many sūtras, and it is certain that Sāgaramati requested one or another of them.

One sūtra tells how to perform the dedication [of merits]: "Share them with all sentient beings." [Maitreya's] *Ornament to Realization* says:

> The dedication to full enlightenment
> Is the most supreme of actions
> And that which has the objectless aspect
> Is characterized as unmistaken.

In other words, do this practice because it is extraordinary: it prevents one from clinging to [ideas of] things being established as true.

The most well-known form of dedicating virtue to one's complete enlightenment is the thought, "Through this virtue, may I achieve complete enlightenment for the sake of others." Just the same, we are sharing these root virtues with all sentient beings, and it is like mixing these virtues in the root virtues of the victorious ones—root virtues that resulted from their extensive deeds for the sake of others and that have never been known to run out. We offer our root virtues to contribute toward these deeds done for others' sakes, and so it is vital to pray that these virtues will take all sentient beings to enlightenment. [Maitreya] says in *An Ornament to the Sūtras:*

> Dedications of the steadfast
> [Are made] with the thought of aspiration.

In other words, before one recites the dedication, one has a thought—a mental factor—that will be responsible for one's root virtues not disappearing.

A word on the witnesses of the act of dedication. You ask the victorious ones and their children to be witnesses, as you would ask someone for assistance. Before you dissolve the secret assembly visualization of the Guhyasamāja tantra, you have to recite certain prayers: their purpose is to ask the assembly to act as witnesses.

We have only a small amount of virtue, but if we dedicate it to our complete enlightenment, this virtue will not disappear before we achieve that enlightenment.

There are three ways to dedicate our virtue: dedicating it to the spread of the Buddha's teachings in others' mental streams and in your own; to being looked after by our spiritual guide in all our future lives; and to achieving peerless and complete enlightenment. You must perform any dedication in one of these three great ways. As it is said: "The prayers of the children of the victors—as vast as the River Ganges..." In other words, upholding the holy Dharma becomes a cause for the teachings to spread. By "holy Dharma" we mean both the transmitted teachings and the realized teachings. So one dedicates one's virtue to the spread of both. And in the *Prayer of Noble Deeds:*

> "What little virtue I have accumulated
> From homage, offerings, confession,
> Rejoicing, requests, and petitions,
> I dedicate it all to my enlightenment.

In other words, this is a dedication to the result: your complete enlightenment. But both the cause—upholding the holy Dharma in your mindstream—and the result of doing this—achieving complete enlightenment—depend on your being looked after by a spiritual guide. So:

> That I have met with the teachings of the supreme Teacher
> Is due to the kindness of my guru;
> Thus I dedicate this virtue so that every sentient being
> May be cared for by holy spiritual guides.

That is, it is enough to dedicate your virtue to being under the care of a guru. So carry out your dedications in any of the above three ways.

The words "little virtue" defeat our inflated opinion of ourself; then we are not proud. "What...virtue I have accumulated" means all the karma we have accumulated. The line "I dedicate it all..." is the actual dedication of that virtue to achieving complete enlightenment.

There is no difference between dedicating something to being a cause and to its resulting in something else—just as there is no difference in asking for barley, the main ingredient, or for tsampa [a meal of roasted barley], the resulting food. All the same, we do not know how to make these dedications properly, so we also recite:

Just as heroic Mañjuśhrī knew how,
Just as Samantabhadra also knew,
I dedicate all this virtue so that
I may learn to follow all their ways.

I dedicate all my root virtues
In whatever way all tathāgatas
Of all three times praise as best;
I dedicate them toward these noble deeds.

We are told that this is the very best prayer ever made by the buddhas of all three times. These buddhas then worked to fulfill this prayer. We are told that these two verses contain the countless hundreds of thousands of prayers made by the children of the victorious ones who dedicated their virtue in the same way as Mañjuśhrī and Samantabhadra did. But note: we must in addition do this limb in conjunction with right perception according to the view.

Here is the way the seven-limbed prayer acts as an antidote to the three poisons. Homage acts against pride; offering, against miserliness; confession, against all three poisons; rejoicing, against jealousy; the request to turn the wheel of Dharma acts against discarding the Dharma; the petition not to enter nirvāṇa against inadvertently disparaging the guru; the dedication is an antidote to anger. Also, the seven limbs include the processes of accumulation, self-purification, and increase. Four and a half limbs build up one's accumulations. The limb of confession is the purification. Half of the limb of rejoicing and all of the limb of dedication increase one's root virtues.

The text books are not clear on this but, according to Kyabchog Dagpo Rinpoche's oral tradition, each of the seven limbs leaves different karmic traces. The limb of prostration leaves traces that go toward giving one the crown protrusion; I have already mentioned this fact [see Day 5, p. 173]. Offering leaves traces that will enable one to achieve wealth or the "space-treasure" siddhi;[31] confession, to achieve complete abandonment of the two types of obscuration; rejoicing, a charismatic body; the request to turn the wheel of Dharma, the Brahmā voice [of a buddha]; traces from the petition not to enter nirvāṇa will enable one to achieve the vajra body or knowledge about how to prolong life; dedication, gaining all the qualities of a buddha in general.

Then you can either offer another maṇḍala before you make the next request, or offer it afterward. This request is:

> I take refuge in the guru and the Three Precious Jewels. Please bless my mindstream. Please bless us so that I and all sentient beings, beings who were once my mothers, stop having any sort of wrong thoughts—from having disrespect for our spiritual guides to our grasping at dualistic signs in the self. Please bless us so that we easily develop every sort of right thought—from having respect for our spiritual guides, and so on. Please bless us and pacify all our external and internal hindering circumstances.

It is, however, the practice lineage to offer the maṇḍala first. If you are going to ask for something vitally important from a great king, you must first give him a huge gift. We want to ask the merit field for three vitally important things, so we should offer a maṇḍala. These three great things are not for our own benefit—having a long life, good health, and the like. One of these three is for us to stop having any sort of wrong thought, such as disrespect for our spiritual guide; another is to enable us to develop all right thoughts; and the third is having our internal and external hindrances pacified. From the tantric point of view, we should rather say "...from having disrespect for our spiritual guides to our having even the subtlest dualistic appearances that occur during the appearances, increase, and attainment phases" [that all occur just before one enters the clear-light state]. The text we use for the preparatory rites does not actually say this after the words "...from having disrespect for our spiritual guides...," but I think we may substitute this tantric version for the words that follow. They say there is nothing Dharmic that cannot be included within the above three things. The hindrances mentioned are as follows. Outer hindrances to practice are wars, kings persecuting the Dharma, and so on. Inner hindrances are illness and so on. Secret hindrances are our minds inability to make use of the Dharma or their not [yet] being fit for this.

It is our usual practice to add the words "Please bless us..."

FURTHER PETITIONS, WHICH FOLLOW THE ORAL INSTRUCTIONS, MADE IN ORDER TO BE SURE YOUR MINDSTREAM IS SUFFICIENTLY IMBUED BY YOUR MEDITATIONS (59)

I have already said that the best method for developing realizations in one's mindstream is to petition one's guru, while regarding him as inseparable from one's tutelary deity. We shall develop experiences and realizations in our mindstreams on the strength of the blessing we receive; and the blessings of the victorious ones and their children will be absorbed into our mindstreams as a result of our petitions.

These petitions are worded in many different ways, but the following passage is the most blessed of all. They say it is a pity not to use this version in one's recitations.

[Petition to the root guru]
My glorious root guru, take your place
On the lotus and moon disc on my crown;
Care for me out of great compassion,
And confer the siddhis of body, speech, and mind.

[Petition to the Lineage of Extensive Deeds]
Our Teacher, the Bhagavān—the peerless savior,
Maitreya the Invincible—the Victor's holy regent,
Ārya Asaṅga—predicted by the Victorious One:
I make petition to three buddhas and bodhisattvas.

Vasubandhu—crest jewel of Jambudvīpa's scholars,
Ārya Vimuktisena—who found the middle path,
Vimuktisenagomin—who still commands faith:
I make petition to three who opened the eyes of the world.

Paranasena—who achieved a most wondrous state,
Vinītasena—who trained his mind in profound paths,
Vairochana—treasured for his powerful deeds:
I make petition to the three friends of beings.

Haribhadra—who spread the path of perfecting wisdom,
Kusali—who held all the victor's instructions,
Ratnasena—who cared for all with love:
I make petition to three captains of beings.

Suvarṇadvīpa Guru—whose mind had bodhichitta,
Dīpaṃkara Atiśha—who upheld the great champions' tradition,

Dromtoenpa—who made clear the noble path:
I make petition to three backbones of the teachings.

[Petition to the Lineage of Profound View]
Śhākyamuni—peerless exponent, supreme savior,
Mañjuśhrī—who embodies all omniscience of the victors,
Nāgārjuna—most exalted ārya to see profound meaning:
I make petition to the three crest jewels of philosophers.

Chandrakīrti—who clarified the ārya's thoughts,
Vidyakokila—Chandrakīrti's best disciple,
Vidyakokila the younger—a true victors' [child]:
I make petition to three powerful intellects.

Dīpaṃkara Atiśha—who rightly perceived the depth
Of mutual dependence and upheld the forerunners' way,
And Dromtoenpa who clarified the noble path:
I make petition to two jewels of Jambudvīpa.

The part beginning "Our Teacher, the Bhagavān—the peerless savior..." refers to the Lineage of Extensive Deeds. "Śhākyamuni—peerless exponent, supreme savior..." refers to the Lineage of Profound View. Both have petitions to our Teacher who initiated both lineages. One passage also refers to the profound part: to his magnificent omniscience. "Peerless exponent" is a way of praising Siddhārtha [the youthful Śhākyamuni] who taught the doctrine of interdependent origination.

When you have to consult an official about a very important matter, you need a well-connected person to act as your advocate. So a duplicate splits off from the figure of your root guru in front of you—the way he appears as you normally see him. This duplicate takes its place on the crown of your head. Imagine that he pleads with the victorious ones and their children on your behalf. When you recite the first repetition of the last line of the verse "My glorious root guru...the siddhis of body, speech, and mind," the duplicate transfers to the crown of your head and petitions the merit field along with you. Purifying nectars descend during the second repetition, and another duplicate of the guru dissolves into you.

Actually, in the preparatory rites for *Mañjuśhrī's Own Words,* one does

"FOR COMPLETE ENLIGHTENMENT, TRAIN IN BODHICHITTA" (SEE P. 36)

not traditionally recite the fourth line of all these verses twice; but in the preparatory rites for the *Swift Path* and the *Easy Path,* one does.

As you recite the last line of the verse "My glorious root guru…" for the first time, imagine you are purified of any hindrances to your developing the stages of both the extensive and profound parts of the path in your mindstream. When first reciting the opening lines of the verses for the Extensive Deeds Lineage, imagine you are purified of the hindrances to your developing the stages of the extensive part of the path in your mindstream; for the Profound View Lineage section, imagine the same thing happening for the profound parts of the path.

When you recite these lines for the second time, imagine that duplicates of the particular gurus mentioned dissolve into you, and you develop realizations into the profound or the extensive paths.

Then come the gurus of the Kadampa Lamrim Tradition.

> *[Petition to the Lineage of the Lamrim Tradition]*
> Goenpowa—that splendid, powerful yogi,
> Neuzurpa—profound single-pointed concentration,
> Tagmapa—who upheld all branches of vinaya:
> I make petition to three lamps lighting these remote regions.
>
> Namkha Senge—who practiced with great diligence,
> Namkha Gyaelpo—who was blessed by the holy ones,
> Senge Zangpo—who gave up eight worldly concerns:
> And I make petition to Gyaelsae Zangpo.
>
> Who with bodhichitta saw all beings as his children,
> Who was blessed and cared for by the god of gods [Vajrapāṇi],
> Who was the supreme guide for beings in degenerate times:
> I make petition to Namkha Gyaeltsaen.

Note that these lineage gurus are put after the gurus of the Extensive Deeds Lineage. This might lead one to wonder, "Do they then belong to the Extensive Deeds Lineage?" No, they do not, even though these gurus came after that lineage.

> *[Petition to the Lineage of the Classical Tradition]*
> Geshe Potowa—the Victor's regent,

Sharawa—whose wisdom has no equal,
Chaekawa—lineage holder of bodhichitta:
I make petition to three who answer the hopes of beings.

Chilbupa—bodhisattva, lord over transmissions and
insights,
Lhalung Wangchug—great scholar steeped in scripture,
Goenpo Rinpoche—protector of beings in all three realms:
I make petition to three great elders.

Zangchenpa—whose ethics were stainless,
Tsonawa—who upheld the hundred thousand sections of vinaya.
Moendrapa—who perfected vast metaphysics:
I make petition to three great saviors of beings.

Lord of vast and profound Dharmas,
Who protected all fortunate beings,
Whose noble works spread the teachings:
I make petition to a glorious guru.[32]

Note that this last verse is a petition to Choekyab Zangpo, the abbot of Dragor [see Day 1, p. 22]. The lineage prayer continues:

[Petition to the Lineage of the Instruction Tradition]
Tsultrimbar—great prince of adepts,
Zhoenue Oe—who cultivated his spiritual guide,
Gyergompa—whose mind trained in the Supreme Vehicle's path:
I make petition to three [children] of the victors.

Sangyaeb Oen—treasure of wondrous qualities,
Namkha Gyaelpo—blessed by the saints,
Senge Zangpo—who gave up eight worldly concerns:
And I make petition to Gyaelsae Zangpo.

Who with bodhichitta saw all beings as his children,
Who was blessed and cared for by the god of gods,
Who was supreme guide for beings in degenerate times:
I make petition to Namkha Gyaeltsaen.

These lineages as set out seem jumbled, but this is not so. This recitation fits in with the following oral instruction. After the Extensive Deeds and Profound View lineages came down to Atiśha, he combined the lineage streams together. Thus Atiśha passed on the Profound View Lineage to his foremost disciple Dromtoenpa; the later Kamdpas are not included. Then, going from the oldest to youngest [of the Kadampa lineages], Goenpawa's Kadampa Lamrim Tradition is the first; this lineage came down to Namkha Gyaeltsaen. Next, the Classical Tradition extends from Potowa to Choekyab Zangpo. The Instruction Tradition extends from Chaen Ngawa Tsultrimbar to Namkha Gyaeltsaen. At this point the streams of three lineages comingle into a single line. So one then begins only the one the petition to Je Rinpoche, a [modified form of] his mantra, to receive a very special blessing:

Avalokiteśhvara—great treasure of right-perceiving compassion,
Mañjuśhrī—master of stainless omniscience,
Tsongkapa—crest jewel of scholars in the Land of Snows:
I make petition at Lozang Dragpa's feet.

In the merit-field visualization, Maitreya and Mañjuśhrī are surrounded by either the gurus of the Extensive Deeds or Profound View lineages, and both lineages end with Atiśha and Dromtoenpa. Visualize the Kadampa Lamrim Tradition directly in front of both the Extensive Deeds and Profound View Lineages; this group consists of Goenpawa surrounded by Neuzurpa and the seven others. They form a sort of teaching group in front of both the Profound View and Extensive Deeds lineages. The Classical Tradition—Geshe Potowa surrounded by the other nine gurus of the lineage—are either to the left or right of the Lamrim Tradition.[33] Visualize Chaen Ngawa, surrounded by the seven gurus [of the Instruction Tradition], to the other side of the Lamrim Tradition group.

Je Rinpoche sits in front of these three groups. The gurus of the neo-Kadampas are in rows on either side of him.

[Petition to the Gelug Lineage]
Jampael Gyatso—great prince of adepts,
Kaedrub Rinpoche—the sun of philosophers and adepts,
Basoje—who held a store of secret instruction:
I make petition to three peerless gurus.

Choekyi Dorje—who attained unification,
Gyaelwa Ensapa—who achieved the three kāyas,
Sangyae Yeshe—who held both transmissions and insights:
I make petition to three great scholar-adepts.

Lozang Choekyi Gyaeltsaen—who held the victory banner of
the teachings,
Koenchog Gyaeltsaen—his closest disciple,
Lozang Yeshe—who shone light on the noble path:
I make petition to three venerable lamas.

Ngagwang Jampa—who spread Śhākyamuni's teachings,
Lozang Nyaendrag—considered his closest disciple,
Yoentaen Tayae—who had infinite good qualities:
I make petition to three kind gurus.

Taenpa Rabgyae—who spread Lozang Yeshe's teachings,
Lodroe Zangpo—who worked for all beings' liberation,
Lozang Gyatso—skilled in the right way to teach:
I make petition to three unequalled gurus.

To my supremely kind root guru [Jinpa Gyatso];
Peerless one, who upheld both teachings and practices,
Who conveyed both transmissions and insights to four types
of receptive fortunates:
With great reverence of body, speech and mind, I make petition.

He who studied much, who extended
The maṇḍala of oral instruction
And revealed hidden practices of the two stages:
I make petition to Taenzin Kaedrub.

Kindest incarnate lama, whose body contained all past, present,
and future refuge;
Whose speech taught with Mañjushrī's eloquence;
Whose mind was an ocean of spontaneous wisdom in the three
high trainings and cause and effect:
I make petition to Lozang Lhuendrub Gyatso.[34]

You are eyes for seeing into all vast teachings,
You are the best gate taking the fortunate ones to liberation,
You, motivated by love, used skillful means:
I make petition to these spiritual guides, givers of light.

This petition is quite short, but each verse is like a distillation of each guru's life story. If you memorize these verses, when you recall these gurus you will be rejoicing [in their deeds] and will develop the desire to study. While you repeat the last line of each verse for the second time, or while you recite the other lines containing the individual brief biographies, feel that you are receiving the same qualities as they did from the transmitted and realized teachings.

Traditionally, one adds one further verse at the end: "Glorious lama, in your biography..." Then, if you are not going to perform a separate review meditation on the lamrim, you should recite [Je Rinpoche's] *Basis of All Good Qualities* as the meditation. If you are going to do a separate review meditation, you need not recite this; it is also sufficient to dissolve the merit-field visualization. The process of dissolution is as follows.

Visualize that light rays stream forth from Guru Vajradhara's heart and illuminate the other figures. Then, rather like the evaporation of condensation on a mirror, the lower figures in the merit field, that is, the four mahārājas and so forth, withdraw progressively into the higher figures; this happens as far as the deities standing on the four petals of the topmost lotus. These four deities withdraw into the Vajradhara figure at Buddha Śhākyamuni's heart. The Profound View Lineage gurus withdraw into Guru Mañjuśhrī; the Extensive Deeds, into Guru Maitreya; the Consecrated Practices Lineage, into Guru Vajradhara; and your personal gurus, from whom you received teachings, withdraw into the figure of your root guru in his everyday form—the one in which you normally see him. Think to yourself while maintaining the clarity of your visualization, "How fortunate I am to have actually seen these buddhas and bodhisattvas." Maitreya and Mañjuśhrī then dissolve into light, which dissolves into the main figure. Vajradhara dissolves into the main figure as a wisdom being. The figure of your root guru in his normal aspect should not, however, dissolve into light—this would be an inauspicious gesture. So, whether he is still alive or not, he dissolves into the Vajradhara at the main figure's heart as one would push a grain of barley into a pat of butter. The wish-granting tree, with the lion throne, dissolves into the lotus base of the main figure.

The main figure itself then dissolves into light, which in turn dissolves into your guru sitting on the crown of your head. Then the lotus base used by the main figure dissolves into your guru's lotus base on your crown. Next, visualize that your root guru on your head turns into our Teacher Śhākyamuni; regard him as the embodiment of all refuges, and perform for him a short seven-limbed prayer and world-maṇḍala offering. Then make fervent petitions solely to your guru. Stick to making these petitions to only one guru—rather like being tethered to one spot by means of a peg driven into the ground. Don't feel it might be better to make the petition to someone else. It is pointless to make this petition to many people.

Make the petition as you would to the embodiment of the Three Jewels and of all refuges. The following verses are taken from the *Miraculous Book of the Gelugpas,* so they are especially blessed.

My most divine guru, lord of the four kāyas,
I make petition to you: Śhākyamuni-Vajradhara.
My divine guru, lord of unimpeded dharmakāya,
I make petition to you: Śhākyamuni-Vajradhara.
My divine guru, lord of blissful saṃbhogakāya,
I make petition to you: Śhākyamuni-Vajradhara.
My divine guru, lord of sundry nirmāṇakayas,
I make petition to you: Śhākyamuni-Vajradhara.
My divine guru, embodiment of all gurus,
I make petition to you: Śhākyamuni-Vajradhara.
My divine guru, embodiment of all deities,
I make petition to you: Śhākyamuni-Vajradhara.
My divine guru, embodiment of all buddhas,
I make petition to you: Śhākyamuni-Vajradhara.
My divine guru, embodiment of all Dharma,
I make petition to you: Śhākyamuni-Vajradhara.
My divine guru, embodiment of all Saṅgha,
I make petition to you: Śhākyamuni-Vajradhara.
My divine guru, embodiment of all ḍākas
I make petition to you: Śhākyamuni-Vajradhara.
My divine guru, embodiment of all Dharmapālas,
I make petition to you: Śhākyamuni-Vajradhara.
My divine guru, embodiment of all refuge,
I make petition to you: Śhākyamuni-Vajradhara.

But note: the lengths of the lines are supposed to be equal; do not spoil the metre by saying, for example, "My most divine guru, lord of unimpeded dharmakāya."[35] During the mind-training practices, when you are training yourself in meditation on the equality and exchanging of self and others, since Ārya Avalokiteśhvara is the supreme deity of compassion, you should change these verses to the following: "My most divine guru, lord of the four kāyas, I make petition to you: Guru Avalokiteśhvara..." Do the same for Mañjuśhrī when you meditate on the view.

This ends the preparations. At this point, you follow a lamrim meditation topic, ranging from the first topic—devotion to your spiritual guide—through to mental quiescence and special insight. Do not dissolve the figure of your guru on your head; he sits there throughout the meditation. If you lose the visualization, revisualize him and offer a maṇḍala.

So now you must begin the main part of the meditation session. Meditate on the lamrim of your choice, either a short or long version—the *Easy Path,* the *Swift Path,* and so on. Then, in addition, purify the mind. Then make petition to develop realization into the particular section of the lamrim you have just meditated on; the stream of five nectars descends from the guru's body: think they purify you of things hindering you in that particular lamrim section. The nectars also make you develop that part of the path in your mindstream. Note that the preparatory rites that come before the words "I make petition to you: Śhākyamuni-Vajradhara" are the same for all the meditation topics to follow.

The passage "Since beginningless time, I and all sentient beings, who have been my mothers, have been born into saṃsāra and for a long while up until now have only experienced the different, powerful sufferings of saṃsāra..." is taken directly from the *Easy Path.* If you are meditating on the great scope, omit the words "been born into saṃsāra and for a long while" when you make this prayer.

HOW TO PURSUE THE MAIN PART OF THE SESSION (60)

One now has to *meditate* during the main part of the session. Familiarization techniques directed toward a single subject is what we call meditation. We have thoughts that lack faith in our spiritual guide, so we turn our attention toward thoughts of faith in him; we use this technique to familiarize ourself with these thoughts and to gain control over them. This is meditation.

Our minds have come under the power of delusions, so we turn our attention to something else to put a stop to it.

There are two sorts of meditation—analytic and fixation meditations. Analytic meditation is thinking many times over quotations, reasonings, formal logic, and so on: this is called familiarization.[36] I'll discuss this on a simple level. We actually do nothing but analytic meditation all the time, but we direct it the wrong way; it is analytic meditation on the three poisons.

Take the example of anger. First you do not recall your enemy and do not develop any anger; you develop anger only if you recollect him. Recollect him and you say, "Last year he said such words to me. He did this to me. Then he did me such wrongs. Finally he gave me such looks!" Externally, your face reddens and your armpits become sweaty. You have developed such anger that if that enemy of yours were there before you, you would doubtless punch him in the head right then. You have performed an analytic meditation, and it is the same for attachment, etc.

When we are thinking over debate arguments, with the exception of thoughts about ways to defeat the others, that inwardly focused analysis is the analytic meditation I am talking about. In a sense we are great meditators—we perform analytic meditation exclusively on delusion and the three poisons, and we will achieve something quite different from the other great meditators: we are said to be in danger of going to a world where all the hills and valleys are red hot. Instead of doing such unbeneficial analytic meditation, we should do analytic meditation on what constitutes the optimum human rebirth, on why this sort of rebirth is so hard to gain, on how it is so beneficial, and so on.

You should be sure about the individual headings of the lamrim. In the section dealing with meditation on the optimum human rebirth and how difficult it is to acquire, you meditate on this alone: it is a great hindrance to pursue meditation on a lamrim topic arbitrarily, doing whatever you please, because you feel, "It's Dharma, nothing can go wrong." This is like mixing soda into a jar of salt. Such meditation is ruined by excitement and dullness; the virtuous practices you then perform all your life will be flawed. If this happens, you may feel, "I have meditated on this [topic]," but you should not trust such thoughts.

Let's take the case of meditation on death and impermanence when not done as above. It is sufficient to meditate on the quotations, reasonings, formal logic, and examples given on the subject—you could even add some items, like the person who died in your village today. Further, take your guru's oral teachings as the root, and add to this even things like the folio you found in a wayside shrine. If you think about the topic from many angles, you will develop realizations with ease, just as you developed feelings of hostility by thinking about things from many angles.

Your meditations are only analytic until you achieve mental quiescence. After you achieve mental quiescence, you can perform fixation meditation, where you direct the mind to one thing. Some people claim fixation meditation is for mendicants, while analytic meditation is for scholars; that analytic meditation is detrimental to fixation meditation, and so on. This is nonsense.

Part Three

The Foundations of the Path

DAY 7

Kyabje Pabongka Rinpoche began, quoting the great bodhisattva Śhāntideva:

> You can free yourself from the great river of suffering
> By relying on the boat of human rebirth.
> Such a boat will be hard to get again;
> O blind one, this time do not fall asleep!

You have gained the perfect rebirth, a human one, a birth that is like a boat to freedom from the great ocean of saṃsāra. The sort of happiness that lasts only until your death is nothing to get attached to, and if you do not achieve the one eternal hope for all your future rebirths it will be difficult for you to find such a physical rebirth again, another boat to free you from this great ocean of suffering. So you must fulfill your one eternal hope now, and to achieve that, you must know how to do it. Set your motivation by thinking, "I will achieve full buddhahood for the sake of all sentient beings, my past mothers. I will therefore listen to this profound teaching on the three scopes of the lamrim and then practice it properly."

Here are the relevant headings...

After discussing the headings already covered, Pabongka Rinpoche continued:

The fourth major heading, "The Sequence in which the Disciples Are to Be Taught the Actual Instructions," has two subheadings: (1) the root of the path: devotion to a spiritual guide, and (2) the proper graduated training you should undertake after you have begun to rely on him. I will now discuss how to devote yourself to a spiritual guide.

I could not cover the material of the preparatory rites four times over, but one must do this four times when teaching the main part of the lamrim discourse—starting from the section on devotion to one's spiritual guide. This includes a summary [at the start of the next day's session]. From now on you should follow this tradition.

You can see for yourselves that carpenters and sculptors, for example, who can learn by watching, must first study with a teacher. So there is no need to tell you that you must rely on a spiritual guide in order to know properly the path that will fulfill your eternal hopes by taking you to the same level as the buddhas. Some people think they can know the path by reading books and not have a guru, but this is not good enough—you must rely on a qualified guru. Suppose you were going to India, for example; you would definitely need to find a guide, and not just anyone would do—you must depend on someone who has been there before. Similarly, a spiritual guide must be a person capable of taking you on the path to buddhahood. If you depend on anyone at all, on bad company and the like, you will not be led on the right path and may go astray. Thus it is vital to depend on a spiritual guide at the outset. Note, too, Je Rinpoche's words [that the spiritual guide is] "the root of the path."

The way to devote yourself to a spiritual guide begins with four headings: (1) the advantages of relying on a spiritual guide; (2) the disadvantages of not relying on a spiritual guide, or of letting your devotion lapse; (3) devoting yourself through thought; (4) devoting yourself through deeds.

THE ADVANTAGES OF RELYING ON A SPIRITUAL GUIDE (61)

Only when you think beforehand about the advantages of relying on a spiritual guide, and about the disadvantages of not relying on one, will you do so enthusiastically.

The benefits of relying on a spiritual guide are discussed in the *Swift Path* and, in accordance with the oral tradition of our gurus, this is treated under eight subheadings.

YOU WILL COME CLOSER TO BUDDHAHOOD (62)

In my own guru Dagpo Rinpoche's oral tradition, we subdivide this heading into two: (1) you will come closer to buddhahood by practicing the instructions he taught you; (2) you will also come closer to buddhahood by making offerings to the guru and serving him.

YOU WILL COME CLOSER TO BUDDHAHOOD BY PRACTICING THE INSTRUCTIONS HE TAUGHT YOU (63)

One general benefit of relying on a spiritual guide is that you will get nearer to buddhahood. Although the other paths and their stages require many countless eons to achieve buddhahood, some people can be led to this state in only one lifetime because they have devoted themselves to a spiritual guide. The highest tantras, too, achieve this extremely quickly, and guru yoga is the very lifeblood of the tantric path. This can be seen, for example, in Je Milarepa's life story.

I could quote you such verses as: "Through his kindness, the state of great bliss..." or, "Through his compassion, the sphere of great bliss..." That is, if you devote yourself to the guru properly, through his kindness and compassion, he will give you the state of dharmakāya—the sphere of great bliss in one short lifetime only, which is but an instant in these degenerate times. The human lifetime is only an instant when compared with the lifespans of beings in the hells below and the gods above.

And to illustrate this, Kyabje Pabongka Rinpoche told the story of Asaṅga's journey to Tuṣhita.[37]

Moreover, the human lifespan is but an instant compared with the length of time we spend in saṃsāra.

If you are not properly devoted to the guru, you will not develop even the slightest realization into the stages and path, no matter what practice you cultivate, be it even the highest tantras. But if you devote yourself properly, you will soon obtain the state of unification, even though this [normally] requires many eons to achieve. As the *Essence of Nectar* lamrim says:

> The great unification is most difficult to achieve,
> Even after perseverance a hundredfold strong
> Over oceans of countless eons. But they say
> One can easily achieve it, in one short life
> In this degenerate age, by relying on the guru's power.

Even in the sūtric tradition, one travels the path quickly if one's guru devotion is exceptional.

Pabongka Rinpoche then told the life story of the bodhisattva Sadāprarudita.

If we were to meet a buddha, say, we would think, "I have met a buddha, higher than my guru." This may be well and good, but Sadāprarudita saw countless buddhas and was not satisfied; instead he searched for a guru. This is a vital point. For no one can benefit us as much as a guru with whom we have had a karmic relationship over all our rebirths. Sadāprarudita might have been satisfied at the time [of meeting his teacher] with offering a wish-granting jewel given he had received from Indra. Sadāprarudita, however, cut the flesh from his own body and bled himself in order to honor and revere his guru Dharmodgata. This was to give the greatest force to his building up the two types of accumulation. Sadāprarudita had already achieved the single-pointed concentration called "continuous Dharma" when he had these visions of many buddhas; he was, in fact, on the great level of the Mahāyāna path of accumulation. Then he met Dharmodgata, who taught him Dharma. Sadāprarudita mastered the eighth bodhisattva level and developed the patience in ungenerated Dharma level [of the path of preparation]. He achieved this so rapidly because of his matchless devotion to his spiritual guide. They say that other bodhisattvas have to spend one interminable great eon building up their accumulations while on the first seven impure levels of the ten bodhisattva levels.

So whether or not you have proper guru devotion determines whether you will reach buddhahood quickly. You will come closer to buddhahood if you rely on him, that is if you put into practice whatever instructions he gives you. And you will reach buddhahood sooner if you rely on someone who can teach the complete path, rather than on a person who can only teach the small scope. If a disciple who is a suitable vessel [in other words, one who can endure austerities] meets up with a guru capable of teaching the whole path, they say that all difficulties will melt away, as if the buddhas had arranged this themselves. Padampa Sangyae said:

> You'll reach any place you desire if the guru carries you there—
> So, people of Dingri, offer him reverence and respect as the journey's price.

Nāgārjuna said:

> If a person fell from the peak of the king of mountains,
> He would still fall, even though he thought, "I shall not fall."
> If you receive beneficial teachings through the guru's kindness,
> You will still be liberated, though you think, "I shall not be liberated."

That is, if you fell from the top of a high mountain, you could not stop even if you felt, "I can go back." Similarly, if your guru devotion is sound, it will lead to your liberation from saṃsāra, even though you might feel, "I will not be liberated." But you cannot travel even the least of the stages and paths if you do not rely on a guru.

YOU WILL ALSO COME CLOSER TO BUDDHAHOOD THROUGH MAKING OFFERINGS TO THE GURU AND SERVING HIM (64)

You must accumulate an immeasurable collection of primal wisdom and merit in order to reach buddhahood. But this huge collection is easily acquired; the best way is to make offerings to the guru. As it is said:

> Offering to a single pore of the guru
> Is superior in merit than offering
> To the buddhas of the ten directions
> And to the bodhisattvas.
> Thus buddhas and bodhisattvas see
> When someone offers to a master.

In other words, as stated in many tantras and commentaries, it is more beneficial to make offerings to a single pore of the guru's body than to all buddhas in the ten directions and their children. Sakya Paṇḍita says:

> The [merit] stock gained by following the [six] perfections
> And sacrificing head, arms, and legs for thousands of eons
> Is gained in but a moment through the guru path.
> Shouldn't you rejoice when made to serve him?

In other words, we may gain a huge stock [of merit] by sacrificing our head, arms, and legs for thousands of eons, but we can acquire the same in a single moment by the little trouble it takes to please the guru. You get closer to buddhahood because it is that much quicker to build up that amount of [merit].

It is more powerful to make offerings to human beings than to animals; it is more powerful still to make offerings to śhrāvakas; even more powerful to make offerings to pratyekabuddhas; and yet more powerful still to offer to buddhas and bodhisattvas; but the guru is the most powerful object of one's offering. Geshe Toelungpa once said:

> I get greater merit by giving food to [my guru] Lopa's dog than by teaching the Saṅgha of Toelung about making offerings.

They say that this geshe used to collect even the congealed butter left in his bowls after meals and give it to Lopa's dog.

It says in a tantra: "It is better to offer to one pore of the guru than to all the buddhas of the three times." Note that the phrase "offering to one pore of the guru" means offering to the guru's horse, his watchdog, attendants, and so on. It does not mean his ordinary body pores.

IT PLEASES THE VICTORIOUS ONES (65)

There are two ways of thinking about this heading:

THE BUDDHAS OF THE TEN DIRECTIONS ARE WILLING TO TEACH YOU DHARMA, BUT YOU ARE NOT EVEN FORTUNATE ENOUGH TO SEE THE SUPREME NIRMĀṆAKĀYA, LET ALONE THE SAMBHOGAKĀYA, BECAUSE THESE APPEAR ONLY TO ORDINARY BEINGS WITH PURE KARMA (66)

Buddha manifested his body for us [in the supreme nirmāṇakāya form], but we were not fortunate enough to receive Dharma teachings from him [in that aspect]. We therefore need an enlightened body suited to our level of good fortune to teach us Dharma. Thus the victorious ones in the ten directions emanate themselves as gurus for our sakes—rather like a modern committee appointing a spokesman. When we properly devote ourselves to the guru, the buddhas know it and are pleased. The *Essence of Nectar* lamrim says this on how they are pleased:

When you properly rely on a holy spiritual guide,
You will soon be liberated from cyclic existence.
Like a mother seeing her child receive help,
All the victors are pleased to the depths of their hearts.

In other words, the victorious ones love us as a mother loves her only child. The buddhas know this and are pleased that their wishes have been fulfilled when we properly devote ourselves to our gurus—the root of all welfare and happiness and the only means to free ourselves from the sufferings of saṃsāra and the lower realms.

IF YOU DO NOT RELY PROPERLY ON YOUR GURU, YOU WILL NOT PLEASE THE BUDDHAS, NO MATTER HOW MANY OFFERINGS YOU MAKE TO THEM (67)

The Fifth Dalai Lama quoted the following lines in *Mañjuśhrī's Own Words.* If you are properly devoted:

I will abide in the bodies of people having these qualifications.
When these other accomplished beings
Accept your offerings and are pleased,
Your mindstream is purified of karmic obscurations.

In other words, you may not have [actually] invoked the victorious ones, but they have still taken their places in your guru's body. When he is pleased by your offerings, they are too. But if you were to make offerings to the victors and their children [alone], you would receive only the benefits of making the offerings, not of pleasing and delighting them as well. Making offerings to the guru brings the benefits both of the offering itself and of pleasing the buddhas.

YOU WILL NOT BE DISTURBED BY DEMONS OR BAD COMPANY (68)

As it says in a sūtra, because of your proper reliance on a spiritual guide, your merit greatly increases. Owing to this increase you will not be bothered by demons and bad company. The *Great Play Sūtra* tells us:

> The wishes of those with merit will be fulfilled;
> They have defeated the demons and will soon reach enlightenment.

Also, we are told: "Gods and demons cannot hinder those with merit."

YOU WILL AUTOMATICALLY PUT A STOP TO ALL DELUSIONS AND MISDEEDS (69)

When you rely on a spiritual guide, you will know how to modify your behavior, and you will actually act appropriately—in the same way that you now automatically stop your misdeeds while you are living close to your spiritual guide or in your teacher's house. The *Laying Out of Stalks Sūtra* tells us:

> The things done by people driven by karma and delusion are difficult for bodhisattvas [who are] under the care of virtuous spiritual guides [to do].

The *Essence of Nectar* lamrim says:

> When you respectfully rely on him continually,
> All your delusion and misdeeds stop of their own accord...

YOUR INSIGHTS AND REALIZATION INTO THE LEVELS AND THE PATH WILL INCREASE (70)

Both Dromtoenpa and Amé Jangchub Rinchen diligently served Atiśha [one as an attendant, the other as a cook]. In terms of concentration and realizations, they had more insights and experiences than Mahāyogi, who practiced only in meditation: they had also developed more on the stages and the path than he. Atiśha could see this by clairvoyance and told Drom, "You traveled the path merely by serving your guru, a grey-haired monk."

Some people think that only famous abbots and people who teach Dharma from high thrones are gurus, such as the vajra masters who give initiations. This is not so. You must also be properly devoted to the teacher who shares the same room, sharing everything, and who tutors you in the books.

When Atiśha was ill, Drom did not regard his feces as something filthy:

he carried them outside in his bare hands. As a result, he suddenly developed such clairvoyance that he could read the subtlest workings of the minds of animals, even ants, at a place so distant it would have taken a vulture eighteen days to reach it. Even today Drom is famed everywhere as "the grandfather Great Forefather of the Kadampa teachings." And the good works, as vast as space itself, of great Atiśha in both India and Tibet came about solely through the power of Drom's proper guru devotion.

Whether a saint's or another's good works are extensive depends on this devotion. Zhoenue Oe, who came from Jayul, relied on Geshe Chaen Ngawa and served him well. One day he was taking out the rubbish. On arriving at the dump, he took only three steps when he developed the continuous Dharma single-pointed concentration.

When Sakya Paṇḍita once asked [his uncle] the venerable Dragpa Gyaeltsaen to compose a work on guru yoga, Dragpa at first said, "You only regard me as an uncle, not as a guru," and did not write the piece. Later, when Dragpa fell sick, Sakya Paṇḍita nursed him well, and so the guru wrote about guru yoga. From that time on, Sakya Paṇḍita regarded him as a buddha, not just an uncle, and became a pandit-scholar in the five sciences.

Taenpa Rabgyae, who later occupied the Gandaen throne, would worry so much whenever his tutor became ill that he almost died himself. Taenpa realized the view because he nursed his tutor so well.

Purchog Ngagwang Jampa one day carried an enormous sack of dried dung [used as cooking fuel] to Drubkang Geleg Gyatso's house. Purchog had undergone much hardship, and Drubkang Geleg Gyatso gave him an ancient skullcup filled with a consecrated "inner offering." Purchog drank the offering and his mindstream was blessed; he then developed an intense renunciation and weariness of saṃsāra.

So if you rely on a guru, your realization in the stages and path will greatly increase. The *Essence of Nectar* lamrim says:

> Experiences and realizations into the stages and path will instantly develop and increase.

YOU WILL NOT BE DEPRIVED OF VIRTUOUS SPIRITUAL GUIDES IN ALL YOUR FUTURE REBIRTHS (71)

Geshe Potowa says in the *Blue Compendium:*

PURCHOG NGAGWANG JAMPA CARRIES FUEL FOR HIS GURU

Avoid unexamined Dharma relationships.
After examining take heed: pay respect to the guru.
Things are such that in the future you will not lack a guru,
For karma does not vanish.

That is, if you are properly devoted to your spiritual guide, that action will give a result similar to it: you will not be deprived of virtuous spiritual guides in all your future lives. If you regard your present spiritual guide, who is an ordinary, average being, as being an actual buddha and devote yourself to him properly, you will later meet with gurus like Maitreya and Mañjuśhrī and listen to their teachings. That is why the *Essence of Nectar* lamrim says:

The result congruous with the cause of paying your guru proper respect in this life
Is meeting with supreme spiritual guides in all future lives
And hearing the completely unmistaken Dharma from them.

YOU WILL NOT FALL INTO THE LOWER REALMS (72)

If you are properly devoted to your spiritual guide, you use up the throwing karma to take you to the lower realms, and you will not be born there. This happens even when he scolds you. Whenever Geshe Lhazowa visited Geshe Toelungpa, for example, Lhazowa would only get scolded. Nyagmo, one of Lhazowa's own disciples, criticized him. But Lhazowa replied, "Don't say that. Every time he does this to me, it is like being blessed by Heruka." Drogoen Tsangpa Gyarae said:

If you are struck, it's an initiation:
If you take it as a blessing, you'll be blessed.
A hard scolding is like a wrathful mantra
That removes every hindrance.

In other words, you use up the karma to be reborn in the lower realms. The *Sūtra Requested by Kṣhitigarbha* tells us:

By doing this, you purify karma that would [otherwise] make you wander in the lower realms for immeasurable millions of

> eons; this karma will occur in this life in terms of things harmful to body and mind—epidemics, famines, and so on. [Karma] is even purified by a scolding, or by nightmares. And you can overcome karma in one morning by giving your generated root merits to immeasurable numbers of buddhas or by keeping your vows.

Think over such quotations.

YOU WILL EFFORTLESSLY ACHIEVE ALL SHORT- AND LONG-TERM AIMS (73)

In short, proper devotion to your guru is the root of all mundane and supramundane qualities. Everything—from the prerequisites for not falling to the lower realms right up to the prerequisites for achieving buddhahood—come effortlessly when you rely on a spiritual guide. Je Rinpoche said: "O kind lord, the foundation of good qualities…"

From the *Essence of Nectar* lamrim:

> Briefly: when you rely upon a spiritual guide, in the short term,
> Free of unfavorable states, you gain good rebirths as gods and humans.
> Ultimately all saṃsāra's suffering will end,
> And you'll achieve the supreme, excellent state.

Atiśha said he had relied on 152 gurus; there was not one he did not hold dear to heart. So his good works in both India and Tibet were as extensive as space itself because of his excellent devotion to his spiritual guides.

THE DISADVANTAGES OF NOT RELYING ON A SPIRITUAL GUIDE, OR OF LETTING YOUR DEVOTION LAPSE (74)

The disadvantages of not relying on a guru are the opposites of the above eight advantages: that is, you will not come closer to buddhahood, and so on.

There are eight disadvantages to letting your devotion lapse. Once you begin to rely on a guru, it is a grave misdeed to then later let your devotion lapse; thus you must receive Dharma teachings only after a thorough investigation into whether that person is worthy or not.

IF YOU DISPARAGE YOUR GURU, YOU INSULT ALL THE VICTORIOUS ONES (75)

The guru is the physical embodiment of all the buddhas and has come in order to subdue you; in a sense he is a delegate. So if you disparage him, you criticize all buddhas. If you must regard just one buddha with reverence, what would happen when you insult all the buddhas!

By *guru* we mean someone who wants to teach, and a *disciple* is someone who wants to listen—even to as little as one verse. We carry out strict guru devotion to our more famous gurus, but treat others such as the one who taught us the alphabet offhandedly. This is not right: Je Drubkang Geleg Gyatso developed no realizations while he still did not see as pure the disrobed monk who taught him the alphabet. The *Essence of Nectar* lamrim says:

> Spiritual guides are the good works of all the buddhas;
> This is so, for they appear to you as your guru.
> Since disrespect to him is said to be
> Disrespect to all buddhas, what action could ripen heavier?

The *Commentary on the Difficult Points of the Kṛiṣhṇayamarī Tantra* says:

> One who upon hearing even one verse [of teaching]
> Does not hold [that person] as a lama
> Will be born one hundred times as a dog
> And then in the lowest of castes.

And in [Aśhvaghoṣha's] *Fifty Verses on the Guru:*

> If you disparage your guru
> After feeling he is your protector and becoming his disciple,
> You disparage all the buddhas.
> Suffering will then always be your lot.

WHEN YOU DEVELOP ANGRY THOUGHTS TOWARD YOUR GURU, YOU DESTROY YOUR ROOT MERITS AND WILL BE REBORN IN HELL FOR THE SAME NUMBER OF EONS AS THE MOMENTS [OF YOUR ANGER] (76)

If you get angry at your guru, you destroy [an equivalent amount of] root merits as the number of moments your anger lasted from start to finish. You must then stay in the Hell of No Respite for the same number [of eons]. From the *Kālachakra Tantra:*

> Count the moments you were angry at the guru.
> You destroy root virtues built up over eons;
> You will experience intense suffering in hell,
> And so on, for that very number of eons.

Suppose you are angry for the duration of one snap of the fingers. [Finger-snaps are said to last sixty-five moments.] You destroy root virtues collected over sixty-five great eons and you must stay in the Hell Without Respite for that length of time. So if you are disrespectful to or disparage your guru, or get angry with or displease him, you must expiate these [negativities] in his presence while he is still alive; if he is not, you should expiate them before some of his clothes, at least.

YOU WILL NOT ACHIEVE THE SUPREME STATE, DESPITE YOUR RELIANCE ON TANTRA (77)

The *Guhyasamāja Root Tantra* states:

> A sentient being may have committed
> Great sins such as the heinous crimes,
> But he can still succeed in the Supreme Vehicle,
> The great ocean of the Vajrayāna.
>
> But someone who despises his master from his very heart
> May practice, but will not succeed.

No matter how great a sinner you may be, having committed the five heinous crimes and so on, you will soon achieve the supreme goal by relying, for example, on the path of the Guhyasamāja tantra. But if you despise your master from your heart, they say you will not achieve the supreme goal, no matter how much you practice.

THOUGH YOU SEEK THE BENEFITS OF TANTRA, YOUR PRACTICE WILL ACHIEVE ONLY THE HELLS AND THE LIKE (78)

No matter how hard a person with lapsed [tantric] commitments to his master may practice, he will achieve only the hells. The *Ornament to the Vajrahṛidaya Tantra* tells us:

> Whoever despises his perfect master,
> Though he be the best practitioner of every tantra,
> Though he give up sleep and all distractions
> And practice well for a thousand eons,
> He will achieve the hells, and so on.

YOU WILL NOT DEVELOP FRESH QUALITIES YOU HAVE NOT ALREADY DEVELOPED, AND THOSE YOU HAVE WILL DEGENERATE (79)

Criticizing your guru prevents you from developing fresh realizations in this life, and those you have already developed will decline. Āchārya Kṛiṣhṇāchārya slightly disobeyed an order of his guru, Jalandharī, and thus did not accomplish the supreme goal in that life. Raechungpa disobeyed Milarepa three times and did not achieve the supreme goal; they say he took three rebirths to achieve it.

Once an āchārya of low caste had a high-caste disciple. This disciple could fly in the air. One day he flew over his guru, thinking, "Not even my guru can do this." His power immediately declined and he fell to the ground. Pandit Nāropa forgot his guru's command and debated with some tīrṭhikas and thus did not achieve the supreme goal in that life but had to wait until he reached the bardo. Mañjuśhrī predicted that two particular novices from Khotan would achieve the supreme goal in that life, but the two developed wrong views about the Dharmarāja Songtsaen Gampo. Because of their doubts about him, instead of achieving the predicted supreme siddhi [of buddhahood], on returning to their homeland, they gained only the siddhi of being able to fill sacks with gold. So if you have wrong views about your guru, it postpones your development of insights and realizations, and the great siddhis you were to attain become lesser ones.

If you mix with bad company, your insights and realizations will be dimmed. You must avoid such things. Most people these days only cling to this life; everybody overvalues this life. Even those who care about us, and those we look upon as helping us, are actually bad company. "Bad company" don't wear coarse sacking, they don't have horns on their heads; "bad company" means people who make you do something nonvirtuous out of a feigned concern for your welfare, or who prevent you from doing something virtuous. Ignore such people, no matter who they may be. Regard them as terrifying, as if they were mad elephants, tigers, or leopards, and avoid them. There are still some who have few wants and are content. Such people say soothing things like, "Don't give up so much! Nothing comes of giving up so much!" People who say such things are in fact bad company. But don't contradict them directly and don't insult them; that is not the right way for us to practice.

IN THIS LIFE, YOU WILL SUFFER UNDESIRABLE ILLNESSES AND SO ON (80)

Fifty Verses on the Guru says:

> Disparage your master and—
> Great fool!—you will die
> From plagues, painful illnesses,
> Spirits, epidemics, and poisons.
>
> Kings, fire, and poisonous snakes,
> Floods, witches, thieves,
> Demons, and vile spirits will kill you;
> Then, sentient being, you go to hell.
>
> Never upset the minds
> Of your masters;
> If you blindly do so,
> You will surely roast in hell.

Those who disparage their masters
Were rightly told they'd stay
In any of the terrifying hells,
Such as the Hell Without Respite.

That is, if you disparage your master, you will suffer many kinds of illness in this life.

At one time in ancient India, Āchārya Buddhajñāna was giving a Dharma teaching. His guru, a mahāsiddha, was a swineherd. The guru arrived during the teaching and Buddhajñāna pretended not to see him. Buddhajñāna later lied to his guru, saying "I did not see you," whereupon his eyes actually fell out and dropped on the ground.

Tsultrim, a neighbor of Dagpo Jampael Lhuendrub Rinpoche, was disrespectful and had no faith toward the Rinpoche. Later a thief smashed Tsultrim's head with a rock at Goeker Pass, and he died.

Kyabje Pabongka told these stories, and also told the story of one of Neuzurpa's disciples who broke his [tantric] commitments, and how he had terrifying visions when he died.

YOU WILL WANDER ENDLESSLY IN THE LOWER REALMS IN YOUR NEXT LIVES (81)

This is the worst penalty for people who disparage their guru, says the *Vajrapāṇi Initiation Tantra.* The sūtras tell many stories about rebirths in the hells, but this tantra does not teach that a person who disparages his guru will be born in these hells; the tantra says:

> Vajrapāṇi asked, "O Bhagavān! What are the ripening effects of disparaging one's master?"
>
> The Bhagavān gave this reply to the request for an explanation of these ripening effects: "O Vajrapāṇi, I will not tell you, for it would terrify the world, gods and all. But, O lord of the esoteric, I will say this much:
>
> Heroes, pay attention, listen!
> I say those people will stay

> In any of the mighty hells I described while teaching
> On the heinous crimes, and so on.
> And this for infinite eons!
> Never, never, despise your master.

In other words, Buddha did not dare go into detail because he knew that the world, gods and all, would be terrified, and even the bodhisattvas and mahāsattvas would faint. He taught only that such people must remain in the Hell Without Respite for many years.

So they say it is never right to disparage your guru. Apart from not actually disparaging him yourself, it is not even right to look at someone else who has done so, as this story shows. Once while Lingraepa, a great adept, was teaching the Dharma, a disciple of Chag the translator turned up. This disciple had broken his [tantric] commitments. Suddenly Lingraepa's mouth became paralyzed; he was unable to teach, and departed.

YOU WILL BE DEPRIVED OF SPIRITUAL GUIDES IN ALL FUTURE LIVES (82)

This is the opposite of one of the above advantages of relying on a spiritual guide. Not only will you not meet with a guru but you will be born only in places where there is no chance of hearing even the word Dharma. In short, as Je Rinpoche says: "Thus, any good fortune you may have..." That is, all your worldly good fortune resulted from reliance on a spiritual guide; any misfortune is the result either of not relying on one or of letting your devotion lapse. If your devotion lapses, you will be deprived of virtuous spiritual guides not only in this life but in future rebirths also. As the *Essence of Nectar* lamrim says:

> Though you may occasionally attain rebirth in the upper realms,
> The results of your disrespect will be congruous with the cause:
> You will be born in places with no opportunity,
> You will not hear a word of holy Dharma,
> Nor a word from a spiritual guide.

Not only do we not think over our guru devotion, our ill-considered and thoughtless actions have subtle [karmic] connections. Various auspicious and inauspicious gestures can occur. It was an inauspicious gesture when Milarepa offered Marpa an empty copper pot; when Marpa first offered him some beer, Milarepa drank the lot—this was an auspicious gesture; when Marpa prostrated himself to a tutelary deity [instead of to his guru Nāropa], it was an inauspicious gesture.

Kyabje Pabongka Rinpoche spoke in detail on how Dromtoenpa relied on Setsuen and Atiśha; on how Atiśha relied on Suvarṇadvīpa; Milarepa on Marpa; how Je Tsongkapa applied gold leaf to the walls of the room where Kyungpo Lhaepa gave him his initiations; and so on.

So devotion to a spiritual guide is vital. Even the smallest auspicious or inauspicious gestures have their consequences.

Kyabje Pabongka then told the story about Gyaeltsab Rinpoche, and how he had intended to debate with Je Rinpoche before the two had ever met, and what happened when he came into Je Rinpoche's presence.[38]

Gyaeltsab Rinpoche's motives were unfortunate, but it turned out to be auspicious. Many things can happen; good motives may turn out to be inauspicious. One must be careful!

When we use our guru's name, we say "Kuzhu [roughly translated as 'Mister'] so and so" or "Kuzhu such and such." Don't do this; you must use some form of honorific with his name such as "His Reverence." Whenever Atiśha used Suvarṇadvīpa Guru's name, he would clasp his hands together and call him "The great Suvarṇadvīpa." He would immediately stand up if anyone else uttered Suvarṇadvīpa's name. I am not trying to put myself forward, but I am unhappy whenever I see my own precious guru's name used casually. If your guru is still alive, you should not use the honorific phrase "whose name I speak with difficulty."

Kyabje Pabongka then reviewed the above headings twice: once in some detail and once quite briefly.

DAY 8

Kyabje Pabongka Rinpoche quoted this verse by Je Rinpoche:

> Anyone unattached to worldly happiness who,
> Yearning to give meaning to their optimum rebirth,
> Follows a path pleasing to the victors—
> O fortunate ones! Listen with clear minds.

The first line refers to the correct view according to the medium scope; the second refers to the small scope section of the path; the third, to bodhichitta and the great scope...

Having given this introduction to set our motivation, he restated the headings we had already covered and revisited the first two main headings of the main body of the lamrim discourse. These headings deal with one's devotion to a spiritual guide. He then continued:

These particular headings treat the subject only as a topic of meditation. The headings in the *Swift Path* and the *Easy Path* are not clear about how one should investigate a [potential] spiritual guide; so I now want to discuss this according to *Mañjuśhrī's Own Words.*

If, as stated above, relying on a spiritual guide has these benefits and if not relying on one has these drawbacks, on whom then should we rely?

Relying on any spiritual guide at all is not good enough; you must rely on one who can teach the whole path. Someone with only a few good qualities—being extremely kindhearted, for example—may not be capable of teaching the whole path. Even though the disciples may have faith, wisdom, and perseverance, if the guru has not fully mastered the sūtras and tantras, the disciples will spend their entire human life practicing just a few things—taking refuge, some sādhanas of deities, meditation on the energy winds and channels, and so on. The disciples' opportune rebirth will not be made meaningful. You must therefore rely on a fully qualified spiritual guide.

There are many individual qualifications: the ability to give pratimokṣha vows, tantric and bodhichitta vows, etc. Here I will deal with the qualifications of a spiritual guide who can teach the complete lamrim. You should investigate to see whether a teacher has these qualifications before you rely on him. Not only should you investigate the qualifications of any guru you wish to rely on as your spiritual guide, but also anyone who wishes to give spiritual guidance in the vinaya, sūtras, or tantras should examine themselves to see if they have the qualifications to be a guru in these subjects. If not fully qualified, they should see to it that they become so. Having all the tantric paraphernalia such as the long-life vase or the ritual bathing equipment [see Day 5], and knowing how to perform the ceremonies by heart do not make a fully qualified guru.

There are individual sets of qualifications: one for being an abbot and ordination master able to teach vinaya, one for being a spiritual guide of the common Mahāyāna, and one for being a vajra master of the secret tantras. I shall mainly describe the qualifications of the guru of the common Mahāyāna. [Maitreya's] *Ornament to the Sūtras* tells us:

> Rely on a spiritual guide who is subdued, pacified, most pacified, Who has more qualities than you, perseverance, a wealth of scripture, Realization into suchness, who is a skilled speaker, Is the embodiment of love, and is not discouraged.

This makes ten qualifications in all: gurus' mindstreams should be *subdued* by ethics. Their mental distraction should be *pacified* by single-pointed concentration. Their grasping at a self should be *most pacified* by wisdom. When a stick of incense is placed among other pieces of wood, the wood acquires its fragrance; you also acquire a guru's faults and good qualities. Gurus should therefore have *more qualities than you. Realization into suchness* is as follows. They have discovered the view by means of wisdom gained through their studies. The "view" is the view according to the Prāsaṅgika school. This is higher wisdom; I am not referring to the wisdom that comes when one discovers the view through the Svātantrika school and below [see Day 22, pp. 623ff.]. The rest of the quotation is easy.

Even if a guru doesn't have all these qualifications, he must definitely have at least these five: a mindstream subdued by each of the three high trainings [ethics, concentration, wisdom], love and compassion, and realization into suchness. Geshe Potowa said:

> Everyone thought my master Zhangtsuen Yerpa hadn't studied much in anything, and because he had no patience when frustrated, he was hardly polite in speech. But Yerpa has the above five qualifications, and anyone who meets him benefits.
>
> Nyaentoenpa has absolutely no speaking skills, although he can discuss all the required topics. One would think that everyone would not understand, but that is not so. He has the five qualifications, and anyone near him benefits.

"Being polite," cited above, means saying "That's all right" or responding with "thank you" or "well done."

Though such people will be rare until the end of time, the point is that you must rely on someone who has mainly good qualities rather than faults, who puts future lives before this life, and others before himself. If you do not do this and instead meet with a nonvirtuous guide, you may become like Aṅgulimālā, who was taught a perverted path by a wrong spiritual guide and was then made to commit horrendous sins. So first thoroughly investigate the guru, and rely on him only if you see he is worthy of it.

Disciples should also have five qualifications: they should be honest and impartial, not attached to their own group and hostile to other groups; they should have the wisdom to know right from wrong; they should yearn [for the teachings]; they should have great respect for their guru; and they should listen with their minds properly directed [that is, have a sound motivation]. If they have these five, they will progress in Dharma.

So how does such a disciple go about devoting oneself to a guru?

DEVOTING YOURSELF THROUGH THOUGHT (83)

This has two subheadings: (1) the root: training yourself to have faith in your guru; (2) remembering his kindness and developing respect for him.

These two headings use both scripture and logic, thus forming an unassailable edifice. If you meditate on them, you will be most happy to devote yourself properly to your spiritual guide. If you don't meditate on them, you will only want to request teachings from him [and have no other relationship].

THE ROOT: TRAINING YOURSELF TO HAVE FAITH IN YOUR GURU (84)

This will have three headings.

Here, "faith" means having the attitude that the guru is actually a buddha. This, and the understanding that all sentient beings have at one time been your mother, are the two most difficult lamrim meditation topics to develop. Although they are difficult, you will not develop the other paths in your mindstream unless you put effort into these two.

Faith is generally the basis or root for the development of all positive things. The *Lamp on the Three Jewels Sūtra* says:

> Faith is the preparation, it gives birth like a mother:
> It protects all good qualities and increases them...

Once a man asked Atiśha twice, "Atiśha, please give me instruction." Atiśha said absolutely nothing and the man made his request yet again—this time by shouting it.

"He! He!" said Atiśha. "I'm afraid my hearing is sound, quite sound! Here is my instruction: Have faith! Faith! Faith!"

The great Gyaelwa Ensapa said:

> In brief: your experiences and realizations will be great or small
> Just as your familiarity with faith is great or small.
> Your kind guru is the source of siddhis.
> Contemplate his qualities and ignore his faults.
> Hold his instructions in your palm,
> And promise to keep them to the last.

In other words, whether you develop realizations depends on whether you have faith and on whether your faith is great or small. You must have the faith of regarding your guru as really being a buddha if you are to achieve the supreme siddhi [of enlightenment]; therefore you definitely must not be mistaken about the instruction you receive.

Even if you get the instruction wrong, you can still achieve the lesser common siddhis if you believe in it. In India, a man asked a guru for instruction. The guru said "Marileja," which means "go away." The man did not understand and took it as an instruction and managed to heal his own and other people's illnesses by reciting the word a number of times.

Another person mistook *oṃ vale vule vunde svāhā* for the mantra of the goddess Cundā. The *v*'s are wrong: they should be *ch*'s. He recited this a number of times and so during a famine was able to cook and eat rocks.

If you lack faith, you will get nothing from your wisdom. There are three types of faith; the faith you should train in during this section of the lamrim is *cleansing faith:* the faith of regarding your spiritual guide as really being a buddha.

A technique to develop this type of faith, in accordance with the lineage stemming from Ketsang Jamyang and his disciples, has three parts. These three are:

THE REASON YOU MUST REGARD THE GURU AS A BUDDHA (85)

You must see him as a buddha because you want a profit, not a loss. You want a profit, so if you regard your guru as a buddha, whether he is or not, you will effortlessly achieve all your wishes in this and future lives—a great profit indeed. To illustrate: an old woman had faith in a dog's tooth [thinking it was a tooth of the Buddha]; the tooth then produced relic pills. The *Blue Compendium* says:

> The guru's blessings are not really
> Great or small: it all depends on you.

That is, the guru's blessing in itself may be great or small but the blessing you receive depends on how far you are able to see him as a buddha, bodhisattva, and so on. Whether you will achieve siddhis or not depends on whether your reverence for him is great or small. Atiśha said that Tibet had no adepts because Tibetans only regarded gurus as ordinary people.

The guru may actually be a buddha, but unless you train yourself to have faith, you will not see his qualities; instead you will only sustain a loss—different kinds of suffering. The Buddha had infinite numbers of qualities, but Devadatta and Upadhāna could see only the aura of light that extended an arm's length from his body; they could not see Buddha's other qualities. So they suffered a loss. Geshe Potowa said:

> If you have no respect for gurus,
> Even relying on the Buddha himself will not help,
> Just as with Upadhāna.

THE REASON YOU ARE ABLE TO SEE HIM THIS WAY (86)

Not only do you need to see your guru as a buddha, but you can in fact do so. There are two means for this: if you focus on the aspect of his good qualities, you can put an end to your lack of faith; and this faith will then overwhelm any trivial fault you may see in him. You should use these two to make the faults you see in him bolster your faith. Think over these two.

In the *Vajrapāṇi Initiation Tantra* we find:

> Seize on your master's qualities;
> Never seize on his faults.
> You will gain siddhis when you seize on his qualities;
> You will not get siddhis when you seize on his faults.

In other words, because of our evil karmic instincts, we dwell only on our guru's faults. Instead, we should dwell on his good qualities, and this will automatically stop any thoughts of seeing his faults, just as the sun outshines the moon in the sky. This is so, just as when you think only about your good qualities, you cannot see your own faults. You may see some small faults in your guru, but thinking of them as his skillful means of subduing his disciples should be enough to bolster your faith. Moreover, at the moment we are beginners, and [to us] our gurus are ordinary people. When we achieve the continuous Dharma single-pointed concentration, we shall meet the supreme nirmāṇakāyas, when on the first bodhisattva level we shall meet saṃbhogakāyas, and so on. One day, even the universe will appear to us completely pure.

HOW TO REGARD HIM PROPERLY (87)

Here we must establish [the guru to be a buddha] using both scripture and logic so that we gain unshakeable conviction. This has four subheadings.

VAJRADHARA STATED THAT THE GURU IS A BUDDHA (88)

There is a danger that some may think, "Spiritual guides are *not* really buddhas, so we must pretend they are during this section of the lamrim on devotion to a spiritual guide." But the point of this heading is that we should not put wrong concepts such as these into the deepest recesses of our minds.

You should think as follows. The guru is a buddha but you do not perceive it. The reason is that Vajradhara is at present among us, taking the form of gurus. *Hevajra's Royal Tantra* says:

> In future times, my physical form
> Will be that of masters...

And:

> Also, in the last five centuries,
> I will take the form of masters.
> Think that they are me
> And develop respect for them.

Also:

> In future degenerate times
> My form shall be that of churls,
> And through various means I will show my forms.

One sūtra tells us:

> O Amoghadarśhī,
> In future times to come
> I will show myself bodily as abbots;
> I will abide in the form of masters.

That is, many sūtras and tantras say that in degenerate times "I, Vajradhara myself, will come in the form of ordinary masters." Out of love he taught, "Don't despair, saying, 'I did not meet him,' for you will recognize me." These literally mean what they say, and you should assume the present time to be these "degenerate times." Vajradhara perceives us with his love and knows how pathetic we have become through karma and delusion, so he manifests like this among our own gurus. In our present rebirth we are capable of knowing how to modify our behavior, to practice the instructions, and so on. So he knows there is no better time for him to work for our sakes.

Further, *all* our present-day gurus are thus. If you think this is not so and put forward reasons for each guru not being one of these emanations of Vajradhara, the process of elimination will leave you with no emanation of Vajradhara at all. This then has the fallacy of contradicting the above quotations—there must be [at least] one emanation of the Buddha among them. If you apply only the reasons for their not being buddhas, you will not find the emanation, so your thinking is at fault. Instead you should feel, "All my gurus are nothing but emanations of the Buddha."

These quotations would be enough for those persons who find it easy to believe. However, it will be much more convincing if we now prove it by logic.

PROOF THAT THE GURU IS THE AGENT OF ALL THE BUDDHAS' GOOD WORKS (89)

As I mentioned in the section above on the merit field, the single moon in the sky appears as separate reflections on the surface of water standing in many different containers. Similarly, the primal wisdom of the minds of all buddhas—the primal wisdom of nondual bliss and emptiness—is of one taste with the dharmadhātu [sphere of truth], and appears in various aspects to the disciple—as śhrāvakas to disciples best subdued by śhrāvakas, as pratyekabuddhas to disciples best subdued by pratyekabuddhas, and [as bodhisattvas or buddhas] for disciples best subdued by bodhisattvas or buddhas. In the *Meeting of Father and Son Sūtra* we find:

> For the sake of sentient beings,
> They disguise themselves as Indra and Brahmā;
> For some, they disguise themselves as demons.
> The worldly cannot realize this.

In other words, buddhas take on various aspects—as demons or Brahmā for people best subdued by demons or Brahmā, and even as birds or wild beasts for people best subdued by birds and beasts, etc. They show themselves to us in accordance with our good fortune as ordinary spiritual guides. They have no other means of guiding us; they might show us such aspects superior to an ordinary guru, as the saṃbhogakāya and so forth, but we cannot see them. And if they were to show themselves in inferior aspects such as birds, beasts, and so on, it would not help because we would not believe in them.

As it is said [in the *Guru Pūjā*]:

> I petition you, compassionate refuge and protector:
> You are the maṇḍala of the jewel of the sugatas' three kāyas,
> But by skillful means you guide beings as an ordinary creature,
> Like a magic net to draw us in.

That is, the three kāyas of all buddhas are contained within the three secrets of the guru [see Day 12, pp. 360 ff.]. The guru is an emanation of all buddhas created in order to perform good works. Suppose a lead dancer in a monastic ritual puts on the āchārya costume [a comic role] and dances the part. Then he dresses as Dharmarāja and dances that part. He has only changed costume; it is still the same dancer. Or you can write many different things with the same red ink, but they all have the same nature: red ink. So think, "Our gurus are nothing but Vajradhara's emanations, which are his skillful means to subdue us."

Tinder catches fire if you use a magnifying glass [to catch the sun's rays]; and you may have different kinds of food, but they will not enter the stomach if they don't go through the mouth. You likewise receive the blessings and white karma of the buddhas' good works by relying on the guru. The guru is the agent of all the buddhas' good works because he makes you perform all your positive actions.

If this is so, do not doubt that he must be a buddha. The buddhas' good works are the blessings they bestow while working for the sake of sentient beings. You must receive these blessings in dependence on the guru. If this is necessarily so, it is impossible that gurus are ordinary: they have to be buddhas. If they were ordinary beings, then the medium for the good works of buddhas would have to be a sentient being. If that were necessarily so, it would mean that buddhas require the assistance of ordinary beings.

Buddhas do not need such assistance. When buddhas work for the sake of sentient beings, they do not even need help from śhrāvakas, pratyekabuddhas, or the great bodhisattvas, so how could we talk of them being assisted by ordinary beings! So buddhas emanate as ordinary beings so that sentient beings are fortunate enough to see them. They also emanate as boats, bridges, and so forth, but these things appear to us merely as the work of carpenters—we can detect nothing else about them.

Sakya Paṇḍita quotes the illustration of the lens:

> Though the sun's rays are hot,
> There can be no fire without a lens;
> Similarly, without a guru, you cannot receive
> The blessings of the buddhas.

And Da Oe Rinchen, a Kagyu lama, quotes the same illustration:

> The rays of the blazing sun
> Focused through a clear lens,
> When nothing shadows in between,
> Will land upon the tinder.

Disciples receive the buddhas' good works in dependence on a guru. If the guru were not a buddha, the buddhas would not require his assistance, just as the rich don't need help from beggars. You must think this over: gurus and buddhas are one and the same, the reason being that buddhas would otherwise be dependent on gurus.

BUDDHAS AND BODHISATTVAS ARE STILL WORKING FOR THE SAKE OF SENTIENT BEINGS (90)

Vajradhara emanates himself at present and definitely works for the sake of all beings. The buddhas unmistakenly know the situation of all sentient beings, love them even more than a mother loves her only child, and always, without interruption, do their utmost to carry out good works. How could they not be similarly working for our sakes in the present times?

Ever since the buddhas first developed bodhichitta, they have worked solely for our sakes. They also built up their [two] accumulations for our

JE RINPOCHE, LAMA TSONGKAPA

sakes. They even became enlightened for the sake of sentient beings. Now that they have achieved the result, it would be impossible for them not to continue benefiting us. All the buddhas would not be so callous as to abandon us by not working for our sakes. So they most surely are benefitting us.

If all the buddhas definitely benefit us, there is no other way for them to do it than as follows:

> The great ones do not wash away sin with water;
> They do not rid beings of suffering with their hands;
> They do not transfer realizations of suchness onto others.
> They liberate by teaching the truth of suchness.

Emanations of the buddhas are doing this; there is no one else to teach the means to high rebirth and definite excellence, the supreme benefits.

In the *Prayer of Ketsang Jamyang* we find:

> The buddhas and bodhisattvas of the past
> Still work for the sake of beings.
> Know that this is not merely an assertion:
> It holds true for qualified gurus.

My own guru said, "There is a complete buddha sittting on the head of every sentient being!"

YOU CANNOT BE SURE OF APPEARANCES (91)

You must assert that your present gurus are actually buddhas and are the agents of all the buddhas' good works. Still, you do not see your gurus as buddhas. You claim, "I see them as ordinary beings because I see this and that faulty aspect in them." Let us analyze this.

What we see is untrustworthy and uncertain. Our perspective follows from our karma. We cannot determine whether we have acquired certain types of karma and not others, and we cannot tell whether we have one karma and not another because we see things in such a way. [Chandrakīrti] says in his *Engaging in the Middle Way:* "A hungry ghost thinks a running river is pus..." That is, when three different types of karmic beings—a god, a human, and a hungry ghost—see a bowl of thirst-quenching liquid, one of them sees nectar, one sees water, and one sees pus and blood. To hungry ghosts the moon in summer seems hot and the winter sun cold. The Kālachakra tantra and the abhidharma [cosmology] were formulated for two types of disciples; in one teaching, Mount Meru is described as being round, in the other square. Ārya Asaṅga saw the venerable Maitreya as a bitch with paralyzed hind legs and infested with worms. Buddhajñāna saw Āchārya Mañjuśhrīmitra as a monk who lived with a woman, ploughed a field, and ate soup made of worms. All the local people thought Tilopa was just a fisherman; they never suspected he was a great adept, and even Nāropa saw him grilling live fish. Kṛiṣhṇāchārya saw Vajravarāhī as a leper woman. So we should be glad our spiritual guide does not appear to us as a horse, a dog, or a donkey—we see him as a human being. Chaen Ngawa Lodroe Gyaeltsaen said:

> [Considering our great] measure of evil karma and resulting obscurations,
> We can draw consolation from our seeing the guru as a human;
> We have great merit not to see him as a dog or a donkey.
> Pay him reverence from your very heart, O child of Śhākyamuni.

Furthermore, appearances are untrustworthy: since everything appears to be established as truly existent, one might draw the wrong conclusion that therefore things truly exist.

Once a thirsty monk went in search of water and had a vision of a hungry ghost. The ghost could not see the Ganges although it was actually walking on the river.

Also, just because you cannot see ghosts is not proof they don't exist. The discussion in [Dharmakīrti's] *Commentary on Valid Cognition,* in the section on the proof dealing with unperceived invisible phenomena, is relevant here.

Here is the proof: You are not fortunate enough to see the guru as a real buddha because you do not have the mindstream of a person fortunate enough to do so. That is, you do not have the valid cognition that permits seeing the guru in that way.

Even when someone does not seem to be a buddha, it need not follow that he is not a buddha; and even when he really appears to be a buddha, you cannot be sure he is one. Once when Arhat Upagupta, the fourth Buddhist patriarch, was teaching Dharma, the demon Kāmadeva caused a disturbance. Upagupta subdued the demon and said, "I have never met the

Buddha, so please emanate an exact likeness of him." The demon emanated a buddha form, complete with the marks and signs, etc., with no omissions or additions. Upagupta was on the verge of prostrating himself because he was now seeing the Buddha in person, but the demon destroyed the emanation too quickly [for him to do so].

In ancient times, great adepts like Nāgārjuna seemed to normal appearances to be ordinary monks, but in truth they were real buddhas.

Still, if misconceptions about the guru's faults arise, you should *not* put an end to them right away. For example, before you wash dirty clothes you must first check every stain. Similarly, you should *allow* such misconceptions [about the guru's faults] to arise. Why? Because you don't know whether the guru has these seeming faults or not. As I have already pointed out, why shouldn't karmic appearances be mistaken? A white conch appears yellowish to someone with bile disease; a person with a wind disease sees a snow-capped mountain as bluish; to someone sitting in a boat, the trees on the shore seem to be moving; people with cataracts have the illusion of seeing falling hairs; and so on.

If even these trivial and temporary causes of error can obscure so much for us, why should we not be mistaken about existing things, since we are thoroughly permeated with immeasurable causes of error—karma and delusions.

I know an incarnate lama who contracted bile disease while on pilgrimage. Three silver relic boxes in his boarding house appeared to him to be gold, but later, when he was free of the bile disease, the boxes appeared silver again.

When Gyaelwa Ensapa visited the great Maitreya statue at Rong, he debated with some Sakya scholars there, but they did not understand a difficult point concerning Buddhist terminology. Ensapa quoted from the *Eight-Thousand-Verse Perfection of Wisdom Sūtra* in Sanskrit to highlight the meaning of these terms, but the Sakyas did not believe him. They said he was an evil spirit, not a man of the Gelug sect. So you must not look at externals; look for people's good qualities, their realizations and renunciations.

Only buddhas themselves perceive one another's dharmakāya [truth body]. Not even the ārya bodhisattvas can perceive it; they can, however, see the saṃbhogakāya. And even to be able to see the supreme nirmāṇakāya adorned with marks and signs, you must definitely be an ordinary being with pure karma. The *Essence of Nectar* lamrim says:

As long as you are not free of the veil of karma and obscurations,
Even if all the buddhas actually came to you,
You haven't the good fortune to see their supreme bodies adorned
with the marks and signs;
You only see what appears to you at present.

Even during Buddha's lifetime, there were tīrṭhikas who could not see his marks and signs, they could see only a mass of faults in him. Devadatta regarded Buddha's deeds as mere fraud.

The right perspective is to see the guru as a measure of our worth. A bandit chief from Upper Golog Arig traveled to Lhasa to see the Śhākyamuni statue in the main cathedral; but he couldn't see even things like the butterlamps, let alone the statue. The previous incarnation of Oen Gyaelsae Rinpoche told him to purify his karma and obscurations. The bandit then had a ten-thousand-fold offering ceremony performed, and did circumambulations and prostrations, but still he could not see the statue. However, he could now see the butterlamps.

When Lozang Doendaen Rinpoche of Gomang College [part of Drepung Monastery] was giving the oral transmission of the *Translated Words of Buddha,* a monk in the audience could not hear the transmission or see the book. Instead he saw a plate of chopped meat placed in front of Rinpoche. While Rinpoche gave the transmission, the monk imagined Rinpoche was eating the meat, and at the end of the day, he imagined he saw people gathering up the meat.

Anything is possible when one's perspective is mere karmic appearances. The amount by which you purify your karma and obscurations determines the level of appearance.

Your perspective is unreliable: so, far from assessing your guru, you cannot assess anyone—your colleagues, friends, and relatives, even your guard dogs, the gods, demons, and so on. You can only assess yourself. Overstep that and you are subject to doubts.

When Gyaelwa Ensapa was about to achieve the unification, there were people who called him Mad Ensa.

The Dharmarāja Karmayama disguised himself as a disciple of Je Rinpoche. Once Je Rinpoche was about to disclose some profound and difficult points concerning the secret tantras to an unsuitable person and Karmayama stopped him. This upset Gyaeltsaen Zangpo, and Kaedrub Rinpoche had to tell him not to make such a fuss.

The Bhagavān Buddha said, "Only I and beings like myself can assess the worth of a person."

In India, a novice monk went to the island of Vachigira to confirm the report that all the men there were ḍākas and the women ḍākinīs. But while he was there he could not see good qualities in anyone and instead developed faith in a charlatan.

Nāro Boenchung said the following about Milarepa:

People who've not seen the famous Milarepa
Say great things about him:
"He's like the great Indian adepts!"
When they go to see him
They find a naked old man asleep...

These stories make a mockery of everything we see. We therefore know nothing about even our most intimate friends and relatives. So, to be on the safe side, train yourself to see everything as pure. Many scholars thought that the great Śhāntideva, a real [child] of the victorious ones, lived for three things only: eating, sleeping, and relieving himself. They could not see his good qualities. Our perspective is similarly untrustworthy.

You cannot be sure that what you see as a fault is really a fault. The way you view things and the way you see things go together. Upadhāna, a monk who knew the three baskets, remained mistaken in his thoughts and views, for he felt, "I see Buddha for what he is; his teachings on karmic causes are self-serving frauds. It isn't true that he has no faults left." If Upadhāna can be wrong, what about us!

When a teacher goes without sleep and does recitations night and day, pupils who are extremely fond of sleep will in their heart of hearts see this as a fault. If the pupils drink beer, they will think themselves lucky if their teacher also drinks beer; they will take it as a good quality. So, not only may the things you see as faults not be faults, but also you can't be sure what things are good qualities. You cannot be sure that the guru is not just simulating a fault as a teaching for your own good. The *Meeting of Father and Son Sūtra* and the *Great Sūtra on Buddha's Nirvāṇa* speak at great length of how the tathāgatas manifest as hostile persons, misers, cripples, madmen, immoral people, and so on, where this will be of benefit.

In general, the sūtras and tantras can be definitive or interpretive; there are various interpretations as to whether a scripture should be taken literally. But when the victor Vajradhara says that in the future he will appear in the aspect of gurus, it is a definitive, literal statement, one that we too should accept. We know that there is no one other than the guru to teach us the path to liberation and omniscience. It would be unconvincing and contradictory for us to think, "My guru, who according to Vajradhara is a buddha, is not a buddha because he has such and such a fault."

Consider the above points from each and every angle, and recognize the guru for what he is—a buddha from the very beginning. Proving this to yourself through scripture and reasoning brings certain knowledge that your guru is a buddha. You have developed realization into how to devote yourself to the spiritual guide when you have that certainty, and the experience arises of a kind of mingling of the guru with all buddhas.

About the mingling of your own mind and that of the guru: when you are fully enlightened, your mind and the guru's mind, which is the dharmakāya great bliss, mingle and become of one taste. At this point you are enlightened, becoming by nature a guru; you achieve the guru's state. Your body, speech, and mind are inextricably mingled with the guru's. This is the point of your having a close relationship with him: your mind must come closer to conforming with the guru's mind.

DEVELOPING RESPECT FOR HIM BY REMEMBERING HIS KINDNESS (92)

According to Ketsang Jamyang and his disciples, this has four headings: (1) the guru is much kinder than the buddhas; (2) his kindness in teaching Dharma; (3) his kindness in blessing your mindstream; and (4) his kindness in attracting you into his circle through material gifts.

THE GURU IS MUCH KINDER THAN ALL THE BUDDHAS (93)

This has two parts.

HE IS MUCH KINDER THAN ALL THE BUDDHAS IN GENERAL (94)

The guru, in terms of good qualities, is the equal of the buddhas; his kindness, however, is generally greater than that of all the buddhas. Infinite numbers of buddhas have guided countless sentient beings for immeasurable eons in the past, but we were not among them. [The *Guru Pūjā* says:]

I petition you, compassionate refuge and protector:
You accurately teach the Sugata's noble path
To the difficult-to-tame beings of these degenerate times
Who were unfit for taming by countless past buddhas.

In other words, 75,000 buddhas, another 76,000 buddhas, yet another 77,000, and so on, came into the world solely to be the object of Buddha our Teacher's build-up of the accumulations. Moreover, in this eon alone, the buddhas Krakuchchanda, Kanakamuni, Kāśhyapa, and so on, have guided boundless numbers of disciples, but they could not subdue us. The guru is teaching us the complete and unmistaken path now—even the previous manifestations of the buddhas could not do better. Thus, although the guru and the buddhas are equals in terms of good qualities, the guru is their superior in terms of kindness.

Geshe Potowa said that the guru is like someone who gives a dying person food during a famine, while the buddhas are like those who give slabs of meat in times of plenty. Suppose we had escaped poverty and, having become rich, someone then gave us food and property. Similarly, we will have visions of many buddhas, receive inspiration from them, and so on when we have already achieved the higher paths, but this is no help to us while we are at present in such a piteous state. The guru, like someone giving us food when we are poor, reveals himself to us and has the means to guide us when we are about to fall over the great precipice into the lower realms, so that we now have some hope of achieving buddhahood. This is the guru's kindness. Kaedrub Rinpoche says: "Supreme unrivaled guru, who is kinder than all the victors..." That is, we may have faith in other buddhas and bodhisattvas, but we have not met them. Now that we are deprived of Dharma, the guru teaches us the same Dharma, so he is more compassionate.

HE IS KINDER SPECIFICALLY THAN EVEN ŚHĀKYAMUNI BUDDHA (95)

Once the Universal Emperor Aranemi had a thousand sons, and each of them developed bodhichitta, promising to look after a particular set of disciples. But they saw that disciples would be difficult to subdue in those troubled times when the human lifespan lasted only a hundred years, so they left them alone. Our Teacher, who was then the Brahman Samandrarāja, also developed bodhichitta at that time and promised to subdue the sentient beings in those troubled times. Śhākyamuni our Teacher was therefore kinder to disciples than the buddhas in earlier times when humans lived to be a hundred. But to ordinary, difficult-to-subdue beings, such as myself and those like me, the guru is very much kinder even than Śhākyamuni.

After Buddha, there were many pandits and adepts in India, such as the seven patriarchs of the teachings, the eighty mahāsiddhas, the six jewels of India, and the two supreme ones.[39] And Tibet has so many saints: in the first dissemination of the teachings there were Padmasaṃbhava, King Trisong Detsaen, Śhāntarakṣhita, and the rest of the twenty-five disciples of Padmasaṃbhava; during the later dissemination there were the five lords of the Sakyas, Marpa, Milarepa, Atiśha and his disciples, Je Tsongkapa and his disciples, and so on. But none of them taught us in person the nectar of the holy Dharma, the means to rescue us from the great ocean of suffering.

In short, as Śhāntideva says in *Engaging in the Deeds of Bodhisattvas:*

> Countless buddhas who worked
> For the sake of all sentient beings
> Have departed, and because of my misdeeds
> I was not among those healed by them.

In other words, we should think as follows: "I was not born in the right places, nor did I go to places they visited; also, every past saint could not guide me and gave up on me. I am the dregs of the dregs. What great compassion my guru has in rescuing me now in this way."

HIS KINDNESS IN TEACHING THE DHARMA (96)

The great bodhisattva once gave himself, his sons, daughters, and relatives to fierce yakṣhas for the sake of one verse of Dharma. When our Teacher was reborn as Vyilingalita, he drove a thousand iron spikes into his body in order to receive Dharma teachings. When reborn as King Ganaśhava he burned his flesh with a thousand oil lamps and jumped into a fiery pit; as

King Paramavarṇa he used his skin as paper and his rib as a pen and listened to the Dharma. Great Atiśha endured great difficulties sailing the ocean for thirteen months to receive these lamrim teachings, heedless of the dangers of storm, sea monsters, and so on. People like Marpa and Milarepa underwent many difficulties to receive Dharma teachings. Even today it is no easy matter to travel to India, but the translators of old risked their lives to go there to receive Dharma teachings; they offered their gurus golden maṇḍalas only to receive the teachings. Even recalling the hardships they had undergone made them shudder. How most kind your guru is, then, to teach you the whole path—not even the buddhas could give you a better teaching without requiring you to endure even the slightest hardship! Atiśha said:

> What great merit you must have to receive such profound Dharma without any hardship! Be serious, and practice it well!

Suppose a person is about to die because he has eaten medicine, food, and poison. A doctor would be showing the most kindness if he made him vomit up the poison, turned the ingested food into medicine, and transformed the ingested medicine into the ambrosia of immortality. Well, we have performed many unvirtuous actions that will take us to the lower realms—this is like the ingested poison. The guru makes us purify these actions. We would normally accumulate virtue for the things of this life: a long life, good health, gifts, and fame. The guru gets us to change direction and have a sound motivation, make pure prayers, and dedicate our virtue. Our virtue has been transformed into something beneficial for future lives. He also makes us transform the virtue we collected to achieve high rebirths and liberation into supreme, complete buddhahood. Who could be kinder? The *Essence of Nectar* lamrim says:

> If they say we cannot repay
> The kindness of being taught one verse,
> Even by offering for as many eons as the verse has letters,
> How to repay the kindness of being taught the entire noble path?

And

How very kind someone would be
To take a man suffering in prison,
Take him out of prison on bail,
And set him up in affluence!

But the guru teaches us
The means to be free of the three lower realms;
He is kind indeed, for we will then enjoy
All desired affluence as gods and humans.

He teaches well the supreme means
To pacify all misfortunes of saṃsāra and nirvāṇa.
He leads us to a holy state: the three kāyas.
What could be a greater kindness?

HIS KINDNESS IN BLESSING YOUR MINDSTREAM (97)

Whatever realizations you develop in your mindstream come from the guru's blessing, because you petitioned him, and so on. If you take guru yoga as the very life force of the path, you will make great progress on the path: this is the very point of the guru's blessing. When Tilopa struck Nāropa in the face with a mud maṇḍala, Nāropa's ability to hold single-pointed concentration immediately extended to seven days. Even the fact that we can still remember different Dharma teachings that we could not remember previously, for example, is due to our guru's blessing our mindstreams.

This year, on the twenty-fourth of the fourth month, I received a clear sign that my precious guru, my refuge and protector, had blessed me; that blessing is making our present lamrim teaching go so well. Once my guru, my refuge and protector, was holding an offering ceremony at Dagpo with about twenty-five geshes. I also participated, and such unbearable, intolerable repudiation [for saṃsāra] arose in me that my eyes were full of tears, and so on, from the start of the *Inseparable Bliss and Void Guru Pūjā*, and continuing for quite a while.[40] Even that was a blessing from the guru.

If you petition the guru, you will achieve all good things and everything you desire in this life and the next. Mahāsiddha Tilopa said: "The most useful thing of all is the guru, Nāropa!" And Gyaelwa Goetsang said:

Many meditate on the developing stage,
But meditation on the guru is the highest.
Many perform the recitations,
But petitioning the guru is the highest.
If you constantly petition him,
You will surely experience inseparability from him.

Kyabje Pabongka told some stories: how once a man from Radreng offered butterlamps to a statue of Dromtoenpa and his wishes were fulfilled; how Atiśha was blessed by Ḍoṃbhīpa; how Drubkang Geleg Gyatso blessed Purchog Ngagwang Jampa; and so on.

HIS KINDNESS IN ATTRACTING YOU INTO HIS CIRCLE THROUGH MATERIAL GIFTS (98)

People these days depend on material goods; the guru therefore first attracts people to his circle with material gifts, and then leads them to the Dharma.

When my precious guru, my refuge and protector, was living in a hermitage, a servant of the Drimé Tengka family, a man from Upper Kongpo, was sent to ask for a dice divination; he was carrying a hide full of butter as an offering. The place where my guru was staying was high up a mountain, which meant that the man was suffering from fatigue. He came into my guru's presence saying, "This lama must be like a wild animal to want to live on top of a mountain like this!" My guru gave him some tea, good food, and consecrated offerings to eat; the man developed faith in him and later had to admit, "But that lama gives a great blessing. His offerings were delicious!" He had been brought into the guru's circle, and he had developed faith.

In monasteries, there is no limit to [the numbers of] teachers gathering students by, for example, taking care of them with material gifts.

Atiśha said, "Any good qualities I have are my gurus'." He meant that we obtain all our good qualities through the guru's kindness.

We do not examine or analyze things, and we arrogantly think that our present happiness, comfort, and reputation have come through our own efforts, but this is not so. Take the example of two brothers; one is put in a monastery and becomes a member of the Saṅgha—an object in which the other brother takes refuge. When the ordained brother meets the other by chance in a temple, they will act according to their different lots: one Dharmic, the other materialistic.

You may be a monk and have few responsibilities; this is through the kindness of your abbot and ordination master who gave you your vows, for you were not like our Teacher who became fully ordained naturally [without the intervention of an abbot]. Now you can read many hundreds of pages a day and analyze their meaning: this is through the kindness of the person who taught you the alphabet. If you have not obtained any initiations to ripen or prepare you, you are not even allowed to read books on tantra. Someone with an initiation has entered the gateway to the secret tantras, something much rarer than even the coming of buddhas. It is through his kindness that the vajra master places into your mindstream seeds that are sure to ripen into results, the four kāyas, within sixteen lifetimes if your vows are still intact. You should count up your guru's kindnesses on your rosary, and think, "He gave me this, this, this..." But this is not all. You have obtained a human body, you may be happy in this rebirth, you may have wealth, and so on. These are all the result of following ethics and of practicing generosity in past lives, and these were the kindnesses of the masters who made you practice them. Thus any happiness you may have is due to the guru's kindness.

You may then think, "It is not always the same guru: many different gurus at different times have each contributed their own individual kindnesses." But these gurus emanated from the same basis, the minds of all buddhas, the nondual primal wisdom of bliss and emptiness, which is of one taste with the dharmadhātu. The gurus are all Buddha Vajradhara himself manifesting in different guises. In Tibet, for example, there was the being who was progenitor of our race;[41] there were people who established the law; translators of the Dharma; kings and their ministers who spread and upheld the teachings; master translators and pandits; the reincarnations of the Dalai Lama; and so on. All these were only different guises for Ārya Avalokiteśhvara, the holder of the lotus. Our gurus are all similarly one entity.

Je Rinpoche says:

> One should understand the foregoing to be the famous instruction called *guru yoga*. But one will go nowhere if one only meditates on it a few times.

That is, in order to understand that the guru is the embodiment of all buddhas, that he is all the buddhas in another guise, you must practice the *Guru Pūjā,* and so on, but if you do not understand this and merely recite the words, you will get nowhere at all.

So when you understand that the minds of all buddhas are of one taste with the essence of dharmakāya, bliss, and emptiness, and that they have arisen from this as the guru, you will understand that all buddhas—the hundred buddha families, the five families, the three families, and the one buddha family—are the guru in different guises. If you don't understand this, you will be dubious about paying great respect even to famous gurus who teach from high thrones; you would also, for example, be in great danger of not respecting the monk in your humble monastery who tutors you in the books. When you have this understanding, training yourself to see one guru as pure will train you to see them all in the same way; then pleasing one will be tantamount to pleasing them all. And so too with displeasing them: displeasing one is tantamount to displeasing them all. You should regard them all as equally kind and show no favoritism in your devotion.

They say we should recite verses on the guru's kindness when we contemplate how very kind he is. The following verses were spoken by Kumāra Maṇibhadra in the section on the kindness of the spiritual guide [from the *Laying Out of Stalks Sūtra*]:

> My spiritual guides, my exponents of the Dharma,
> Are qualified to teach me all the Dharma;
> They came with but one thought: to fully teach me
> The tasks facing the bodhisattva.
>
> Because they gave birth to me, they are like my mother;
> They are like wet nurses feeding me the milk of good qualities;
> They have thoroughly trained in the branches to enlightenment.
> These spiritual guides keep me from that which harms.
>
> They are like doctors who free me from death and old age,
> Or like Indra the celestial lord raining down nectars;
> They increase white Dharma like the waxing moon
> And, like the shining sun, show the way to peace.

They are like mountains, unmoved by friend or foe.
Their minds are undisturbed like oceans.
They are dear ones who protect completely.
These were the thoughts that made me go to them.

Bodhisattvas, who are developing my mind,
Children of the buddhas who bring me enlightenment—
They guide me, the buddhas sing their praises.
I came to them with these virtuous thoughts.

They are like heroes for they shield me from the world;
They are my captains, my refuge and protection;
They are my very eyes, my comfort;
With these thoughts honor your spiritual guides.

From the *Essence of Nectar* lamrim:

I have given up family life, that pit of fire,
And carry out in solitude the Sage's deeds;
I taste the succulent nectar of the Dharma.
This is the kindness of my venerable gurus.

I have met the teachings of Tsongkapa,
Hard to find in a thousand eons of searching,
And gained faith in the way he taught—
This is the kindness of holy tutors.

Therefore my spiritual guides
Are protectors shielding me from lower realms,
Captains to free me from saṃsāra's ocean,
Guides to lead me to high rebirth and liberation.

Doctors to cure me of chronic delusion,
Rivers to douse the great fires of suffering,
Lamps to remove the darkness of ignorance,
Suns to light the path to liberation.

Liberators from the close prison of saṃsāra,
Clouds that gently rain the holy Dharma,
Dear friends who help me, dispelling harm,
Kindly parents who are always loving...

Contemplate these verses as you recite them, and remember the kindness of your own gurus.

Devoting yourself through deeds will be discussed as in *Mañjuśhrī's Own Words* at the end of the fourth preparatory rite, so you must not confuse it [with the topics presented elsewhere].

You should, for this and every topic, begin with petitions, [visualize] the descent of purifying nectars, and conclude by believing you have fulfilled [that meditation topic].

BANDIT CHIEF IN FRONT OF ŚHĀKYAMUNI STATUE

(SEE P. 250)

DAY 9

Kyabje Pabongka Rinpoche gave a short talk to set our motivation, quoting from peerless Atiśha:

> There is much evidence this life will be short,
> But one cannot know its exact length;
> Take from it the most desirable things,
> As a swan separates milk from water.

He restated the headings already covered and then briefly reviewed the subject of devotion to the spiritual guide.

DEVOTING YOURSELF THROUGH DEEDS (99)

In *An Ornament to the Sūtras* we find:

> Through gifts and reverence, through service,
> And through practice, rely on a spiritual guide.

In other words, there are three ways to devote yourself through deeds: the least [gifts and reverence], middling [service], and best [practice]. When, for example, pupils rely on their teacher, they are carrying out all three of these; so proper devotion to a teacher or guru is guru yoga. If your reliance on a guru is based on a personal relationship, you need not emphasize the visualization side of your guru yoga. When he is not with you in person, you should generate the merit-field visualization, perform the bathing ceremony, and make petitions, prostrations, offerings, etc.

The best means of pleasing your spiritual guide is to offer him your practice of his instructions. Milarepa said:

> I have no material wealth or gifts to offer.
> My practice repays my kindly father-guru...
> I practice with courage, ignoring hardship;
> This is service pleasing to my father-guru.

The two traditions of *Mañjuśhrī's Own Words,* the brief [Southern Lineage] and the more extensive [Central Lineage] versions, teach that devotion through deeds comes under the fourth preparatory rite; devotion to the spiritual guide through thought is covered by the third preparatory rite.

[According to this text], when you are somewhere without your guru, you devote yourself through deeds by performing the last three preparatory rites: that is, you invite the guru to the merit field at the start of devotion through deeds, then make offerings, and so on. In this way, you please your guru with material gifts.

To do this, you consecrate the earth's surface as above [Day 5, p. 154]; you then invoke the power of truth. Visualize the earth's surface as lapis lazuli with vajra crosses drawn in gold, which seem to stand out in relief, but if you were to touch them you would find them to be flush with the surface.

[In the lineages of the Central Province] in the center of the ground surface there is a square palace. This has four entrances and no ornamental façades, so it resembles the palace in the Medicine Buddha maṇḍala. The palace is huge; at its center there are four platforms on a large throne supported by lions—like a stūpa without the pot-shaped dome.

Visualize on the first [highest] platform three lion thrones. They are to the rear of the platform; on the middle throne sits the victor Śhākyamuni. Maitreya sits on the throne to his right, Mañjuśhrī on the one to his left. The lineage gurus of the Extensive Deeds and Profound View lineages sit behind each of these two. There are three lion thrones on the front portion of the platform; Atiśha, Nagtso the translator, and Dromtoenpa sit on these.

There is a group of three lion thrones on the second platform. Tsongkapa the victorious one sits on the middle throne, Sherab Senge to his right, Genduen Drub [the First Dalai Lama] to his left.

On the third platform is a group of three lion thrones. The great Fifth

Dalai Lama sits on the central throne; to his right, Jinpa Gyatso; to the Dalai Lama's left, Jampa Choedaen, himself a truly glorious guru.

On the fourth platform your root guru sits on the middle throne. The text says his chief disciples should sit to his right and left, but according to the oral instruction, his guru sits to his right and his guru's guru to his left. Your other gurus sit on silken cushions.

One tradition has all the gurus of the three baskets sitting on the remaining three sides of the platforms, and the buddhas, bodhisattvas, śhrāvakas, pratyekabuddhas, Dharma protectors, etc., at the rear of the platforms.

In another tradition, you visualize the lineage gurus of the Extensive Deeds and Profound View lineages placed, in their proper order, to the right and left of the trios of gurus. Visualize other vinaya-basket lineage gurus on the right side of the platforms, abhidharma-basket gurus on the left, and sūtra-basket gurus at the rear of the platform. You do not have to visualize tutelary deities, etc.

If you wish to do this meditation, it is enough to think these figures are present in person even though you cannot see them clearly. The figures on the rear parts of the platform are not hidden by the lion thrones [of the front groups of three gurus]; these rear figures also face toward you.

The bathhouse has four entrances. Inside is a full complement of thrones for the merit field. There is no pool inside, and the center of the floor is raised. The seven-limbed prayer and the rest are the same.

The Southern Lineage is quite different. Visualize in front of you a great lion-supported throne with seven platforms; this is like the [form of the] Kadampa altar. The stages are made of seven precious substances: refer to the recitation text for details. The lions stand on the ground. Three stairways have been built going up the front of this lion throne. The top platform has a scrim or backdrop-like cloth that resembles the backrests of the thrones of high lamas and has two finials on the top corners, which are called *twisted-metal arrows.* These decorations look like handles and are made of a precious substance. Each platform also has small golden stairways that go down the sides of the platforms and lead down to the other stairs in front of the lion throne.

The top of the scrim curves up to the center and is surmounted by a golden gañjira pinnacle with victory banners to the left and right. In the middle of the first [and highest] platform is a throne with backrest for Śhākyamuni. The throne is supported by six creatures—a nāga, a garuḍa, etc.[42]—to symbolize the six perfections. There are five brocaded cushions stacked on Śhākyamuni's throne. Maitreya sits to his right and Mañjuśhrī to his left, on thrones with three cushions each. These thrones are not supported by lions. Your guru sits in front of them in his normal aspect, on two cushions and doesn't need a throne. His guru sits to his right; his guru's guru to his left. They each sit on only one cushion. Your other gurus who are still alive sit on mats. The central portion of the platform is left empty as if to leave a pathway.

Your guru in his normal aspect makes the Dharma-teaching gesture with his right hand. He holds a Tibetan loose-leaf book in his left hand, which is in its wrapper with an ornamental bookmark of five layers of silk.

The gurus of the Extensive Deeds and Profound View lineages sit on Maitreya's right and Mañjuśhrī's left respectively. The Kadampa Lamrim Tradition continues at the end of the Extensive Deeds Lineage and, as an important symbolic gesture, the last place of the lineage is left empty. Your other gurus who are not on the first platform occupy the second and third platforms.

The Kadampa Instruction Tradition gurus sit in a row on the fourth platform, with Chaen Ngawa at the head of the row. The bodhisattvas sit on the fifth platform. The buddhas sit at the left and right corners of the first four platforms. The śhrāvakas and pratyekabuddhas sit on the sixth, the Dharma protectors on the seventh.

This is a sūtric tradition, so you do not visualize the gurus of the Lineage of Consecrated Practices. If you want to include them, imagine they are there in an unmanifest form.

The two lineages of *Mañjuśhrī's Own Words* are sūtric traditions, so you need not generate the visualization of commitment beings and the like. The figures are invoked, or invited, as guests. To illustrate: before we invite our dinner guests to sit down, we should first provide seats for them. So you consecrate the offerings [see Day 5] and then invite the wisdom beings, who take their places on their own seats. You invite them, and the way in which you visualize them coming to you and so on resembles the way Buddha and his retinue came when invited by Sumagadhā.

Kyabje Pabongka Rinpoche then told this story and discussed the practice in greater detail.

Next you wash their bodies. The bathhouse, unlike the above, has four glass doors, one for each cardinal direction. It has no central pool, but there are many ewers. Its ceiling has a system of beams and a pagoda from which hang sachets of fragrant lotion or paste. Imagine that the water descends directly from these into the ewers. During the washing ceremony, the monks [in the merit field] come down in groups of three. They take their places on the thrones [in the bathhouse] as above, and the clothes collected from them are in the form of yellow light rays. The figures are then washed. The rest is the same as above.

If you do not typically have the necessary ewers and other implements on hand, you need not always do the washing ceremony every time you do the preparatory rites; even if you do it only occasionally, doing so will rid you of obscurations, [mental] impurities, and so on. The rest of the washing ceremony follows the section I taught from the *Swift Path* [Day 5].

When one gives a teaching based solely on *Mañjuśhrī's Own Words*, one should at this point discuss the practice of *not* dissolving the merit-field visualization. When, for example, you are doing a number of repetitions of the preparatory rites, you should recite up to [Tsongkapa's] *Basis of All Good Qualities* in your final session. Without going on to the dissolution of the merit field, begin the next repetition of the text of the rites after reciting the spell for a profusion of offerings. To shorten further, perform the seven-limbed prayer only, a number of times.

At present, I have discussed the preliminary rites according to *Mañjuśhrī's Own Words* and associated [texts]. For your regular practice, you should perform the preparatory rites according to *An Ornament for the Throats of the Fortunate,* because it is a particularly profound and blessed piece of instruction and better than any other.

WHAT TO DO IN THE LAST PART OF THE SESSION (100)

At the end of a particular lamrim meditation topic, recite the name and mantra of Śhākyamuni, the king of the Śhākyas, and make prayers and dedications.

WHAT TO DO BETWEEN MEDITATION SESSIONS (101)

There is no time that cannot be included in either the meditation session itself or the interval between sessions. It is vital to make proper use of the between-session period. If you train your mind during the meditation session and then allow it to become distracted between sessions, it will play havoc with your practice when you return to the meditation session. But if the period between sessions goes well, your optimum human rebirth becomes meaningful. That is why Je Rinpoche placed such emphasis in his teachings and writings on the time between sessions as well as on the meditation session itself.

Let us take this particular meditation topic as an example. Between sessions you should read the accounts in the authentic commentaries on devotion to the spiritual guide, on how, for example, Nāropa devoted himself to Tilopa, Milarepa to Marpa, Dromtoenpa to Lama Setsuenpa and Atiśha. They say your wisdom will slacken if you read other kinds of books. Reading stories, for example, causes your hostility to increase—so, in order to increase your wisdom, don't read them.

To prevent delusions from arising at all between meditation sessions, we could become so restrained that our senses do not even see the object that gives rise to delusions. We have not yet achieved this however, so we should be vigilant all the time with our three doors, and even if, for example, we see something attractive, not allow our mind to be led astray. We need to constantly guard the three doors of our senses with vigilance.

You should refer to the chapter "On Maintaining Vigilance" in Śhāntideva's *Engaging in the Deeds of Bodhisattvas* for more details. The gist of that chapter is:

> Time and again examine
> The state of your body and mind.
> In short, that alone
> Is the definition of maintaining vigilance.

That is, it is vital to maintain vigilance.

You should perform the actions of your three doors—the movements of your body, the things you say, and the trains of thought that go through your mind—while giving these matters their due consideration. Suppose you go into a room that has only two doors. There can be only two ways to enter or leave the room—by these two doors; so by guarding these doors, you bar thieves from the room. Similarly, if you guard your three doors and do not give up any remembrance of them, you shut the door against committing misdeeds.

There is a story about Geshe Baen Gung-gyael: he safeguarded his mind and refused the curd.[43] He shouted, "I'm a thief!" We ought to be on our guard in the same way. If we are forever daydreaming, we are in danger of having the following happen to us. A man decided to call his son Dawa Dragpa before the child was even born. In his joy the man started to dance and immediately died.[44]

Atiśha said: "Check your speech when with company; check your mind when alone." We commit sins while we are distracted and without recollection. At the time we do not even know whether it is a sin or not. While we are sitting down or walking, we might absentmindedly kill a louse while in conversation, say, whereas we would have refrained from killing it had we been vigilant and thought, "Don't do that, it is sinful." Similarly, when we are in a large gathering of friends, and various conversation topics come up, we should check with a part of our mind, "What exactly am I about to say?" If we are about to utter harsh words or idle talk, we should hold our tongues. When we are alone, we should mentally check, "What am I recalling?" We should maintain our recollection and vigilance by thinking, "If I forget to safeguard my mind, I will not be immediately aware that this has happened. Therefore I must not forget."

Geshe Karag Gomchung once wrote notices everywhere, putting them even on the walls around his room. He wrote, "No distracted thoughts!" But we are not like him: we put up signs like "I need to get some cash from a certain person," and these are our only reminder notes.

The time between meditation sessions is extremely important, even in a retreat. You might have a stone beside your door to show you are in retreat [see Day 4, p. 113], and stay on some snow-capped mountain, but your thoughts might not be mindful. My guru said, "The mind of the practitioner is in retreat and meditates on vigilance in the retreat house of the body." You can become skilled in this method of not being distracted by always being vigilant.

Je Milarepa said that worldly trivia can act as your books. In other words, everything you see ought to stimulate your love, compassion, renunciation, and so on. For example, Je Drubkang Geleg Gyatso saw an ant bite a bee, and thereby gained conviction in the law of cause and effect.

When we go to the market we develop delusions like attachment; sins accompany every step we take. By the time we return home, we are carrying a very heavy sack of sin. But if we are properly analytical, and go to the market together with vigilance, this can be the supreme stimulus for our renunication and [realization of] impermanence. We need to turn everything trivial into a stimulus for Dharma practice along these lines.

Kyabje Pabongka Rinpoche talked about food and how to regulate our intake. He also talked about offering daily ritual cakes to the hungry ghosts. The text that most clearly discusses this is called Daily Schedules, *and we should follow it. He told of the great benefit even the crows [who eat the cakes] would receive.*

THE PROPER GRADUATED TRAINING YOU SHOULD UNDERTAKE AFTER YOU HAVE BEGUN TO RELY ON YOUR SPIRITUAL GUIDE (102)

This has two major headings: (1) the stimulus to take the essence from your optimum human rebirth; (2) how to extract that essence.

THE STIMULUS TO TAKE THE ESSENCE FROM YOUR OPTIMUM HUMAN REBIRTH (103)

The stimulus comes from thinking about the great benefits of the optimum human rebirth and how difficult it is to acquire. There are two subheadings here: (1) a short discussion to convince you; (2) a brief teaching on how to pursue the practice.

A SHORT DISCUSSION TO CONVINCE YOU (104)

The last two headings form a scheme that applies to all the meditation topics that follow; this is the traditional way to combine the formal discourse material with material from informal discourses. You should substitute each meditation topic, such as the one I shall now discuss under the above headings, for the heading on how to pursue the main part of the meditation session. You must do what I explained in the section on devotion to your spiritual guide: join that meditation topic to the end of the preparatory rites, and then follow it by the last part of the session, and so on.

We find nothing wrong in our mouths being open all the time indulging in idle gossip—that's because we don't think about the great benefits and the rarity of the optimum human rebirth. Thinking about these things would be a strong stimulus for us to practice Dharma.

When you think about the great benefits and the rarity of the optimum human rebirth, you will feel involuntarily happy, and when you think of death and impermanence, you will feel involuntarily sad.

There are three headings here: (1) identifying the optimum human rebirth; (2) thinking about its great benefits; (3) thinking about how difficult it is to acquire.

IDENTIFYING THE OPTIMUM HUMAN REBIRTH (105)

This has two parts: (1) the freedoms; (2) the endowments.

THE FREEDOMS (106)

You must identify the optimum human rebirth before you can want to extract the essence from it. Your hearthstones may be made of gold, but if you don't know it, you will still be a pauper. So you must also from the beginning identify the freedoms—that is, being free of the eight states unfavorable for Dharma practice. These eight unfavorable states are mentioned in Nāgārjuna's *Letter to a Friend:*

> Upholding wrong views, being an animal,
> Hungry ghost, or being born in hell,
> Being without a victor's teachings,
> Being born in a remote place as a barbarian,
> As an idiot or mute, or as a long-lived god:
> Any of these rebirths is one of the eight faulty unfavorable states.
> Because you have gained a favorable state free of these,
> Strive to block your future rebirths.

There are four unfavorable states as nonhuman creatures, and four as human beings.

The four unfavorable nonhuman states are as follows. The hells are unfavorable for Dharma practice because of the intense sufferings of heat and cold there. If someone put a glowing ember on your head and ordered you to meditate at the same time, the pain would prevent you from even beginning to meditate. If we were now born in hell, we would feel one hundred thousand times more suffering than a [live] rat placed in a red-hot iron frying pan. So far as practicing the Dharma, or even hearing one word of the Dharma, our minds would only be filled with suffering, and all we would do is stay there and be without Dharma. We should feel lucky not to have been born there.

A rebirth as a hungry ghost is unfavorable for Dharma practice because of the great hunger and thirst. When we are extremely hungry and thirsty, and our guru, for instance, urges us to practice Dharma, instead we only yearn for food and drink first. This rebirth is therefore also unfavorable for the practice of Dharma. How lucky we are not to be born as hungry ghosts!

A rebirth as an animal is unfavorable for Dharma practice because of animals' stupidity and benighted ignorance. For example, if someone told a dog, donkey, or whatever, "Recite *oṃ maṇi padme hūṃ* once, and you will then be enlightened," they wouldn't understand at all. And if they don't know how to recite even a syllable of *oṃ maṇi padme hūṃ,* how could they understand any other Dharma? So, animals only experience their particular forms of suffering, and this is unfavorable for Dharma practice. How extremely lucky we are not to have been born as one!

At present, whenever we say "How lucky!" we are referring to some money we might have made, but this is not really being lucky at all. When we look at animals such as dogs and donkeys, we should not treat them as objects of curiosity; we should feel, "How lucky I am not to be like that!"

The long-lived gods are as follows: being born in the form and formless realms is one of the greatest [karmic] results you could have, yet when the gods are born in these realms they feel, "I have been reborn a god," and when they finally leave that rebirth they feel, "I am dying and am leaving this rebirth as a god." The rest of the time they are engrossed in such single-pointed concentration that it is like being asleep—they waste their whole rebirth in this utterly meaningless way. As Asaṅga's *Shrāvaka Levels* tells us, the gods in the other celestial realms may have some great instincts for virtue, but, except for a few of them, they normally spend the whole time engrossed in pleasure and so will receive no Dharma. The king of doctors, Kumārajīvaka, when he was still a human being, was a disciple of Shāriputra. Whenever Jīvaka was out riding an elephant and happened to see Shāriputra, without a moment's hesitation he would jump off his elephant. Later, Jīvaka was reborn in the god realms and Shāriputra went there to teach him Dharma, but Jīvaka was so engrossed in celestial pleasure that he merely raised a finger [in recognition] and then returned to his amusements, giving Shāriputra no chance of teaching him Dharma. This is how it is that the gods have absolutely no thought of practicing Dharma or renunciation. They only have celestial drums, magic birds, etc., that speak to them about the Dharma; they do not have gurus like ours to give them detailed instructions.

The four unfavorable human states are the following. If you are born in a remote, that is, barbarian region, you will not hear a word of the Dharma. If you are born in a place where a buddha has not come, you will not know how to practice Dharma, or even if you do practice it, you will not do so properly. What would we do if we were now born in these ways? Think how lucky we are not to be like that!

Even if you are born in a central [that is, Buddhist] place, if you are born an idiot with a defective or unclear mind, or a mute with defective speech, you will either not understand the real purpose behind the Dharma or only go through the motions and not practice properly.

Being a person with wrong views is the greatest hindrance to taking up the Dharma—that is why Nāgārjuna's *Letter* mentions this first. It is most unfortunate if you are born like today's Muslims, for example, because you will never acquire so much as the root virtue of reciting *oṃ maṇi padme hūṃ* once, even if your life is a long one.

If there were eight difficult but trivial things to achieve, and if we achieved them all, we would be inclined to say: "What good fortune!" With something so much more important, are we not that much more fortunate still to have assembled these eight things so difficult to assemble?

THE ENDOWMENTS (107)

There are ten endowments; five are personal and five relate to others.

THE FIVE PERSONAL ENDOWMENTS (108)

The *Śhrāvaka Levels* says:

> Born a human, in a central land, having all one's faculties;
> Not perverted by the heinous crimes; and having enduring faith.

The first personal endowment is being a human being. This is particularly superior to the other migrations in its potential for carrying out the practices that benefit one's future rebirths. We are now most definitely human beings—but it doesn't seem to have helped us.

Being born in a central land means being reborn in a central place that is under the influence of the words of Dharma, and that has at least four members of the Saṅgha. Having all one's faculties means having all one's [sense] organs from birth. Also, hermaphrodites, eunuchs, and so on, are not suitable candidates for pratimokṣha vows, and as you have not been born as one of these, you have all your faculties. Not being perverted by the heinous crimes means that one will not achieve arhatship in this life if one has committed these crimes. We have not committed these, so we are "not perverted by the heinous crimes." Enduring faith is said to be faith in the vinaya, but here it should be faith in all three baskets and the lamrim system.

Since one must possess these endowments oneself, they are "personal endowments." We all certainly have these five.

THE FIVE ENDOWMENTS IN RELATION TO OTHERS (109)

> A Buddha has come and taught the Dharma;
> The teachings remain and are followed;
> People have love in their hearts for others.

If no Buddha has come to a particular world, there will be no holy Dharma there. If a Buddha does come but, for example, dies before teaching the Dharma, his coming will have been to no avail. These first two endowments, strictly speaking, are not fulfilled, but our gurus are still alive and substitute for the Buddha and teach the Dharma, so these two endowments are virtually fulfilled.

The teachings are supposed to remain in an undegenerate state and will be put into practice so that through them people will actually acquire the path of the āryas. At present the five thousand years of transmission [of the Buddha's teachings] have not run their course. All the same, although the teachings are still being transmitted, the fruit of the teachings will only flourish in your own mindstream if you develop realization into the teachings. As the Kadampas of old tell us, this has not happened: we don't have the external teachings in our mindstream, so we must not let our own share of the teachings die out. That is, even if the Buddha's teachings flourish externally, but the teachings die out in your own mindstream, your share of the teachings has died out.

Not only should the Buddha's teachings remain, they should also survive intact. Of all the tenets of the Indian and the early and later Tibetan sects, the most precious and stainless are those that combine the pure view and the practices of both sūtra and tantra—for example, the teachings of Je Rinpoche the reformer, the embodiment of Mañjuśhrī the protector, teachings that are the purest, polished, refined gold. You have met with them. For such a thing to happen to you is rarer than rare. Je Rinpoche's teachings on sūtra and tantra are of unprecedented eloquence. Tagtsang the translator, for example, came to see the special features of Je Rinpoche's teachings late in his life and said he was won over, that they hit the mark. There have been many other such praises, but even after days of telling you in detail how these teachings on both sūtra and tantra are superior to the others, I would still not be finished. Once a Mongolian gave the Paṇchen Lama a gift and made prayers for a human rebirth and to meet with the Buddha's teachings. The Paṇchen Lama told him this would happen. When he also made prayers to meet with Je Rinpoche's teachings [in the future], the Paṇchen Lama did not say this would happen.

You have met with such teachings, and not only that: the fourth of these endowments is also fulfilled—the teachings are being followed—because, there being no other hindering circumstances, it is easy for you to give up your secular life and become ordained. Actually, "the teachings...are followed" means that you can manifestly see that people obtain one of the four results [as a stream-enterer, once-returner, never-returner, or arhat]. So the fourth endowment relating to others, as actually discussed in the *Shrāvaka Levels*, only applied to people like the monk Udayī,[45] and not to the Protector Nāgārjuna, for example. During the period of "realized teachings" [the earliest period of the teachings], the people who obtained the four results set the example; even now, the deeds of saints set us an example, so this fact serves as a substitute for fulfilling the fourth endowment.

The fifth endowment relating to others—that people have love for others in their hearts—means benefactors, etc., provide favorable conditions for Dharma practitioners. So this endowment is also fulfilled. Except for a few, all eighteen of these most beneficial things are extremely rare to achieve, yet we have them. Moreover, we achieved them because we made all the right prayers in our past human lives: we prayed to receive ten things and not to receive the other eight. Thus we now have the eight freedoms and ten endowments.

THINKING ABOUT THE GREAT BENEFITS OF THE OPTIMUM HUMAN REBIRTH (110)

This has three headings: (1) its great benefits in the short term; (2) its great benefits in the long term; (3) in short, thinking on how even every moment of it can be most beneficial.

ITS GREAT BENEFITS FROM THE SHORT-TERM POINT OF VIEW (111)

No matter which of the upper rebirths you desire, be it human or divine, or which of the lower rebirths you want to avoid, you can succeed. To achieve a high rebirth you must have ethics, and you can guard them in this life; to be affluent in a high rebirth you must practice generosity, and you can accomplish that in this lifetime; and to have a magnificent retinue you need to practice patience, with which you can familiarize yourself in a life such as this. You might wonder, "How could I ever achieve a high rebirth of a wealthy and happy god or a human?" But there is no doubt that you can—all you have to do is practice.

If you wish to achieve your next rebirth as Brahmā, Indra, or a universal monarch, you can. If you want a rebirth that has the eight good qualities from karmic ripening [effects] [see Day 13, pp. 414ff.], or a high rebirth with the seven good qualities, or the right physical rebirth for the four wheels of the Supreme Vehicle [the four classes of tantra], you can achieve them.

In this rebirth you can also achieve causes to be born in the pure lands, Sukhāvatī, Śhambhala, and so on. Longdoel Lama made his optimum human rebirth meaningful by practicing in a hermitage; he showed little interest in even a single bowl of barley flour. He practiced in order to collect the causes to be reborn as the king of Śhambhala. After he had made these prayers, he thought he should now make an offering to the Paṇchen Lama Paeldaen Yeshe. He asked the Paṇchen Lama, "Will I achieve my aim?"

The Paṇchen Lama knew what he meant and said, "The old lama is being really greedy! You will achieve your aim."

ITS GREAT BENEFITS FROM THE ULTIMATE POINT OF VIEW (112)

In order to achieve liberation, you must cultivate the Dharma path for achieving it, that of the three high trainings, the first of which is ethics. Let us take the pratimokṣha vows as an example. You must cultivate renunciation in order to develop [or imprint] these vows in your mindstream, but it is difficult to develop things like renunciation in other migration states, for example as gods and so on. The inhabitants of Kuru [the Northern Continent] are not suitable candidates for these vows. And, of the humans on the other three continents, those on Jambudvīpa [the Southern Continent] are the best candidates.

One develops the most powerful bodhichitta in the human rebirth. [Chandragomin's] *Letter to a Disciple* tells us:

> Humans achieve the strongest bodhichitta;
> The gods and nāgas do not achieve this on the path;
> Neither do demigods, garuḍas, knowledge bearers, or
> python-spirits.

The same applies to the vows of the secret tantras.

The human form is also the best and most powerful rebirth in which to reach omniscience. Even a beginner in this sort of rebirth can, through the secret tantric path, become enlightened in one lifetime, in the one body. This is because one must karmically possess the six physical constituents and be born from the womb of a human of the Southern Continent. We have received such a rebirth.

We should pray to receive such a rebirth again; even the bodhisattvas in Sukhāvatī pray to be reborn on this continent. We could not have found a better rebirth than our present one—the only exception being those of us who were not born as males.[46]

The Śhākyamuni statue in Lhasa Cathedral is supposed to have a wish-granting jewel in its knees.[47] Some people circumambulate the statue and say, "May I achieve whatever I pray for!" They make such trite prayers! If you had many hundreds of thousands of wish-granting gems and turned some of them into cushions and some into pillows and sat on them, they would not help you to stay out of the lower realms when you die. But, by means of this rebirth, you can achieve the great, eternal aim, as I explained above. Just as it is better to have a jewel that will benefit you for a hundred human years than it is to have one that will benefit you for just one year, our present life is one that can accomplish lasting happiness.

Each of us has received the same rebirth as Je Milarepa, except that we do not practice the Dharma. No qualitative distinctions can be drawn between Milarepa's rebirth and ours. For example, we can understand that there is a difference between Milarepa and the king of the nāgas. The king of the nāgas has piles of wish-granting gems in his hoard, and he wears jeweled ornaments on his head and so on; but he was not even able to close the gate to the lower realms, let alone reach enlightenment. Milarepa was so poor that he did not even have barley flour to eat, but he had received this precious optimum human rebirth and so was enlightened in that very life.

Such thoughts give meaning to this optimum human rebirth; Mahāyogi told Geshe Chaen Ngawa to take it easy, but Chaen Ngawa replied that he was working as hard as he was because this optimum rebirth was so hard to find. What a great shame if this rebirth you have gained is not used meaningfully; this is like a pauper finding a sack full of gold and losing it before spending even the smallest amount.

THINKING BRIEFLY ABOUT HOW EVEN EVERY MOMENT OF IT CAN BE MOST BENEFICIAL (113)

The literature is not clear about this heading, which supplements the other two on the ways in which the optimum human rebirth is so very beneficial. The oral instruction is as follows. This rebirth has the additional great benefit of "holding great benefit every day, every moment; you will create immeasurable causes for your liberation and omniscience if you do not let even the short time it takes to burn a stick of incense go by without making use of it and, for example, work hard to build up the accumulations or purify yourself of obscurations. It is a mistake not to regret wasting our optimum human rebirths and yet to regret wasting one or two silver coins. Āryaśura [Aśhvaghoṣha] said: "Like a trader gone to an island of jewels returning home empty-handed." In other words, the trader goes to an island of jewels, does not acquire any jewels, gets heavily into debt to boot, and returns home empty-handed. We only acquire this optimum human rebirth once. There would be no greater pity than if we failed to practice Dharma, just accumulated sins, and then went to the lower realms.

THINKING ABOUT HOW DIFFICULT THE OPTIMUM HUMAN REBIRTH IS TO ACQUIRE (114)

This section has three headings.

THINKING ABOUT THE CAUSES FOR ITS BEING SO HARD TO ACQUIRE (115)

So your optimum human rebirth, which could be most beneficial, is extremely difficult to acquire: you do not receive it again and again. If it were not so difficult to obtain, you could let it now go by without using it meaningfully; then when you obtained it another time, it would be enough to make sure you used the next rebirth meaningfully. But this fully endowed human rebirth that you have received was created out of many causes and conditions. You have been lucky by virtue of your merit and the prayers you made. It will be difficult to receive the same thing in future.

Once, when a Mongolian lama was giving a Dharma teaching, a Chinese man said, "That's because the lama has never been to China himself—there are many people there!" This is quite wrong. Though there are many people in general, what good is that to you if you go to the lower realms? Regardless of whether there are many human beings in the external world or not, you must look with valid inferential cognition to see if you do not have in your mindstream all the [necessary] causes for the optimum rebirth: you can then tell whether or not it will be hard for you to receive such a rebirth in future. For example, in the external world, the autumn harvest of barley, wheat, and so on, are the outcome of the spring planting. Further, you won't get any flowers growing in a flowerpot if you don't plant any seeds in it beforehand. To receive an optimum human rebirth, you must similarly gather together very many causes.

Generally, in order to receive merely a high rebirth in the upper realms—that of a god for example—one must follow some form of ethics. As Nāgārjuna says, to obtain such an optimum human rebirth, the causes are: "Generosity, which will give wealth; ethics, which will give happiness"; and the *Short Perfection of Wisdom Sūtra* says:

> Through ethics, one abandons
> The eight unfavorable states and
> The forms of many animal migrations;
> One then always receives an opportune rebirth.

From this we come to know that the basis is pure ethics; generosity and the rest assist. They say that you should also set up karmic connections by making endless, unsullied prayers and being untainted by craving for this life. If you do not keep to your ethics but practice generosity, you will be reborn as a nāga. If you keep to your ethics but do not practice generosity, you will be reborn poor. And so on.

We are now not self-critical and claim our ethics to be pure white, but as a Mongolian geshe once said: "When you have the vows, you don't know the vinaya. You know the vinaya when you no longer have the vows."

If we analyze properly, we will see that we have rarely kept one type of ethics to our satisfaction. Our only thoughts are delusion, our only actions, sin. If we recite the lists of root transgressions and minor infractions of tantric vows, bodhisattva vows, etc. but don't understand them properly, how can we talk of keeping these vows?

Hoping for a resulting optimum human rebirth when you do not have the causes to receive it is like hoping for a harvest of barley in autumn when you planted the seeds of poisonous plants in spring.

In *Engaging in the Deeds of Bodhisattvas,* [Śhāntideva] says:

> If they say a single moment's sin
> Will keep one in the Hell Without Respite for eons,
> What can be said of going to the upper realms
> When one has collected sins throughout beginningless saṃsāra?

In other words, if just one sin can throw you into the lower realms like that, you have no hope of reaching the upper realms when you consider that you have in your mindstream a pile of sins as big as a king's treasure hoard that you have built up since beginningless time.

We might feel, "But won't my next rebirth be faultless owing to the kindness of my precious gurus?" But if we fail to practice the Dharma, there will be nothing our precious guru can do for us, just as the Buddha could not save his cousin Devadatta from falling into hell.

Wasting this good rebirth, which you have received just this once, and then wanting to receive another optimum human rebirth to use beneficially is like a poor man who finds a nugget and throws it in the water, thinking, "If only I had another, then I'd make use of it!"

It is difficult to make prayers without any expectations [of benefit] in this life. When we see the Śhākyamuni in Lhasa Cathedral and make prayers, we straight away only make prayers for long life, no illness, and all going well. As *Engaging in the Deeds of Bodhisattvas* says:

> Because of such actions as these
> I will not receive a human body;

If I don't receive a human body,
I will only sin and have no virtue.

In other words, it is usually certain that we will not practice Dharma properly in this rebirth, and if this happens, when we fall into the lower realms, we will then in that rebirth only achieve causes to be reborn yet again in the lower realms, and so wander endlessly in these realms. We will not have even the slightest virtue such as faith, wisdom, or renunciation; we will have things like attachment, hostility, and pride that lead us to our downfall. We can understand this, for example, by looking at dogs.

Once you have been reborn in the lower realms, it is even more of a struggle to regain a human rebirth than it is to achieve enlightenment in your [present] rebirth. Receiving a human body now is like carrying a copper boulder up from the halfway point up a mountain. You can go higher with the boulder from the halfway mark. If you can't go any higher, you must not let the boulder fall, for then it will be even harder to reach halfway again. Similarly, if in this rebirth you do not manage to achieve realization into higher paths, such as liberation and omniscience, at least do not fall into the lower realms. Then your chances for the optimum rebirth are next to nothing, for once you fall you will wander from lower realm to lower realm; you will be virtually without any chance of liberation. When you take the wrong path, you get progressively farther from where you should be going; that is why, in just the same way, you must not use this present rebirth to go the wrong way. Do not blame anyone if you do not [heed me]. If you do [heed me], do not despair, even if you're getting old. Take the case of the householder Śhrījāta [see Day 14, p. 432].

SOME ANALOGIES FOR THE DIFFICULTY OF ACQUIRING IT (116)

Geshe Potowa says in his *Analogies:* "Grass on the roof of a tower; the neck of a turtle...," which means the following.

Rebirths into the upper realms are generally as frequent as the grass that grows on the mountain slope. But a human rebirth with all the freedoms and endowments is extremely rare—as rare as blades of grass on the roofs of houses.

The "neck of a turtle" means this. Suppose there is a golden yoke floating on the great ocean, being blown by the wind. The yoke has only one hole, and a blind turtle living in the ocean pokes its head out of the ocean's surface just once every hundred years. The turtle's head would [probably] not come up through the yoke. We are similarly in the great ocean of saṃsāra; owing to the power of our delusions, the eyes of our wisdom are closed, and we normally wander from one state in the lower realms to another. Occasionally we get free of the lower realms and attain the odd rebirth in a human state by virtue of the laws of probability. But the world is enormous, and there are worlds in all the cardinal and intermediate points of the compass; one cannot be sure where in these worlds the buddhas' teachings flourish or where they will be going. These teachings are like the golden yoke, and meeting with them is also extremely rare.

If the turtle constantly swam to the ocean's surface, he would probably meet with the yoke from time to time; but if he only surfaces every hundred years, he will only [ever] meet it once. If we, as in the analogy, received human rebirths frequently, we could possibly meet a Buddha's teachings wherever they occur. But this is not the case: only occasionally do we receive one or two human rebirths.

If the golden yoke stayed in one place for a long time, the turtle would not surface at the exact place, but at least there would be a chance he might hit the right place a few times, and so meet with the yoke. But this is not in fact the case: the yoke moves at random in all ten directions on the huge expanse of the ocean's surface. And, as in the analogy, if the Buddha's teachings always stayed in the same world, we would possibly meet with them a few times when we gained human rebirth. But we cannot be sure that a Buddha's teachings will remain in a particular world, and [in any case] such teachings would only remain there a very short while.

One cannot claim that the yoke and the turtle will never meet, but this is very nearly the case. Receiving an optimum human rebirth is even rarer, but this does not stop it from occurring before the end of saṃsāra.

The elements of this analogy are taken to mean the following. The ocean is our saṃsāric state; the turtle is ourselves; his blindness, ignorance; the yoke, a Buddha's teachings; and so on. This interpretation of the contemplation on the difficulty of receiving this optimum rebirth is said to be an oral tradition stemming from Je Drubkang Geleg Gyatso.

Again, Geshe Potowa's *Analogies* says: "Loding's boy..." Drom Loding had a son who knew how to prospect for gold. This boy went on a trading trip with some friends. The local people came to hear of Loding's son's reputation and were saying, "Ah, if only I were Loding's son! If only I could find a mountain of gold!" On hearing this, he abandoned ideas of going on the business trip and had a mind to go prospecting. We similarly have received such a good rebirth that it is the subject of the prayers of bodhisattvas in Sukhāvatī. But what a great pity if, after receiving this, we waste away its benefits.

Geshe Potowa says: "And the Tsang man's fish." Once a man from Tsang went to the Central Province and ate some fish. In fact he gorged himself on it and was at the point of vomiting. He said, "What a pity to vomit up such a delicious meal!" and tied up his neck. If it's a shame when you sometimes vomit up tasty food, how much more of a pity it would be not to benefit from a rebirth that is so difficult to receive you will only get it once in many eons.

Geshe Potowa then speaks of: "An earthworm prostrating itself…" It sounds impossible that a red, slimy earthworm could surface out of the ground and prostate itself to the Buddha. That is how impossible it has been for us earthworms to surface from the lower realms, take human forms, and even to go through the motions of studying and contemplating the Dharma.

Think over these various analogies showing how the optimum human rebirths we have acquired are so very rare and difficult to achieve.

IT'S DIFFICULT BY NATURE TO ACQUIRE (117)

Many beings practice nonvirtue, few practice virtue. When beings leave their rebirths in the higher and lower realms, the vast majority go to the lower realms. So very few leave rebirths in either realm and go to the upper realms that the Tathāgata, in his basic teachings on the vinaya, said the beings who go from the upper realms to the lower realms, or who go from the lower back to the lower, are like the dust particles in the vast earth. The number of beings who go from the lower to the upper, or from the upper back to the upper, are like the dust particles that fit on the tip of a finger. Among the six types of rebirth, there are generally very few beings who are human. There are fewer hungry ghosts than hell beings; still fewer animals; and fewer land animals than marine. This is like the fact that hundreds of millions of flies can fit into a space that will not hold ten humans. There are very many beings in the bardo: so many that it is like the many hundreds of thousands of flies that immediately gather round a dead horse's corpse; or even a hundred such corpses: there are still just the same [number of] flies [for each] at the ready.

Even among human rebirths, it is extremely rare to be born during the eons of illumination, that is, in an eon when buddhas come to a world. And each eon of illumination is separated by many tens of thousands of eons of darkness. Even within each eon of illumination there are eighty minor eons: twenty minor eons of void and twenty each of formation, stasis, and destruction. Buddhas do not come to a world during sixty of these minor eons—during the eons of void, formation, and destruction. Nor do they come to a world at certain times during the twenty minor eons of stasis—during the first and last of these twenty minor eons when humans have immeasurable lifespans, and at those times when human lifespans are on the increase. Buddhas only come during the "dark ages" when human lifespans are decreasing.[48]

Let us talk about this present time of our birth in the Southern Continent. Buddhas come during the eighteen intervening minor eons when human lifespans follow a cyclic pattern. We could have been born when a previous Buddha had, to common appearances, gone to nirvāṇa and his doctrines died out. Birth during this period before the coming of the next Buddha is no different from birth in an eon of darkness. But we were not born at such a time. They say that after these teachings die out, 4.9 billion human years will elapse before Maitreya Buddha comes, but we were also not born during this intervening dark age: the Buddha's teachings still exist, and we were born in the Southern Continent, the only place where these teachings can be found. We were born in one of the few countries in this continent where the teachings are widespread, and such countries, like Tibet and Mongolia, are in the minority, only a few. We were born in Tibet, one of the foundations allowing the Dharma to thrive. But here is an example of what happens in Tibet. Gushri Kaelzang [a Mongolian] once said:

> When I went to Tashikyil Monastery in Amdo, there were several thousand monks. Of these, about five hundred were geshes, about five hundred were traders, about five hundred were neither…

In a single family there may be ten brothers, but only two or three of them will enter monasteries. And even among people in monasteries, those who practice Dharma purely, by putting the lamrim into practice, are most rare. But in spite of all this, we were not born in a place with no freedom [to practice].

According to my own precious guru's oral tradition, the optimum human rebirth is hard to acquire because it is difficult to achieve, because it is by nature something difficult to create, and because its probability is shown by analogy to be low.

Kyabje Pabongka Rinpoche then discussed how to think over these three reasons.

This rebirth we have acquired can fulfill our fondest wishes, be they good or evil. We are on the border between the upper and lower realms. We ought not to put our hopes in anything else. The choice lies in our own hands, so we must make no mistake about which choice leads to happiness and which to misery. If we are mistaken, the mistake will not be for a day or two—it will spoil our eternal hopes for all our rebirths.

It is so good you have not yet died! You now have only so much of this life left: two years, three years, or whatever it may be. If you now do not perform austerities day and night and practice some holy Dharma, you must consider: "Dare I risk going back to the lower realms?"

It is vital that we do not let this opportune rebirth of ours be wasted; a precious rebirth we get only once, like a priceless jewel created out of eighteen things. Suppose a merchant goes to an island of jewels and instead of taking any of the precious stones just spends his time singing, dancing, and so on, even getting into much debt to other merchants. What could be more insane than eventually returning with no jewels? At such a time as this, you could gather the jewels of liberation and omniscience with your own hands. By not doing so, and by creating instead the causes for going to the lower realms, you could make no greater show of blindness or stupidity.

Śhāntideva says:

> If I do not cultivate virtue,
> After obtaining such an opportunity,
> There is no greater self-deception.
> Nothing could be blinder!

You should extract some essence from this good rebirth you have acquired—this rebirth is all you need to extract the essence. Build up your accumulations and do some self-purification for at least the time it takes to drink a full bowl of tea! At best, you could be enlightened in one lifetime, in the one body. If not, then you may achieve liberation. Failing that, you ought at the very least to strive not to go to the lower realms. The *King of Single-Pointed Concentration Sūtra* says:

> Yet the patient does not take much wholesome
> And precious medicine, the potential cure.
> Do not blame the doctor; The medicine's not at fault.
> Rather, the patient himself is to blame.
> So, too, with people ordained into this doctrine:
> They may know full well about the [ten] forces,
> The dhyāna concentrations, the [ten] powers,
> Yet they make no true effort to meditate.
> How could nirvāṇa come without proper effort?…
> Though I have taught you the Dharma well.
> If you have heard it and do not practice well,
> You are like the patient who left the medicine in its case,
> Thinking, "This cannot cure my disease."

Engaging in the Deeds of Bodhisattvas says:

> Physically make use of these;
> What do mere words accomplish?
> Will the sick be helped
> Just by their reading the prescriptions?

In other words, your virtuous spiritual guide may teach you the path leading to liberation and omniscience properly, but if you do not put these things into practice, you are like a patient who does not take the many medicines a skilled doctor has prescribed—and so cannot be cured. It is entirely up to you whether you practice your guru's instructions and teachings. You should strive to make your optimum human rebirth something meaningful and integrate the Dharma into your life right to the very end.

Now I shall review the above and teach you briefly how to follow this practice. Make petitions to the figure of your guru you are visualizing above your head. Then meditate according to the above headings. The criterion for having developed realization into this topic is as follows. Geshe Potowa said:

> How could you waste your life, slacker,
> When you understand how hard it is to get the optimum human rebirth?

Je Tsongkapa says:

> If you knew how hard it is to acquire, living the average life would be impossible.
> If you saw its great benefits, you would be sorry if it passed meaninglessly.
> If you thought about death, you would make preparations for your future lives.
> If you thought about cause and effect, you would stop being reckless.

That splendid yogi Goenpawa did not pause to extract an extremely painful thorn that had lodged in his thigh but continued to meditate instead. When this happens to you, you have developed realization into how beneficial the optimum human rebirth is and into how difficult it is to receive.

Part Four

THE SMALL SCOPE

DAY 10

Kyabje Pabongka quoted the following praise from the writings of Genduen Taenzin Gyatso, a great adept:

> This is not false, invented Dharma, because it is the pith of authentic oral teachings.
> This is not foolish talk, because it comes from classical texts by the great champions.
> This is not a shimmering mirage, because saintly scholars and adepts have experienced it.
> This is not a perilous cliff, because it is the highway to highest enlightenment.

He quoted this as part of a short talk to set our motivation. He restated the headings we had above and then reviewed the material that comes after the subheading "Devoting Yourself through Deeds," part of the section on "The Root of the Path: Devotion to a Spiritual Guide."

Between meditations, mainly read books that teach about the optimum human rebirth. If, after thinking about the difficulty of obtaining this most beneficial human rebirth, you develop a wish to extract some essence from it, you should train your mind through the three scopes of the lamrim. The extent to which you train your mind in these three scopes determines how much of the small, medium, or great essence you will eventually extract.

If we want to achieve buddhahood, we must first develop realization into the earlier sections of the path; if not, we will not develop realization into the later parts. For example, Khampas coming to see the Śhākyamuni statue in Lhasa Cathedral first leave their homes, arriving finally at the statue. The road leads them here bit by bit; it is impossible for them to skip any part of the way. Nor can you develop realization into such higher parts of the path as compassion until you have first achieved the lower parts—renunciation and so on. [Śhāntideva] says in *Engaging in the Deeds of Bodhisattvas:*

> If you have not even dreamed
> Of benefiting yourself
> Before dreaming of this for sentient beings,
> How could you be of benefit to others?

When we speak of small and medium scopes, we mean training the mind in the stages of the path *shared* with the small and medium scopes; we do not mean training the mind in the actual small and medium parts of the path. Suppose there are three people: one going to Tashi Lhuenpo, one to Rong, and one to Chushur. The first wants to go to Tashi Lhuenpo but must first share some of the road with the other two. The three have three different things in mind: two are traveling to either Rong or Chushur, and the first intends to continue on to Tashi Lhuenpo.

So, in the small- and medium-scope sections of the lamrim, you must focus on achieving buddhahood for the sake of sentient beings. Developing bodhichitta is the actual practice; the small- and medium-scope parts of the path are preliminaries to developing bodhicitta. You may be wondering, "In that case it must be sufficient to teach the great scope from the outset. I doubt that the so-called small and medium are needed." There are two reasons for discussing all three. There are people who cannot train their minds in the great scope initially, so they need to practice in stages through the small and medium scopes. This approach is more beneficial for people with good, mediocre, or inferior minds. Also, without some familiarity with the earlier parts of the path, you will have no renunciation at all in your mindstream, so you need to defeat any pride you may have about being a Mahāyānist or follower of the secret tantras.

To develop bodhichitta, which is the actual practice, you need to develop such compassion that you simply cannot bear others being tormented by suffering. But in order to develop this compassion, you must know exactly how you yourself are plagued by suffering. And you must understand that the whole of saṃsāra is by nature suffering. But first you must fear the lower realms, for without this you will have no repudiation of celestial and human happiness. You must therefore train your mind in the small- and medium-scope parts of the path. This training is like the foundations and wall-supports of a house.

We have not yet achieved advanced results like previous practitioners. Je Milarepa trained in the common path under Marpa, and many of his songs are about his development of these realizations. And you need the lamrim to make the especially rapid progress promised by the secret tantras. This is the implication of the names the *Easy Path* and the *Swift Path*. That Milarepa achieved the unification in one lifetime was not due to tantra alone; he had already trained in the path of the three scopes in former lives. In one former life, for example, he was the Kadampa Chagtrichog, as said in the introduction to mind training.

Although people who embark on the secret tantras must have trained in the shared part of the path beforehand, we did not do this: we embarked on the secret tantras first, did not keep our tantric commitments, and thought we meditated on the two stages. They say that many such people will go to the Vajra Hell.

You must be farsighted from the beginning. You must feel, "I am prepared to use my entire human life to pursue just one meditation topic of the lamrim." But we are farsighted about worldly things, which is the wrong way round. Lack persistence in worldly things, not the Dharma. If you feel, "It's impossible not to achieve anything in the Dharma" and practice with courage, you will not have to spend a month or a year on a single meditation topic.

Geshe Kamaba said:

> We say, "Our contemplations achieve nothing." Why do you think that is? Don't lie: you are distracted in the daytime and fall asleep at night!

In other words, never mind our spending a month on a meditation topic; we have not even meditated on a single topic for the length of a single meditation session. How unrealistic to feel, "Even now I haven't developed realizations!" We don't make determined practice our starting point, yet we roll our eyes into the top of our head [and pretend to meditate] when we do just one recitation of, for example, [Tsongkapa's] *Basis of All Good Qualities*. If we act in this way, our wish to develop insights and realizations into the lamrim is an extremely greedy one. This is where the fault lies.

Karag Gomchung Rinpoche, a Kadampa, said:

> Look far ahead. Be farsighted. Be in tune.

These three things are vital. The meaning is that you must look far ahead to the goal of omniscience; be farsighted about the small and medium scopes; and meditate to reach the right pitch or tension. Your practice, too, should be at the right pitch. When you receive Dharma orally from your guru and then practice frantically for a few days with superficial renunciation, this is a sure sign that you will make no progress.

HOW TO EXTRACT THE ESSENCE FROM YOUR OPTIMUM HUMAN REBIRTH (118)

This has three sections: (1) training your mind in the stages of the path shared with the small scope; (2) training your mind in the stages of the path shared with the medium scope; (3) training your mind in the great-scope stages of the path.

TRAINING YOUR MIND IN THE STAGES OF THE PATH SHARED WITH THE SMALL SCOPE (119)

This has two subheadings: (1) developing a yearning for a good rebirth; (2) teaching the means for happiness in your next rebirth.

DEVELOPING A YEARNING FOR A GOOD REBIRTH (120)

This has two subdivisions: (1) remembering that your present rebirth will not last long and that you will die; (2) thinking about what sort of happiness or suffering you will have in your next rebirth in either of the two types of migrations.

RECALLING THAT YOUR PRESENT REBIRTH WILL NOT LAST LONG AND THAT YOU WILL DIE (121)

This has three subheadings: (1) the drawbacks of not remembering death; (2) the advantages of remembering death; (3) the actual way to remember death.

THE DRAWBACKS OF NOT REMEMBERING DEATH (122)

There are six sections here.

THE DRAWBACK THAT YOU WILL NOT REMEMBER DHARMA (123)

If you do not recollect death, you will think about only this life, get caught up in its many demands—food, clothes, and so on—and thus not practice Dharma. If you recollect death well, you will work hard to prepare for your next lives, just as a Khampa about to go on a journey would work only at preparing and packing. Your enormous craving for food, fashion, reputation, and so on, can be blamed on your not remembering impermanence. Every day that passes without your recalling impermanence is a day of your life wasted.

THE DRAWBACK THAT YOU WILL REMEMBER [THE DHARMA] BUT NOT PRACTICE IT (124)

Je Tsongkapa said:

> Everyone thinks, "Death will eventually come." Yet they keep the evil thought, "But I will not die today, I will not die today," right until they are on the point of dying.

You grasp on to the idea that you are not going to die, and think, "Oh, I could practice Dharma next year or the year after." You are forever procrastinating. You think about Dharma but do not practice it; you remain engrossed in thoughts such as, "I want this valuable object." Meanwhile, while you are not practicing Dharma, your human life is running out.

[THE DRAWBACK THAT] YOU WILL PRACTICE BUT NOT PRACTICE PROPERLY (125)

At the moment we are Dharma practitioners, but because we do not ignore this life's trivia, our practice is not at all pure. We study and contemplate, yet unintentionally want to be scholars, or famous. We meditate, do recitations, and so forth, thinking this will remove life's unfavorable circumstances. Even great meditating hermits are not free from involuntarily wanting to be famous, and so forth. As great Atiśha said:

> Ask me what the results of thinking only about this life are and I will tell you: they are merely the results of this life. Ask me what will happen in your next lives and I will tell you: you will be reborn in hell; reborn as a hungry ghost; reborn as an animal.

In other words, you will achieve a few resultant benefits in this life, and your next lives will result in your going to the lower realms.

If you act like this, you are no different from a lay person. A Dharma practitioner must first of all ignore this life. I am not saying you should become a pauper; even paupers in their wanderings do not ignore this life. The things you should ignore are the eight worldly concerns. Anything mixed with these concerns is not Dharma. The yogi Chagtrichog asked Atiśha, "Should I meditate? Should I teach? Or sometimes teach and sometimes meditate?" Atiśha said to each, "This will not help." Chagtrichog then asked what he should do and was told, "Give up worldly things."

Lama Gyamaba said:

> You fools, you haven't succeeded in a single type of practice,
> Yet you are proud of being Dharma practitioners!
> See whether you have the first of all Dharmas
> In your mindstreams: ignoring this life.

As Geshe Toelungpa once told another: "It is good, my lord, if you practice generosity, but better still to practice Dharma itself." In other words, Dharma and worldly things are opposites—even in such actions as these.

Geshe Potowa said you cannot sew with a two-pronged needle. If you do not think about death, you will not ignore this life. If you do not ignore this life, you will be controlled by the eight worldly concerns: being happy if you acquire and unhappy if you do not; being happy if comfortable and unhappy if not; happy if famous and unhappy if not; happy if praised and unhappy if criticized. Nāgārjuna said of these eight:

> By the eight worldly concerns we mean:
> the worldly thoughts of acquiring or not,
> Comfort or discomfort, fame or notoriety, praise or criticism.
> Keep a level head: These are not subjects for your thoughts.

Compare this with the story about Geshe Potowa and the offering of turquoise. Lingraepa said:

> In saṃsāra, the city of preconceptions,
> Wander the zombies of the eight worldly concerns.
> You are in a terrifying charnel ground;
> Have your guru perform an exorcism.

So ignore this life and devote yourself wholeheartedly to the Dharma. If afterward you wonder whether you will be able to support yourself, feel that it would be all right even if you cannot, and be prepared to become a pauper. Our Teacher left his home and became a homeless monk; he renounced all the wealth of his royal position, wore clothes he found in rubbish heaps, and so on. He devoted himself wholeheartedly to the Dharma. He was prepared to become a pauper. Je Rinpoche did the same. But you might wonder, "If I become a pauper from devoting myself wholeheartedly to the Dharma, won't I die because I will not get any food?" You should be prepared to die as a beggar and say to yourself, "If I die while undergoing hardships for the sake of the Dharma, then so be it."

Should you ignore this life like that, there are no stories of Dharma practitioners starving to death after they stopped earning their livelihood. Our kind Teacher dedicated to us merits [worth] 60,000 [rebirths as] universal emperors so that his followers would not starve to death, even in times of such famine that pearls have to be bartered for flour. As they say:

> If the great meditator does not roll down the hill,
> Noodles will roll up to him.

Geshe Baen Gung-gyael also said:

> When I was a layman I wore a sharp sword, arrow, and spear at my belt, but I had many enemies and few friends. When I was a bachelor I had fields that could yield forty bushels of wheat, so people gave me the nickname the "Forty-Bushel Bandit." I used to hold up people by day and rob villages at night; but even so, food and clothes were scarce, and my cows gave no milk. Now that I practice Dharma, I am short of neither food nor clothing, and my enemies are at peace.

As he said:

> If craving rots like a human corpse,
> The things you desire gather round it like vultures.

The good works of people like Je Tsongkapa were as vast as space; this is because they ignored this life and practiced Dharma properly. According to one story, a Sakyapa [who didn't realize this] thought [instead] that Je Rinpoche had achieved the power to amass wealth, and so [even] asked him, "What is the deepest power of all for amassing wealth?"

When you die and your corpse has been disposed of, do you need even the smallest material possession? At the time of death, completely resign yourself to it and say to yourself, "I'm going to die no matter what I do, so let me die."

Kyabje Pabongka Rinpoche went on in more detail, telling us of the need to have the ten most closely guarded possessions of the Kadampas.[49] *He also talked about the full contemplation described by Milarepa: that we will have no mourners, and our bier no followers.*

You might think that people will have to be paid to get rid of your corpse; in fact they will be nauseated by it and will do anything to get rid of it. Have no doubt that your body will be taken from your deathbed!

Thus, make up your mind to ignore the eight worldly concerns, and you will receive this life's comforts, happiness, and fame as if by the load-ful. So, if you yearn for the eight worldly concerns, you are a worldly person; if you ignore this life you are a Dharma practitioner. Geshe Potowa asked Dromtoenpa, "What is the fine dividing line between Dharma and non-Dharma?"

Drom replied, "It is Dharma if it becomes an antidote to delusions; it is not Dharma if it does not. If all worldly people do not agree with it, it is Dharma; if they do, it is not Dharma."

The point is that Dharma and worldly things are opposites: who has time both to do their recitations and maintain a household? Our bodies are pale reflections of those of Dharma practitioners, and our minds are no different from those of worldly lay people: we make the eight worldly concerns our basic practice.

Having turned away from this life, the main technique for practicing

Dharma purely is to meditate on death and impermanence. If you do not ignore this life, any Dharma you practice will involuntarily slip back into this life. You must not let your head be turned by the eight worldly concerns. You must ignore your craving for food, clothing, and reputation. The criterion for having done this is if you want to be like the Seventh Dalai Lama Kaelzang Gyatso or the Paṇchen Lama Lozang Yeshe. The Seventh Dalai Lama said that he owned only his vajra, bell, and three robes—nothing else. And there is a story that even an offering of one hundred ingots of silver did not please the Paṇchen Lama Lozang Yeshe.

We might not necessarily crave all three—food, clothing, or reputation. Some of us may be fettered by just one of them; others by two; others indeed by all three. But the hardest of the three to abandon is the desire for reputation. Many people, no matter who they are—scholars, monks, teachers, meditators—want a good reputation or to be famous. Drogoen Rinpoche, Gyer Drowai Goenpo, said:

> In this life, you may be a scholar, monk, or great meditator;
> But you want to be called "scholar" or "monk."
> You may place a notice on your door that you are in retreat,
> You may be a great meditator who shuns other people,
> But, great meditator of this life,
> You want people to call you "great meditator"...
> Even the offerings you make to the Three Jewels
> Are made only to be seen by others...

Some people fancy themselves as great meditators or adepts; they give up food and clothes, and work hard at such austerities as taking only the essence of flowers or pebbles.[50] Yet people who deep down have absolutely no desire for reputation are rare. Geshe Potowa's *Analogies* said: "The fox and monkey [lurk near the] doorstep of the grouse..." In other words, instead of examining the fiery pit that lies on your own doorstep, you explore faraway places; that is, you explore the higher paths, the buddha levels, tantra, and so forth, while not noticing your craving for this life's trivia. You are not free of these fetters. This is one of the drawbacks of not recollecting death.

THE DRAWBACK OF NOT PRACTICING SERIOUSLY (126)

If you do not recollect death, you will not practice Dharma seriously, nor will you be able to practice continually. At present we do not have great perseverance in our virtuous practices; we only practice until we get bored. Our not recollecting death and impermanence is to blame. Because Geshe Karag Gomchung recollected impermanence, he never even got round to cutting down the thorn bush on his doorstep. Milarepa used to wear pieces of cloth and barley-flour sacks, and when they eventually fell to pieces, he did not even bother to sew them together; he did virtuous practices instead. If we were to have a similar recollection of impermanence, we would not strive hard at other activities; we would work hard at virtuous practices and not feel downhearted each time we start: we would be only too glad to do them.

THE DRAWBACK OF ACTING VULGARLY (127)

When you do not recollect death, your craving for the things of this life increases, and in order to achieve them, you help some people, harm others, and so forth; you develop attachment, hostility, or benighted ignorance; and you fight and argue with people. You become the butt of others' vulgar talk, and eventually your own vulgar behavior even leads you to get head wounds: all things leading in the future to your total degradation.

THE DRAWBACK OF HAVING TO DIE WITH REGRETS (128)

If you do not recollect death, your Dharma practice will be only a pale reflection, and it will be diluted by your yearning for the things of this life. Then, one day, you will suddenly be confronted by an enemy called "dying without having practiced Dharma." You will see that your possessions, the things you yearned for so much in the past, are of no benefit whatever, and you will know that you have obtained none of the divine Dharma, something that would surely have been of help. You will develop much unbearable regret, but all will be over, except your misery—like Moendro Choedrag, who when stricken with a fever knew he was going to die, and said words of regret. Geshe Kamaba said, "We should fear death now. We wish to die a painless death, but it will be the opposite for us: we are not afraid now, but at the time of death we will be flaying our breasts with our fingernails." In other words, we must be afraid of death and impermanence from the start, then we needn't be afraid when we die. But we do it the wrong way round. We never think, "I could die right now," and so we remain complacent. What a horrible death we will have!

You may be rich with one hundred pieces of gold, or you may be a king who reigns over every country, but these things are of no benefit at all at the time of death—they are only hollow.

We might suddenly be seized by some virulent and fatal disease, but we have not yet achieved a single thing we can confidently count on at the time of death. If we did not die right away, we would feel, "I will now definitely practice Dharma"—but our life would be coming to an end. This would be as helpful as holding some food in our hand and not getting to eat it; then, to no avail, we think to eat it when a dog has already come along and carried it away.

These are the six drawbacks.

THE ADVANTAGES OF REMEMBERING DEATH (129)

There are six of these.

THE ADVANTAGE OF BEING MOST BENEFICIAL (130)

Recollecting death is most beneficial. As Buddha, our Teacher, said in the *Great Sūtra on Buddha's Nirvāṇa:* among animal tracks, that of the elephant is best; among all attitudes, that of death and impermanence is best. In other words, you will practice the Dharma faultlessly when you recall death; wanting to achieve a good rebirth in the future, you will practice generosity, uphold your ethics, and so forth. In short, recollection of death will lead you through the whole lamrim, through the three scopes, right to the unification.

When Yungtoenpa's benefactor died, this inspired Milarepa [Yungtoenpa's disciple] to practice Dharma. Many of the great adepts used to hold skullcups, trumpets made of human thighbones, and so on, to improve their awareness of death and impermanence. The vinaya speaks of keeping drawings of skeletons in bathhouses and the like for the same reason. Geshe Chaen Ngawa said: "If you do not do at least one meditation session on impermanence in the morning, I think you will devote the whole day to this life."

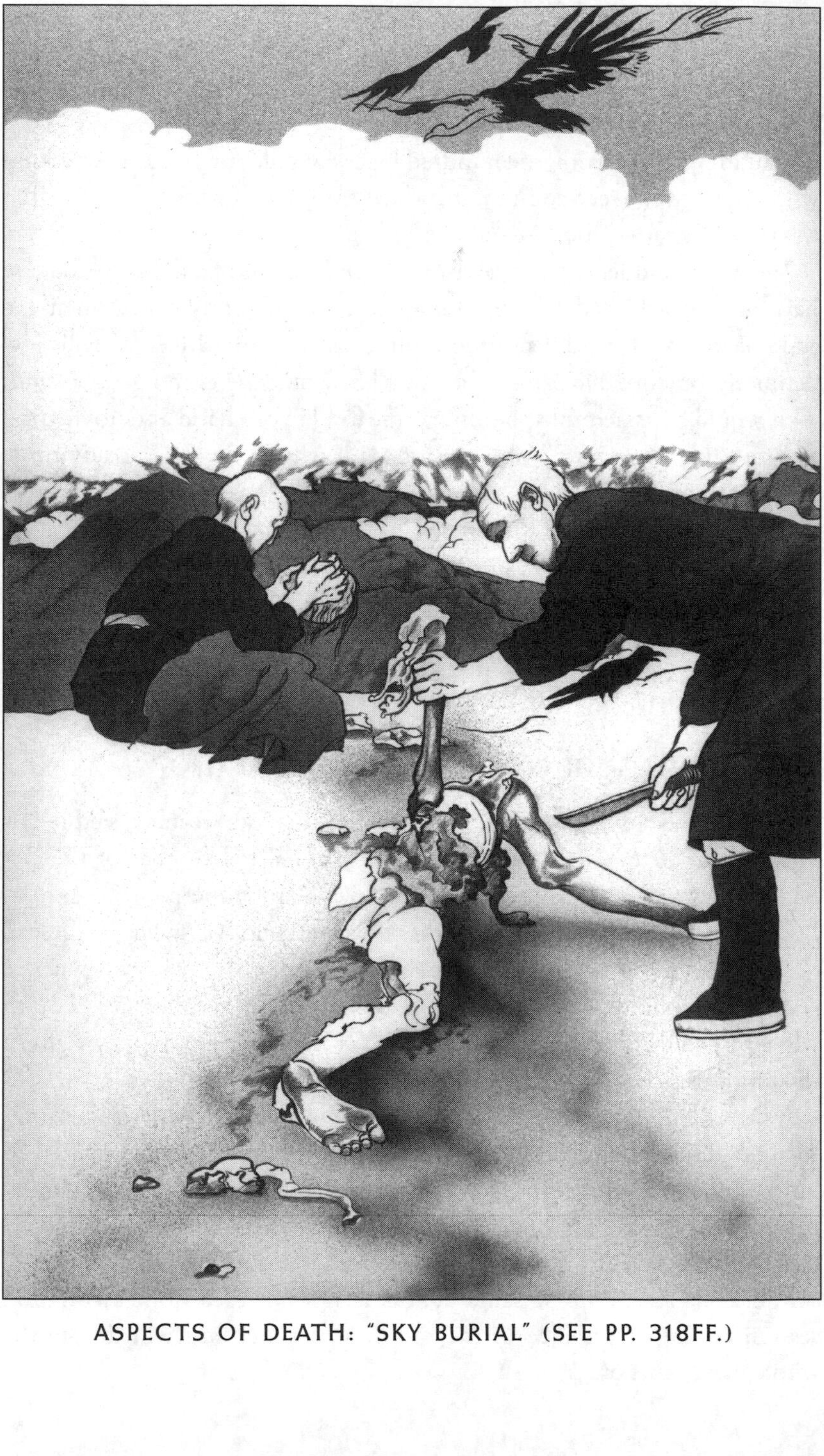

ASPECTS OF DEATH: "SKY BURIAL" (SEE PP. 318FF.)

Zhangtsuen Yerpa said that if you did not recall impermanence in the morning, you would devote the morning to this life, and if you did not develop this recollection at noon, you would devote the afternoon to this life. If you devote yourself to this life, whatever you do will not be Dharma.

THE ADVANTAGE OF BEING MOST POWERFUL (131)

If you recall death and impermanence, they say you will destroy the non-Dharmic: attachment, anger, and so on. You will have great power to complete the accumulations, and it is like a hammer to destroy all your delusions and misdeeds at one stroke.

IT IS IMPORTANT AT THE BEGINNING (132)

Recollecting death at the beginning acts as a cause for you to embark on the Dharma.

IT IS IMPORTANT IN THE MEANTIME (133)

In the meantime, it acts as a condition to stimulate you to work hard at the Dharma.

IT IS IMPORTANT AT THE END (134)

At the end, it will bring your Dharma practice through to completion by consummating the result.

THE ADVANTAGE THAT YOU WILL DIE HAPPILY AND GLADLY (135)

At death, you will have the confidence that comes from practicing Dharma faultlessly and be like a son returning to his father's household. Longdoel Lama Rinpoche said:

> I am not afraid of being impermanent. I will be an old monk in the morning and get the body of a god that night.

So, the best Dharma practitioners are happy to die; the middling die gracefully; the least have no regrets. They will feel, "I managed to practice

Dharma well; it will be easy for me to die now," and have no regrets. As Je Milarepa said:

> I fled to the mountains because I feared death.
> I have realized emptiness, the mind's primordial state.
> Were I to die now, I have no fear.

THE ACTUAL WAY TO REMEMBER DEATH (136)

This has two sections: (1) the nine-part meditation on death; (2) meditation on the aspects of death.

Not even the early Kadampas had this detailed treatment: it consists of instructions taken from Je Tsongkapa's works. These works have many unique, profound, and detailed instructions. They contain the thoughts of the classical Indian treatises on tantra, they have special points drawn from [Tsongkapa's own] experience, their headings are not in a muddle, and so forth.

THE NINE-PART MEDITATION ON DEATH (137)

This has three roots: (1) thinking of the inevitability of death; (2) thinking about the uncertainty of when you will die; (3) thinking of how nothing can help you when you die except Dharma. Three reasons are given for each root, making nine parts in all.

THE FIRST ROOT: THINKING ABOUT THE INEVITABILITY OF DEATH (138)

The first of the three reasons given for this is:

THE FIRST REASON: THE LORD OF DEATH WILL INEVITABLY COME, AND NO CIRCUMSTANCE AT ALL CAN PREVENT THIS (139)

Inevitably you will die. No matter what sort of body you have, no matter where you go, no matter what method you employ, you cannot stop the Lord of Death. Not even a sound body will stop him. The *Sayings of the Buddha on Impermanence* tells us:

If all—even the buddhas, pratyekabuddhas,
And śhrāvaka disciples of the buddhas—
Abandon their bodily remains,
Need I speak of ordinary beings!

In other words, when we now tell stories about the Bhagavān Buddha who achieved the vajra body, and about the many adepts of India and Tibet who achieved the unification, it might seem that they are still with us, yet they have gone to nirvāṇa. If, to common appearances, our Teacher Buddha and others have died and their vajra bodies been destroyed, why should people like ourselves not die?

When our Teacher was about to pass into nirvāṇa, many tens of thousands of his retinue, Śhāriputra and others, went before him into nirvāṇa. Then Buddha, our Teacher, while in Kuśhinagarī, commanded that his last sleeping platform be built between two sāla trees. He then subdued his last two disciples, Pramudita, the king of the celestial musicians, and the Brahman priest Subhadra, who was not a Buddhist. They could not bear to see Buddha pass into nirvāṇa, and Subhadra immediately passed away himself. When our Teacher was just about to pass away, he removed his upper garments and urged people to take a good look, because it was difficult to get to see the body of a tathāgata. His last teaching centered on impermanence. Then, in order to show that this meditation was fundamental, he said:

All conditioned phenomena are impermanent.
This is the last teaching of the Tathāgata.

He then passed into nirvāṇa. When most of the arhats who had achieved partial or complete [karmic] freedom understood what had happened, they too passed away; their number was one short of five hundred.

Moreover, Indian pandits like the seven hierarchs of the teachings, the eighty great adepts, the six ornaments, the two supreme ones, and so forth, and in Tibet, Śhāntarakṣhita, Āchārya Padmasaṃbhava, and the Dharmarāja Trisong Detsaen, Atiśha and his disciples, Mañjuśhrī's embodiment Lord Tsongkapa and his disciples, and so forth, have all passed to nirvāṇa; now only their reputations remain. How could we escape death?

When Lama Tsechogling Rinpoche, a tutor to the Dalai Lama, gave lamrim teachings, they say there were many thousands in the audience;

now not one of these lamas or disciples is still alive. And they say Chuzang Lama Rinpoche and others gave teachings very like our present one at this very spot; now only the reputation remains. In a mere hundred years, all those sitting in this assembly will be dead, and the only remnant will be the report that something happened on this spot. If after only a hundred years all the people now in the Southern Continent—in China, Tibet, Mongolia, and so forth—even the babies born today—are sure to be dead, and not one left alive, then no better karmic result awaits us. Likewise, if your time has come, there is no place that will not mean death for you. The *Sayings of the Buddha on Impermanence* tells us:

> Wherever you stay, there will be no place
> That does not mean your death:
> Not in the sky, not in the sea,
> Not even if you stay in the mountains.

Once Prince Virūḍhaka, King Prasenajit's son, intended to slaughter the Śhākyas. Maudgalyāyana thought to use his miraculous powers to cast Virūḍhaka and his army beyond the iron mountains [that enclose this world], but Buddha said it was impossible to stop them. Some Śhākya men and women were concealed inside the Tathāgata's begging bowl; some were put inside the palace in the sun, but even those Śhākyas were still killed, and that day was such that they were going to die.

Running away, bribery, force, etc., will all be quite useless. From the *Sayings of the Buddha:*

> Anyone with the five clairvoyant powers
> Of great ṛiṣhis, able to go far into the sky,
> Cannot go to a place that is
> Not under death's jurisdiction.

In other words, if fleeing could free you from death, then having miraculous powers or the five clairvoyant powers of the ṛiṣhis would be sufficient to run from the Lord of Death, but even such people cannot escape him and will die.

Even force cannot stop the Lord of Death. The most powerful lion can defeat elephants by clawing their heads, but when death comes, lions die with their claws drawn in. Even a powerful universal emperor must die: all his power cannot help. We tote up our beloved wealth and property, and we suppose that these things will be enough to bribe the Lord of Death; but if, as they say, he cannot be bribed with the precious jewels of a universal emperor, how can we speak of other people bribing him? In the *Instruction Given to the King Sūtra* we find:

> Suppose there are four great mountains in the four cardinal directions; they are firm, stable, with solid cores, are uncracked, indestructible, extremely hard, uniformly dense, they touch the sky and thrust into the ground. On they come, grinding all to powder: all grass, trees, twigs, branches, and leaves, all animals, insects, and elementals. They cannot be stopped by fleeing, by force, by wealth, by substances, mantras, or medicines.
>
> Great king, the four great terrors are similarly coming; they cannot be stopped by fleeing, by force, by wealth, by substances, mantras, or medicines. What are these four? Old age, sickness, decay, and death. Great king, old age will come and destroy you in your prime. Sickness will come and destroy your health. Decay will come and destroy all your splendor. Death will come and destroy your life force. These four will not be pacified or placated by fleeing, by force, by wealth, by substances, mantras, or medicines.

In other words, if the four great firm and swift-moving mountains were to come from the four cardinal directions and crash together, they would pulverize grass, trees, and so forth; they would be difficult to stop, no matter what you did. The four mountains of old age, sickness, decay, and death are just as hard to stop.

THE SECOND REASON: THINKING HOW NOTHING IS BEING ADDED TO YOUR LIFESPAN AND IT IS ALWAYS BEING SUBTRACTED FROM (140)

You will definitely die. Anything that is precipitated by past karma can have no further additions made to it [and this applies to your lifespan]. Each moment you are getting closer and closer to the Lord of Death. [Śhāntideva] says in *Engaging in the Deeds of Bodhisattvas:*

Why should one like me then not die,
If every day and night, without fail,
This life is always getting shorter
And no additions to it come from anywhere.

From the *Sayings of the Buddha:*

Suppose one stretches out a string
And a child follows it bit by bit;
The child will eventually come to its end.
So it is with people's lives.

The Seventh Dalai Lama Kaelzang Gyatso said:

After birth, you don't have the freedom to rest a moment
In the race you run toward Yama, the Lord of Death.
What we call "living" is but a journey on the highway to death.
Unhappy is the mind of the criminal being led to his place of
execution!

In other words, once you are born, you rush even faster than a racehorse to death's state, and get no rest even for the time it takes to draw a few breaths. It is possible the riders in a horserace may get a little rest, or whatever, but the people fated to die do not get even a moment's rest in their course to death: each moment brings them closer to their deaths. From the *Sayings of the Buddha:*

Those up for slaughter
Get closer to their executioner
With every step they take.
So it is with people's lives.

Just as a sheep being led to the slaughter yard gets closer to death with every step it takes, at no time, once we are born, do we deviate from the direction of our death. We have already used up so much of our lifespan, there is little of it left. Further, we use up our breaths, hours, days, months, and years; the day is coming for us to die. The so-called time to go comes suddenly, so we should not be complacent and think, "I will not die." Even when we sleep, we may be relaxed and happy, yet we are still rushing directly toward the Lord of Death.

THE THIRD REASON: THINKING ABOUT HOW YOU WILL DEFINITELY DIE BEFORE GETTING ROUND TO PRACTICING DHARMA (141)

Life is extremely short, and you will in the end meet your death before you can get round to practicing Dharma. Assume you live for sixty years. You sleep the whole night, so half your life is used up. The other thirty years are interrupted by the time you spend eating and so forth. This leaves only five years or so to devote to Dharma practice, even if you spend the whole time in retreat and perform, say, the four-session yoga. At New Year we say, "Let's have a party!" and celebrate. Every month is named after some holiday, such as the Great Prayer Festival; the whole year passes swiftly in a blur of distractions. Gungtang Rinpoche said:

> Perhaps twenty years of being unaware of practice,
> Perhaps twenty years of "Going to, going to" practice,
> Perhaps another ten years of "Never did, never did" practice;
> That's the story of an empty and wasted human life.

In other words, in the beginning as a child you were unaware of Dharma. Later, you may have wanted to practice Dharma and felt, "I must practice, I must practice," yet you did not take on a practice, and did not manage to carry out the Dharma. Then, when you are old, you do nothing but say, "All I can do now is recite prayers for my next rebirth."

Some people are now engrossed in this life and feel, "Going to, going to practice"; many people have already reached the time when they regret not having practiced Dharma. When we see these people, we should see the damage their actions did them; we should have the courage not to attach any importance to the meaningless actions that, every day, leave us no time for Dharma practice. We must practice as much Dharma as we can before Yama, the Lord of Death, shows up on our doorstep. Purchog Ngagwang Jampa said:

> Suppose there is a huge pile of barley standing in the middle of a great plain. The local women can see that a flood is coming from the top of the valley and that it will carry away the pile—yet they remain in their tents. The flood will sweep the pile away before they can take a single grain. Instead, if they themselves work hard the whole time and do not get distracted and carry off as much as they can, they may in the end take away a quarter or even a half of the pile. If they are lucky, they may even take the lot and thus fulfill their great needs. Similarly, we must practice as much as we can of the path of the three scopes before death comes.

Think over these three reasons and you will feel, "I am definitely going to die"; then you will decide you must practice Dharma.

THE SECOND ROOT: THINKING ABOUT THE UNCERTAINTY OF WHEN YOU WILL DIE (142)

There are three reasons for this.

THE FIRST REASON: IN GENERAL THE LIFESPAN OF PEOPLE FROM THE SOUTHERN CONTINENT IS NOT FIXED, AND THIS IS ESPECIALLY SO FOR LIFESPANS DURING THESE DEGENERATE TIMES (143)

If you could be certain when you will die, you would first carry out your worldly work—subduing your enemies, protecting your dear ones, and so forth. Then, while living happily, you could practice Dharma before dying. But you cannot be certain, so it is vital to think about the uncertainty aspect of when you will die. The *Treasury of Metaphysics* says:

> The inhabitants of Kuru [live] a thousand years; On two [of the other continents the lives] decrease by half and half again.

In other words, on most of the other continents the lifespans of the inhabitants are fixed.

> Here [the lifespan] is not fixed: At first it is immeasurable, and it ends up being ten years.

It is said that, in the beginning, the inhabitants of the Southern Continent had lifespans so long that they could not be measured in years; eventually their lives will last only ten years. Thus, in general, the lifespans of the inhabitants of the Southern Continent are not fixed, and this is especially true during degenerate times.

Generally we don't think, "I will never die"; but until we are dying, we always have the thought, "I will die, but not this year." There may be reasons for feeling this way. Some of you may think, "I will not die yet, because I am young." But being young is of no help. The order in which death strikes is not according to age: many children die young, and their parents have to bury them. Also, many people younger than you have already died. Some even die as soon as they are born.

Some think, "I will not die, because I am not ill." Even this is not definite. Patients may be confined to their beds and yet not die, while many healthy people die sudden deaths. Some people die in the middle of a meal, without ever having had the slightest premonition that they would die before they had finished eating. Some people present at large ceremonies [in a monastery] went to the temple on their own two feet, only to be carried out by others as corpses on a stretcher. Many government officials draw up grand political programs but never get round to carrying them out, because they die before completing their work. In many saints' collected works, the notation "left unfinished" appears: they were able to compose only the title along with some fragments of verses and died before finishing.

From among the relatives and friends who surround us in our valley, we can say that so-and-so has died, but we do not think, "This will also happen to me." We treat it merely as an object of curiosity. We even hear people say, "He has a nice saffron robe. Here's hoping I get it next!"

Such a death will definitely strike you down at some point, though when is uncertain. As they say:

> There is no telling which will come first:
> Tomorrow or your next rebirth.
> Do not put effort into tomorrow's plans;
> It is right to work hard for your next life.

From the *Sayings of the Buddha:*

Some of the many people you see in the morning,
You will not see in the evening.
Some of the many people you see in the evening,
You will not see in the morning...

How can you be so sure that you will not die tomorrow?

We make no preparations for the death we are sure to experience but whose time of coming is uncertain. It is not certain that we will live to an old age. Think that it is definitely a mistake to make a lot of preparations for an enjoyable old age.

If you cannot think about death coming today, tomorrow, or the next day, at least you must think how death can strike anyone between now and next year. You cannot be certain which of the people sitting here will die first—someone sitting in the front row, or in the middle, or at the back.

You will not get a message, and so on, warning you, "Now get ready to die." Death will strike suddenly one day, and you will just have to leave whatever you are doing. Even simple monks have to stop drinking butter tea, eating barley flour or noodles, and go to their next life: this shows how uncertain is the time of leaving to the next life.

Grasping at permanence tricks you into thinking you have many years left, but the day will come: "Now get ready to die." People who will die from illness today are still thinking, "I will not die today." Some, when they reach an astrologically unfavorable year, might remember death and wonder, "Will I die this year?" But even if you have no such year, there is no year from your first to your hundredth when you can say, "I will not die this year." Suppose you are twenty-eight. You must think, "I may die this year. So-and-so and such-and-such died at this age."

We might say, "I swear that I will definitely not die this year," but we cannot make such an oath—and none could be more dubious.

We are not analytical and might get led astray when we live in big towns or communities. Death and impermanence are [therefore practical subjects for meditation because they are] not difficult to understand like selflessness. They are things we can see for ourselves; they are tangible.

My own precious guru, my refuge and protector, said:

Pray that if you don't die in a month or two, you may achieve some benefit for your next rebirths; and if you don't die in a year or two, may you achieve your eternal hope for all your rebirths!

You must think this section over in the way stated, quotations and all.

THE SECOND REASON: WHEN YOU WILL DIE IS UNCERTAIN BECAUSE THERE ARE MANY FACTORS CONTRIBUTING TOWARD YOUR DEATH AND FEW TOWARD YOUR LIFE (144)

We are now protected by our past prayers, our merits, and the buddhas' compassion. There are besides a great many contributory factors toward our deaths. Like flies buzzing around rotten meat, 80,000 different types of hindering spirits and factors contributing to death surround us. They wonder, "When can we eat you? When can we take your breath from you?" The 404 types of disease swarm around us like a fog. The 360 types of evil spirits, the 15 great evil spirits who attack children, the 360 devouring spirits, and so forth, are greedy for our lives.

You do not just have these external contributory factors. If you put four snakes into a container, the strongest snake will eat the rest; if the humors, such as wind, bile, and phlegm, or the four elements, get a little out of balance, this can be a contributory factor toward you losing your life.

> Many more factors contribute to your death.
> Very few contribute to your life—
> And even these all contribute to your death.
> Therefore, always practice Dharma.

Not only are there many internal and external contributory factors to death, but many of the factors contributing to life may also contribute to death. Houses can collapse, boats can break up or overturn, horses can buck and trample you, your friends can trick you, food can disagree with you, and so on. Many things can act as contributory factors toward death.

Our life force is like a butterlamp in a draft; as Nāgārjuna says:

> We live surrounded by the factors of the Lord of Death
> Like an oil lamp in a draft.

THE THIRD REASON: WHEN YOU WILL DIE IS UNCERTAIN BECAUSE THE BODY IS EXTREMELY FRAGILE (145)

If our bodies were firm and hard,[51] then even though there were many things contributing toward death and few toward life, there would be no problem. But our bodies are like bubbles on water: we do not need major contributory factors in order to die; we can die merely from being pricked by a thorn. Anyway, even if our bodies were firm and hard-wearing, it wouldn't help; Nāgārjuna's *Letter* says:

> The earth, Mount Meru, the oceans,
> And seven suns will burn, and all saṃsāric beings
> Turn to ashes—nothing will remain.
> What need I then say about
> So-very-fragile man and such…
>
> Much can harm this life, more impermanent
> Than bubbles on water blown by the wind.
> How amazing that we wake up breathing
> After we have gone to sleep!

In other words, when you go to sleep, the inhalation and exhalation of your coarse breathing is suppressed, and the subtle wind element can move freely in your nostrils; how amazing that you do not die when you resume your breathing of the coarse wind element.

Think about this: when you will die is uncertain. This is like being certain that an enemy is coming to kill you but not knowing when—that from today on you will try to stop him. Then you should feel that you must practice Dharma now. If you want to practice Dharma but instead have some work that will last this year or the next, and you think, "I will practice Dharma after I finish the work," you are deceiving yourself. Gungtang Rinpoche said:

> "It seems this work will only take a month, or year;
> When it's finished,
> Then I will practice pure Dharma."
> This thought is the demon that tricks everybody.

We feel, "I will practice Dharma after I've finished this or that project," [but]

> Unfinished work is like the old man's moustache:
> The more it's cut, the more it grows.

In other words, you never have time to finish one project; then, another project comes and so you need to get *that* done. Then there will be another, and you will think, "I'll just finish this." Worldly work is like a river: it never *stops.* As Gungtang Rinpoche said:

> The great risk is: before the tomorrow when
> You were going to practice Dharma comes,
> The time for you to die will come today.
> So do not let your head be turned;
> If you would practice Dharma, do it from today.

If you put things off and say, "When this is finished I will practice Dharma," or "I will practice Dharma tomorrow," the work will never finish, but the day when you are ready to die will surely strike like lightning.

Think over the three reasons why it is uncertain when you will die, and right away you will abandon worldly work and decide to waste no time in practicing Dharma. But there is no need for students [in monasteries] to interrupt their studies or group debating practice and go off to some mountain cave: instead you must convert such Dharma you do now into [real] Dharma. Suppose formerly you only recited the words of texts; you may have recited the verse "Until enlightenment, I take refuge in Buddha, Dharma, and the Supreme Assembly…" thousands of times, but check if you have properly thought over the verse even once: you will see that you have rarely done so.

No matter what efforts you put into business, farming, and so forth, they will never turn into Dharma; but those of us who are ordained must convert what we do into Dharma. It's a pity if we don't normally practice Dharma; it's no pity if we merely do not know facts.

THE THIRD ROOT: THINKING OF HOW NOTHING CAN HELP YOU WHEN YOU DIE EXCEPT DHARMA (146)

THE FIRST REASON: WEALTH CANNOT HELP YOU (147)

You may be like Brahmā, Indra, or a universal emperor, for instance, but when you die you will not take a single servant with you; you will not be free to take even a single possession with you—these are no help at such a time. You may be the most powerful king, ruling every country, but when death comes you will not be able to take even a grain of barley with you. If you are a beggar, you will not be allowed even your walking stick. "The king will leave behind his trappings; the beggar will leave behind his stick." The *Living Tree Sūtra* says:

One may have enough food for a hundred years,
But come death's morning, one goes hungry;
One may have enough clothes for a hundred years,
But come death's morning, one goes naked.

From *Engaging in the Deeds of Bodhisattvas:*

I must leave everything;
Yet I do not understand this
And sin in various ways
For dear ones and those not [so] dear…

When born, you are born alone,
When you die, you are just as alone.
What can your meddlesome friends do
If they won't take on another share of suffering?

A man once carved a great rock into a cube. Another person asked him what he was going to do with it. "Oh nothing," he replied, "I'm just going to leave it behind." So too will you leave behind all the wealth and all the possessions you have acquired in this rebirth.

THE SECOND REASON: FRIENDS AND RELATIVES CANNOT HELP YOU (148)

A dying man may be surrounded by servants, disciples, and his most intimate friends, some of them holding his arms and some holding his legs, but they cannot help him from dying. He cannot take a single one of them with him; he will travel the perilous road of the bardo alone. Mitrayogi, a great adept, said:

Your majesty! No matter how wealthy you may be,
When you depart and go to another world,
Like a man attacked by enemies in the desert:
You will be alone, without your sons, or your concubines…

From *Engaging in the Deeds of Bodhisattvas:*

> When you are caught by Yama's messengers,
> What help are your dear ones? What help are your friends?

As the Paṇchen Lama Lozang Yeshe said:

> You will be forever separated from your loving, mournful friends…

Some people now are sure to die in the middle of the coming winter; then how many of their plans for next year will they carry out?

If we were now going to India, China, or somewhere else, we would treat it as something most important. We would prepare our luggage, and travel with horses, mules, and servants. But when we make the great move to our next rebirth, we will be without friends, alone, and unable to take even one hair of our possessions.

THE THIRD REASON: EVEN YOUR BODY CANNOT HELP YOU (149)

When you die, it will be of no help if all the mountains turn to gold and all become family. Quite apart from your wealth, possessions, and relatives, you will have to leave behind your body—the thing you call "my body," which was born from the womb with you, which you protected from hunger and cold, which you wouldn't even dare prick with a thorn, and which you guarded and cherished like a wish-granting gem. As the Paṇchen Lama Choekyi Gyaeltsaen said: "This body you so cherished and protected will prove deceptive when you most need it." In other words, think about how you will be completely separated from even this body that you have so cherished and protected.

Having thought over these three reasons, it does not help to stay afraid and depressed. As Gungtang Rinpoche Taenpai Droenme said:

> Dharma is the guide to the undeceiving path;
> Dharma supplies you for the long track;
> Dharma is your captain on the difficult journey;
> From this moment practice Dharma with your three doors.

Je Milarepa said:

> Ange Nyama Paeldarbum!
> Listen, lady of wealth, you who have faith:
> Have you enough supplies
> For the long road of future lives after this one?
> If you do not have enough supplies at hand,
> Practice generosity—that will be your supply…
>
> Ange Nyama Paeldarbum!
> Have you enough companions
> To face the great terrors in future lives after this one?
> If you do not have enough companions at hand,
> Practice divine Dharma—that will be your companion.

In other words, Dharma is your guide, captain, and provisions for your journey when you die. If you have not practiced Dharma, think on how poor your death will be: no different from that of an old stray dog in some alley.

People going to visit their homeland do not make preparations for staying [where they already are]: they put all their energies into packing their luggage and nothing else. You too must also decide to practice the Dharma only, something untarnished by the obscurations of this life.

MEDITATION ON THE ASPECTS OF DEATH (150)

This is an instruction from my precious guru. Although it mainly centers on how to pursue meditations on a *practical teaching* [see Day 1], it is said to be good to contemplate in this way.

You should recall the things said in either the text *Compassionate Refuge* or Paṇchen Lama Lozang Choekyi Gyaeltsaen's *Petitions Made to be Freed from the Perilous Road of the Bardo.*

Examine just what will happen when you die. Then, when you are approaching death, as it says in [the Paṇchen Lama's] *Petitions for the Bardo:*

> When the doctor gives me up and rituals no longer work,
> When friends have given up hope for my life,

When anything I do is futile,
May I be blessed to remember my guru's instructions.

In other words, the sickness gets worse despite proper medical treatment or rituals; the things the doctor tells you are not the things he is telling everyone else; your relatives and friends tell you only nice things to your face but get together in secret behind your back and agree that you will die; you display various nasty internal and external symptoms—your body heat dissipates, your breathing is labored, your nose becomes constricted, your lips are contorted, your complexion is pallid, and so on. You regret your past sins but have not sufficiently expiated them, or refrained from repeating them, or practiced virtue purely. Your fatal illness causes you suffering, and the signs of the progressive dissolution of the elements appear. Diverse terrifying hallucinations are blocking the immediate appearances of your present life. Your [bodily] aggregates are rolled up in a blanket, put in a corner of your room, and hidden behind a curtain. People light a cheap butterlamp for you. If you are a lama or the like, they will dress you in your initiation costume to make you look presentable.

You may now work hard to have a good house or warm, soft clothes and carpets, but when you die, your body will be folded in three, trussed up with a leather strap, left on the bare earth or rocks, and so on. At present you may enjoy the most delicious food, but in the future you will have to live on the smell of burnt offerings made for the dead. At present you may be called such nice things as "Geshe," "Sir," or "Venerable monk"; in the future, a time will come when your body will be called "corpse," and you will be called "the late Mister So-and-so." Whenever you lamas see your initiation costume, it should remind you that when you die, your remains will be decked out in it. When we see our blanket, it should remind us that our corpse will be wrapped in it. This is how much remembrance we need. Je Milarepa said: "The terrifying thing called *corpse* now lives in the channels of the yogi's body." This is what the body is indeed.

After death you will go to the bardo, where you will be unimaginably frightened and will have hallucinations of duststorms and firestorms, of being buried under avalanches or mounds of earth, of being surrounded by whirling firebrands, of being swept away by water or winds, and so forth.

Some lamas claim to give [dead people's consciousnesses] a sound introduction to the bardo and perform the introduction ritual next to the corpse's head, yet the time to give a true introduction to the bardo is now; it is more beneficial to do this before one dies. We can always be sure of enjoying food and drink, but when we are dying we won't even have the chance to say, "Help me sit up." How certain that we will not practice Dharma at such a time, since we do not practice even now, when we are alive and well. All the same, these rituals [of introducing the corpse's consciousness to the bardo] may be slightly helpful, because the blessings of the buddhas are inconceivable.

A source for the meditations on the aspects of death is *Engaging in the Deeds of Bodhisattvas:*

> Go into charnel grounds:
> Other people's skeletons and my own body
> Are subject to decay.
> When will I see that they are the same?

When someone dies and his bones are scattered in a charnel ground, consider that his bones are no different from your own—in time you will judge them to be the same. "The corpses in the charnel ground were originally like your body: a human being used to cherish them." The great adepts of India used to hold human thighbones or skulls; they did not do this because they wanted to look terrifying or threatening. It was to increase their awareness of the aspects of death. Even a skullcup was once in a person's head; he so cherished his head that even when his fingernail slightly scratched it, he would say, "Ouch"!

If you are an ordinary monk, you will leave your monk's cell empty when you die, and someone else will move in, saying, "Oh, he died that number of days ago."

Someone else will wear your saffron robes and say, "They used to be so-and-so's. I bought them." Likewise, a time will definitely come when other people will buy the furniture, clothes, and so on, that you cannot use any more, and use them. This is why the Seventh Dalai Lama Kaelzang Gyatso said: "In time I will lose even these possessions: I am pleased with these borrowed gems." In other words, they are things on loan to you for just a short time.

If you cannot bring yourself to think about your own death, go and witness someone else dying; it is impossible that you will not recall this instruction at such a time.

Unless we have never thought about this, how could we not be afraid when we see a strap [used to bind corpses]? This is the amount of fear we need to have. We may die before we wear out one saffron robe, for example. Think about it: our lives are extremely short.

These things are discussed in the *Instruction Given to the King Sūtra.* [Genduen Taenzin Gyatso's] *Red Hat* lamrim discusses how meditation on impermanence can be an antidote to getting fat at a time when you have access to magnificent clothes, food, and so forth. Whenever you see your possessions, that is, your clothes and so forth, always think: "These are only masquerading as my things. There will come a time when other people will divide them up among themselves, and I don't doubt they will say, "These belonged to the dead person." I now cherish my body and look after it, but a time will come when it will turn into what is called a corpse. If I were to see it then, I would be terrified; I would be nauseated if I touched it. It will be tied with a rope, and they will do all manner of things to it." Think how your leftover barley flour will be used in offerings, how the rituals of introduction to the bardo will be performed next to your head, and so on. Some other person will handle your skull, saying, "This is his skull. The quality is not too bad." Such a time is coming, and from now on you ought to do things you will not regret.

The criterion for having developed realization into death and impermanence in your mindstream is if you want to be like Geshe Karag Gomchung [see pp. 269, 300].

Kyabje Pabongka Rinpoche then reviewed this material in moderate detail.

DAY 11

Kyabje Pabongka Rinpoche told us we should adjust our motives:

The *Great Play Sūtra* says:

> The three realms are as impermanent as autumn clouds.
> Beings die and are born: it is like watching a play.
> Beings' lives run like lightning flashes in the sky,
> Or rush on like high mountain waterfalls.

In other words, the three realms—the earth, Mount Meru, and all—are like autumn clouds. Beings are born and die; it is like watching a play, for the characters can change from moment to moment. Our lives do not last long: they are mere flashes of lightning. They undergo cessation from moment to moment, are not stationary, and rush by like high mountain waterfalls. You should therefore think, "I will practice Dharma immediately." The lamrim is the best gateway to the one path followed by all buddhas of the three times. You should therefore attend this discourse on the lamrim so as to achieve buddhahood for the sake of all sentient beings; then you must put it into practice…

He then restated the headings already covered, and reviewed yesterday's material on impermanence.

The section "Developing a Yearning for a Good Rebirth" has a second subdivision:

THINKING ABOUT WHAT SORT OF HAPPINESS OR SUFFERING YOU WILL HAVE IN YOUR NEXT REBIRTH IN EITHER OF THE TWO TYPES OF MIGRATION (151)

The contemplation on the sufferings of the upper realms will come later in the medium scope. I will now discuss the sufferings of the lower realms.

You will surely die, but it is not certain when. After you die, your consciousness does not end: it must definitely take rebirth. There are only two places in which it can take rebirth, the upper or the lower realms. You can assess inferentially to which of these two you will be going. As I have already said, we get divinations and horoscopes made to tell us where we will be reborn next, but these are unnecessary. Buddha has already predicted that we will go to the upper realms if we have been virtuous and to the lower realms if nonvirtuous. From the *Jātaka Tales:*

> Be quite certain: your rebirth to the next world
> Will be happy or unhappy according to virtuous or nonvirtuous karma.
> Therefore abandon sin and adopt virtue.

We examine the happiness and unhappiness of this life a great deal, calling it "thinking about the future." It is nothing of the sort. Be even more farsighted: investigate where you will be reborn next. If you do so, you will see that you cannot escape going to either the upper or the lower realms, and that you are not free to choose which. If we had a choice, who would be in the lower realms? Thus, where you are reborn next depends on karma.

If you have a mixture of karma, some virtuous, some nonvirtuous, the stronger will ripen first. If both types are equally strong, the type you are most familiar with will ripen first. If you are equally familiar with both types, then the type produced earlier will ripen first. Vasubhandu's own commentary to his *Treasury of Metaphysics* says:

> In saṃsāra, ripening through karma,
> From their ripening first [to last]:
> Whatever is heaviest, the nearest,
> The most familiar, and that done earliest.

For us, nonvirtuous karma is the stronger of the two. Our thoughts are normally only of attachment, and so forth. That being so, all the karma produced from these thoughts is nonvirtuous. Even our virtuous actions inadvertently come under the power of nonvirtuous thoughts, and very few of these actions are dedicated toward our future lives.

Take the example of your scolding a disciple. Your motive is extreme anger. So, as the actual deed, you use those words that will hit home. As the final step, you rejoice over what you have done. So the *motive,* the *actual deed,* and the *final step* are all very powerful.

The majority of our sinful actions are similarly most powerful, but our virtuous actions are as follows. There was once a man who used to be distracted by other thoughts whenever he recited the *Hundreds of Gods of Tuṣhita.* He would converse with others while reciting the text many times from start to finish. We also mouth the words of texts, but meanwhile our minds are engrossed in worldly matters. What little virtue we have is destroyed by anger or wrong views. Even our smallest nonvirtues double in size every passing day. Further, in past lives, when reborn as insects, creatures, sea monsters, ferocious beasts of prey, and so forth, we committed many enormous sins. These, in addition to the above-mentioned sins we have committed in this life, constitute the vast number of very powerful sins we have accumulated. We are not capable of remedying all these before our deaths by expiating them and by refraining from repeating them. We know this is beyond our present capabilities. This proves by direct valid cognition that we are more familiar with nonvirtue than with virtue; the only possibility is that we shall go to the lower realms in our next rebirth.

We cannot be confident of not going to the lower realms until we have achieved the patience level of the path of preparation. They say that even mahātma bodhisattvas have been reborn there.

Suppose you go to sleep tonight as a monk in your nice room on your soft bed; you then die because of some sudden, unfortunate occurrence. By the time you would normally have awoken the next morning, you may already have arrived at a place where all the hills and valleys are filled with fire. What would you do then?

You will not be sufficiently moved to develop renunciation if you simply meditate on how you may be born in the lower realms in the same way that you stare at some object out of curiosity. As Nāgārjuna said: "Recollect the great heat or cold of the hells as if you had spent a day there." That is, you should meditate to produce experience of having been born in this or that lower realm—rather like the generation-stage meditations on a tutelary deity. You must then be terrified.

We hold in high regard those meditations on having the divine body of a tutelary deity, but it would be much more beneficial in the beginning to meditate for a while on having a hell body. The sufferings of the hot hells will facilitate our first mental transformation and will produce our first development of renunciation. This is a wholesome result. We will also become sad; sadness has great qualities, it gets rid of arrogant pride, and so on. As Śhāntideva said:

> The good quality of suffering is that
> It removes arrogance through sorrow.
> One develops compassion for the beings in saṃsāra,
> Avoids sin, and rejoices in virtue.

It is easier for us to develop renunciation and compassion while in this optimum rebirth as a human being. For this reason we must [carry out] their primary cause, meditation on suffering.

The meditation on the suffering of the lower realms has three sections: thinking about the sufferings of (1) the hells; (2) the hungry ghosts; (3) the animals.

THINKING ABOUT THE SUFFERINGS OF THE HELLS (152)

This has four subheadings.

THINKING ABOUT THE SUFFERINGS OF SENTIENT BEINGS IN THE GREAT, OR HOT, HELLS (153)

The hot hells are located as follows. The Hell of Continual Resurrection is thirty-two thousand yojanas under Bodhgaya in India. The other hot hells are below this hell, with four thousand yojanas between each of them. All the ground and all the mountains in these hells are composed entirely of red-hot, intense burning iron; the ground, like that in the human realms, is not at all flat, not at all like the palm of your hand.

When you are about to be born into the hot hells, as Gungtang Rinpoche says:

> Human life is impermanent, a short bout of sleep
> Crowded with meaningless dreams—some happy, some sad.
> When you suddenly awaken to a life
> In the pit of the lower realms, what will you do?

That is, at the point of death you have hallucinations of being cold, so you develop a craving for heat, which activates karma leading to rebirth in the hot hells. You die; this is like falling asleep. You experience the bardo as you would a dream. Then you suddenly find yourself in the hot hells, which is like waking up.

Hellfire is seven times hotter than fire in the human realms. Let us compare these two types of fire. Human fire is so cold compared to hellfire that it is like water cooled by Gośhīrṣha sandalwood.[52]

Maudgalyāyana once carried a small ember from the hells to the human realm and placed it on the ocean shore. All human beings were driven mad by the heat, and they could not bear to have it left where it was. If you were born in the midst of such fire, it would be bad enough if your body were so small that it was immediately consumed by the fire. But your body is huge, as large as a mountain range. This would still be bad enough if the soles of your feet were as calloused as the skin on the feet of some of us. This doesn't happen: your body is like the body of a child still suckling [at its mother's breast].

So the sufferings of the hot hells in general are quite unbearable: the suffering of having a body—the thing being burnt—that is enormous; the suffering of having flesh with as little tolerance [to pain] as a newborn child's; the suffering that the thing doing the burning, the fire, is extremely hot; and so on. There are eight such hot hells:

THE HELL OF CONTINUAL RESURRECTION (154)

There are no hell guards here. People born in this hell are sentient beings who have taken rebirth here under the power of evil karma. When these sentient beings see others, they immediately get angry. Anything they pick up turns into a weapon. They keep hacking each other to pieces; all faint and collapse on the ground. Then a voice from the sky tells them, "You will now be revived." A cool wind strikes their bodies, a contributary factor for their scattered flesh and bones to come together. Their bodies heal and become as they were before. Then they do the same thing again. Every day they fall into these death faints; every day they have many hundreds of these deaths, and they are revived many hundreds of times. We must develop insight into what it would be like to be born there now, to be hacked by weapons, to faint, to be revived, and so forth. In this life we are afraid to be stabbed by a small knife and die the once—and we still suffer inconceivable terror and pain. In this hell we would die many times each day and would experience this [terror and pain] each time, and our lifespans there would also be very long: our former human lives would bear no comparison. Nāgārjuna said in his *Letter:*

> The suffering of being violently jabbed
> Three hundred times by a spear in a single day
> Cannot compare to the least suffering in hell,
> Cannot rival it, cannot come anywhere near it.

THE BLACK LINE HELL (155)

From this hell downward there are guards, such as "Elephant-headed Ava" and "Pig-headed Yakṣha." These labor as hell guards, are as huge as mountains, have bloodshot eyes, and are horrifying; they shout words like "hit" and "kill." [In your meditations] you should experience the terror that they are going to destroy your body. The hell guards seize you and lay you supine on the burning iron ground; they make many weals on your huge body with ropes of burning iron that leave black marks. Some of the guards saw along these as a carpenter would saw a piece of wood. Other guards chop along the lines with axes; others use hatchets. After you have been dismembered in these ways, the bits of flesh and drops of blood that fall on the burning iron ground surface are still connected to your consciousness, and they add to the suffering you experience.

The causes for being born in this hell are committing the ten nonvirtues, horsewhipping people, and so forth.

THE ASSEMBLE-AND-BE-CRUSHED HELL (156)

Rebirth here is usually the [karmic] ripening of killing. Two mountains resembling, say, goats' or rams' heads race together, and you are crushed between them; there is no avenue of escape. The two mountains separate, and your body regenerates to its former state. The process is repeated again and again. Some beings are ground to powder between grindstones; some are pounded with pestles like sesame seeds; some are squeezed in iron vices. You could be crushed, or whatever, between many different instruments: these take the form of whatever killing instrument you used in the past. Suppose you kill a louse between your fingernails. Later in hell you will be killed by being crushed between two mountains that look like fingernails.

THE HELL OF LAMENTATION (157)

You are placed inside a house of burning iron. It has no doors, and it is all on fire, inside and out. You suffer, thinking, "I will not find any means of escape." Your great mental suffering makes you wail.

THE HELL OF GREAT LAMENTATION (158)

You are placed in an iron house, which is contained within another, each similar to the one above. Your suffering is also twice as great. You think, "I may escape from one of these iron houses but not from the other," and so you suffer.

Committing the ten nonvirtues, or recklessly drinking alcohol, can cause rebirth in these hells. A sūtra tells us much the same thing:

> Drink alcohol and you'll be born in a place of lamentation.
> People who serve [drink] are born in its surrounding hell.

THE HOT HELL (159)

You are impaled on a flaming iron skewer that runs through your anus and emerges out of the top of your head; all your insides burn, and you burn through roaring flames issuing from your mouth, eyes, and so forth. You are cooked in a huge copper cauldron of boiling water. Then your bones are reassembled, your body is restored to its former condition, and you are cooked all over again.

THE EXTREMELY HOT HELL (160)

This is twice as hot as the previous hell. Your flesh, muscles, and insides all cook and come off the bone. When only your bones remain, you are reassembled and restored to your former state. Some beings are stretched longer, and their bodies flattened between plates of burning iron. Burning-iron wire is wrapped around the bodies of some beings; their flesh and bones ooze out like dough under pressure. Some are impaled on three-pronged skewers of burning iron that run through their anuses and out of the top of their heads; their tongues are stretched till they are many yojanas long, then furrows are made in them by ploughs and so forth. Some beings are held between two pieces of burning iron resembling bookcovers, and their bodies are squashed like books. There are, thus, very many ways to experience suffering.

Kyabje Pabongka Rinpoche told a story of how Kokalika, one of Devadatta's circle, was born in this hell.

THE HELL WITHOUT RESPITE (161)

In this hell there is no chance to rest, and so the suffering here is greater than in all the above hot hells. When we burn rocks or iron in a fire, they become indistinguishable from the fire. The bodies of beings born in this hell are similarly indistinguishable from the fire. One can tell that there are sentient beings in this hell only by the pathetic sounds they make. They are burned by eleven fires: the fires in the four cardinal points of the compass, the four in the subpoints, the fires in the zenith and nadir, and the fire within their own bodies. They are like the charred wick in an offering lamp. Their suffering is limitless. From Nāgārjuna's *Letter:*

> Among all happiness,
> The elimination of craving is the lord of happinesses.
> And so, among all suffering,
> The suffering of the Hell Without Respite is the most intolerable.

In other words, the Hell Without Respite contains more suffering than the total suffering of all the rest of the three realms—including the Extremely Hot Hell.

Though the hells contain these sufferings, we think, "I shall not be reborn there." But we can never be sure of not being reborn in these hells as soon as we leave this life. We cannot be confident of not going to the lower realms. We have accumulated many causes for definitely being born

CHARNEL GROUNDS (SEE P. 320)

in hell; these causes are very powerful and have in no way degenerated. The worst cases of our committing any one of the ten nonvirtues will cause our rebirth in hell; each medium instance could cause our rebirth as hungry ghosts; and each of the least, rebirth as animals. They say we will be reborn in the Hell of Continual Resurrection because of committing minor misdeeds against the pratimokṣha vows and not caring, and in the Hell Without Respite because of not caring whether we break major pratimokṣha vows. So we must beware. We have in our mindstreams many extremely grave misdeeds: breaking minor vows and misdeeds against the pratimokṣha and tantric vows, getting angry at bodhisattvas, being disrespectful to gurus, and so forth. If we have broken a root tantric vow, we will be reborn in the Hell Without Respite for a number of eons equal to the moments that elasped before we restored the vow by confessing [the sin] and renewing [the vow]. We did not care in the past when we broke minor pratimokṣha vows, we have transgressed the rules, and have already accumulated the karma for being reborn in each of the eight hot hells in turn.

Once reborn there, we must experience suffering until the results of the evil karma run out, for we will not be able to detach our consciousnesses from our bodies. Nāgārjuna's *Letter* tells us:

> Such sufferings are utterly intolerable.
> One will experience them billions of times;
> So long as the nonvirtue has not run out,
> One will not stop living that life.

The lifespans in the eight hot hells are also very long. The shortest lifespans are those of beings in the Hell of Continual Resurrection. Fifty of our human years constitute one day for the gods in the Realm of the Four Mahārājas; thirty of these days are reckoned to be one of their months; twelve of these months, one of their years. Five hundred of these years make a lifetime for a being in the Realm of the Four Mahārājas, yet this is only a day in the Hell of Continual Resurrection. Thirty of these days are reckoned to be a month in this hell; twelve such months make a year. A lifetime in the Hell of Continual Resurrection is five hundred of these years—one could say this is 1.62 trillion human years. The old woodblock edition of *Mañjuśhrī's Own Words* states that it is 60 billion years, but this is a printer's error. You should consult either the Meru Monastery woodblock masters of this text or lamrims of the Southern Lineage.

It might seem strange to say these hot hells are so many yojanas away, but no great distance lies between you and the lower realms—only the fact that you still breathe. Think about it closely: you can't be sure you won't have gone to these hells by next year, or even by tomorrow. If you go to these hells, what will you do?

As it is, we cannot bear having our bodies burnt by a little fire or pricked by a needle. How then could we bear it when being born in these hells? As the Kadampas of the past have said, it is as if only one of our feet stands in the human realm; we have already put the other on the lip of a hell cauldron; we have already created the causes for being born in hell.

Once born in the lower realms, it is impossible to get free of them or to find any refuge. Thus, before being reborn there, we must work hard while we still have a little of our lifespan left. If we do not gain the best thing, buddhahood, or the next best, becoming an adept or a siddha, we should at least work hard at some way of preventing ourselves from being born in the lower realms, by expiating our sins and so forth.

THE SURROUNDING HELLS (162)

Round the outside of the hot hells, like the iron fence [that encircles this world system], are four surrounding hells: the Fiery Trench, the Swamp of Putrid Corpses, the Plain of Razor-sharp Knives, and the Uncrossable Torrent.

The time comes when the karma of the beings born in the hot hells weakens; these beings then escape the hot hells and go to the surrounding hells. There are also beings who are born straight into these surrounding hells.

When some of the beings are ready to escape from the hot hells, they get the idea of running away; they leave by the gates of the hot hells and arrive at the Fiery Trench. Their legs burn up to their knees, and as they pull their legs out of the trench, they heal. The legs get burnt this way every time they take a step. They spend many hundreds of thousands of years crossing the Fiery Trench, being continually tormented by this great suffering, hoping to escape from it.

They finally escape the Trench but come upon the Swamp of Putrid Corpses. They sink into it up to their necks and writhe about; many worms with sharp birdlike beaks penetrate their bodies and eat them, leaving their bodies like sieves.

The beings spend many hundreds of thousands of years crossing the swamp, hoping they will escape from this too. They reach the Plain of Razor-sharp Knives. This plain is completely full of sharp iron knives whose tips point upward. They long experience the suffering of the knives penetrating and cutting up their legs. Eventually they escape the plain and come to a forest where the trees have swords for leaves. Mistaking these for living trees, they walk under them. The sword-leaves cut into their bodies, which then heal and are cut again. Such are the sufferings they experience. When the beings emerge from the forest, they come upon the "Śhālmala" tree trunk, which has many sharp iron blades. The beings hear the cries of family and friends, the beloved people who were most dear to them, coming from the top of the Śhālmala. But as they scale it, the tips of the iron blades point downward, penetrating their bodies. Undergoing these sufferings, they make their way up. When they get to the top, terrifying birds pluck out and eat their eyes and brains. Then the cries come from below, and the beings climb down; the iron blades point upward and penetrate their bodies. When they reach the bottom, dogs and other predators eat them from the feet up. The beings experience the suffering of going up and down like this until their karma runs out.

They say that these three different types of assaults from weapons should be counted as the one surrounding hell.

When the beings get free of these, they arrive at the Uncrossable Torrent. The moving water is mixed with fire; it burns and cooks their bodies as boiling water cooks peas. They must experience this suffering for a long time.

We are all set to be reborn in the hot hells. It is vital, therefore, to work hard henceforth at the means to not be born there—by modifying our behavior.

THINKING ABOUT THE SUFFERINGS OF THE COLD HELLS (163)

The cold hells are on a level with the hot hells and lie to the north, which is why this land of ours is so very cold. The cold hells are separated from each other vertically by two thousand yojanas. You may be wondering, "In that case, the cold hells could not be on a level with the hot hells because the hot hells are separated from each other vertically by four thousand yojanas." There may be four thousand yojanas between each ground surface of the hot hells, but each of the cold hells has snow-covered mountains that are two thousand yojanas high, so the cold hells are in fact level with the hot hells.

When about to be born there, you desire cold bodily sensations at the point of death; this activates the karma to be reborn in the cold hells. You experience the bardo as if it were a dream; you are then reborn in the cold hells, which is like waking up. There are snow-covered mountains in these places, each many yojanas high. There is no light from sun, moon, fires, and so forth. It is so dark that you cannot see the movements of your own arms. The ground below is a glacier; a blizzard rages on high; between these two, a cold wind blows. There is no means of keeping warm—no fire, no sun, no clothes, nothing.

There are eight such cold hells, each one progressively colder. There is the Hell of Blisters, where you develop blisters on the body. The Hell of Burst Blisters is even colder: here the blisters burst, dripping blood and lymph. The next hell is even colder: the body stiffens rock hard, you can't move, and all you can ever say is "Brrr."[53] In the next hell, which is even colder, you can't even say this, you can only make the faint sound "Hue" from the back of your throat. In the next hell, you can't even make this sound; the mouth is tightly closed, the teeth clenched. The next hell is even colder; your body is as stiff as a corpse, turns blue in color, and makes a cracking sound; it cracks like a blue lotus. The next is even colder; your flesh cracks like red lotuses. In the next, your flesh develops a hundred or a thousand times more lotuslike cracks. In the Brrr Hell and the hells below it, the bodies of the hell beings dot the ice field and the snow-covered mountains like the jeweled studs that decorate stūpas; the bodies are so frozen that they can't move. Chandragomin's *Letter to a Disciple* says:

> A wind that has no equal seeps into their very bones.
> Their emaciated bodies shiver and are bent into a crouch.
> Insects grown from hundreds of burst blisters feed on them,
> And fat, lymph, and marrow drip out.

That is, many flies with poisonous beaks gather round the lymph dripping from the cracks in the hell beings' bodies and they attack them. Even the drops of blood falling on the ground are still connected to the beings' consciousnesses. They experience the suffering of the drops freezing and cracking. And, in addition, the beings experience such sufferings as being tormented by various infectious diseases.

The *Jātaka Tales* mentions the causes for being born in these hells:

> Holders of nihilistic views will, in all their future lives,
> Dwell in these places of darkness and cold winds.
> They will contract diseases that rot their very bones;
> What good then lies in my dabbling in these?

In other words, the cause is such things as holding wrong, nihilistic views, for example, the view that the law of cause and effect does not exist.

We have accumulated many causes for being born in these hells, and they have not degenerated since. These causes are stealing other people's clothes, removing covers from statues, or throwing sentient beings such as lice out into the freezing cold.

The lifespans of beings in the cold hells are as follows. Though Asaṅga's *Śhrāvaka Levels* states that these sentient beings have lifespans half as long as those born in the great [or hot] hells, [Vasubhandu's] *Treasury of Metaphysics* says:

> Emptying a bin of sesame
> By taking out a seed once every hundred years
> Gives the lifespan in the Hell of Blisters.
> The other lifespans increase twentyfold each.

In other words, the lifespan is as long as it takes to completely empty a bin holding eighty Magadha standard bushels of sesame by throwing out one sesame seed every hundred years. One eightieth of a bushel holds about fifteen thousand sesame seeds [and so it would take 9.6 trillion years to empty the bin]. This is the lifespan of beings in the first of the cold hells, the Hell of Blisters. In the hells below this it increases twenty times each.

THINKING ABOUT THE SUFFERINGS OF THE OCCASIONAL HELLS (164)

These hells are in the human realms, on the ocean shore, and so forth.

At one time some merchants invited Ārya Saṅgharakṣhita to accompany them to an island. He straggled behind the others and walked to the ocean shore, where there was a beautiful temple. The five hundred members of the Saṅgha there invited him inside. The monks quarreled at noon, but when noon passed everything returned to normal. He asked for the cause and was told that it was the result of their not being friendly to each other at the noonday meal and fighting in the past when the teachings of Buddha Kāśhyapa were still in existence. The Ārya also saw hell beings in the form of walls, pillars, pestles, ropes, brooms, water pipes, and cooking pots. Later, when the Ārya returned from his journey, he asked Śhākyamuni about all this. We have already dealt with Buddha's reply concerning the pillar-like beings in the section on the preparatory rites [Day 4, p. 140]. The pestle-like creature, however, had been a monk in the time of Buddha Kāśhyapa's teachings and had lost his temper and said to a novice, "You ought to be pounded with a pestle." The monk had become the pestle-like creature as a result of these insulting words.

Kyabje Pabongka Rinpoche told how these beings had been experiencing these things from the time of the teachings of Buddha Kāśhyapa till the present.

Once there was a ship's captain named Koṭikarṇa who had been born with an earring set with a gem worth ten million gold pieces. Captain Koṭikarṇa had sailed away to obtain jewels. He fell asleep by the ocean shore, and the other merchants went on without him. He awoke to find that a strong wind had erased the path, and even his pack animal, a donkey, could not pick up the scent. Koṭikarṇa wandered around, unable to find the path. There was a house like a palace, and in it a man surrounded by four goddesses. The captain saw that at night the man had such bliss, it was like that of the gods. But by day, the house became burning iron licked by fire, the women turned into four ferocious dogs, the man fell down on his face, and the dogs ate his flesh bit by bit. Then, after the sun had gone down, things reverted to their former state. He asked the man what the cause was. The man said he used to be a butcher in the town of Sthirā, but on the advice of Ārya Kātyāyana he had taken vows not to kill at night. He had not been able to take these vows for the daytime, and this was the result. The man said he had a son in Sthirā who was a butcher. Koṭikarṇa was to give the son a message: "You should not kill; when you give alms to Ārya Kātyāyana you should dedicate the root virtues to me." As proof, the man told Koṭikarṇa he had hidden a pot of gold in the place [in his son's house] where the swords were kept.

Koṭikarṇa moved on. There was a fine house where a man and two beautiful women enjoyed the peak of happiness and bliss. But the captain saw it was quite the opposite at night, when the women turned into snakes and ate the man, starting from the top of his head. Koṭikarṇa asked the man why this was. The man said that when he was a Brahman in Sthirā he used to be an adulterer, but he took the vow from Kātyāyana not to do this during the day. This was the result. He said, "Go and talk with the son I have in Sthirā," and gave Koṭikarṇa a similar message to the previous one to take back. And, as proof, he told Koṭikarṇa he had hidden a pot full of gold under the stove.

Then the captain moved on further and saw a four-legged throne. A hungry ghost held up each leg…

And Kyabje Pabongka Rinpoche told the rest of this story.

These are some of the occasional hells. There are also occasional hells in the human realms. Once in India, when venerable Śhrīmān was going about his daily business, he saw the form of a beautiful house in the sky; the house was ablaze with fire, and in it there was a man, the rebirth of a butcher. The butcher's servant was reborn as a mountain of bones and underwent much suffering.

There is a story of a castrator of animals who was reborn with a body as huge as a mountain. This was the serious karmic result of his actions.

We have already accumulated many instances of karma, the results of which we are sure to experience in these ways. We bought a ticket to the effect that all these things are certain to happen to us.

One great adept saw a huge fish in Lake Yardrog. The fish was the rebirth of a man called Tanag Lama of Tsang Province. While he was alive, he used to eat many of the offerings made to him. The fish's body was half the circumference of Lake Yardrog and was being eaten by many parasites. The adept pointed the fish out to to his followers and said, "Don't eat offerings. Don't eat offerings." We say "monks eat offerings and peacocks can eat poison," but if we haven't practiced Dharma and do not know how to eat offerings for sure, it is not good enough to take the easy way out and eat offerings just because you are ordained. The *Transmission of the Vinaya* says:

> It is better to eat pieces of iron
> Burning with tongues of flame;
> People with loose ethics who lack proper restraint
> Should not eat the district's alms.

That is, when people with loose ethics eat the food offerings of the faithful, it is as if they were eating pieces of molten iron. However, those who keep ethics and put the right effort into their studies and the abandonment [of delusions] may eat such offerings. If you are not putting effort in these directions, eating offerings is like taking a loan. It is all too easy not to do things properly and just put donations and offerings into your purse, but a difficult time will come in a future life when you repay the loan with the flesh of your body. Even when lamas get a request to say prayers for someone, if they merely write out a receipt for the money and do not say the prayers and dedications, they will definitely have to repay the loan with flesh from their bodies [in a future life].

Here is such a story. A large frog, with many smaller creatures feeding on it, was found inside a boulder. And a Derge lama once asked his attendants to bring and show him anything washed down the river that day. It happened to be a tree trunk, and when they removed the bark, they discovered a huge frog being eaten by many smaller creatures. They say the first creature was a lama who had eaten the offerings made to him, and the second was the chief attendant of some Derge lama.

My guru, the embodiment of Vajradhara, personally told me that when he went to Kham there was a huge animal resembling a yak-hair tent in Doshul Lake. The creature was submerged in the lake during the summer, but in winter, when the lake iced over, its back would protrude from the surface, and many creatures, birds and the like, would feed on it.

These are occasional hells, and we have created, and are still creating, countless causes for such rebirths. We must therefore think again and again about how we will have to experience such suffering.

THINKING ABOUT THE SUFFERINGS OF THE HUNGRY GHOSTS (165)

Mañjuśhrī's Own Words discusses animals first. Hungry ghosts have greater wisdom than animals, so are higher. If one were to teach Dharma to some hungry ghosts, they could understand it. Animals are dull and stupid; it is an inferior rebirth and a bigger hindrance to practicing Dharma than being a hungry ghost. So the sufferings of animals were taught first. However, the *Swift Path* puts hungry ghosts first: generally they have greater suffering than animals.

There are two subsections at this point: (1) thinking of the general sufferings of hungry ghosts under six headings—heat, cold, hunger, thirst, exhaustion, and fear; and (2) thinking of the sufferings of particular types of hungry ghosts.

THINKING OF THE GENERAL SUFFERINGS OF HUNGRY GHOSTS UNDER SIX HEADINGS—HEAT, COLD, HUNGER, THIRST, EXHAUSTION, AND FEAR (166)

Think as follows: "At present, I have not been reborn in hell, but if I were born a hungry ghost, I would be so tormented by intolerable sufferings—heat, cold, hunger, thirst, exhaustion, and fear—that I would not even be able to recollect that I should practice Dharma, let alone actually practice it. I have not taken such a rebirth, owing to the kindness of my gurus. What great merit I have to be able to meditate even perfunctorily on the Dharma of the lamrim! How lucky I've been!" But we have accumulated in our mental streams much karma that will throw us into these rebirths; this karma is still powerful and undegenerated. We know it is beyond our present capacity to purify it all before we die.

There is more, though. Usually our thoughts at the point of death are crucial. Sinners may have committed great sins during this life, but if they die with only virtuous thoughts on their minds, they will activate virtuous karma from a past life. If Dharma practitioners are angry, for example, at the point of death, their nonvirtuous karma will be activated. Normally, the thoughts with which one has the greatest familiarity in this life will be the ones that manifest at the point of death. We have always had the strongest familiarity with delusions—the three poisons—so our nonvirtuous karma is sure to be activated at death.

One may be revolted by food and drink at death, and feel, "May I never hear the word food again." This would trigger off karma to be reborn as a hungry ghost by either attachment or hostility. You cannot be sure that you will not be reborn in the unfortunate state of a hungry ghost; in fact, most of us will be reborn as one.

The hungry ghost rebirths are located in Kapilanāgara, the city of the hungry ghosts, which is more than five hundred yojanas underground. This place has absolutely no grass, trees, or water; the whole ground is copper slag, as if scorched by the sun. The bodies and limbs of hungry ghosts are most ungainly. Their hair is matted on their large heads, their faces wrinkled, and their necks extremely thin and unable to support their heads. They have huge mountainlike bodies, and an uneven number of legs and arms, which are as thin as stalks and unable to support them. They have a hundred times more difficulty in walking than old people do in our human realm. For many years they have found nothing to drink, so there is absolutely no moisture in their bodies, no blood, pus, and so forth. Their muscles and veins are wrapped in their dry skin like a dry log wrapped in brown leather. When they move about, the joints in their arms and legs creak like dry wood or like two rocks tapping together, giving off sparks. Since ghosts have had no food or drink for hundreds or thousands of years, they have enormous suffering. On top of this, there isn't a place where they haven't been in search of food and drink. Their bodies are feeble, so they are exhausted. They are in terror of seeing Yamasujana [king of the city of the hungry ghosts], fearing for their very lives. In the heat of summer, moonlight burns them, and sunlight makes them cold in winter, so they have great suffering.

THINKING ABOUT THE SUFFERINGS OF PARTICULAR TYPES OF HUNGRY GHOSTS (167)

This has three parts.

GHOSTS WITH EXTERNAL OBSCURATIONS (168)

These hungry ghosts see water, trees laden with fruit, and so forth, for which they wearily trudge long distances, but when they get there, the things vanish. When some hungry ghosts reach them, the hungry ghosts are prevented from enjoying them by armed men standing guard. In addition to their sufferings of hunger and thirst, therefore, they also experience inconceivable suffering due to physical exhaustion and mental depression.

THOSE WITH INTERNAL OBSCURATIONS (169)

These hungry ghosts occasionally obtain food, but it does not get past their mouths. Their necks have knots in them that make swallowing food very difficult. Some ghosts have to drink rancid pus from their own goiters. As it says in the full version of the above-mentioned story about Koṭikarṇa, the food they eat takes various forms corresponding to the different types of karma the ghosts have accumulated: burning pieces of iron, grain husks, pus or blood, their own flesh, and so forth. The ghosts must endure these unbearable karmic results according to whatever is their accumulated karma. Food and drink may go down some hungry ghosts' necks, but it turns into boiling iron when it reaches the stomach, which as well as not slaking their thirst, creates limitless suffering. There is one type of hungry ghost that this sort of thing does not happen to, but their stomachs are so huge that the food doesn't fill them. Sheets of flame, the fires of hunger, come out of the mouths of some of these hungry ghosts; the "will o' the wisp" is merely fire from the mouths of such ghosts.

THOSE WITH OBSTRUCTIONS FROM KNOTS (170)

Once, when Ananda was going about his daily business, he saw a female hungry ghost. She had three knots in her neck, and she shouted the five kinds of terrifying words. Hungry ghosts of this type have a vertical row of three knots in their necks, which causes them infinite suffering. [Nāgārjuna's] *Letter* says:

> Hungry ghosts are also bereft of the things they desire.
> This gives rise to continual suffering,
> Aggravated by most intolerable
> Hunger, thirst, cold, heat, fatigue, and fear.
>
> Some have mouths as small as the eye of a needle,
> Yet their stomachs, the size of mountains, are plagued by hunger
> But lack the power to digest
> the smallest speck of filth.
>
> Some go naked, though their bodies are but skin and bone.
> They are as thin as palm trees.
> Some are aflame at sex and mouth;
> Food put into their mouths is burnt.
>
> Most cannot obtain even filth for food—
> No pus, feces, blood, and so on.
> They touch their faces together
> And take rancid pus from the goiters at their throats.

For hungry ghosts, in the two hottest months of summer,
Even moonlight is hot, the sun cold in winter,
And trees become fruitless.
They have only to look at rivers for them to dry up.

Chandragomin's *Letter to a Disciple* says:

Unending thirst: if they see afar a clear stream,
And wish to drink from it, they go there,
Yet the water is mixed with old hairs, fish gills, and rank pus.
The water is full of mud, blood, and feces.

A wind whips up waves, and the spray is mountain-peak cold.
When they go to the green sandalwood forests of Malabar,
These become burning woods, a field of sharp-tipped flames;
Many burning fragments drop and gouge them with pocks.

Even when they go to a lake, its terrifying waves
With dazzling foam at the crests,
The water turns into a mirage of desert sands,
A tormenting place with sandstorms swept by fierce, hot winds.

When the longed-for thick stormclouds gather,
They rain a fog of impaling iron darts upon them.
Flinty diamond nuggets of golden color
And orange lightning chains rain upon their bodies.

While they are tormented by heat, even sleet to them seems hot.
When made pathetic by wind, even fire makes them cold.
The intolerable ripening effects of karma completely blind them;
They have various utterly mistaken hallucinations.

Their mouths are small as the eye of a needle; their terrifying
  stomachs, many yojanas round.
Were these pathetic creatures to drink,
Even the water of great oceans could not go down their cavernous
  gullets:
Their poisonous mouths would dry the water to the last drop.

Kaelzang Gyatso, the Seventh Dalai Lama, said similarly:

> Stomachs like mountains; necks blocked; limbs as thin as grass;
> Dry bodies covered in dust; joints give off sparks;
> Their merest glance dries up rivers; always weary, tormented by hunger:
> May a shower of food, drink, and nectar rain down upon these hungry ghosts.

We can't be sure that this time next year we won't be reborn as one of these hungry ghosts. The causes for such a rebirth are being miserly with one's possessions; enormous covetousness; such great attachment to one's possessions that one fondles them over and over again; preventing other people from practicing generosity; stealing other people's possessions; stealing; stealing offerings made to the Saṅgha [see Day 4, p. 140]; abusing charity; and other forms of taking what is not given. Another cause is calling people hungry ghosts; and especially, if you call a member of the Saṅgha a hungry ghost, you will take rebirth as one yourself five hundred times.

When hungry ghosts of the type with obscurations from knots receive a drop of water, it is due to their not having been miserly about giving water in the past. The others do not have the fortune to enjoy any water.

Āchārya Buddhajñāna went to the realm of hungry ghosts. An extremely pathetic hungry ghost with five hundred children gave the āchārya a message to take back to her husband when the āchārya returned to the human realms. "Twelve years ago," she said, "my husband left to search for food, and I have meanwhile given birth to five hundred children. I have not had so much as a drop of water and so have undergone great hardship and suffering. Āchārya, tell my husband to help me by returning quickly from the human realms with any food he has found."

The āchārya said, "What if there are many hungry ghosts there? I won't know which is your husband."

"He has some identifying marks that set him apart from other hungry ghosts. He has lost one eye, and one of his limbs is deformed."

When the āchārya returned to the human realms, he saw some hungry ghosts. One of them was just like the ghost to whom he was to give the message. The āchārya told his story and gave the message.

The hungry ghost said, "I have gone such a distance, but in twelve years

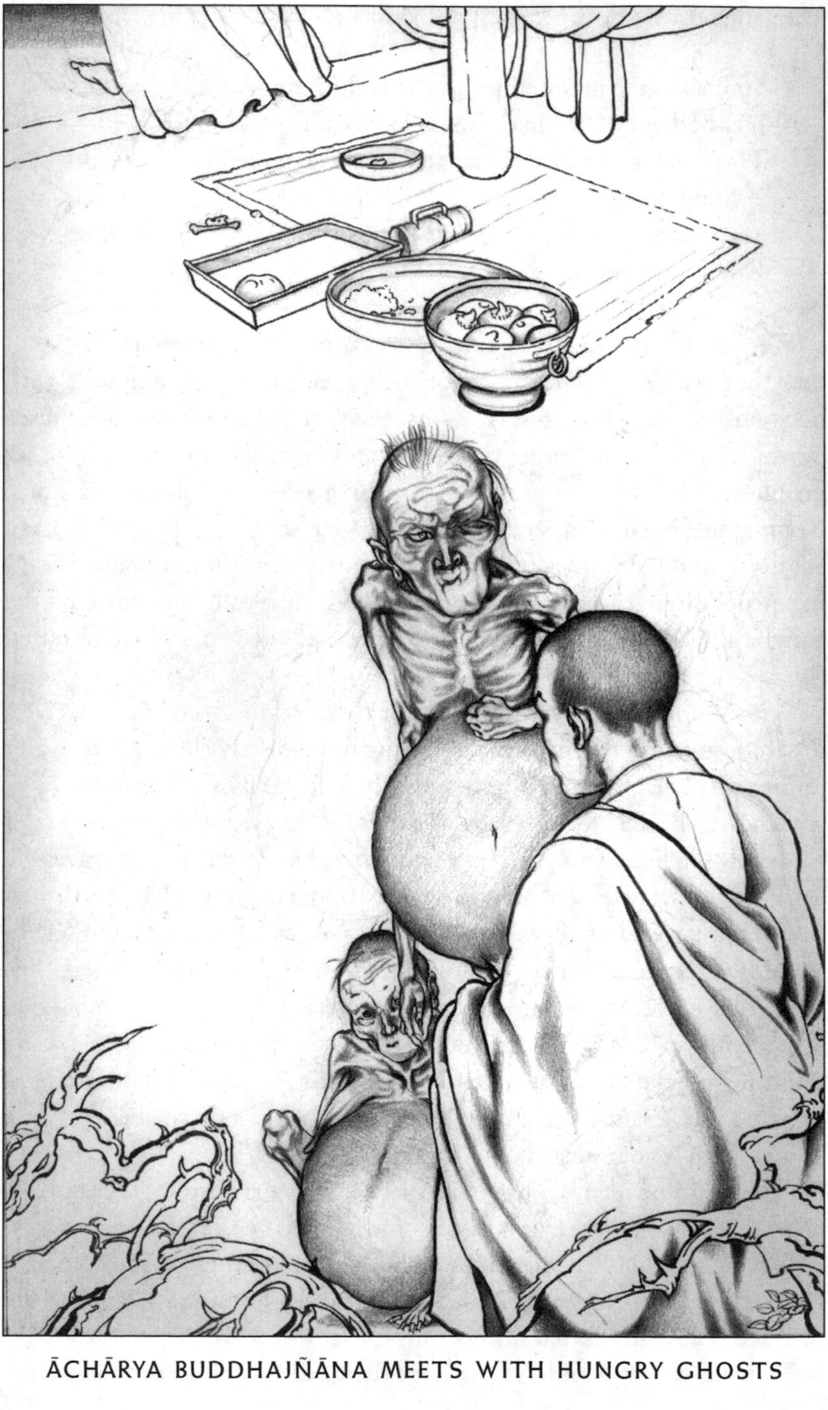

ĀCHĀRYA BUDDHAJÑĀNA MEETS WITH HUNGRY GHOSTS

all I found was this food." He was holding a small piece of dry spittle with the claws of his clenched fist; this was his most prized possession. "A monk who maintained his ethics spat this out and dedicated it [to the hungry ghosts]. Many hungry ghosts fought for it, and I won."

Unless we are careful, we can never be sure there won't come a time when we will have to make lunch out of dry phlegm.

Twenty-five years after the mother of the novice monk Uttara died, he saw a terrifying hungry ghost. The frightened Uttara was about to flee in terror, when the ghost said: "Don't run away!" "Who are you?" Uttara asked. It replied:

> My only son, I'm your loving mother
> From whom you were born,
> Reborn among the hungry ghosts
> Who have no food or drink.
>
> Twenty-five years have passed
> Since the time of my death.
> I have not seen any water;
> Where will I see anything like food?

The novice asked Buddha to dedicate prayers to her. Buddha used his skillful means, and when the ghost left that rebirth she was reborn as a hungry ghost called Mahardhikā, who was extremely rich. Her miserliness was six times worse than before, and she would not practice generosity. The novice persuaded her to offer Buddha a bolt of cloth, but she regretted the action and stole it back. According to the story, this happened many times.

Kyabje Pabongka Rinpoche told the story of a monk who had a beautiful saffron robe. He became so attached to it that after his death he was reborn as a hungry ghost wearing a saffron robe.

These days miserly people are praised as being "clever," but miserliness especially is the cause for being born as a hungry ghost. We act in a miserly way, so it is almost certain we will be reborn as hungry ghosts next year, or at most in forty or fifty years' time—that is, if we do not get a rebirth in hell.

THINKING ABOUT THE SUFFERINGS OF THE ANIMALS (171)

This has two sections: (1) thinking about their general sufferings; (2) thinking about the sufferings of particular types of animals.

THINKING ABOUT THEIR GENERAL SUFFERINGS (172)

Animals experience five kinds of suffering: eating one another, being stupid and benighted, experiencing heat and cold, experiencing hunger and thirst, and being exploited or made to work.

The sufferings of animals are the least of the three lower realms, yet in such rebirths they eat one another and suffer. Animals with huge bodies, sea monsters and the like, have bodies many yojanas long. Some sea monsters are types of fish, others are whales that are capable of swallowing them, and there are even whales that can swallow other whales. Many smaller animals infest the bodies of the monsters and eat them. There comes a point when the monsters can no longer bear this, and they rub their bodies on [underwater] rocky mountains; this kills the parasites living on their bodies, and the oceans are made red for many yojanas.

The larger creatures devour the smaller ones, while many smaller ones feed on the larger ones.Though they cannot bear to remain there, they cannot even wiggle free of the spot they live on. The animals of the great oceans are heaped on top of each other and must live with the one eating the other from the behind. Creatures reborn in the dark depths of the oceans between the continents do not recognize each other—mothers do not recognize their offspring just after giving birth, and vice versa; they eat whatever falls into their mouths, and so must live by feeding on each other.

Even the animals in the human realms eat each other: hawks eat little birds, birds eat worms, beasts of prey and deer kill each other, hunting dogs stalk deer and kill them, and so on.

You should not look on all this suffering as if it were some spectacle happening over there; you must meditate on it in order to gain insight into what happens when you are reborn as one of these sentient beings.

Animals are stupid and benighted: they do not even know whether they are being led to a place to be slaughtered or to be fed, much less know anything else. They suffer from heat and cold. They are scorched to death in summer, frozen to death in winter, and so on.

Kyabje Pabongka Rinpoche told us more of the inconceivable sufferings they experience.

Once a lama picked up a long red worm in his hand and asked it, "Aren't you a Khampa monk?"

"I am," it said in human speech.

We cannot be certain we won't be reborn as such worms. One can cite this story. The father of a Boenpo villager died, and Milarepa predicted that the father would be reborn under a piece of dung in the valley's heights. We might wonder, "How could we ever get such a rebirth?" But this might in fact be only an hour away. When we are reborn as worms, we have to live wriggling under the ground—just to keep breathing. Or we might get eaten by birds. But even if they ate our upper half, still we would not die: our lower half would continue to wriggle. How can we be certain that we will live like this or not? Even if we do nothing else, we must work hard at preventing our rebirth in such a base state.

Most animals, moreover, are ugly in shape and coloring. They also get hungry and thirsty and spend the whole day on the ground in search of food, suffering because they do not find any.

If we cannot stand it now when someone calls us a mangy old dog, what would we do if we were actually reborn as one? Look at the food, drink, sleeping places, and so forth that dogs have. The only places they can find food are inside human dwelling places; yet when they go inside, everyone says, "A dog's come in!" and for no reason they act like a demon has come inside! What else could this be but the result of the dog's evil karma? In some monasteries dogs howl when the horns are sounded for the monks to assemble. This is a sign that some monks have been reborn as dogs.

Some animals are coin-like in shape, with no arms or legs at all.

Once a lama in Dagpo regularly received butter from one family that sponsored him and meat from another, but the lama had not consecrated them. He died and was reborn as a she-yak that used to give a lot of milk in the household of the family that offered the butter. Later the yak fell down a ravine and the river carried it off. The layman who had given the meat found the yak. When he had eaten its meat, he discovered writing engraved on one of the ribs: "I have repaid my debt of meat to the so-and-so family, and my debt of butter to family such-and-such."

Lamas, monastic officials, geshe-scholars, and the like, may get exemptions in monasteries, but the law of cause and effect makes absolutely no exceptions. If we are not careful now, it wouldn't be difficult for the head of a family to change places with his donkey or his guard dog. There is a story of a family that used to sacrifice animals to the tīrṭhika idol behind their house whenever their luck was bad; things would then go very well. The father of the family's dying words were: "Make more animal sacrifices." The father was later reborn as a bull, and his own son performed a "sixfold sacrifice" on it. There is also the story of how the head of a family was reborn as a fish in the lake behind his house. We cannot be certain these things will not also happen to us.

The suffering of being exploited is as follows. Take the case of a donkey. He is made to carry loads even though his back may be covered with sores. When he is close to death, he is abandoned where he drops, and he dies while the crows pluck out his eyes even before he has stopped breathing.

We must think about these things in order to develop insight into how impossible it is to bear these sufferings in such a rebirth.

THINKING ABOUT THE SUFFERING OF PARTICULAR ANIMALS (173)

This has two divisions: thinking about (1) the suffering of animals living in overcrowded environments; and (2) the suffering of the more dispersed animals.

THINKING ABOUT THE SUFFERING OF ANIMALS LIVING IN OVERCROWDED ENVIRONMENTS (174)

Most of these animals live in the depths of the great oceans, the dark depths between the continents. Some of them live in the lower reaches and others in the higher, like piles of discarded dregs from beer-making. The higher animals press down on the lower ones, who have difficulty even in breathing.

[THINKING ABOUT THE SUFFERING OF] THE MORE DISPERSED ANIMALS (175)

These are the animals in the human realms, and they have limitless ways of experiencing suffering.

We have all possible causes for taking these rebirths; they are still powerful and many in number. The most powerful of them are, for example, being disrespectful to the Dharma and its exponents, and celibates calling each other animals. These are illustrated by the story of Mānavakapila [see Day 4, pp. 141ff.].

Once, in India, someone acted as benefactor for those members of the Saṅgha observing the monsoon retreat, but the benefactor gave shoddy goods. He was reborn in foul-smelling mud as a worm with a monk's head, and so endured suffering. Once someone said a certain monk looked like a monkey; for saying that, he took five hundred monkey rebirths. These stories come from the sūtras.

Great sins take us to hell rebirths; medium sins to hungry ghost rebirths; and small sins to animal rebirths. The way a sin becomes great depends on the intention, the merit field or material object involved, and so on. By great sins we do not mean obvious things like killing a human being. We will in future lives disappear into the lower realms because of the karma of inadvertently joking about karmically potent beings [such as our parents], or insulting them under our breath. The assurance of not being reborn in the lower realms will only come when we have achieved the patience stage of the path of preparation. *A Treasury of Metaphysics* says:

> Those who have gained the patience stage will not fall into the lower realms.

This does not apply to us. We know our present capabilities; before we die we cannot expiate the causes we have already accumulated that lead to the lower realms. And once we are born in the lower realms, we will not gain any means or a refuge to free us from these realms. *Engaging in the Deeds of Bodhisattvas* says:

> "Who will protect me
> From these great terrors?"
> With staring eyes
> I'll scour the four directions for a refuge.
>
> But when I see no refuge in the four directions,
> I will give way to utter despair.
> If these places have no refuge,
> What will I do then?

Observe and you will know that the animal realm is the best of the three lower realms; but it is still impossible for animals to recite even one *oṃ maṇi padme hūṃ.* It is second nature for them to have powerful delusions or the three poisons; they therefore accumulate fresh evil karma and migrate from lower realm to lower realm. *Engaging in the Deeds of Bodhisattvas* also says:

> If I do no virtue
> When fortunate enough to practice virtue,
> What will I do when completely blinded
> By the sufferings of the lower realms?
>
> If I then practice no virtue
> And accumulate much sin,
> I will not even hear the words
> "Upper realms" for billions of eons.

In other words, if we do not at least work hard at achieving some refuge or means of being free of the lower realms in our future lives before this rebirth of ours has come to an end, it will be too late once we have actually fallen into the lower realms.

The only thing lying between us and the infamous three lower realms is the mere fact that we haven't stopped breathing. In a short while—later this year, or next, or at most in a few years' time—some of us could be reborn in hell and live with our bodies indistinguishable from fire. Others could be reborn as hungry ghosts and live while not finding even a drop of water or a speck of food. Others will be reborn as animals with sharp horns on their heads and shaggy fur on their bodies. We can't be sure we won't get such rebirths, like waking up from a dream.

When we recall these things, we should not think of them as stories happening far away or as mere objects of curiosity. The point is to have insight into what it would be like to be reborn in these realms already and, afterward, the certainty that we will be reborn in these realms after this life. Suppose we were spectators when many criminals were being punished by a king's edict; then suddenly we ourselves were seized, led from the mob, and received punishment like the criminals before us. Similarly now we just feel that many, many sentient beings undergo such suffering in some place called "the lower realms," and we look on with curiosity like watching a butcher at a sheep slaughtering yard; but imagine the suffering and fear we would experience if we suddenly arrived in the lower realms, or turned into a sheep and were held down by that same butcher and actually felt his blade going between our ribs. We should have this sort of insight. The Buddha, the Bhagavān, gave us this prediction:

> My śhrāvakas, in the future, [beings] will go to the lower realms like sand running out of an overturned sandbag.

We are like the criminal sentenced to be hurled over a cliff who relaxes by the cliffside. We are unaware of this and act as complacent as an arhat who "has done what needs to be done": this is an omen that we will be going to the lower realms.

You must see if you think you will be like the small quantity of sand that remains behind in the seams of the overturned sandbag.

If our meditations give us insight into what it is like to be reborn in the lower realms, we will develop renunciation. So sometimes it is better to meditate on the sufferings of the lower realms than on tutelary deities.

The amount of recollection of the sufferings of the lower realms needed is as follows. Two sons of Ānanda's sister were put under Maudgalyāyana's care. The lads would not study their books, so Maudgalyāyana showed them the hells; they developed a natural repudiation because of their recollection of the hells.

Kyabje Pabongka Rinpoche reviewed this material at some length, and also taught briefly how to pursue this practice.

DAY 12

Kyabje Pabongka Rinpoche gave a short talk to set our motivations, quoting from the works of great Dharmarāja Tsongkapa:

> The optimum human rebirth is difficult to acquire; this life does not last long.
> Familiarize the mind with this, and turn away from this life's trivia…

Then, after restating the foregoing headings, he reviewed the material on the sufferings of the lower realms, part of the section on "Thinking About What Sort of Happiness or Suffering You will Have in Your Next Rebirth in Either of the Two Types of Migration."

Such things lead you to want to extract the essence from your opportune rebirth. When you think about the sufferings of the lower realms, you will be terrified and will want to seek some refuge to protect yourself from them, as well as some means of being happy in your future lives. The refuge you take, as a protection from the lower realms, is in the guru and the Three Jewels. The means [to be happy in your future lives] is to develop faith in the law of cause and effect—this faith is the root of all health and happiness—and then to modify your behavior accordingly.

TEACHING THE MEANS FOR HAPPINESS IN YOUR NEXT REBIRTH (176)

This has two subheadings: (1) taking refuge, the holy gateway for entering the teachings; (2) developing faith in the law of cause and effect—the root of all health and happiness.

TAKING REFUGE: THE HOLY GATEWAY FOR ENTERING THE TEACHINGS (177)

This has five sections: (1) the causes on which one's taking refuge depends; (2) what object to take refuge in; (3) the criterion for taking refuge sufficiently; (4) the benefits of taking refuge; (5) advice after one has taken refuge.

THE CAUSES ON WHICH ONE'S TAKING REFUGE DEPENDS (178)

Our proper taking of refuge depends on whether we have within our mindstream the proper causes for taking refuge. These causes are discussed in [Lozang Choekyi Gyaeltsaen's] *Melodious Laughter of Lozang—Answers to "Questions on the Whitest Altruism of All,"* which says:

> The true nature of taking refuge:
> Taking refuge because one is most afraid
> And because one knows the Three Jewels are able to protect.
> This is what you meant, omniscient one.

In other words, we need both causes: personal fear of saṃsāra and the lower realms, and the belief that, if we are able to put our trust in them, the Three Jewels will have the ability to protect us from these terrors. If we do not have both these causes, we will not take refuge purely. If we do not fear suffering, we will not think of seeking a refuge. If we do not believe in the object of refuge, we will not remember our reliance on it as a refuge—or we might recall it, but only in words, because our heart will not be in the act of entrusting ourselves to that refuge. Each of the three scopes contains its own version of the [first] cause for taking refuge. For the small scope it is: fear of going to the lower realms ourselves. For the medium scope: fear of saṃsāra. For the great scope: such love and compassion that we cannot bear others suffering in saṃsāra. In this particular section of the lamrim, the cause for taking refuge is fear of the lower realms.

WHAT TO TAKE REFUGE IN (179)

This has two parts: (1) the actual identification of the things to take refuge in; (2) the reasons why they are fitting refuges.

THE ACTUAL IDENTIFICATION OF THE THINGS TO TAKE REFUGE IN (180)

The *One Hundred and Fifty Verses of Praise* says:

> Take refuge in whoever does not have,
> And never will have, any shortcomings
> And in whom resides
> Every aspect of all good qualities.
>
> If one with such a mind exists,
> Take refuge in him,
> Praise him, and venerate him.
> It is right to abide by his teachings.

In other words, when we think of how to distinguish between what should be a refuge and what should not, we will want to take refuge in the Buddha, the teacher of Buddhism, in his teachings, and in those who abide by his teachings. The average worldly person seeks refuge in worldly creatures—spirit kings, gods, nāgas, spirits, and so forth. Non-Buddhists seek refuge in Brahmā, Indra, etc., but these themselves are beings in saṃsāra, so they are not fitting refuges.

Who then is a fitting refuge? From the *Seventy Verses on Taking Refuge:*

> Buddha, Dharma, and Saṅgha
> Are the refuge for those desirous of liberation.

That is, the only refuge is the Three Jewels: Buddha, Dharma, and Saṅgha. But if we do not identify these three properly, we will not take refuge purely. We are not critical and so pretend to be Mahāyāna knowledge-bearers, yet when things go wrong, sickness comes and so forth, or when we have some important work to do, we seek refuge in worldly Dharma protectors, in spirit kings, local gods, etc.—we carry an armload of aromatic wood for a smoke purification and rush off to the shrine of any deity having a statue in the neighborhood. Inwardly we should entrust ourselves to the Three Jewels; instead we cling to spirit kings. The external reality indicates our inner state. We may have actually gained admittance to a monastery, but we do not even qualify to be Buddhists, let alone Mahāyāna knowledge-bearers.

Nāgas, spirit kings, and others do not have these three qualities: omniscience, love, and ability. They don't even know when they are going to die. Normally they are categorized as animals or hungry ghosts, and their rebirths are inferior to ours. No matter how badly off we are, we are still human. What plan could be worse than to seek refuge in them? Forget about protecting us from saṃsāra and the sufferings of the lower realms, or even giving us little temporary help—they may do us great harm instead. Here is a story to illustrate this. A man with a goiter once went to a place haunted by flesh-eating rock spirits. A tax in flesh that these rock spirits paid to other creatures was due, so the spirits removed the man's goiter. Another man with a goiter heard of this and went to them and took refuge in them hoping for the same result, but the spirits did not destroy his goiter—they made it larger. Similarly, worldly gods and evil spirits are sometimes helpful, sometimes harmful, they can never be trusted.

Non-Buddhists make Brahmā, Indra, Śhiva, Rudra, Gaṇeśha, and so forth, their refuge. This is an improvement on the above, yet these gods are still not liberated from saṃsāra and the lower realms so they cannot protect other beings. But Buddha, the Teacher of Buddhists, is not like these. *Praise to the Praiseworthy* says:

> You proclaimed, "I am friend
> To you who are without protection."
> Your great compassion
> Embraces all beings.
>
> Teacher, you have great compassion,
> You have love; you act by your love.
> You are diligent, you are not lazy.
> Who else could be like you?
>
> You are the protector of all sentient beings;
> You are a kind relation to all.

I will discuss the Buddha's qualities individually in another section. According to that section he has three magnificent qualities: omniscience, love, and ability. Not only do spirit kings and so forth not have even a portion of these good qualities, but also the sum of the good qualities of worldly refuges, gods, nāgas, and the like, cannot rival even the good qualities of a single Buddhist śhrāvaka stream-enterer.

Buddha is the ultimate refuge because he has taken the two benefits [benefit for self and for others] to their most developed state. Our Teacher has eliminated all faults and possesses all good qualities.

Simply put, the ultimate jewel of Buddha is assumed to be the two dharmakāyas, or "truth bodies"; the relative jewel of Buddha, the two physical kāyas [the saṃbhogakāya, or "enjoyment body," and nirmāṇakāya, or "emanation body"].

The jewel of Dharma is as follows. The ultimate jewel of Dharma is anything that comes under the truth of cessation or the truth of the path—these are the [two] purifying truths [in contrast to the two truths of suffering and the origin of suffering] in the mindstreams of āryas. As a guide, we take the *truth of cessation* partly to mean a freedom from [or the "cessation" of] some particular obscuration, this freedom being a function of a particular unhindered path. The *truth of the path* is taken to be the means for āryas to achieve these cessations [and realizations in their mindstreams]. For people who have not studied the classics and who think at a lower level, it is enough to identify the three scopes of the lamrim as a rough approximation for the ultimate jewel of Dharma.

Such things as the twelve divisions of scripture are the generally accepted jewel of Dharma.

The jewel of Saṅgha is as follows. The ultimate jewel of Saṅgha are ārya beings who have any of the eight good qualities of the liberated mind.

A group of four ordinary beings holding the monk's full ordination vows is the generally accepted jewel of Saṅgha. If we help or harm these beings, we will receive virtuous or nonvirtuous karmic results in relation to the Saṅgha.

One doesn't need all three of these refuges in order to be protected from some types of danger; each of the Three Jewels can protect one. Once a man in Dokham petitioned Avalokiteśhvara while he was being dragged off by a tiger. The tiger immediately put him down, and the man was freed from threat from the tiger.

After Pūrṇa had become ordained and gained arhatship, some relatives and merchants went to sea to obtain choice sandalwood, but their defending deity began to destroy their boat. The relatives petitioned the arhat Pūrṇa [in their prayers] and were saved from the waters.

The king of the nāgas caused a rain of weapons to fall on King Prasenajit; Maudgalyāyana turned it into a rain of flowers.

However, all Three Jewels are needed to protect one completely from saṃsāra and the lower realms. To cure a patient of a severe illness, three things are needed: a doctor, medicine, and nurses. Similarly, in order to be freed from the serious illnesses of the sufferings of saṃsāra and the lower realms, the danger of the peace [of Hīnayāna arhats], or [saṃsāric] existence, one definitely needs all of these: the Buddha, the teacher of the liberating path, who is like the doctor; the Dharma, the liberating path of the three scopes, which is like the medicine; and the Saṅgha, the friends of the Dharma practitioners, who are like the nurses. So, these three are the objects to take refuge in.

THE REASONS WHY THEY ARE FITTING OBJECTS OF REFUGE (181)

The main reasons are the good qualities of the jewel of Buddha. There are four reasons for this.

THE FIRST REASON (182)

Buddha has freed himself from all dangers. People drowning or trapped in quicksand cannot rescue each other. If the buddhas, the guides in whom we take refuge, had not freed themselves from all dangers, they could not free others. Buddha, our Teacher, is liberated from all dangers. Devadatta once wanted to murder the Buddha and used a mechanical device to hurl rocks at him, yet he could not harm him. In Rājagṛiha, Ajātaśhatru let loose Dhanapāla, a mad untamed elephant. All the other arhats were terrified and flew into the sky but Buddha was not afraid and subdued Dhanapāla. A householder named Śhrīgupta devised a plan to throw Buddha into a pit of fire, but Buddha did not come past. Śhrīgupta poisoned Buddha's food, but this did not succeed either.

After Pabongka Rinpoche had told this story at length, he continued:

Śhrīgupta, his wife, and the rest, regarded our Teacher as a mere ordinary being who could be intimidated by fiery pits or poison. One can readily compare this with the section on devotion to one's spiritual guide that tells how one cannot be sure of appearances. This indicates that Buddha has freed himself from all danger because he has abandoned the two types of obscurations together with their karmic instincts.

THE SECOND REASON (183)

He is skilled in the means to free others from danger. If he were freed from all personal danger but not skilled enough to know how to protect others, he would be as unable to protect others as a mother with amputated arms is to save her drowning child. But the Bhagavān, the Buddha, is skilled in the means of subduing his disciples. He liberated such great sinners as Aṅgulimālā, who [was consumed by feelings of] hostility; Pramudita, the king of the celestial musicians, and Uruvilvākāśhyapa, who were consumed with pride; such powerful creatures as the yakṣha Hārītī and yaksha Āṭavaka; such people with dull faculties as Cūḍapanthaka, who [was consumed by] benighted ignorance; such people who were old and had few root merits as the householder Śhrījāta; and such people with great lust as Nanda. That is how skilled Buddha is in the means of subduing disciples.

THE THIRD REASON (184)

He reacts compassionately to all, without feelings of intimacy or distance. If he did not do this, he would help only those dear to him and not his enemies. Buddha, however, has no feelings of intimacy or distance toward any being. There was no difference in the help he gave and the intimacy he felt toward Devadatta, a sworn enemy, and Rāhula, his own son. Devadatta ate a vast amount of medicinal butter in order to compete [with a similar feat of the Buddha's], but he could not digest it and became very sick. Buddha, our Teacher, freed Devadatta from the illness by swearing that he loved Devadatta and Rāhula equally.

Śhākyamuni Buddha was the Buddha who came to our present world system, but if we were to compare, we would see that other Buddhas share the same qualities.

THE FOURTH REASON (185)

The Buddha works for the sake of all others, whether they have helped him or not. We do not do this: when we gain a little power or wealth, we do not judge the downtrodden worthy enough to hold a conversation with them or say a few kind words to them, let alone help them. We work for the sake of people who have helped us and not for people who have not; so we do not protect the downtrodden. Buddha is not like this; he works for the sake of everyone, whether they have helped him or not. Buddha nurses the sick. For example, he once nursed and washed the body of a monk who was so ill that his body was covered in his own feces and urine. He looked after people like the ugly Brahman who had the eighteen signs of ugliness and was an outcast even among beggars. Buddha protected and looked after people who were ugly, such as King Prasenajit's daughter, Vajrī, who was deformed and had a face like a pig's, or the householder Bodha's son Svāgata [Welcome], who had such a small amount of merit that his family gradually lost all its wealth after he was born. Svāgata became a beggar, but whatever group of beggars he joined never got any food. He was renamed Durāgata [Unwelcome]. Wherever he went, no one gave anything away, so he became an outcast even among beggars. Even when he went on pilgrimage he was not allowed to return.

Kyabje Pabongka Rinpoche spoke in greater detail on how Buddha offered his protection and cared for these most unfortunates.

Thus the Buddha has great compassion for all and has no feelings of intimacy or distance. Furthermore, he works for the sake of all, whether they have helped him or not. But he loves pathetic wretches especially. If he were not loving or did not have great compassion, he might not offer his protection even when sought. But the Buddha has these qualities, and they say he definitely offers protection even when it is not sought.

After this short discussion on the reasons for taking refuge and the beings in whom to take refuge, Kyabje Pabongka Rinpoche continued.

THE MEASURE OF HAVING TAKEN REFUGE (186)

This third section has four subsections.

TAKING REFUGE BY KNOWING THE GOOD QUALITIES OF ONE'S REFUGE (187)

One must take refuge knowing the qualities of each of the Three Jewels. So this has three parts: (1) the good qualities of the Buddha; (2) the good qualities of the Dharma; (3) the good qualities of the Saṅgha.

THE GOOD QUALITIES OF THE BUDDHA (188)

Buddha has four types of good qualities: the good qualities (1) of his body; (2) of his speech; (3) of his mind; (4) of his good works.

THE GOOD QUALITIES OF HIS BODY (189)

The *Ornament to Realization* says: "His hands and feet [are] marked by wheels, his tortoise feet..." In other words, his body is adorned by thirty-two signs. The same text also speaks of "The Sage's copper-colored nails..." That is, he is also adorned by eighty marks.

The *signs* signify that he has the mindstream of a great personage. The marks indicate the sort of qualities he has inside. It is very powerful to think about the natural qualities of the marks and signs, the good qualities of their causes, and so forth. Nāgārjuna's *Precious Garland* tells us that if one added up all the merits in the world, of the pratyekabuddhas, the learner and no-more-learner śhrāvakas, the world emperors, and so on, all this merit would produce a single pore on the body of a buddha. All the merit needed to produce all the pores of a buddha, multiplied by a hundred, would produce one of the marks. All the merit needed to produce all eighty of these marks, multiplied by a hundred, would produce one of these noble signs. The merit needed to produce thirty of these signs, multiplied by a thousand, would produce the ūrṇa hair-curl [between a buddha's eyebrows]. The merit needed to produce this last sign, multiplied by a hundred thousand, would produce the uṣhnīṣha. The merit to produce this, multiplied by a quadrillion produces the Brahmā voice of a buddha. Further, every part of a tathāgata's body, the signs and marks, is a teacher of Dharma and so performs the deeds of enlightened speech. Even his uṣhnīṣha, his pores, etc., perform the deeds of the enlightened mind and so perceive the relative and ultimate [aspects] of all knowables.

According to the tradition of past lamrim lineage gurus, there are three lines of verse [from Tsongkapa's *Songs from Experience*] each relating to the qualities of the enlightened body, speech, and mind respectively:

> Body born of ten million virtues and excellences,
> Speech that fulfills the hopes of infinite beings,
> Mind that sees all knowables as they are:
> I pay homage to the head of the Śhākya tribe.

This is why the enlightened body pervades all knowables.

Whatever is pervaded by his body is also pervaded by his speech and mind. Hence, "All buddhafields appear in his body, and his body pervades all buddhafields." These are the inconceivable mysteries of the enlightened body. A sūtra tells us:

> Wherever their primal wisdom pervades,
> So, too, do their bodies pervade.

Usually, whenever one sees the famous uṣhnīṣha on a buddha's head, it is only four inches high; but when it was measured by the bodhisattva Vegadharin, he rose upward to immeasurable world systems through his miraculous powers, yet still failed to see the top of the tathāgata's crown protrusion, and he was too weary to complete the measurement. This is told in the *Sūtra on the Inconceivable Mysteries.*

A buddha's clothes maintain a distance of four inches from his body, yet when seen externally they follow the shape of his body. His feet do not touch the ground, yet they leave the outlines of wheels as footprints. Earthworms under his feet have great bliss for seven days, and when they leave their animal state, they are reborn in the celestial realms. From the *Praise in Similes:*

> Your body is adorned by the signs;
> So beautiful, it is nectar for the eyes,
> Like a cloudless autumn sky
> Adorned with constellations.
>
> Sage, you are a golden color,
> And beautifully draped in robes,
> Like the peak of a golden mountain
> Rising above a bank of clouds.
>
> You, Protector, are not adorned with jewels;
> Your maṇḍala face is full of lustre.
> Not even the full maṇḍala
> Cloudless moon can equal it.

Your lotus face
Is a lotus opened by the sun.
Disciples, like bees, see the lotus
And unhesitatingly fly to it.

Your golden-colored face
Is beautiful with white teeth,
Like a golden mountain range
Bathed in pure autumn moonlight.

O one worthy of our offerings, your right hand
Is made beautiful by the sign of the wheel;
It gives encouragement to people
Frightened of saṃsāra's wheel.

Sage, when you walk,
Your two feet are like glorious lotuses;
They leave outlines on the ground.
O Lotus One, how beautiful you are!

Remember these qualities. If you need more detail on this section, you will have to consult the discussions in *An Ornament to Realization* and other texts.

THE GOOD QUALITIES OF HIS SPEECH (190)

His speech has sixty nuances; one tantra says of its fundamental [characteristic]: "Though he may say only one thing, it appears individually to the multitude." Tsongkapa, the embodiment of Mañjuśhrī, said in his *Verses on the True One:*

Should all the sentient beings of the world
Ask him, all at once, to resolve their doubts,
He would, in front of each,
Simultaneously, with corresponding bodies and voices in an array,
Perform the deed of resolving their misconceptions.

This means that if various beings asked the Tathāgata different questions simultaneously, he would with one utterance simultaneously answer all the questions in each being's language and at the level of each one's faculties. Buddha taught the three versions of the *Perfection of Wisdom Sūtra*—the long, medium, and brief—simultaneously. These three versions came about because of the extensive, medium, and narrow faculties of the disciples.

Also his speech can be understood regardless of distance. The *Sūtra on the Inconceivable Mysteries* says that Maudgalyāyana traveled past many buddhafields by means of his miraculous powers to measure the carrying power of Buddha's speech, but no matter how far he went, he could still hear it as though in front of him. Maudgalyāyana therefore could not measure the carrying power of his speech.

His speech has other qualities, as the *One Hundred and Fifty Verses in Praise* tells us:

> Your face is most fair to see;
> To hear the sound that from it comes:
> A voice like nectar
> Dripping from the moon.
>
> Your speech is like a raincloud
> To settle the dust of attachment.
> It casts out the snake of hostility
> Like the garuḍa.
>
> Like a parasol it conquers over and over
> The mirage of ignorance.
> Like a vajra it truly destroys
> The mountain of pride.
>
> You have seen reality, and so do not deceive.
> Because you do not err, you are consistent.
> Well-constructed, so easy to comprehend,
> Your speech is eloquent.
>
> Your speech towers over others.
> It wins over all who hear it;

Even on later recollection
It removes attachment and benightedness.

It inspires the destitute,
Protects the reckless,
And sobers the ecstatic;
Thus your speech is suited for all.

It gives the scholars joy,
Develops the minds of the mediocre,
And destroys the mental haze of the inferior.
Your speech is medicine for everyone.

However, this is not all: the mysteries of enlightened speech are infinite, such as also performing the actions of enlightened body and mind.

THE GOOD QUALITIES OF HIS MIND (191)

As discussed in more detail in the classics, the good qualities are to be understood as the twenty-one divisions of unsullied primal awareness, the ten powers, the eighteen unique qualities, and so forth. People who study and contemplate the classics need to contemplate these extensive teachings in order to derive some benefit.

In short, there are two types of good qualities: those that come from omniscience and those that come from love. Because buddhas are omniscient, even when in meditative absorption on ultimate truths, they are aware of and perceive all knowables as plainly as they would a myrobalan fruit resting in their hands. One can know this from *Praise to the Praiseworthy:*

Bhagavān, all phenomena throughout time,
All [karmic] sources and all places,
Come under the jurisdiction of your mind,
Like a myrobalan in your palm.

To all phenomena, mutable or immutable,
whether single or multiple,
Your mind is open without obstruction,
Like the wind blowing in the sky.

Once a Śhākya called Nandaka died. The priests summoned the dead man while they performed the funeral rites. The dead man's form manifested, and the priests gave it food and drink; it behaved just like Nandaka. The man's relatives thought it was really Nandaka, but our Teacher told them it was a likeness of the dead man created by the celestial musician Vyāpaka, the yakṣha Paryāsannakāma, and so forth. But the relatives did not believe the Buddha. So our Teacher invited each of the Śhākyas to bring a small packet of grain. Each was to put his household's own identifying mark on his packet. So many Śhākyas offered packets of grain that they would have loaded down an elephant. Buddha identified each one, saying, "This is so-and-so's" without making a single mistake. This caused everyone to believe.

The *Transmission of the Vinaya* tells us that if all the trees in the world were burnt by fire and their ashes stirred under the ocean for a long time, they could be given to the Buddha and he would recognize each correctly, without confusing one with another. He could state that the ash was from the wood of such and such a district, from such and such a tree, and know everything, even whether it had come from the top or the base of the tree.

The miraculous power of the manifestation of the enlightened body is its ability to show an emanation to each of however many disciples there may be, ten million, one billion, or whatever. The miraculous power of enlightened speech is its ability to speak to all; as I have already said, it teaches Dharma simultaneously in each sentient being's language and according to each one's wishes. The "miraculous power of the enlightened mind's single-pointed concentration" is as follows. When our Teacher has a worldly thought, the minds of other sentient beings, even ants, come to know the thoughts of others and understand what the Tathāgata means. But when he has a supramundane thought, even bodhisattvas in their final incarnation cannot understand the Buddha's thoughts. When Buddha taught the three Perfection of Wisdom sūtras, he made all the worlds turn into pure worlds. Thus they say Buddha's mind has an infinite number of such good qualities.

His good qualities of love are described by the Seventh Dalai Lama:

> Some persons may be evil. Others may be ruled by anger and
> intend to murder.
> But you always think of beings as your children;
> You have put far away any thoughts of doing harm.

> The love I have for myself cannot compare with your mind's rain of compassion.

In other words, the sort of love we have for ourselves does not compare with even a fraction of Buddha's love for sentient beings. Also, his love is not like the intermittent compassion we feel: we feel compassion only when we see a suffering sentient being and not when we don't see one. A buddha always perceives that all sentient beings are tormented by suffering; his great love and compassion toward them is uninterrupted, always operating, for a buddha's compassion comes ultimately from the force of his familiarization with the trainings since he first entered the path. This is what is meant when the *One Hundred and Fifty Verses of Praise* says:

> All these beings are no different:
> They are bound by delusions.
> You have been bound a long while by compassion
> To liberate deluded beings.

From *Verses on the True One:*

> All beings' minds are always veiled
> By the darkness of benightedness.
> The holy Sage sees all inmates
> Of saṃsāra's prison, and develops compassion.

THE GOOD QUALITIES OF HIS GOOD WORKS (192)

[Maitreya's] *Sublime Continuum of the Great Vehicle* says:

> Like Indra, the drum, clouds, Brahmā,
> The sun, a precious gem.
> Tathāgatas are like echoes,
> Like space, like the earth.

Your contemplations should follow the teaching of this text on these nine similes: the reflection of Indra appears—without any dependence on effort or conceptualization [on Indra's part]—on the lapis-lazuli surface [at the top of Mount Meru].[54] When the lesser gods see the reflection, they think, "I shall act so as to obtain the same." They will then amass the causes to gain the state of an Indra, lord of the gods. Likewise, when we see the body of Buddha, adorned with the marks and signs, we think of gaining such a state, and attempt to accumulate the causes for this to happen. These are the good works of the Buddha's body.

In the Realm of the Thirty-three Gods is a great drum named Vegadhārin, produced from the gods' merit. Without need of a player, the drum emits sounds that teach the four seals of the Dharma; these sounds stimulate the gods to seek liberation. Buddhas, similarly, without the effort associated with motivation, make their speech extend to all beings, leading them to high rebirth or definite excellence. The good work of enlightened speech is its ability to teach Dharma to suitable fortunate beings.

Rain falls from the clouds and the crops grow. The good works of the enlightened mind are similarly their ability to make the crop of virtue grow in the mindstreams of disciples.

The miraculous body is revealed in order to subdue sentient beings. The good work of enlightened speech is teaching Dharma. Buddhas perform the good work of enlightened mind in dependence upon undeluded concentration.

In short, bodhisattvas on and below the eighth level have to make coarse efforts; the bodhisattvas above this level have to make the subtle [effort of having] motivation. Because of this, their good works do not extend to all sentient beings simultaneously; but the Buddha's good works do not depend on the motivation of thinking "I shall work for the sake of sentient beings," or on effort. As an illustration: the moon in the sky has no conception of us, yet its reflection appears on dew on the tips of blades of grass and on the surface of the water in many hundreds of thousands of containers, provided the water is clear and still. The Buddha's good works take effect spontaneously and effortlessly in the mindstreams of disciples when the time is right for them to be tamed. In fact, the cause of the phrase "Buddha's good works" itself is the primal wisdom truth body *[dharmajñānakāya]* acting as the environmental condition; these [good works] thus arisen are taken to be one with the Buddha's perfectly pure good qualities.

THE GOOD QUALITIES OF THE DHARMA (193)

If you have studied the classics, think of the Dharma as the way in which obscurations are abandoned as a function of, say, the uninterrupted paths during the path of seeing. If you do not understand this, think as follows. From where did the buddhas, who are supposed to have these above-mentioned inconceivable qualities, arise? They arose, and will arise, in dependence on the realized Dharma, that is, the path of cessation and the like, and on the transmitted Dharma. Think that the Dharma has the quality of producing these buddhas.

One can generally take the jewel of Dharma to be the ten levels, the five paths, and so on—in other words, the truth of cessation, and the uninterrupted paths within the paths of seeing and meditation. However, the most important thing is subduing one's own mindstream; so, in simple terms and to give you a rough illustration, it is all right to take the lamrim as the jewel of Dharma. I have already said this.

THE GOOD QUALITIES OF THE SAṄGHA (194)

Let us take the example of a śhrāvaka on the path of accumulation. He was moved to renounce cyclic existence and then entered the path of accumulation, he built up the thirteen prerequisites for [his type of] enlightenment, achieved the first three [of the thirty-seven] wings of enlightenment, emanated himself for the good of others, received the clairvoyant powers, and so on. Śhrāvakas on the path of preparation have understood the sixteen aspects of the four truths through firsthand mental images. Śhrāvakas on the path of seeing have directly understood emptiness; on the path of meditation they abandon sequentially the eighty-one orders of objects to be abandoned. When śhrāvakas gain arhatship, they have many more good qualities: they can combine many physical objects together; they can produce many emanations through single-pointedly meditating on earth, water, fire, wind, and space to the exclusion of all else; they can go to any place where there is a disciple; and so on.

In fact the śhrāvaka arhats have immeasurable good qualities. After our Teacher had gone to nirvāṇa, Ānanda subdued the tīrṭhikas, leading eighty thousand people to the truth in the space of seven days. There is a story about Upagupta. Once when he was giving a teaching, Kāmadeva made it rain food and jewels, and emanated dancers as well. Ārya Upagupta garlanded the dancers with flowers just before they began their dance; he consecrated the flower garlands, which then turned into extremely repulsive things. People these days hold śhrāvakas to be inferior, but anyone with their good qualities would have to be considered a great adept.

Pratyekabuddhas have built up their collections over one hundred eons, etc., and have one hundred thousand times more good qualities than śhrāvakas.

A bodhisattva's good qualities are infinite by comparison. While still on the paths of accumulation and preparation, and still acting out of faith, they ascertain the meaning of emptiness through study, contemplation, and meditation. They train themselves in compassion, bodhichitta, and the profound view, thus weakening their manifest dualistic conceptions of perceiver and perceived, and complete their collection of merit for the first immeasurable eon. When bodhisattvas are on the first level, they achieve the extraordinary form of the practice of generosity. When they are on the ninth level, during the path of meditation, those ninth-level bodhisattvas achieve the extraordinary form of the remaining perfections just by virtue of their proper perception of suchness.

Bodhisattvas on the first level emanate hundreds of bodies, each of which is surrounded by hundreds of other bodhisattvas. These first-level bodhisattvas see into hundreds of eons, they can make hundreds of worlds tremble, they enter the doors of hundreds of single-pointed concentrations, see hundreds of buddhas, receive these buddhas' blessings, emanate hundreds of buddhafields, travel to hundreds of these fields, open the doors to hundreds of Dharmas, ripen hundreds of sentient beings, and live for hundreds of eons. Every single moment, these first-level bodhisattvas manage hundreds [of examples] of these twelve kinds of qualities.

One can make a comparison of these twelve qualities for bodhisattvas on the other levels. Second-level bodhisattvas achieve thousands of each of these qualities; third-level bodhisattvas hundreds of thousands; fourth-level bodhisattvas, billions; fifth-level, tens of billions; sixth-level, quadrillions; seventh level, ten billion trillions; eighth-level, a number equal to the atoms in one hundred billion worlds; ninth-level, a number equal to the atoms in one million countless billions of worlds; and tenth-level bodhisattvas achieve a number of these qualities equal to the atoms in one billion inexpressibly countless billions of worlds. In short, bodhisattvas on the first seven impure levels spend two countless eons building up their [two] accumulations, while bodhisattvas on the three pure levels take one more countless eon to complete the remaining accumulations.

The great classics discuss such things at length. So, the Saṅgha has immeasurable good qualities.

TAKING REFUGE BY KNOWING THE DIFFERENCES BETWEEN THE THREE JEWELS (195)

There are six types of differences.

The difference between the characteristics of the Three Jewels is as follows. Buddhas have the characteristic of complete enlightenment: they starkly and unobstructedly perceive the mode of existence of all phenomena, no matter what. One suspects the syllable *jang* [in *jangchub,* the Tibetan for "enlightenment"] has the conventional meaning of "to train," as in memorizing a piece to be recited; so one could say a buddha has achieved the most fully developed realization. The Dharma has the characteristic of being the result of a Buddha's coming. When the Buddha turned the wheel of the Dharma of the four truths, his first five disciples developed various realizations in their mindstreams: the path of seeing, and so forth. The same happened in other situations [where Buddha turned the wheel of Dharma]. The Saṅgha has the characteristic of being the practitioners of that Dharma.

The difference between the good works of the Three Jewels is this. The Buddhas teach Dharma by giving the oral transmissions. The good work of the Dharma is different: it causes one to abandon the things one ought to abandon. The Saṅgha practice the Dharma, and when they gain Dharma's results, others see this and engage in these practices. So those who are the Saṅgha and those who are not together help one another. This is the good works of the Saṅgha: they manifestly rejoice in virtue.

There are different ways of regarding the Three Jewels when one takes refuge. To rescue someone from the water, for example, you need a boatman, his leather coracle, and the assistants accompanying him. Similarly, one should regard the Buddhas as objects of one's offerings and service; the Dharma as the thing to be made manifest in one's mindstream; and the Saṅgha as one's true friends.

The different practices [associated with the Three Jewels] are the means for putting these three different ways of regarding the Three Jewels into practice.

The different ways of recalling them are to remember the different qualities of the Three Jewels. This is explained in the *Sūtra on the Recollection of the Three Jewels* in the passage beginning "Thus the Bhagavān Buddhas..."

The differences in how the Three Jewels increase one's merit are as follows. With Buddhas, merit increases in dependence on the one person only; with the Saṅgha, merit increases in dependence on many people. So, in the case of the Buddha and the Saṅgha, merit increases by virtue of persons. With the Dharma the difference is that merit increases by virtue of something impersonal.

When you take refuge you do so because you want to make offerings, serve the Buddha, and develop the Dharma in your own mindstream.

TAKING REFUGE OWING TO ONE'S BELIEFS (196)

One's beliefs are: the Buddha teaches refuge, the Dharma is the actual refuge, and the Saṅgha assist practitioners who take refuge. This is illustrated by the different ways in which patients pin their hopes on their doctor, the medicine, and their nurse. If, through the processes of realization and abandonment, one develops each part of the Dharma in one's mindstream, one is freed from every type of danger. Dharma is therefore the true refuge.

TAKING REFUGE AND NOT ASSERTING ANOTHER [RELIGION] (197)

In ancient India, Āchārya Udbhaṭasiddhasvāmin and his brother were at first both non-Buddhists. The two went to the Himalayas to make offerings to Śhiva, but they saw the great god Śhiva taking refuge in the Buddha, so they became Buddhists and great āchāryas in the Mahāyāna. Udbhaṭasiddhasvāmin composed the *Supreme Praise,* which tells about the great qualities of Buddha.

As this work says, we have taken refuge in our Teacher and are disciples of his teachings; we have taken this refuge for good and cannot exchange it for some other refuge. The dharmas of Boenpos, tīrṭhikas, and so forth are non-Buddhist and should not be taken as our refuge. There is a difference in superiority between Buddhist and non-Buddhist teachers, their teachings, and their disciples. As the *Supreme Praise* says:

> I have abandoned the other teachers,
> And take refuge in you, O Bhagavān.
> Why did I do this?
> Because you have no faults and have good qualities...

The more I consider
The tīrṭhika commentaries,
The more my mind grows faithful
To you, my Protector.

And *Praise to the Praiseworthy* says the same:

What should one enter, and what should one forsake?
What is deluded, and what is most purified?
The difference, O Hero,
Between your words and those of others.

Here in Tibet there are no true tīrṭhikas, but there are some big mouths who claim to be practitioners and scholars yet see nothing wrong in dabbling in Boen or barbarian dharma to curry favor with others, gain a big following, or help themselves out when they meet with difficulties. By taking two refuges, they have evicted [the act of] taking refuge from their mindstreams and cast themselves out of the ranks of Buddhists.

Some people say, "We like Buddhists, we like Boen," but there is no reason why the Boen teachers, their dharma, or their adherents should be worthy enough to be refuges; the three do not have all the required qualities. Their teachers do not have the required qualities, that is, having abandoned all faults, and so forth. Their dharma is not even a means of reducing delusion. They claim their Saṅgha is based on the pratimokṣha vow, but their vows do not have the lineage. Boen is not a refuge for Buddhists; it is not worthy of being a refuge. All the same, Buddhists and Boenpos say things to each other out of attachment or hostility, and this hardly makes for honest debate. It is vital that you should know the sources of the Boen religion. They are discussed in the authentic histories in the writings of past scholars. You must know these things from such works as the *Crystal Mirror on Eloquence* by Tukaen Dharmavajra; this discusses what the various teachers assert and the sources of all their tenets.

Boen teachers, their teachings, and [philosophical] views have been corrupted by non-Buddhist meditations and views. They have also plagiarized the Buddhist scriptures. Their false dharmas were invented a very long time ago, and this evil system is now prevalent everywhere; but it is not a fitting refuge for people who yearn for liberation, nor is it trustworthy. With this in mind, Drigung Jigtaen Goenpo said:

> As for the Boen meditations and [philosophical] views: in their system there seems to be the systems that the universe was born from eggs or created by the Cha deities, Śhiva, and so on. These are borrowings from tīrṭhika views.

The *History of the Later Kadampas* says:

> Tīrṭhikas and Boenpos soon gain siddhis.
> Happy now, they later go to the lower realms.
> Tīrṭhikas and Boenpos are like fire:
> You feel comfortable when somewhat near,
> But really touch them and you'll be burnt.

Je Milarepa, the lord of yogis, says:

> The source of Boen is perverted Dharma.
> A creation of nāgas and powerful elementals,
> It does not take one to the ultimate path.
> Boen is a most inferior lineage.
> The difference between Buddhism and Outsiders
> Hinges on the refuges:
> The refuge of Buddhists is the Three Jewels;
> Of non-Buddhists, Brahmā and Indra.
> The fully enlightened Buddha
> Is himself freed from saṃsāra,
> So is able to liberate others.
> Worldly gods such as Śhiva and the like
> Are themselves bound to saṃsāra;
> They can give others short-term siddhis,
> But how could they give
> The freedom of complete liberation?...
> They say, "May I achieve buddhahood
> In the maṇḍalas of the five nāga families
> Found in the *White Nāga Anthology*."
> Yet nāgas are counted among the animals.
> Most of the Boenpos make idols such as Kuenzang
> And construct various maṇḍalas; but I feel
> It is just perverted Dharma invented by
> Āchārya Blue Skirts...

Kyabje Pabongka Rinpoche discussed these at length.

These days some people say that the Boen gods Shenrab and Oekar are one with the Buddhist deity Avalokiteśhvara. They claim, "In order that all sentient beings be disciples of the buddhas, many emanations of buddhas and bodhisattvas have appeared among the ranks of the Boenpos. So, following the Boen system not only does no harm, it can only be a good quality." They make such high-flown claims out of their great blindness, for their mindstreams have been affected by evil instincts formed from perverted views. If what they say were so, then it would follow that imitating the actions of dogs and pigs does no harm, it could only be a good quality, because it is possible that emanations of buddhas and bodhisattvas have appeared among the animals. People who want the best should completely abandon such nauseating and evil systems as they would discard the stones they use to wipe their arses. The only refuge for Buddhists is the Three Jewels. Buddhists should take refuge purely, and it is vital that they surrender themselves to their refuge.

In short, we do not mean merely reciting words when we speak of "taking refuge." Just as a criminal seeks the protection of an influential official, we must fear the lower realms, saṃsāra, and so forth, and must be convinced that the Three Jewels have the power to protect us. Then we must think most sincerely, using our primary mind and its mental factors, that we are entrusting ourselves to the Three Jewels, our only friend and helper. This is the criterion for taking proper refuge. Whether we have developed refuge in our mindstream depends on whether we have developed these thoughts in our mindstream. So don't be like the people who have recited the formulas for taking refuge billions of times but haven't once produced [the entity of] refuge in their mindstreams. You must work hard at the techniques to genuinely develop the causes and the refuge itself in your mindstream.

There are two different ways of taking refuge: merely seeking protection and regarding the Three Jewels as something that others have achieved in their mindstream, and the special form of refuge, regarding the Three Jewels as something that can be developed in one's own mindstream and then deciding that one will achieve this. There are ways of taking these two types of refuge in each of the three scopes of the lamrim, but since we are people who study and contemplate the classics, we must mainly try to take the special form of refuge. However, doing a lot of study may not be much help when it comes down to taking refuge if our taking refuge turns out no different from that of an old, unexceptional lay person, because our study and contemplation has never turned inward. Yet even when we know nothing of the classics, we should have both causes for taking refuge and should surrender ourselves to the Three Jewels. Here is the way to do so.

Think about the way patients entrust themselves to their doctor, medicine, and nurses, and their mental state. If you have all the causes for taking refuge and entrust yourself to the Three Jewels from your heart, you will develop refuge properly in your mindstream. These, then, are the main things. Without them, nothing will come of reciting the refuge formula many times and of claiming to be a bodhisattva or knowledge-bearer. As the Kadampas of old said: "That elder facing you [in the temple] may not yet have joined the ranks of Buddhists."

THE BENEFITS OF TAKING REFUGE (198)

There are eight of these: you become a Buddhist, you become a candidate for all vows, you will use up obscurations acquired from previously accumulated karma, you will easily accumulate a huge amount of merit, you will not be bothered by the harmful actions of humans or creatures, you will not fall to the lower realms, you will effortlessly achieve all your temporary and longterm aims, and you will soon be enlightened.

When you take refuge, therefore, don't merely repeat the same words as other people, or take refuge only verbally—take refuge from your heart. You become a Buddhist only when you develop the act of taking refuge properly in your mindstream. Reciting the refuge formula hundreds of thousands of times doesn't make you a Buddhist. People these days say, "You must recite the refuge formula a number of times"; people who instead say "You must develop it on your mindstream" are rare.

In Dagpo once, a monk named Atar was doing a retreat with friends in which they were to recite the refuge formula a [prescribed] number of times. Atar gave proper thought to the meaning behind taking refuge and so took a long time. The others were much quicker because they only repeated the words of the refuge formula; they had nearly completed a billion repetitions. Fearing that Atar would not complete the required number they asked him how many he had done, and Atar said, "Have you only been totting up some number for the refuges formula?" So, if you recite the formula while keeping your attention on taking refuge, you will be significantly ripened by it.

When you take any of the three types of vows, you must precede this by taking refuge. If you do not, you will not receive the vow. Just as the ground supports houses, crops, walls, trees, forests, and so on, the act of taking refuge serves as the basis for receiving all vows.

You may have committed many karmic actions in the past and accumulated many obscurations—for example, the major heinous crimes such as when Ajātaśhatru killed his own father Bimbisāra, who had achieved the result of a never-returner, or the minor heinous crimes—but when you have taken refuge, you purify such karma and the [resulting] obscurations because you have taken refuge in the Buddha. Thereafter, saying the names of buddhas or even reading the set of the Perfection of Wisdom sūtras once will purify many eons' sins and obscurations. The sūtra basket speaks of these benefits again and again. The *Short Perfection of Wisdom Sūtra* says: "If the merit from taking refuge had form, the three realms would be too small to hold it." In other words, the merit accruing from the act of taking refuge is immeasurable.

Moreover, the buddhas are such karmically potent beings that root virtues generated in relation to them will definitely become the cause of one's achieving full enlightenment—even if this is done without pure motives. From the *White Lotus of Compassion Sūtra:*

> "Ānanda, it is like this. Suppose a farmer householder has a field that has no stones, tree stumps, or brambles. It has no pebbles or rubble, and has rich topsoil. He plowed it well, and prepared it with hand implements. He did right by planting his seed while it was still fresh and fertile. The sun and wind have not been harmful; the seed has not been cracked open, nor has it rotted. The seed was planted at the right time in the furrows of the field. Sometimes it was watered, sometimes left dry, and safeguarded against everything. Ānanda, this householder at some other time goes to the field, stands on the edge of it and says, 'O seeds, be seeds no longer! O seeds, do not sprout, do not grow. I do not want the fruit. I do not want the rewards!' Ānanda, what do you think? Would those seeds no longer be seeds because of those words?"
>
> "No, Bhagavān," he replied. "No, Sugata."

> The Buddha said, "Would the fruit no longer become fruit? Would he reap no rewards?"
>
> "No, Bhagavān," he replied. "No, Sugata."
>
> Then the Buddha said, "Ānanda, when people who praise saṃsāric existence, who rejoice in saṃsāric existence, make offering to the buddhas, even though they may say, "By these root virtues may we never go to nirvāṇa," it is quite impossible that they will never go to nirvāṇa. Ānanda, these root virtues generated in relation to the Buddhas will result in nirvāṇa, although they do not want it. I tell you, these virtues will be transforming until their eventual nirvāṇa. Therefore, whenever one develops root virtues by having a single thought about the Bhagavān Buddhas, the fruit of all such root virtues will be nirvāṇa. I tell you, these root virtues will be transforming until one's eventual nirvāṇa."

One will not be bothered by the harmful actions of humans or creatures. Here are some stories to illustrate.

A tīrṭhika once made a noose out of energy wind and tried to catch a Buddhist upāsaka with it, but did not succeed.

A man from India was sentenced under the law of a certain king and was to be abandoned in a charnel ground. All other people abandoned there had disappeared: they had been carried off by creatures, a species of ghost, and been eaten. Not one had come back alive. The man placed on the crown of his head a patch taken from the robes of a member of the Saṅgha; then, he took refuge. He was not bothered or harmed by the creatures.

Once a nomad was left alone for a day in an uninhabited spot and was attacked by a yeti. He nearly died. His head was still scarred, and so a lama asked what had caused these scars; the man told his story. The lama gave him instruction on taking refuge. Later the man again encountered a yeti. He took refuge; the yeti merely sniffed the air, did not pick up the human scent, and went away.

The householder Anāthapiṇḍaḍa recited some verses on taking refuge one night when he saw that a road had taken him into a charnel ground. The creatures there could not harm him. Anāthapiṇḍaḍa then prostrated himself before a tīrṭhika idol and lost his protection, so the story goes.

A thief once saw someone give a monk some cloth. The thief returned at night to steal it. The monk outwitted him, tied his hands together, then beat him three times with a stick while saying the names of the Three Jewels. The thief ran away; he repeated what the monk had said while staying under a bridge frequented by demons.

"I'm lucky there were only three of them," he muttered under his breath. "If there had been any more, I would have been killed!" That night, the demons were unable to cross that bridge.

These were some of the stories Kyabje Pabongka Rinpoche told.

We should not be afraid when we get into difficulties: we must take courage from the Three Jewels and be satisfied with taking only this one kind of refuge.

Taking refuge will also stop us from being reborn in the lower realms. A god was certain he was going to be reborn as a pig and so sought Indra's protection, but Indra could not save him. The god asked the Buddha, who gave him instruction on taking refuge. The god died while taking refuge according to these instructions. Later Indra investigated where this god had been reborn. Now the gods can see mentally only into levels below their own but cannot see higher; Indra could not find the god, so asked Buddha. The Buddha announced he had been reborn in the Tuṣhita celestial realm.

That god not only prevented his certain rebirth as a pig, but was also reborn in a very high celestial state—all through taking refuge. Yet we do not appreciate that taking refuge is so important. During public ceremonies we sit distracted, fidgeting while we recite "Until enlightenment, I take refuge in Buddha, Dharma, and the Supreme Assembly. When it comes to the part *"Oṃ svabhāva śhuddhaḥ sarva dharmāḥ svabhāva śhuddho haṃ,"*[55] we pretend we're in deep meditation and roll our eyes. This is a sign that we don't know what the gateway to Buddhism is and what a marvelous means it is for preventing rebirth in the lower realms.

Atiśha saw that taking refuge and the laws of cause and effect were alone important, and so he taught them. He was called the "Taking-refuge Lama" and the "Cause-and-effect Lama." Atiśha heard about this and said, "Those names of mine will also help the teachings."

When we are about to die, practicing the generation and completion stages may be beyond our capacities, but if we take refuge properly, it is certain that for once we will not fall to the lower realms. As Sangyae Oen says:

> In short, if I have not developed
> Death and impermanence in my mental stream,

Even the Guhyasamāja would not be profound.
But three verses on taking refuge are profound
When produced in my mindstream at death.

There is also no better means of fulfilling one's wishes than taking refuge. Jangsem Retrengwa said:

Do not put your hopes in people—petition the divine!

In other words, past saints achieved their temporary and longterm aims by petitioning the divine Three Jewels. Once Retrengwa was embroiled in lawsuits; he won them by depending on the Three Jewels.

You will soon be enlightened. Your taking refuge now will result in the future in actions that correspond to it. In this life, whenever unfavorable circumstances arise, you will automatically take refuge right away. And because the mind characteristically follows whatever it is familiar with, you will recall Buddha when you die. The *King of Single-Pointed Concentration Sūtra* says:

Also, construct images of the victors
And recall Śhākyamuni, whose primal wisdom is immeasurable.
If one grows accustomed to always remembering him,
One's thoughts quite automatically turn to him...

With cleansed body, speech, and mind,
Always sing praises to the Buddhas.
Accustom your mindstream to thoughts like this,
And you will see the world's protector day and night.

If you are ever ill, or unhappy,
Or meet with misery at your death,
Your recollection of the Buddha will not decline;
Feelings of misery will never take this from you.

Not only this, but we will also gain optimum human rebirths in all our lives, we will meet with a refuge, and we will never be separated from people who take refuge. And when we train in the ultimate path, we will achieve the Three Jewels in our own mindstream. Thus we will soon be enlightened.

ADVICE AFTER ONE HAS TAKEN REFUGE (199)

This has two parts: (1) advice concerning each of the Three Jewels in turn; (2) advice concerning all three in common.

ADVICE CONCERNING EACH OF THE THREE JEWELS IN TURN (200)

This has two subheadings: (1) advice on what not to do; (2) advice on what to do.

ADVICE ON WHAT NOT TO DO (201)

Once you have taken refuge in the Buddha, you should not do things like seeking refuge in worldly gods. There are even now some monks who, if driven to desperation when things go wrong, will grovel abjectly before the idols of worldly gods. They are a disgrace to Dharma practitioners. As I have already told you, by taking only two refuges you cast yourself out of the ranks of Buddhists, because you destroy the refuge vows in your mindstream [see p. 384]. All the same, it is all right to offer ritual cakes, perform smoke purifications, make burnt offerings to gods, nāgas, spirit kings, and so forth, if you merely invoke their help in Dharma matters. However, you must not take refuge in them. It's like giving someone a bribe and asking them to help you: you don't have to take refuge in them.

Because you have taken refuge in the Dharma you should not harm sentient beings. Apart from not harming beings by killing, whipping, or robbing them, and the like, you should not even levy unfair taxes or, for example, put a heavier than normal load on an animal. These things are injurious and therefore not right.

Because you have taken refuge in the Saṅgha you should not associate with tīrṭhikas [those holding wrong views]. Here in Tibet there are no true tīrṭhikas, but there are people who resemble them. These people say, "Do you think there are such things as the Three Jewels or the law of cause and effect? They are only things talked about by smooth-tongued lamas and geshes." It is not right to associate with such people. We have not yet achieved any stability in our minds, so there is a danger that these people could turn our heads and change our thinking. We ought to keep our distance from such people.

Someone, while in Geshe Potowa's presence, said that it wasn't true that the Buddha had come to the world. The geshe got the better of him by saying, "In that case, your ancestor Teu Nagong never existed either."

"Yes he did!" the man said. "There is evidence of it. You should know that there are documents!"

Potowa then said, "One can draw an analogy here. There is evidence that the Buddha came into the world—his scriptures." The man then became firmly convinced that Buddha had indeed come.

ADVICE ON WHAT TO DO (202)

RESPECTING ALL BUDDHA IMAGES, EVEN THOSE POORLY CRAFTED (203)

Because you have taken refuge in Buddha, then, as Nāgārjuna's *Letter* tells us: "No matter how a sugata's image is constructed, even of wood, the wise make offerings." In other words, a Buddha image may, for example, be badly made or of poor materials, or there may be many fragments of Buddha images in a wayside shrine, but you must still have the attitude that these images are real buddhas.

We have greater faith in images made of brass, gold, or Indian bronze; we put such images in the middle of temples. We have little faith in images made of clay and the like, or in damaged ones; we put them by boundary fences [made of dung in Tibet] and later take them to some wayside shrine. But the lamas of the past said that carrying such images out of one's house is like carrying one's merits outside. Also, it is a sign that your faith and respect for the Three Jewels is rotten to the core if you take the brocade border off paintings and store the central canvas rolled up when they get old.

RESPECTING EVEN A SINGLE LETTER AS IF IT WERE THE REAL JEWEL OF DHARMA (204)

Since you have taken refuge in the Dharma you should respect even a single letter N, for example, as if it were the real jewel of Dharma. It is highly damaging if you do not do this—you will be thick and stupid and so on, in rebirth after rebirth. As Geshe Sharawa said:

> We treat Dharma as a joke, and our disrepect for Dharma or its exponents is a cause for our wisdom to slacken. We are already

> blind enough; let's not accumulate causes to be even blinder. What would we do if we were blinder than we are already!

We have a higher regard for five *ngulkar* [the lowest unit of Tibetan currency] than we have for a page of writing. If we see some money fallen down a drain or whatever, we try to fish it out and will even resort to using a long stick. We wouldn't bother if it were some writing. We should emulate the following story. Once, when Gyaelwang Choeje was made government auditor, he was ordered by the central government to present a financial report for the Iron-Tiger Year. While he was carrying this out he had many ledgers of the many government districts spread out [on the floor]. Whenever he went outside—to relieve himself, say—he would clear a path through the documents first [so that he would not tread on them].

RESPECTING PIECES FROM SAṄGHA MEMBERS' CLOTHES, OR EVEN MAROON-COLORED RAGS FALLEN ON THE GROUND, AS YOU WOULD THE PEOPLE WHO WORE THEM (205)

Because you have taken refuge in the Saṅgha, you should show the same respect as did Geshe Dromtoenpa Rinpoche and Mahāyogi. They would not step over a yellow rag even if it were lying on the footpath; they would shake it out and carry it to a clean place. You should pay as much respect to pieces from Saṅgha members' clothes, or even to maroon- or yellow-colored rags fallen on the ground, as you would to the people who wore them. The *Ten Wheels of Kṣhitigarbha Sūtra* says:

> Even the remains of a champaka flower
> Is still much better than other flowers;
> A monk's ethics may have declined, and he may be a sinner,
> But he's still superior to all the tīrṭhikas.

If that is so, what sort of misdeed does one commit by not paying respect to such a person? As the *Plea for Altruism Sūtra* says:

> Those who seek good qualities dwell in forests.
> Do not point out the faults of others;
> Do not have any thoughts of
> "I am superior, I am better."

Such actions are the root of all recklessness;
Do not despise the lowly monk:
For an eon you would not gain liberation.
So it is taught; this is the hierarchy.

ADVICE CONCERNING ALL THREE JEWELS IN COMMON (206)

There are six pieces of advice.

You should repeatedly take refuge by recalling the good qualities of the Three Jewels. As I have already said, recall the difference between Buddhist and non-Buddhist teachers, and between their teachings. Also recall the good qualities shared by the Three Jewels, then take refuge in them repeatedly.

Recall the kindness of the Three Jewels, offer the first part of whatever you eat or drink: every time you eat or drink, offer the first portion, so as not to forget that the Buddha, Dharma, and Saṅgha should be the subject of your thoughts. Such offerings are extremely beneficial because there can be no higher merit field than the Three Jewels. But you should not spoil such offerings by apathy, carelessness, laziness, and so forth. Even when you offer water bowls, you are in the presence of the omniscience of the victorious ones, so it is said that you must be like a new kitchen manager pouring tea [before his employer].

Lead others to take refuge. You should stop people from accumulating evil karma when, for example, they take refuge in such tīrṭhika teachers as Pūrṇa, or Boen teachers like Shenrab, in their dharma, their followers, and other such bad company, out of admiration for them. Also, you should lead people who have no faith or respect for the Three Jewels, but who might be suitable for the path, by talking indirectly about the qualities of the Three Jewels in conversation.

You should recall the benefits of taking refuge and take it three times in the day and three times at night. That is, grasp that the Three Jewels are the perfect refuge, develop faith in them with all your heart, and take refuge in them six times a day.

Whatever action you do, trust in the Three Jewels. No matter whether the things you do are great or small, trust in the Three Jewels, conscientiously make offerings to them, and your work will be accomplished. Do not instead have evil thoughts, harbor guile, or take refuge in local spirits, spirit kings, or in Boen and the like.

Do not abandon the Three Jewels even if it costs you your life, or even as a joke. If you give up the refuge you have taken, you cast yourself out of the ranks of Buddhists. And if you are no longer a Buddhist, you are no longer a novice, fully ordained monk, one of the bodhisattva family, or a practitioner of the secret tantras. Giving up your refuge vows might not seem a big thing, but it also means you give up all your other vows. So, as I said, do not give up your allegiance to the Three Jewels even if it means your life or even to merely swear an oath or as a joke. From [Tsongkapa's] The *Great Stages of the Path:*

> Do not abandon these, even at the cost of your life. If you violate this you have truly given up your refuge. Likewise, you may not have given up the Three Jewels but still take a second refuge in teachers and the like who go against the Three Jewels. You would then violate [the instruction that you should not] subscribe to another religion or give up your trust in your refuge.

Here is an example of someone not forsaking the Three Jewels, at the cost of his life. Once some tīrthikas told a Buddhist lay-vow holder they would not kill him if he gave up his refuge. The upāsaka did not, so they killed him. He was reborn in the celestial realms.

Kyabje Pabongka Rinpoche then reviewed this material.

DAY 13

Kyabje Pabongka Rinpoche quoted from Tsongkapa, that great Dharmarāja:

> You have no assurance that you will not go to the lower realms after death...

After this short introduction, he restated the headings already covered and reviewed the first subsection of the heading "Teaching the Means for Happiness in Your Next Rebirth." This first subsection deals with taking refuge. He then briefly taught how to pursue this practice:

When people give oral discourses there are separate headings for contemplating the sufferings of the lower realms and for taking refuge. However, when one is taking a "practical teaching," one must meditate on a combination of these two headings, as explained below.

This is how it is done. After you petition [the visualization of] your guru above the crown of your head, he emanates from his heart a complete refuge visualization, for example the merit field, and this stands before you in space. Then think deeply about the individual sufferings of each of the hells and the sufferings of animals and hungry ghosts; after each, as you become terrified of each lower realm, take refuge. This is the integration [of the two headings]. An illustration: if in this world a petty criminal gets the support of an influential official, it sets the criminal's mind at rest, and he thinks, "I cannot do much by myself, but I have the backing of a great official." That is why he sought his support. Similarly, if you are terrified of the lower realms you will want to take refuge and take confidence from the thought: "I have come under the protection of the Three Jewels, a refuge that won't prove deceptive."

If you are taking refuge a number of times, it is enough to repeat the beginning of the preparatory rites. However, in this section of the lamrim you should combine three lamrim meditation topics together, although it is still all right to repeat only "I take refuge in the guru, the tutelary deities, and the Three Jewels" for your accumulations. Let us take the section on thinking about the suffering of the Hell of Continual Resurrection as an example. The three meditation topics would go as follows.

First, once you have insight into being reborn in this hell, you think how it would be impossible to endure it. At this point you will have the thought: "I have not now been reborn there."

The second meditation topic comes in at this point. Think that though you have not taken rebirth in this hell now, you have accumulated very powerful karma to be born there; this karma has not declined [in strength], and you will not be able to purify it before you die. And as you cannot purify it, you are certain to be born there. This should terrify you.

Then comes the third meditation topic. You think: "These refuge objects to protect me from this lower realm should have immeasurable numbers of good qualities—omniscience, love, ability, and so forth. How lucky I am to have found such a refuge!" And then take refuge.

Follow the same process for the other lower realms.

After giving three excellent versions of the teachings on taking refuge—an elaborate version, a medium-length version, and a short version—Rinpoche continued.

DEVELOPING BELIEVING FAITH IN THE LAW OF CAUSE AND EFFECT—THE ROOT OF ALL HEALTH AND HAPPINESS (207)

Because you have taken refuge in the Three Jewels, you can be sure that you have prevented one or two rebirths in the lower realms, but not that you will be free of the lower realms forever.

If you want to be absolutely confident of never again going to the lower realms, you must try to follow the advice that goes with taking refuge [see Day 12, pp. 380 ff.]. Here is an illustration of what happens when you do not. When a criminal seeks the protection of an influential official, the official may tell him: "From now on, you should do this and not do that." If the criminal does not listen and instead only commits more crimes, there is no way that even that official can protect him: the criminal will again run afoul of the law.

Similarly, if we do not keep the advice that accompanies taking refuge, there is nothing the Three Jewels can do for us at all. This is why our Teacher taught that Dharma is the actual refuge to protect us from the lower realms. Dharma itself is the act of modifying our behavior according to the law of cause and effect.

If you do not develop believing faith in the law of cause and effect, you will only want to practice a little virtue and to abandon a little nonvirtue. As long as you do not properly modify your actions according to the law of cause and effect, you could still go to hell, despite being well versed in the three baskets or being a great adept and yogi. Once Guru Avadhūtipa looked back at Atiśha while they were crossing a bridge and said: "Until you abandon grasping at a self, and while you still place little value on the law of cause and effect, [always] remember that even scholar so-and-so and yogi such-and-such were reborn in hell." They say that even great Ra the translator had to spend a few moments in hell—about as long as bouncing a ball of yarn [on the floor].

A yogi in the Yamāntaka tantra was reborn as an evil hungry ghost that physically resembled this tutelary deity; the ghost traveled from India to Tibet. Great Atiśha said, "If it remains here, Tibet will be harmed," so he dedicated ritual cakes to the ghost and made it go away.

Devadatta knew one [of the three] heap[s] of Dharma, but this did not help him, as he was reborn in the Hotter Hell. A Brahman named Chanakya had achieved visions of Yamāntaka and had killed many people through his paranormal powers. They say he was reborn in the Hell Without Respite.

If you do not keep to the law of cause and effect, even doing a tantric retreat will not be of any help. A yogi in the Yamāntaka tantra from Lower Paenpo was also reborn as a hungry ghost, taking the form of the tutelary deity. He turned up to beg at a burnt-offering ceremony performed by some of his fellow practitioners.

Kyabje Pabongka Rinpoche told how an elder of Vikramaśhīla Monastery was reborn as a hungry ghost with a deformed hand.

So, if you are unable to modify your behavior out of a belief in the law of cause and effect, being a scholar or adept will be of no help at all. And it is said: "Karma ripens in inconceivable ways—even lords of love are born as animals." In other words, they say that even mahātma bodhisattvas have taken rebirth in the lower realms when they ignored the law of cause and effect. This is why setting one's motivation is the start of all meditations, why the optimum human rebirth is the start of the lamrim, and why the law of cause and effect is the start of putting the Dharma into practice. The law of cause and effect has even been called "the correct view for worldly people." Here "worldly people" is taken to mean ordinary beings; the whole phrase means that ordinary beings should act principally according to these laws. A great many people these days pretend to esteem the view highly, but you must first develop believing faith in the law of cause and effect and then modify your behavior accordingly. If you not do this, you may mumble your recitations three times every day and every night and pretend you are recalling the Dharma, or work hard at imitating meditative absorption and pretend that this is meditating on the view, but these are just signs that you do not know what Dharma entails.

Some people commit sins all day and night and even order others, servants and pupils, to carry out many sinful actions all over the place. These people may go through the motions of getting up early and going to bed late after doing their recitations, but this is the wrong way to go about a practice.

So you must think about the law of cause and effect in order to develop this believing faith in it. There are three sections here: (1) thinking about cause and effect in general; (2) thinking about the specifics; (3) after thinking about these things, the way to modify your actions.

THINKING ABOUT CAUSE AND EFFECT IN GENERAL (208)

This has two subsections: (1) the actual way to think about cause and effect in general; and (2) thinking about some specific points.

THE ACTUAL WAY TO THINK ABOUT CAUSE AND EFFECT IN GENERAL (209)

This has four subheadings: (1) how karma is fixed; (2) karma shows great increase; (3) one does not meet with something if one has not created the karma for it to happen; (4) karma once created will not disappear of its own accord. The Bhagavān himself spoke of karma in these four ways, so they are most vital.

HOW KARMA IS FIXED (210)

The *Transmission of the Vinaya* says:

> Whatever karma is created
> Will bring a corresponding result.

In other words, the result of some virtuous action—the cause—can only be happiness; this cause does not bring suffering. The result of some nonvirtuous action—the cause—can only be suffering; this cause does not bring happiness. This is the fixed aspect of cause and effect. For example, it is fixed that from the seed of a hot-tasting plant comes hot-tasting fruit. Likewise, it is certain that from the seed of a bitter plant comes bitter fruit; from a sweet plant's seed, sweet fruit. Now, at the time that we create karmic causes, we must exercise care, for it is impossible to put things right once the cause has produced its results.

When we get sick, for instance, having rituals performed may sometimes not help; the cause and effect go their individual ways. It's like if you plant the seed of a hot-tasting plant, chili for example, and then once it has started to grow you plant grapes and apricots and so on around the chili as a way of making it turn sweet. You can't make the chili sweet, because the plants' growth is separate.

Cause and effect is extremely subtle, because any cause one accumulates will bring its corresponding result. The monk Priyabhadra had an extremely ugly body and an extremely sweet voice. Both of these were caused by the following. In a past life he had been born a coolie when a certain king was building a huge stūpa. The stūpa was so enormous that he criticized it, saying, "Why are they building this stūpa so big? It will never get finished." Later, when the stūpa was completed, he offered it a bell to expiate what he had said.

While Atiśha was in Tibet, a Tibetan man was unconcerned when he committed some trivial sin in his sight. This proved too much for Atiśha, who said, "Alas, you should not be so brazen. Cause and effect is subtle! Cause and effect is deep!"

Once a monk spilt some grease over a cushion used by the Saṅgha in assembly. In his next life he was reborn as a man with a black back.

Another time, when a monk was dying his robes, they turned into pieces of calf's flesh; he was accused of stealing a calf and had to spend six months in prison. This was said to be the result of the following. In a past life he had accused an innocent pratyekabuddha of stealing a calf. The pratyekabuddha was thrown into the king's prison for six days.

Sagama, mother of Mṛigaradhara, a minister of the city of Śhrāvasti, had thirty-two athletic young sons. Another minister of King Prasenajit caused them to fall out of favor; the king had all the sons put to death and the pile of their heads taken to their mother. This resulted from thirty-two thieves in the past stealing a bull and killing it. Sagama herself had been the thieves' landlady when they killed the bull.

Kyabje Pabongka told these stories in more detail.

This is how karma is fixed.

KARMA SHOWS GREAT INCREASE (211)

Internal causes produce much greater effects than external causes. Even so, here is an analogy using an external cause and its results: a great tree grows from but a single tiny peach stone, and every year the tree yields hundreds of thousands of things—leaves and fruit. Though this is a big increase, internal causes yield even bigger results.

When the Bhagavān visited the city of Nyagrodhikā, a woman gave him a handful of sweetmeats made of sesame called *ladus*. The Buddha predicted that in a future life the woman would be reborn as a pratyekabuddha called Supraṇihita. Her husband irreverently said, "Please don't tell a lie just for food, Buddha." The Buddha gave the illustration of the seed of the pipal tree, which is only the size of a mustard seed, yet from it grows such a huge tree that its shadow falls over five hundred chariots, placed so that they do not touch each other. Buddha then said that small karmic actions have great results. And so the husband came to believe.

Once a monk told some people, "Your voice is like a dog's bark," or "like a frog's croak," or "like a monkey's chatter." That monk had to take five hundred corresponding rebirths for each insult.

In China, a man once wrote, "Scholars these days are like snakes," so his book was called the *Snake Simile Treatise*. This author's body later became racked with pain; his legs and arms fused to his body, which turned into a snake's. A snake's head then worked its way out of a crack in his head. In that rebirth the author was actually transformed into a snake.

In India, five hundred fishermen once caught in their nets a huge fishlike animal with eighteen heads. The Buddha said this was the result of the following. The animal had once been Mānavakapila, and his mother had encouraged him to say to members of the Saṅgha, "You are like a dog," and so on. But when the Bhagavān arrived to give this pronouncement on the causes for the creature's karma, he was criticized by tīrṭhikas, who said, "Gautama the holy man is fond of vulgar spectacles." I have already told you this in greater detail in the preparatory rites section [see Day 4, pp. 141ff.]

These things arose from trivial insults—not from, say, killing a man and making off with his horse.

Before the nun Utpalavarṇā became ordained she had two sons. One of them was drowned, the other was eaten by a wolf. Her husband was killed by a snake. Her parents and their household perished in a fire. She then married a priest. While she was giving birth to a son, her husband got drunk with another man. He then came home, killed her son, and made her eat the flesh. She ran away and came upon another householder whose wife had died. The householder took Utpala as his wife, but he, too, died, and she was buried alive with his corpse, as was the local religious custom. A grave robber dug her up, and she became his wife. Later the king killed this husband, [who was also] a bandit chief; she was yet again buried with the corpse. It is said that she underwent these miseries as a result of the following. In a former rebirth Utpala had been a king's chief concubine. She had killed the queen's son but had sworn many oaths denying it.

There are very many such stories. Cause and effect is even subtler and more obscure than emptiness. Śhrāvaka and pratyekabuddha arhats can understand and teach the subtle details of emptiness but the subtleties of cause and effect come under the jurisdiction of buddhas alone, and one must assess it solely through their authentic pronouncements. This law, in fact, is so subtle that one should avoid even the smallest sin. From the *Sayings of the Buddha:*

> Do not think "The small sins I do
> Will not return in my future lives."
> Just as falling drops of water
> Will fill a large container,
> The little sins a churl accumulates
> Will completely overwhelm him.

A trivial virtue will also grow into a good result. The universal emperor Mābhvātā ruled over the four continents, celestial realms and all. They say this was the result of his having thrown a handful of lentils [as an offering to] Buddha Vipaśhyin. Four of the lentils landed in Vipaśhyin's begging bowl, and one stuck to his crown protrusion.

Once, while Buddha was still alive, there was a Brahman named Suvarṇavasu. Gold coins would come out of his hands. There was an inexhaustible supply of coins, said to be a result from an action in his past life as a timber merchant, when he had once received a gold coin in payment for some wood and offered it, dropped in a clay pot full of water, to Buddha Kāśhyapa.

Kanakavatsa was an elder of the Saṅgha. At the time of his birth, seven golden elephants appeared spontaneously in his family's treasure vaults. All the elephants' droppings and urine were gold, so Kanakavatsa was well provided for. Seven times King Ajātaśhatru had the elephants stolen, but this did not succeed because the elephants would sink into the ground, and things became as they were before. This was said to have been the result of a past life when Kanakavatsa had restored and gilded a clay statue of Buddha Kanakamuni's elephant mount.

When the nun Śhuklā was born from her mother's womb, she was already wearing clothes of fine linen. When she was ordained, the clothes were transformed into robes. These are said to have been results from a past life when she had been a beggar, and she and her husband had had only one garment between them and had to take turns going outside. Yet they offered this garment to Buddha Kanakamuni, though it could have meant their deaths. The act ripened into a tangible result for both of them in that very life: the king and his concubines gave them clothes.

One must not belittle the practice of even small virtues. From the *Sayings of the Buddha:*

> Do not think "A small virtue
> Will not return in my future lives."
> Just as falling drops of water
> Will fill a large container,
> The little virtues the steadfast accumulate
> Will completely overwhelm them.

These two sections on how karma is fixed and on how it increases make one decide that one should definitely practice virtue and abandon sin, and that one should practice even the smallest virtue and abandon even the smallest sin.

ONE DOES NOT MEET WITH SOMETHING IF ONE HAS NOT CREATED THE KARMA FOR IT TO HAPPEN (212)

When there is a war or other conflict, some people claim, "I had no talisman against weapons, yet when people fired many guns I came to no harm." You might take this to be something amazing, but it is a case of their not meeting with something for which they had not created the karma.

Some people are at first unscathed by weapons but later get killed. Not understanding cause and effect, some will say, "Their talisman must have weakened." It was nothing of the sort: initially these people had not met with [a situation created by their] karma. Later on, they did. When one does not meet with [a situation created by one's] karma, one will not die, despite being burnt in a fire. Once the householder Agnibhu was burnt in a fire together with his mother's corpse, but he did not die and later gained arhatship. Ajātaśhatru stole [Kanakavatsa's] golden elephants seven times but he derived no benefit, because the elephants sank into the ground each time.

King Udayana's concubine Śhyāmavatī had achieved the results of a never-returner [and so could fly]. Her retinue of five hundred ladies had seen the truth [that is, gained the path of seeing]. Yet when Mākandika the Brahman set fire to her apartments, [because in a previous life they had burnt down a Brahman's hut] they could only fly a small distance away. Śhyāmavatī said, "Who rules us but our own karma, which we ourselves created and accumulated?" They all dived into the fire like moths into a flame and were burned. There was also a woman servant named Kubjottarā, who had not achieved any magic powers [but did not share this karma]. She escaped from the fire by fleeing into a well.

When Virūḍhaka waged war against the Śhākyas, all seventy-seven thousand of them were stream-enterers, but this did not save them from being killed. A few who had not created the appropriate karma fled far away and escaped, while the great name of Śhākya was brought low.

The city of Rāvaṇa was buried under a rain of earth. The king, his ministers, and subjects were all buried, but two ministers escaped.

KUBJOTTARĀ ESCAPES FROM THE FIRE

These are some of the examples of people not meeting with something because of not possessing the karma for it.

KARMA ONCE CREATED WILL NOT DISAPPEAR OF ITS OWN ACCORD (213)

As a sūtra tells us:

> The karma of embodied beings
> Does not vanish over hundreds of eons.
> If the prerequisites and the time are right,
> Karma will ripen to results.

Karma does not grow stale after a long time, nor does it lessen, become nonexistent, and so on. Though small, it will sooner or later ripen into a result, as in the story of Ārya Vibhudatta, who had achieved arhatship yet could not obtain alms, or if he did, the alms would vanish for some reason. Just as he was about to die, he took some soup of ash and water, and then he left his body.

The householder Śhrījāta had in his mindstream so few and such small root virtues to contribute to his liberation that an arhat [Śhāriputra] could not see them. Though extremely small, they were to give a result. He had received these root merits in the following way. Śhrījāta had taken rebirth as a fly in a past life. Following the scent of a dry animal dropping, he landed on it, and by accident had circumambulated a stūpa when the dropping was swept away by some water.

A pig was once chased around a stūpa by a dog; it was reborn as a god after its death.

When King Virūḍhaka was persecuting the Śhākyas, the Bhagavān Buddha himself had, to common appearances, a back ailment. Once, in a past life as a child of a fisherman, a number of fishermen had caught two huge fish and eaten one alive, and he had rejoiced over this. The back ailment was the result. The story goes that Virūḍhaka himself was burnt to death in a fire, despite living completely surrounded by water.

The Buddha predicted that a Jain named Duḥkhitaka would die from ill-digested food. The Jain went on a fast but died anyway from undigested water and sugar cane.

Nāgārjuna had gained knowledge of immortality, but in a past life he had sliced through an ant's neck while cutting grass, and because of that karma he died by losing his head.

The śhrāvaka Maudgalyāyana was the best at working miracles, yet some staff-bearing priests, whose heads were shaven except for the small lock of hair at the crown, managed to beat him with their staffs. "All his flesh and bones were thrashed like bullrushes": his entire body was crushed like reeds. Śhāriputra asked him why he had not shown them his miraculous powers. Maudgalyāyana replied that he had been completely under the power of his karma; how could he create a miracle if he could not even remember to be miraculous! In a past life he had said something insulting to his mother; the karma had not disappeared of its own, and this was the result.

As for the results of evil karma, if you cannot purify the evil karma itself through the four powers of confession and restraint, it will not let you go, even in your last life [as a bodhisattva]. As the *Sūtra on the Wise and Foolish,* the *One Hundred Verses on Karma from the Sūtras,* the *One Hundred Life Stories,* the *Transmission of the Vinaya,* and so forth tell, after you have accumulated either a sin or a virtue, the result will not disappear. It is impossible for the karma to become nonexistent, which is why they say you must modify your actions even on the subtlest level.

The next two sections are a discussion of sin and a contemplation of techniques to ensure that your virtue will not be destroyed by anger. In any case you must decide to modify your behavior properly according to the law of cause and effect. The above four headings were mainly to promote faith in cause and effect. When you want thereby to modify your behavior according to cause and effect, you should think about the tenfold paths [of virtuous and nonvirtuous] karma—a rough overall scheme describing virtue and sin—because this makes the task of modifying your behavior easier. From *Engaging in the Middle Way:*

> Apart from ethics, there is no cause of high rebirth or definite
> excellence:
> [Not] for ordinary beings, [for śhrāvakas] produced by
> enlightened speech,
> For beings certain to gain enlightenment by themselves,
> Or for children of the victors.

In other words, the tenfold path of karma is the foundation of high rebirths for people who have not yet entered the path; it is the foundation for the sort of enlightenment enjoyed by people inclined toward being śhrāvakas and pratyekabuddhas; and it is the foundation for the supreme, perfect, full enlightenment of bodhisattvas. It is therefore vital for ordinary beings initially, in this small-scope section, to keep the ethics of modifying their behavior according to the black and white sides of cause and effect.

THINKING ABOUT SOME OF THE SPECIFICS OF CAUSE AND EFFECT (214)

This has three sections: (1) thinking about the black side of cause and effect; (2) thinking about the white side of cause and effect; (3) teaching about the doors that unintentionally lead to powerful karma.

THINKING ABOUT THE BLACK SIDE OF CAUSE AND EFFECT (215)

This itself has three sections: (1) the actual black karmic process; (2) the differences that make for heavy or light karma; (3) teaching what the results of these karmas are.

THE ACTUAL BLACK KARMIC PROCESS (216)

If the law of cause and effect is so important even on a very subtle level, what then is the basis for modifying one's behavior? The *Treasury of Metaphysics* tells us:

> To approximately summarize,
> Be it virtue or be it nonvirtue,
> The paths of karma are taught to be tenfold.

This says that virtue or nonvirtue can be roughly summarized under ten types. Even ordinary lay people, and not just the ordained, must modify their behavior. That is why Longdoel Lama Rinpoche had woodblocks for a quarto edition on confession of the ten nonvirtues carved and printed.

Engaging in the Deeds of Bodhisattvas says:

> Though you think you want to avoid suffering,
> You actually hasten on to suffering itself.

You want happiness, but through benightedness
You destroy your happiness like an enemy.

In other words, we may desire happiness, but we don't understand how to create virtue, the cause for our having happiness. We may not want suffering, but we don't understand that we must abandon sin, the cause of suffering. So we destroy happiness—the very thing we want—as if it were our enemy. We modify our behavior the wrong way round.

Some people who think at a low level might feel, "I do not know the ten nonvirtues." But if we can learn twenty or thirty songs and tunes, it is impossible that we cannot know the ten nonvirtues after being introduced to them. We will go to the lower realms not because we don't know the Dharma or haven't studied it, but because we know the Dharma but do not put it into practice. It is *vital* to put Dharma into practice.

The ten nonvirtues, the things to abandon, are:

Karma of the body has three aspects,
That of speech has four,
And those of mind three.
Expiate each of these ten nonvirtues.

In other words, *killing, taking things not given to you,* and *sexual misconduct* are the three nonvirtues of body. *Lying, divisive speech, harsh words,* and *idle gossip* are the four of speech. The three of mind are *covetousness, harmful intent,* and *wrong views.*

Each of these nonvirtues has four components: the *basis, intention, deed,* and *final step.*

KILLING (217)

The *basis* of killing involves another being, quite distinct from oneself, that is to be killed—a sheep for example. The *intention* itself has three parts: the *recognition, motive,* and *delusion.* Here, *recognition* is to recognize unmistakenly that a thing is what it is. The *motive* is wanting to kill. The *delusion* is any of the three delusions [or "poisons"]. An example of killing out of hostility would be getting angry at, say, an enemy and striking him with a weapon. An example of killing out of attachment is killing a sheep because one is attached to its meat, hide, and so forth. An instance of killing out of benighted ignorance is the intentional killing of a sentient being by a tīrṭhika or any such person to make an offering of its meat and blood, with the thought or claim that this is not a misdeed. The *deed* is carrying out the killing using poison, weapons, mantric charms, or whatever else may be used. Killing need not be something obvious like stabbing with a knife: it could also be done through black magic, mantras, and so forth. The *final step* is the other being's death before one's own.

When there is a full set of all these, the karmic process of killing has been completed. Ordering someone else to do the killing is no different from doing it yourself. *A Treasury of Metaphysics* says: "It is all one for armies and so forth: all of them have equally done the deed." That is, if eight people kill a sheep, each of them does not receive a *share* of the sin: each one receives the full sin of killing a sheep. When a general sends out many soldiers to the slaughter and a thousand men are killed, each soldier commits the sin of killing as many men as an individual soldier is capable of doing; the general, however, gets the full sin of killing all one thousand men.

We may set a good example here in the Central Province, but everywhere in Tibet I believe ordained people are making others slaughter cattle for them, claiming, "They are our serfs." But the slaughterer and the person who made him do it each commits the sin of taking a life. If the monk had done the killing with his own hands, only one person would have committed the sin. I would be happier if he had not asked the other person to assist and had instead done the killing himself—the other person would not have acquired the additional sin.

We may think that we do not acquire the sin of actually killing a living being, but we do; for though we do not judge it so, it is still a great sin to make others kill for us. Once some monks and novices herded a goat, a sheep, and a bull into a pen. When the animals were about to be slaughtered, the goat said to the other two: "They want to kill us."

"But they take refuge every day," said the bull. "They fold their hands together, shut their eyes, and say, 'May all sentient beings have happiness and its cause.' They will not kill us!"

"They are disciples of the Buddha," the sheep said. "When they embarked on the teachings, they promised to keep the advice that goes with taking refuge. The main advice is not to harm sentient beings. Surely they will not harm us!"

The animals talked among themselves a great deal. Then, early that morning, a vile butcher went to the monks' doorstep. The goat saw him and listened.

"I'm busy today," the butcher said with some heat. And though he implored them, "Please ask somebody else," the monks insisted.

"I've run out of things for lunch," one monk insisted. "Help me out by butchering these three today—it has to be today."

The butcher had to promise to do it.

The goat heard that they were certain to die and told the other two. The three of them were miserable and crying helplessly. Just then the monk came, telling the beads on his rosary, taking refuge, and reciting *oṃ maṇi padme hūṃ;* he had come to see if the goat, sheep, and bull were fat enough.

The three said that it was not right for monks to kill sentient beings, or to get others to do so. "It would be best if we were not killed. If we must die, monk, you yourself should kill us."

The monk did nothing. The butcher returned and bound the legs of the three animals with a rope. He knocked the bull unconscious with a mallet, thrust a sharp sword into the goat's and sheep's ribs up to the hilt, and used his sharp fingernails to cut their main blood vessels. Thus the animals went through inconceivable suffering. The bull cried out in a pathetic voice: "Hear me, all the buddhas of the ten directions. I have evil tidings. In such-and-such a place, the monks of this land are only pale reflection of monks, for they have sentient beings killed—sentient beings who were once their mothers of old." The victory standard of the Dharma was lowered, and the standard of the demons raised on high; all the buddhas and bodhisattvas were saddened.

This was the dialogue between the monk, goat, sheep, and bull—and all for the sake of lunch for a few monks! *A Clear Mirror* gives a longer version.[56]

Such things detract from the teachings; it is vital to avoid killing living beings. My own guru, my precious refuge and protector, delighted in making others give up killing other beings, and was better at it than anyone else. And when I went to Kham I was able to put an end to the annual mass slaughtering of animals that Sog Tsaendaen and other monasteries used to carry out to raise funds. I think this is the best thing I have done in this life for the Dharma.

TAKING WHAT IS NOT GIVEN (218)

The *basis* is a possession that another holds to be his. The intention is made up of three parts: the *recognition* should be unmistaken; the *motive* is wanting to take the thing that is not given to you; the *delusion* is any one of the three [poisons]. An example of anger would be stealing property from an enemy. An example of attachment is being attracted to someone else's property and stealing it through subterfuge. An example of benighted ignorance is the tradition among non-Buddhists that "When a Brahman's fortunes decline, we claim it is Dharma for him to steal." In other words, they do not count it as a misdeed.

The *deed* need not be skulking around at night, for example. Taking what is not given could be an ordained person's abuse of charity, an official's meting out of an undeserved punishment, the sort of practice of generosity that gives away a penny in the hope of receiving a pound, and so on. When a monk breaks the monastic rules he is made to do prostrations and the like; the point of doing these is so that none of the above misdeeds will occur.

To sum up: you have the thought of wanting to obtain a particular piece of property even though the other person does not want to part with it. You obtain it through various deceitful means, making that person powerless to withhold it from you. We are in great danger of committing this sort of theft. Not only that: we could let someone have another person's property or possessions, even if these are worth only a few *zho.* Or we could be lent something and much later take possession when its owner has forgotten about it. Or we could think, "Wouldn't it be good if he has forgotten" and find out that he has.

The *final step* comes when you think you have received the thing—you are then nothing less than a thief. If you are a novice, it is tantamount to breaking a major vow; if a fully ordained monk, you break a major vow.

SEXUAL MISCONDUCT (219)

For lay people the *basis* is: any wrong orifice, in other words, all orifices except the vagina; any wrong time, such as when the woman is pregnant or during one-day vows; at any improper place, such as before one's guru or a stūpa; any wrong partner, such as one's own mother, and so on.

For ordained people, all sexual activity becomes sexual misconduct.

The *recognition* is: one must be in no doubt that the act is sexual misconduct; but when you break a major monk's vow of celibacy, they say it does not matter if you are mistaken or not.

The *delusion* is one of the three poisons. The *motive* is wanting to engage in perversion. The *deed* is the two organs coming into contact, and so forth. The *final step* is completed when one experiences orgasm.

LYING (220)

One can lie about eight things: something (1) seen with your own eyes or (2) not so seen, (3) heard with your own ears or (4) not so heard, (5) perceived or experienced by your own nose, tongue, or body consciousnesses or (6) not so perceived or experienced, and (7) experienced or known by your mind consciousness or (8) not so experienced or known. You must be speaking to a human being who knows how to speak and who understands what you are saying.

The components of the *intention* are as follows. The *recognition* is recognizing that you are, for example, saying you did not see something when you in fact did. The *motive* is wanting to say such a thing. The *delusion* is one of the three poisons.

The *deed* is speaking lying words, or lying by some movement of your head without saying anything, for example. The *final step* is when the other person understands what you mean.

It would not be right, however, to give an honest answer if some potential killers ask you, "Where has our victim gone?" However, those who still have some misgivings over this must do the following. When asked, "Did the man go this way?" you should say something irrelevant to throw them off, like: "I'm going round to see what's-his-name tonight."

DIVISIVE SPEECH (221)

The *basis* can be either people who get along or those who do not. The *recognition* should be unmistaken; the *motive* is wanting to cause division; the *delusion* is one of the three poisons. The *deed* is as follows. You wish to divide people who get along, or to prevent a reconciliation between those who do not; it makes no difference if your divisive speech is the truth or lies. Some people consider doing these things to be good. Not only is it not, divisive speech causes great harm and so can't be right.

The *final step* is when people understand the meaning of your words, and the karma is complete when the divisive words have been spoken and the other person has understood and split off in opposition. If the words were not understood and the opposed parties did not divide, or whatever, this becomes idle speech, not divisive speech.

HARSH WORDS (222)

The *basis* of harsh words could be either a sentient being that serves as the basis for the development of harmful intentions, or an inanimate object such as a thorn.

The *recognition* should be unmistaken. The *delusion* is one of the three poisons. The *motive* is wanting to say such words. The *deed* is speaking about faults in another person's ethics, race, body, and so on. You could tell the truth or lies; for example, you could say, "You're blind" to either a blind person or to someone not blind. When you talk about faults in the other person's ethics, race, body, and so forth, even if you say it pleasantly, you have committed the misdeed of harsh words if the other person's feelings are hurt.

The *final step* is when the meaning of the words is understood. The words must be understood; the karmic process is therefore incomplete if you say them to inanimate objects.

IDLE GOSSIP (223)

The *basis* is something frivolous. The *recognition* is recognizing that whatever it is you want to talk about is this [or that] thing. The actual basis of idle gossip may be anything at all, anything that enters the conversation by virtue of being recalled and that is made out to be paramount. The *motive* is wanting to talk. The *delusion* is one of the three poisons. The *deed* is talking about the king, the army, or whatever.

These days we monks discuss a range of topics—the government, China, India, and so on—when a large group of us gets together in the monastery grounds or goes circumambulating. This is idle gossip. Idle gossip is the least of the ten nonvirtues, but it is the best way to waste our human lives. The evil of idle gossip bedevils even the seating rows of public [religious] ceremonies, and monks regularly get together in their rooms and spend the whole day making much frivolous conversation, and the time is frittered away in idleness. Atiśha said: "When in company check your speech." In other words, you must be careful even if you are with only one friend.

Stories and discussions on non-Buddhist treatises are idle gossip.

Although you can get other people to do six of the nonvirtues of body and speech for you, except for sexual misconduct, you yourself are also involved in the karmic process.

COVETOUSNESS (224)

The *basis* is another's property or possessions. Suppose you go to the market, see an attractive piece of merchandise, and think, "If only I had that!" and are almost sick with desire.

The *recognition* is recognizing the particular object serving as the basis of your covetousness as being that particular object.

The *motive, deed,* and *final step* must be assumed to be functions of the one thought. The *motive* is thinking, "If only this or that valuable thing were mine." The *delusion* is one of the three poisons. The *deed* is when the thought becomes stronger: "I will make it mine." The *final step* is when the thought becomes stronger still and you decide that you will employ some means of making the valuable object your own.

You can even covet your own possessions.

When we go to the markets in Lhasa, we develop covetousness hundreds of thousands of times, because we are without remembrance about whatever arises in our mind. We should apply the antidote to covetousness and think how these illusory goods are without essence.

HARMFUL INTENT (225)

The *basis, delusions,* and so on, of harmful intentions are the same as those previously discussed in harsh words. The *motive* is either wanting to inflict harm by, for example, beating and killing the basis of the harmful intentions, or wishing things like, "Wouldn't it be good if that other person were ruined." The *deed* is putting [more] effort [into the thought]. The *final step* is deciding [to harm that person].

We perform the tantric activities of peace, increase, power, and wrath; if we do not do these with good motives or solely for the sake of the teachings and sentient beings, there is a danger that they can become covetousness, harmful intent, and so on. We must therefore be careful.

WRONG VIEWS (226)

The *basis* must be something that exists: cause and effect, the four truths, the Three Jewels, and so on. A wrong view is to view these things as nonexistent; denying these things, for example, is saying they do not exist.

One example: the tīrṭhika ṛiṣhi Akṣhapāda lusted after his own daughter and wanted to sleep with her, so he composed the *Hundred Thousand Verses,* in which he claimed that there were no past or future rebirths. He also fabricated sixty evil views of his own, and so forth.

The *recognition* is like the other nine forms of recognition except that one does not recognize that the thing being denied is in fact true. The *deed* is actively denying the thing serving as the basis. The *final* step is to decide that it does not exist.

There is little chance that we would actually [hold wrong views], but there is a danger that people with only small amounts of merit could be swayed into doing so by bad company.

Now that we can identify these ten properly, it is vital that we scrupulously avoid doing them.

THE DIFFERENCES THAT MAKE FOR HEAVY OR LIGHT KARMA (227)

There are six of these:

HEAVY BY NATURE (228)

The seven karmic actions of body and speech range from the heaviest first, killing, to the lightest last of all. The reason is that the order reflects the magnitude of suffering that other beings will have. An illustration: no matter how different we may be from each other, none of us cherishes our possessions as much as we do our lives. Killing therefore causes more suffering to another person than taking something not given. However, with the three nonvirtues of the mind, the lightest is first and the heaviest last of all.

HEAVY BECAUSE OF THE INTENTION (229)

When the intention is due to a very strong delusion but the nonvirtue, using insulting words, for example, is by nature light, as when one says "You mangy old dog" out of very great anger, this act then becomes heavy.

HEAVY BECAUSE OF THE DEED (230)

An example of this is killing sadistically, with intense torture. Also, killing an elephant, for example, is a heavier sin than killing an insect. Killing animals with huge bodies or with great physical strength is a bigger sin because they experience greater suffering, and this is heavy due to the deed. In some lands they burn live frogs, poultry, and insects; these acts are heavy both because of their nature and because of the deeds themselves.

HEAVY BECAUSE OF THE BASIS (231)

It is a heavy sin, for example, to cast dirty looks at karmically potent beings such as one's guru, ordination master, bodhisattvas, members of the Saṅgha, parents, and so forth.

HEAVY BECAUSE OF ALWAYS BEING DONE (232)

Idle gossip, for example, is heavy because one is always doing it.

HEAVY BECAUSE NO ANTIDOTE HAS BEEN APPLIED (233)

The sins in the mindstream of a person who never performs a single virtue are extremely heavy.

There are one to six types of heaviness involved [in any action]. Casting a dirty look at a bodhisattva when one is very angry, for example, or killing an animal sadistically both incur two heavinesses. Singing and dancing out of great attachment has only one type of heaviness. All six types of heaviness are present if, say, a butcher who always sins and never does anything virtuous gets very angry with his parents and kills them sadistically.

None of our sins are not heavy, and we are always adding to their heaviness.

TEACHING WHAT THE RESULTS OF THESE KARMAS ARE (234)

There are three types: ripened results, results congruent with the cause, and environmental results.

When one commits any of the ten nonvirtues, one has to undergo four results instead of three, because results congruent with the cause are subdivided into two types: experiences congruent with the cause, and behavior congruent with the cause.

Great nonvirtues will lead to rebirth in hell; medium nonvirtues to rebirth as a hungry ghost; small ones to rebirth as an animal. Let us take killing as an example. The ripened result could be rebirth in hell. Later one gets free of the hells and is reborn as a human being, but one's life is short, with much sickness: the experiences congruent with the cause. One may also have liked killing ever since childhood: the behavior congruent with the cause. The environmental results occur in the surrounding world: food, drink, medicine, and so on, have little power. After we have been born in hell and lived with our bodies indistinguishable from the fires there, we could then be born among humans as an evildoer who likes to kill. Our killing perpetuates this process, and we are again thrown into the lower realms. The most disheartening results of all are the behaviors congruent with the cause; that is why they say we must work hard at the means to prevent behaviors congruent with nonvirtuous causes from occurring, and to promote the behaviors congruent with virtuous causes.

Now, we will deal with the other nonvirtues—taking things not given, and so on—in order. Experiences congruent with the cause are: [for stealing] you will lack possessions, or have to share them with others; [for sexual misconduct] you will be unable to keep your followers, servants, or spouses; [for lying] others will not believe you; [for divisive speech] you will have few friends, be without followers, servants, and so forth; [for insulting words] others will speak ill of you; [for idle gossip] your words will carry little weight because others will think little of what you say; [for covetousness] you will not achieve your aims; [for harmful intent] you will be terrified; and [for wrong views] you will be blind to the right view.

Some sinners have long lives in which all goes well for them; some Dharma practitioners have illness, short lives, and so on. There are many causes for this: the causes for these effects are in past lives. When something undesirable happens to us in this rebirth, we think that other more immediate circumstances, ourselves, or others are responsible, but this is not so. Normally these things are created by karma from past lives.

Behaviors congruent with the cause are as follows. Due to taking what is not given, in this life there are those who, since childhood, have liked stealing things, even needles. Rats and mice and so on are skilled at stealing; they are fond of taking what is not given, and do so. Other actions congruent with the cause are analogous and easy to understand. The behaviors congruent with the causes of covetousness, harmful intent, and wrong views are an increase in attachment, hostility, and benightedness.

The environmental results due to taking things not given are: few crops and fruit; frost, hail, drought, and so on; few offspring, little milk, or curds, etc. [Due to sexual misconduct] you have to live in places that are muddy or filthy, for example; [due to lying] there will be many cheats about; [from divisive speech] you will have to live in places where the ground is uneven; [from insulting words] you will be born in a place where there are many tree stumps and brambles; [due to idle gossip] the crops will fail or appear at the wrong times; [due to covetousness] all your pleasures will be overshadowed; [due to harmful intent] there will be much war, sickness, and famine; [due to wrong views] your sources of water and precious things will dry up.

So, if you have studied and know what happens through the results of nonvirtue and yet still indulge in them knowingly, it is like jumping off a cliff with your eyes wide open.

Some land was once quite good but now it is no good at all; the essence has been leached out, and so on. Karma did this. Earlier in this fortunate eon the ground was spacious and magnificent, but it has gradually declined and is now eroded with gullies and ravines.

THINKING ABOUT THE WHITE SIDE OF CAUSE AND EFFECT (235)

This has two sections: (1) teaching the actual white karmic process; (2) teaching its results.

TEACHING THE ACTUAL WHITE KARMIC PROCESS (236)

Merely refraining from committing the ten nonvirtues will not complete the white karmic process. The complete process is defined as: identifying the ten nonvirtues, refraining from doing them after seeing their drawbacks, and then having the thought of abandoning them, the ultimate form of restraint. The virtue of not killing, for example, has four parts: the basis, motive, deed, and final step. Take the white karmic action of not killing a sheep. The sheep is the *basis* of the karma. You see the drawbacks of killing the sheep and want not to kill it, thinking, "It would not be right." This is the *motive*. When this thought becomes even stronger and you see that killing the sheep would be a misdeed, you try to entirely refrain from killing it; this attempt is the *deed* of the white karma of foregoing killing the sheep. The karmic process is complete when you decide that you will not kill it: you see the drawbacks of killing the sheep and think you will completely refrain from killing it—this is [equivalent to] a karmic action of the body. This is the *actual* or *final step* to the white karma of not killing a sheep.

When you are going to steal something not given, for example, the *motive* for not taking it would be the thought: "This valuable thing is the basis for my suffering and degradation; to do this evil action for this purpose will be the cause of my going to the lower realms, so to do it would not be right." The *deed* is your attempt to give up this karmic action. The karmic process is complete when you are quite decided on abandoning [the deed]. Apply the same principles to the other nonvirtues, such as sexual misconduct.

TEACHING ITS RESULTS (237)

This has three sections.

THE RIPENED RESULT (238)

You take rebirth as a god of the higher realms [that is, in the form and formless realms] because of highly virtuous karma; as a desire-realm god owing to medium virtuous karma; and as a human being owing to small virtuous karma.

RESULTS CONGRUENT WITH THE CAUSE (239)

There are two types of these. *Experiences congruent with the cause* are: longer life, greater wealth, harmony with your spouse, people heeding what you say, harmony with your friends, and so on.

Examples of *behaviors congruent with the cause* appear in some people—reincarnations of saints, for example—who right from birth develop renunciation and compassion on their own.

ENVIRONMENTAL RESULTS (240)

These are easy to understand: they are the opposites of the above environmental results for the ten nonvirtues—food, drink, medicine with great power, and so on.

TEACHING ABOUT THE DOORS THAT UNINTENTIONALLY LEAD TO POWERFUL KARMA (241)

This has four sections.

POWERFUL OWING TO THE FIELD (242)

Generosity becomes more and more powerful when practiced toward ordinary people, one's parents, monks [and nuns], lay or ordained bodhisattvas, buddhas, and one's gurus respectively. It is a much greater sin to give a bodhisattva a scornful look than to throw all the sentient beings of the three realms into prison and pluck out their eyes. It is more beneficial to fold one's hands out of faith as a sign of respect for a bodhisattva than to release all those sentient beings from prison and give them eyes. Similarly, if a monk kills an animal, he breaks only a minor vow. If he kills a human being, he breaks a major vow.

POWERFUL BECAUSE ONE HAD BEEN A CANDIDATE FOR VOWS (243)

A sūtra says one's virtue is much more extensive if one has taken vows than if one has not. And the same holds for nonvirtues: it is a heavier sin for someone ordained to commit a trivial misdeed than for a lay person to indulge in the ten nonvirtues. This is why it is so heavy when people who hold bodhichitta, and even more so, tantric vows, commit misdeeds. Some might claim, "Take a vow and the sin is great," and avoid them, but this is definitely not so. From *Engaging in the Middle Way:* "There is no cause for high rebirth other than ethics." That is, in order to gain a human rebirth in a future life, you must definitely take vows and then maintain ethics. If you do not, and merely practice generosity, say, you may be reborn as an animal, a nāga, for instance.

If you take a vow you will receive virtue continuously. And if you take an unvirtuous vow, you will continuously receive nonvirtue: the local butcher and a woman who serves alcohol are examples of people who have taken unvirtuous vows, and their sins will continually increase, even while they are sleeping or relaxing.

Two people may live together, and one of them may have taken a vow not to kill while the other has not. Both of them may equally not kill the whole time, but the person without the vows does not receive the virtue that comes from abandoning killing, whereas the virtue of the person with the vow will increase every day. Similarly, people with lay, novice, or full ordination vows may not make any special effort to create root virtues but at the very least they still see an increase in five, thirty-six, or two hundred and fifty-three types of virtue respectively, even when they sleep. And this applies to an incalculable degree, more than for any of the above, for people holding the bodhichitta vows. As *Engaging in the Deeds of Bodhisattvas* says:

> Thereafter, even in their sleep
> Or in unguarded moments, the merit has power.
> Much merit comes to them continually
> And will become as enormous as space itself

People with tantric vows see one hundred thousand times more increase than even this. Thus someone who has not taken any vows does not create these special root virtues unless he does so specifically; contrast this with someone holding vows who every day sees an increase in virtue and so profits greatly. The narrowminded should therefore not have wrong views: even lay people must be encouraged to take one-day vows, one-day fasting vows, and bodhichitta vows.

There are two types of prohibitions: natural and declared prohibitions. Prohibitions of the first type are assumed to be as follows. One of their features is their cause: one's actual motives are nonvirtuous ones. Another feature is their nature: their natures are sinful and they embody nonvirtue. Yet another feature is their result: a part of their nature is that they are capable of ripening into an unpleasant result. No matter whether someone has taken vows or not, if these basics are present, that person will generate a prohibited sin.

The second, the declared prohibition, is any karmic action or [resulting] obstacle that goes against a ruling made by the Buddha. They are assumed to be as follows. One of their features is the cause: one's actual motives are virtuous or neutral thoughts. Their nature is another feature: they embody a neutral nature. Another feature is their result: part of their nature is that they are not capable of ripening into unpleasant results.

If you break a minor vow and the cause—that is, your motivation—is linked to something nonvirtuous—thoughts of ignoring your instructions, and the like—you will then commit a sin and break a minor vow: that is a natural prohibition and a declared prohibition. If you break the minor vow with only a neutral motive, you break the minor vow by going against a ruling of the Buddha, but you do not commit the sin—the natural prohibition. If a monk kills an animal he commits a sin—the natural prohibition of killing an animal—and breaks a minor vow—the declared prohibition, for killing an animal is a minor transgression of the monk's vow.

Such sins and broken minor vows may have the same nature, but they have different designations. No matter how much one applies some antidote, such as the four powers, to the broken [minor] vow, and although one may be able to completely purify the sin having the same nature, doing this still does not properly restore the broken [minor] vow that has the same nature as the sin. Also, even though one may properly restore the broken [minor] vow, if one does not expiate the sin through the four powers, one has still not purified it.

One takes pratimokṣha vows from one's abbot, ordination master, and members of the Saṅgha; one must therefore restore these vows in the presence of monks or members of the Saṅgha. Misdeeds against the bodhichitta vows must be confessed and purified before one's gurus, the victorious ones, and their children; misdeeds against tantric vows must be confessed and purified in the presence of the set of deities of the particular maṇḍala.

It is much more beneficial to hold, at minimum, Mahāyāna one-day vows when creating great root virtues by, for example, making offerings or building up our [merit] collection.

POWERFUL BECAUSE OF THE THINGS BEING DONE (244)

Generosity with Dharma is better than generosity with material things; offering one's practice is better than offering material things; and so forth.

POWERFUL BECAUSE OF THE INTENTION (245)

If in conjunction with bodhichitta one makes a single prayer to Tārā or offers a single butterlamp, one's virtue will become very powerful, even more than offering one hundred thousand butterlamps without bodhichitta.

These headings teach in summary the things you must principally avoid—nonvirtue—and the things you must practice—virtue.

If you are to become skilled at doing a practice, you must know how to build up a huge amount of virtue without much trouble and how to reduce your nonvirtue. If a monk, for example, performs the preparatory rites once in conjunction with bodhichitta thoughts, it is powerful in all four ways owing to the field, his having been a candidate for vows, the thing being done, and the intention.

There is also a difference between *throwing* and *completing* karma. Throwing karma is either virtue that throws one to [i.e., causes one to be reborn in] the upper realms, or nonvirtue that throws one to the lower realms. Completing karma is not as fixed: one can have virtuous throwing karma and the completing karma be either virtuous or nonvirtuous. Or the throwing karma can be nonvirtuous and the completing karma either virtuous or nonvirtuous. So there are four possibilities.

For a happy human rebirth—for example, rebirth as a universal emperor—both types of karma must be virtuous. A human rebirth marred by unpleasantness and hardship—rebirth as a beggar, for example—is a case of virtuous throwing karma and nonvirtuous completing karma. Rebirth in hell is an example of nonvirtuous throwing and completing karma. And examples of nonvirtuous throwing karma and virtuous completing karma are being the horse or mule of the Dalai Lama or Paṇchen Lama, or being their pet dogs.

A single karmic action can throw one into many bodies in succession, for example, insulting someone once with the words "You're like a frog" can result in taking five hundred rebirths as a frog; or many karmic actions can result in one taking a single body; and so on.

There are other types of karma: karma one is obliged to undergo, karma one is not obliged to undergo, karma one has accumulated through some action, actions done that accumulated no karma, karma that one accumulated without doing anything.

The results of karma that one is certain to undergo can occur in three different time periods. With visible results: owing to some special motive or merit field, one experiences the results during the same life that the karma was accumulated. With karma to be undergone after rebirth, one experiences the results of a karmic action in the next rebirth. With karma to be undergone in a number of rebirths' time, one undergoes the results of a karmic action in the rebirth after next or in subsequent rebirths. You should refer to such works as [Tsongkapa's] *Great* or *Medium Stages of the Path* to understand these in more detail.

THINKING ABOUT SOME OF THE SPECIFICS (246)

We should therefore fear the results of nonvirtue and keep the ethics of abandoning the ten nonvirtues. If we practice the ten virtues properly, we will not fall into the lower realms and instead merely achieve an unexceptional rebirth as a human being or god. Yet this alone is insufficient for us to achieve liberation and omniscience. If we could gain the special high rebirth that has the eight ripened qualities, however, we could cover more ground on the path than would otherwise be possible. We must therefore achieve such a rebirth with these eight ripened qualities. Great Tsongkapa said:

> You will not cover much ground until you achieve a rebirth
> With all the characteristics for practicing the supreme path.
> Train yourself to have causes for them all.

There are three headings here: (1) the ripened qualities; (2) their functions; (3) the causes to achieve them.

THE RIPENED QUALITIES (247)

There are eight of these qualities: long life, a handsome body, high family, great wealth, trustworthy speech, great power and fame, being a male, being strong in mind and body.

To take an example: in this world, good fruits in a field come from good seed. Make no mistake: our wealth, the fact that we have such a sound high rebirth, and so on—all in truth come from karmic actions in our past lives. And merely having the fruits of this year's harvest is not much help; one must make an effort to plant the seed for next year's. Similarly, it is not helpful to have no curiosity about one's future rebirths, or to think about them and then get terrified. One will get nothing at all if one simply achieves the cause for an ordinary high rebirth; one must achieve the causes to obtain a special type of rebirth suitable for the practice of Dharma. Even more, one must have the eight ripened qualities—long life, a handsome body, and so forth.

THE FUNCTIONS OF THE RIPENED QUALITIES (248)

The first of these eight qualities [long life] will allow you to progress in the Dharma because you can spend a lot of time creating root virtues for your own and for others' sakes.

Because of the second [a handsome body], you will attract disciples merely through your looks. Atiśha was an example of this.

The third [a high family] will make others pay proper heed to your orders.

The fourth is great wealth. Because you will have great resources and a large retinue, you will firstly attract sentient beings through your material possessions, then you will ripen them with Dharma. So this quality gives great impetus to your work for others' sakes.

The fifth [trustworthy speech] enables others to apprehend the truth [emptiness].

The sixth [great power and fame] makes others follow your orders quickly and not disobey them, as if they were the king's command.

The seventh [being a male] means that you will not be afraid in a crowd and that when you live in deserted places you will have few hindrances and interferences in practicing Dharma, and so on.

The eighth [being strong of mind and body] has these functions. You need a strong body to practice great austerities as Milarepa did; you can then practice Dharma during adversity. With a strong mind you will not despair, no matter what may be involved in benefiting yourself and others—you will always be most happy to do whatever is necessary. You will gain powerful conceptualizing [wisdom], and this will act as a cause for your rapidly gaining clairvoyant powers.

THE CAUSES TO ACHIEVE THESE RIPENED QUALITIES (249)

Although it is good for Dharma practitioners to receive these eight, you may wonder, "Will I receive them?" You definitely will; it is like farmers, who plant seed in the spring, knowing that they will get the fruit in autumn. That fruit will then definitely come in autumn. If in this rebirth we create the causes for our receiving the eight ripened qualities and make pure prayers that carry over into future lives, we will certainly get these eight as a result in future lives. This is because it is the nature of things that results happen when a full set of causes [has been assembled].

Let us go through the eight qualities. The causes for long life are giving up killing or harming sentient beings; saving a life; sparing the life and ending the suffering of, for example, minnows left high and dry; giving food; freeing prisoners; giving medicine to the sick or nursing them; and so on.

The main cause for having a handsome body is practicing patience. However, there are other causes: offering bright butterlamps to images; erecting new objects to represent the enlightened body, speech, and mind; restoring these objects when they fall into disrepair; renewing their gilt and decorations; providing them with new cloth coverings; giving away new clothes and jewelry; and so on.

One cause for being born into a high family is not having an inflated opinion of yourself—no matter whether you are a lay person or ordained—or of your good qualities, race, ethics, wisdom, retinue, clothes, etc. Other causes are acting with humility and abandoning all pride or feelings of superiority; and showing great respect to karmically potent beings such as your guru, ordination master, abbot, and members of the Saṅgha. Ordained people should respect any monks senior in ordination to themselves. Scholars must also gladly accept the service or prostrations that the junior pay them out of respect for the learning in their mindstreams; and when a young man is about to receive monk's vows, he should similarly respect those who have preceded him in ordination. It may be the custom to pay respect to practitioners or to the reincarnations of lamas, but you should respect those with senior ordination, and so forth; such things must be done as properly as they were in the time of the Buddha.

The Tibetan government, the government of the Tuṣhita Palace, uses the sixteen unsullied laws of humans and Dharma that contain many extremely important things: the young should respect the old; one should esteem people with good qualities or people who have been most kind to oneself—for example, one's parents; one should help people brought low by sickness or poverty; and so on. If these are followed it will help the general happiness of the land. A story is told in the *Transmission of the Vinaya*, and so on, of four animal friends who respected each other according to their ages. Because of these animals' ethical behavior, the people of Kaśhi [near Varanasi] enjoyed great happiness. These four friends were animals, and yet this is what happened when the younger animals respected the older ones; need I say that we practitioners of Dharma, ordained people, and so on, should also do the same—it will bring even greater happiness!

The causes for being wealthy are presenting the symbols of enlightened body, speech, and mind with new coverings or repainting them; giving clothes, food, drink, jewelry, and so on to people asking for them; helping people who do not ask for help but who are still in need; and making offerings or practicing generosity as much as you can to people with good qualities or to those tormented by suffering.

Causes for having trustworthy speech are being punctilious in one's speech and taking pains to abandon nonvirtue.

The causes for having great power are: being respectful and making offerings to karmically potent beings such as one's abbot, ordination master, the Three Jewels, one's parents, people older than oneself, and so on; making prayers to receive these various qualities; and so on.

Causes for being born a male are preferring the male rebirth; not liking the female state because one can see enough drawbacks to repudiate such a state and feel it is not good to take such a rebirth; disabusing women of the attitude that it is good to have a female body. Another cause is to invoke the names of great bodhisattvas, as in the verse:

> I pay respect and homage
> To Jñānottara, Prabhāketu,
> Praṇidhānamati,
> Śhāntendra, and Mañjughoṣha.

Other causes are not speaking ill of people censuring one, saving beings from being castrated; and so on.

The causes for being strong of mind and body are performing chores that others are too busy to do, or are physically, mentally, or otherwise incapable of doing; helping others; not beating or whipping others; giving others food and drink; and so on.

If you make prayers that your rebirth with these eight ripened qualities may also become an instrument of virtue, you could become like Atiśha or the Dharmarājas of old. If you don't make these noble prayers, your rebirth could be nonvirtuous: though you obtain a physical state that has the eight

MAN MEETS YETI (SEE P. 377)

ripened qualities, you might through it become a great force working for nonvirtue—a king of some remote region, for example. It is therefore vital to make strong prayers for this not to happen so that one may not have such a nonvirtuous rebirth.

Although the Dharma teachings on impermanence are important first, last, and in the meantime, the underlying fundamental practice in this section of the small scope is that of modifying one's behavior according to the laws of cause and effect.

AFTER THINKING ABOUT THESE THINGS, THE WAY TO MODIFY YOUR BEHAVIOR (250)

This is in two parts: (1) the general teaching; (2) in particular, how to purify oneself with the four powers.

THE GENERAL TEACHING (251)

During your meditations you should repeatedly think over the discussions on virtue and sin. In between sessions you should vigilantly and scrupulously modify your behavior. Geshe Baen Gung-gyael used to count up his virtuous actions and his sins [at the end of each day] with white and black pebbles; he then modified his behavior accordingly. You must do the same. From *Engaging in the Deeds of Bodhisattvas:*

> How right for me to think diligently
> All the time, both day and night:
> "From nonvirtue comes suffering;
> How, then, to be free of nonvirtue?"...
>
> The Sage said that belief
> Is the root of all things virtuous.
> The root of this belief has always been
> Meditation on [karmic] ripening effects.

In other words when you come to know the white and black sides of cause and effect, you will always cultivate vigilance and scrupulousness. When you are in danger of taking a life, of lying, or whatever, you will immediately draw the line.

If you purify yourself of even the subtle sins you have done, expiate yourself of them, and refrain from doing them again, then, as we find in Nāgārjuna's *Letter:*

> Whoever was once reckless,
> May later become scrupulous;
> They are then as comely as the cloudless moon,
> Just like Nanda, Aṅgulimālā, Ajātaśhatru, and Udayana.

I have already discussed this verse in the preparatory rites section [Day 6, p. 184]. Nanda was dominated by lust, Aṅgulimālā killed 999 men, Ajātaśhatru killed his father who was a nonreturner, and Udayana killed his own mother, yet they purified these sins. Your previously accumulated sins will also be purified, so it is vital to combine expiation of these sins with refraining from repeating them.

To sum up, in this small-scope section you should place high value on the law of cause and effect by putting the main points into practice. Even great Atiśha put special emphasis on this.

Once in Paenpo there was a man who used to recite the *Seal of Pangkong*[57] and a man who had pawned a copy of the *Hundred-Thousand-Verse Perfection of Wisdom Sūtra.* Immediately after their deaths, Yama's minions led them under the ground and brought them into his presence. The second man lied, but to no avail: he was shown Yama's mirror. The mirror revealed who had sold the sūtra, who had bought it, the lentils the man had bought with the proceeds, and even the child who picked up the lentils when they were spilt. The man was thrown into a giant cauldron. The man who used to recite the *Seal of Pangkong* took refuge and so returned from the dead. Geshe Potowa told him: "Tell your story to others!"

You might think, "In my next rebirth the sins I've accumulated will not harm me because my abbot, ordination master, and so forth, don't know about them." But the *King of Single-Pointed Concentration Sūtra* says:

> The stars, moon, and all may fall,
> The earth, its mountains, its cities may perish,
> Space itself may be transformed into something else,
> But you [Buddha] will not speak words untrue.

In other words, Buddha's discussion of the law of cause and effect is the truth and will never deceive.

Not even the smallest virtue or sin will disappear of its own accord; you should therefore modify your behavior properly. Even so, because of your excessive familiarity with every small sin since beginningless time, you have been tarnished by them and should therefore expiate and refrain from these sins by using the four opponent powers.

IN PARTICULAR, HOW TO PURIFY ONESELF WITH THE FOUR POWERS (252)

Although I have already covered this in the above section on the preparatory rites, it is so important that I shall briefly go over such familiar headings again.

The first is the *power of repudiation;* this means having strong regret for one's sins of the past. This is the most important of the four powers, for if one has it the others will follow of their own accord. This power is the result of having faith in cause and effect.

The *power of applying all antidotes,* as I have already told you, has six types, all of which were mentioned in Śhāntideva's *Compendium of Instruction.* All the same, any virtuous practice done to purify the sin becomes an example of this power.

The *power of refraining from the misdeed* involves firmly resolving to refrain from it and thinking, "Even at the cost of my life, from now on I will not do it again." It will be difficult at first to be able to abandon all your misdeeds for good, but there will be some things that you can abandon from the root. For the things that you cannot abandon in this way, you should cultivate a resolve to refrain from doing them; think, "*I will not* do them today," and repeat this every day.

The *power of the basis* is taking refuge and developing bodhichitta. This is the point of having these two prayers at the beginning of meditations on Vajrasattva and recitations of his mantra or of the *Confession of Transgressions,* and so on.

We have accumulated every sort of sin since beginningless time; our collection of sins is like the treasure hoard of a king. Even so, as I have already mentioned in the preparatory rites section, if we vigorously expiate them by means of the four powers, and refrain from repeating them, we will be able to purify even karma whose consequences we would otherwise be certain to undergo. It is best to do this using *Ākāśhagarbha's Confession* (found in the *Compendium of Instruction*), the *Confession of Transgressions,* combined with full prostrations; or *Suvarṇabhāsottama's Confession Sūtra,* as discussed in the volume of miscellaneous works in *Tsongkapa's Collected Works;* and the like.

They say that the process of purification is particularly effective if, at the conclusion of the expiation, one feels each and every sin has been purified, and if one visualizes, as hard as one can, unfocused emptiness.

It is not helpful to be either indifferent to one's sins or to remain afraid of them. It is vital that we beginners expiate them and that we do so vigorously for a long time, until the signs that we have purified ourselves mentioned in the *Spell of Kaṇḍakāri* appear repeatedly. As I said, ordinary monks will purify sins by attending public ceremonies or debating practice, by pursuing their studies and contemplations, and even by participating in a series of debating tournaments between the various houses of their college—if such things are done with the aim of accumulating merit and as a self-purification. The actions would then build up their accumulations. Analyzing the contents of the scriptures or going to assembly is also a form of analytic meditation: *meditation* need not mean retiring to some cave with our bodies set in a certain posture. However, if we go to assembly or study merely to receive an alms distribution, or to defeat others in debate, this is not Dharma.

When we debate, we should not take it as merely siding against the person being examined; we should take it as a sign that we also have to take sides against our own mindstreams. This means that we who are ordained could be practicing Dharma the whole time; if we think in this way, these things will become Dharma, and we don't necessarily need to go off on our own or do anything else to become Dharma practitioners. On the other hand, worldly people must direct some special effort toward the Dharma. The ten virtues, however, are given as a practice for everyone, including lay people.

My own precious guru said, "The parts of the lamrim to follow, the medium scope and so on, are an extension of the practices related to the law of cause and effect."

Here is how to take up this practice. Abandon what little sins you can as best you can. When about to kill a louse, for example, even as your fingernail is poised over it, abandon the action with the thought, "It would not be right." When you intend to tell a lie, remember to hold your tongue.

You must gradually build up your practice of virtue—many a mickle makes a muckle.

Some people think that committing trivial sins does no harm, for sins can readily be expiated. But there is an enormous difference between not committing a sin in the first place and expiating it after it has been committed: as great a difference as between not breaking a leg and mending it by binding it after it has been broken. In other words, one does oneself grave harm by distancing oneself from gaining the higher stages on the path by wandering in saṃsāra for as much as eons, even though one need not experience the ripening effects of the sins if one purifies them by refraining from them and by strenuous expiation. Sinning, therefore, does great damage.

This ends the discussion. In the past you regarded this life as paramount, and had no yearning at all for a good rebirth. Now you have studied Dharma about the optimum human rebirth, impermanence, the sufferings of the lower realms, taking refuge, and cause and effect. If you now feel, "I must work only for my future rebirths," yearn for good rebirths only, and lose interest in this life's trivia, you have developed your first type of realization into the small scope of the lamrim. Even if you develop this you must still familiarize yourself with the topics repeatedly, as Je Tsongkapa said: "You must still stabilize this; you should still work hard and train yourself, despite already having this [realization]." This is why I have worked toward your developing the first type of realization into the lamrim during this teaching.

Then Kyabje Pabongka Rinpoche taught this material at medium length. Next he taught how to pursue the practice.

First perform the preparatory rites. Then petition your guru, visualized sitting above the crown of your head. Then think over the generalities and particulars of cause and effect as laid out in the headings. Modifying your behavior, however, is a practice you should do all the time; it need not therefore be pursued as a meditation topic.

Between sessions, you must repeatedly refer to discussions that teach about cause and effect: the *Sūtra on the Wise and Foolish,* the *One Hundred Verses on Karma,* the *One Hundred Life Stories,* the *Sūtra on Having Much Remembrance,* the set of four texts that make up the *Transmission of the Vinaya,* and so on, for I have given you only a short teaching on this.

Part Five

THE MEDIUM SCOPE

DAY 14

Kyabje Pabongka Rinpoche quoted two verses from the great Tsongkapa, the king of Dharma. They begin: "One's life and body are like a bubble on water..." He then gave a short talk to set our motivation and mentioned the headings already covered. He also reviewed "[Developing Believing Faith in the Law of] Cause and Effect"—the actual means to have happiness in your next rebirths.

TRAINING YOUR MIND IN THE STAGES OF THE PATH SHARED WITH THE MEDIUM SCOPE (253)

There are two sections to the mind trainings shared with beings of medium scope: (1) developing thoughts of yearning for liberation; (2) ascertaining the nature of the path leading to liberation.

DEVELOPING THOUGHTS OF YEARNING FOR LIBERATION (254)

There are two subsections here: (1) thinking about the general sufferings of saṃsāra; (2) thinking about its specific sufferings.

As I have already said, when you cultivate the part of the lamrim shared with the small scope and uphold the ethics of abandoning the ten non-virtues, you will get a rebirth in the upper realms and be temporarily free from the sufferings of the lower realms. But this alone is insufficient. Suppose a criminal has been condemned to die in one month; people go and see a man of influence for him, and for a few days he no longer receives other minor forms of punishment—being flogged, burnt with hot wax, and so forth. But he is still not released from the ultimate execution.

Similarly, one would not be free of saṃsāra forever. As it says in *Engaging in the Deeds of Bodhisattvas:*

> You could go again and again to upper realms
> And continue to enjoy so much bliss.
> When you die, you fall to the suffering of the lower realms,
> Where the suffering is unbearable and lasting.

In other words, you are certain to go to the lower realms when you run out of the right throwing karma. If you want to stop the flow of suffering for good, you must be freed from saṃsāra for good.

In this medium-scope section of the lamrim, you must develop thoughts of yearning for liberation. There are two ways of developing these: by thinking about the nature of the four truths, or by thinking about the twelve links.

Here *liberation* means being released from bondage. Suppose you were freed from the ropes binding you; you would then be "liberated from them." We are similarly bound by karma and delusions to the aggregates with which we are inflicted. We are bound in the following way. Owing to karma and delusions, the aggregates are formed. In terms of the realm, there are three realms in which this happens, that is the desire realm, [form realm, and formless realm]; in terms of migration, there are five or six types of migration[58] in which this happens; and in terms of birth, there are four modes of rebirth, that is, rebirth from a womb, etc.[59] That is the nature of this bondage, and liberation means being freed from it.

People generally assume *saṃsāra* to mean taking on bodies from the Peak of Existence down to the Hell Without Respite. People who have not studied think *saṃsāra* means circling between temporary residences, or circling between the six types of migration. This may be the correct usage of the word, but it is not the real saṃsāra. Some scholars claim that saṃsāra consists of such things as being conceived again and again; however, the Seventh Dalai Lama Kaelzang Gyatso's claim is the best—that saṃsāra is one's continuum of rebirth into the contaminated, afflicted aggregates. One is therefore liberated from saṃsāra when one has broken the continuity of being reincarnated and being brought into existence under the power of karma and delusion.

Prisoners must develop the wish to be free of their prison before they can escape from it. They will not develop this wish unless they consider the drawbacks of being in prison. If you likewise do not want to be free of saṃsāra, you will not make any effort to be liberated. And when you develop the wish to be liberated, as Āryadeva's *Four Hundred Verses* says: "The wise are just as afraid of high rebirth as they are of the hells." In other words, you must be weary of saṃsāra. You must think about saṃsāra's sufferings.

There are said to be two ways of doing this: by thinking about the four truths or the twelve links. I shall now discuss it as per the first of these. When the Bhagavān Buddha first taught at Varanasi and first turned the wheel of Dharma for his five earliest disciples, he said:

> Monks! That is the noble truth of suffering. That is the noble truth of the source [of suffering]. That is the noble truth of cessation. That is the noble truth of the path…

He discussed the four truths three times each, making twelve versions in all. This was his turning of the wheel of Dharma on the four truths. They are called *truths* because they are true according to how āryas [noble beings] perceive things.

In terms of causes and effects, the truth of the source of suffering should be discussed first; however, the four truths here do not follow this order, for the truth of suffering was discussed first. The point of doing this was as follows. Suffering was taught first because you should be moved to renounce it. If you are not so moved, you will not want to abandon its causes. When you first want to achieve some separation from these causes, you will work hard at the path—the cause for this achievement. So the four truths were discussed in this order so as to reflect the disciple's practice. Thus these four are the fundamental things that determine how people seeking liberation should modify their behavior.

Venerable Maitreya taught some similes in his *Sublime Continuum of the Great Vehicle* on knowing about the need to destroy the cause of suffering, and so on:

> The illness is to be diagnosed,
> Its cause is to be abandoned,
> Health is to be achieved,
> The medicine is to be relied on.

Likewise, suffering, its cause,
Cessation, and path are to be
Diagnosed, abandoned,
Reached, and relied on.

When we are sick, we diagnose the cause of the illness and rely on a medicine to remedy this cause.

The great Fifth Dalai Lama gave a water analogy: when you sleep on a comfortable piece of ground and your underside gets wet, you want to first find out from where the water is coming and then stop it.

You must want to be without the cause of suffering if you are to work hard at the means to be free of the disease of suffering. To develop this wish you must investigate the causes of suffering, and for this to happen you must understand how you are tormented by suffering. Great Tsongkapa said:

If one does not think hard about the true drawbacks of suffering,
One will not develop any yearning for liberation.
If one does not think of the source—the gateway to saṃsāra—
One cannot know proper cutting of the root of saṃsāra.
Be moved to renounce this existence, weary of it,
And cherish the knowledge of what binds one to saṃsāra.

Each of the four truths has four features. For the truth of suffering they are: impermanence, suffering, emptiness, and selflessness. For the source of suffering: cause, source, contributory cause, and intense production. For the truth of cessation, they are: cessation, peace, splendor, and definite outcome. And for the path, they are: path, correctness, accomplishing, and definite deliverance.

Contaminated, afflicted aggregates have three types of feeling: happiness, suffering, and equanimity. Although you do recognize the contaminated [feeling of] suffering for what it is, you do not realize that the other two are also suffering.

Once a tantrist told his women, "Someone like me is all set to go to the pure lands of knowledge bearers the moment you do wrong." He later fell sick, and his women asked him, when he was about to die, "Master of the tantras, you are all set to go to the pure lands of the knowledge bearers. Did we do wrong?"

He replied, "It's only because I am powerless to keep living. If I were not, instead of going to these pure lands, I would rather stay with you."

Like the story about Āchārya Manu, we think there is happiness in saṃsāra; we do not know this is merely attachment and that its nature is suffering.[60] When we come to know that it is the truth of the origin—the very cause of suffering—we will want to abandon it.

There are two origins: originating karma and originating delusions. The truth of cessation is the thing resulting from an absence of suffering; the truth of the path is the means to achieve the truth of cessation. In order to achieve the truth of cessation one must put the truth of the path into practice.

In order to understand suffering one should think about the eight, the six, and the three kinds of suffering.[61] These are discussed in [Tsongkapa's] *Great Stages of the Path.* Human suffering comes under the eight kinds. The three sufferings include the suffering that pervades all conditioned phenomena.

THINKING ABOUT THE GENERAL SUFFERINGS OF SAṂSĀRA (255)

This has six sections.

THE BANE OF UNCERTAINTY (256)

You may sometimes be reborn in the upper realms, but as long as you have taken rebirth in saṃsāra, you have not transcended suffering at all—because saṃsāric happiness is totally untrustworthy.

Let us take the example of our past and future rebirths. Our enemies, friends, parents, and so forth, change places. Once a family's old father always used to eat fish from the pool behind the house. He died and was reborn as a fish in the pool. The mother was attached to the house, so she was reborn as the family's dog. The son's enemy had been killed for raping the son's wife; because the enemy was so attached to her, he was reborn as her son. The son caught his father, the fish, and killed it. While he ate its meat, the dog, his mother, ate the fishbones, and so was beaten by her son. His own little son, his enemy, was sitting on his knee. Shāriputra saw this and said:

He eats his father's flesh and hits his mother.
The enemy he killed sits on his knee.
A wife gnaws her husband's bones.
Saṃsāra can be such a farce!

Also, as Nāgārjuna's *Letter* says:

Fathers, sons, mothers, wives: persons can change;
Enemies become friends and change back again.
After death, those in saṃsāra
Have no shred of certainty.

In other words, although we are sure our enemies, friends, etc. will always be that way, we cannot really be so certain. Friends in the early part of our lives can become our enemies later on in our lives; our enemies can become our friends. And this holds for wealth and poverty: someone who was rich yesterday could become a beggar today because he was robbed by enemies, and so on. These are obvious: things change from moment to moment.

Pabongka Rinpoche then told in detail the story of the householder Śhrījāta.

Śhrījāta saw a snake coiled round the corpse of a woman, a great tree being eaten by insects, a man being hit by many of Yama's underlings wearing different masks, and the skeleton of a sea monster the size of a mountain chain and so large that it could blot out even the sun.

Then Maudgalyāyana told him:

The first of these was the rebirth of a woman much attached to her own body. The second was a man who irresponsibly misused the Saṅgha's wood. The third was the rebirth of a hunter, and the fourth—that was the skeleton of a past life of yours, Śhrījāta.

Once a king's ministers asked the king how to deal with a certain criminal. The king was engrossed in a game of chess and absentmindedly said, "Execute him according to the law." Because of that the man was put to death. When the king finished his chess he asked what they had done with the man. His ministers told him the man had already been killed. The king felt great remorse, but was still reborn as a sea monster because of the sin of having the criminal executed. A long time passed. Some merchants who had gone to sea in a ship were sailing toward the sea monster's mouth. The merchants were terrified and took refuge in the buddhas. The sea monster heard them taking refuge. It shut its mouth and died of starvation, and its corpse was carried to the shore by the ocean nāgas.

Thus Śhrījāta was first reborn a king, then a sea monster, and then a human being again. This is how uncertain saṃsāra is.

THE BANE OF BEING DISSATISFIED (257)

Butterflies are destroyed by their attraction to visual form, deer to sound, bees to smell, and elephants to physical sensations. In the same way saṃsāric happiness is like drinking salt water—no matter how much of it you obtain, it does not satisfy. Suppose a man has but a single coin. He will think, "When will I get ten coins?" When he gets ten, he then wonders when he will get a hundred. If he ever does, he'll wonder when he will get a thousand. No matter how many he gets, he will not be satisfied. As the *Great Play Sūtra* says:

> O king, if a man were to receive
> All celestial pleasures there be,
> All noble human pleasures there be,
> It would not be enough: he would seek even more.

Let us take the example of celestial and human happiness. King Mābhvātā ruled over the four continents and the celestial regions, yet he was still dissatisfied. Eventually his merit ran out; he fell to this continent of Jambudvīpa and breathed his last. Desires do not satisfy, and there can be no greater fault than this.

If you ruled over one land you would think, "If only I ruled over two!" You would not be satisfied, no matter how many you ruled. No matter how much wealth you get you still wonder if you can get more, and you are prepared to wear yourself out to achieve this. If you lack contentment, no matter how much wealth or how many possessions you have acquired, you will be no different from a beggar. Once in India, Sūrata the beggar found a priceless jewel and said he must give it to another beggar. He gave it to King Prasenajit, saying, "O king, you lack contentment, and so are the poorest!"

If you are content you may not have any possessions, but you are still rich. From Nāgārjuna's *Letter:*

> Always be content.
> If you know contentment,
> Though you have no property
> You have the purest wealth.

Drogoen Tsangpa Gyarae said:

> In the gatehouse of the contented,
> A rich man dozes by the door.
> People with desire cannot experience this.

In other words, if you are not content, your dissatisfaction is boundless. This is why discontent and dissatisfaction are the greatest fault.

THE BANE OF REPEATEDLY LEAVING BODIES (258)

No matter what body you take, it will prove untrustworthy. From Nāgārjuna's *Letter:*

> Gain the enormous bliss and pleasure of the god realms,
> Gain the bliss free of attachment of Brahmā himself,
> And later you will fuel the fires of the Hell Without Respite,
> Where the suffering is unbroken and constant.
>
> When you were the sun or moon gods,
> The light from your bodies shone on all the worlds.
> Later you went to pitch-black darkness,
> Where you could not even see your own outstretched hands.

In other words, in the past you had numberless rebirths in the bodies of a Brahmā, an Indra, and so on, yet derived no benefit at all. Later you were born in the Hell Without Respite and so forth, or as a slave, etc. From time to time you were born as sun or moon gods, and the light from your body illuminated the four continents. Then you died, left that rebirth, and were born in the dark depths of the oceans between continents, where you could not even see the movements of your limbs.

There are no celestial or human riches that you can claim not to have experienced in the past, but none of these riches proved trustworthy. You have already been born in the god realms, and sat on thrones encrusted with diamonds, and the like; even your house has been made entirely of precious substances. You have enjoyed such things many times, but now all you sit on are leather cushions. Even though you were even born as an Indra, you then became a beggar; your rebirths as Indra were of no help to you.

> In the high rebirths you spent much time in pleasure,
> Caressing the breasts and waists of women;
> Then in hell, you felt the unbearable touch
> Of instruments of torture that crushed, cut, and tore you.

In other words, you have already been born in the god realms and for a long time experienced pleasure with the goddesses there. Then you left that life, were reborn in hell surrounded by the terrifying hell guards and experienced suffering. You drank and drank the celestial ambrosia of immortality; then you left that rebirth and had to drink the molten metal of the hells. You have already been made universal emperors, had power over many hundreds of thousands of human households, had the seven signs of regal power at your disposal, and so forth. Now you have nothing to show for it, no trace of benefit. As I have already told you, the drawback is that your attachment to objects of the senses increased, leaving you discontented; you then accumulated sins for the sake of those things, and went from lower realm to lower realm.

My own guru, my refuge and protector, told me this story. Once a lama was dying and someone asked him if he had any last thing to say. The lama repeated over and over again, "The things in saṃsāra have no essence."

No matter what wealth or riches we have, we will derive no essence from them, just as in the past. When we were reborn as universal emperors, all this world's wealth could not compare with the value of one of our shoes. We had the experience of wearing many such clothes and it did not benefit us.

When a king and a beggar travel the perils of the bardo they are equals, treated neither better nor worse.

Geshe Chaen Ngawa said:

> O Lord Toenpa, since beginningless time, no matter what kind of body we received, we have not experienced Mahāyāna Dharma practice as now. Therefore, we must work hard!

In other words, be careful.

THE BANE OF BEING CONCEIVED AND BORN OVER AND OVER AGAIN (259)

From Nāgārjuna's *Letter:*

> If you counted all your mothers
> With juniper-berry–sized balls of earth,
> The earth would not be enough...
>
> Instead of ridding yourself of sorrow,
> You have time and again in hell
> Drunk so much boiling, molten brass;
> Even the water in the oceans
> Would not equal it.

That is, you have already been born in hell and drunk more molten brass than there is water in the great oceans—and if you do not break the continuity of your rebirths into saṃsāra, you will have to drink even more.

> When you were dogs and pigs,
> The amount of all the filth you ate
> Would be much greater
> Than Meru, king of mountains.

You have already been dogs and pigs and have eaten more filth than Mount Meru—and if you do not break away from saṃsāra you will have to eat even more.

So many tears have you shed in saṃsāra's realms
When separated from your dearest friends
That the teardrops from your eyes
Would overflow the basins of the oceans.

You have already been separated from parents, children, brothers, and so on, and shed more tears than the oceans—and if you do not break away from saṃsāra you will cry still more.

Since people fight among themselves,
The pile of all your lopped-off heads
Would be so high
It would exceed the world of Brahmā.

You have already been involved in fighting, and the pile of your heads cut off by enemies would be higher than even Mount Meru. And if you do not break the continuity of your rebirths into saṃsāra, you can be sure even more in future will be cut off.

When you were earthworms you were so hungry,
All the manure and earth you ate
Would more than fill
The great milky oceans.

In other words, we have been born as muddy earthworms and have already eaten so much filthy earth and manure that the quantity would not fit into the great ocean basins. But if we do not free ourselves from saṃsāra, we will have to eat even more.

Nāgārjuna said:

Each of you has drunk more milk
Than the four oceans, and yet,
As you are still ordinary, a being following saṃsāra,
You will be drinking even more.

In other words, you have already continuously received bodies in saṃsāra and drunk more milk at your mothers' breasts than the four great oceans.

Yet if you cannot stop being reborn into saṃsāra, you will have to drink even more.

If, according to the above contemplations in the small-scope section, you have so much suffering and undergo such terrors every time when reborn in the lower realms after you die, what can you say of the even greater sufferings and terrors you will have, for you are certain to re-experience such births, deaths, and so on, countless times more.

We are afraid whenever we see a scorpion, but if we were to make a pile of the scorpion bodies we have had, the pile would be the size of Mount Meru. Yet we are certain to have even more of such scorpion rebirths so long as we cannot break the continuity of our rebirths into saṃsāra.

THE BANE OF MOVING FROM HIGH TO LOW OVER AND OVER AGAIN (260)

From the *Transmission of the Vinaya:*

> All collections end up running out,
> The high end up falling,
> Meeting ends in separation,
> Living ends in death.

This speaks of the four ends of conditioned phenomena: collections of wealth and property end up running out, a fall ends our high position, the end of coming together is being separated, and death is the end of a rebirth. No matter what you acquire of saṃsāra's affluence, not one bit of it will be exempt from decay or will not end. As Geshe Sangpuba said: "In saṃsāra, one must hoard a great many things, but do not pin your hopes on them—they will decline."

Further, we make a great effort to build a house and amass wealth, but we may well not see them through to completion—enemies could steal them or we may die.

We lamas and disciples gathered here today are sure to be separated after only a few years' time.

As Kaelzang Gyatso, the Seventh Dalai Lama, said: "In but a short while, the high become downtrodden slaves." And from Nāgārjuna's *Letter:*

> You may be Indra, to whom the world makes offerings,
> But still, through karma's power, you will fall to the ground.
> You may be a universal emperor,
> But in the cycles of saṃsāra, you'll become a slave.

In other words, this is what happens to the high—Brahmā, Indra, and the like.

As for the lowly: any worldly gains, status, or good fortune are without essence. Gungtang Rinpoche said:

> As you climb farther and farther up
> That dead tree called "name and fame,"
> It will bend and break. Alas!
> Best stay only halfway up…

In other words, not only are past and future lives untrustworthy, but so also is this one: there are kings who have to stay in prison, and so forth.

Once Sangyae Gyatso, a regent of Tibet, instituted many reforms in the central government. He was a rich and powerful man, and one of the greatest scholars as well, but in the end he incurred the displeasure of Lhazang Khan and was beheaded. His severed head was left for days in the middle of the Trizam Bridge at Toelung, and no one dared claim it. His wife and sons had to wander the ends of the earth as beggars. Lhazang Khan himself was later killed when the Dzungarian armies invaded.

THE BANE OF HAVING NO COMPANION (261)

In the beginning, when you were born from your mother's womb, you were born alone. In midlife, when you get sick, for example, only you can experience it. In the end, when you die, you go through death [utterly] alone, like a hair drawn out of a butter pat. There is no one to help you. *Engaging in the Deeds of Bodhisattvas* says:

> When born, you are born alone,
> When you die, you are just as alone.
> What can your meddlesome friends do
> If they won't take on another share of suffering?

Great Je Tsongkapa said: "The splendors of existence are untrustworthy; [bless me to] know their drawbacks..." In other words, no matter what you obtain of the splendors and happiness of saṃsāra, these are untrustworthy, and not one saṃsāric friend is reliable in the long run.

Think on how you experience the suffering of saṃsāra, and how, if you consider how endless it is, that must make you weary of it. So, regardless of whether saṃsāra in general has an end, you must employ some means to end your *own* saṃsāra. If you want to set some limit on your suffering and bring your own saṃsāra to an end, you must, as I have already said, manage to break the continuity of your saṃsāric rebirths.

THINKING ABOUT SAṂSĀRA'S SPECIFIC SUFFERINGS (262)

This has two subheadings: (1) thinking about the sufferings of the lower realms; (2) thinking about the sufferings of the upper realms.

THINKING ABOUT THE SUFFERINGS OF THE LOWER REALMS (263)

You have already thought about the first of these in the small-scope section, and it would revolt you as alcohol revolts someone with a hangover.

THINKING ABOUT THE SUFFERINGS OF THE UPPER REALMS (264)

This has three sections: (1) thinking about human suffering; (2) thinking about the sufferings of the demigods; (3) thinking about the sufferings of the gods.

THINKING ABOUT HUMAN SUFFERINGS (265)

There are seven subheadings.

THINKING ABOUT THE SUFFERING OF BIRTH (266)

If the sufferings of the lower realms are as I described above, you might think, "Aren't the sufferings of gods and humans small?" But when you are born in saṃsāra, even gaining a higher rebirth is nothing but suffering. We have been reborn as humans, but if we ignore the fact that we can derive great benefit through practicing Dharma, we will suffer as enormously as the rest. Owing to the trauma of being born from a womb, we have completely forgotten about the way we have already undergone the sufferings of birth. If we manage to take a human rebirth again, we must again experience all the sufferings of birth, although we do not remember them now.

After you enter the mother's womb, and until you are born in the outside world, you have each of the sufferings associated with both the five stages of development in the womb and the periods when each part of the body develops. First, when your consciousness is placed in the center of your parents' drops of blood and sperm, your body is only like a speck of yogurt, and when your consciousness enters it, the suffering is like being boiled in a giant hell-cauldron. When the head and the swellings for the limbs appear, you suffer as if you were being stretched out on the rack. Each limb adds only more suffering. When your mother drinks something hot, when she moves, sleeps, and so on, you suffer as if you were being boiled in a hot spring, carried off by the wind, or crushed under a huge mountain. As Chandragomin's *Letter to a Disciple* says:

> Enclosed naked in a most intolerable stench,
> You live enveloped in pitch blackness;
> After entering this hellish place, the womb,
> You must endure great suffering with your body all hunched up.

In other words, imagine you are placed in an iron pot filled with various kinds of filth and the lid is put on. There is no way you could stay in it even for a day, yet you have had to stay in your mother's womb, in its smelly filth and its black darkness, for nine months, ten days.

You then develop five attitudes concerning the nauseating aspects of the womb's interior that make you want to emerge. Yet even as you are being pushed through the cervix, as the *Letter to a Disciple* says:

> You are gradually squeezed as hard as one crushes sesame.
> Then, somehow, you are born.

In other words, the suffering is like having your body squeezed in a vice. When you emerge your skin is like raw flayed cowhide; and when you are placed on a cushion, no matter how soft, it is like being thrown on a bramble patch. When you feel an outside wind it is like being penetrated by a sword. When your mother takes you in her arms and carries you, it is like a sparrow being carried off by a hawk. These things terrify you.

All your learning from past lives is veiled, and you have absolutely no wisdom at all. You even have to learn from scratch how to eat, sleep, walk, and sit.

When you meditate on your birth from the womb, it should not be like goggling at someone else at an entertainment: you should meditate to develop insight into how you yourself are certain to have such a birth again, and into what it would be like. You should think about the sufferings mentioned in the *Sūtra for Nanda on Entering the Womb.*

Some may think that the sufferings of birth do no harm because the experience is over. But until we set a future limit on our saṃsāra, we must experience the sufferings of birth an infinite number of times.

And Pabongka Rinpoche told how this would be difficult to endure, and so on.

THE SUFFERING OF AGING (267)

From the *Great Play Sūtra:*

> Age makes a beautiful body ugly;
> Age takes radiance, age takes strength;
> Age takes happiness, age humiliates;
> Age kills, and age robs the complexion.

In other words, the sufferings of aging are: one's handsome body deteriorates, one's strength declines, one's faculties decline, one's enjoyment of objects of the senses declines, one's lifespan declines, and so on.

Your sense faculties, wisdom, etc. gradually dim; your body gets bent like a bow; your complexion declines; it is difficult for you to sit down and get up; your hair whitens; you have many wrinkles—you become as ugly as one already departed. As Milarepa said:

> One: you will get up like someone tethered to a stake.
> Two: you will walk as if stalking birds.
> Three: you will sit like a crumbling clod of earth.

When the time comes for you, grandmother, to have all three,
The decay of the body—that mirage—will depress you...

One: outside, your skin creases into many wrinkles.
Two: inside, your flesh and blood thin out, so bones protrude.
Three: between these you're dull, stupid, deaf, blind, and senile.
When the time comes for you, grandmother, to have all three,
You will look ugly, wrinkled, and wrathful.

All these things are defects of being in saṃsāra. Kadampa Geshe Kamaba said:

How good that old age comes bit by bit!
It would be impossible to take if it came on all at once.

In other words, if a healthy young man in his prime went to sleep tonight and woke up tomorrow with unclear faculties, with a bent and ancient body, and so on, it would be impossible for him to bear.

You must practice Dharma now, before your faculties, wisdom, and body decline. Later, when the sufferings of old age dominate you and you are about to leave your human body, your physical condition will have changed. Your faculties will have declined, and you will not even be able to get up or sit down. How could you practice Dharma then? Gungtang Rinpoche Taenpa Droenme said:

It is as if the old received
Initiation water on their heads.[62]
Their hair is conch-shell white
But not because it's pure of filth:
It's been spat on by the Lord of Death
And has taken on a frosty look.

Wrinkles crisscross their foreheads.
This is not from baby fat:
Time's messengers made these tally marks
To count the many years gone from their lives...

Drops of mucus dribble from their noses.
These do not look like necklaces of pearls:
Their youth, their carefree times,
Are glaciers melting in the sun.

Their rows of teeth have fallen out,
But no replacement teeth await to grow:
They have eaten all this life's food,
So their cutlery's been confiscated...

Their drawn faces and poor color
Are not because they're wearing monkey masks:
Their loan of youth has been called,
And now their true colors show.

Their heads are nodding, nodding,
But not because they're sniggering at others:
Yama prods them with his club's tip,
And they can't help shaking their heads.

Their faces look down, bent toward the road,
But they're not searching for lost needles:
Their memory and jewels of youth
Have spilt on the ground—hence the posture.

They use all four limbs when they get up,
But not because they pretend they're cows:
Their legs cannot support their bodies,
So their hands have to assist.

They sit down with a thud,
But not because they're furious with a friend:
The rope of health and sling
Of mental happiness are now severed.

When they walk, they sway and lurch,
But not because they're walking like a lord:

They're under a great burden from their age,
And the weight has upset their sense of balance.

Their hands clutch at things and tremble,
But they're not scooping up some gambling wins:
They're afraid that Yama will steal
Everything in their reach.

Their eating very little food and drink
Is not because they're stingy with their meals:
The fire in their bellies has declined,
So old people fear they may faint.

They wear only thin, light, clothes,
But don't so dress to go out dancing:
They have lost their inner body strength,
And even clothes have become a burden.

They wheeze and puff for breath,
But are not blowing mantras [like a lama]:
The gurgling sound they're making when they breathe
Foretells their disappearance into thin air.

Everything that they do
Isn't just to act the fool:
The evil spirit of old age has captured them,
And they aren't free to do as they would wish.

They forget to do all their work
But not because they're shallow or don't care:
Their faculties have declined,
Dimming their memories and minds.

In other words these wrinkles and white hairs are omens that they will be killed by Karmayama. And there are yet more sufferings: mental anguish from the fear of death, and so forth.

THE SUFFERING OF ILLNESS (268)

From the *Great Play Sūtra:*

> In the dead of winter, great winds and falls of snow
> Rob grass, trees, forest, and shrubs of brilliance;
> Sickness likewise robs beings of their brilliance,
> And their bodies, strength, and faculties decline.

In other words, you suffer: the nature of your body changes; your suffering and mental anguish increase and remain high; you no longer want things that delight the senses; you have to experience unpleasant things that you don't want; you suffer mental anguish at the prospect of losing your life; and so on. And as it is said: your body loses strength, your mouth and your nose dry and are constricted. That is, you may be at the prime of life, but if you are bedridden, your body loses its strength, your lustre fades, and so on.

If you require more detail, think how each disease torments, and think how you may not even have time to make a will when you come down with a fatal disease.

Pabongka Rinpoche then told how the young Prince Siddhārtha achieved liberation through his meditations after seeing a sick man, an old man, a dead man, and so on.

THE SUFFERING OF DEATH (269)

The *Great Play Sūtra* tells us:

> Time makes for death, leaving, and leaving in death.
> Forever you are separated from dear and pleasant people.
> They will not come back, there will be no reunion.
> How like falling leaves or the flow of a river.

In other words, you will be separated from beauty and from affluence—from your property, relatives, retinue, and your body. When you actually die, you experience fierce suffering and mental anguish. When it is time for you to die, you cannot prevent it, as the *Instruction Given to a King Sūtra* tells us. I have already discussed this in the section on remembering death.

THE SUFFERING OF BEING SEPARATED FROM THE BEAUTIFUL (270)

You will be separated from your guru, disciples, relatives, friends, parents, and dear ones—the cherished people from whom you cannot bear separation for even the time it takes to drink a bowl of tea—and from your position, power, wealth, possessions, and affluence. Some ordained people even have such sufferings as having to be without their ethics.

Such things are not some injustice done us: they are a sign that we are still within saṃsāra.

THE SUFFERING OF MEETING WITH THE UGLY (271)

By "ugly" we mean unpleasant. Meet with your enemies, and you get beaten or robbed; meet with diseases or evil spirits, and you undergo torments, illness, or insanity. There are an infinite number of sufferings—meeting with lawsuits, punishment by the king, thieves, and the like.

If some unfortunate circumstance arises and you suffer great mental and bodily fatigue while still in the middle of your duties, even this fault is due by nature to your still being in saṃsāra. For example, when a donkey has to carry a heavy load that makes sores on his back, it is by virtue of his own karma—if it were [karmically] impossible, it would not happen. Geshe Potowa wrote:

> So long as we are born in any of the six types [of rebirth], we will suffer from heat, death, and so on. Who is to get sick, gets sick; and who is to die, dies. These are not just random injustices—they are characteristic of and in the nature of saṃsāra. For as long as we remain in saṃsāra, we have not transcended the saṃsāric state. We must be moved to renounce these things and so abandon rebirth. For that, we must abandon their causes.

In other words, if we do not wish to undergo the sufferings of saṃsāra we must use the means to be liberated from them.

THINKING ABOUT THE SUFFERING OF SEEKING THE THINGS WE DESIRE BUT NOT FINDING THEM (272)

This is suffering from heat and cold, or from ignoring the heat, cold, fatigue, fear, and so forth that go along with earning a living.

It is like the example of asking something important of an official. First your hopes of getting what you want tire and trouble you; then you suffer when you do not attain your aims.

Some may think that landowners are happy because they possess the causes of affluence, but they have not transcended suffering either. Farmers have to get up early in the morning, at the crack of dawn, for their work; during the day they are burned by the sun and tormented by the wind, in the midst of dust. Once the seeds have been planted, the grain must be brought in, but until the grain is safely in its storage vessels, farmers worry that frost, hail, blight, and drought may come. Even if they prepare the ground, they may not get any crops. These worries continually cause them to suffer.

You may think traders are happier than farmers, but traders suffer too. They have to leave their parents, friends, wives, and children behind and risk their lives by wandering through remote lands. They don't dare to lie down and sleep at night. They cross rivers, passes, narrow paths, and so on. Some show no profit from their trading, and lose all their capital as well. Enemies, bandits, robbers, or thieves could even take their lives.

Even if you don't have any wealth or property, you still suffer its lack. Beggars suffer. If they eat this piece of food today, they wonder what they will eat tomorrow. This makes them unhappy, so they go off in search of food, yet they may suffer by not finding any.

Even when you have wealth and property, you suffer because of it. Beggars accost the wealthy, those with possessions, and carry some of the wealth away; others borrow and carry some of it away; officials take from you and carry some of it away; even rats and cats rob you and carry some of it away. The rich suffer because they accumulate wealth and cannot protect it.

You can worry about losing something and suffer. You can suffer because people slander you. People who ply a trade for a living—carpenters and tailors, for example—may not earn enough for their food, clothes, and rent; they suffer because people don't respect them; they suffer from pride and jealousy; and they may not be able to acquire, or even steal, a piece of wood or cloth.

We may be ordained, but if we do not solely practice Dharma properly by having contentment and few wants, even performing funerals and rituals in people's homes is a form of suffering.

When officials investigate they think their citizens are happy, but their citizens have not transcended suffering either. Their clothes are in rags on their pale bellies; they have no freedom over their property because they are taxed and must do compulsory service; they may be insulted, whipped, and so on. Some have no time even to eat and must herd the animals near, far, and in between. Some don't even have the means for making barley flour, yet they are still taxed. Disaster can befall them, they can be heavily punished, and so on. In short, they worry day and night, and they must waste their human lives in suffering and exhaustion.

And these citizens may think the officials are happy, but it is not so. From [Āryadeva's] *Four Hundred Verses:*

> The high have mental suffering,
> The ordinary have physical suffering.
> These two sufferings conquer the world
> Every single day.

In other words, you may be a great king of a country, but you still suffer: you carry the burden of the country's suffering, because the country's disputes and other unpleasant topics are usually brought before you. You fear any enemies still unsubdued; you fear for any unprotected friends; you fear the people the law cannot suppress; you worry about loss of power; and so on.

We [ordained people] only eat at lunchtime, yet we have to wear ourselves out with a great deal of work.

In short, even if you only have one horse, that's a horse-worth of suffering.

When people first meet they say nice things to each other, no matter who they are; on further acquaintance they will only argue and make sarcastic remarks. Kaelzang Gyatso, the Seventh Dalai Lama said:

> Whoever you see—high or low, ordained or lay, man or woman—
> Except for their dress, appearance, and haughtiness of manner,
> Each has an equal share of ugly human life.
> How sad to see friends and family sharing the same burden.

In other words, externally people may have good or bad clothes and surroundings, but internally all experience suffering equally.

Our living place may be unsatisfactory and there may be various other things wrong: we may have no furniture, friends, and so on. Yet even if we have the best of places, friends, and amenities, we still have not transcended suffering. Even if we replace all our hundreds or thousands of servants, pupils, and friends, still they will all be unsatisfactory. Not one will be truly like-minded, and this is a sign that whoever we befriend will increase our suffering.

Whatever you enjoy, even tea, is an enjoyment of suffering. Wherever you stay, even in monasteries, it is a place of suffering.

When we first stay in a monastery we are unhappy. So we go to another, hoping this will be better, but its not, and so we go to a hermitage. But even there we don't get along with someone. So we go on a pilgrimage. Even this doesn't make us happy, so we go back to our homeland thinking this might be better, and then we get restless.

Whomever we speak to, we only complain about such tiresome things as food, fashion, and people's reputations—and this is the fault of saṃsāra.

I have acquainted you with human suffering. When you do not have this acquaintance, there is a danger that you might think that it is your particular location or friends that create your suffering, or that "saṃsāra" is somewhere far off over there. For this not to happen, you must know that the root of suffering—as I have already explained—is the fault of saṃsāra. Until you turn away from saṃsāra, you will only experience infinite sufferings, no matter where you go.

THINKING ABOUT THE SUFFERINGS OF THE DEMIGODS (273)

You may think, "Still, if I'm reborn as a demigod, won't I have some happiness?" But even in this rebirth you experience only suffering. From Nāgārjuna's *Letter:*

> The demigods, by nature, have great mental suffering,
> For they hate the glory of the gods.
> Though they are discerning, they will not
> See the truth, for this migration is obscured.

The demigods are located on the part of Mount Meru that lies under the ocean. They have four cities: Bright, Moon-garland, Noble Place, and Immutable. These four levels are the same distance apart as the gods' [four levels on Mount Meru].[63]

The demigods cannot generally compete with the gods except in a few things where they are similar. And the gods steal the beautiful demigod women. The gods have greater riches—for example, the ambrosia of immortality—and therefore the demigods are forever tormented by the fires of suffering of enormous jealousy. If we get so unhappy when we are jealous of the petty affluence of our enemies, need I say how unbearable the great affluence of the gods must be for the demigods. When the demigods can no longer stand their sickening jealousy, they go to war. Airāvaṇa, the gods' great elephant, hurls rocks at them with his trunk. The demigods throw weapons, but the gods die only when their necks are severed; the demigods may die when a weapon hits any part of their body, so they are always defeated, and at no time do they win. We are terrified when two armies of similar strengths fight in the human realms, but are the demigods afraid when they must wage such a war against the gods? They are absolutely terrified! Demigod armies must wage these wars continuously till they die; so they suffer. The demigod women back home are also tormented by suffering, for they can witness everything in the surface of Lake Ādarśha—the defeat of the demigod armies, the deaths of their companions, and so on.

Though the demigods have wisdom, their rebirth is so veiled by karma that in that birth they are not fortunate enough to see the truth.

THINKING ABOUT THE SUFFERINGS OF THE GODS (274)

In that case, you may ask, "Are these so-called gods happy?" No, the desire-realm gods also experience suffering: from falling when they leave that rebirth, from being intimidated, and from being maimed, killed, and banished. The first of these is as follows.

Nāgārjuna's *Letter* says:

> Their body color becomes ugly,
> Their thrones do not please them,
> Their flower garlands fade, their clothes pick up stains,
> And their bodies sweat for the first time.
> These, the five omens of death, signal departure from paradise.
> When these happen to gods in the celestial realms,
> They are like omens of death proclaiming
> That even people beyond the earth will die.

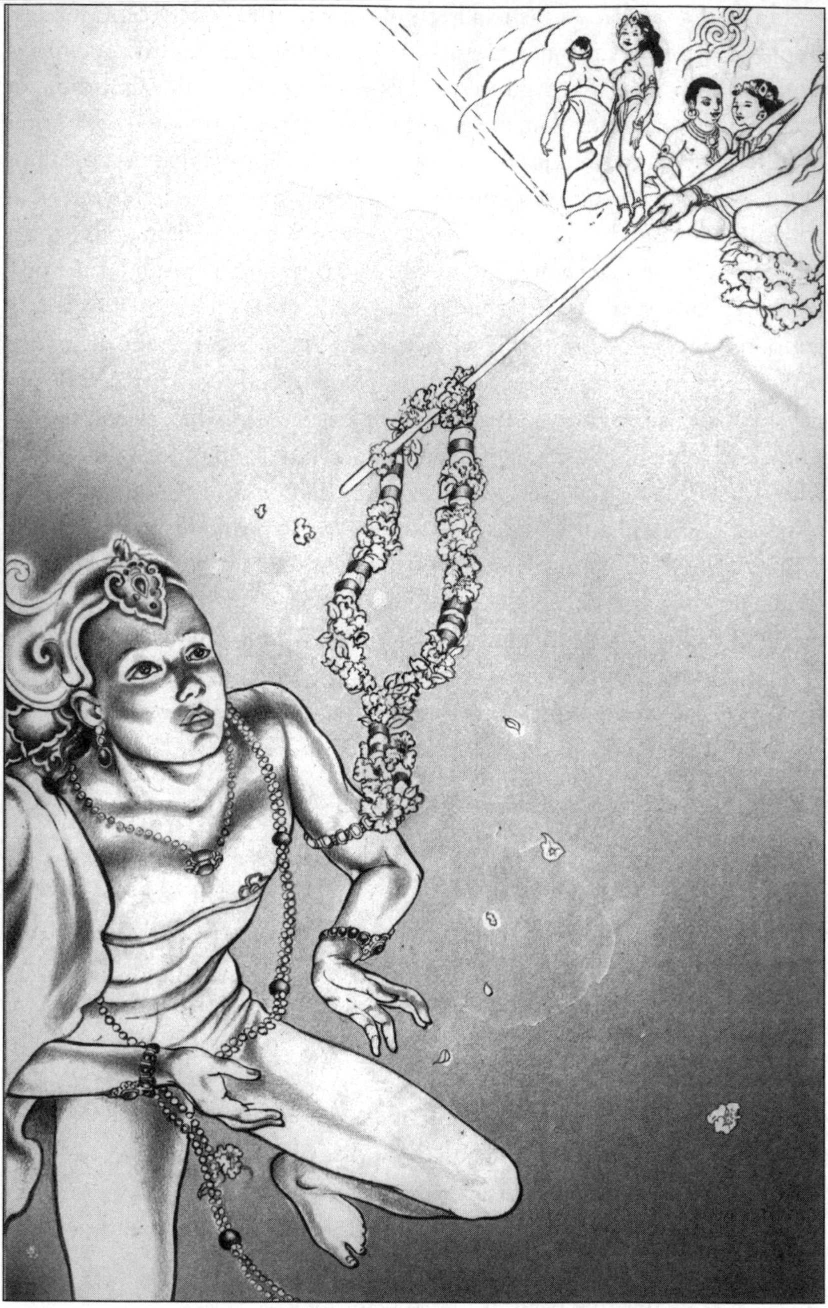

THE GODS' SUFFERING OF DEATH

In other words, there are five signs of distant death and five signs of approaching death, and the gods suffer when these ten omens appear. The luster of their body fades; they refuse to sit on their thrones; the flowers they wear fade; their clothes pick up stains; they sweat, and so on; their bodies give off less light; water adheres to their bodies when they wash; the jewelry on their bodies gives off an unpleasant sound; their eyes blink; and they keep to one place. When these ten signs appear, they wail in some forsaken place, writhing like fish out of water. Gods undergo this suffering for seven of their days. In the Realm of the Four Mahārājas of the cardinal directions, for example, this lasts for three hundred and fifty human years.

The gods undergo three phases: the previous rebirth that caused them to be reborn as gods, their present situation as gods, and wherever they will be going after they die. The gods know all three, so they know where they will be reborn next. The gods did not use the early part of their rebirth to create even one kind of virtue, such as considering their own suffering and developing renunciation, or considering the sufferings of others and developing compassion, thus their previously accumulated merit is running out, having been used up. Suppose you wear a monk's shawl that cost ten *sang,* while other monks wear shawls that cost only one *sang.* That means you have squandered ten times as much of the results of your merit. Similarly, bliss in the god realms is so intense that it uses up a lot of merit, and hence the gods are normally reborn in the lower realms. This is why they say that now is the time for us to accumulate merit, not the time to squander the results of merit. The gods know they will fall and it increases their suffering. They see that they will be without their affluence—the celestial realms, their body, possessions, friends, and so forth—and will be reborn in the lower realms. Their mental suffering is sixteen times greater than that of the hells. We have such suffering and mental anguish when we die, even though we are uncertain whether our next rebirth will be good or bad. They are certain, however, for they see that they are sure to be reborn in the lower realms. They say things like, "Alas [I shall not see] the Grove of Chariots [again]."

The other gods and goddesses cannot even bear to look at those displaying the signs of death; they avoid them as they would shun a corpse and leave them in solitude. Those about to die say to their companions, "I have only a short while to live and then will move on to my next rebirth, which will be miserable, so I want to see you now." They make these heartrending pleas, but the others cannot bear even to look at them with their own eyes.

Their old companions and once-firm friends put flowers on the end of a pole, and so on, and, keeping their distance, place these on their heads. They pray for them, "After you die and leave these rebirths, you will be reborn in the human realm; may you then accumulate merit and so be reborn as a god." This is all they do, and it only adds to the misery [of the dying gods], making their mental anguish even greater.

The gods with smaller amounts of merit see the majesty and affluence of the gods with greater merits; this is intimidating, and they have even greater suffering and mental anguish thereby.

When the gods and demigods fight, they experience the suffering of having their limbs cut off, of being maimed, and of dying. The less powerful gods suffer because the more powerful gods drive them out of their dwellings.

In a rebirth as a god of the higher realms [of form and formlessness], one does not have the sufferings of displaying the signs of death, but one is still oppressed by the suffering of all conditioned phenomena: one still has delusions and obscurations, and one will suffer by taking bad rebirths because one is powerless to remain in this rebirth, powerless to control one's death or where one will go afterward. [Vasubandhu] says in his *Instruction for the Accumulations:*

> Those in the form and formless realms
> Transcend the suffering of suffering for a while,
> But these lords of single-pointed concentration
> Remain motionless for eons.
> So it is most certain they'll not be liberated
> And will later fall from there.

In other words, when you are born as, for example, a formless-realm god, you know that you have been reborn. Then you enter meditative absorption for many eons, and eventually die and fall to a lower state. You therefore suffer because you are powerless to maintain your state. These rebirths as gods use up merit, and when there is no more accumulated merit left, the gods must leave that life and are reborn in a lower state. But because the continuity of their conceptual wisdom has been broken, they will be very stupid and more lacking in wisdom than other beings.

Some people mistake the actual dhyāna-concentration states for liberation and think that when they attain these states they have gained liberation. Later, when they see they are going to take rebirth, they deny that there is liberation, and so are reborn in the Hell Without Respite. This is why being reborn in these states is no different from staying in a cauldron in hell—all you have done is lost your direction temporarily. Far better to be in the human realm as some old beggar woman reciting *oṃ maṇi padme hūṃ* instead!

Kaelzang Gyatso [the Seventh Dalai Lama] said:

> The famous so-called three realms of saṃsāra
> Are a house of molten iron:
> Go in any of the ten directions
> And you'll be burnt by suffering.
>
> Your heart aches,
> But these are your surroundings.
> You wander in such an evil place,
> And sad are your surroundings.

In other words, you may be reborn anywhere in saṃsāra, from the depths of the Hell Without Respite to the heights of the Peak of Existence, but it is like staying in a six-story house of molten iron—you have not transcended suffering at all. Once during a famine some children asked for barley flour but were given several varieties of turnip instead. The children wouldn't touch any of them and said, "Ugh! They're only turnips!" Similarly, wherever you are reborn, its nature is suffering, only certain aspects are different, and everyone is equally happy or unhappy.

To summarize, you are endlessly tortured by the three types of suffering.

Kyabje Pabongka Rinpoche then brought the discussion of suffering to a close by teaching the three types of suffering.

We in saṃsāra have such thoughts as, "I am happy," but these thoughts are really suffering in their very nature. Our thoughts of "I am indifferent" are in their very nature suffering. When we pour cold water on a burn, we seem temporarily happy. All our contaminated happy feelings eventually change into suffering, and thus are the suffering of change. Not only these contaminated happy feelings, but all their concomitant primary minds and mental factors and any contaminated object that serves to develop [the happy feelings]—all are the suffering of change.

When you first receive a burn, you are not actually tormented by heat, although the nature of the burn is heat. This is only temporary, however, so long as nothing hot or cold to the touch, like water, etc., comes into contact with the wound. Likewise, contaminated feelings of equanimity—together with their concomitant primary minds, mental factors, and their objects—are under the power of past karma and delusions. They are linked to the seeds of future suffering and delusion; they are also linked to the everpresent evil mental states. Feelings of equanimity are therefore the suffering that pervades conditioned phenomena.

When hot water, say, comes into contact with a burn, you develop manifest suffering from the sensation of heat. Suffering such as this is the worst suffering, these feelings of pain. Contaminated feelings of suffering that torment mind and body—together with concomitant primary minds, mental factors, and the objects of these feelings—are the suffering of suffering. When we feel "I am suffering," it is the suffering of suffering.

Your notion of happiness is itself the suffering of change. A sign that it is not truly happiness but only your notion of happiness is the fact that if it goes on too long, your suffering will increase. Your suffering had at first only dropped below a threshold level; later it will rise above the threshold, and the intervening period is your notion of happiness.

Suppose we are now sitting in the shade for too long. We feel cold, so we move out into the sun. We seem to feel happy for a while, but this is not happiness. If it were, it would be like suffering: the more we encounter, the more it would increase. If going out into the sun were happiness, no matter how long we sat there, our happiness must grow the more, not become unhappiness. This is not what happens: we suffer again a little later and have to go back into the shade. Our suffering has gradually risen above its threshold, although this is not in fact obvious.

The same thing happens when you go walking: when you get tired, you sit down and seem to be happy for a while, but the suffering from standing up has only dropped below its threshold; the smaller suffering from sitting is not yet apparent although it will soon rise above its threshold [when you tire of sitting]. Similarly, after you sit for a while, the suffering becomes apparent. Then you will say, "I want to go for a walk." When you get up again, your suffering from sitting falls below its threshold, and your suffering from standing again has not yet actually risen above its threshold, and so on. From [Āryadeva's] *Four Hundred Verses:*

You can see that no matter how much
Happiness increases, it will end.
Similarly, suffering also increases,
But there is no end to it.

The contaminated aggregates are a case of the suffering that pervades all conditioned phenomena: the creation of these aggregates causes one to become a vessel for all suffering. You experience the sufferings of the heat and cold of the hells because you have received the aggregates of a hell being; you experience the sufferings of a hungry ghost's hunger and thirst because you have received the aggregates of a hungry ghost; when you create for yourself the body of an animal—a donkey, say—you carry a load on your back, get whipped, and so on, because you have created for yourself the vessel in which to experience these sufferings.

In short, even the unbearable pain of being pricked by a thorn happens because you are inflicted with a set of aggregates. Just as a man carrying a load of brambles on his naked back will never be without suffering until he puts his load down, you will never be without any type of suffering until you are free of the burden of the contaminated aggregates.

Kyabje Pabongka Rinpoche told of Śhrījāta the householder, and how Maudgalyāyana, Śhrījāta's abbot, took him to the ocean shore to show him the bones, human corpses, and so on, from peoples' past lives, and how Śhrījāta was moved to develop renunciation.

They are called inflicted "aggregates" for three reasons:

Fire issuing from brambles is called "bramble fire" The [inflicted] aggregates come from past delusions—the inflictor or substantial cause—so the result has been named after the cause.

A man dependent on the king is called "the king's man." Delusions—the inflictor or substantial cause—are an outcome of [inflicted] aggregates; the thing being bolstered is given the name of the bolsterer.

A tree that produces a medicine or a type of blossom is called "the tree of this particular medicine" or the "tree of that particular blossom." Your own actions arose from your inflicted delusions—so the name of the result has been given to the cause.

These aggregates are the suffering that pervades all conditioned phenomena, because the evil states of suffering and delusion are forever adhering to them. As long as one has these aggregates, each time one does not have the feeling of suffering one will immediately afterward be made to develop much suffering by various means. The suffering that pervades conditioned phenomena therefore pervades all suffering, and is the root of the other two kinds of suffering.

The aggregates created the vessel for the suffering of this rebirth because they create the future rebirth that leads to suffering. Among all sufferings, the aggregates are the worst: *saṃsāra* is a state of helplessness in which one receives the burden of contaminated, inflicted aggregates by virtue of karma and delusion. This means that one takes rebirth from the Peak of Existence down to the Hell Without Respite, and circles between these over and over again. This is why it is correct to see the contaminated, inflicted aggregates themselves as saṃsāra. In order to weary of saṃsāra one must weary of the contaminated, inflicted aggregates. Until one wearies of the suffering that pervades conditioned phenomena, one will not truly weary of saṃsāra.

Kyabje Pabongka then discussed all this at some length.

DAY 15

Kyabje Pabongka Rinpoche quoted from the great pandit Āryadeva:

> You churl! How could you not be afraid
> That you will be bound here
> When there is no end at all
> To this ocean of suffering.

After giving a short talk to set our motivations and naming the headings he had already covered, he revised the section "Developing Thoughts of Yearning for Liberation." He then taught how to pursue this practice.

As in the preparatory rites, you should think about the sufferings of saṃsāra while meditating that your divine guru sits above the crown of your head. Between meditation sessions, refer to sūtras that teach the drawbacks of saṃsāra—the *Sūtras on Having Much Remembrance* and others.

After such contemplations, the criterion of having developed renunciation is: whatever you see—saṃsāra's happiness, power, riches, and so forth—you think, "These are fraudulent things; they are suffering."

You may be moved to renounce such things when you suffer a few saṃsāric problems, like punishment, degradation, and so on. But this is only a superficial renunciation, only a pale reflection. So long as you are born into saṃsāra, its nature is nothing but pure suffering; if you want never again to undergo suffering, you must break the continuity of your rebirths. You develop a yearning for liberation when you weary of saṃsāra and wish to gain some certainty—in other words, renunciation. Great Tsongkapa said:

> After such meditations, when you do not long
> For the splendors of saṃsāra for even a moment,
> When your thoughts day and night always yearn for liberation,
> You have developed renunciation.

And:

> When others construct fine thrones for me, show me deference, pay me respect, and so on, I think, "These are all impermanent, they are all suffering," and I am uncontrollably moved to renunciation. I have had this for some time.

No matter how much of saṃsāra's magnificence you see, it ought to increase your weariness of it.

When people die, they suffer mental anguish when they realize that they will be separated from this life's wealth, friends, and so on, but this is a superficial sense of impermanence, prompted by the trivia of this life. It is vital to use some means to develop in our mindstreams the pure thoughts of being moved to renunciation. The main thing we should yearn for is buddhahood. For us to receive buddhahood, we must have bodhichitta; to have bodhichitta, we must first have compassion; and to have this, we must first recognize that all sentient beings have been our mothers. We must develop renunciation by meditating on our own saṃsāric suffering, and then develop compassion by meditating on others' sufferings. Thus it is certainly not the case that the great-scope section has no meditation on renunciation.

Nevertheless renunciation is the principal path in the medium-scope section. Following the development of renunciation in our mindstream, any virtue we create will be a cause for our liberation. As long as we have not developed even a contrived form of the principles of the path, such as renunciation, any virtue we create will usually only turn saṃsāra's wheel. An exception to this is virtue created in dependence on the power of a [merit] field. If we do not take the three fundamentals of the path seriously or if we ignore them, any profound Dharma we put effort into—meditation on the energy winds and their channels, meditation on the deities, recitation of the mantras, and so forth—will not become even part of a path leading to liberation or omniscience. It would just be a pointless waste of energy. So for now, put aside the so-called profound; it is vital that we first work as hard as we can on renunciation, bodhichitta, and the correct view.

ASCERTAINING THE NATURE OF THE PATH LEADING TO LIBERATION (275)

This has two sections: (1) thinking about the source of suffering—the entry to saṃsāra; and (2) actually ascertaining the nature of the path leading to liberation.

THINKING ABOUT THE SOURCE OF SUFFERING—THE ENTRY TO SAṂSĀRA (276)

This has three subheadings: (1) how delusions are developed; (2) how karma is accumulated through them; (3) how one leaves one rebirth at death and is conceived in another.

HOW DELUSIONS ARE DEVELOPED (277)

This has four sections: (1) the identification of the delusions; (2) the stages in their development; (3) the causes of delusions; (4) the drawbacks of delusions.

There are two ways of fitting [into the lamrim scheme] the heading "Thinking about the Source of Suffering—The Entry to Saṃsāra." One way is to attach it to an earlier heading; the other—the way used here—follows the traditional discourses on the *Swift Path* and the *Easy Path* and puts the heading under the next, "Actually Ascertaining the Nature of the Path Leading to Liberation."

You should first think about the general and specific drawbacks of saṃsāra, become moved to renounce it, and develop a wish to be liberated. You will then wonder, "What is the cause of saṃsāra?" After investigating the cause and becoming acquainted with it, you will then want to break its continuity.

The origin of suffering has two parts: originating delusions and originating karma. You must carry the burden of the inflicted aggregates, and karma is responsible. Karma developed because of delusions. You have accumulated immeasurable karma in the past, but without the delusions of craving and clinging as an attendant, subsidiary cause, karma cannot on its own throw you into another rebirth: it would be like a seed without moisture. Even if you have no accumulated karma from the past, if you have delusions, you will immediately accumulate fresh karma because of these delusions, and so take on a set of saṃsāric aggregates in your next rebirth. [Dharmakīrti said in his] *Commentary on Valid Cognition:*

> For those beyond craving for existence
> Karma cannot precipitate another birth
> Because the attendant causes have been destroyed.

Also:

> [But] if one has craving,
> It will happen again.

The root, therefore, of being reborn into saṃsāra is delusion itself. By *delusion* we mean something that, through its own power and whenever we develop it, has the function of immediately making our mindstream—our personal mental continuum—unpeaceful and unsubdued.

Thus we must identify the delusions, for not doing so would be like not identifying the poison in a deadly arrow: we would not know what antidote we need to apply.

THE IDENTIFICATION OF DELUSIONS (278)

This has two parts: (1) the root delusions; (2) the secondary delusions.[64]

THE ROOT DELUSIONS (279)

From Vasubhandu's *Treasury of Metaphysics:*

> The six subtle and extensive roots
> Of [saṃsāric] existence are:
> Attachment, anger, pride,
> Ignorance, wrong views, and doubt.

That is, there are six root delusions.

ATTACHMENT (280)

When we see an attractive jewel, body, food, drink, or whatever, we develop thoughts such as not wanting to be separated from it. Other delusions are like dust on a piece of cloth—easy to remove; but attachment, which means clinging to or being fixated with something, is like oil that has soaked into a piece of cloth—difficult to remove, because it spreads out farther and farther. When, for example, one wants to look at an object, touch it, and so forth; craving and clinging to this object of one's attachment penetrates the mind; these then spread and are difficult to remove.

> The lasso of craving and attachment confines you to saṃsāra's prison.

In other words, because attachment is the root that prevents us from being sufficiently moved to renounce saṃsāra, it is the main thing binding us to saṃsāra.

Its antidote is meditation on the ugly, and so on. Here, ugliness meditation is as follows: you develop the attitude that the body [as a corpse] has a bloody aspect, an aspect of being scattered [to feed the vultures], a swelling aspect, and an eventual future as a skeleton. When you are attached to someone, for example, consider how that person is just a sack full of thirty-six kinds of filthy substances. When you are attached to eating meat, think how the main ingredient is filthy, how it was prepared by taking a life, and so on. Your attachment and craving will then diminish.

ANGER (281)

Anger is the highly disturbed aspect of the mind that arises when we see something unpleasant—enemies and so forth. The objects of anger could be sentient beings or inanimate objects; when we focus the mind on them, the mind is disturbed and tormented. The wish to do the object utter harm is anger.

Anger does great damage. It does things like destroying your root merits as if they had been burnt in a fire. Anger is responsible for people taking lives, stabbing or beating others, and so forth.

Nowadays some people apply sweet-sounding names to anger: "Our lama is cross," they say. These people may not reckon that anger is damaging, but as it is said: "There is no sin like hostility. There is no austerity like patience." Or: "Anger is the weapon to murder your high rebirths." In other words, of all the delusions, anger has the greatest strength to destroy root virtues and is the main thing that throws you into the lower realms. It therefore does great damage. There are different ways in which root virtues can be destroyed, and these ways depend on the object [of the anger: see Day 6, pp. 197–98]. You must apply the antidotes to anger—being patient, etc. I will talk about anger further in the section on the six perfections below.

It is permissible, however, to beat your pupils if you do it solely with their benefit in mind, and not out of anger.

PRIDE (282)

Pride is your inflated opinion of yourself and can manifest in relation to some good or bad object: your power, wealth, good qualities, family, wisdom, your pure ethics—even your pleasant voice or physical prowess. When you look down from a high mountain, everyone below seems to have shrunken in size. When you hold yourself to be superior to others, and have an inflated opinion of yourself, you take on a superior aspect. It requires only a trivial object to serve as a cause for your developing pride. As the Kadampas of old said: "Does the snow on mountaintops melt in springtime? See if it happens to the snows in the ravines below!"[65] They also said that the mountaintop of pride won't get flooded with the water of good qualities. In other words, it is difficult to develop any good qualities at all when one has pride. Also, a guru may teach Dharma to a person who has pride, but it will do no good.

The antidote to pride is to think over some list you don't understand, especially the full classification of the sense elements.[66] Occasionally you should think over every individual internal and external thing that exists from the crown of your head down to your feet; you will not know very many of these, and it ought to kill your pride.

IGNORANCE (283)

Generally, ignorance [*marigpa* in Tibetan] is the opposite of the word "to know" *[rigpa]*, with the negative particle *[ma]* added—like the verbs "to see" and "not to see" or "to know" and "not to know." Ignorance is not knowing, not seeing, not understanding, being unclear, and so forth. Like the pitch black we see when our eyes are shut tight, or not seeing objects in total darkness, ignorance is the blindness of not seeing the nature or mode of existence of something: the four truths, cause and effect, the Three Jewels, and the like. Ignorance is the root of all delusions.

There is one system that asserts that ignorance is the same as the view that equates the self with the perishable [that is, the aggregates and so on], and in that system, that view itself is ignorance. Another system asserts that ignorance and this view are separate. For example, the mistake of thinking a rope is a snake is like the view that equates the self with the perishable [aggregates]. The cause for this is that because the striped rope is covered in darkness, there is a lack of clarity about the mode of existence of the rope. Ignorance is like this [lack of clarity about the mode of existence of the rope].

The first system was asserted by the splendid Chandrakīrti, by Dharmakīrti, and others; the second by Asaṅga and his disciples.

DOUBT (284)

This is directed toward the four truths, the Three Jewels, cause and effect, and so on; one wonders whether they exist or not, whether they are true or not. Doubt in the Three Jewels is a condition to prevent us from developing realizations. As the First Dalai Lama Gendun Drub, said:

> Save me from doubt, that terrible ghost,
> That cruel one who flies in a sky of utter blindness,
> Who harms my yearning for conviction,
> Who murders my liberation.

When you doubt the law of cause and effect, it prevents you from attaining high rebirth; doubt about the four truths serves to block you from gaining liberation. Doubt, then, is most harmful. As such, it is assumed to be one of the five nonviews [that is, the first five root delusions].

[DELUDED] VIEWS (285)

There are five deluded views:

THE VIEW THAT EQUATES THE SELF WITH THE PERISHABLE (286)

This is a deluded view directed toward the collection of the aggregates—which have the property of being perishable—regarding them to be the self and to belong to the self, that is "I" and "mine."

An illustration: when people through praise or insults help or harm you, the thought "Why did they do this to me?" presents itself most vividly to your mind; you grasp at [this] as if it existed in this way. This is the root of misdeeds.

Even ants hold this view equating the self with the perishable. If you poke an ant on the nose with a blade of grass, it will immediately think, terrified, "Something is happening to me!" hunch up, and play dead. Later it will turn around and run away. The view of equating the self with the perishable caused it to do this.

EXTREME VIEWS (287)

These views are directed toward anything grasped at by the above view of equating the self with the perishable; extreme views take such things to be permanent, stable, independent, established as being true, and so on. Views such as regarding the continuity of the "I" as being discontinued at death are also extreme views.

Although it is mainly non-Buddhists who hold these views, we may also [wrongly] regard things as being established as true, or have nihilistic views, etc.

THE VIEW OF HOLDING THE AGGREGATES TO BE SUPREME (288)

This is a deluded view deriving from any of the abovementioned wrong views, those equating the self with the perishable, or those holding things to be permanent or nonexistent. This delusion is directed toward the aggregates of the holder of these views, and it takes these aggregates to be supreme.

HOLDING AN ETHIC OR CODE OF BEHAVIOR TO BE SUPREME (289)

This view is taking, for example, the cultivation of the five fires, jumping over tridents, the ethic of standing on one leg,[67] and so on, to be paths to liberation. It could also be holding some code of behavior to be supreme, such as sitting on an animal hide. Some people perceive by subtle clairvoyance that they were a dog in their previous life and this blinds them: they want to receive a human body again in their next life, so [mistaking this as the cause], they imitate many dog actions, bark, and so forth. They take this to be supreme, and so make their body and speech perform these evils.

People pursue these evil ethics because, for example, they hold that such things are the main cause of liberation.

WRONG VIEWS (290)

These mainly comprise the view that the four truths, the Three Jewels, cause and effect, etc. do not exist.

Two things should be considered here: exaggeration—where something nonexistent is supposed to exist—and denial—where something existent is supposed not to exist, or where one holds the view that things do not exist at all. Some non-Buddhists claim that the world was created by Vishṇu, who incarnated ten times into the world; the Sāṃkhyas divide all knowables into twenty-five categories and hold that the general primary principal created this world; others assert that that the world was created by Īśhvara; and so on. These people claim that something was created when it was not—so these are exaggerations. Wrong views, however, are denials.

Count these five types of wrong view as one, add to them the five nonviews, and the resulting six make up the subtle and extensive root delusions.

When any of these are generated, you should apply their antidotes. Still, as [Āryadeva's] *Four Hundred Verses* says: "Just like the sense faculties in the body, benighted ignorance resides in them all." In other words, benighted ignorance pervades and acts as a cause for all the other delusions. However, benighted ignorance is difficult to identify, so I will discuss it below.

THE STAGES IN THEIR DEVELOPMENT (291)

The six root delusions, in fact all delusions, derive fundamentally from grasping at the self [see Day 22] and the view of equating the self with the perishable. All suffering, all karma, and all delusion therefore derive from this view of equating the self with the perishable—if you assert that this view is one with ignorance. According to the system that does not assert this, ignorance itself is the key element.

According to the Prāsaṅgika Madhyamaka system, the view of equating the self with the perishable is the root. There are intellectual and instinctive views, and here this view is the latter kind. There are two types of instinctive views: grasping at "I," and grasping at "mine." The view of equating the self with the perishable is a grasping at "mine." When someone compliments *you,* or whatever, you think, "How nice of him to say that of *me.*" This "I" and "me" are very vivid and very deep-seated within the mind; because you have these [thoughts], you take them to be the self, and [the notion that this self] is the experiencer arises. Because of this [notion], you cling to the "I," grow attached to those who help you, hate people who harm you, and have benighted ignorance toward strangers. From *A Commentary on Valid Cognition:*

> You know people as "others" because you have a self;
> You grasp at the pair—self and others—and become hostile.
> These are completely related;
> All misdeeds derive from them.

From [Chandrakīrti's] *Engaging in the Middle Way:*

> May my mind perceive that
> Every faulty delusion derives
> From views that equate
> The set [of aggregates with the self]...
>
> At first I clung to the self, the "I";
> And I developed attachment to things, to "them"...

Although the root of the six subtle and extensive root delusions is ignorance, one develops attachment, hostility, doubt, and so forth, in dependence on the view of equating the self with the perishable. And in dependence on attachment, etc., one accumulates karma. And in dependence on this karma, one cycles in saṃsāra. The roots of saṃsāra are ignorance, the view that equates the self with the perishable [set of aggregates], the instinctive grasping at an "I." To abandon delusion for good, one must work hard at applying the antidote to ignorance and to grasping at a self—that is, the wisdom that understands selflessness. This wisdom that understands selflessness is therefore like the "white panacea" medicine that can destroy hundreds of evils. From the *Four Hundred Verses:* "That is why all delusions are conquered when benightedness is conquered." From the *Sūtra on the Ten Stages:*

> In this world, all misdeeds ever committed, arose, or to be found, came from manifest clinging to a self. Without manifest clinging to a self, these would not happen.

All the same, until one understands selflessness, one must employ some means to suppress delusions in order to be temporarily rid of them. One must prevent their cause. And so:

THE CAUSES OF DELUSIONS (292)

There are six.

THE FIRST CAUSE: THEIR FOUNDATION (293)

This foundation consists of seeds or latencies. Just as when one is unable to uproot the seeds of illness, even the smallest piece of food will provoke illness, so when one meets with a certain condition, one will readily develop delusion in one's mindstream because one has the seeds of delusion. These ready-to-sprout seeds are the foundation or instinct for this to happen.

THE SECOND CAUSE: THEIR FOCUS OR OBJECT (294)

This could be something pleasant, unpleasant, or whatever. When we meet with these things, because we have not abandoned the seeds of delusion, as [Vasubhandu's] *Treasury of Metaphysics* says:

Not abandoning [delusion]
Both subtle and extensive;
Remaining in proximity
To their subjects;
And carrying out
Unrealistic thinking—
These are the full set
Of causes for delusion.

In other words, we must distance ourselves as far as possible from the objects of delusions, since we will otherwise develop delusions. Ordained people should avoid them by living in monasteries, hermitages, and so on. It will benefit us beginners, and allow us to avoid delusions, if we do not see these subjects of delusion for a while. We should therefore avoid them as much as we can. In the mind-training texts, we find:

He who still applies antidotes
Should chiefly abandon these evil objects.

And Togme Sangpo said:

Abandon evil objects, and delusions gradually subside.
Free from distractions, virtuous practices gradually increase.
Your mind cleansed, you gain conviction in the Dharma.
Cultivating solitude is a task of a child of the victorious ones.

In other words, it is vital to abandon the objects that develop delusions and to stay in some place congenial for this.

THE THIRD CAUSE: SOCIETY (295)

You should abandon the diversions of bad company. However, everyone involved in this life is bad company, since their conversations are about things that cause delusions—alcohol, games, and so on. You should not heed such people, or be influenced by them. If you don't do this, and fall under their influence, they will increase your delusions, and you will participate in unbecoming actions. An illustration: there were once two people from the kingdom of Paenpo; one drank alcohol and the other did not.

The drinker went to Radreng; the nondrinker, to Lhasa. The one in Radreng met the Kadampa geshes. The one who went to Lhasa fell in with bad company. The two men later met, and because of the influence of good and bad company, the man who used to drink had now given it up and the former nondrinker now drank.

We call miserliness "thrift," and anger "being cross," "being rash," and so on. We give them these sweet-sounding names, but they still do great damage. When pupils depend on a thrifty teacher who is tight-fisted with all his possessions, the miserliness of the pupils increases. And the same goes for anger-prone teachers. It is all too easy to understand the activities of bad company, so we must abandon such company.

All the same, although almost everyone these days yearns for the things of this life, and so usually there is nothing but bad company, we cannot forsake everybody, so it is vital we treat such people with caution and do not associate with them too much. There was once a country where everyone drank the water of madness and became insane. Only the king was left sane, but the others only said, "The king is mad." Similarly, these days Dharma practitioners do not conform with the common herd, but this does no damage, for they wish to reach out, to pursue, and to succeed in their practices. When bad friends advise you, do not contradict them; be like a stubborn old yak and practice the "ten most prized possessions of the Kadampas," which include: send the invulnerable vajra ahead of you, associate yourself with the primal wisdom vajra, and put behind you the vajra of shamelessness.

THE FOURTH CAUSE: DISCUSSIONS (296)

This involves reading books which give instructions that seem plausible but still generate delusions. When you read these evil works—such as the [folktale] exploits of Gesar Ling, treatises on love, anthologies of tantric spells or sex positions, and so forth—they make your attachment, hostility, and benighted ignorance increase and spread. But if you think over the deeds and life stories of holy beings, this can implant the seeds of liberation in you; you should therefore read such stories.

When many people get together, they talk about many things that increase attachment or hostility—about the king, the army, women, lawsuits, and so on. This is also a cause to develop delusions.

THE FIFTH CAUSE: FAMILIARITY (297)

Zhangpa Rinpoche said: "You are as if wrapped in instincts from your familiarity with evil thoughts..." In other words, owing to your great familiarity with delusions, you develop attachment, hostility, and so on as a matter of course, even when distracted.

We have great or small delusions according to our great or small familiarity with them in past lives. Some people develop great attachment, hostility, or whatever, at the slightest pretext. For example, people familiar with anger can't even tolerate a dirty look, and so on. There is nothing for such people but to apply some antidote, and do what they can to prevent these delusions continuing.

THE SIXTH CAUSE: UNREALISTIC THINKING (298)

Unrealistic thinking involves the constant exaggerations that one makes concerning the object of one's attachment, hostility, and so forth. Regarding the object of one's attachment—clothing, for example—one thinks that it has fine colors, a beautiful cut, a lovely belt, and so on. Regarding the objects of one's hostility, an enemy for instance, one thinks, "They did me this and this harm, and afterward did that and that to me." One thinks over and over again about these pleasant or unpleasant objects.

A person may be a Dharma practitioner, but he will still suffer or experience problems, and so may doubt the law of cause and effect, etc. He will develop delusions if the above causes arise, so he must do what he can to prevent them. If he does not apply the antidotes, his delusions will increase; they will be overshadowed if he applies the antidotes. So work hard at this.

THE DRAWBACKS OF DELUSIONS (299)

From *An Ornament to the Sūtras:*

> Delusions destroy you, destroy sentient beings, and destroy ethics.
> Lesser people disparage you; you lose guardians and gain your teacher's reproach.
> You gain disputes and infamy, and then rebirth to unconducive states.

> You lose both what you possess and have yet to acquire, and you gain great suffering.

In other words, delusions have many drawbacks. When you develop a delusion, your mindstream becomes a nonvirtuous entity; you then act perversely toward the objects [of the delusions]; this makes the latent seeds of the delusion take hold; so you will continually develop the same sort of delusions—that is, attachment, hostility, or whatever—and enter those forbidden states deprecated by the saints. Your unfortunate karmic actions will increase because of these last two drawbacks. You stray away from both liberation and omniscience, becoming distanced from them. Delusion causes your virtuous actions to decline, and so on; so it makes you wrong yourself and others. It makes your ethics decline; you will be given fewer gifts and be paid less service. Even the buddhas and Dharma protectors will criticize you. Other beings as well as you will suffer because your delusion may make other people want to kill you, and so on. In this life you develop a worse reputation because of becoming embroiled in lawsuits, arguments, and so on. And in future lives you will be reborn in remote lands, or in the lower realms. To summarize, there are an infinite number of drawbacks, and they are all said to be produced by delusions.

So when you develop these delusions, you must immediately recognize them clearly as your enemies and employ some means of putting a stop to them. From *Engaging in the Deeds of Bodhisattvas:*

> If all the gods and demigods
> Were to become my enemies,
> Even they would be unable
> To lead me to the fires of the Hell Without Respite.
>
> These powerful delusions are an enemy:
> When I encounter any, they could throw me
> In an instant into fires that would consume
> Mount Meru until not even ash remained.

In other words, no enemy is more powerful than these. When you accommodate your foe, it may pacify his anger and he will not harm you. When you accommodate delusions, they harm you in return. All the myriad sufferings you had, even when you were burned by the fires of the

Hell Without Respite, were created by delusions. Henceforth, delusions make your experiences; they are what will force you into misery in saṃsāra, and so they are more powerful than all your enemies in the three realms. The Kadampas of old said:

> Train to stand at the ready against delusions and do them harm but to extend your hands to sentient beings and do them benefit.

Geshe Baen Gung-gyael said:

> I guard the entrance to the fortress of my mind with a spear—the antidotes. At no time am I not doing this. When delusions are at the ready, so am I. When they relax, so do I.

In other words, you must clearly see delusions as your worst enemy and apply their antidotes right away.

HOW KARMA IS ACCUMULATED (300)

There are two types of karma: mental karma and intended karma.

MENTAL KARMA (301)

[Asaṅga's] *Compendium of Metaphysics* says:

> What is mental karma? It is a karmic action of the compositional factors aggregate that makes a thought manifest. Its function is to engage the mind in the virtuous, the nonvirtuous, or the neutral.

In other words a mental karmic action is, for example, the primary mind that provokes us to feel we should speak insulting words; or it is a karmic action of the secondary mind that provokes or encourages us while we are saying these insulting words.

INTENDED KARMA (302)

This consists of the actions of body and speech motivated by mental karma. As *A Treasury of Metaphysics* says:

> Karma: it is mental or created by the mind.
> Mental karma is mental action;
> It gives rise to karmic actions of body and speech.

Delusions give rise to three types of karma: unmeritorious, meritorious, and immutable. To take them in order: *unmeritorious karma* is karma accumulated from yearning for the things of this life, and then [acting upon this by] killing, etc. This type of karma makes one take rebirth in the lower realms. *Meritorious karma* is karma accumulated from yearning for sensual happiness in a future life. This karma makes one take rebirth as a desire-realm god or human.

Immutable karma is as follows. One repudiates sensual pleasure in future lives, indulges in the happy feelings that come from single-pointed concentration, and is thus reborn as a god in the first three dhyāna-concentration states. Or, one could even repudiate the happy feelings that develop from single-pointed concentration and so, yearning for feelings of equanimity, accumulate karma that acts as a cause to be reborn in the fourth dhyāna-concentration state or higher.

Both meritorious and unmeritorious karma throw one into a rebirth in the desire realm, and their results are mutable. For example, one may have already achieved the bardo state of a being on its way to the hells, but through the power of one's guru, of rituals, of the secret tantras, and so on, one's bardo state can be changed so that one is able to receive rebirth in the upper realms. Drom Rinpoche said,

> If all the people of Radreng with lay vows were to hold their property in common, it would be particularly helpful in the creation of root merits after one of their deaths.

In other words, because these lay people would all have the same property, root merits [created in relation to this property] would be especially beneficial to any of their dead colleagues still in the bardo.

The throwing karma to be reborn into the higher realms is as follows.

Suppose one has already accumulated karma to be reborn in the first dhyāna-concentration state. The karma will not change instead into karma to be reborn in the second dhyāna-concentration state, or whatever. This is why such karma is called "immutable." From *A Treasury of Metaphysics:*

> Virtuous karma is merit to be born into the desire realm.
> Karma to be born higher is immutable;
> This karma is immutable because
> It will ripen [only] in these [higher] levels.

Any karma not accumulated in conjunction with any of the three fundamentals of the path will only be cause for saṃsāra; any karma created when you are moved to renounce the three realms [of saṃsāra] could only become cause for your liberation. When you give up this life with the thought that you will practice Dharma but do not do this in conjunction with renunciation and so on, you may stay and meditate on mental quiescence in some hermitage, but even if you are lucky you will only receive causes to be reborn in the formless realms or the form-realm dhyāna-concentration states. This is why, if you want to practice Dharma, it is vital to seek some totally unmistaken instruction.

HOW YOU LEAVE ONE REBIRTH AT DEATH AND ARE RECONCEIVED IN ANOTHER (303)

This has three sections.

WHAT HAPPENS AT DEATH (304)

Your lifespan may run out. Your merit may run out. You have not rid yourself of danger. The *Sūtra on the Factors Contributing to Death* mentions nine such factors for death. These and others can kill you.

Your dying thoughts activate the karma that will throw you into the next rebirth after that death. The activators of this karma are craving and clinging, and this is what happens: You might feel, "I am going to be separated from this body," and cling to your present body. Craving includes things like desiring heat when you are to be reborn in the hot hells.

The object of this triggering process is your most powerful karma, be it black or white. If your black and white karma are equal, then the triggering object is whichever of these two types is the more familiar. If the two types are still equal, then whichever type of karma was carried out first will be triggered.

The time when this triggering takes place is while the mind is still active and still has the coarse form of recognition [or attitude]—an either virtuous or nonvirtuous phenomenon, that is faith, compassion, attachment, anger, etc.—and you can still recall such things by yourself or can be reminded of them by other people. When coarse recognition ceases, and while your dying thoughts are subtle, your thoughts are neutral, and you are unable to remember any virtue or nonvirtue.

If your dying thoughts are of faith, and so on, your virtue will be activated. It is therefore vital to pray with virtuous thoughts when your dying thoughts are on the point of being activated. You could be a Dharma practitioner who continually creates virtue, but if you get angry, etc., when you are dying, you activate nonvirtuous dying thoughts and go to the lower realms owing to the ripening effect of past nonvirtues. And the same principles would apply to a sinner who continually sins.

At this point one will be going to either the upper or the lower realms. If one is going to the upper realms, one's body heat dissipates from the lower parts of the body and collects into the heart. If one is going to the lower realms, the opposite happens: heat dissipates from the upper reaches of the body and collects in the lower. Also, you can know which of these two will happen by such signs as the degree of discomfort the person experiences during his fatal illness. "Discomfort during the illness" refers to when a major part of the body fails.

Some people hallucinate when they die: for example, they may imagine being squashed under bricks of tea or by people.

Kyabje Pabongka Rinpoche told how in Lhasa he saw a steward of the central government die. He had stolen tea; when he died he had hallucinations and thought he was being squashed under boxes of tea.

When an official from Tsang Province died, he said, "I am being crushed by many people," and he left that life in a state of terror. And so on.

This also happens to people who have performed virtuous actions. Once a beggar who lived by the side of the road had visions of a palace and white light rays when he died.

Kyabje Pabongka Rinpoche also told how an old woman in Chuzang who had recited oṃ maṇi padme hūṃ *a lot had virtuous visions when she died.*

Such signs are but a prelude to death.

THE WAY ONE ACHIEVES THE BARDO (305)

Like the swinging of the arms of a balance, your present incarnation ends simultaneously with your adoption of the physical form of the preliminary incarnation—this refers to the phantom that resembles the aggregates of your next rebirth; the next rebirth or incarnation, wherever it may be, is preceded by this phantom. Some people claim that the dead live in the bardo with the appearances and costumes they had when they were alive and that there are ways of sending messages to them. This is a fallacy. It is possible there have been one or two such sightings, but they are not the dead person; they are said to be some creature taking the form of the dead person, done to deceive ordinary worldlings.

Kyabje Pabongka referred here to the story from Je Milarepa's biography about the death of the head of a Boenpo family.

Bardo beings have all their faculties; they are clairvoyant and can perform paranormal acts; nothing—except for sacred reliquaries or their birth sites—bars their way. The bardo beings who are to be reborn in hell are the color of burnt logs; beings to be reborn as hungry ghosts are of a watery color; those about to become animals are smoke-colored; those about to become humans or gods of the desire realm are the color of fine gold. Those about to become form-realm gods are of a white color in the bardo. There is no bardo for beings taking rebirth in the formless realms.

The bardo incarnation state appears as black night to the nonvirtuous; to the virtuous the state appears as a night punctuated by white strips of cloth or lit by moonbeams.

Many claims have been made about the lifespans of bardo beings, usually said to be seven days—days of the same duration as those in the next life. After these seven days, bardo beings undergo a small death, and they can have up to seven such small deaths before they find a birth site.

THE WAY ONE IS CONCEIVED AND REBORN (306)

Take the case of being born from a womb. Conception occurs within the sperm and blood of the parents. The bardo being sees the father and mother sleeping together; its anger and attachment nauseate it, and it sees only the sex organs of the parents. Its anger kills it, and it is conceived into [its next] incarnation.

This completes the heading "Thinking About the Source of Suffering—The Entry to Saṃsāra," following [Tsongkapa's] *Medium Stages of the Path,* the *Swift Path,* and the *Easy Path.* I shall now discuss this heading according to the twelve interdependent links, which are also discussed in [Tsongkapa's] *Great Stages of the Path.* The *Swift Path* and the *Easy Path* lamrims are not clear on this topic. I shall teach this according to its treatment in *Mañjuśhrī's Own Words,* giving little more than its headings.

The above brief version of the way to think about the entry to saṃsāra—that is, the source of suffering—is sufficient. People who, for example, have studied the classical debate texts, however, should think about this starting with the twelve interdependent links. This is the best thing for certain exceptional people.

Kyabje Pabongka Rinpoche told how once the king of Magadha on the advice of the Buddha explained the process of taking rebirth to the foreign king, Utrayana, by using a drawing of the wheel of life. Utrayana developed a weariness of saṃsāra. Rinpoche also told us how Geshe Puchungwa made a study of the twelve links and taught the small and medium scopes according to these links.

So you should think further about the drawbacks of the origin of suffering and the drawbacks of saṃsāra by means of the twelve interdependent links in order to strengthen your weariness of saṃsāra, and so forth. The Buddha discussed these links when he taught the *Rice Seedlings Sūtra.* As it was said:

> Because this exists, that will occur. Because this has arisen, that will arise. Similarly, because of ignorance, the compositional factors…

In other words, there are twelve interdependent links, as follows.

IGNORANCE (307)

This is the root of our going round in saṃsāra. We are ignorant of how to apprehend selflessness with our wisdom; when we perceive persons or phenomena, we hold that they have a self or that they can be established by their nature. *Ignorance* is our perverse manner of apprehension that contradicts the cognition of primal wisdom. This is like being benighted and blind.

There are two forms of ignorance: ignorance of cause and effect, and of suchness.

COMPOSITIONAL FACTORS (308)

Ignorance motivates the compositional factors as if this were its job. The aggregates manifest in our [next] reincarnation, and this is the function of the compositional factors. Thus we are motivated by the ignorance of being blind to the law of cause and effect, thereby creating unmeritorious karma; or we are motivated by the ignorance of being blind to the mode of existence of things, and we create unmeritorious or immutable karma. All these types of karma are compositional factors.

CONSCIOUSNESS (309)

This refers to two consciousnesses: the consciousness at the time of the cause, and that at the time of the result. The first type is the consciousness immediately after the instinct or latency of the compositional factor, that is the karma, has been imprinted. The second type is the consciousness immediately after conception into the [next] incarnation.

An illustration: suppose that, motivated by ignorance, you take a life. When you commit this karmic action, or compositional factor, its instinct or latency is imprinted as soon as the karmic process has been completed. This is the consciousness at the time of the cause. By virtue of this karma you are conceived into an incarnation as a hell being; immediately after this conception, the situation of your consciousness constitutes the consciousness at the time of the result.

Each nonvirtuous karmic action is capable of throwing one into many rebirths in the lower realms. Apply the same principles to meritorious karma and so on.

The instincts of these karmic actions enter the consciousness as oil soaks into sand or the ink of an official seal soaks into paper. Craving and clinging are able to activate these latencies, which then become potent enough to effect rebirth.

NAME AND FORM (310)

In the case of rebirth from a womb, the name link is the four aggregates of feeling, recognition, compositional factors, and consciousness. The form link is the blood and sperm in their first stage of development, etc., into which the consciousness has been placed. Such links, where they apply, are called the link of name or of form.

THE SIX SENSES (311)

Once the six sense faculties—the eye, ear, [nose, tongue, body, mind]—have formed, this link only applies as long as one still cannot discriminate between objects whenever a certain object, a faculty, and the sensory consciousness are present. The physical and mental faculties are said to exist from the period of initial fetal development. With the example of a transformational rebirth into the two inferior realms [the desire and form realms], the name and form link and the link of the six senses occur simultaneously. In the formless realm there are only the name link and the link of the mental sense; there are no links of form or of the five physical senses.

CONTACT (312)

Once the previous link has been formed, the [potential] object, the [appropriate] faculty, and the [appropriate] sense consciousness are present and touch [that is, interact] as well; one can then discriminate between pleasant, unpleasant, and neutral objects. This is the contact link.

FEELING (313)

The contact link serves as the condition for the development of one of the three types of feeling: happiness, suffering, or equanimity. For example, we develop happy feelings on meeting with a pleasant object.

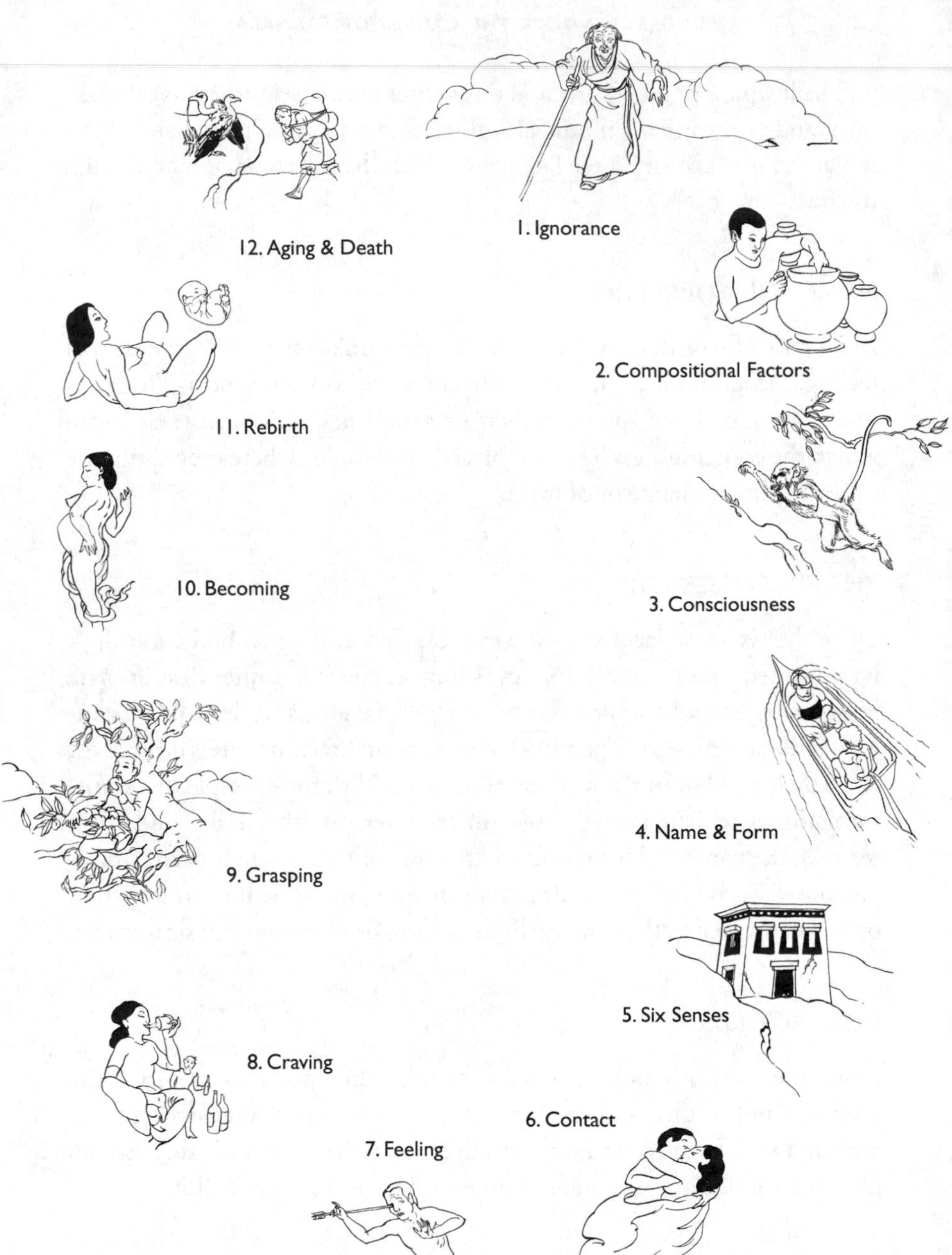
1. Ignorance
2. Compositional Factors
3. Consciousness
4. Name & Form
5. Six Senses
6. Contact
7. Feeling
8. Craving
9. Grasping
10. Becoming
11. Rebirth
12. Aging & Death

THE TWELVE LINKS

CRAVING (314)

Craving is wanting not to be separated from happy feelings. It is also wanting to be separated from suffering and clinging to this separation. We can also crave that our equanimity does not decline.

Feelings are said to serve as a subsidiary cause for the development of craving. This should be understood to mean that ignorance is present and that contact then serves as a contributory factor for the feelings that then occur, which in turn produce craving. So when we do not have ignorance, we may still have feelings, yet craving will not develop.

GRASPING (315)

Our craving increases, so we desire the object and become attached to it. There are four types of grasping. *Grasping at the sensual* is being attached to the objects of the senses. *Grasping at views* is being attached to [all] evil views except the view that equates the self with the perishable. *Grasping at ethics and modes of behavior* is being attached to inferior ethics and modes of behavior linked to evil views. *Grasping at assertions that there is a self* is a fondness for [notions of] true existence: it is fundamentally a fondness for [the view of equating the self with the] perishable aggregates.

BECOMING (316)

In the past, the compositional factors [link] implanted the instinct of some karmic action into the consciousness. Craving and grasping activate this instinct, which then becomes potent enough to throw one into a body in a future rebirth.

REBIRTH (317)

This link extends from just after this activation—when the [now] potent karma, which will be responsible for our reincarnation, serves as the basis for our being conceived in one of the four types of rebirth—until just after our conception into this rebirth.

AGING AND DEATH (318)

We receive, where applicable, the links of aging and death in order. Aging is the maturing of the aggregates, the gradual changing of their condition. Death is what we call the destruction of the aggregates or their ceasing to function.

Once you have properly recognized these twelve links and can distinguish between them, you must know how to group them properly into limbs. There are four of these limbs: the *precipitating limb,* the *establishing limb,* the *resultant precipitating limb,* and the *resultant manifested limb.*

Ignorance is like a sower of the seed. The karmic action—the compositional factor—motivated by ignorance is like the seed. And, like the earth into which the seed is planted, the consciousness at the time of the cause has the instinct of this accumulated karma put into it. So the precipitating [throwing] limb is the first two and a half links: *ignorance, compositional factors,* and the *consciousness at the time of the cause*—not the other division of the consciousness link, that at the time of the result.

Just as the seed is nurtured by water, manure, heat, and moisture, so craving and grasping activate karma into being able to produce a result. Like a seed being made potent enough by water, manure, heat, and moisture to develop into a sprout, karma that has been activated by craving and grasping is made certain to precipitate the aggregates of one's next incarnation by the link of becoming. Thus *craving, grasping,* and *becoming* are the establishing limb.

Just as the sprout has grown from the seed, so the link of *rebirth*—that is, being conceived into one's incarnation—is one component of the resultant manifested limb.

Five and a half links make up the resultant precipitated limb: the *consciousness at the time of the result,* which I have already described, *name and form* where applicable, the *senses, contact,* and *feeling.*

Aging and death, where they apply, are another component of the resultant manifested limb. So the resultant manifested limb is made up of the link of *rebirth,* plus that of *aging and death.*

Let us take the example of rebirth as a god. Through the power of our ignorance, that is, being blind to suchness, the instinct of some karma we accumulated—karma that will throw us into rebirth as a god—is placed in our consciousness. Then we feel, "How I would welcome rebirth as a god," and aspire to this in our prayers, and so on: this is craving. Then we put even more effort into increasing this aspiration: this is grasping. At death, these last two make up the karma certain to throw us into this rebirth: this is becoming. So the three components of the precipitating limb and the three of the establishing limb (the links at the time of the cause)—six in all—are completed in this life. Then we are reborn as a god. The other six links at the time of the result are completed in this next rebirth as the god; four of them—name and form, the senses, contact, and feeling—are the resultant precipitating limb; and two—birth, plus aging and death—are the resultant manifested limb. This is how one set of twelve links is completed in two lifetimes.

Take the example of rebirth in the lower realms. The same principles apply: because of our blindness to the law of cause and effect we accumulate nonvirtuous karma, which is activated by craving and grasping, etc.

It is impossible for one set of links to be completed within the one lifetime under the power of one karmic action. The fastest is definitely two lives.

It takes longer when we have been unable to activate some karma through craving and grasping; then, the three components of the precipitating limb will be completed in one life; the three of the establishing limb in another life; and the four of the resultant precipitating limb, as well as the two of the resultant manifested limb, will be completed in yet another life, taking three lifetimes in all. An illustration: in this lifetime, we accumulate evil karma to be reborn in the lower realms, and the instinct is implanted. However, at death the guru and others induce virtuous thoughts in us; this activates a karma for a human rebirth, and we are next reborn as a human being. When we die, we activate the previous evil karma through craving and grasping and are then reborn in the lower realms.

In our example there could be many intervening rebirths between the precipitating and establishing limbs, but they are lives that belong to other sets of links, and so do not count.

So to summarize: the fastest we can complete a set of links is in two lives, and the slowest, in three. It is not possible to do it any faster or more slowly. Each link gives rise to the link that follows it, so all suffering—rebirth, aging, death, and so on—is experienced as a cycle. While we follow the links that resulted from a single karmic action, we may develop various other sets of links in their cause phase. Aging and death derive from rebirth; the compositional factors derive from ignorance; and so on. So one link follows another, and ignorance is, therefore, fundamental in causing the wheel of saṃsāra to turn.

Nāgārjuna said:

> Two of them derive from three;
> Seven of them derive from the two;
> From the seven the three occur again.
> That is the wheel of life, and so it turns and turns.

In other words, the three delusion links give rise to the two karma links, and from these come the seven links of suffering. And from these seven links come the three delusion links, and so on. The cycle is repeated, and the wheel of life turns without interruption. This is the revolving of the wheel of suffering.

The twelve links can be dealt with in another order. If we practice a path that is able to put a stop to them, we impede the compositional factors link by preventing the ignorance link from occurring; this will put an end to all the sufferings intervening before aging and death.

To summarize: the twelve interdependent links can be brought under the three types of links: the karma links, the delusion links, and the links of suffering. Ignorance, craving, and grasping are the three *delusion links.* The two *karma links* are compositional factors and becoming. The remaining links are the seven *links of suffering.* As Nāgārjuna said:

> The first, eighth, and ninth are delusion;
> The second and tenth are karma;
> The remaining seven are suffering.

The first line of the verse discusses the three links of motivation; the second line, the two karmic links of karmic actions of body and speech,[68] that is, the compositional factors and becoming; the third line, the links that one will experience.

You have developed renunciation when, as a result of your meditation on the general suffering of saṃsāra and the twelve interdependent links, you yearn to be liberated from saṃsāra as a prisoner yearns to be freed from prison. When you develop the mind with such yearning for liberation, you will then want to train in a path leading to freedom.

[ACTUALLY] ASCERTAINING THE NATURE OF THE PATH LEADING TO LIBERATION (319)

This has two sections: (1) the sort of rebirth that will stop saṃsāra; (2) the sort of path that will stop saṃsāra.

THE SORT OF PHYSICAL REBIRTH THAT WILL STOP SAṂSĀRA (320)

You have thought about the drawbacks of saṃsāra. The nature of saṃsāra is that its environment is impermanent and perishable, just as the image of the moon on water whose surface is being blown by the wind does not stay still even for a moment. Saṃsāric happiness and wealth are like the shadow of a hooded cobra: great risk for little profit. Once you see that any of the five kinds of rebirth are an uninterrupted torment of suffering, just as people in prison or in a burning house do not wish to remain there in those places and want to be freed from them, you will develop unforced thoughts of wanting to be liberated from saṃsāra. You will investigate the causes of saṃsāra. There are two causes: karma and delusions. When you understand, out of these two, the delusions—and their root, ignorance—you will want to work hard at some means to defeat them.

The rebirth to have is the optimum human rebirth; and now that we have gained an optimum human rebirth in which we can follow the three high trainings and other wholesome endeavors, we must turn away from saṃsāra. Geshe Potowa said:

> When you wandered so much in the past, saṃsāra did not stop by itself, nor *will* it stop by itself—you must stop it. And the time to stop it is now that you have gained the optimum human rebirth.

In other words, there is no better rebirth to have than this one.

THE SORT OF PATH THAT WILL STOP SAṂSĀRA (321)

We should sever the root of saṃsāra: that which must be extirpated is the root of saṃsāra, the ignorance of being blind to suchness—the instinctive form of grasping at the "I." When we do not sever this and cultivate other antidotes instead, it merely dulls a few delusions a little but does not destroy them forever. Other virtues cannot affect this instinctive grasping at the "I"; only thoughts directly opposing its manner of grasping can stop it.

The wisdom that understands selflessness realizes that the "I" does not exist by way of its nature; this wisdom is therefore directly opposite to the thoughts and manner of grasping that take the "I" to be established by its nature. You therefore need the wisdom that understands selflessness in order to extirpate the instinctive grasping at a self. When you do not have this wisdom, and work hard at other virtues, it will only bolster your grasping at a self; the virtues will be unable to harm it.

To develop this wisdom properly in your mindstream, you need the following. You will not develop it without the high training of single-pointed concentration. For example, you need two things when you chop a tree trunk: a sharp axe and a steady arm. If your axe isn't sharp, it cannot cut into the tree trunk. If your arm is unsteady, the axe will not fall on the same place on the trunk. Or, to see a mural at night you must have a bright butterlamp that is not disturbed by the wind. The wisdom that understands selflessness is like the sharp axe, or the butterlamp illuminating how things are; grasping at true existence is the trunk to be cut; properly seeing the mode of existence is like the steady arm wielding the axe. You must develop in your mindstream stable single-pointed concentration that is free of subtle internal mental distractions—like the butterlamp not flickering in the wind. In order to develop in your mindstream single-pointed concentration devoid of internal mental distractions, you must free your mind of gross external distractions; that is, you must first take up the higher training of ethics.

To summarize, the *Sūtra Requested by Brahmā,* as quoted in [Asaṅga's] *Śhrāvaka Levels* tells us:

> The things to have:
> A very stable root,
> Rejoicing in a pacified mind,
> And the ārya view.
> Things not to have:
> The views of the sinful.

That is, in order to develop the antidote to grasping at a self—the special insight that possesses the ārya view, understanding the true mode of existence, emptiness—you must first achieve mental quiescence. And if you do not follow the high training of ethics, you will not have all the requisite causes for mental quiescence.

From Nāgārjuna's *Letter to a Friend:*

> If your hair or clothes should suddenly catch fire,
> Give up putting them out:
> Strive instead to stop reincarnation.
> No other aim can be as great.
>
> Through pure ethics, wisdom, and concentration
> Achieve peaceful, subdued, stainless nirvāṇa,
> A state immortal, ageless, inexhaustible,
> Beyond earth, water, fire, wind, sun, and moon.

The things to be practiced in the medium scope are the three high trainings, so I would have to discuss all three at this point were I not going to teach the great-scope Dharma topics. However, this is only a teaching on the path shared with the medium scope, not a teaching on the actual medium-scope path. So I will discuss two of the high trainings—single-pointed concentration and wisdom—in the mental quiescence and special insight sections of the great scope. That leaves only the high training of ethics to be discussed; this is the traditional way of teaching.

As it says in [Nāgārjuna's] *Letter:*

> Like the earth supports the animate and inanimate,
> So ethics were said to be
> The foundation of all good qualities.

In other words, ethics are most vital because they are the basis of all good qualities. They are the root of the Buddha's teaching. Ethics are most beneficial if one keeps them, but there are enormous drawbacks if they are not kept; the benefit is in the keeping of them.

The fundamental thing that determines whether the Buddha's teaching will continue to exist is the ethics of the pratimokṣha vow. The teachings exist if there are fully ordained monks upholding the vinaya. If not, any teachings still in existence are ineffective, despite there being, for example, knowledge-bearers and bodhisattvas. From the *Pratimokṣha Sūtra:* "When I go to nirvāṇa you should call *this* your teacher." That is, you should feel that the ethics in your mindstream stand in for our Teacher; you should cherish these ethics and uphold them.

Out of the three high trainings, the difficult ones for us beginners to practice right away are wisdom and single-pointed concentration; but the ethic of the pratimokṣha vows in our mindstreams is an insight into the teachings that we can definitely put into practice, that we definitely have in our mindstreams. This is why they say it depends on the Saṅgha whether the Buddha's teachings continue to exist or not. Also, the pratimokṣha vows are like the basis or medium for the two higher sets of vows.

By "upholder of the teachings," we do not only mean someone who teaches Dharma from a meditation throne. You are an upholder of the teachings if you keep properly the vows you have in your mindstream. If you study and contemplate the transmitted Dharma, you uphold the transmitted Dharma. If you keep your vows of ethics pure, you are an upholder of the realized Dharma.

Of the three types of vows, we can definitely put the pratimokṣha vows into practice. A sūtra says, "A monk having ethics is luminous..." And:

> Wherever there is a monk upholding the vinaya, that place has illumination, it has light. See this as a place where I am not absent. Such a place will not give me much cause for concern...

This is a vital feature of vows.

Our Tibet, the Land of Snows, has features not generally found in other countries; and the only root of our immediate and longterm happiness is Buddha's teaching. Whether or not these teachings still flourish is not due to our houses, population, or our colorful offerings; it depends on the ethics of the pratimokṣha vows—the root of the teachings. If we do not have these ethics purely, it shows that our ethics have died out in our own mindstreams and our own share of the teachings has died out, even though externally the teachings may be as widespread as the rocks and ground itself.

From the *King of Single-Pointed Concentration Sūtra:*

> One may, with cleansed mind,
> Honor ten million buddhas with food, drink,
> With parasols, banners, and rows of lamps
> For as many eons as there are grains of sand in the Ganges;

> But whoever, at a time when the holy Dharma is utterly destroyed,
> When the Sugata's teachings will end,
> Practices a single training day and night
> Will receive much greater merit.

In other words, it is more beneficial in these degenerate times to uphold one's ethics than to make offering constantly, throughout the day and night, to the buddhas of the three times. It is more beneficial to keep the ethics of our Teacher Śhākyamuni's doctrine for a day in this human world of sorrows than to keep our ethics for eons in Buddha Īśhvarāja's pure land of the northeast quarter. They say it is more beneficial to keep just one form of ethics now than to have completely kept the basic trainings during the earlier parts of this eon; this is a greater act than making offerings to many buddhas for tens of millions of eons.

Every fortnight we recite the passage "Those who still have their ethics will meet with the coming buddhas..." The point is not to pass an oral examination, or to repeat the passage a required number of times, and so on. We do it to stimulate our remembrance [of the vows].

Think about what comes of keeping your ethics. Keep properly within the bounds of your commitments. Though you recite "Long may I illuminate the heart of the teachings," or "May victorious Lozang Dragpa's teachings spread," the heart of the teachings must first flourish in your *own* mindstream.

When you do not keep your ethics, as the *Sūtra Delivered to the Monks* says:

> For some, ethics mean happiness;
> For some, ethics mean suffering.
> Those who keep their ethics will be happy.
> Those with loose ethics will suffer.

And as the *Sūtra on Having Pure Ethics* says:

> Monks: it is easy to give up your life and die—but not so for the decline or destruction of your ethics. Why so? If you give up your life and die, then the life of this rebirth comes to an end; but owing to the decline or destruction of your ethics, you give up happiness for tens of millions of eons, you separate yourself

> from the lineage, you abandon happiness, and experience a great downfall.

You will undergo suffering for many hundreds of thousands of rebirths. As the *Systematized Vinaya* tells us:

> Whoever makes light of the compassionate Teacher's doctrine
> Or makes light of departing slightly from it
> Comes instead under the power of suffering,
> Just as the mango grove will decline when the bamboo grove is cut down.
>
> When some disobey the king's commands,
> They may at times not receive punishment.
> When one does wrong and departs from the Sage's commands,
> One becomes an animal, as happened to Elapatra Nāga.

In this world, if you disobey the order of a powerful king, sometimes you'll be punished, sometimes not; but if you break the rules laid down by the Compassionate Teacher, you undergo punishment when you depart from this life, as happened to Elapatra Nāga. Elapatra had disregarded only a minor vow, yet was reborn as a nāga. When we disregard so many major, minor, and ancillary vows, what will our next migration be like?

Though we may not have received an extensive amount of some other famous most profound or most extensive Dharma, if we properly keep the novice or full-ordination vows that we have in our mindstreams, we will be members of the Saṅgha, we will be upholders of the teachings. This does not only apply to the novice vows and full-ordination vows; lay people can also keep one-day vows, and the great benefits of doing this are made clear in stories already covered from the *Transmission of the Vinaya,* the *Sūtra on the Wise and Foolish,* and the like.

You should take only vows you think you will be able to keep: the one-day vows, all five lay vows, four of these, three of them, only one, or whatever. Even the ordained have good reason to take one-day Mahāyāna precepts as often as they can: they are vows for one day only, so you will be able to keep them purely.

We always pretend to follow the three high trainings, but we have only a pale reflection of the other two in our mindstreams. But we could actually keep the pratimokṣha vows, so we must try hard to do so. But in order to keep them, we must shut the doors that lead to breaking them. There are four such doors.

The first door leading to broken vows is *ignorance.* If you do not know what basic commitment you must keep, you will not know whether you have broken it. So in order to shut this door, you should be informed: refer to the classical texts on vinaya, verse summaries of the vows, any advice on the three basic practices, summaries of the basic vinaya instructions, and the like. You should then at least know the lists of rules to be followed.

Disrespect is also a door leading to broken vows. You should respect our Teacher, what he taught, and your wholesome friends whose actions accord with Dharma. Moreover you should have the attitude that the vows in your mindstream represent our Teacher the Buddha, and so must be respected. Don't be indifferent to your vows; they are like a substitute for our Teacher after his nirvāṇa.

Another door leading to broken vows is *the biggest delusion.* Breaches of vows also follow from whichever delusion—attachment, hostility, and so on—is greatest. To suppress your enemies, you must first subdue whichever of them is strongest—some hero, general, or whoever it may be. Similarly, you should apply the antidote to the predominant delusions in your mindstream. When attachment is your greatest delusion, meditate on the ugliness [of the body]: that it is a sack full of filth; and develop the attitude that it will have a bloody aspect, a swelling aspect, that it will be eaten by worms, that it will be a skeleton, and so on. As an antidote to hostility, meditate on love. As antidotes to pride, think over the saṃsāric banes of sickness, aging, and death, of uncertainty, of moving continually from high to low, or over the full classification of the sense elements. Meditate that if there are so many things in your own body about which you know nothing—the aggregates, the sense elements, sense faculties, the contact interaction that exists between your faculties and your body, etc.—how many other things must there be that you do not know! The antidote to benightedness is meditation on interdependent origination; meditation on the view concerning emptiness is the general antidote to delusion.

Recklessness is a door to broken vows. You should have remembrance and not forget to modify your behavior at all times during your daily routine—when you walk, sleep, sit, eat, drink, and so forth. From time to time check if your body, speech, and mind have been tarnished by misdeeds or broken vows.

You should shut the doors leading to misdeeds or to transgressing vows: do this by means of remembrance, vigilance, shame, and decency. You may occasionally still become tarnished by transgressions, so attend the purification rites, etc., frequently, to expiate them. The classical literature on vinaya states that you must expiate your ancillary vows by three things: taking a lowly position in the assembly, paying respect to other members of the Saṅgha, and by being formally reinstated. However, Ensapa and his disciples claimed that one could purify the ancillary vows and other lesser vows if one had sufficient regret and exercised sufficient restraint.

The peerless Atiśha and great Tsongkapa, who was the embodiment of Mañjuśhrī, their disciples, and so on, completely prevented their ethics from becoming tarnished by misdeeds; we cannot keep our vows like this or exercise such restraint, but we could keep the four root lay vows, together with giving up alcohol, and keep them as we would protect our very lives.

Since you take the pratimokṣha vows from your abbot, ordination master, and the Saṅgha, you must expiate any sins or transgressions of your commitments to them in the presence of the Saṅgha. This is why when you perform the expiation on your own you are able to purify only the sin; you are unable to purify the broken vow in this way, so it is not beneficial. Do not be indifferent to [minor] vows: if you cannot even rinse your mouth out after meals, if you don't remove your shoes when you should, or if you wear robes with sleeves, how can you keep the other vows? Those who do these things, even though they do not break the major vows or some of the auxiliary vows, still do great damage to the regard people have for the Dharma. You should perform the consecration rites [that allow you to relax certain minor restrictions] as often as possible.

In this world, when you prepare your lunch, tea, and so on, you need a number of things at hand—butter, salt, meat, and so on. Likewise, to achieve the rebirth we most yearn for in our next lives, it is not good enough to perform just a few things, such as keeping our ethics, or practicing generosity, or whatever. Even ordained people must also practice generosity, etc., besides keeping their ethics pure.

Some people claim: "The disciplines of the pratimokṣha vows come under the jurisdiction of people with inferior faculties. So people with sharper or superior faculties need not be cramped by such things: the secret tantra path is a rapid one and permitted for them because it takes the three poisons as part of the path." They do not value their vows at all and act recklessly, but even if you follow the secret tantras and have taken the pratimokṣha vows, you should keep those vows properly. From the *Tantra Requested by Subahu:*

> I, the Victorious One, taught the pratimokṣha vow;
> Do not forsake its pure ethics.
> Lay tantrists, abandon the signs and rituals [of monks]
> But practice all the rest...

The *Mañjuśhrī Root Tantra* says:

> Śhākyamuni did not teach
> That people with loose ethics will succeed in tantra.
> That is not the way and place
> Leading to the city of nirvāṇa.
>
> How could these evil churls
> Succeed in tantra?
> How could people with loose ethics
> Go to the upper realms?
>
> They will not even go to a high rebirth;
> They will not have supreme happiness.
> How, then, can one speak of their success
> In tantras taught by the victors?

There are some who have absolutely no renunciation, bodhichitta, or correct view, yet spend their whole lives meditating on the conscious operation of the mind [see Day 22, p. 620]. This is useless effort: at best it could become immutable karma.

Then Rinpoche reviewed the above topics.

PART SIX

THE GREAT SCOPE

DAY 16

After the traditional reading of today's part of the text, Kyabje Pabongka Rinpoche spoke on how we should adjust our motivation. He stressed that we need bodhichitta in addition to renunciation, quoting the words of the king of the Dharma and the three realms, great Tsongkapa: "When you have developed pure bodhichitta as well as renunciation..." He went over the headings already covered and then reviewed the material under the heading "Ascertaining the Nature of the Path Leading to Liberation."

What is it that makes you go round on the wheel of saṃsāra? It is karma, and this karma is developed through delusion. Among delusion, ignorance is the root, so ignorance produces karma. To root out ignorance you have to practice the high training of wisdom. You have to prepare yourself for this practice with the high trainings of single-pointed concentration and ethics; this is why ethics is said to be the basis of any good qualities.

When you are still at the stage of applying antidotes to delusions, you should allow a delusion to develop and apply its antidote only after identifying it. The whole point of doing this is to eventually be able to identify delusions even when you are distracted.

TRAINING THE MIND IN THE GREAT-SCOPE STAGES OF THE PATH (322)

This has three headings: (1) teaching that the development of bodhichitta is the sole gateway to the Mahāyāna, and teaching its benefits as well; (2) how to develop bodhichitta; (3) how to set about training yourself after the development of bodhichitta.

TEACHING THAT THE DEVELOPMENT OF BODHICHITTA IS THE SOLE GATEWAY TO THE MAHĀYĀNA, AND TEACHING ITS BENEFITS AS WELL (323)

In the above sections dealing with the small and medium scopes, you had to be motivated by renunciation. When you put your effort principally into the three high trainings you will achieve merely a state of liberation for yourself, and merely put an end to your own saṃsāra. This is not good enough: you will be of only partial benefit to yourself and others because you will not have abandoned all that has to be abandoned or achieved every good quality. Later you will have to enter the Mahāyāna at its most basic level. As it says in the *Short Perfection of Wisdom Sūtra:*

> Forsake forever the two vehicles
> Futile for benefiting the world
> And enter the compassion vehicle taught by the Victorious Sage,
> Whose very nature smacks of benefit for others.

As Geshe Potowa said:

> Don't carry your load across the river twice!
> Enter the Mahāyāna at the outset!

It would be like having to cross the same river twice. But there is more. Arhats experience such inconceivable bliss when they are absorbed in their sphere of peace that they stay in this absorption for many eons and have no wish ever to leave it. Meanwhile, someone who had been living in hell might achieve an optimum human rebirth, enter the Mahāyāna path, and take about the same amount of time to achieve enlightenment. Thus these arhats set themselves at a great distance from buddhahood. Suppose someone had studied the Mahāyāna, developed a propensity for it, but been reborn in hell because of developing wrong views. Such a person would be enlightened quicker than anyone of Mahāyāna propensities who had entered the Hīnayāna path and achieved arhatship. It is therefore better to be of the former type.

For example, when the śhrāvaka Kāśhyapa was giving teachings on Hīnayāna Dharma, there were sixty monks who would have gained arhatship. But Mañjuśhrī had already gone to them and taught them Mahāyāna

Dharma. This teaching proved too much for them, and they developed wrong views, thus taking rebirth in hell. Kāśhyapa asked Buddha, our Teacher, for some explanation, and Buddha said, "That was the skillful means of Mañjushrī! Such an excellent teaching!"

In the same way, when the buddhas rouse the śhrāvaka and pratyekabuddha arhats from their blissful absorption and force them into the Mahāyāna, these arhats will not try hard to develop such qualities as bodhichitta in their mindstreams because of their great familiarity with absorption in the taste of bliss. Even when they do try, it is hard for them to feel compassion, and so on, because they have already been liberated from their own suffering. The two major disciples of Buddha, Śhāriputra and Maudgalyāyana, said, "The Teacher has taught both the Mahāyāna path and its results. These are most wondrous, but we are like wood already consumed by the fire: we could not have done more." But note: this does not really apply to people like Ārya Śhāriputra, because they were emanations [of buddhas] taking the form of śhrāvakas. It is said that this statement refers to more typical śhrāvakas, who do have these great hindrances to enlightenment.

Hence, when we have gained some insight into renunciation, we must then definitely enter the Mahāyāna path. We train the mind according to the part of the path we share with the medium scope expressly so as to develop renunciation in our mindstreams, not actually to tread the medium-scope path. Training in bodhichitta in accordance with the great-scope section is the main body of the path; the small and medium scopes are an introduction, a supplement to the general tasks [of a bodhisattva].

Since the first thing to be done in the study of the path of the great scope is to rejoice, the oral tradition deals first with the benefits [of bodhichitta]. What follows is according to the way in which these benefits are discussed in *Mañjuśhrī's Own Words.* I will speak about these benefits under ten headings: (1) teaching that the only way to enter the Mahāyāna is to develop bodhichitta; (2) you gain the name "child of the victors"; (3) you outshine the śhrāvakas and pratyekabuddhas; (4) you become a supreme object of offering; (5) you amass an enormous accumulation of merit with ease; (6) you rapidly purify sins and obscurations; (7) you accomplish whatever you wish; (8) you are not bothered by harm or hindrances; (9) you soon complete the entire path and its levels; (10) you become a fertile source of every happiness for other beings.

TEACHING THAT THE ONLY WAY TO ENTER THE MAHĀYĀNA IS TO DEVELOP BODHICHITTA (324)

The thing that determines whether you have joined the ranks of the Mahāyāna is whether you have developed bodhichitta in your mindstream. Je Tsongkapa said:

> It is not enough that the Dharma be Mahāyāna—the person must also belong to the Mahāyāna. You become a Mahāyānist by having bodhichitta. If you merely understand bodhichitta, you are not much of a Mahāyānist.

If you do not have this bodhichitta in your mindstream but practice, for example, the generation and completion stages of the Guhyasamāja tantra, the pinnacle, the king of tantras, apart from such a practice not becoming a cause for your enlightenment, you would not even be able to embark on the Mahāyāna path of accumulation. And, aside from this, such a practice would not even become a Mahāyāna Dharma! But if you have bodhichitta, even saying a single *oṃ maṇi padme hūṃ* would be a Mahāyāna Dharma and a cause for your enlightenment. In the *Precious Garland,* Nāgārjuna says:

> If you desire supreme enlightenment
> For yourself and the world,
> Know that its root is a bodhichitta
> As firm as Meru, king of mountains.

If you do not have this mind, your meditations on the generation stage of the secret tantras are like staring at the spectacle of the deity's mansion [in the maṇḍala]; and as for your meditations on the completion stage, it is said: "Breathing in, holding it, expelling it..." In other words, such energy-wind practices, etc. would be no better than working a pair of bellows!

The unique rapidity of the secret tantras is due to the fact that they increase one's bodhichitta so very much. Changkya Roelpai Dorje said this in praise:

> I have studied the Dharma under Purchog Ngagwang Jampa. Even when Lama Jampa gives a major initiation, he talks only

> about the lamrim in the explanatory parts of the initiation. If someone else were to see this, he would take it that Lama Jampa could not discuss the secret tantras, but this lama speaks from his understanding of the whole point of the complete path.

A yogi in the Hevajra tantra who had no bodhichitta had achieved the state of a stream-enterer. Atiśha was astonished to hear this story and said, "Blame it on his not having bodhichitta. People who have meditated on Hevajra can even go to hell!" That yogi had done relatively well, for there were many more people reciting the mantras of wrathful deities while lacking bodhichitta that were reborn as malevolent spirits or in hell.

There is a story about the local deity of Chushur. He was formerly a person who did major retreats but later took rebirth as a local god. If the Hevajra yogi who achieved the level of a stream-enterer had had bodhichitta, he would have been enlightened in that very lifetime. Instead, he achieved a Hīnayāna result and not a single cause to become enlightened; his lack of bodhichitta was to blame. [Bodhichitta] is something we might well call "profound Dharma."

I have already told you similar stories, such as the one about the Brahman Chanakya, the other about the Indian yogi who practiced the Yamāntaka tantra and was reborn as an evil spirit that went to Tibet, only to be evicted by Atiśha's offering of ritual cakes. We also had the story of the yogi of the Yamāntaka tantra from Paenpo who was reborn as a hungry ghost in the shape of the deity and went to hang round a burnt offering ceremony for the dead that was being held at the home of his former neighbors and benefactors.

These days most people prize things like visions of deities, clairvoyance, or miraculous powers; but without bodhichitta you could still go to the lower realms, and any clairvoyance or having such powers would be of no benefit. When you have this bodhicitta mind, you may not make much effort in other things, but you will have the very root of Mahāyāna Dharma. Any topic, be it sūtra or tantra, is Mahāyāna or not depending on whether you have this mind. If you already have this mind, even giving a ball of barley flour dough to an animal will be a cause for you to gain full enlightenment. This would also apply to everyday activities that are normally neutral in character. Great bodhisattvas can even convert nonvirtue into virtue because they do all things in conjunction with bodhichitta.

When you do not have this mind but meet with the right conditions to develop the wisdom that understands emptiness, such conditions act only as a cause for any one of the three types of enlightenment [as a śrāvaka, pratyekabuddha, or buddha]; so that wisdom is like a mother. But when you have bodhichitta, such conditions act as cause for your full enlightenment only. Bodhichitta is therefore like a father [see p. 515]. This is why the former is called "mother."

To sum up: unless you have absolutely no yearning for enlightenment, you must make bodhichitta your basic practice. Anything of value—such as good qualities in any of the three vehicles—in the end comes from bodhichitta. If someone were to ask us what our basic practice is, we might reply, "I recite Hayagriva," "Vajrapāṇi," or "Yamāntaka," but in fact most of us have usually made the three poisonous delusions our basic practice! Atiśha was a scholar of all these Dharmas, but this did not satisfy him. Instead, he sailed the oceans for thirteen difficult months to hear the complete instructions on bodhichitta from Suvarṇadvīpa Guru, and made this his basic practice. He paid much more respect to this guru who taught him these instructions than to his other gurus. Yet Suvarṇadvīpa was a Chittamātrin and so his views [concerning emptiness] were inferior.

For these reasons we must see if we can develop this bodhichitta in our mindstreams. We could have no better rebirth to use for its development than our present one. There is no better single Dharma instruction on training ourselves in bodhichitta than this Dharma, the lamrim. Given these considerations, it would be a great pity if we did nothing to develop bodhichitta in our mindstreams. There are people everywhere who spend their whole lives cultivating the difficult practice of living on pebbles for food. They may pride themselves on being the cream of practitioners, but they have strayed from the paths leading to full enlightenment, because they care little for bodhichitta. There are many tangible instances of this.

We must see if we think we can genuinely develop this mind in our mindstreams, as this is the best thing we can do. Failing that, we must see if we can gain some sort of contrived experience of it, or failing even this, see if we can gain a low level of insight into it. This is why they say that if we do not pursue this as one of the topics of a particular meditation session, effort in only deity meditation or recitation of the mantra will just be pointless hard work. What a great pity.

YOU GAIN THE NAME "CHILD OF THE VICTORS" (325)

As it is said [in *Engaging in the Deeds of Bodhisattvas*]:

> From the moment pathetic beings trapped
> In saṃsāra's prison develop bodhichitta,
> They are given the name "children of the sugatas."

and:

> Today I have been born into the buddha race.
> I have become a child of the buddhas.

So, whether or not you become a child of the victorious ones depends on this very thing. If you have not developed bodhichitta, you are not a bodhisattva, or a child of the victors, although you may be clairvoyant, able to work miracles, learned in the five sciences, have gained direct understanding of emptiness, or have completely abandoned all delusions. You will not have joined the ranks of the Mahāyāna. But if you have developed this thought in your mindstream, you have joined the Mahāyāna ranks, even though you are an animal, for example, a dog or pig, or even a simpleton without any other accomplishments and as stupid as a donkey.

When you develop bodhichitta, the earth quakes and all the thrones of the buddhas shake. Because the great earth was produced by the collective karma of sentient beings, when someone develops bodhichitta it proves too much for the earth, which then quakes because that person with bodhichitta will lead many sentient beings and cause a commotion in saṃsāra.

The bodhisattvas regard anyone who has developed this mind as their brother or sister. The buddhas of the ten directions are as happy as is a universal emperor when he becomes the father of a new heir. Hence that person becomes a child of the victorious ones. Should they ever forsake that mind, they would shut themselves out of the Mahāyāna. We have in the past attained many types of clairvoyance and miraculous powers that did us no good in the long run; it is better to understand the lamrim. Being clairvoyant and having miraculous powers is neither unusual nor beneficial: it is said we receive these powers in the bardo after we leave each rebirth.

YOU OUTSHINE THE ŚHRĀVAKAS AND PRATYEKABUDDHAS (326)

The *Laying Out of Stalks Sūtra* tells us that:

> As the jewels from the ocean outshine all the baubles of the Southern Continent, those who develop bodhichitta in their mindstreams outshine the whole group of śhrāvakas and pratyekabuddhas.

The *Sūtra on Maitreya's Life Story* says that just as a small prince outshines even a group of elderly ministers, or just as a garuḍa chick outshines a group of other birds, a fledgling bodhisattva who has developed bodhichitta in his or her mindstream outshines the whole group of śhrāvakas and pratyekabuddhas. This happens through the power of altruism. Moreover, a diamond may develop a flaw, but it will still be called a diamond, still outshine golden jewelry, and still dispel poverty. Similarly, those who have developed bodhichitta in their mindstreams may not be capable of training themselves in the tasks of the victorious ones' children, but they are still called children of the victors because of the bodhichitta in their mindstreams; of all precious collections of virtue, theirs is the best. It will even outshine such golden jewelry as the [merit and wisdom] collections of the śhrāvakas and pratyekabuddhas. And they say that all saṃsāric poverty is dispelled by it.

Bodhichitta alone should be recognized as the essence of the 84,000 heaps of the Dharma. As Atiśha said, "Give up this life! Meditate only on love, compassion, and bodhichitta."

YOU BECOME A SUPREME OBJECT OF OFFERING (327)

When you develop bodhichitta in your mindstream, "Humans and the worldly gods fold their hands in respect..." In other words, you become a supreme object for the offerings of gods and humans. However, you do not develop this mind by training in it a short while. Even great Atiśha trained in it for twelve years. Just look at the people who merely meditate on deities and recite mantras, persevering at these things for many years! How much more valuable it would be for us to try even harder to develop bodhichitta. The Kadampas of old said that everyone has images of deities to meditate on, everyone has mantras to recite; the trouble is no one has any Dharma to contemplate.

It is vital to instill in yourself as many instincts for this mind as possible. Once five hundred geese merely heard the voice of the Buddha and thus came to be reborn as gods and see the truth. King Ajātaśhatru had an enormously strong instinct for emptiness. One day at noon he tried to offer Mañjushrī robes worth a thousand ounces of gold but did not succeed, because the recipient of the offering simply vanished into emptiness. The king himself then put on the robes and he, too, vanished. This gave him realization of emptiness. These things happened by virtue of some instinct for emptiness having been instilled into him in the past.

Brahmā, Indra, etc., come and make offerings when a person develops this mind. They lend them their brilliance and help them to fulfill their wishes. It is also said that even the buddhas respect bodhisattvas because such fully enlightened beings were once bodhisattvas themselves, and being a bodhisattva depends on bodhichitta. It also says in the sūtras:

> You should pay homage to the new moon and not to the full moon. Likewise, anyone who draws inspiration from me should pay homage to the bodhisattvas and not to the tathāgatas... When a bodhisattva mounts a chariot, they [the buddhas] will provide delights for their five senses and entertain them. Should there be no one else to pull the chariot, the buddhas themselves will even draw that chariot by a rope tied around their own heads.

It is said that āryas like Śhāriputra will remain in the absorption of utter serenity for eons but the tathāgatas will not pay them this much respect.

Even stories like the following are told. The Buddha once did not offer Mañjuśhrī the first portion of the alms from his begging bowl, so the bowl was swallowed into the earth.

YOU AMASS AN ENORMOUS ACCUMULATION OF MERIT WITH EASE (328)

Nyugrumpa said:

> When someone manages to develop some bodhichitta, that in itself builds their first accumulation of merit, purifies their obscurations, and rids them of hindrances.

Je Tsongkapa said:

> It is like a philosopher's stone for the two collections:
> It gives you the merit to gather a huge stock of virtue.

And to amass an enormous stock of merit easily [as Shāntideva explained]:

> It is like the supreme philosopher's stone:
> For it will turn your impure body
> Into something priceless—the body of a buddha.
> Thus, always maintain this thing we call bodhichitta…
>
> Other virtue is like the plantain tree,
> For it is barren once fruited.
> Bodhichitta is a living tree
> That continues to fruit and grow.

In other words, you could have nothing better than bodhichitta in order to complete your merit collection. If you were to be generous without bodhichitta to hundreds of thousands of beings for many hundreds of thousands of eons and fill the billion worlds with jewels, the [karmic] results of this would eventually come to an end. This would also not be a deed of a child of the victors, and would not act as a cause for your buddhahood. But with bodhichitta, if you were to give a ball of barley dough to an animal, the results of your action would never come to an end. It would be a deed of a child of the victorious ones, and would act as a cause for your buddhahood. If, with this mind, you offer only one stick of incense, they say that it confers the same benefits as offering the same number of sticks as there are sentient beings. If you have this mind and recite a single *oṃ maṇi padme hūṃ,* it will be as beneficial as reciting this mantra as many times as there are sentient beings.

Once, during the Buddha's lifetime, a beggar with this mind offered a small oil lamp to the Buddha. Ānanda could not put it out, and the Tathāgata said that even the wind of destruction at the eon's end could not blow it out due to the continual growth in the merit.

From *Engaging in the Deeds of Bodhisattvas:*

Whenever one truly takes up,
With an irreversible mind,
This thought to completely liberate
The infinite realms of sentient beings,

Thereafter, even in one's sleep
Or in unguarded moments, one's merit will have power.
Much merit comes continually
And will become as enormous as space itself

In other words, once you have adopted the engagement form [of the bodhichitta] vow, you will receive a continual flow of virtue, even while asleep or when negligent. If there is great benefit in wanting to rid one sentient being of a headache, how could the wish to free all sentient beings of all their immeasurable suffering from illness not be greatly meritorious? Much the same thing is said in *Engaging in the Deeds of Bodhisattvas:*

If the thought to free beings
Of only their headaches
Is such a beneficial thought
That it brings one boundless merit,

Then need I speak of the wish to free every being
Of all their boundless miseries,
And wanting each of them
To develop every good quality?...

Give ordinary food to a few beings,
And that act of generosity with food lasts but a moment.
Yet the person who perfunctorily fills bellies for half a day
Is praised as "a person of virtue."

What then to say of he
Who, over a long time, has always
Tried to fulfill all wishes of infinite numbers of beings
With the peerless bliss of the sugatas?

In short, it is said that when you are motivated by this mind, any virtue you create will provide you with the same benefit as the total number of sentient beings.

YOU RAPIDLY PURIFY SINS AND OBSCURATIONS (329)

Nothing is better for the purification of sins. *Engaging in the Deeds of Bodhisattvas* says:

> Any sin of great and intolerable force
> Will overpower any virtue
> Other than sublime bodhichitta.

That is, you may have committed some huge sin that could not otherwise be expiated, but it would be consumed if you were to generate this mind. This is illustrated by the story of Ārya Asaṅga. Just one instance of generating compassion purified far more sins and obscurations than he could in twelve years of virtuous practice. Further:

> You might have some intolerable sin,
> But when you rely on this [mind] you will immediately be free of it,
> Just as you would of some great danger when you rely on a hero.
> What prudent person would not then rely on this?

In other words, just as you need not fear [an ambush] when the road runs through a narrow gorge if you are in the company of a very heroic friend, you need not fear the results of your sins and obscurations if you have bodhichitta.

> Great sins are sure to be consumed in a moment,
> As if by the fire at the end of time.

That is, no matter how big your heap of sins, it will be purified like kindling burned in the fires at the end of the eon.

For these reasons, in order to destroy your sins, it is better to meditate on bodhichitta for one session than to try for a hundred years to purify these sins by some other means divorced from this mind.

YOU ACCOMPLISH WHATEVER YOU WISH (330)

When you develop this mind, you effortlessly achieve all your desires, both temporary and ultimate. The best thing to wish for would be that all sentient beings abandon their unwanted suffering and achieve their desired happiness. *Engaging in the Deeds of Bodhisattvas* says:

> It is said that, with this, the boundless mass of beings
> Will easily reach supreme happiness.

If you have developed bodhichitta in your mindstream, you will easily succeed in all things, both ordinary and extraordinary: the knowledge mantras or tantric spells described in the tantric canon and so on. We have not accomplished the set of trival deeds described in sūtras and tantras, in certain anthologies, and so on—making it rain, stopping hail, and so forth. Blame this on our lack of bodhichitta. Thus if you want to rid yourself and others of obstacles like sickness, etc., and want to have greater abilities, you must develop this mind. It is wrong to think an instruction taught on some tantric spell is at fault if it does not work for you.

You need not resort to mantras—*hūṃ hūṃ phaṭ phaṭ,* for instance—or tantric paraphernalia. You can do these things by merely swearing an oath: Bodhisattva Sadāprarudita made his body whole again by such an oath. Once in Lhasa the Kyichu River was about to overflow its banks and no one could stop it. Je Moenlam Paelwa wrote these words on a stone: "If it is true that I, Moenlam Paelwa, am a bodhisattva, may the waters quickly subside!" He took the stone to the riverbank, and the river immediately went down. He had prevented the flood simply by swearing this oath.

Thus with bodhichitta you will achieve the highest thing, your main desire, the state of omniscience; you will also succeed in these minor spells at the very least.

YOU ARE NOT BOTHERED BY HARM OR HINDRANCES (331)

Even when a universal emperor goes to sleep, he is guarded by Vajrapāṇi, Brahmā, Indra, the four mahārājas, etc. But the bodhisattvas get twice as many protectors as universal emperors, and they are protected both day and night. They are never harmed, never bothered by evil or interfering spirits. If we do not have this mind and invite the protection deities with drums, cymbals, and so on in amelioration rites [to please them and request their help], we cannot be certain that they will come. But if we have developed this mind, then even though we might not have invited the four mahārājas, for example Vaiśhravaṇa, they would still guard us like faithful servants. The *Laying Out of Stalks Sūtra* tells us:

> If you apply the all-healing balm to your body, no disease, etc., can harm you. If you apply the king of balms—which we call "water"—to your body, snakes will avoid you. If you apply the king of balms that incapacitates others, your enemies can do nothing to you. Likewise, when you have bodhichitta, the delusions are incapacitated, and so forth.

When Geshe Kamlungpa was living at Yungwai Pur in Paenpo, spending his time in meditation on bodhichitta, the nonhuman spirits of that place began to attack him; but one of these spirits said, "He holds us dearer than he does himself. He cries all the time. How could you think of harming him?"

Our Compassionate Teacher defeated the army of demons through the power of his love. Five yakṣhas could not kill the herdsmen in King Maitrobala's kingdom [because of his great love].

[King] Pehar presented Butoen Rinpoche and Lama Dampa with iron styluses [to write on slates], but as the story has it, he was unable to make a similar offering to Ngulchu Togme Sangpo [see Day 21, p. 598]. Also once when Butoen Rinpoche was ill, he invited Ngulchu Togme Sangpo to come. Togme Sangpo meditated on bodhichitta and this helped Butoen Rinpoche.

These stories illustrate the infinite benefits that accrue from not being bothered by dangers and hindrances. Suffice it to say that people who have meditated on this mind have experienced no trouble from such creatures.

YOU QUICKLY COMPLETE ALL THE STAGES OF THE PATH (332)

When you pursue meditation on the view without bodhichitta, you will be able to complete only your accumulation of primal wisdom, not your merit accumulation. It is mainly through the power of relative bodhichitta that you complete both accumulations and rid yourself of the two types of obscurations, together with their instincts. If you have this mind, you can become enlightened in one lifetime through the secret tantras; but without it, you will not be able to gain the lowest level of the Mahāyāna path of accumulation, even using tantra.

In short, it is said that because bodhichitta is the root of development of all virtuous Dharma, even giving a piece of food to a crow acts only as a cause for your buddhahood; that is why you will complete the stages and paths so quickly.

YOU BECOME A FERTILE SOURCE OF EVERY HAPPINESS FOR OTHERS (333)

It says in *Engaging in the Middle Way:*

> The powerful buddhas produced
> The śhrāvakas and middling buddhas,
> But the buddhas developed from bodhisattvas...

In other words, all the happiness of this world, all śhrāvakas, pratyekabuddhas, universal emperors, and the like come from the power of the buddhas. The buddhas developed from bodhisattvas. The bodhisattvas come from bodhichitta, so not only is bodhichitta the sole root of all the happiness of beings, it is also the essence of all the [84,000] bundle-divisions of Dharma. It is the main practice of the children of the victors. The superiority of the secret tantras derives from the power of this mind.

Geshe Dromtoenpa asked a man for news of the three Kadampa brothers. The man told Drom about each of them [and their many Dharma activities]. "How wonderful!" said Dromtoenpa. "That's really something."

Then the man told him of Geshe Kamlungpa: "He lives at the head of a ravine. Sometimes his eyes are half closed. Sometimes he cries. That's all he ever does!"

Drom folded his hands and said by way of praise, "He is *really* putting Dharma into practice!"

Engaging in the Deeds of Bodhisattvas tells us, "It is the quintessence of butter churned from the milk of holy Dharma." That is, bodhichitta is like the essence of all Dharma. Thus I urge everyone to do whatever they can to employ the methods to develop it.

Whether a particular teaching is Mahāyāna depends on whether it has bodhichitta in it. For the moment, put aside Dharma everyone calls profound and practice bodhichitta seriously. But many are the Sakya, Gelug, Kagyu, and Nyingma practitioners who do not understand this point yet still want buddhahood. They meditate on the two stages of the secret tantras, dispense with bodhichitta, and still hope to make rapid progress on the path. They act, to use a colloquial expression, like a man "with an unwanted goiter on his precious neck." No buddha of the three times became a buddha without developing bodhichitta. A [potential] buddha not needing bodhichitta is something unheard of. Therefore someone without any bodhichitta will not receive the buddhahood they want; they haven't a hope of achieving buddhahood if they lack this. So you must take it seriously.

Rego Āchārya said to Drubkang Geleg Gyatṣo, "Whenever you come round, I hope we can praise bodhichitta to our heart's content. Such talk is quite lost on the rest of our contemporaries." Just so, few of us actually practice it. Some of us say on the one hand, "Bodhichitta is far too difficult for us to develop," and therefore put it aside, while others say, "That's the common part of the Mahāyāna. We meditate on more profound things, such as the two stages [of highest yoga tantra]," and put it aside. This is like a man searching for a wish-granting jewel in a puddle left by the hoofprint of a bull instead of in the ocean. Je Tsongkapa said:

> Because they understand that this is so,
> The heroic children of the victors
> Make this supreme and precious mind
> Their foremost practice.

So only bodhichitta is praised as being the basic practice. These days some would say they take a certain deity as their basic practice. Others would say they specialize in Chinese astrological texts; still others say they do "The Spell for Pacifying Disputes," or whatever. But the time when you achieve buddhahood will never come if you do not have bodhichitta.

Atiśha thought Suvarṇadvīpa the best of his gurus. And when Atiśha himself was ill, he said to Dromtoenpa, "Your mind is very wholesome. Give me your blessing." Atiśha meant this in praise of bodhichitta.

Kyabje Pabongka told a story of Guru Dharmarakṣhita, originally a Vaibhāṣhika who became a Mādhyamika by virtue of his bodhichitta.

Atiśha's good works spread far and wide, both in India and Tibet. This happened through the power of his devotion to spiritual guides and his bodhichitta. As the Kadampas of old said:

> You might have such concentration that you cannot hear a drum beaten right beside your ear, but it will go nowhere if you do not have this mind.

Guru Rāhulagupta also said:

> Seeing visions of tutelary deities, achieving clairvoyance and miraculous powers, and having mountain-range-firm concentration get you nowhere on their own. Meditate on love and compassion!

In the sūtras, bodhichitta is said to be like the precious wheel of the universal emperor, like a being's life force, or like hands.

It says in the *Sublime Continuum of the Great Vehicle:*

> Esteem for the Supreme Vehicle
> Is the seed of wisdom;
> It is the mother of the
> Development of buddhahood.

This is illustrated as follows. A father acts as the determinant cause of a particular family line, while the mother is an indeterminate cause. Precious bodhichitta is similarly the determinant cause for buddhahood; the wisdom that realizes emptiness is the indeterminate cause for any of the three types of enlightenment. Therefore this emptiness wisdom will act as a cause for the particular enlightenment of whatever vehicle—Mahāyāna or Hīnayāna—you happen to meet with. Thus someone who merely has some understanding of bodhichitta will be enlightened sooner than someone lacking bodhichitta who meditates on, for example, the mahāmudrā, the great completion [dzogchen], the two stages [of tantra], or receiving visions of many sets of deities. Bodhichitta is vital, and this was the message of great

Atiśha, someone who knew all the holy Dharma and practiced it. He said: "Meditate on love, compassion, and bodhichitta."

For this reason, do not pin your hopes on just meditating on deities and reciting mantras. You must work hard at bodhichitta. It is meaningful to take pains to develop this essence of the Dharma in your mindstream: the effort is most worth it. And you are sure to develop bodhichitta if you meditate on it, because conditioned phenomena do not just remain static [so the right cause will produce the desired effect]. Yet, before the arrival of Atiśha, a ceremony existed in Tibet to confer the development of bodhichitta. At the start of the ceremony, people would recite, "I will achieve buddhahood for the sake of all sentient beings, once my mothers." They had replaced bodhichitta by a mere formula! To develop bodhichitta in your mindstream, you must train the mind: it is difficult even to be acquainted with bodhichitta, let alone have it develop in your mind, in the way that you are given pratimokṣha vows without [any] mind training [beforehand]. Once Atiśha said sarcastically to the Tibetans, "The people you Tibetans take for bodhisattvas have no acquaintance with either love or compassion!"

The Tibetans asked him, "In that case, what must we do?"

"Train yourselves in stages," was his reply.

It is quite impossible to develop bodhichitta without having experienced the great compassion and that is why you have to train the mind in stages.

THE WAY TO DEVELOP BODHICHITTA (334)

This has two subheadings: (1) the actual stages in training for bodhichitta; (2) how to develop bodhichitta by means of a ceremony [i.e., through the ritual of taking vows].

THE ACTUAL STAGES IN TRAINING FOR BODHICHITTA (335)

There are two further subheadings here: (1) training the mind by means of the sevenfold cause-and-effect instruction; (2) training the mind through the interchange of self and others.

The sevenfold cause-and-effect instruction works by seeing all sentient beings as attractive. It was the system used by Āchārya Chandrakīrti, Chandragomin, Śhāntarakṣhita, and others. Śhāntideva's system was to train the mind through the interchange of self and others. You will be able to develop bodhichitta if you train by means of either of these instructions, for they are lineages that stem from the Teacher himself, and came down through Maitreya and Mañjuśhrī.

Atiśha's *Lamp on the Path,* and other works of his, set forth the instructions of Suvarṇadvīpa, the guru who held both of these instructions. The sevenfold cause-and-effect system was popular during the ancient Kadampa period, but the instruction on the interchange of self and others was passed on in secret. In this way the entire lineage came down to Je Tsongkapa. His own teachings told how to train the mind in both types of instruction; you should practice this combination of the two. However, although they must be combined in your meditations when you train your own mind for bodhichitta, these two have to be discussed separately when taught.

There are eight sections in *Training the Mind by Means of the Sevenfold Cause-and-Effect Instructions* (335A): (1) immeasurable equanimity, (2) understanding all sentient beings to be your mother, (3) remembering their kindness, (4) repaying their kindness, (5) love through the force of attraction, (6) compassion, (7) altruism, and (8) bodhichitta.

The six from "understanding all beings to be your mother" to "altruism" are the causes. They result in the development of bodhichitta. This is how these all act as cause and effect; but before you can develop the wish to achieve buddhahood to benefit all sentient beings, you must have the altruism to take responsibility for others' welfare. Further, you will not develop this altruism if you do not have such compassion that you are unable to bear the fact that all sentient beings are tormented by suffering. In order to generate this compassion, you must generate love through the force of attraction—an attraction to all sentient beings whereby they seem to be as attractive as your own dear cherished children. You must precede such love by regarding all sentient beings as dear ones to whom you have the sort of attraction you have at present for people you hold dear but do not have for your enemies. Because the ultimate form of dear one is the mother, you will love and cherish as valuable all sentient beings if you can prove that they have indeed been your mothers, remember their kindness, and wish to repay them.

That is why this is known as the "cause-and-effect" instruction, as each step is the necessary preliminary to the next, bringing each succeeding one into being. Don't be shortsighted and don't think this process too long:

you will definitely be able to develop bodhichitta if you train in stages. Kadampa instructions are in general profound, and this is especially so for the teachings of Tsongkapa: inspired by the living presence of Mañjuśhrī, and they contain the full range of sūtra and tantra quite stainlessly. They were even more profound than their predecessors. As my own precious guru, my refuge and protector, said:

> It is as if the past teachings in Tibet had prepared the ground for those of Je Rinpoche that followed and that were like refined gold.

Tagtsang Lotsawa, being frank, said:

> I praise your stores of unprecedented eloquence
> On all sūtra and tantra, but especially on Vajrayāna;
> On all types of tantra, but especially the highest;
> On all parts of the two stages, but especially the illusory body.

Or, as Dzogchen Paelge said, "O Tsongkapa, eloquent source of sūtra and tantra…" Such examples are sincere praise.

"Conferring buddhahood" seems rather high flown; it is hard enough to confer even the lowest level of the path of accumulation. But you will be handed buddhahood if you depend on the lamrim. However, you will not develop buddhahood if you do not train yourself in the proper sequence of the path. So first train yourself to understand that all sentient beings have been your mothers. If you do not take the training in such thinking seriously, you will be as perverse as those people who sin although they desire happiness. If you do not put any effort into it, even though your desire may be buddhahood, your practice will be back-to-front. You may be working hard at the secret tantras, a path of great rapidity, but you must take pains in the techniques of training the mind in bodhichitta. If you do not, you will be like a man who wants to go to Tsang Province who mounts his horse or whatever and rides off, under the impression that he is going to arrive at Tsang. But he may never reach Tsang, ending up at Kongpo or Rong instead!

How you begin to develop this understanding that all sentient beings were once your mother can be illustrated as follows. If you do not make the drawing surface smooth, flat, and even, the drawing will not come out. If you likewise do not develop equanimity toward all sentient beings, even though you meditate on love, or compassion, or whatever, you will develop only a prejudiced form of these. Therefore you must first develop immeasurable equanimity.

Mind training through the sevenfold cause-and-effect instruction does not include everything contained in the interchange of self and others training, whereas mind training through the interchange of self and others does contain the complete sevenfold instruction within it.

IMMEASURABLE EQUANIMITY (336)

The equanimity first meditated on in the sevenfold cause-and-effect instruction is immeasurable equanimity. On our side, we need to have equanimity of mind toward all sentient beings, but at present our mind-streams do not react equally to all: we get angry at some and attached to others. We could take neutral beings as our first object of mind training, then move on to our friends, and then to our enemies. Or we could take all three together as our object. I think the latter of these two has the wider application.

We should meditate on our enemies, friends, and those neutral, visualizing them in front of us. We have three different reactions toward them: hostility, attraction, and indifference. In the first place, we become angry with the people we currently take to be our enemies. We then look into what our grievances are and think over their cause—that these people have harmed us. Next we meditate on how nothing is certain, as discussed in the above section on "Thinking about the General Sufferings of Saṃsāra." We contemplate how these enemies had been dear to us in many past lives. This will stop us being hostile.

We experience involuntary happiness toward those we now take to be our friends. Then we examine the reasons for this: that they now give us food, clothing, and so on. These are only trivial, short-term reasons. Our attachment to them would come to an end if we were to recall that they have been our enemies countless times over.

We ignore those sentient beings we call "neutral," those neither enemies nor friends; but in the past they have been both enemies and friends. Thus all have been our enemies, all have been our friends; and if they are all the same, then all three of them—enemies, friends, and strangers—are equivalent. To whom should we be attached, with whom should we be angry?

Reflect on how senseless it is that our friends are the subjects of our attachment: in the past they were many times our enemies. It is also senseless that enemies are the subjects of our hostility, for they have also been dear to us many times in the past. Moreover, everyone we see now only appears to be our enemy or friend. There is no certainty that any will always remain so.

There are two points of view: that of ourselves and that of others. Not only is it senseless to be attached or hostile to others for our own part, but equally for their own part as well. They are all equally pitiable, all equally want happiness and do not want suffering. Thus, from this other point of view, all sentient beings are equal and should be treated impartially.

From another point of view, you may think there are differences between them because some of them have benefited you in this life while others have done you harm. This is not so. Benefit done in the past is equal to benefit done now. Harm done in the past is equal to harm done now. For example, the damage is the same if someone beat you on the head with a stick last year, or if they beat you on the head with a stick this year. Giving you a brick of tea last year is equal to giving you a brick of tea this year. Take the example of ten beggars. When they come to you and ask for alms, from their side they are all equally to be pitied for their hunger and thirst and they are all demanding the same things. From your side, they have all equally neither hurt nor harmed you.

If you gain equanimity toward enemies, dear ones, and those neutral through this contemplation, you can then extend it to all sentient beings. When you have such an equanimity toward them, you will not categorize them into enemies or friends. It will stop you forever from doing such evil, worldly actions as subduing enemies and upholding friends. Without it, you will single out beings, feeling that this or that one of them should be left out of "all sentient beings." People who make such distinctions will never develop bodhichitta. You must work hard solely at equanimity for months or years on end, because if you spend only a few meditation sessions on it, you will not progress. Your hopes of laying the foundations for your enlightenment will then only be wishful thinking. If you work hard at this bodhichitta training, I can assure you it is more worthwhile by far than working hard at and meditating on all sorts of less beneficial things that can fritter away your human rebirth, such as meditating on deities, reciting mantras, or trying to improve your meditative abilities.

Then Kyabje Pabongka Rinpoche reviewed the above material.

DAY 17

Kyabje Pabongka Rinpoche spoke about some of the benefits of bodhichitta.

As Śhāntideva, a great child of the victors, said:

> Homage to the enlightened bodies of those
> Who have developed this holy, precious mind.
> I take refuge in them, the source of happiness;
> Anyone who harms them is still brought to happiness.

In other words, someone who has developed bodhichitta in their mindstream may be abused and so forth, but still they will work for the sake of the person who wronged them and lead them to eternal happiness.

Then he gave a short talk to set our motivations properly.

In short, whatever action you do in conjunction with bodhichitta becomes Mahāyāna Dharma and a cause for your buddhahood. Thus, merely meditating on deities or reciting mantras is not the way to carry out effective practice, and you should not do things this way. The lamrim is the basis of an effective practice; and within this, the practice of bodhichitta is mandatory. If, lacking bodhichitta, you spend your entire life on some empty mountain, whatever other meditations you do will be merely perfunctory, and you will not get a whit closer to buddhahood.

Kyabje Pabongka Rinpoche told us how we need to make bodhichitta our major practice, how the mind training instructions are indispensable for the development of bodhichitta, and so on. After giving this short talk to set our motivation, he then restated the headings already covered and reviewed the benefits of bodhichitta and the equanimity meditations.

The first section of the sevenfold instruction on training the mind for bodhichitta is "Understanding All Sentient Beings to Be Your Mother." This is very difficult to develop indeed, but without it, the causes and effects that result, such as "Repaying the Kindness of Sentient Beings," will not follow. So take this section seriously!

THE FIRST CAUSE: UNDERSTANDING ALL SENTIENT BEINGS TO BE YOUR MOTHER (337)

You must understand that all sentient beings were once the ultimate form of friend or relative—your mother. You have no chance of gaining bodhichitta if you do not develop such an understanding. You can think over other profound topics, such as emptiness, using many different logical arguments, so those topics are not difficult to understand. But here it is difficult to be convinced by simply thinking deeply about a single scriptural quotation. Still, the sharp-witted follow ideas [Dharma], and for them things need to be proved by logic. It will be hard to gain realization in this section since it has but one solitary line of reasoning. This reasoning is given in [Dharmakīrti's] *Commentary on Valid Cognition:*

> When someone has been reborn,
> [How absurd it would be]
> For his breathing, organs, and mind
> [To have developed from the body alone,]
> And not in dependence on
> [Things] of their own class…

What needs to be proved here is the beginningless nature of our consciousness. Today's mind is the continuation of yesterday's mind, and this in turn is a continuation of that of the day before. This much is understandable. The mind just after birth is the continuation of the mind that lay within the mother's womb. The mind immediately after it has entered the womb is the continuation of the mind immediately before entering the womb. As saṃsāra goes back limitlessly in time, you cannot find anything that is "The starting point for the mind." This proves that your rebirths must also go back limitlessly in time.

It then follows that the number of your rebirths is infinite. You have therefore had a limitless number of rebirths. Just as you had a mother in this life, you must have had a mother each time in the past, whether you were born from a womb or from an egg. To take such a birth, you had to have a mother; and similarly, for one hundred such rebirths, you must have had one hundred such mothers; for one thousand rebirths, one thousand mothers, etc. You must have had countless mothers, and so it is impossible that all sentient beings have not been your mother.

You may object, "Granted I must have had many mothers, but all sentient beings could not have been my mother, because they are infinite in number." In general, you have had many rebirths. Moreover, you have been born numberless times in the physical shape of each animal species, such as deer, antelope, earthworms, and so on. You have therefore received countless bodies of each of the countless types of sentient beings. You have even taken rebirth many more times than there are sentient beings; and for each of these rebirths, you needed an equal number of mothers. So not only have all sentient beings been your mother, but also there are not enough beings for them to have been your mother only once. As it says in Nāgārjuna's *Letter:*

> If you counted all your mothers
> With juniper-berry–sized balls of earth,
> [The earth would not be enough...]

This passage is taken to refer to one's direct line of mothers, that is one's grandmother, great-grandmother, and so on. However, here I shall reinterpret this passage according to the oral tradition of our gurus. Take the whole of the earth and roll it into juniper-berry–sized balls. One of these stands for your mother of this life, one for the mother of your previous life, one for the life before. When you run out of balls of earth, you still have not reached even one hundred thousandth of the number of mothers you have had. If all sentient beings had not been your mothers, there would be a discrepancy. Further, because all sentient beings will definitely become enlightened, a time will come when there will be no more of them left. But as cyclic existence is limitless, you have had more rebirths than there are sentient beings. Thus, if all sentient beings had not been your mother countless times, there would again be a discrepancy. All sentient beings, therefore, have been your mother, and many times over at that.

There is no form of sentient being that you have not taken rebirth as; think how you have taken rebirth countless times in these forms. Let us take human rebirth as an example. There is no place in this continent where you have not taken rebirth as a human being, and countless times at that. And in the same way, you have taken countless rebirths in every world system to the east, west, north, south, and so on. Since you have therefore had more rebirths than there are sentient beings, not only must they have been your mother, but also every single one of them must have been your mother in human rebirths. Thus it is reasonable [to conclude] that all sentient beings have truly been your mother.

If you have not developed understanding after this contemplation, ask yourself, "Have I ever had a mother?" You will then think, "Obviously I have: my mother in this rebirth." You then extend this to the mother of your immediately preceding rebirth, and so on, going back as far as necessary to convince you.

The *Easy Path* and the *Swift Path* lamrims deal only briefly with how to meditate on the understanding that these beings have been your mother. But I shall expand this heading using instructions, the hard-wrought inheritance of my guru. If the practices are not to degenerate, it is vital that people who practice regularly or who have made the teachings their responsibility should, in order that the practices not decline, do the following meditation, which greatly facilitates people's development of realization of the lamrim.

First meditate on how your mother of this life has been your mother many times over in previous rebirths. Then meditate on how your father has been a mother to you. Then do this for all your friends and dear ones; then, for those neutral. Then, if you have managed to gain some insight from all this, meditate on how your enemies have been your mother. Only then should you carry out this training with respect to all sentient beings. Even so, you may feel, "If all sentient beings had been my mothers, I would recognize them as such. I do not, they can't have been my mothers." But the buddhas themselves have observed that not one sentient being has not been your mother. In reality they have all been your mothers, only you do not recognize them as such. Our true mother of this life may later be reborn as a dog, but we would not be able to tell this; we would not even recognize her as our true mother of this life. This is illustrated in the story of the nun Utpalavarṇā and in the quotation:

> He eats his father's flesh and hits his mother.
> The enemy he killed sits on his knee.
> A wife gnaws her husband's bones.
> Saṃsāra can be such a farce![69]

So your mere nonrecognition of a being is no reason for it not to have been your mother; nor is that being no longer your mother just because she was your mother in the past. If that were the case, the mother of the earlier part of your life would not be your mother in the later part of your life; nor would yesterday's mother still be your mother, because that, too, was in the past. This is a subtle facet of impermanence and is difficult to realize if you have not done any study. Take this shawl, for example. A year ago when it was new, it wasn't stained and it had no holes. But its continuation, the shawl of today, is stained and is moth-eaten. Such is the distinction between the two. And so you must think over the fact that there is no difference between mothers of past and future lives in their being your mothers. Similarly, if someone had saved your life last year, you would surely remember that kindness this year!

Here is the criterion that determines whether you have developed this understanding after repeated training: if you see a sentient being—even an ant—you will involuntarily remember that you were once that being's child and that all your happiness and suffering depended upon it.

And Kyabje Pabongka Rinpoche talked about how we need to develop—as Atiśha did, for example—the understanding that all sentient beings are our mothers.

THE SECOND CAUSE: REMEMBERING THEIR KINDNESS (338)

When you have insight into the fact that sentient beings have been your mother, you ought to think of the enormous kindness they showed you as your mother. Take the case of your mother in this life: [while you were in her care,] she showed you great kindness at the beginning, in the middle, and at the end. In the beginning she carried you in her body for nine months and ten days, cherishing you and protecting you. She was careful about the things she ate or drank, and careful when moving and sitting, for fear of harming her child. If our mothers had not known how to look after us so well, we would not have been able to meet with the holy Dharma or study it now. This did not happen because we could fend for ourselves: it was through our mothers' kindness.

In the meantime, just after your birth she handled you carefully with both her hands, even though you were completely unaware and looked as repulsive as a maggot. She felt as happy as if she had found a treasure. She kept you warm with her own body, laid you on a soft bed, smiled lovingly at you, and even wiped your runny nose with her own mouth because she feared that you would be hurt if she used her hands. She feared that wiping away your excrement using a piece of wood, or whatever, would hurt you—although they would have sufficed—so she used her own hand. She could not leave you alone for a day, or even an hour. Each day she saved you from hundreds of things that would probably have killed you: a dog might have eaten you, a bird nearly pecked you, or you could have fallen off a cliff. If her child suffered, don't you think she suffered too? Her only thoughts were for her child, even in her sleep: she no longer dared sleep as soundly as she used to. Also, she gradually taught her child how to stand, speak, even how to eat and drink. That is why we can now move about, speak, and so on, without difficulty.

She didn't care about the sins, bad reputation, or suffering she acquired to earn the money to keep you. She cherished you more than her own flesh, and so didn't spend any of her savings on herself—she spent them on you. Whoever you may be, a man or woman who has married or been given in marriage, or someone who has been sent off to be ordained, your standard of living is due to the kindness of your mother. In short, she did the best she could within her power and knowledge for your welfare. There was no end to the kindness she showed in keeping you from all harm and suffering.

All other sentient beings, such as your father, have also shown you the same kindness. As all sentient beings have been your mother in human lives—not just once but countless times—they have shown you much the same kindness as your mother in this life has. When other sentient beings were your mother and you were reborn as some wild animal, for example, those mothers treated you with loving kindness and looked after you. They even licked you with their tongues. When your mother was a bird, for example, she shielded you with her wings for nearly a month. And if enemies threatened, such as a man with a stick, she would protect her precious chick with her life although she herself could have flown away. Later, she would feed you, and even if she only managed to find a single worm, she would give it to you.

Therefore, sentient beings have not been kind to you just once or twice: they have shown you kindness in every type of situation. Their kindness is beyond reckoning. Once a bandit from Golog stabbed a mare in the belly. The dying mother delivered her foal on the ground and licked it to show her love. The bandit saw this, and it reformed him. How could you be sure that you weren't that foal? And just as your own mother has shown you such kindness in this rebirth, think on how all sentient beings have also shown you the very same kindness.

THE THIRD CAUSE: REPAYING THEIR KINDNESS (339)

It says in [Śhāntideva's] *Compendium of Instruction:*

> You and the others always have grounds for suffering;
> The sufferings of sentient beings are all equal.
> For made mad by delusion, blinded by benightedness,
> Every step they take treads the path to many an abyss.

You should think in this way: Suppose your mother of this life were blind, had no one to guide her, and were mad. She is about to fall over a cliff, yet her child is near at hand. If she cannot turn to her child for help, to whom can she turn? If the child will not save its mother, whom will it save? All sentient beings likewise lack eyes to discriminate between Dharma and non-Dharma in order to see how to modify their behavior. Every single moment their steps are guided by their vices—they commit their misdeeds due to their perverse desires and practices. They have no spiritual guide, no one who will instruct them to do this and not do that. Their minds are disturbed and bedeviled by the three poisonous delusions; so they have no control over their minds and are mad. They will fall down that great cliff leading to the lower realms, and for many eons their bodies will be indistinguishable from the flames there. We, on the other hand, have met with spiritual guides, we have come in contact with Mahāyāna Dharma. We know a little about how to modify our behavior. We are, therefore, in a much better position than they are, and the responsibility has fallen on us to do something to save them.

In Chandragomin's *Letter to a Disciple* we find:

> Like kinsmen stranded in saṃsāra's ocean,
> They seem to have fallen into the ocean's rip;
> Not recognizing them due to birth, death, and leaving rebirths, you ignore them.
> There is no shame greater than freeing only yourself.

That is, for our meditations on repaying their kindness we should feel that we have the means of freeing these sentient beings stranded in the ocean currents of saṃsāra. The responsibility for rescuing them now rests with us, and we would be utterly contemptible if we did not do so.

The *Heart of the Middle Way* has this to say about repaying their kindness:

> Up till now I was possessed
> By the devil of delusion;
> Like an irritant poured on a wound, or like being struck—
> What makes me suffer the disease of suffering?
>
> Is there some way
> Other than nirvāṇa
> To repay those who loved me,
> Respected me, or helped me in my other rebirths?

Think as follows: "By merely giving them food, clothing, and so forth, I will only free them from temporary hunger and thirst. It would not bring them any lasting benefit. They would benefit greatly and permanently, however, if they had every possible happiness and were rid of every suffering. If I could lead them to buddhahood they would achieve a state that has every happiness and is free of all suffering. Thus I will lead all sentient beings to buddhahood!

Suppose your mother were mad, carrying a knife, and trying to kill you, her child. You would not be angry with her; you would surely try to rid her of her madness. This is how you must repay the kindness of your enemies.

THE FOURTH CAUSE: MEDITATING ON THE LOVE THAT COMES FROM THE FORCE OF ATTRACTION (340)

This love appears in the form of a heartfelt cherishing, an affection for sentient beings. "Love through the force of attraction," said Geshe Potowa to an old woman, "is just like the love you have for your son Toelekor."

In other words "love through the force of attraction" is being attracted to all sentient beings as if they were your own children. This love does not need a separate meditation topic: you will develop it automatically when you have developed some feeling for the preceding three sections: "Understanding All Beings to Be Your Mother," "Remembering Their Kindness," and "Wishing to Repay Their Kindness." So contemplate as follows:

"I can discount the uncontaminated happiness in the mindstreams of all sentient beings; they have only the contaminated sort. Even the thing they take to be happiness has not transcended the nature of suffering. How wonderful if all sentient beings had happiness! May they come to have it! I will procure for them such happiness!"

Nāgārjuna's *Precious Garland* mentions the following benefits of meditation on this type of love:

> The merit of giving the three hundred types of food
> Every day in the three times
> Cannot compare with the merits gained
> From meditating once for a short while on love.
>
> Though such a person might not be liberated,
> He will achieve love's eight cardinal virtues.
> Gods and humans will come to love him
> And will give him protection;
>
> He will have mental ease and much happiness;
> Poison and weapons will not harm;
> He will achieve his aims effortlessly
> And be born in Brahmā's world.

The benefits are enormous, such as achieving these eight cardinal virtues of love. You will be reborn as a universal emperor or as Brahmā the same number of times as the number of living beings you took as objects for your meditation on love. That is why the meditation is called the *brahmāvihāra* or "stages of Brahmā." But if you take all sentient beings as your object, all beings, who extend to the limits of space, you will achieve the nonabiding [or dynamic] form of nirvāṇa—the mahābrahmā state [that is, the Mahāyāna nirvāṇa—buddhahood].

THE FIFTH CAUSE: THE GREAT COMPASSION (341)

This is a potent determinate cause for buddhahood. Je Tsongkapa paid special attention to the great compassion in "The Stages in Training for Bodhichitta" section of his *Great Stages of the Path.* He gave the following headings: "Showing that the Great Compassion Is the Root of the Mahāyāna Path," and "The Way the Other Causes and Effects Act as Either Cause or Effect for [the Great Compassion]." Also in a sūtra we are told that the whole Mahāyāna path and its results depend on the great compassion, just as the universal emperor [or wheel-turning king] is dependent on his chakra [wheel], or a man on his life-force. Chandrakīrti, in the verse preface of his *Engaging in the Middle Way,* says:

> Love is the seed for a magnificent crop—the state of a victor.
> Like water, love makes that crop grow
> And matures it for abiding enjoyment.
> That is why at the outset I praise compassion.

It is as important as a seed, since it ensures that the path is Mahāyāna at the outset, and is the root of developing bodhichitta. In the meantime, it is as vital as water and manure, because it produces a perseverance along the way that acts as armor against despondency at the tasks facing a child of the victors. Finally, it is as important as the fruit to be enjoyed, because it is responsible for your continual good works for the benefit of others after you achieve buddhahood. The degree of strength of your bodhichitta is also a function of your great compassion; and the various speeds at which bodhisattvas travel the lamrim fundamentally depend on the strength of their compassion. Bodhisattvas enter the secret tantras in search of a rapid path, and they complete this path quickly through the power of their compassion. An illustration: when a child falls into a burning pit, his parents will rescue him instantly, whereas even other relatives do not have the will to rescue him as unhesitatingly. This is due to the strength of their compassion.

In your early meditations on compassion, take as your object a sheep being slaughtered by a butcher; you will easily develop compassion. You must contemplate the way the sheep dies, the sadistic way it is killed, and how it dies in a state of unbearable agony and terror. The sheep is turned upside down and thrown on its back. Its legs are tied together with rope. It struggles but is helpless. It can tell its life is threatened but cannot escape, and has no protector or refuge to turn to. Its eyes are full of tears, and it stares into the butcher's face.

Nevertheless, when we see a sheep being slaughtered like this, we wonder if it is intelligent enough to know what is happening. Once a butcher was slaughtering a number of sheep. After killing the first few, he bound up one of them for slaughter. Another sheep happened to be standing close to the butcher's knife, and it kicked up dirt to conceal it. This story shows that animals do experience unbearable terror and suffering. For the sheep now grazing on the grassy mountainside who have not yet been led to the slaughteryard, sooner or later the same will befall them. For your meditation on compassion, think how they have been your mothers in so many of your past lives. Once you have developed some insight into this, recall your meditations on the sufferings of the lower realms that you yourself may have to undergo, and then meditate on how other sentient beings will also undergo—and are undergoing—these sufferings. Some of your mothers will be burnt by flaming iron and boiled in molten copper in these hells. Some will be reborn as hungry ghosts and tortured by hunger and thirst. And so on. Develop compassion for them, and then think as follows:

"The only thing that distinguishes the sheep on the mountain from the sheep being slaughtered is when it is killed; those who now sin in the human realm may look like people who can look after themselves, but they are certain to fall to the lower realms; they are thus no different from those who have already gone to the lower realms."

Then meditate on compassion for your mother in this life by considering the causes of suffering she has created and the suffering she will have to undergo. Meditate as follows to develop great compassion:

"Others, such as my relations, work hard to earn a living—but this only means sinning and breaking their vows. They are temporarily in high rebirths, but they undergo the three forms of suffering and later will experience the much greater sufferings of the lower realms, since [unknowingly] they are preoccupied with acquiring the causes for this to happen.

Further, *all* sentient beings are creating suffering and the causes for suffering. How welcome it would be if these kind ones, these mothers of mine, were without suffering and its causes! This is what I shall work for!"

Then do the more difficult meditation of taking as your object those beings for whom it is harder for you to develop compassion. If you find it difficult to develop compassion toward beings like Brahmā, contemplate according to the medium-scope section; then you will develop it.

Here are the criteria for having developed the great compassion in your mindstream. You have developed it if, even while eating or drinking, you think about all sentient beings, and want them all to be free of suffering just like a mother worrying about her beloved child who has been struck down by a virulent disease.

However, the compassion merely wanting beings to be free of suffering is common to śhrāvakas and pratyekabuddhas. The compassion of actually wishing to *save* them from their suffering is exclusive to the Mahāyāna. You should develop this latter type. Still, these are hard things to develop, and you must work very hard indeed at the techniques. If you have had a serious illness in the past, when you see people with the same sickness you will feel compassion for them, since you have gone through the same thing yourself. So it should also be easy to develop compassion after you undergo some excellent meditation on the sufferings of saṃsāra and the lower realms, as described in the small and medium scopes.

Love through a force of attraction so strong that it makes you cherish sentient beings and hold them dear is as much a form of love as the love that wishes them happiness. However, the slight difference is that one form is general and the other is specific. Love through the force of attraction is the sum of three things: understanding that all sentient beings are your mother, remembering their kindness, and wishing to repay their kindness. It necessarily precedes the great compassion, for it brings about the generation of this great compassion. Compassion and the love that wishes happiness do not have such a fixed cause-and-effect relationship. One section of the *Great Stages of the Path* dealing with the repayment of the kindness of sentient beings tells how to meditate on the love that wishes happiness, and it is appropriate for you to sometimes meditate on this type of love *before* you meditate on compassion. However, meditating on this type of love *after* the compassion meditations accords with the traditional instruction on pursuing the practice.

Next we will deal with altruism. At this stage we meditate mainly on the love that wishes all beings to have happiness. However, according to the headings in the *Great Stages of the Path,* we ought to contemplate a little this type of love combined with the force-of-attraction type before contemplating compassion.

THE SIXTH CAUSE: ALTRUISM (342)

You have a responsibility toward your mother. Likewise you should take responsibility for relieving all sentient beings of their suffering and making them totally happy. You should resolve: "I myself will lead them to buddhahood." This is being more altruistic than either śhrāvakas or pratyekabuddhas. Suppose you saw a man about to throw himself off a cliff. This unbearable sight might move you to feel, "Is there no one to save him?" Such a reaction is one of love and compassion, but instead of leaving things at this, you could decide to rescue him yourself. That would be analogous to this altruism. Śhrāvakas and pratyekabuddhas have, in general, only love and compassion—not altruism.

My precious guru has said that the difference between this altruism and the way you take on responsibility during the section on "Repaying Their Kindness" is illustrated by the example of a trader either intending to buy some goods or having already closed the business deal. One has similarly made up one's mind in the one section but not in the other.

DEVELOPING BODHICHITTA (343)

After taking on this responsibility, see if you are able to carry it out yet. You are unable to help even a single being! You are forced to look for someone who can do this effectively and then see if you too can achieve such a state. Some great worldly beings, Brahmā or Indra, for example, are of no help at all to sentient beings. And the śhrāvakas, pratyekabuddhas, and arhats can do little better since they have not abandoned all their fetters. The first-level bodhisattvas can help sentient beings to a much greater extent, but they can only do a fraction of what the bodhisattvas who will reach enlightenment in their next rebirth can achieve. Even the things these bodhisattvas do cannot compare with a fraction of what bodhisattvas in the very last stages perform for the sake of sentient beings in one day while they sit under a bodhi tree. And even the deeds of those under the bodhi tree do not bear comparison with what buddhas achieve. It is like the difference between the palm of your hand and the whole of space. The buddhas are incomparable in the spontaneous and effortless way they benefit others in accordance with others' dispositions, wishes, and mental capacities. If you were to achieve such a state, you too would have these qualities [cf. the section on taking refuge, Day 12, pp. 359–66].

Thus you will develop the conviction that it is not possible to benefit others until you have achieved omniscience yourself. You must develop a yearning for complete enlightenment in order to benefit others. "Equanimity," "Understanding All Sentient Beings to Be Your Mother," "Remembering Their Kindness," and "Wishing to Repay Their Kindness," all constitute the basis needed for the development of a yearning to benefit others, while "Love," "Compassion," and "Altruism" actually produce this yearning and the wish to achieve full enlightenment. As it has been said [in the *Ornament to Realization*]:

> Development of bodhichitta is
> Desiring full enlightenment to benefit others.

In other words, wanting to achieve buddhahood by merely seeing the need to benefit others is not sufficient for the proper, fully characterized development of bodhichitta. You must want to gain that state because you see that you yourself have not yet achieved buddhahood, so you do not have its magnificent realizations and abandonments; however, you do not merely want this for your own benefit: just as you developed a yearning to benefit others in the "Love," "Compassion," and "Altruism" sections, you must also develop the wish to achieve this complete enlightenment for the sake of others.

But you may wonder: can I succeed if I meditate in this way? Definitely you can. There is no better time for you to develop bodhichitta than the present, since this physical form you have acquired is quite sufficient for gaining buddhahood. The Dharma you follow is the Buddha's teachings. Within these teachings you have met with the Mahāyāna Dharma, and more importantly, the teachings of the secret tantras that can enlighten you in a single lifetime. This is something that holds for all the [Tibetan] sects. The lineage of Je Tsongkapa's secret teachings can bring you enlightenment in only twelve human years, and many have achieved the state of unification much faster—in only three years and three months. This can be seen in the life stories of past holy beings such as the [second] victorious one [Tsongkapa] and his disciples. We call the present time "a degenerate period," but we have never had a better opportunity than now. The body that Milarepa or Ensapa had was no better than the form we have. We are like the crippled child riding the wild ass: now is the time to work hard![70]

We would rather die than meditate on the lamrim! People like to waste their lives reading books, becoming academics, or doing recitations. They are missing the point! We cannot know whether we are going to get such a rebirth again in future: and even if we did, it is still going to be extremely difficult to meet with the teachings, and especially with teachings so completely free of error as, for example, those of the second victorious one.

So you must check whether you will be able to develop bodhichitta, the cause for your complete enlightenment, while still in this present rebirth. Once you develop this one thing, it will bring benefit to both yourself and others. Once there was a famine, and a man and his family were on the brink of starvation. One day this man found a piece of meat. "If I were to divide this meat up," he thought, "and my whole family were to eat it, there would not be enough to go around. They would still be hungry, and I know it would be only a temporary measure. I am going to eat all of it myself. Then I will have the strength to go and look for more food and provide for them all." So the father ate all the meat, went in search of food, and saved everyone. Thus, when you practice the secret tantras, or just repeat a rosary of *oṃ maṇi padme hūṃ*—or when, for example, you attend a debating practice or offering ceremony as an ordinary monk—do so in conjunction with this mind.

When you experience the conscious desire to achieve buddhahood for the sake of sentient beings, you have developed a bodhichitta that resembles the outer layer of a piece of sugar cane. But when you experience an involuntary desire to achieve full enlightenment for the sake of any sentient being you see, you have developed true bodhichitta in your mindstream. You have thus entered the Mahāyāna path of accumulation and begun the three great eons of amassing [the two collections]. You will acquire infinite qualities and gain the names "child of the victorious ones" and "bodhisattva." When you practice after achieving this insight, you are sure to be enlightened quickly if you add the mantric [i.e., tantric] path.

The development of bodhichitta has two types according to its nature—the aspiration and engagement types; four types according to one's location on the path—the belief type of bodhichitta or the analytic type, etc.; three types according to the mode of development of the bodhichitta—the kingly type, etc.; and there are another twenty-two types of development of bodhichitta. It is said to be most important to know these various presentations.[71] This completes the section on developing bodhichitta by means of the sevenfold cause-and-effect instruction.

Now I shall discuss the mind-training system that uses the interchange of self and others (335B). This was the system of Śhāntideva, a great child of the victorious ones. Although you will develop bodhichitta if you train your mind according to the above sevenfold cause-and-effect method, we will still cover this system of interchange of self and others, because this thought is so powerful. The earlier Kadampas used this technique.

What we usually call *mind training* refers particularly to the interchange of self and others, and to giving and taking. This Dharma of interchanging self and others derives from *Engaging in the Deeds of Bodhisattvas:*

> Anyone who wishes quickly to protect
> Both himself and others
> Should practice the holy secret:
> Exchange of self with others.

In other words, since this practice would have been beyond the mind of an unfit vessel, from the time of Atiśha until that of Geshe Chaekawa, the teaching was kept under a seal of secrecy.

There are many texts about mind training, such as the *Poisons Conquered by the Peacocks Mind Training;* but the high point of this genre is the famous *Seven-Point Mind Training.* If you practice this teaching, it will be even more beneficial than the one already covered. So now I shall teach this seven-point training using an older variant of the root text. [See pp. 726ff. for the entire text.]

There are many ways of presenting this text. I shall follow the teaching lineage derived from Ngulchu Dharmavajra and his disciples.

First, the greatness of the authors of this teaching. The lineage came from Buddha Śhākyamuni down to great Atiśha; he passed it on to Dromtoenpa under a seal of secrecy. Drom gave lamrim teachings to his disciples in public but passed this mind training down to Potowa and others in secret. Potowa passed it on to Langri Tangpa and Geshe Sharawa. Sharawa gave his disciple Geshe Chaekawa all the teachings on bodhichitta. These teachings were made public during Chaekawa's lifetime.

Geshe Chaekawa was born into a family of great Nyingma tantrists and became very learned in the five sciences, and so on, but this did not satisfy him. He happened to see Langri Tangpa's *Mind Training in Eight Verses,* which says:

> Give the gains and victories to others;
> Take the losses and defeats yourself...

Chaekawa then sought out the meaning of this, but Langri Tangpa had died. He met Langri Tangpa's successor, Sharawa, requested instruction on mind training from him, and through his meditations developed bodhichitta in his mindstream. Chaekawa gave this instruction to many lepers, who cured themselves through their meditations. The teaching was even known as the "Lepers' Dharma." Chaekawa thought it a great pity that this teaching was being kept so secret and taught it in public. He committed it to writing as this *Seven-Point Mind Training,* dividing the teaching into seven sections. It has been called the "Essence of Nectar Instruction" because this is the ultimate instruction on training the mind and will enable you to achieve the immortal state of buddhahood.

The greatness of this Dharma can be seen by referring back to the section on the benefits of bodhichitta and how bodhichitta is like a diamond. It is similarly able to dispel the darkness of self-cherishing, just as even a fraction of the rays of the sun can dispel darkness. It can dispel the disease of self-cherishing just as even a part of the medicine tree can dispel illness. In these times when the five types of degeneration are commonplace and Dharma paths may not be effective, this mind training will assist you and you will not be bothered by unfortunate circumstances. This Dharma has so many greatnesses.

It starts with "Homage to the Great Compassion." This homage is not being made to Ārya Avalokiteśhvara [the Great Compassionate One]: just as Āchāryā Chandrakīrti honored compassion in the opening of *Engaging in the Middle Way,* it is the great compassion that is being honored here. Now follow the seven sections of the main body of this mind training [see p. 726 for a summary of these seven].

TEACHING THE PRELIMINARIES ON WHICH THIS DHARMA DEPENDS (344)

This section is the training of the mind in the part of the path shared with the small and medium scopes. I do not have to teach this all over again as there is no difference between the way they are treated here and in the lamrim.

TRAINING YOURSELF FOR THE TWO TYPES OF BODHICHITTA (345)

Developing (1) ultimate bodhichitta, and (2) relative bodhichitta.

ULTIMATE BODHICHITTA (346)

The preserved teachings of the past say that the sharp-witted of the Mahāyāna lineage should train their minds by developing ultimate bodhichitta first. However, the story of the mahāsiddha Hastikovapa could repeat itself if you first discuss training the mind through development of ultimate bodhichitta before you have taught the other part that deals with method.[72] So I will not speak on the ultimate-bodhichitta mind training first. This follows the practice of Tutor Tsechogling. I shall be dealing with it later, for it is included below in the section on the six perfections.

TRAINING THE MIND IN RELATIVE BODHICHITTA (347)

The source for this instruction is the story of Maitrakanyaka and other stories. These tell of a previous life of our Compassionate Teacher while he was a still-learner on the path. Although he had been born in hell as a wrestler forced to pull a cart, he developed bodhichitta. And so on.

There are five subsections.

MEDITATING ON HOW SELF AND OTHERS ARE EQUAL (348)

This is preceded by the same early sections we had above, that is from "Equanimity" up to "Love that Comes from the Force of Attraction."

Then you should contemplate as follows. As the *Guru Pūjā* says:

> There is no difference between myself and others:
> We do not want the smallest suffering,
> Yet happiness never satisfies.
> Bless me to be glad at others' joy.

In other words, at present we cherish and value the thing we call the "self" but do not regard others in this way, so the self and others are not equal. It is not right to make such an enormous distinction between these two. We ought to feel, "I and others are equal because we both want happiness and don't want suffering."

At this initial stage [in the technique], hardly any other reasoning is used. There is no difference between this stage of the mind training and the "Understanding All Sentient Beings to Be Your Mother," "Remembering Their Kindness," and "Repaying Their Kindness" parts of the above sevenfold cause-and-effect technique. This also holds true for the final sections, "Altruism" and "Bodhichitta." However, there are differences in the strength of your compassion and your love through the force of attraction. These two aspects receive special treatment here. The above section on "Remembering Their Kindness" only gave a method of recalling the kindness sentient beings showed you when they were your mother. This new technique has a way of recalling their kindness when they were *not* your mother. Before moving on to the "Interchange of Self and Others," you must think that self-cherishing is a fault and an unfavorable condition, and that cherishing others is a favorable condition and a good quality.

CONTEMPLATING THE MANY FAULTS RESULTING FROM SELF-CHERISHING (349)

The *Guru Pūjā* says: I see this chronic disease of self-cherishing is the cause to produce unwanted suffering... In *Engaging in the Deeds of Bodhisattvas* it says:

> All worldly sufferings that have occurred
> Stemmed from wanting happiness for oneself...
>
> Anything that befalls the worldly,
> Any fear and suffering,
> All stemmed from self-cherishing.
> Why should I have this great devil!

Our root text says:

> *Put the blame on one thing alone.*

That is, all your unwanted sufferings come from your self-cherishing. Coming to grief through weapons, poison, and nonhuman evildoers such as gods and nāgas; being reborn in hell, as hungry ghosts, animals, etc.—these are due to killing other beings in the hope of some gain for your own happiness, or to being miserly, or to treating others with contempt. Likewise, succumbing to the diseases of the humors, wind, bile, phlegm, etc.; fearing enemies; getting into quarrels; or fearing prosecution by the authorities—all these are due to gorging yourself on food because of self-cherishing, or to not abandoning your obsession with food, fashion, and fame. It alone is at fault with unbearable illness. When at the top of the ladder kings, ministers, and whole countries fight, or when on the bottom rung their subjects, families, etc., argue—or even when monks squabble—self-cherishing is at fault. Don't have self-cherishing; instead have an attitude of "I don't care, you do what you like," and none of these problems will occur. Your self-cherishing created all your troubles with thieves, bandits, and even with mice making holes in your bag of barley flour. When you die from poison, or from undigested food, you do not really die of poison: because of your self-cherishing you ate far too much. Your self-cherishing killed you. When you are innocent but get accused of being a thief, it is the direct [karmic] result of having harmed others due to self-cherishing.

Self-cherishing is like a butcher who kills your chances of high rebirth or liberation. It is like the burglar who carries a swag full of the three poisons on his back and steals your crop of virtue. It is like the sower who sows the seed of evil karma in the field of ignorance, thus reaping the harvest of saṃsāra; like the glory-seeker who braves the arrows, spears, and swords in the thick of battle in hope of some personal gain. It is a reckless ne'er-do-well who will desert even his guru, abbot, or parents in a crisis. It is the empty-handed wretch who, right from the beginning, never achieved any good qualities. It makes you have hopes, or fears, for things you shouldn't. It makes you be jealous of those above you, compete with your equals, and snub those below you; it makes you arrogant when praised and angry when criticized. It brings everything second-rate in the world. It is the source of all nonvirtue, the thing that since beginningless time has brought you suffering—an old owl-faced ill-omened one. It is an evil talisman lying buried in the center of your heart. If we must take control of anything and throw ritual cakes at it, we should throw them at this. When we throw out ritual cakes, we do it to sentient beings—our former mothers—while saying, "This is for anyone who is my enemy." What a misunderstanding that is!

This is the point brought out by the quotation, "Self-cherishing is a blue-headed bird of ill omen; mind training is the way to dismiss this demon."

Once, a man who practiced *choed*[73] usurped a place where a spirit lived. Because of the magic employed to stay there, the man's two benefactors one day fell into a quarrel; the man went to heal the dispute, and one of them took up a weapon and killed him. I heard this story from my precious guru. The ultimate root of such violent deaths is nothing but self-cherishing. *Engaging in the Deeds of Bodhisattvas* says:

> O mind, eons beyond counting have passed
> With you working only for your own ends.
> Such great labors
> Have achieved you only misery.

That is, the thing that has brought us suffering since beginningless time in saṃsāra is our own self-cherishing. Self-cherishing and grasping at the self are two quite distinct things, but they are discussed in this mind training as if they were the same, for there are some resemblances. To be brief, both are at the root of all problems. One of them operates by taking the "I"—your feeling of "I"—to be established as true. The other operates by not giving up ideas of "I" and then assiduously cherishing it.

To sum up, all problems come from the deep-seated thought "I want some happiness," but if you cannot subdue this self-cherishing, you will have no happiness. You have never before checked to see what is at root to blame for your suffering, but it is self-cherishing. From now on, check what is to blame and look on your self-cherishing as an enemy. Practice the techniques to abandon it.

CONTEMPLATING THE MANY GOOD QUALITIES RESULTING FROM CHERISHING OTHERS (350)

Śhāntideva said:

> All worldly happiness to be found
> Comes from wishing others happiness.

And the *Guru Pūjā* says:

I see that cherishing these, my mothers,
Is a thought that leads to happiness,
The door leading to infinite qualities…

Our text on mind training says:

Meditate on the greater kindness of all.

In other words, having the body and wealth of a high rebirth or having magnificent surroundings results from cherishing others. Virtue from abandoning killing because you cherish the lives of others will ripen into a resultant rebirth in the upper realms, long life, and so on. Practicing generosity, abandoning the taking of that not given, and so on, out of cherishing others will result in great wealth, etc. In short [as Śhāntideva said]:

What more need be said?
Look at the difference between the two:
Churls who work for their own ends
And the Sage who benefited others.

And in the *Guru Pūjā* we find:

In short: the infantile work only for their own good,
Śhākyamuni worked solely for the good of others.
May I realize which is the fault, which the good
quality…

Once our Teacher was like us, wandering in saṃsāra. But at some time in the past, that supreme Sage began to cherish others and progressed to fulfill both his own and others' aims by eradicating his faults and gaining the consummation of all good qualities. We, however, from beginningless time in saṃsāra, have cherished only ourselves. We have toiled and toiled, thinking "I want some happiness," but gained nothing in return. We were not able to gain the least benefit nor in the end gain any means to avoid the lower realms. Even now all we have is such tormenting suffering. If the opposite had happened, and at some time in the past we had acted as our Compassionate Teacher, all our suffering would have been eradicated by now. Undoubtedly we would have had supreme happiness and been able to fulfill the needs of others magnificently. That is not what happened, however, and so we are in our present predicament.

During the amelioration ceremony [for protector deities], a geshe of Dagpo inserted into the ceremony some of the curse lines found in the *Wheel of [Sharp] Weapons*. An example:

> That is how it is: I know my enemy!... I lay in ambush and caught you, sneak thief! Hypocrite! You have fooled me with your lies! O self-grasping! I've no doubts this is how you are.

He slipped these in at one monastery and this created quite a stir. But the point was made: recognize your true enemy.

A tantrist once practiced sorcery and killed many thieves. Gyaelwa Doendrub, the spiritual heir of Machig Labdroen, prayed that the sorcerer might cast a spell on his own self-cherishing. But he had no self-cherishing, and the sorcerer's magic was unable to harm him.

Drugpa Kuenleg once made ritual cakes while performing a ritual for his younger brother Choegyael [to dispel obstacles]. Instead of throwing the cakes outside, Kuenleg had an idea: why not throw the cakes at self-cherishing? So he threw them on his brother's lap!

Our Compassionate Teacher also cherished others [in his former lives]. Once he took rebirth as King Padmaka. He died of a plague and was reborn as the rohita fish, whose flesh cured many sentient beings struck down with plague. When he was reborn as a tortoise, he rescued five hundred merchants who had fallen into the sea; then he gave his body to eighty thousand flies. He gave away half his body when he was King Śrīsena. When he was Mahāratnachūḍa he had a jewel on the crown of his head, and he actually cut it out of his flesh to give it to another. As Prince Prakṛiti he gave his body to a hungry tigress who was just about to eat her own cub. As Chandraprabha he gave his head.

After telling these stories at length, Pabongka Rinpoche continued:

These were the deeds of our Compassionate Teacher. We only ever think of ourselves, yet although these things are difficult to do, we should prepare ourselves for them now by at least making prayers.

Cherishing others is the right thing to do. Since we depend on sentient beings for our daily food and drink, they are like a field that grows magnificent crops, or like wish-granting gems. Not only have all sentient beings shown us great kindness when they were our mothers, but also even when they were not our mothers, we stayed alive only through their kindness. For example, a single bag of barley flour is the result of immeasurable hard work. First, some sentient beings had to plough the field; others watered it; others threshed the grain; and so on. This building we are in is the result of the kindness of sentient beings: many animals and people had to carry earth, build the walls, do the carpentry, fetch water, and so forth. This shawl of mine is now ready to wear, but a large number of sheep had first to produce the wool; then some beings wove the cloth, and others sewed it.

It is through the kindness of all sentient beings that we temporarily have this optimum human rebirth; and ultimately through their kindness we shall develop bodhichitta, train in the [bodhisattva] tasks, and even gain buddhahood. We gain all these things through their kindness, because sentient beings are the objects of our compassion, of our development of bodhichitta, and of our generosity. They are the basis of our ethics and the object of our patience.

From *Engaging in the Deeds of Bodhisattvas:*

> The victorious ones and sentient beings
> Are both necessary to practice Buddhadharma.
> While you honor the victors,
> How could you not revere sentient beings as well?

In other words, you will achieve buddhahood half through the kindness of your guru and half through that of sentient beings. Thus Langri Tangpa said:

> By contemplating how I shall achieve
> Supreme benefit due to all sentient beings—
> More than I could attain from any gem—
> May I cherish them all the more.

That is, sentient beings will achieve all your ends for you, both temporarily and ultimately. Thus, they are like the wish-granting gem, and that is why it is only right to cherish others.

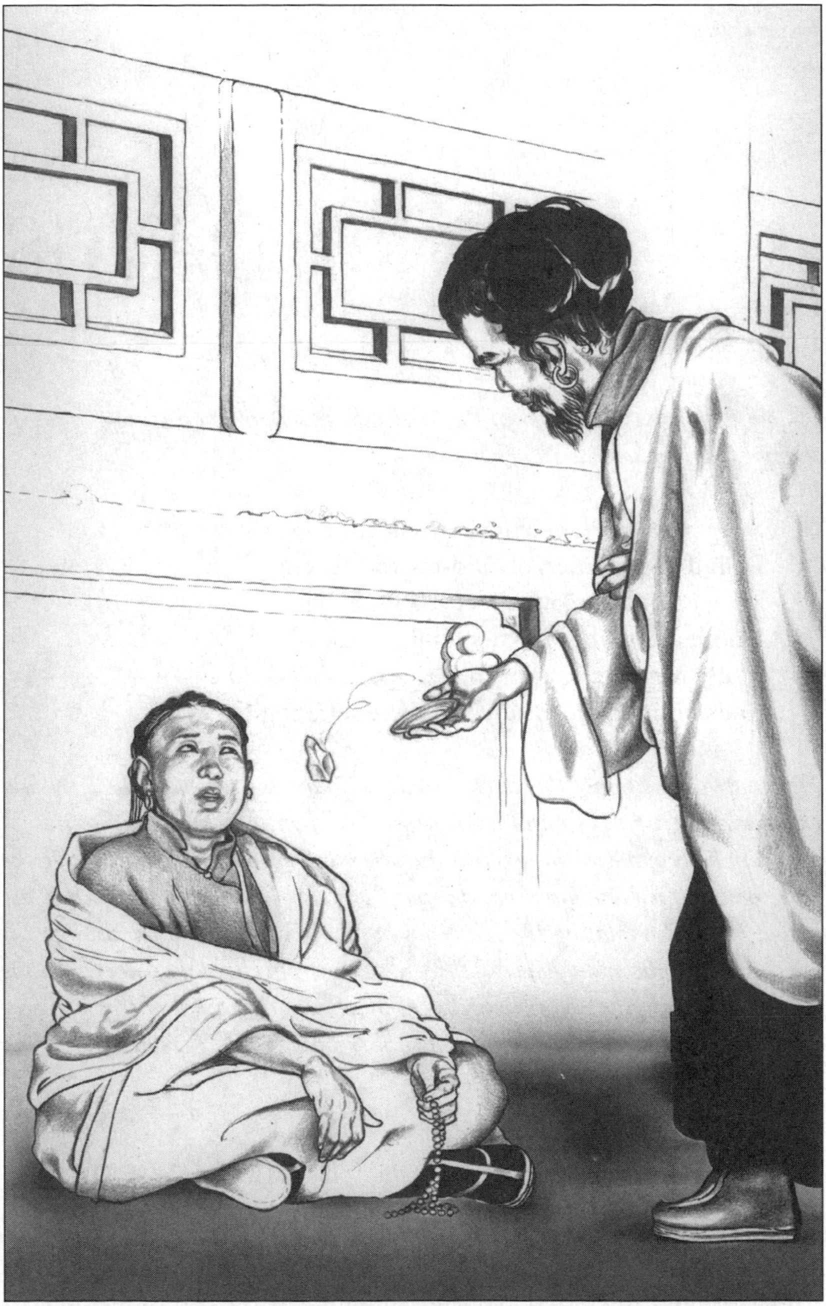

DRUGPA KUENLEG THROWS CAKES IN HIS BROTHER'S LAP

(SEE P. 543)

DAY 18

Kyabje Pabongka Rinpoche gave a brief talk to set our motivations, quoting that great Dharmarāja, Tsongkapa:

> Swept in the stream of four strong currents,
> Bound by the fetters of hard-to-stop actions,
> Trapped in the iron mesh of self-grasping,
> Smothered in the blackness of ignorance,
> They are endlessly born and reborn in the world
> And continuously tortured by three sufferings...

He restated the titles of the above headings, and then reviewed the sevenfold cause-and-effect type of mind training for bodhichitta. This second section of the main body of the teaching is training the mind for bodhichitta [through the interchange of self and others] and it has five parts: (1) how self and others are equal; (2) contemplating the many faults resulting from self-cherishing; (3) contemplating the many good qualities resulting from cherishing others; (4) the actual contemplation on the interchange of self and others; (5) with these serving as the basis, the way to meditate on giving and taking. He reviewed the first three of these, and continued:

THE ACTUAL CONTEMPLATION ON THE INTERCHANGE OF SELF AND OTHERS (351)

We have already covered the contemplation on the faults resulting [from self-cherishing] and the good qualities resulting [from cherishing others]. This same teaching is contained in four verses [in the *Guru Pūjā*]: "I see this chronic illness of self-cherishing..." After seeing what these resulting faults and good qualities are, you should interchange the self with others, that is, thoughts of self-cherishing should change places with thoughts of ignoring the needs of others. But this does not mean you should think that the self is now others, and that others have become the self. In the past you have ignored others because you cherished yourself; now these two attitudes should change places. Thus, this "interchange" is a term for the transference of your self-cherishing onto others. You train the mind by feeling: "I used to ignore others, but from now on I shall ignore my own needs; I have been cherishing myself, but from now on I shall cherish others." Through this sort of familiarization process you will be able to effect such an interchange. Think in terms of this analogy: when you stay a while on the far side of a mountain, you think of that side as being the "near side."

WITH THESE SERVING AS THE BASIS, THE WAY TO MEDITATE ON GIVING AND TAKING (352)

Taking is done to build up compassion; giving, to build up love. Our root text says:

> *Train alternately in giving and taking.*

This is to increase [the effect of] the preceding contemplations. In many written teachings on giving and taking, the former is treated first. However, in practice it is the latter that is carried out first. In fact, it may be appropriate to do only the taking and omit the giving. It would not be of benefit to give away happiness before having taken away suffering. So practice as follows in order to build up your compassion.

Think, "I shall remove all suffering from all sentient beings, my mothers," and generate compassion. Then visualize all their suffering being shed like hair shaved off with a razor, and taking the form of black rays that dissolve into the self-cherishing at your heart.

You could do this in more detail. Think that the suffering due to the heat of the hot hells dissolves, fire and all, into your heart on inhalation and that it dissolves into the demon of your self-cherishing. Contemplate that you take on the sufferings, sins, and obscurations, etc., from the beings in the cold hells, hungry ghosts, animals, demigods, humans, gods, and so forth, right up to the tenth-level bodhisattvas. Now visualize that they are without suffering and have been purified of sins and obscurations. Pray, "May these ripen on me." But when you do this taking, do not take from either your gurus or the buddhas.

There are many types of people with different degrees of ability. Some beginners find that they are not capable of meditating on giving and taking. For these types of people [the text says]:

Build up your taking by starting with yourself.

In other words, meditate in the morning that you are taking on the suffering you will experience that evening; then move on to taking the next day's suffering; then your suffering for the rest of the month; then the rest of the year; then the rest of your present rebirth; then your next rebirth; then all your future rebirths. Move on to your parents, your relatives and friends, strangers, enemies, and so on, until you include all sentient beings. Train yourself in each of the steps, and then move on to the next, taking on the suffering, sins, obscurations, etc. [of each particular level]. You ought to follow these steps because you will not be inclined at first to take suffering from such people as your enemies. So sometimes meditate starting with yourself, moving outward in this way; and sometimes work your way from the hells up to the tenth-level bodhisattvas. Sometimes start with the men and women in the upper part of your valley and work down; sometimes start with those at the bottom and work up. Take on even the sufferings of a dog being hit by a stone. Visualize that the things you take do not disappear or get put to one side—they are taken right into the center of your heart. It is good if this makes you fear for your very life!

You may not really be able to take these things when you do the meditation, but it will give you great impetus to complete your merit collection; and if your mind becomes more familiar [with the process], it is said that eventually you actually *can* take on these things, as illustrated by the story of Maitrīyogi.[74]

Giving in order to build up your love is as follows:

In order to benefit sentient beings,
My body shall become whatever they desire.

In addition, the *Vajra Victory Banner Sūtra* and the *Laying Out of Stalks Sūtra* speak of giving away your body and possessions. So, in accordance with these sūtras, think that you emanate replicas of your body, which become whatever these beings desire, and send them out to the universal environment and its beings. First, for the beings in the universal environment, these things emanate out in the form of soothing rains to the denizens of the hells, for example, thus easing their sufferings. You send out bodies that transform into the optimum human rebirths, which they obtain through your agency. You send out bodies that transform into beautiful locations and mansions for them to enjoy. You send out bodies that turn into delightful things for them to enjoy, an abundance of food and drink to satisfy them, and clothes for them to wear. The bodies even become spiritual guides to teach them Dharma, through which they come to the very point of reaching enlightenment. Then the bodies take the form of sunlight, clothes, and so on, for the beings in the cold hells; food and drink for the hungry ghosts; wisdom to differentiate phenomena properly for the animals; armor for the demigods; the five objects of the senses for the gods. But humans have the greatest desire, so send them bodies that become whatever they want. Send out your possessions, root virtues, and so on, in the same manner; and make profuse offerings of such bodies to your gurus, thinking that these will increase their deeds, good works, and lifespan. Although it is fine to give away your root virtues of the three times, or your bodies and possessions of both present and future, do not give away any of your bodies or possessions from the past. When practicing this giving you will principally develop love—as I have already pointed out—because you will be thinking about how these beings are so lacking in happiness. You ought to make this mind-training visualization your main practice.

In your everyday life,
Train yourself with verses
To stimulate remembrance.

In other words, to improve your remembrance of the practices of giving and taking, recite some verses on the subject at all times. There are a few such verses in the *Golden Rays Mind Training,* but if you do not know these it is sufficient to recite these lines [from the *Guru Pūjā*]:

Venerable, compassionate guru:
Bless me: may all the sufferings,

Sins, and obscurations
Of all beings, once my mothers,
Ripen on me now without exception;
May I give my happiness and virtue to others,
And may all beings have happiness.

There are even stories of past lamas who used to recite this verse on their rosary.

You must also employ some method to increase your bodhichitta while you go about your daily routine. You should refer to the *Avataṃsaka Sūtra* and the *Sūtra on the Jurisdiction of Utterly Pure Endeavor.* Those of you who wish to make bodhichitta your main practice should constantly consult and contemplate the *Avataṃsaka Sūtra,* just as the great Tsongkapa did, according to the biography of this embodiment of Mañjushrī.

The root text then says:

Mount these two on the energy winds.

In other words, when you have mastered this giving-and-taking visualization a little, combine giving with breathing out, and taking with breathing in. At first you may not be able to mount these on the energy winds, but with continued familiarity you will manage it. The mind and these energy winds go together, and so this device of interchanging self and others greatly facilitates the development of bodhichitta. It also has its direct counterpart in the tantric context, where the vajra recitation is discussed. When Kaedrub Rinpoche praised Tsongkapa with, "O protector! Even the very breath from your mouth became a balm for all beings..." it was to be understood this way.

There are other instructions at this point, but it would not do to give them to people who will not practice them constantly without interruption.

CONVERTING UNFORTUNATE CIRCUMSTANCES INTO A PATH TO ENLIGHTENMENT (353)

These degenerate times can be most beneficial. When a practitioner meets with many hindrances and is unable to rid himself of them, he ought to be able to turn such unfavorable circumstances into favorable ones. If he does not do so, he will give up Dharma in the face of both favorable and unfavorable conditions. Some Dharma practitioners become arrogant when they are promoted, and so on, and then give up the Dharma. Some acquire a little wealth and then give up the Dharma in order to maintain their income. Some despair when faced with unfavorable conditions and then give up the Dharma. When such things happen it is difficult to practice Dharma. Nothing could be worse than slavishly practicing a little Dharma and then giving it up. That is why it is necessary to be able to turn unfavorable circumstances into the path and into something that will not harm the Dharma. This has two headings: (1) converting [circumstances] through thought; (2) converting them through actions.

CONVERTING CIRCUMSTANCES THROUGH THOUGHT (354)

The first has two further subheadings: (1) converting them through analysis; (2) converting them by means of the view.

CONVERTING THEM THROUGH ANALYSIS (355)

It says in the *Guru Pūjā:*

> When the universe is completely filled with the fruits of sin...

Our root text on mind training similarly says:

> *When the universe is full of sin,*
> *Turn these unfortunate conditions*
> *Into the path to enlightenment!*

That is, at present, whenever the disagreeable occurs, like illness, enemies, spirits, etc., we put the blame on others. Because we do not understand that all sickness is the outcome of our karma, we claim that it is due to food, evil spirits, and so on. However, when we look into the thing or root to be blamed, we find that everything undesirable comes about through karma, just as I have taught in the cause-and-effect section of the small scope. And even that karma came about through our self-cherishing; so self-cherishing is fundamentally to blame.

When a thief robs you of your valuables, do not blame the thief. Blame instead your evil karma and the thing that made you develop such karma—your self-cherishing. Thus whenever you are faced with sickness, suffering, unfavorable circumstances, etc., you must think how these *help* you to achieve enlightenment. As was said:

> Sickness, sins, and obscurations are a broom.

That is, whenever you fall sick and so on, feel that this evil karma, these sins and obscurations—the results of which you would normally be obliged to experience in the lower realms—have ripened instead while you are still in this present rebirth. This should make you feel very happy. Further, you should be glad and feel, "I have already been practicing giving and taking by [visualizing myself] taking on the sins and obscurations of sentient beings. Now I have actually managed to achieve this." Pray that the rest of their suffering may ripen on you and imagine in your meditation that this successfully relieves sentient beings of all the suffering they would otherwise have experienced for themselves. Wholeheartedly think while you are doing this taking, "How welcome it would be if I could now actually take on the suffering of sentient beings!" If you practice in this way, even sickness will not be a hindrance for you. Your virtuous practices will increase, as in the story of the disciple of Kuenpang Draggyaen, who contracted leprosy and was cured at Kyimo Dzatreng.

It has been said:

> Unfavorable conditions are an incentive to virtue.

That is, you will strive to accumulate your [two] collections and purify your obscurations when you dwell on the fact that you ought to abandon sin if you do not want to have suffering. We are perfectly happy as long as no unfortunate circumstances crop up, and do not recollect Dharma. But when unfavorable circumstances such as insults, degradation, and sickness arise, we are sufficiently jolted out of our apathy to engage in virtue.

> Spirits and devils are apparitions of the victorious ones.
> Suffering is the abundance of suchness.

When you are harmed by spirit kings, spells, evil spirits, and so forth, consider that they are doing you a great kindness, since this harm will act as an incentive for you to practice Dharma, whereas formerly you were quite lost in worldly matters and had no recollection of Dharma. It is even possible for suffering to act as a contributory factor for your realization of suchness when you know how to direct your thinking. As sickness is the result of your self-cherishing, you should feel that the illness, evil spirits, and so on are being very kind to you because they help you to subdue your enemy, self-cherishing—something you could not manage to do on your own. When some unfavorable circumstance befalls us, we immediately curtail our practice. But do not do this. Just as you have to beware while traveling when you come to a narrow gorge, you should be even more careful not to give up your practice when you get sick or when conditions are bad. This is why they say it is so important to take seriously this giving and taking, and so on. As it says in *Engaging in the Deeds of Bodhisattvas:*

> The good quality of suffering is that
> It removes arrogance through sorrow.
> One develops compassion for the beings in saṃsāra,
> Avoids sin and rejoices in virtue.

When faced with suffering, you become unhappy, and this removes pride; you also feel compassion for others by reason of your own suffering, and will want to abandon its causes. When suffering does not come our way, we feel that things are going well and are happy. We should not be like this, for it is said:

> Do not be glad when happy, rejoice when sad:
> Happiness uses up accumulated merit,
> Unhappiness purifies sin and obscurations.

Holding a high position is tantamount to being under house arrest, as in the case of high lamas and officials who cannot go wherever they wish. Drubchog Lozang Namgyael said:

> They say that high rank is like being under house arrest! Low rank is a royal dwelling of the victorious ones!

That is, all the scholar-adepts of the past occupied low positions and reached the state of buddhahood. Even Drom Rinpoche prostrated himself before [his minor] Zhangtreng Kaber Chung. We ourselves should be like him and take a low position, just as water always finds the lowest level. That way, it will be easy for us to keep friendships.

> Do not be glad when praised.
> Be happy when censured:
> Criticism highlights your faults.

In other words, your pride increases enormously when others praise you. But this will let you down in this and in future lives. You cannot see your own faults, and although being criticized is not pleasant now, afterward you will examine your actions, and this will make you careful to modify your behavior.

It is said:

> Slander is a favor from the gods.

That is, slander is a divine boon. So whenever you get entangled in bad circumstances such as upsetting slanders, think of them in that way.

When you are happy, feel that it is the result of virtue, and this will make you very happy to meditate on bodhichitta and so on.

CONVERTING CIRCUMSTANCES THROUGH THE VIEW (356)

Our present text says:

> *Regard all deceptive appearances as being the four kāyas.*

However, such a statement follows the old style of explanation from the first dissemination of the teachings, and on examination we find it to be a little unsatisfactory. When we look into the nature of any suffering that has arisen, we are told it is in the first place dharmakāya [wisdom truth body] because it was not produced from anything, and so forth, but I feel this misses the main point. To be brief, our happiness and suffering may have arisen from either good or bad circumstances, but when we examine their nature, these things are found to have arisen out of a mere set of causes, conditions, and mutual interdependence. Thus, good or bad circumstances, suffering or happiness are all merely labels, and such things cannot be established by way of their nature, even though they undeniably appear to be real. When we look into the way "I" and "others" do not truly exist, this will readily prevent our being unhappy, attached, and so on.

If you do not understand the view, you must think, "When I die, all the happiness or sadness I may now have will only remain as memories, as if I had dreamt them. It is meaningless to be attached or to be hostile in this short life."

DAY 19

Kyabje Pabongka Rinpoche gave a short talk to set our motivations. For his text he took the Prayer of Maitreya, *in which it says:*

> I prostrate to bodhichitta,
> Which blocks the paths leading to lower realms,
> Which teaches well the paths leading to upper realms,
> Which guides the way to the deathless and the ageless.

Then he restated the above headings, and reviewed "The Actual Contemplation on the Interchange of Self and Others," and "With These Serving as the Basis, the Way to Meditate on Giving and Taking." He also went back over the first two parts of this seven-part teaching:

The self and others are the bases on which you build your thoughts of either cherishing or ignoring things, respectively. Now these two bases should change places. Then, as I have already told you, in order to develop further, you should visualize taking on suffering in order to build up your compassion; and you should visualize giving away your body, possessions, and root merits in order to build up your love. Also, you should practice combining such giving and taking with breathing in and out. Further, so that you do not forget to do this, you should jog your memory with some verses during routine activity.

There are a number of different ways discussed for combining these two instructions on training yourself for bodhichitta in your practice. These treatments have different headings and sequences, and even divide up the teaching in different ways, but here briefly is the way to do it under eleven topics of meditation.

Begin by contemplating these four:

1. equanimity;
2. recognition that all sentient beings were your mothers;
3. both the ordinary and the special ways of recollecting their kindness;
4. the wish to repay their kindness.

They are followed by:

5. the equality that exists between self and others;
6. contemplating the manifold faults resulting from self-cherishing;
7. contemplating the manifold good qualities resulting from cherishing others.

Now comes the actual contemplation on the interchange of self and others:

8. taking, involving a visualization that will build up your compassion;
9. giving, involving a visualization to build up the love that wishes others happiness—one of the two types of love.

And, at the end of all this, comes:

10. the development of altruism.

When you examine whether you have in fact managed to do any giving and taking, you will find that it has only been a visualization. You have not at present actually achieved anything substantial for the sake of other beings. Now feel, "I shall do something to actually bring this about," and, by shouldering this responsibility, you will develop altruism.

Then, for the above reasons comes:

11. developing the actual wish to achieve full enlightenment.

These eleven meditation topics constitute a synthesis of both the sevenfold cause-and-effect instruction and the interchange of self and others. This is how it should be practiced.

At the conclusion of the sequence, there is another step, an auspicious gesture to facilitate your complete success in the secret tantras and their maṇḍalas. This also resembles the prayers made by the Brahman Samandrarāja and the Universal Emperor Arenemi for their future rebirths [Day 8, pp. 253–54]. What you do is imagine that all sentient beings achieve every happiness; this will be a great asset in helping you complete your two collections. You do this by transforming yourself into the form of Śhākyamuni Buddha, then radiating out light rays that purify all sentient beings of suffering. Visualize that all sentient beings also transform into Śhākyamuni Buddha. Then meditate on joy. In this way, you both visualize the fruits of your development of bodhichitta and use this visualization as part of the path.

Our text says:

> *Three objects, three poisons, and three root virtues.*

The three objects are the things we find attractive, repulsive, or neutral. When we direct our attention to such objects, we develop attachment, hostility, and so forth. When other sentient beings direct their attention to any of these three types of objects, they likewise develop such delusions as attachment, hostility, and so forth. Their rebirth in the lower realms depends on all such delusions and these three objects. [Imagine yourself] taking on all these things, together with the causes for these beings' suffering in saṃsāra; think, "I have relieved all sentient beings of attachment, hostility, and benighted ignorance, so that now they have only root virtues." Do this for each [of the three poisons]. Regard their self-cherishing as being to blame for all their unfavorable circumstances, troubles, illnesses, etc. Cause the results of their karma to come to an end and take from them their sufferings. Understand that these things you have taken will ripen on you, and let this be a cause of delight.

By doing this, someone familiar with mind training will never be unhappy, because all unfavorable circumstances will seem to them to be helpful. That is why mind training is termed "the well of the citadel of happiness." It makes you tolerant of even trivial unfavorable circumstances. For example, when a trader takes to the road he has to take things philosophically. If it rains, at least he will not be robbed. If he is snowed in, at least his pack animals will not go lame. *Engaging in the Deeds of Bodhisattvas* says:

If something can be put right,
Why be unhappy?
If a thing cannot be put right,
What good is being unhappy?

If you are plagued by suffering, it is quite useless to be unhappy: you should turn this into something helpful. Moreover, you can see for yourselves that there are people who have gained insight into impermanence on their own after nearly dying from an illness or whatever, despite their never having studied such things as the lamrim.

Thus, when beset by bad circumstances, think, "Whatever happens to me is alright. May the things to which all sentient beings fall victim descend on me." Nothing could be more beneficial than thinking in this way.

Kyabje Pabongka Rinpoche then gave us another review of the heading "Converting Unfavorable Conditions into the Path to Enlightenment."

CONVERTING SUCH CONDITIONS THROUGH ACTION (357)

There are four types of action involved here: amassing the [two] collections, purifying obscurations, giving ritual cakes to the elementals, and invoking the good works of the Dharma protectors.

If, when you are thoroughly familiar with this mind training, you chance to fall ill, you should invoke the good works of Dharma protectors as follows: "My practice of giving and taking has gained new meaning because the suffering of all sentient beings is now ripening on me. May my sickness be even worse than it is already!" When you offer ritual cakes to the elementals, think thus: "You have been most kind to me for you have harmed me. This has proved advantageous for my practice. I have purified my sins and obscurations and have built up my collections even further. Now do me even more harm than ever before!" Those not sufficiently brave, who are frightened by such a thought, will find themselves incapable of doing this. They should do the more usual things of invoking the aid of elementals so as *not* to get sick, and so on.

If your home were flooded, you would look for the root of the problem and put a stop to it. When you are subjected to suffering, you should likewise abandon sin—the cause of suffering—and build up your two collections—the cause of happiness. If you expiate your sins by reciting the

General Confession [see p. 713] after finishing a hundredfold offering ceremony, you will fulfill all four types of action; it is also appropriate to make mind training prayers at the end of this ceremony.

The text says:

> *Immediately apply your practice to whatever you encounter.*

In other words, you must resort to mind training as soon as some favorable or unfavorable circumstance occurs, so as to convert it to the path immediately.

TEACHING A PRACTICE TO BE APPLIED TO YOUR WHOLE LIFE (358)

First, there are five powers: (1) the power of the white seed; (2) the power of familiarity; (3) the power of determination; (4) the power of repudiation; (5) the power of prayer.

The *power of determination* is the most important of these powers. As soon as you wake up in the morning, you must forcefully make this resolution: "I shall not let my life become meaningless in general, and I must especially not let this happen this year and, even more, not today. I shall do something meaningful—I shall subdue my self-cherishing, my true enemy!" Your determination initiates all your actions, making them virtuous or nonvirtuous, Mahāyāna or Hīnayāna. When you are determined to kill a louse or to prepare your lunch, then that is what you will in fact do. [Usually,] by the time we have got up each morning and put on our belt, we have determined to make the things of this life—things like food, fashion, and fame—the means for our happiness. Instead, as you knot up your belt in the morning, remind yourself to make the former resolution and make it from the very depths of your heart.

The *power of the white seed* means building up your two collections and purifying your obscurations by means of the preliminary rites and so forth. These are done to increase your bodhichitta. The virtue we perform normally is misdirected to this life, and it is vital not to let this happen.

The *power of familiarity* means practicing all the time, no matter what we may be doing—walking, sleeping, or sitting—by using methods that increase both types of bodhichitta. The thoughts of mahātma bodhisattvas are beyond us, as are their deeds, such as sacrificing one's head, arms, and legs. Yet these are the result of familiarity. We may at first not know how to do metalwork or carpentry, but we can come to understand these things, and they will no longer prove difficult for us. Similarly, sacrificing our lives would be easier even than giving away a dish of greens when we have gained some familiarity with [the thought of] giving our lives. It is said, "Nothing does not become easier through familiarity." Some great beings of the past could do a complete retrospection meditation on the lamrim while mounting a horse: they did this as they put one foot in the stirrup and the other over the saddle, before it too went into the stirrup. This is also a result of familiarity. Meditation and familiarity are synonymous. How could it be easy for us to even drink tea out of a full bowl were we not already familiar with doing this?

The *power of repudiation* is as follows. At present, self-cherishing is the only thing you develop, and you should stop doing this. You must repudiate self-cherishing: striking out at it whenever it shows its face, just as you would hit a thieving dog.

The *power of prayer* is dedicating, just before you go to sleep, the root virtues you have acquired that day so that they serve to increase your two types of bodhichitta.

These five powers apply to this life. There are also five powers at death; they are a mind-training transference practice [to direct your mind to its new rebirth].

The Mahāyāna instruction on transference
Concerns the five powers. Cherish this activity!

The mind-training transference technique doesn't employ [the mantras] *hik* and *phaṭ*[75] but it is more profound than any other transference technique.

Your *determination* here is the resolve not to become separated from bodhichitta while in the death state, the intermediate state, and so on.

The *power of the white seed* is this: suppose you are most attached to your possessions. Destroy your attachment to them by giving them all away as an offering, etc. Give them as a votive offering to karmically potent recipients; or bequeath all your goods and chattels to be just given away. Nothing, not even another person creating root merits on your behalf, could be more helpful after your death. The following may happen if you do not.

A monk was attached to his begging bowl and was reborn as a snake.

The Buddha drove him into the forest. This angered the snake, and the fires of his anger destroyed both the forest and himself. He was then reborn in hell, and his three bodies [that is, the corpse of the monk, the snake corpse, and the body of the hell being] burned simultaneously.

A person was obsessed with some gold hidden under the ground. He, too, was reborn as a snake, and was forced to offer the gold to the Buddha.

These stories demonstrate what happens if you do not assign away your possessions. But you can also be attached to your own body and be reborn as a worm living inside it, for example. Once a woman's corpse lay on the ocean shore. A worm that looked like a snake lived in the corpse and would slither constantly in and out of the mouth, nose, eyes, ears, and so on. The creature was said to be the rebirth of a girl who had been attached to her own body and was always looking at herself in the mirror. So, at death, build on your [two] collections and make strong prayers to increase your bodhichitta. It is vital foremost to not be attached to our own bodies.

A lowly monk was extremely attached to some money. He died and became a frog that would spend its time clutching this money with its paws.

There are some people who, due to powerful attachment, cannot die when they should. An old monk from Amdo was attached to fat [in his food and tea] and so was having a hard time dying. Gungtang Jampaelyang used his skillful means and said, "Make a wish to go to Tuṣhita pure land. The fat there will be even better than the fat we get during the holy festivals in the seventh month of each year." The monk immediately breathed his last. There is some risk that this could also happen to us. It is vital that we abandon such things as attachment.

The *power of repudiation* is to confess and then retake broken vows at death. These must be done forcefully. If you practice the secret tantras, you should restore your broken tantric and bodhisattva vows by either performing a self-initiation or by receiving the initiation again. Even if you do not, at least purify and retake the vows as best you can. While it is important to do this all the time, it is especially important to do it when you die. If you do not, its shadow will hang over you: you may not be able to go to places like the pure lands, etc., despite being otherwise ready for such a journey.

The *power of prayer* is not praying to go to pure lands, etc. Instead, you make prayers that will aid in the development of bodhichitta and pray that the suffering, sins, and obscurations of all sentient beings may ripen on you.

The *power of familiarity* is as follows. Having always familiarized yourself with bodhichitta, you leave that rebirth while in meditation on it by virtue of your mental familiarity. You could do nothing better.

You should adopt the position of lying on your right side in the lion-like sleeping posture while transferring your mind to its new rebirth. This is how our Compassionate Teacher entered nirvāṇa, and doing even just this makes a big difference in helping you to reach the pure lands.

In general, people should perform the transference by taking refuge according to the small scope. However, someone practicing the great scope must do the transference and the like while in meditation on bodhichitta. You may think this latter method is no way to reach the pure lands, but this is definitely not the case. When Chaekawa was dying he told his attendant to quickly make offerings. "I have prayed to go to the Hell Without Respite for the sake of all sentient beings," he said, "but this is not going to happen: I am having visions of the pure lands!" There is also a similar story about Geshe Potowa. A mother and her child were both swept away by a river. They developed kind thoughts toward each other and both were born in Tuṣhita. Once, the leather coracle that served as the ferry at Jasa in the south was overloaded and about to sink. A messenger developed thoughts of kindness and so jumped into the river. A rainbow appeared until he died. Bodhichitta is a superior form of kindheartedness; thus, if you activate even a contrived form of bodhichitta, there can be no doubt that you will be born in a favorable state.

We attach more importance to the mind-transference practices that employ the mantras *hik* and *phaṭ* than to bodhichitta. We place far too much importance on receiving the signs of accomplishment of such practices. If you practice saying *hik* many times without doing any visualization whatsoever, the signs of having gained the ability to transfer the mind may manifest themselves [as a swelling] on the crown of your head, but this is merely the action of the energy winds and not anything to be marveled at. This mind-training form of directing rebirth does not involve *hik* or *phaṭ,* yet it is the most profound of all mind-transference practices. After practicing the other forms of mind transference, it is still uncertain whether you have shut the door on rebirth in the lower realms. If you direct your rebirth through these five powers, you can be quite certain of not being reborn in any of the unfortunate states.

THE CRITERIA OF HAVING TRAINED THE MIND (359)

All Dharma comes within one thought.

The Bhagavān gave a vast number of individual teachings, all of which boil down to being antidotes to self-cherishing. The fine dividing line between what is Dharma and what is not is said to be whether a thing is an antidote to delusion. Thus the best sign of accomplishment is how much you have reduced your delusions. If you have not managed to do this, other signs of accomplishment do not mean a thing—even vultures and so on can fly in the air, even mice can burrow underground, and even fish can glide through water. They say you should test whether a thing is Dharma by using this mind training as your set of scales. A reduction in self-cherishing is evidence of having practiced Dharma.

Uphold the chief of the two witnesses.

There are two witnesses: yourself and others. Your practice may be far from perfect, but you can give the impression that it is. Others may take you at face value and respect your seemingly pure ethics. There are said to be four states of ripeness for mangoes. These have to do with the ripeness or lack of it on the inside and outside of the fruit. You could be like the mango that is ripe externally but green inside. In this case, your movements would be as studied as a cunning cat stalking its prey, and you would be thought a good person by people who know no other Dharma. Do not act like this! Also, do not be ripe inside and green outside. If you display outward discipline, others will not be offended. When you are inwardly disciplined, your mindstream is enriched by your practice. So both outside and inside must be sound. It is said that: "Bodhisattvas do not abandon ill repute." In other words, although you should take care to abandon those actions that could serve as the basis of a poor reputation, the most important thing is to retain your self-respect.

Always cultivate mental happiness.

If you become rich, do not make yourself mentally unhappy with preconceptions of increasing or safeguarding your wealth. If you are not rich, give up worrying about your livelihood. Think about the disadvantages of being wealthy. Be happy and content: know how to convert both favorable and unfavorable conditions into the path.

Do not let the eight worldly concerns rear their [ugly] heads when you are praised or condemned; check over the reasons for your being happy or sad, and then, they say, you will not have mental unhappiness.

The criterion for having trained your mind is as follows:

You have mastered it if you are capable while distracted.

The less experienced rider is not thrown by his horse if he keeps his mind on the job, but when his mind wanders he will be thrown. The experienced horseman is never thrown, even while distracted. Someone who has not mastered the mind training is like the inexperienced rider. If someone insults him, badmouths him, and so on, when he is off his guard, he will at first get angry, and only after that will he recollect himself and pacify his anger. A person with a trained mind will not get angry when others strike or insult him even when his mind is distracted. This is the criterion of having trained the mind.

The criterion for having been trained is when you have reversed it.

In other words, a criterion for having trained your mind in the meditations on death and impermanence or on renunciation is the fact that you stop being preoccupied with the trivia of this life or aspiring to the affluence of saṃsāra. Similarly, you have mastered mind training if you have reversed your self-cherishing.

You will have the five great signs of mastery.

With familiarity you will receive five signs with this type of mind training: you will be a *great ascetic* because you are able to be patient. Your mind will not tend to delusion, no matter what suffering, harm, and so on, may befall you. You will be a *great personage* because you cherish others more than yourself. You will be a *great practitioner of virtue* because, in all your activities, you never depart from the practices of the ten types of Dharmic behavior. You will be a *great upholder of the vinaya* because you remain calm, composed, and untarnished by the least sin or nonvirtue. You will be a *great yogi* because you practice the real Mahāyāna path.

THE EIGHTEEN COMMITMENTS OF THE MIND-TRAINING PRACTICE (360)

Always keep to three general points.

The first of these is never to transgress the precepts of mind training. Do not use mind training as a pretext for ignoring the more basic vows, such as those in the vinaya.

The second is not to let your mind training become a mere travesty. Do not use mind training as a pretext for not refraining from upsetting creatures and humans by cutting down sacred trees, and so on, because you pretend to have no more self-cherishing. You must not let your behavior be a travesty.

The third is not to let your mind training become partial. Do not be patient with friends and impatient with enemies, or tolerant of humans while intolerant of creatures, and so forth.

Those are the three general precepts.

Change your aspirations, but preserve your old manner.

Do not leave the old, obstinate thoughts you have in your mindstream the way they are: employ some remedy to improve them a good deal. The best type of person sees improvement in a day; the medium in a month; and the most inferior in a year. You must see which of these you can manage. If even this much is beyond you, then, even though you have already received ordination and since become old, you will still have preserved the thoughts you had before you were ordained. Do not be like the rocks behind your house [that never change from year to year]. Change your aspirations! For anything to be transformed, they must be changed into bodhichitta, renunciation, [realization of] impermanence, and so on. But do not modify your external behavior at all. There are those who do not have even two *annas'* worth of good qualities developed internally, yet pretend to be practicing and externally wear a "holier-than-thou," far-away look in their eyes, and so on. You should only develop insights and improve your mind: do not make any outward display. Nor should anyone know you have made great progress; you should be like those high sons of the victorious ones, Śhāntideva or Ārya Chūḍapanthaka, who abandoned [delusion] and developed realization. Even glorious Chandrakīrti only seemed to be an unexceptional pandit, and no one paid him much attention. Yet inwardly he had achieved siddhis and was able to milk a drawing of a cow. Such beings did not make themselves conspicuous. And the past lamas of the Kadampa tradition also did not court fame by practicing in public, revealing their signs of accomplishment, and so on. Follow their example! You meet with many hindrances when you advertise yourself—it is like boasting to others about your wish-granting gem. We are no different from worldly beings, and we slip back into the things of this life. Yet if we ever do even one Dharma practice, we make sure everyone knows about it, as if we had hoisted a flag on a mountaintop. Don't be like this. In this tradition of Atiśha and the Kadampas, you must hide your good qualities like a butterlamp concealed inside a pot.

Do not mention others' withered limbs.

That is, do not speak about others' defects.

Do not think of others at all.

That is, you should analyze your own faults and not look into the faults of others at all. Otherwise you will only look for faults in your fellow practitioners, the members of your monastic college, or the monks in your house at college, etc.; you will then naturally find fault even in buddhas. Do not attribute faults to others, for if you do, you will only ignore people, belittle them, and so on all the more.

Purify the greatest delusion first.

Purify whichever delusion in your mindstream is the largest. If your attachment is the largest, purify it by the application of antidotes such as meditation on the ugly aspects [of the body].

Abandon all hopes of a result.

When you do something virtuous, expect neither reward nor some favorable ripening [of karma].

Abandon food with poison in it.

Do not cultivate any "food" of virtue that is mixed with the poison of self-cherishing.

[The remaining verses will be covered without directly quoting the root text.]

Should you develop a delusion, apply its antidote right away and do not allow it to persist—*treat it unfairly.*

The text talks about the four Dharmas to be performed by practitioners of virtue, for example, *not repaying an evil action with an evil action.* You are not a practitioner of virtue if you do not carry out these four, for you promised before your abbot and ordination master to practice them.[76] If someone says to you, "You mangy old dog!" do not retaliate with "You thief!" If someone hits you once, do not hit him twice in return.

Do not bide your time waiting to avenge some wrong, as if you had been *waiting in ambush,* where the road runs through a gorge, to harm that person in return. Foolish worldly minded people think it is best to smile though secretly harboring resentment. This merely shows that Dharma and worldly actions are opposites.

If you know of some gross defects in another person, do not belittle them in front of many others or *attack their weak spot.* Do not bring up any of their faults. In the same way, do not recite wrathful mantras in order to destroy creatures, and so forth.

When you do something wrong, do not deceitfully blame someone else. Also, do not be clever and blame others when things go wrong: *do not put the load of a dzo on an ox.*

The mind is trained in order to subdue self-cherishing. But if your meditations are done to prevent harm by nonhuman creatures or to gain fame, gifts, and so on, this will only cause an increase in your self-cherishing—the *spell has gone awry.* Do not do this.

Do not be in a hurry to get possession of something that is common property, or try to get the best for yourself by being there first—that is, *do not run a race.*

Do not let the god become a devil means do not let your mind training act no longer as an antidote to self-cherishing but bolster it instead.

Do not think, "If only my enemy would die or suffer ruin—then I would be happy!" This would be *seeking happiness in unhappiness.*

These make the eighteen commitments.

THE TWENTY-TWO PIECES OF ADVICE (361)

All yogas are practiced through the one.

That is, the practitioner need not perform a variety of virtuous practices, because they are all included within thoughts of interchanging self and others. When you eat, think "I have already given my body to sentient beings. Thus, in order to work for their sakes, I shall keep it nourished." And do the same thing with all your daily routine. Do everything in this way—reciting knowledge mantras, petitioning protector deities, and the like.

If the medicine is not proving beneficial, the doctor may both bleed the patient and perform a moxibustion. The thought of interchanging self and others will likewise serve in hundreds of cases, for it is an antidote to all illness and delusion.

Set your motivation before all virtuous actions and follow them with a dedication [of the merit]. It is also most important to determine every morning what you will and will not be doing.

You must not give up your mind-training practice, come what may, either happiness or sorrow. Some people drop the Dharma when made happy by promotion or acquisition of wealth. Some give it up when they suffer from their enemies. But you must not give up your practice of mind training in either event.

Safeguard the commitments of your mind-training practice, and those of your other practices in general, as you would value your very life.

There are three ascetic practices that you should know and devote yourself to. They are: the asceticism of identifying delusions, that of applying antidotes, and that of breaking the continuity of the delusions.

Pray to be able to assemble the three main causes for practicing Dharma: meeting with the right guru; being mentally fit [to practice]; and having all the necessary conditions, such as food and clothing.

Do the three things that should not degenerate: holding the guru in awe and respect, rejoicing in mind training, and keeping these pieces of advice through remembrance and vigilance.

Do not leave, your body, speech, and mind idle. Occupy them with virtue. The virtues of the body are not merely prostrating yourself or performing circumambulations, and so on—you should even turn your posture into something virtuous by straightening your spine.

Do not divide up the objects of your mind training into "friends" and "enemies," or into sentient beings and buddhas. You must master this practice in the very depths of your heart to include all possible objects, as Geshe Chaekawa did. In order to completely master it, emphasize meditating on enemies with whom you find it difficult to be patient, and so on; also reserve a special place for objects that could prove [karmically] dangerous for you, such as your guru, parents, and roommates.

Continue to meditate, regardless of whether you have all the necessary conditions such as food and clothes. Do not let this apply to you:

> Looking like a practitioner when your belly's full and the sun's shining,
> And an ordinary type as soon as things go wrong.

From today meditate on bodhichitta, which is hard to develop but most beneficial. You must do this in order to work for your own and others' sakes and not for the things of this life. You should work mainly toward your next life rather than this one; toward Dharma rather than worldly things; and on your meditations on mind training rather than on the other Dharmas taught and practiced.

The text continues, "*Don't misunderstand.*" There are six ways of misunderstanding. (1) *Mistaken patience:* this is being tolerant of problems met while doing something worldly but having no courage to face the difficulties encountered in Dharma practice. (2) *Mistaken taste:* you have to taste the Dharma through study, contemplation, meditation, etc. When you have no conception of Dharma but can understand the concepts of worldly conversation, business, military affairs, etc., and can analyze things, you have tasted the worldly. This is tasting the wrong thing. (3) *Mistaken compassion:* this is not meditating on compassion for those who sin yet having compassion for those who undergo difficulties for the sake of Dharma. (4) *Mistaken aspiration:* not wishing to practice the pure Dharma but aspiring to worldly happiness, power, and wealth. (5) *Mistaken yearnings:* this is encouraging people who trust in you not to practice Dharma, which would benefit their future lives, but encouraging them instead to study business, the law, etc., which will prove very harmful for their future lives. (6) *Mistaken rejoicing:* this is not rejoicing in your own or others' virtue or in others' happiness. Not to do this is nonvirtuous. Also, mistaken rejoicing is to rejoice when your enemies suffer. An illustration:

once a monk rejoiced when his rival broke a major vow. Geshe Potowa heard of this and said, "The one who did the rejoicing committed a greater sin than the one who broke the vow."

When we do things like study under a lama, we may develop a superficial renunciation and for a few days frantically practice virtue, practicing this, that, and whatever. After a while, we get fed up and give virtue a wide berth. So do not be intermittent in your practice. As Geshe Karag Gomchung said:

> Look far ahead.
> Be farsighted.
> Keep in tune.

In other words, when you practice virtue, you should always maintain the right pitch, neither too intense, nor too relaxed, so as to last. From the yoga of getting up each morning onward, you should practice the right amount. Later, increase this, and you will cover a wide range. This is like the story of the louse and the flea.[77]

The text says,

> Train with determination.

One interpretation of this is: devote your mind fully to this training.

When a doctor lets blood, he cuts deep, through blood vessels and skin together. In the same way, your mind training should wear down your mindstream as a rock will wear down a bone.

Train yourself thoroughly through analytic meditation on mind training by means of both conceptualization and analysis.

Apply the antidote to whichever delusion you deem greatest.

Working for the sake of sentient beings is only right, and something you have already promised to do. So do not make a big deal of it to anyone.

Suppose someone belittles you in front of others. Do not get angry and so on; that is, do not be spiteful.

Do not be as changeable as spring weather, changing from happiness to sadness for the slightest reason.

Do not offer your help in the hope of receiving praise and so forth.

This completes the advice.

If you follow it, you will be able to convert unfavorable circumstances into the path to enlightenment, despite the fact that the five degenerations—the degeneration of lifespan and so forth—are commonplace.

The lineage of this instruction comes from Suvarṇadvīpa. It delighted Chaekawa, who said he could now die with no regrets.

Except for the part covering the view, this completes the teaching. In many commentaries on this text, the view is dealt with according to the earlier dissemination of the teachings, and so is not made clear. The *Rays of the Sun Mind Training* follows the Madhyamaka Prāsaṅgika system when it discusses the view, and your contemplations must be along Prāsaṅgika lines. Suvarṇadvīpa originally followed the Chittamātrin version of the view but later changed to the Madhyamaka system.

When giving an informal discourse on lamrim, one does not, as with earlier material, follow the tradition of repeating three or four times the material below this section on the development of bodhichitta.

DAY 20

Kyabje Pabongka Rinpoche spoke a little in order to set our motivations. He quoted these lines from the Summary of Precious Good Qualities:

> The path of all victorious ones past, yet to come, and present,
> Is that of the perfections and no other.

That is, all the buddhas of the three times have followed in each others' footsteps, never deviating from the tasks of the six perfections. There is no other path in either sūtra or tantra, and texts like ours also teach this path.

Then Rinpoche listed the headings we had above. And, beginning at the heading "Teaching a Practice to Be Applied to Your Whole Life," he reviewed the material on how to convert unfavorable circumstances into the path to enlightenment.

This completes the discussion on the way to develop the wish for complete enlightenment.

DEVELOPING BODHICHITTA THROUGH THE RITUAL OF TAKING VOWS (362)

I shall teach this section later, so we shall leave it for the time being.

If you have no bodhichitta, no matter what meditations you do in the hope of achieving buddhahood—be they on mahāmudrā or dzogchen, the middle way, or the generation and completion stages, etc.—they will not get you one bit closer to buddhahood. And as if this were not enough, you will not even enter the gateway to the Mahāyāna. Thus everybody must concentrate on the practice of bodhichitta. The buddhas have perceived things for many eons with the primal wisdom of their omniscience, but they have not seen any better method or any other gateway to the path.

THE ACTIVITIES TO TRAIN IN AFTER DEVELOPING BODHICHITTA (363)

After having developed bodhichitta you must train in certain activities. It is not sufficient merely to develop bodhichitta. Just as someone going to India will not get there unless they physically begin the journey, you also have to train in the [bodhisattva] deeds. You should gather both the merit and the primal wisdom types of collection in conjunction with each other in order to achieve both the physical and wisdom truth bodies of a victorious one; your training therefore has to be a balance of both method and wisdom. The deeds of the children of the victors come down to two things: method and wisdom. The first five perfections come under method. The last perfection, which includes special insight, comes under wisdom.

AFTER DEVELOPING BODHICHITTA, THE WAY TO TRAIN IN THE DEEDS OF THE CHILDREN OF THE VICTORIOUS ONES (364)

I will discuss this under two headings: (1) how to train in the six perfections in order to ripen your own mindstream; (2) how to train in the four ways of gathering disciples in order to ripen the mindstreams of others.

HOW TO TRAIN IN THE SIX PERFECTIONS IN ORDER TO RIPEN YOUR OWN MINDSTREAM (365)

This has three subheadings: (1) the general way to train in the deeds of the children of the victors; (2) in particular, the way to train in the last two perfections; (3) the way to train in the Vajrayāna.

THE GENERAL WAY TO TRAIN IN THE DEEDS OF THE CHILDREN OF THE VICTORS (366)

There are six headings: (1) generosity; (2) ethics; (3) patience; (4) perseverance; (5) [dhyāna] concentration; (6) wisdom.

GENEROSITY (367)

Generosity is, by nature, the thought wishing to give away one's body, possessions, and root virtues. It is classified into three types.

BEING GENEROUS WITH MATERIAL THINGS (368)

This type of generosity ranges from giving a spoonful of barley flour, to sacrificing one's life and body. If you cannot give something away, think how you have been born in the past as Brahmā, Indra, the universal monarch, and so on. At those times you were very wealthy, but because you failed to practice generosity, you extracted no essence from those rebirths, and this put you in your present situation. Also you must practice giving without expecting anything in return, or any [karmic] ripening effects. If your generosity is motivated by bodhichitta, then your giving a morsel of food or a little clean barley flour to beggars, the poor, and so on—or even to worms and ants—would be a [true] practice of generosity, and a deed of a child of the victorious ones. You should also satisfy the wants of the recipient, so that the karmic fruits will not be insignificant.

When we make a huge offering as a sign of respect to the Three Jewels, we feel we have done a great deal, which makes us puff up with pride. This is not a pure form of generosity! However, it is not right to feel regret after giving away material things, thinking, "I gave too much," or "I gave it to the wrong person." When you give something away, set your motivation both before and afterward: the thing is being done for the sake of all sentient beings. Also make strong prayers. No matter whether the act of generosity is large or small, do not hope for benefit in return through offerings or respect, and so on.

BEING GENEROUS WITH THE DHARMA (369)

This form of generosity could even be teaching a single four-line verse of Dharma to someone who wishes to listen, if done with that person's benefit in mind. Even tutoring our pupils in their textbooks is being generous with the Dharma. To do this you need not be called a lama and give discourses from the heights of a meditation throne. Generosity with the Dharma is better than the other forms of generosity. Also, your memorization, recitation, or study of texts will become an act of generosity with the

Dharma if you imagine yourself to be surrounded by gods who uphold virtue and by all sentient beings, who are listening in. What more need I say about this, except that when earthworms, etc., hear the words of Dharma, it puts [virtuous] imprints in their mindstreams? Think in this way, even when just performing a reading in the home of your benefactor.

You have to be particularly careful when you go into the village to perform a ritual. Our Compassionate Teacher taught the secret tantras as a means of gaining enlightenment in one rebirth. If you exchange this for the gifts received for performing these rituals, you have sold the Dharma for material goods. This is like dragging a king off his throne and forcing him to sweep the floor. So do these rituals with the right motive.

Being generous with the Dharma does not just mean teaching it formally. It could also mean using your conversation and so forth as a direct or indirect means of leading others to the Dharma. Those who are ordained should practice generosity mainly by giving Dharma; but they ought also to be generous with material goods if this is not too much trouble. However, the Kadampa Geshe Sharawa once said to a group of the ordained:

> I am not going to speak about the benefits of giving things away,
> for I have already told you the drawbacks of grasping.

THE GENEROSITY OF GIVING OTHERS FEARLESSNESS (370)

This could be, for example, liberating prisoners from jail or rescuing the drowning. Even saving creatures such as earthworms from heat in summer or cold in winter is a form of this type of generosity. You do not have to go far to practice this "generosity of bestowing fearlessness"—you can do it with the lice on your body! Saving insects from drowning, for example, is very easy to do. It only involves moving one of your hands. The visualization of giving found in the section dealing with the practice of mind training is a practice of generosity, too.

Engaging in the Deeds of Bodhisattvas tells us fundamentally what "the perfection of generosity" is:

> If the perfection of generosity
> Were ridding all beings of poverty,
> How would the previous protectors, the buddhas, have perfected it,
> Since even now the poor exist?

In other words, generosity cannot be merely ridding sentient beings of poverty; nor can it be freedom from miserliness, since śhrāvakas, pratyekabuddhas, and arhats have this. *Engaging in the Deeds of Bodhisattvas* says:

> They say the perfection of generosity
> Is the state of mind that gives to all beings
> All your possessions and all your karmic fruits.
> Thus generosity must be mental.

This says that the perfection of generosity is a complete familiarity with the thought of giving your body, possessions, root merits, and all their [karmic] results to others; and it means giving these things from the very depths of your heart without any miserliness, while thinking about the various benefits [of giving sincerely] and the drawbacks of not doing so.

Thus the important point being made here is that you should increase your thoughts of giving. If a beggar asks you for your three monk's robes, say, and you immediately think, "Should I risk giving them away?" this is an outcome of familiarity with being generous. You will eventually be able to sacrifice even your body after training yourself in a lower level of generosity. Until you reach such a level of familiarity, increase your thoughts of giving.

This is how you increase such thoughts. Contemplate how all things are impermanent. When you die, you will not take a single item of your property with you. Those things you leave behind will then fall into decay, etc. Bequeath them to others from the very depths of your heart; then there will be less chance of your breaking the minor vows concerned with ownership. This would be practicing generosity.

But do not take thinking alone to be sufficient; you must also *actually* give things away as much as possible. You should be as generous as possible to beggars, but it is not right to give things acquired through wrong livelihood, [even] when you have nothing else to give.

In general, the first three perfections should be the main practice of lay people. It has been said:

> The three Dharmas of generosity and so forth are for the majority:
> The Tathāgata recommends them to lay people.

It may not be right to give your body, for example. Do not give your body while you are still at the stage of undergoing the process of familiarization and merely increasing your thoughts of giving. Only later is it right to give your body, when, as mentioned in *Engaging in the Deeds of Bodhisattvas,* it has become as easy for you as is giving away a dish of vegetables.

There are things that should not be given away. Do not practice generosity with certain exceptional things disallowed on account of the recipient, the time, the thing being given, etc. If the giver is ordained, he should not give away his three types of robes, etc. Nor should the ordained be offered food in the afternoon. You should not give unclean food, such as garlic or onions, to people like Brahmans, who are bound by [caste] rules of cleanliness. You should not give away anything putrefying, or give books to people who merely want to create controversy, or give poison or weapons to suicidal people. You should not teach the secret tantras to an unfit vessel or shield a criminal from the law if you can be sure he will harm either sentient beings or the teachings. And so on.

It is a wrong view to think "an act of generosity is without results." It is also of little benefit to support one sentient being and ignore the needs of many others. Train yourself to be unsullied by the above things, as well as by the following: having wrong views that lead you, for example, to sacrifice cattle, belittle others, act competitively, have an inflated opinion of yourself, wish for fame, feel regret, be defeatist, or act in a partisan manner.

Śhāntideva's *Compendium of Instruction* speaks of three things: giving, protecting, and keeping pure. In other words, you increase your thoughts of giving your body; but until the time is ripe, you should *protect* your body from harmful conditions and *keep* the body *pure* by not using it nonvirtuously. The text also discusses a fourth: you should accomplish causes with this present body so that your next rebirth will have the eight qualities that result from [karmic] ripening—that is, increasing.

There is another group of four, with respect to possessions: *giving* away your possessions and increasing your thoughts of giving; *protecting* them until you encounter a karmically potent recipient [of other people's offerings]; *keeping* [your wealth] pure by not letting it be sullied by wrong livelihood or sin; *increasing* the extent of your giving so that you will have possessions to give away in your next rebirth.

Another group of four is discussed: *giving* away your virtue to sentient beings from the depths of your heart; *protecting* your virtue from being destroyed by anger; *[keeping]* the purity of being unsullied by impure motives, such as yearning for the happiness of this life, or merely wanting to prevent your rebirth in the lower realms; *increasing* your sense of rejoicing. And so on. In fact the text discusses four groups of four. You must train in the way set out in this text.

THE PRACTICE OF THE PERFECTION OF ETHICS (371)

As it says in *Engaging in the Deeds of Bodhisattvas:*

> They say the perfection of ethics
> Is to gain the abandonment of certain thoughts.

That is, you reverse thoughts of harming others along with the basis of such thoughts, turning them into the thought of abandoning [these actions]. Complete familiarity with this abandonment becomes the perfection of ethics.

There are three types of ethics.

THE ETHIC OF REFRAINING FROM MISDEEDS (372)

An example of this is the three types of vows. The *Lamp on the Path* says:

> Those who hold one of the seven pratimokṣha vows
> May always hold another vow.
> They have the good fortune to receive bodhisattva vows;
> Others do not.

At first sight this seems to be saying that you must have the ethic of the pratimokṣha vows in order to be a candidate for the bodhisattva vows. But this also means, in the tantric context, that the best candidates for practicing the secret tantras are monks and nuns. Although this might also be interpreted as saying that monks and nuns are the best candidates to follow the trainings of the bodhisattvas, this does not cover all cases: there are gods and nāgas who are suitable candidates for the bodhisattva trainings [but they are barred from receiving pratimokṣha ordination].

In that case, what should you do? When you have the pratimokṣha vows and are able to follow the bodhisattva trainings, you should in this context recognize the ethics of vows as being abandonments and restraints conforming with the pratimokṣha vows. If you do not have the vows, you should take the ethics of restraint to be abandonment of and restraint from the ten nonvirtues. The bodhisattva vows are distinct from either the pratimokṣha vows or the ethics of abandoning the ten nonvirtues in the mindstreams of bodhisattvas.

THE ETHIC OF GATHERING VIRTUOUS DHARMA (373)

This ethic means all the effort you make with your three doors to perform virtue while having the bodhisattva vows. This includes making offerings and prostrating before karmically potent recipients; paying respect; offering your services; studying, contemplating, meditating, and practicing; teaching or listening to Dharma; etc. In short, it is all the tasks that belong to the six perfections performed in order to ripen your own and other beings' mindstreams.

All the deeds of the children of the victors come under the three types of ethic. In general the entire lamrim serves to increase these three types of ethic.

THE ETHIC OF WORKING FOR THE SAKE OF SENTIENT BEINGS (374)

This consists of the four ways of gathering disciples [see Day 23, pp. 650–51] and so forth.

There are eleven further ways of working for the sake of others: (1) helping those who toil and those who suffer; (2) working for the sake of those blind to the right methods; (3) working for the sake of people by benefiting them; (4) working for the sake of those threatened by danger; (5) working for the sake of those afflicted with miseries; (6) working for the sake of the deserted; (7) working for the sake of the homeless; (8) working for the sake of those without like-minded people; (9) working for the sake of those on the right path; (10) working for the sake of those on the wrong path; (11) working for the sake [of all these people] through miracles.

We can carry out ten of these, the exception being working through miracles. To summarize: this ethic includes all the actions of your three doors motivated by thoughts of benefiting others.

You must follow such ethics as abandoning the ten nonvirtues even when you have not taken the pratimokṣha vows. You train in the six perfections so as to ripen your own mindstream; the system of following the three types of ethics trains you in deeds of any benefit to others.

HOW TO TRAIN IN PATIENCE (375)

Patience is by nature the mind being undisturbed by any harm that is inflicted, or being undisturbed by suffering. It says in *Engaging in the Deeds of Bodhisattvas:*

> Unruly sentient beings cannot all be subdued,
> And they are as vast as space.
> If you defeat this angry mind,
> It is the same as defeating them all.

In other words, anger is what should be defeated. Anger, if not defeated, is most dangerous and heavy. As [Śhāntideva] said:

> There is no sin like hostility;
> There is no austerity like patience.

There are three types of patience.

THE PATIENCE OF REMAINING CALM IN THE FACE OF YOUR ATTACKERS (376)

When others, such as your enemies, harm you, be patient and do not get angry. Be aware of the drawbacks of anger: for it is the worst of all the nonvirtues. It is said that each time you get angry, you destroy the root virtues of one thousand eons. When we come to understand the damage wrought by anger, we will always want to persevere with the meditation on patience. You cannot know who is a bodhisattva. If you get angry with someone who is a bodhisattva and your bodhichitta is weaker than his, you destroy the virtue of one hundred eons. If you yourself are not a bodhisattva, and the person you are angry with is, you destroy the virtue of one thousand eons. This is mentioned in *Engaging in the Middle Way* and *Engaging in the Deeds of Bodhisattvas.* Thus the drawbacks are heavy indeed.

You must cultivate patience, but do this before you get angry; once you are angry it is too late. You must be patient and think about the drawbacks of anger. If you do not, you will make everyone, including yourself, unhappy. Aside from anything else, anger can even drive you to suicide and so on. Anger results in your having many enemies.

You might feel, "All this may be true, but how can I be patient when there are so many potential objects of anger?" *Engaging in the Deeds of Bodhisattvas* says:

> How could I find enough leather
> To cover the earth?
> Having leather on the soles of your sandals
> Is the same as covering the whole earth.

Check whether or not you could ever completely subdue your enemies. You will [find that you would] never run out of enemies or subdue them all before the time came when there were no sentient beings left. But if you subdue your anger you will not have a single enemy, and it will be the same as subduing all your enemies.

Once you thoroughly understand how the types of patience are classified by their nature, plus the drawbacks of anger and so forth, will you ever again let your whole body be possessed by anger? Once a lama tried to separate his disciple and a thief in a fight. He did not succeed and the disciple was hitting the man. The lama put his finger on his disciple's nose and said, "Patience! Patience!" Immediately the disciple recalled his lost patience. What use is it to pretend to be patient if your anger has already done its work?

It will be difficult at first to be patient; it will become easy if you familiarize yourself through mind training.

There are reasons why it is not right to get angry with someone who does you harm. Suppose a man hits you on the head with a club. Think as follows to stop yourself becoming angry: "If I must be angry with the thing that actually causes the pain, I should be angry with the club. But the club itself is powerless, it is being used." The man hitting you is powerless, too. He is being forced to do this by the delusions in his mindstream. It profits you little to be angry with them, so it is wrong to be angry. It all comes down to one thing: the wrong way you behave is the most immediate causal factor for your being hit with the club. The root, however, is the evil karma you acquired through hurting people in the past, and so forth. So,

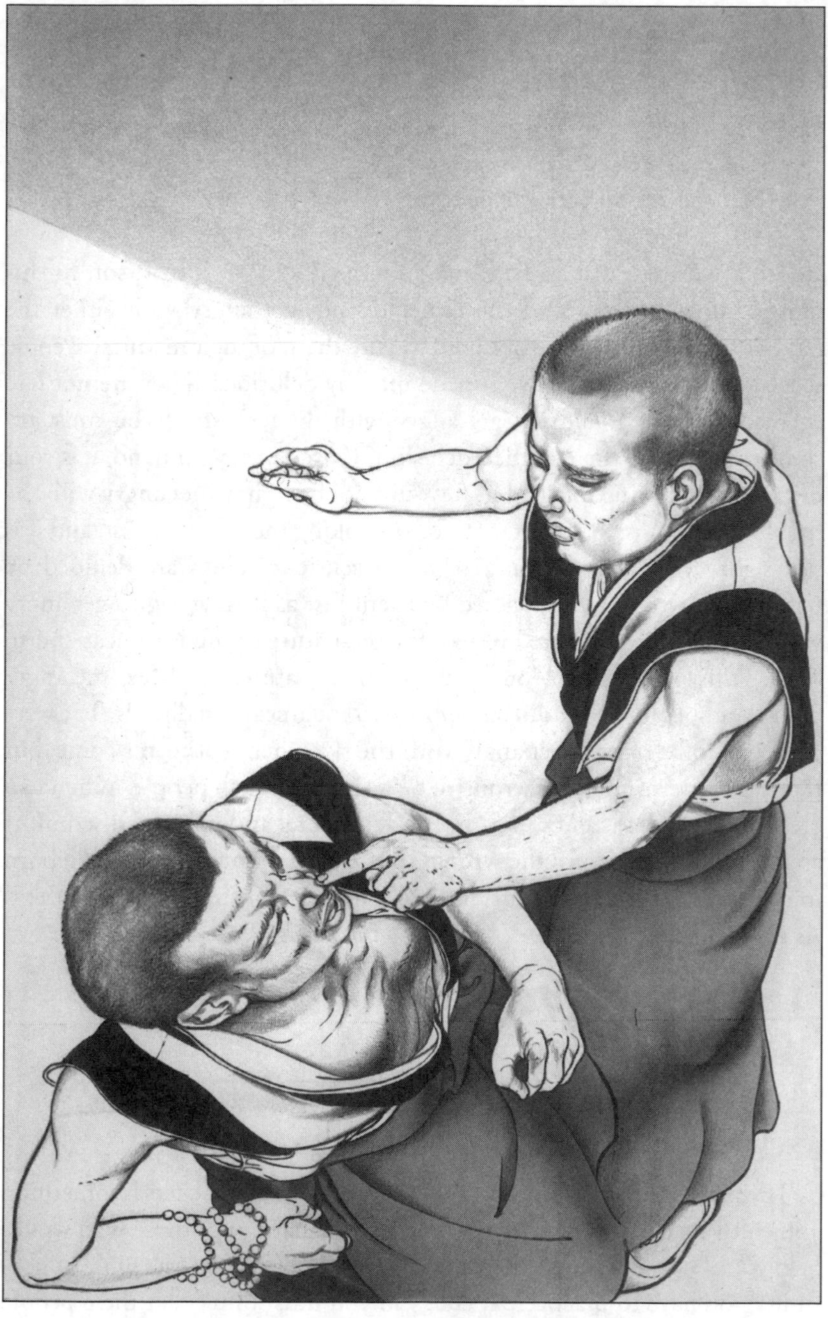

"PATIENCE! PATIENCE!"

since this resulted from the ripening of your own actions through cause and effect, with whom should you be angry?

The *Four Hundred Verses* says:

> The sage sees the delusions,
> Not the person with the delusions.

In other words, a mad patient may hit the doctor or a mad son hit his father, but the doctor and the father do not get angry with either the patient or the son—they work hard to cure them of their madness. People who do you harm are likewise made mad by delusions. They are not free agents, and you should not get angry with them. Instead you must try some means to rid them of their delusion. If fire burns your hand, it is your own fault for having touched it. It would not be right to get angry with the fire. Likewise, it is your own fault for provoking the other person, and it is not right to be angry with him. Since sentient beings are deluded by nature, it is wrong to be angered by them just as it is wrong to get angry with the fire when you are burned, for the nature of fire is to heat and to burn. Still you may feel, "Such may be their nature, but I became angry with them because they did something to me unexpectedly." If that were so, it would be right to get angry with the sky when hailstorms come, but that is pointless. Thus it is wrong to be angry with such people. When you are struck, insulted, and so on, and suffer mental and physical discomfort as a result, do not return the wrong, thus creating causes for being reborn in the lower realms. Apply antidotes to your anger instead, and be patient. As it says in *Engaging in the Deeds of Bodhisattvas:*

> If at present I cannot tolerate
> Even this much suffering,
> Since anger is the cause of suffering in hell—
> Why not stop being angry?

The patience of remaining calm in the face of your attackers is something you cultivate toward those who would do you harm, not those who would help you. The more people there are who would harm you, the more opportunity you have to practice patience. So you must think that these people are an aid to increase your patience. Atiśha always used to be accompanied by King Asaṅgavyaya's jester, a difficult fellow to get along with. When

Atiśha was asked to get rid of him, he replied, "With him around, my patience has a chance to fully develop its qualities!" In short, feel, "If even the śhrāvakas, who work for their own sakes, do not get angry in the face of adversaries, how much more must it apply to me, someone who claims to be a Mahāyānist." You must study the story of Ṛiṣhi Kṣhāntivadin.[78]

THE PATIENCE OF ACCEPTING SUFFERING (377)

Not only should you be unattached to happiness, but you should also regard suffering as a form of adornment and use it as a medicine. As in the preceding section on the mind-training practices, whenever you are beset by suffering—while enduring ascetic practices for the sake of Dharma, when sick, when beset by unasked-for enemies, or even when suffering in a nightmare—turn them all into things that will help your Dharma practice; think about how they will use up evil karma; increase thereby your love and compassion for others; think about the faults of saṃsāra; and so on—be patient. When you experience suffering, think, "This replaces the suffering that I would otherwise have experienced in the lower realms." This ought to make you happy. Suppose a man who was to be executed had his hand amputated instead. He would rightly feel happy about his escape. Also one can put up with the suffering of being bled or having a moxibustion in order to pacify the sufferings of an illness, so when you undergo difficulties for the sake of Dharma, think, "Good. This replaces much suffering in the lower realms." At such a time, recall the good qualities of suffering. *Engaging in the Deeds of Bodhisattvas* tells us:

> The good quality of suffering is that
> It removes arrogance through sorrow.
> One develops compassion for beings in saṃsāra,
> Avoids sin, and rejoices in virtue.

Furthermore, you must accept suffering and cultivate a state in which you will increase your wholesome activities. Do things like practicing contentment and having few wants. Think while carrying out such practices of asceticism, "Because I have been ordained, I should not expect anything better than an inferior place to stay, inferior food, clothes, etc. How fortunate I am to train myself in the four things suited to the āryas, such as being content with the bare necessities: robes, alms, a bed, and so on." If you do not do this, you will desire better food, more wealth, etc., and will always be looking for ways to increase your possessions. You will not think about Dharma; you will not transcend the meaninglessness of human life.

Once a timber merchant heard our Teacher say: "After buried treasure is discovered, a poison quickly pervades it. That poison is potent!" Later the merchant located some treasure he had been seeking and became a rich man. The king asked him to give the cause for his wealth. The merchant lied and the king knew it. Just before being executed, the merchant said, "It was quickly pervaded by poison. That poison was potent!" When he said this, he was asked again for the reason, and so told his story. Wealth is just such a poison. If even we simple monks have few wants and are content, conditions will be favorable for us. When Je Rinpoche left for Jadrael, he and his disciples had only eight *zho* between the nine of them; but their wants were few, and they were content. Their clothes were not too bad, and they were content with whatever happened. Their food, clothes, and so on did not harm their practice. Similarly, you should enjoy and be satisfied with your possessions, for you acquired them through your merit.

Be patient if something unpleasant such as others criticizing you happens. Accept sufferings in your normal activities—such as the asceticism of holding an erect posture, etc. Accept the sufferings that go with upholding the Dharma—making offerings to the Three Jewels, etc. Accept the suffering that goes with your livelihood: do without sensual pleasures, abandon ostentatious desirables, and make do with whatever you already have, even though you may look ugly and your clothing be of poor quality, etc. Accept the suffering of practicing virtue till you are worn out. Accept the suffering of working for the sake of sentient beings, such as having patience, although you know you will have to suffer in preventing someone from being killed, etc. And accept the sufferings that go with living hand-to-mouth after abandoning the means of increasing your wealth through commerce, farming, etc. And so on.

Thus the patience of accepting suffering is a vast subject.

THE PATIENCE TO GAIN ASSURANCE IN THE DHARMA (378)

The *Swift Path* lamrim talks about this in detail. You gain assurance in the Dharma by: (1) meditating on the key points of practices to perform virtue; (2) learning how to modify your behavior by memorizing and reciting texts; (3) analyzing the significance of the good qualities of the Three

Jewels, the meaning of your goal of enlightenment, the path leading to that goal, what is meant by selflessness, and what the profound and extensive baskets of the teachings mean. Or in this context you could do this by becoming sure of the meaning of the words in this lamrim, for example. This type of patience resembles the comprehension acquired by logicians from their debates.

The first of these three forms of patience is to be exercised when you are provoked by your adversaries. The other two are to be practiced all the time. You should be patient during the teachings—no matter how long they may go on for, and so forth. Listen single-pointedly; think over the meaning. Be careful about your behavior while attending debating sessions or assembly: endure the hunger and thirst. Let your mind be single-pointed when you memorize or recite texts. The last two types of patience always apply, even when you are going off to the village to do a ritual in someone's house.

PERSEVERANCE (379)

> What is perseverence? Gladness in virtue.

Perseverance is, by nature, gladness for performing virtue. It is the best means of carrying a virtue through to completion. *An Ornament to the Sūtras* tells us:

> Perseverance is the best among the whole range of virtues:
> When you cultivate it you will later succeed.
> Through perseverance you will soon reach the best of happy states
> And have both the worldly and the transworldly psychic powers.
>
> Through perseverance, you will obtain your mundane aims.
> Through perseverance, you will come to be pure.
> Through perseverance, you will be freed and transcend your views
> of equating the self with the perishable.
> Through perseverance, you will gain supremely enlightened
> buddhahood.

Thus this text says that perseverance is the best of all virtues; everything up to buddhahood derives from it. *Engaging in the Middle Way* says:

> Every good quality follows from perseverance.

Thus do not behave like a stubborn donkey digging in its heels when you should be doing your recitations, etc. Commence these activities by taking great delight in performing virtue. Accustom yourself to doing only a little in the early stages; increase this as your perseverance increases.

There are three types of laziness that hinder perseverance.

THE LAZINESS OF SLOTH (380)

This means losing the chance to perform virtue because you keep putting it off. You continually procrastinate because your heart is not in it. As its antidote you must meditate on death and impermanence or on the difficulty of gaining the optimum human rebirth.

THE LAZINESS OF CRAVING EVIL PURSUITS (381)

This is craving mundane pursuits and engaging in them, and in nonvirtuous actions as well, because you have not yet tired of them. Reputation, society, idle gossip, farming, business, sewing, and spinning are examples of such things. We do not talk of perseverance in relation to such things: we call it obstinacy. *Engaging in the Deeds of Bodhisattvas* mentions its antidote:

> Happiness' cause is the infinite, holy Dharma;
> But you are lost among the causes of suffering
> And abandon supreme happiness.
> Why do you delight in ruin and the like?

In other words, the pursuits of saṃsāra are without essence and cause suffering. Think in this way and you will prevent this form of laziness.

THE LAZINESS OF DEFEATISM (382)

This is a deep-seated form of laziness. Examples of it are: "How could someone like me achieve buddhahood?" or "How could I work for the sake of all sentient beings?" or even "How could someone like me possibly sacrifice my body, arms, or legs?"

Feel instead, "I shall be patient even though it may take my whole life to train in just one meditation topic, such as the difficulty of obtaining an optimum human rebirth." Or think, "I can persevere with such worldly pursuits as trading, and how patient I can be with such hard work for so small a profit. Thus if I can manage this much, I must be able to persevere and work hard enough to achieve enlightenment!" It says in *Engaging in the Deeds of Bodhisattvas:*

> Don't be despondent and say,
> "How could I be enlightened?"
> The Tathāgata, who speaks truly, has spoken this truth:
> Anyone, be they flies, bluebottles, and bees,
> Can, if their perseverance be strong,
> Gain supreme but hard-to-procure enlightenment!
>
> Someone like me has been born in the human race;
> I recognize what helps and what harms.
> If I do not forsake the bodhisattva tasks
> Why should I not achieve enlightenment?

That is, think, "Our Teacher, who spoke the truth, said that even flies can be enlightened. A person like myself has been born a human. I know how to talk, I comprehend. How could I not become enlightened, too? I can achieve it."

You may feel, "Granted, but I cannot perform such ascetic practices as giving my head, arms, and legs." But as *Engaging in the Deeds of Bodhisattvas* says:

> When I say, "I'm afraid to give away that which I must:
> My arms, legs, and so on,"
> I am ignorant of what is light and heavy
> Because I have not analyzed.
>
> Our Guide in the beginning practiced generosity
> By giving away vegetables, and so on...
>
> When I regard even my own body
> As worth no more than things like vegetables,

I could then sacrifice my flesh, and so on.
What would be hard about that?

In other words, after beginning your meditations on giving at a low level, you would later be as unconcerned at giving away your head, arms, and legs as at giving away a dish of vegetables. When you have reached that level, you would rejoice and not feel it difficult to make such a sacrifice.

You may think, "Buddhas have infinite good qualities, and these would be difficult to achieve." Contemplate that you can surely achieve these if you practice, because the path used to achieve them is infinitely profound and vast.

Still, you may object, "It would be difficult for me to go to the lower realms, for example, for the sake of sentient beings." *Engaging in the Deeds of Bodhisattvas* says:

Because sin was abandoned, you will have no suffering.
Because you were skilled, you will not be unhappy.

In other words, you may stay in the Hell Without Respite for the sake of sentient beings, but because you have abandoned sin, you would not suffer nor be unhappy, for, as it is said, you cannot meet with something if you have not created the karma to do so. You should therefore feel, "I will not be unhappy there—it would be like going to the pure lands."

There are three types of perseverance.

ARMOR-LIKE PERSEVERANCE (383)

It says in the *Guru Pūjā:*

Bless me to perfect perseverance:
Even if I have to stay
In the fires of the Hell Without Respite
For oceans of eons
For the sake of each sentient being.
May my compassion not flag,
May I strive for supreme enlightenment.

In other words, train yourself to feel that you could even endure having to stay in the Hell Without Respite for hundreds of thousands of eons for the sake of each sentient being. In the tantric context, you should enter tantra with the thought: "For my own part, I would be able to endure this. But sentient beings would still be left suffering for a long time." Your wish is to rescue sentient beings as soon as possible from their suffering, just as a mother would rescue her beautiful boy from drowning.

In this section on the armor-like perseverance, you train yourself to think you could endure going to the Hell Without Respite for the sake of sentient beings. Contrast this with the medium scope, where you develop thoughts of wanting to be free of saṃsāra. You may wonder: are these two opposites? But there is no contradiction. Bodhisattvas are also afraid of being reborn in the lower realms under the power of karma and delusion. That way they would not even be able to benefit themselves, let alone benefit others. They have continually trained themselves in bodhichitta and have gained the courage not to be afraid for themselves; instead, they would be most happy to take rebirth there through the power of compassion and prayer. They would not suffer there, nor would they have the slightest mental anguish. This training is called the *armor-like perseverance* because you face difficulties for the sake of others at a time when the Dharma has so degenerated that people no longer practice such things.

THE PERSEVERANCE TO COLLECT VIRTUOUS THINGS (384)

This perseverance is collecting [merit], purifying yourself, making offerings, persevering in the practice of the six perfections, etc.

THE PERSEVERANCE OF WORKING FOR THE SAKE OF SENTIENT BEINGS (385)

An example of this is persevering with the practice of the four ways of gathering disciples. It is a training that resembles "The Ethic of Working for the Sake of Sentient Beings." You may possibly view the last two types of perseverance, of ethics, of patience, and so on, as amounting to much the same thing, but leave them separate: do not confuse them, even though you take delight, you practice, and you wish to abandon contrary factors all in relation to the one basis.

If, for example, you were to meditate for one session on the generation stage [of the highest yoga tantra] in conjunction with the generation of bodhichitta, you would be practicing all six of the perfections.

Then Pabongka Rinpoche merely introduced the last two perfections of single-pointed concentration and wisdom. He then said he would be dealing with these last two in detail in the following parts of the teaching.

DAY 21

Kyabje Pabongka Rinpoche gave a short introductory talk on Dharma. He quoted the following verse, which comes from the works of Gyaeltsab Rinpoche Jampa Goenpo:

> First, due to your study, your thinking becomes realistic.
> Because of your realism, you will gain primal wisdom into the
> purest matters.

He then listed the headings we have already covered and briefly reviewed the first four items—generosity and so forth—that come under such headings as "[After Developing Bodhichitta, the Way] to Train in the Deeds of the Children of the Victorious Ones."

IN PARTICULAR, THE WAY TO TRAIN IN THE LAST TWO PERFECTIONS (386)

There are two subheadings here: (1) how to train in the very essence of concentration—mental quiescence; (2) how to train in the very essence of wisdom—special insight.

HOW TO TRAIN IN THE VERY ESSENCE OF CONCENTRATION—MENTAL QUIESCENCE (387)

This has six further headings: (1) cultivating the prerequisites for mental quiescence; (2) the actual way to achieve mental quiescence; (3) taking this way as the basis, how to achieve the nine mental states; (4) the way the mental states are achieved through the six powers; (5) how there are four types of mental process; (6) the way true mental quiescence develops [from this point].

Since Kyabje Pabongka did not deal with the high trainings of single-pointed concentration and wisdom in the medium-scope section, he now discusses them in this section on the last two perfections.

Mental quiescence is something we share with non-Buddhists. The most inferior forms of it are the non-Buddhist practices of the form-realm dhyāna states of concentration and the practices involving the formless realm. We could turn such practices into a cause for our liberation by carrying them out in conjunction with thoughts of renunciation. We could also make them into Dharma by practicing them in conjunction with taking refuge. Without mental quiescence we will not develop any of the great realizations that come through the sūtric types of meditation on emptiness, or tantric types on the generation and completion stages, and so on. Any good quality you may wish to develop through one of the single-pointed concentrations in either sūtra or tantra is out of the question if you do not have mental quiescence. Mental quiescence is like a container to hold the water you have poured into it. It is therefore vital to develop firm mental quiescence in the early stages.

You must develop special insight into the understanding of emptiness in order to sever the roots of saṃsāra, or achieve mere liberation; but, to do this, you must have already gained firm mental quiescence. In order to see things as they are—and clearly—you must first have stability and firmness. Suppose you are viewing a mural. Two prerequisites are needed to dispel the darkness [obscuring the painting]: a bright butterlamp and no drafts that would make it flicker. Similarly, if you have already achieved mental quiescence, it is much easier to develop realization through meditation on everything from the difficulty of gaining an optimum human rebirth to meditation on impermanence. Atiśha's *Lamp on the Path* speaks of the development of mental quiescence in order to achieve clairvoyant powers. Be that as it may, the fundamental thing to understand about all this was said by Śhāntideva:

> Knowing that through special insight having great mental quiescence
> You will destroy your delusions,
> First seek mental quiescence.

Thus, you must achieve mental quiescence early on. You need not necessarily develop it only after achieving bodhichitta, because you may gain it either before or after this achievement. If you manage to achieve mental quiescence, you will make great progress in your meditations on any of the practices of the three vehicles.

You must first cultivate the prerequisites of mental quiescence; without them you will not achieve it. The *Lamp on the Path* says:

> When the limbs of mental quiescence have withered,
> You will not achieve single-pointed concentration
> Despite most diligent meditation
> For thousands of years.

Which leads to:

CULTIVATING THE PREREQUISITES FOR MENTAL QUIESCENCE (388)

There are six of these: (1) dwelling in a conducive place; (2) having few wants; (3) being content; (4) completely abandoning the many demands of society; (5) having pure ethics; (6) completely abandoning conceptual thoughts such as desire.

DWELLING IN A CONDUCIVE PLACE (389)

The place where you carry out your practice should have five features. The sort of place needed was described in *An Ornament to the Sūtras:*

> Any place where the wise practice
> Has excellent provisions, is a wholesome place,
> Is a healthy location, has noble friends at hand,
> And has facilities to satisfy the yogi.

If it is not easy for you to be self-sufficient from a livelihood that accords with the Dharma, you will have to keep going down to the town. But you must be well supplied in a way that accords with the Dharma; otherwise you may acquire supplies through a wrong livelihood or obtain sinful things. Our lamas say that these kinds of provisions are dangerous. So you need easily obtainable provisions that have not been tainted by some great sin—in other words "excellent provisions."

The place where you live should be a consecrated one where, for example, the feet of saints of the past have trod. When beginners dwell in such a place, the place itself will be a blessing for them. If you cannot find such a place, wherever you stay should not be the dwelling of someone who has, for example, broken his vows or caused dissension within the Saṅgha.

It should also be a wholesome place—that is, not a place where there are beasts of prey, thieves, or wrathful spirits. It should also have people willing to act as benefactors. If it is not like this you may think you can live there in safety, but you will later come to grief.

Kyabje Pabongka illustrated this with the story about a past lama who was tricked by spirits.

The place where you will be living may be the home of spirit creatures, so it is vital to employ some gentle means of subduing their mindstreams, not something that will expel them.

A "healthy location" means a place where you will not develop chills or fever and where the water is fit to drink.

Your friends, too, should be friends conducive to both view and deeds. As they say, these friends' two shadows should form but one silhouette. This, of course, is not to say that you should have only two friends or that you have to live alone. It simply means that you and they should be like-minded. It is very damaging for beginners to live alone without friends. You should have at least three friends at hand; and if they are Dharmic friends, it is better to have even more. However, no matter how many friends you have, they must be people who command your respect; do not befriend the disrepectful or unscrupulous.

It is also said: "Because sounds are irritants to concentration..." In other words, the place must not have the sound of people by day or the sound of dogs or running water at night.

As my own guru said, you should be someone who can stand on your own two feet: through study and contemplation you have eliminated inaccuracies about the meaning of the things you are to meditate on. Such a person is equipped to gain satisfaction. However, this could also mean you have made all the necessary preparations—such as having the initiations, teachings, books, etc. The main thing is to become skilled at doing your practice. These days, people's main preparation seems to be working hard at making a living, so when it comes time to actually practice, they have no idea what to do and so are compelled to request dice divinations and so on. Do not act like this. Make proper preparations for your Dharma practice.

HAVING FEW WANTS (390)

Having few wants means having no attachment to large quantities of fine clothes, good food, etc.

BEING CONTENT (391)

Contentment is making do with the bare necessities of food and clothing. You will be attached to sensual things if you are not content and do not have few wants. You will not develop single-pointed concentration because you will be distracted by the need to protect your possessions, and so on.

HAVING PURE ETHICS (392)

In general, ethics are the basis of all good qualities. Pacification of the subtle internal distractions depends on the abandonment of gross external distractions. Ethics restrain and pacify your misdeeds of both body and speech, and do this by taking you out of the mental yoke of your grossest conceptual thoughts.

ABANDONING THE DEMANDS OF SOCIETY (393)

This means restricting the time you spend on meaningless actions, conversations, etc. You must have very little to do with such meaningless actions in order to be completely undistracted by them. Development of concentration is much more important, and so you will automatically have little to do with these things, because you have few wants and have contentment. In order to be one-pointed about your practice, you must abandon astrology, medicine, throwing dice divinations, and going off into the village to perform rituals in people's homes, because these are the demands of society.

This does not merely apply to beginners like ourselves. It can be quite ruinous even for holy beings. Butoen Rinpoche and Lama Dampa were favored by King Pehar, who used to give them iron styluses to write with. They used up thousands of these, and it is said that in those rebirths they did not gain the supreme achievement because they were immersed in the practices of astrology. But Togme Sangpo, a real child of the victorious ones, remained in meditation on love and compassion, and Pehar's ruse did not succeed with him.

Je Tsongkapa wrote eighteen volumes, but he did not put the three lines of [Sanskrit] calligraphy at the beginning of each, not because he did not know the *vṛtta* and *jāti*;[79] he did not do these because he thought they would not help his practice. For one year I myself studied only Sanskrit calligraphy. This study wore away the surface of two or three slates, and my fingers were rubbed raw [from wiping the slates]. Yet even *this* was giving in to the demands of society. It did nothing to help my practice.

If you work hard at such things, then, apart from the mere instinct you gain for the subject, you will not be able to instill in yourself instincts that will result in either a high rebirth or definite excellence. You will achieve nothing of essential meaning and will be like the person attached to sugarcane who does not extract any of the juice. Some of the lesser of the ten sciences are of so little benefit; why bother mastering them?[80]

Somebody said, "Even you are bent over with old age, your state is pitiful as long as you still strive after sensual objects." This was the reason that Sūrata the beggar gave the wish-granting gem he found to King Prasenajit, saying, "O king, in this whole kingdom you have the most desire and are the poorest."

Pabongka Rinpoche also told the story of Geshe Baen Gung-gyael repairing the rug.

COMPLETELY ABANDONING CONCEPTUAL THOUGHTS SUCH AS DESIRE (394)

Turn your mind away from these thoughts by thinking about the drawbacks of desire and about impermanence.

When you have fulfilled all the above prerequisites and make effort in your practice, you will take no more than six months to achieve mental quiescence.

THE ACTUAL WAY TO ACHIEVE MENTAL QUIESCENCE (395)

It says in [Maitreya's] *Distinguishing Between the Extremes and the Middle Way:*

> Abandon five pitfalls, cultivate eight adjustments,
> And that will cause you to achieve it.
> I claim the five pitfalls are:
> Laziness; forgetting the instruction;
> Excitement and dullness;
> Nonadjustment; and readjustment.

In other words, they say you must cultivate the eight adjustments, which are antidotes to the five pitfalls. There are no better instructions on how to achieve single-pointed concentration than those to be found in the classical treatises—the works of Maitreya, Asaṅga's studies on the various levels, texts on the middle way and its stages of meditation, etc. We must seek this sort of instruction and then meditate on it. Instead of doing this we might put a higher value on some lama's oral instruction that does not accord with the Dharma as presented in the classics, or we might value short miscellanies on spells, or class notes, short pamphlets, etc. This is searching for something in a place where it cannot be found and not where it can. However, there is no danger of this happening if we follow chapter and verse the section on mental quiescence in Je Tsongkapa's *Great Stages of the Path.*

So if you do not refer back to these classical treatises, you might put your trust in what any lama you come across may say, claiming these to be "instructions." If so, even though you spend the rest of your life in some mountain cave, you will mistake subtle dullness for meditation. Far too many have been mistaken, directing their attention to the mind itself as the most secret path of gaining mental quiescence. They have missed their big opportunity. Putting effort into such instructions will only make your human rebirth hollow. Many famous Tibetan scholars have been mistaken about the view, how to meditate on it, etc. The discerning should look in detail into each of the traditions and texts of such scholars, and they will then come to understand that this is so.

Witness how any part where Je Tsongkapa deals with the view, its meditations, and the tasks involved agrees with the works of all the ultimate Indian pandits and adepts. Further, Mañjuśhrī himself cleared up

Tsongkapa's doubts and gave him permission. So we should depend on such instructions because they were formulated with these authoritative scriptures in mind—scriptures that are quite without the taint of error. But if you pin your hopes on some instruction that does not accord with these texts, or that says things not to be found in them, there is the danger of developing some unheard-of realization! This applies to the generation and completion stages of the secret tantras down to the most trivial level of concentration. All are impossible to achieve without this instruction on how to achieve mental quiescence, whose source is the śhastras and which deals with the methods for extricating yourself from the five pitfalls by cultivating the eight adjustments.

THE FIRST PITFALL: LAZINESS (396)

This has four antidotes: (1) faith due to seeing the good qualities of single-pointed concentration; (2) yearning and wishing for single-pointed concentration; (3) perseverance in seeking single-pointed concentration; (4) the result of seeking single-pointed concentration—meditative suppleness.

What is the goal of our meditation? It is single-pointed concentration. The faith that comes from seeing the good qualities of single-pointed concentration is as follows. The pitfall of laziness is not having any heartfelt desire to enter single-pointed meditation or not being able to continue with it on entering such meditation. The true end result of your training [in this concentration] is meditative suppleness. Although you do not have this at present, you must think about the good qualities of single-pointed concentration. *Engaging in the Deeds of Bodhisattvas* says:

> You may persevere a long while
> At recitation and all types of asceticism,
> With a mind distracted by other things,
> But the Knowledgeable One says it is meaningless.

In other words, think about the damage a distracted mind does to you. If you develop mental quiescence, you will be able to focus your attention on a subject quite firmly whenever you perform some virtuous practice, and because of this firmness will soon gain actual attainments, even the common clairvoyances and so forth; your sleep will become single-pointed concentration; your delusions will become very slight indeed. More importantly, it will be easier for you to quickly develop [realization] into the path, from devotion to your spiritual guide all the way up to the generation and completion stages. And so on.

Think about these good qualities. You will then have faith due to seeing the good qualities of single-pointed concentration. With this faith you will achieve the wish and perseverance to seek single-pointed concentration. With these you will wish to have meditative suppleness. This is how these four antidotes act as causes and effects—the latter ones developing from the earlier in an orderly fashion.

THE SECOND PITFALL: FORGETTING THE INSTRUCTION (397)

This is what we term no longer recalling the meditation device. It is highly damaging to the practice of single-pointed concentration. The *Heart of the Middle Way* says:

> Securely tie the wayward elephant of the mind
> To the firm pillar of the visualization
> With the rope of memory;
> Break it in with the hooks of wisdom.

You have to tie the elephant of your mind to the pillar of the visualization that you employ, so you need something that you can fasten the mind onto—that is, the visualization employed to develop mental quiescence. The meditation device can be almost anything—a visualization or a physical object. Non-Buddhists use stones and pieces of wood for their visualizations. The Boenpos visualize the letter A. Thus people who set about achieving mental quiescence employ various devices, but these are mental objects only—such people do not practice by looking at the devices with their eyes. On the other hand, there are people who do actively look at their meditation devices, but this practice is inferior to the other two already mentioned, for mental quiescence must be achieved with the mind, not with the eyes. The Great Fifth Dalai Lama, and so on, have repeatedly refuted that mental quiescence must be achieved with the eyes, not the mind. Once someone who came here from India used a bull's horn as his meditation device. He did not employ the other purely mental types of device, yet he nonetheless achieved mental quiescence. This shows that you can achieve it no matter what device you meditate on.

Nevertheless, when *we* go about achieving mental quiescence, we visualize the form of the Buddha in accordance with the oral tradition deriving from Tsongkapa. One major feature of this visualization is that it allows you to build up your [merit] collection and purify obscurations. Another major feature: it accustoms you to the deity yoga to be found in the secret tantras. It is also most beneficial to be reminded of the Buddha. And so on.

From your guru, visualized on the crown of your head, emerges Guru Śhākyamuni, about the size of your thumb. He comes to rest in front of you, about level with the gap between your eyebrows. Alternatively, you could put him level with your navel—whichever you prefer. Or you could visualize that you transform into Śhākyamuni.

Some people find it easier to imagine formlessness as their meditation device rather than visualizing something physical; so the Paṇchen Lama Lozang Choekyi Gyaeltsaen began a tradition in his teachings on the *Gelugpa Mahāmudrā* that is in keeping with Tsongkapa's thoughts in the *Medium Stages of the Path*. In this tradition you achieve mental quiescence by focusing on the mind itself, and these people could readily use it. It even has its counterpart in other sects, where you investigate the conscious operation of the mind. It is also possible to achieve mental quiescence by visualizing the form of the deity, as in the generation stage, or by visualizing the letter A or a vertical stroke, as in the completion stage. There are further mental quiescence visualizations that involve pervading [everywhere with the visualization], employing some trick or a certain activity, or even visualizing that some delusion has been purified. In practice, use whichever of these is easiest for you to imagine, and meditate on it until you achieve mental quiescence. Do not substitute some other visualization. You need not meditate on all four of the focal objects described in the sūtras [the body, feelings, mind, and phenomena]. You must fix your mind on one thing, and this should be something that you feel comfortable with. As Āchārya Aśhvaghoṣha said:

> Be firm in your contemplation:
> Always use the one visualization.
> With many visualizations in succession,
> Your mind will be excited by delusion.

In other words, fix the mind on the one visualization when you meditate. You will not achieve mental quiescence if you change the visualization.

Suppose you rub two sticks together; you will not make a fire if you shift to another stick. Further, you must meditate continually for mental quiescence, except when you eat, sleep, or move your bowels, just as you have to rub the sticks together without interruption until they catch fire. Do this continuously until you achieve mental quiescence—in six months, a year, or whatever. You will not attain it if you get sick of it and move on to something else, or if you take a couple of days off to rest, and so on.

The "instruction" [in "forgetting the instruction"] means you memorize the features of a drawing or statue of the Victorious One for your meditation device so that you can imagine it as your mental object when you enter meditation or, as your guru has acquainted you, recall the image of the meditation device in your mind's eye. You have begun to utilize your meditation device when you are able to partially imagine your visualization as a rough mental image.

We say that you have forgotten the instruction when you have lost this object of your recollection. This is the second pitfall. Its antidote is the fifth of the eight adjustments—memory. Very strong memory is necessary to maintain the continuity of your meditation device, rather like a hand holding a rosary. An individual's memory may be strong or weak, and this will make it easy or difficult for him to achieve mental quiescence. [Asaṅga's] *Compendium of Metaphysics* says on the subject of memory:

> What is memory? Something that functions so as not to allow the mind to forget a thing with which it has been made familiar.

In other words, memory necessarily has three properties. It must *distinguish its object*—that is, you have previously looked at your meditation device and familiarized your mind's eye with its aspects. Subsequently, when you direct your mind to these aspects, memory necessarily has the property of *retention*—that is, you have not forgotten these aspects of the meditation device, and they present themselves to you continually. This is like your vivid recollection of food when you are hungry. Lastly, memory has another property of the *function it performs*—the mind is made not to stray or unfocus from the object it is directed toward.

If these three are present, you will be able to visualize the form of, say, the Victorious One, clearly in front of you, in your mind's eye. Do not become distracted—retain a tight hold on the visualization. You must imagine the visualization and nothing else.

THE THIRD PITFALL: EXCITEMENT AND DULLNESS (398)

You will fall prey to the third pitfall—excitement and dullness—during your actual meditation period while recalling your meditation device. If you do not differentiate between dullness, mental fog, and excitement, it will be like not recognizing enemies bent on murdering you; since they are great faults, you must recognize them.

Mental fog can be either nonvirtuous or neutral. It obscures the consciousness, weighing down both mind and body, as when you want to go to sleep. It acts as a cause for dullness and is never virtuous.

There are two types of dullness: subtle and coarse. When you recall your meditation device, its image may be steady but unclear. This is coarse dullness. Subtle dullness is as follows: you have not lost the retained features of the visualization, you even have steadiness and clarity of image, but the force of your retention has slackened, and its clarity is not intense. Subtle dullness is the main obstruction to meditation. What do I mean by "not being intense?" I mean that there is clarity but the mind has become somewhat slack. At such a time, though the image's stability is quite firm, this slackness has acted as a cause for subtle dullness. If the image has intense clarity, the mind is sharp, fresh, vital, and still on the meditation device.

I can illustrate the fact that you can have both clarity and stability but that the clarity may or may not be intense. Suppose you are holding your rosary and bowl in your hands. You may hold them differently, one tightly and one loosely. Or, more generally, we can always have faith in a guru, but this may not be particularly strong. From time to time we may develop more or stronger faith in him; the way we retain our faith is then more acute than before. That is the difference between the two situations. They say this will become very clear in the light of experience in contemplation—it is impossible to put it into words.

Note: clarity and brightness are not due to the object. Whether or not there is any clarity or brightness is necessarily a function of the subjective consciousness. When there is no clarity, it is as if a darkening shadow has fallen over the image.

Subtle dullness and single-pointed concentration may both have clarity and stability; thus it is difficult to tell the difference between single-pointed concentration and subtle dullness. Air may even have stopped flowing through your nostrils and your mind may remain stable for a whole day, but you have merely built up subtle dullness. Many of the early

Tibetan scholars mistook this state and praised it as "deepest meditation in deepest relaxation." They had not understood this key point in meditation. If you mistake subtle dullness for meditation, your meditations will not even act as causes for [rebirth in] the form and formless realms, and even in this life you will be more absentminded. Because your wisdom becomes unclear, the practice is no better than doing, say, a great deal of meditation on a sādhana where you visualize yourself as an animal!

A Compendium of Metaphysics says this about excitement:

> What is excitement? A disturbed aspect arisen in the conceptual mind of attachment led astray by beautiful signs. It functions by interrupting mental quiescence.

Beautiful objects or the objects of your attachment unfocus the mind. Thus they are the beautiful signs referred to here. Suppose you watch an opera one day and that night you vividly recall the scene: this is an example of recalling an attractive object of your attachment.

There is a big difference between lack of focus and excitement. You can become unfocused through an unpleasant object, such as your enemy. At such a time, you undergo lack of focus due to mental distress. Or while meditating on mental quiescence you can become unfocused by some virtuous object, such as generosity, ethics, and so on. These may be forms of lack of focus, but they are not excitement.

Nevertheless, both lack of focus and excitement may interrupt your mental quiescence. Why then is only excitement assumed to be the thing that interrupts mental quiescence? Lack of focus occurs less and is of shorter duration when its object is either the object of your hostility or when your attention is being directed to something virtuous. Usually, lack of focus is much greater when the object is one of attachment. So lack of focus is usually of the latter type [i.e., excitement] because it is easier to develop than the other forms. It has been given pride of place, and we speak of excitement alone. But note: when you meditate on mental quiescence, your mental state will be interrupted by the two other types of lack of focus: unfocusing due to either pleasant or unpleasant objects; and lack of focus due to, for example, recalling some generosity you may have performed, prostrations you may have made, etc. When you meditate for mental quiescence, you have to put a stop to these forms of unfocusing whenever they occur.

We may lose track of the meditation device such that it is no longer our mental object. For example, when meditating on the form of a deity, we may forget about our visualization for a while. Coarse excitement is just such a loss of the meditation device.

Subtle excitement is as follows: the mind does not lose track of the device, but something subliminal with a pleasant aspect arises in a portion of the mind below the level of conceptual thought, like water flowing under a sheet of ice.

Though the actual antidote to both of these adverse conditions is not vigilance, vigilance is still a component of the antidote, just as the army has its spies. You must cultivate vigilance—number six of the eight adjustments—in order to detect whether you have any excitement or dullness. If you apply vigilance continuously it becomes a hindrance to your meditative state, but if you do not apply vigilance regularly you may develop some serious faults in your single-pointed concentration and not be aware of it. The thief, as it were, has already carried off your possessions. It says in the *Gelugpa Mahāmudrā:* "Turn off vigilance when this seems right." In other words, keep your vigilance in check. You must apply it only as a sentry to know if you have any excitement or dullness. In *Engaging in the Deeds of Bodhisattvas* it says:

> Time and again examine
> The state of your body and mind.
> To be brief, just this:
> The nature of vigilance is to be a guard.

This is like holding a bowl of tea in your hand: you both hold it firmly and look to see if the bowl has tilted. Similarly, you hold the meditation through memory while retaining its image firmly, and maintain the visualization while using vigilance to check whether you have any excitement or dullness. By the way, vigilance is included as a part of wisdom.

THE FOURTH PITFALL: NONADJUSTMENT (399)

When you get excited or dull, one of the antidotes—nonadjustment—becomes a pitfall and it has its own antidote. If your vigilance has detected any dullness or excitement—whether in coarse or subtle form—you must immediately apply the antidotes without further ado. The seventh of the eight adjustments—readjustment—is actually the antidote to the eighth of the adjustments—equanimity [also known as nonadjustment]. Adjustment has to be mentally applied against nonadjustment. These two are like enemy scouts: as soon as one sees the other, he tries to stop him.

So how should this antidote be applied? Subtle dullness is a state of depressed mental activity. Thus both depression and dullness have much the same consequences. With subtle dullness you have clarity and stability of the image, but the quality of its retention has dropped, and the clarity, therefore, is not as intense. Whenever you develop this form of dullness, there is no need to quit your meditation session or break off visualizing since it is sufficient to tighten up your retention of the image. However, when your hold becomes too tight, you develop excitement, and you should then loosen your hold. As the Bhagavān said:

> If the vina's string is too taut, loosen it; tighten or loosen it as needed, making sure that it does not get too slack. In the end the sound will be sweet.

You should do the same thing: loosen a little when you feel you will develop excitement, and tighten your hold a little when you feel that dullness will ensue if you loosen any more. Experience dictates the border between these two. If you do not analyze intelligently through your vigilance, it will be very hard for you to put your finger on it. Āchārya Chandragomin said:

> Apply effort and you get excited;
> Abandon it and you develop depression.
> "If this is true, and it is so hard to gain absorption,
> Why do this: it will only disturb my mind!"

Doing this sort of thing may be mentally fatiguing; but among all types of enemies, an enemy you mistake for one of your family is the hardest of all to identify. Because of this, they are more dangerous. Likewise, there is great danger in mistaking this type of dullness for single-pointed concentration; so you must be skilled in this fine-tuned state.

Thus, in spite of having fine-tuned your mind, you may again lose the intensity of the image's clarity. When this happens, the retention lapses as though the thought has died, and the image is no longer clear. If this will not go away, coarse dullness has returned. It says in the *Heart of the Middle Way:*

When depressed, meditate on expansive visualizations
And thus open yourself…

That is, the fault is that your mind is in a great knot; so you should meditate, broadening the visualization somewhat. If the problem does not then go away and your mind becomes depressed when you resume the visualization, try a method to be uplifted, or cheer yourself up by contemplating how difficult it is to find the most beneficial optimum human rebirth. Or you could contemplate the good qualities of the Three Jewels, study the benefits of devoting yourself to a spiritual guide, contemplate the benefits of bodhichitta, etc. These will uplift your mind. You could imagine rays of light shining on you, or meditate on things like the giving visualization. Such meditations will raise your mind to a higher plane, and it will then retain the visualization again.

Our minds have not been familiar with this sort of thing in the past, and it will be difficult to gain immediate benefit from these techniques. But when we become familiar with them, the contemplation of things such as how hard it is to gain a human rebirth will be like splashing cold water on our faces. The difficulty will disappear.

If your dullness will still not go away, employ a more forceful means of removing it. Visualize your mind as being a white light at your heart. As you utter the syllable *phat,* your mind comes out of the fontanelle on the top of your head and penetrates the depths of space. Think that your mind and space have become inextricably mixed. Do this as many times as seems best.

If still the problem will not go away, terminate your meditation session. Mental fog is causing you to develop dullness. Use some means to make the mental fog, sleepiness, or grogginess go away. Settle down in some cool spot, go for a walk on some high, open place, go for a visit, splash water on your face, and so on. If these clear your mind, resume your visualization as before.

Subtle excitement is when you do not lose track of the meditation device but the mind is distracted. When this happens, the fault is that the mind is too tight. Slightly loosen your retention of the image. If this does not help and your mind is still distracted, you now have a coarse form of excitement. This has developed only because of your happy state of mind, so you should not increase your happiness any more. Over-happiness is damaging, as shown by the story of King Śhuddhodana [Buddha's father], who could not attain the state of a stream-enterer [because he was so elated by his son's return]. In this kind of situation, don't stop the meditation session, for, as it is said in the *Heart of the Middle Way:*

> Calm your excitement by
> Thinking of impermanence and the like.

In other words, contemplate things that cause mental depression, weariness, or renunciation. Death and impermanence or the sufferings encountered in saṃsāra and the lower realms are just such things.

If this does not clear up the problem, employ a more forceful method to rid yourself of excitement. Because your conceptual thinking has increased, you should do the following visualization when you breathe in or out. When you breathe, think, "I am breathing out" or "I am breathing in." Also think, "That's the first time," and continue to count mentally the number of times you have been breathing out and in. At first you will only be able to manage up to three or four cycles. Just resume counting from one again. Being able to keep this up till you get to twenty-one without the mind becoming distracted is the criterion for having achieved the first mental state.

There is a story about the great adept of Yerpa, Puentsog Gyatso. He had a nephew who was a servant to the regent, Sangyae Gyatso. The servant was expelled from office together with the regent [at the hands of Lhazang Khan]. Puentsog Gyatso could not keep his mind on his meditation. He counted his breathing, and only then could he resume his practice.

If doing this does not cut your excitement, take a bit of a break from the session. Then meditate in shorter sessions, preceding these by a firm resolve. If you lengthen your sessions, the very sight of your meditation mat may make you feel lethargic or nauseated. It is most important to break off your meditations at the right point, "while it is still a pleasure to meditate," as it is said. To illustrate: if two people part at the right moment, they will later be pleased to see each other again. As it is said, if the image is still clear, you should stop; but if the image is unclear, you should stop in any case. If you draw the line while you still feel, "It would be fine if I meditated a little more," you will want to meditate again from the depth of your heart. This is the best way to meditate. Even if you are unfocused, if you do things this way, your meditation will be excellent. However, while you have no clarity and keep trying to fix it, if it does not go away and you stubbornly persist in fixing it, you will fatigue yourself; later the lack of clarity will grow even worse. Here is a story to illustrate. There was once a brilliant adept named Lozang Namgyael. He was giving an oral transmission of miscellaneous Kadampa works. "In these degenerate times," he read, "now is the time to tame your own mindstream, not the mindstreams of others." He broke down and wept, and had to stop the teaching. For the next two days he was unable to teach whenever he reached these words.[81]

Although our hope is for an image that remains stable for long periods of time, all we can do at present is to evoke the visualization; it will not persist. Thus we should make each session quite short. We are told to have eighteen sessions each day. If after some time you do not lose your dullness or excitement, you should have a larger number of very short sessions. These should be of the highest quality. Do this and the image will begin to persist of its own accord. Only when this happens should you lengthen your sessions.

THE FIFTH PITFALL: [READJUSTMENT] (400)

When you have put an end to your dullness or excitement, readjustment becomes a pitfall, although it is in fact an antidote. The antidote to readjustment is number eight of the adjustments, nonadjustment. You must cultivate this equanimity.

You will be subject to interruptions from dullness or excitement until you get to the eighth mental state. At that stage you may have pacified dullness and excitement, but all the same you have to investigate to see whether they are present or not. But if in your zeal you apply an antidote, you will interrupt this mental state; and so readjustment is a pitfall. Nevertheless, do not put effort into your vigilance: it is best to loosen up a little and to cultivate the adjustment of equanimity. Everyone says that you need to be loose at this point because you were so tight before. By the end of the eighth mental state, you do not fall under the power of mental dullness or excitement, and it is said that you should only loosely apply vigilance. But it was quite a different matter before you reached this point, and the looseness referred to here is not that referred to in the discussion on memory and on loosening the intensity of the retention of the visualization. The Tibetans of the past did not recognize the right point to slacken off, and they claimed that they had "deep meditation in deep relaxation." Their mistake was to slacken their hold on memory too soon. So do not fall into the same trap that they did. Why should you not do as they? Because it would take you far away from the sort of single-pointed concentration that would allow you to gain stability of the image quickly and shed subtle dullness.

So this is the way to pursue other visualizations as well. It is the same from the completion stage downward.

Now I shall discuss the way to pursue this practice. Fulfill the prerequisites for the development of mental quiescence—for example, a location that has the five characteristics. Then sit on a comfortable mat in Vairochana's posture with the seven features. From the visualization of your guru on the crown of your head, imagine that a Śhākyamuni image splits off. Place it in space at about the level of your navel. At first this visualization will not be clear, but it is not yet necessary to achieve clarity. All that appears may be, for example, a flickering yellow blob of just some part of him, such as the head, feet, hands, etc. Do not let these slip from your memory; tighten your retention and do not allow the mind to become distracted. This system of nurturing your recollection alone will be all that is needed to interrupt dullness or excitement. This is why this is the supreme instruction that the great adepts hold in their hearts. Moreover, dullness is cut short by tightening up your image retention. Excitement is cut short by your lack of distraction. When you meditate in this way and achieve a measure of stability, you are most in danger of falling prey to dullness; so be wary of dullness and keep a tight hold on your retention of the image and its clarity. Once you have achieved some clarity the danger is excitement. Take the required measures against excitement and seek further stability.

Though you slavishly do the practice, you are not practicing at all if you do not know what is required to achieve single-pointed concentration. You must definitely achieve single-pointed concentration with the two features: great clarity together with some stability, and a tight image retention.

As in the detailed section on mental quiescence above, the meditation device is retained by your memory not losing the image. At that stage you are set to to fall prey to whichever of sutble or coarse dullness or excitement. As soon as you detect these through vigilance, immediately apply the appropriate antidote and put a stop to them. Do not employ any antidote after cutting short either dullness or excitement: just remain single-pointedly on the visualization while still maintaining most lucid, vivid clarity.

Note: according to the mahāmudrā, the focal object and the mind apprehending this focal object should be taken to be the same thing. A shepherd has to look into two things: which sheep or goats have been lost on the mountain and which have not. When you develop conceptual thoughts, there are similarly two ways mentioned to cut them short. You could look into the nature of the thought and let it cease of its own accord, or you could apply an antidote to the conceptual thought to cut it short and then direct your attention to the mind's clear intelligence. You will receive more details on this in a teaching on the *Gelugpa Mahāmudrā.* Those who wish to achieve mental quiescence by using the mind as the focal object will need to know these.

TAKING THIS AS THE BASIS, HOW TO ACHIEVE THE NINE MENTAL STATES (401)

If you wish to meditate you must experience mental states for yourself. In order to do that you must know what these nine mental states are. They are: (1) fixing the mind, (2) fixation with some continuity, (3) patchy fixation, (4) good fixation, (5) becoming disciplined, (6) becoming peaceful, (7) becoming very pacified, (8) becoming single-pointed, and (9) fixed absorption.

FIXING THE MIND (402)

This is achieved by the power of studying the instruction on visualization with your guru. However, you are only evoking the visualization at this stage. It does not stay, and you cannot make it persist for any length of time. At this point, through the power of the mind's mental processes of conceptual and analytical thinking, you can detect that you are under the power of a lack of focus or excitement. You feel that your conceptual thoughts have increased, but in fact these thoughts have not increased; you have only had the insight of gaining some acquaintance with your conceptual thoughts.

FIXATION WITH SOME CONTINUITY (403)

After meditating in this way you are able to evoke the image and can even make it persist a while—you can meditate for about the time it takes to say a rosary of *oṃ maṇi padme hūṃ* without being distracted. At this point your conceptual thoughts are sometimes peaceful and sometimes they develop. This gives you some insight into what it is like to be cured of conceptual thinking. This state is achieved through the power of contemplation.

Both these first two mental states have a great deal of dullness and excitement, and the image does not remain for long. At this time you are using the first of the four mental processes—forced fixation—but your distraction lasts longer than the image persists.

PATCHY FIXATION (404)

This state is like a garment with patches on the material. Though the image basically persists, the mind becomes distracted from the visualization. But you are immediately aware of this and "patch up your fixation" on the meditation device. The duration of your distraction is shorter than in the previous two states. At this stage you are developing a more powerful memory.

GOOD FIXATION (405)

You have developed powerful memory and you can fix your mind on the meditation device. From now on it is impossible for you to lose the meditation device, and so this state is far more forceful than the previous three. Just the same, while you are not losing the meditation device, you fall prey to the strongest forms of dullness and excitement, and you must apply antidotes to these two.

Both the third and fourth mental states are achieved through the power of memory. But from now on, memory is like a man at the height of his powers, for the power of memory has reached maturity, or has been perfected.

BECOMING DISCIPLINED (406)

In the fourth state, the mind is overly knotted up inside. Now at the fifth, the greatest danger is from subtle dullness. Here you develop powerful vigilance. Vigilance stands on guard; you think this [vigilance] is a quality of single-pointed concentration, and it buoys up your mind.

The difference between the fourth and fifth states is that only the former has coarse dullness and excitement.

BECOMING PEACEFUL (407)

In the fifth state, the mind has been uplifted rather too much, and under these circumstances the greatest danger now is from subtle excitement. When subtle excitement arises, you develop a more powerful form of vigilance in order to detect it. You see that even this subtle excitement is a fault and that you need to prevent it.

The difference between this state and the fifth is that subtle dullness is not the main danger here. Both the fifth and sixth are achieved through the power of vigilance. At this point the power of vigilance has been perfected.

BECOMING VERY PACIFIED (408)

In the seventh state, it is very difficult to develop dullness or excitement because the power of your vigilance and memory has been perfected. You develop the power of perseverance at this point, for you wish to abandon dullness and excitement as much as possible—because you have looked into the damage that they cause.

The difference between the sixth and seventh states is this: in the sixth you must be very wary of the danger of falling prey to subtle dullness and excitement. This is not the case with the seventh.

At this stage there is no danger from subtle dullness or excitement. All the same, you must make an effort in the techniques to abandon both of them. In the fifth and sixth states, there was concern about the harm excitement could do to you. Now at the seventh you persevere and are able to put a stop to excitement or dullness whenever they occur; they cannot then interrupt you for long.

The five mental states starting with number three and going up to number seven, are single-pointed concentration for the most part, interrupted by excitement and dullness. At these stages the mental process is that of interrupted fixation.

BECOMING SINGLE-POINTED (409)

At the beginning you apply the antidote of memory, and though this involves a slight effort, you are then able to pursue the whole length of the meditation session without the subtlest excitement or dullness. Here is an illustration to show what happens in the later mental states. First your enemy was powerful. Then some of his strength declined, and then his power left him completely. This is how the power of your excitement and dullness declined. By the eighth state, you do not have to put effort into the application of vigilance. After the slight [initial] effort during the eighth mental state, the whole session is not interrupted by dullness, excitement, and so on; thus the mental process at this stage is that of uninterrupted fixation.

The seventh and eighth are achieved through the power of perseverance.

FIXED ABSORPTION (410)

The fixation is now effortless. You spontaneously achieve this effortlessness by repeated cultivation of familiarity with the eighth state. You need not exert the slightest effort to slip into single-pointed concentration, just as a person who is good at reciting verses can start a familiar passage. You are now completely absorbed in single-pointed concentration. This state corresponds to the single-pointed mental quiescence of the desire realm. This ninth state is achieved through the power of complete familiarity.

In the first state, your insight acquaints you with your conceptual thoughts. In the second state, you gain some insight into what it is like when your conceptual thoughts take a rest. In the third state, it seems as if these conceptual thoughts have exhausted themselves.

To summarize: In states one and two, the image remains only a short while. In states two and three, your distraction lasts only a short while. The difference between states three and four is whether or not it is possible for you to lose the meditation device. In the fourth state you develop coarse dullness, but not in the fifth. In the fifth you have to beware of subtle dullness, but not in the sixth. Though you develop subtle excitement in the sixth, it is less than you had before. In the sixth you have to be particularly on your guard against slipping into subtle dullness or excitement. There is no need for this in the seventh. In the seventh you have excitement and dullness, but not in the eighth. In the eighth you depend on effort, but not in the ninth.

In the seventh state, you merely put a stop to your excitement and dullness. There is no need to be very wary of falling prey to them. Suppose you are going into battle against an enemy. If his strength has already become inferior to yours, you do not have to take great precautions; it is sufficient just to pin him down.

DAY 22

Pabongka Dorje Chang gave us a short talk in order to set our motivations.

Glorious Chandrakīrti said:

> The king of swans spreads his broad white wings,
> One relative, one of suchness, and flying at the head of his flock.
> Propelled by strong winds of virtue,
> He crosses the lake of good qualities to the supreme shore of
> the victors.

That is, with the two types of bodhichitta—the relative and ultimate forms—together with the two collections, you will reach the level of the victorious ones. You must study how to do this.

He then reviewed the above headings on: the way to train for mental quiescence by cultivating the five or six prerequisites; the actual way to go about achieving mental quiescence; the five pitfalls and the way to cultivate their antidotes, the eight adjustments; and, with the foregoing serving as the basis, the way to achieve the nine mental states.

THE WAY TO ACHIEVE THE MENTAL STATES THROUGH THE SIX POWERS (411)

The first mental state is achieved through the *power of study;* the second through the *power of contemplation.* The third and fourth are achieved through the *power of memory;* both the fifth and sixth come through the *power of vigilance.* The seventh and eighth are achieved through the *power of perseverance;* the ninth through the *power of familiarity.* I have already dealt with this in more detail in the above sections that discuss the nine mental states individually.

HOW THERE ARE FOUR TYPES OF MENTAL PROCESS (412)

The first two mental states are a forced type of fixation. The next five are an interrupted type of fixation. The eighth state is an uninterrupted form of fixation involving some effort. The ninth is a spontaneous, effortless form of fixation. Each of these mental processes is distinguished by the following features:

Both the first and second mental states are chiefly dullness and excitement with hardly any single-pointed concentration. They are not considered worth labeling interrupted—or even uninterrupted—single-pointed concentration. At this stage you must force yourself into these mental states through vigilance and memory.

While it is not the case that you do not need to force yourself into the next five mental states by vigilance and memory, your single-pointed concentration does become progressively more stable. Thus the mental process here is one of interrupted fixation, because your mental state is being interrupted by dullness and excitement.

In the eighth state you apply a little of the antidote of effort at the beginning of the session; the rest of the session is uninterrupted by excitement or dullness.

In the ninth you effortlessly evoke the visualization; thus the fixation is spontaneous.

THE WAY TRUE MENTAL QUIESCENCE DEVELOPS FROM THIS POINT (413)

When you reach the ninth state, your single-pointed concentration is free of subtle dullness and excitement. You are able to remain in this state effortlessly for long periods, and yet this state is *not* true mental quiescence: it only resembles it. In order to achieve true mental quiescence, you must meditate single-pointedly again and again to gain further familiarity with it. You must then attain the exceptional bliss that comes with mental and physical suppleness.

Mental suppleness is the first of the two types to develop, but the bliss due to physical suppleness is the first of the two blisses to develop. The deleterious energy winds within the body are pacified, and you feel comfortable, although you feel a kind of pressure in the scalp or brain, rather like the sensation of a warm hand touching your newly shaven head. You immediately pacify the deleterious states of mind that stand in the way of carrying out any of the virtue you may wish to perform. You have developed mental suppleness.

You then develop physical suppleness as a result of this mental suppleness, and the energy winds are now well adapted and circulating throughout the body. The body is now free of any deleterious states and feels no discomfort while you perform virtuous practices. It can be put to any use you want. The body is supple and as light as cotton wool; you thus experience great bliss from this physical suppleness, and the body has extremely blissful natural physical sensations.

Then, whenever you enter meditative absorption, you have the experience of your body dissolving into the meditation device, and nothing else appears to you, not even your own body, etc. This is the experience of the great ecstasy of mental suppleness, and the mind is so flooded with mental bliss that it is almost unable to stay on the visualization. This problem of the mind being flooded with bliss will clear up, and you then feel that the bliss has lessened somewhat. While in this state, you have gained the immutable type of suppleness that corresponds to the single-pointed concentration which always stays on the visualization.

At the same time, you have also gained the mental quiescence associated with the mandatory access level of the first dhyāna state of concentration. This particular access level is termed "mandatory" because it is a path without which it is quite impossible to achieve many types of mundane and supramundane realizations. From this point you are able to achieve the other access levels that follow and are achieved serially—in fact you can achieve all eight of the levels associated with the form-realm dhyāna states and the formless-realm states.

There is little need for this, however, so we do not develop these latter levels. Non-Buddhists abandon manifest delusions associated with the levels up to and including the Nothingness plane of the formless realm. And when they gain the mental state of the Peak of Existence, they take it to be liberation; but this has not liberated them from saṃsāra at all. As *Praise to the Praiseworthy* says:

These people, blinded by benightedness,
Do not endorse your Dharma.
They may ascend to the Peak of Existence
But will suffer yet again—they merely achieve samsaric existence.

One sūtra says:

Worldly beings meditate single-pointedly
But have not destroyed their attitudes toward the self;
And for all their pains, their single-pointed meditation
Is such that their delusions will return.

We are told of an example of this. One practitioner, after taking many pains, remained for many years in the Peak of Existence meditative absorption. The rats ate up his long hair. Later he noticed this and lost his temper! His dhyāna concentration declined and he went to the lower realms.

When you achieve excellent mental quiescence, you experience such clarity of mind that you can even count the atoms in walls, etc. Whenever any of these ten signs appear before you—that is, the five objects of the senses, external visual form, for example; the three poisons; men; and women—you will recall their drawbacks and come to dislike them. You will develop fewer delusions, and those you do develop will be weaker. You will develop good qualities, such as thinking you are combining your single-pointed concentration with your sleep, because this stability is so solid.

These days there are people who pretend they seek the view found in the mahāmudrā or dzogchen teachings by referring to short and simplistic texts instead of relying on the great classics. Such people will find it difficult to achieve anything of real value discussed in the classics, even common mental quiescence, for example. Yet we share mental quiescence [with non-Buddhists]. According to the root text of the mahāmudrā, observation of the conscious workings of the mind is said merely to acquaint you with the relative truth of the mind. So you may think your meditations along these lines are sound, but it is like believing a lump of brass to be gold. You deserve only to wander aimlessly on wrong paths. You may increase your dullness and mistake this for meditation, but such meditation will not even precipitate your rebirth in the higher realms [of form and formlessness]. You will merely create the cause for rebirth as, for example, an animal. Sakya Paṇḍita says:

The blind usually turn meditation on the mahāmudrā
Into the cause for becoming an animal,
Or, better, fall into the cessation of śhrāvakas,
Or are reborn in the formless realms.

You may analyze the nature of the mind as having no color or shape, and do this not in conjunction with any of the three fundamentals of the path; or perhaps you are familiar with the instruction, "Do not retrace the past; do not anticipate the future" [that is, dwell only in the present in your meditations]. Such slavish meditations only cause a human life to become empty and hollow; they cannot lead you to any of the paths and levels. But in conjunction with bodhichitta, renunciation, correct view, and taking refuge, such a practice becomes, respectively, Mahāyāna, a practice leading to liberation, a Buddhist Dharma. You must enter such an unmistaken path. If you don't, the mere realization that the nature of the mind is clear, empty, and without grasping [at meaning] cannot make inroads on your grasping at a self. At best, such meditations threaten to have the same effect as those extreme practices of the tīrṭhikas. Do not, therefore, hold such inferior paths to be sound. You must know how to distinguish between the correct path and those that only seem to be correct.

HOW TO TRAIN IN THE VERY ESSENCE OF WISDOM—SPECIAL INSIGHT (414)

This has three subheadings: (1) ascertaining the nonexistence of a personal self and (2) ascertaining the nonexistence of a self of phenomena; (3) then, the way you develop special insight.

ASCERTAINING THE NONEXISTENCE OF A PERSONAL SELF (415)

There are two more headings here: (1) how to pursue the absorption resembling space; (2) when not in absorption, how to pursue the attitude that things are like an illusion.

HOW TO DEVELOP THE ABSORPTION RESEMBLING SPACE (416)

Here there are four key points to be determined: (1) what is to be refuted; (2) what are the full set of possibilities; (3) how the self and the aggregates

RATS EATING THE YOGI'S HAIR (SEE P. 619)

cannot be truly the same; (4) how the self and the aggregates cannot be truly different.

After achieving very stable mental quiescence, we do not meditate on things like the special insights found in worldly paths to the gross mental peace [of the form and formless realms]. These would only suppress manifest delusions. The thing we most yearn for is liberation, so we must develop the supramundane type of special insight that analyzes the meaning of selflessness. This will sever the root of cyclic existence for us. Were we to develop such insight, we would systematically prevent all the banes of cyclic existence without ever having to resort to any special meditation in the higher planes. As is said in *Praise to the Praiseworthy:*

> Although people who follow your doctrine
> Do not gain the actual dhyāna planes,
> They prevent their rebirth existence,
> While Māra looks on helplessly.

Thus we must ascertain what is meant by profound emptiness. If we gain no realization into it, it is quite impossible to gain liberation; and even the other tasks of a child of the victorious ones would only become something associated with grasping at dualistic signs.

If you have only part of the combination of method and wisdom, you will not be able to travel to the state of a victorious one. You will be like a bird with only one wing. The method is bodhichitta; wisdom is [realization of] emptiness. You must not train in one without the other. Just as Je Rinpoche said:

> If you do not have the wisdom that understands the way
> things exist,
> You cannot eradicate the roots of existence,
> Despite [your] acquaintance with renunciation and bodhichitta.
> Thus, work hard at the means to realize interdependence.

Although while still tending to believe in emptiness you may have some doubts, they say emptiness will tear to shreds your grasping at a self. It is like a hailstorm flattening crops. The *Four Hundred Verses* says:

Even those with few merits
Have no doubts about this Dharma.
Even those who still have their doubts
Will tear existence to tatters.

Now this practice is something that also has its necessary prerequisites: in order to develop the correct view in your mindstream, you must have all the following causes and prerequisites. You should devote yourself to a holy being who has correct understanding of the key points of the scriptures, and you should obtain from him instructions on emptiness; you should also accumulate your [merit] collection and purify your obscurations; you should petition your guru and hold him to be inseparable from your tutelary deity; and so on. If you do not have a complete set of these, you will not be able to gain any realization.

There were many different versions of the view among the four schools of tenets asserted in the noble land of India, but foremost among these views is that put forward by the Prāsaṅgika Mādhyamikas. They were the only ones to explain that the meaning of interdependent origination is emptiness, while the meaning of emptiness is interdependent origination.

Our Compassionate Teacher taught at various levels for disciples with inferior to superior mentalities. Hence he first taught that the person is empty of substantial and autonomous existence. He did this in order to prevent his disciples from clinging to a personal self. To disciples with better minds, he made the distinction between phenomena that truly exist and those that do not. To people with even better minds, he taught that phenomena do not truly exist but that they can be established by their natures. To those with still better minds, he taught that all phenomena by nature do not exist. This last version is the best and the Bhagavān's ultimate thought on the matter.

As our Teacher himself said:

A most famous and glorious monk,
Born in the land of Bhaita in the south,
Who will be named Nāga,
Will destroy nihilism and substantialism.

The Protector Nāgārjuna is here predicted as the peerless interpreter of the thoughts of the Victorious One on how to abandon the extremes of nihilism and substantialism. Thus we must seek the view by following in his footsteps. Many are the views that are newly fabricated by people's mere whim that have been declared to be profound, but the ultimate view accords with Nāgārjuna's thoughts, and it is certain that to alter them is to misrepresent the thoughts of the Victorious One. And this does not merely apply to the stupid Tibetans! People like the great Indian scholar Āchārya Bhāvaviveka and the great Tibetan Jonangpa pandits were mistaken about key points of the view. There were also others who followed Nāgārjuna but did not understand his thinking. There were even those who not only did not follow Nāgārjuna but who tried to refute him as well. Of those who do not depend on the philosophical system of Nāgārjuna and his successors, and who teach views they themselves invented and that fall outside his system, Chandrakīrti says:

> Paths other than those Āchārya Nāgārjuna trod
> Are outside his system, and are not the means to peace.
> They debase relative and ultimate truth.
> With these debased, liberation is unattainable.

So, unless there is a second gateway to the peace of liberation, such a peace is impossible for those who do not follow his system. Atiśha said:

> How can emptiness be realized?
> Chandrakīrti, disciple of he who was predicted by the Tathāgata,
> Of he who saw the true suchness of phenomena: Nāgārjuna.
> Through his lineage of instruction you will see the true suchness of phenomena.

That is, Āchārya Chandrakīrti was the best of Nāgārjuna's followers. Many Tibetan āchāryas of particular sects followed Chandrakīrti during the earlier dissemination of the teachings in Tibet. The thoughts of many of these earlier āchāryas remained in the Prāsaṅgika camp; but the āchāryas taught in various ways to suit the mentalities of their disciples, and later, many of their followers did not comprehend the true thoughts of these masters and gradually fell into error. There were few authorities on the ultimate version of the view, and Je Tsongkapa, the embodiment of Mañjuśhrī, did not trust what most of these other Tibetans were saying about the view. So he set off for the noble land of India to meet Āchārya Nāgabodhi, the great adept Mitra, and so on. The great adept Lhodrag Namkha Gyaeltsaen begged him to abandon this plan. With the adept himself acting as intermediary, Tsongkapa asked Vajrapāṇi questions on the view. Vajrapāṇi's teaching was written down in the form of questions and answers and called the *Rosary of Supreme Healing Ambrosia.* This teaching made Je Rinpoche doubt all the more the views expressed in the books available at that time. He was still completely dissatisfied. And so he made petitions to his guru while regarding him as indivisible from Mañjuśhrī; he worked hard and long at building up his accumulations and at purifying himself, and pursued a variety of meditation topics. He practiced these intensively and later received the direct vision of Mañjuśhrī.

In general there are three types of vision. One is seeing a hallucination of the deity, experienced when the energy winds enter the energy channels. There is another type of vision where the deity appears to the mental consciousness, and this type is experienced in meditation. Lastly is the type where one actually sees the deity with one's sense consciousness—man to man, as it were. Je Rinpoche had this last type of vision of Mañjuśhrī and was able to meet Mañjuśhrī as a disciple meets his guru. Mañjuśhrī's answers to the questions Je Rinpoche put concerning difficult points on the view were too profound. Whenever Je Rinpoche did not understand something, he would debate these doubtful points with Rendawa. Yet even this did not clear up all his doubts. Mañjuśhrī declared that Tsongkapa should take his teachings as his starting point, and then if he took pains, he would come to realize the profound and undistorted view by relying on the learned classics. So it came to pass: Later, by virtue of his stack of accumulations and purification of obscurations, he had the vision of Buddhapālita; he then went through this author's commentary, the *Pursuit of Buddhahood,* and so the ultimate view of the Prāsaṅgika arose in his mindstream. During these periods of his life, he had visions of many Indian pandits and adepts but paid scant attention to them. Mañjuśhrī told Je Rinpoche—with a highly realized lama [probably Umapa] acting as intermediary for the deity—that he should heed these visions, for it would be most beneficial for others and himself if he were to depend on their masterpieces.

When Je Rinpoche came to realize the undistorted view of the Mādhyamikas, his faith in Buddha the Teacher welled up, and he composed a poem in praise of the doctrine of interdependent origination that Buddha had expounded. This work is called *In Praise of Interdependent Origination* or the *Brief Essence of Eloquence.* Choglae Namgyael of Badong heard a nearby beggar on a pilgrimage singing this poem. At first Namgyael thought it was the work of Nāgārjuna, or perhaps that of Chandrakīrti. But then he heard the author at the end of the work discuss how he had depended upon the classics of Nāgārjuna and Chandrakīrti. From that Namgyael understood that they could not have written the poem. He asked the beggar, who replied, "Great Tsongkapa wrote this." Namgyael developed unshakable faith in Je Rinpoche and set off to meet him. He discovered that Je Rinpoche had already departed—he had gone to the pure fields for the sake of other beings. Unable to see him, Namgyael prayed they would meet and threw pieces of gold and silver into the air. These landed in the grounds of Gandaen Monastery. This and other wonders can be found in Je Rinpoche's biography.

So the great Je Rinpoche's eloquent works are the supreme clarification of the meaning of these profound teachings, which disentangled the thoughts of these masters. Yet he did not regard a text as authentic merely because it came from the noble land of India. He did not make use of the major body of writings that could fulfill this criterion for his ascertainment of the view. Instead he asked his own tutelary deity Mañjuśhrī for advice. Mañjuśhrī told him that Chandrakīrti was a courageous and discerning bodhisattva of high degree who had come here from a buddhafield with the intention of spreading Protector Nāgārjuna's teachings on the profound view, and that his writings were error free. Thus Je Rinpoche regarded Mañjuśhrī's words together with the corpus of Chandrakīrti's writings as authoritative.

Je Rinpoche's writings concerning the view set forth in the scriptures are difficult for us to comprehend or to realize during our study and contemplation of them because they are so tremendously deep and profound. So we do not easily develop understanding, and so on. And yet, if we study them over and over again in detail, we will develop the wisdom born of studying emptiness, for these texts are exceptionally profound in many ways, with clarity not found elsewhere. His teachings impart greater understanding than other [writings].

THE FIRST KEY POINT: WHAT IS TO BE REFUTED (417)

Now I shall teach this topic briefly, based on the thoughts of Je Rinpoche. He first discussed how to ascertain personal selflessness. [Āryadeva's] *Four Hundred Verses* says:

First, reverse your meritless state;
Next, refute the self;
Finally, the one view refutes all.
He who knows this is skilled.

This accords with the instructions concerning the order in which you should carry out this practice. In the small and medium scopes, you must refute such views as regarding cause and effect as nonexistent. Next you must refute the personal self and, finally, the self of phenomena.

There is no difference between the nonexistent selves dealt with in the doctrine of the two selflessnesses. All the same, I shall first teach selflessness in relation to a particular object in question: the person. It is easier to determine this type of selflessness. Also, there are a number of arguments about emptiness to be ascertained: arguments based on mutual interdependence, the argument that looks at the components of a chariot in seven ways,[82] and so on. The easiest of these for beginners to understand is the argument of the self being neither one with nor different [from its basis of imputation, the aggregates]. At this point, Je Rinpoche and many of his followers discuss four key points to this argument.

The first of these is to determine just what is to be refuted. In *Engaging in the Deeds of the Bodhisattvas* we find:

When you do not touch on the imputed thing,
You will not grasp its absence.

In other words, if you cannot identify what the self is—the thing to be refuted and that does not exist—you will not recognize the negation having no further implications that remains after the process of refutation. Some analogies: you cannot shoot an arrow if you cannot see the target, and you will not catch a thief if you cannot identify him. You must identify the self to be refuted. This truth that does not truly exist, the nature that is not established by its nature, the independent entity denied in "lack of independent existence," is described in [Chandrakīrti's] *Commentary to the Four Hundred Verses:*

> The thing known as the *self* is the entity or nature that is not the outcome of any other functional phenomenon. *Selflessness* is its nonexistence.

Thus the self is supposed to be something distinct in itself, for it is not the outcome of other conditions. It is also said to be self-sufficient as an entity, for it is independent of anything else; it is not the outcome of anything else.

You could use those words in debate and they would serve to silence your opponent, but you have not identified the object of refutation until you have determined it through experience. For example, you will not identify a thief if you just go by descriptions such as "the thief is a man" or "he was wearing white." Likewise, you will not comprehend this object through somebody else's description or through mental images derived from mere words and terms. You must recognize the object of refutation through vivid, naked, personal mental experiences brought on by an analytic process.

If you have not determined the object of refutation, you are in danger of falling into the nihilistic view disproving the mutual interdependence [of phenomena], despite making use of the many arguments that prove they are not established as true. For example, the convention of a pot is entirely familiar to you. So you might say, "The mouth of the pot is not the pot. The base of the pot is not the pot," and so on, eliminating each part of the pot and finally slavishly meditating on the emptiness of merely not being able to find the pot anymore. But [this way] you still lack the precision to properly refute the object of refutation upon the basis of that particular emptiness, and so you only destroy the *conventionality* of the pot and fall into complete nothingness. This emptiness you have imagined is quite on the wrong track.

In seeking the object to be refuted, we must investigate the way we instinctively grasp at an "I" that is supposed to be established by its very nature. When we investigate just how the "I" instinctively appears to the mind, and just how the mind grasps at the "I," we find that we feel: "This 'I' is *not* merely something our minds impute upon the set of aggregates—it is established along with this set." Such instinctive grasping at the "I" is to be found even in the mindstreams of ants, in the deepest recesses of their minds, and even in their dreams.

In general there are three ways of grasping [intellectually] at the "I" based upon the person. They are: (1) the sort of grasping carried out by people who have developed the view concerning emptiness in their mindstreams. They merely impute the "I" conceptually upon the basis of imputation. There are also people who hold the doctrine that things do not truly exist, and they have [the same] form of grasping at the "I." (2) The way ordinary people, whose mindstreams have not been influenced by tenets, grasp at the "I." This manner of grasping at the "I" is found in people who couldn't care less whether or not the "I" can be established by its nature. (3) The form of grasping at the "I" found in people whose concern is to establish the "I" by its nature.

The second of the above three modes is a valid mental cognition that assumes the conventional "I." Its subject is merely this type of "I," something that exists conventionally. It is also correct that cause and effect operate on this conventional "I."

The third of these three types of grasping at the "I" is a mistaken consciousness and should be destroyed by some antidote. It is this aspect of the "I" that is the object to be refuted in the various arguments. When you are led astray by the way in which the "I" instinctively appears to you, you are clinging to the "I"—for example, when you feel, "I have eaten."

The mind, when it is being uncritical, is satisfied with an "I" that is a mere imputation. Actions and agents, such as in going or sitting—as in "I'm going" or "I'm sitting"—are only imputed labels. This is how we accommodate activities and agents [in our philosophical system]. Part of the way that the "I" instinctively appears to you is this thinking that assumes the conventional "I." Nevertheless, this instinctive appearance of the "I" does not present itself in any precise way that is clear and not confused with any other object appearing to you [at the time]. You must know how to distinguish between these two: the way the "I" seems to be established as something self-sufficient by nature and the way the [conventional] "I" itself appears.

This instinctive form of grasping at the "I" is something we have always had in our mindstreams, even when dreaming. As long as we do not meet with certain circumstances, we will not be clear on how it appears. The "I," however, manifests clearly when there are powerful conditions for you to be happy or sad—such as when you are praised or criticized. Suppose someone accuses you of being a thief and this makes you upset. Great hostility arises within you, and you feel, "I'm innocent, and he accused *me*!" You say, "That's the last straw for me!" You cannot refute the accusation on the spot and instead lose control of yourself. The subject of the accusation of theft: the feeling of "me" in "That's the last straw for me"; the "I" that rises vividly out of the very center of your heart in all its glory—this is the way the object of refutation will present itself to you.

Whenever this thinking manifests in any circumstance making you glad, afraid, happy, or sad, let this instinctive grasping develop strongly, and then examine on the spot the way it appears to you.

Suppose two people are traveling side by side on the same road, each keeping an eye on both the road and their companion out of the corner of their eye. This illustrates the following. While your mind continues to act instinctively, and while you let the object to be refuted present itself to you, you must examine the instinctive mode of appearance of this object with a minute part of your mind. If this mind examining the mode of appearance of the "I" is too strong, part of your grip on the "I" will be destroyed and will become void or unclear. Thus it is vital to examine the "I" skillfully.

In this process, while you are looking into exactly how the "I" appears to your instinctive grasping at a self, the "I" may present itself in various ways. Sometimes the "I" may seem like something imputed on the body, sometimes on the mind. This is not the genuine way the "I" presents itself to the instinctive grasping of the "I." The body and mind, which are the bases of imputation, as well as the person—the imputed phenomenon—all merge into the one undifferentiated set. The self-evident "I" plainly appears to not be just some name imputed on this set. It appears instead to be something established as being self-sufficient. If the "I" seems to be like this, you have rightly perceived the way the object to be refuted appears to you. Once recognized, it is easy to refute.

This key point is a subtle one; sometimes the mistake is in taking it too far and at other times in not taking it far enough. If you do not identify the object of refutation, it will always present itself to you; when you try to identify it, it stays hidden among the set of mind and body, and you will not find it. If you were, for example, to go to the edge of a high cliff, in your fear you would think, "I might fall," not "My body might fall" or "My mind might fall." The body and mind are inseparable, like a mixture of milk and water. The self-evident "I," which is the thing that might fall over the cliff, will arise on top of the mind and body—that is *it*. Likewise, when you go for a gallop on a horse, you do not mean the horse's mind or body when you say "horse." "Horse" is not merely a name imputed on the set of both of them. You apprehend the horse to be the self-evident thing covered by [the term] "horse." When you speak of Sera or Drepung, you are not distinguishing between the external buildings such as the main temples, and the monks, etc., that are inside them. The basis of imputation is the collection of the physical environments of these monasteries together with their contents. Over this collection will arise the self-evident thing equal in size and extent to "Sera and Drepung"—it is *it.* When you talk of a scholar, the basis of imputation is merely the set of his mind and body. But something self-evident and quite independent of anything else presents itself to you.

In short, as Ketsang Jamyang Monlam says, any and every phenomenon is said to be "this" or "that." "This" or "that," equal in size and extent to the basis of imputation, presents itself. This is the ultimate object of refutation by logic. It has been described as "the thing to which you direct your grasping at true existence," or as "the object of negation that is supposed to be established as true when one does not recognize that it only appears to be true." When you recognize only part of the object of refutation, and slavishly make use of the many different arguments put forth in the Madhyamaka classics, your analysis will only be through the medium of mental images gained secondhand of "being established as true" or "self-sufficient." Everything will be mere words. You will make no inroads into your grasping at true existence at all. If you do not allow the object of refutation to present itself to you of its own accord and instead merely refabricate the thought of "I" for your fresh object of refutation to be used in analysis, you will arrive only at some theoretical form of the view.

To sum up, venerable Lozang Choekyi Gyaeltsaen said:

> The way things now present themselves to us ordinary beings is nothing but the way the object to be refuted through logic would appear to us. All consciousnesses within the mindstreams of ordinary beings have been affected by ignorance; because of this, any object that appears to us seems to be true.

That is, at the moment, all phenomena, any things that appear to us—the self, the aggregates, Mount Meru, houses, etc.—present themselves to us ordinary people in such a way that their appearance is a mixture of an appearance of relative truth and true [existence]. So we have no way of dividing things into "those that appear to exist truly" and "those that do not appear to exist truly." *Everything* appears to exist truly; and so the way everything impresses itself on the mind appears to us, without exception, mixed with the object to be refuted. Thus the way things appear to us is the way the object of refutation appears, or [if you like] the way things established as true would appear. Leave it at that, because it is futile to seek the object of refutation elsewhere. Changkya Roelpai Dorje said:

> Now a few of us with clearer minds
> Cling to slogans such as "self-contained" and "established as true,"
> Yet leave self-evident appearances alone.
> They seem to seek a thing to be refuted with horns [on its head]!
>
> Do not say these blurry things
> Are the shadowless face of the Mother.
> If you do much talking but don't hit the target to be refuted,
> I fear the old Mother will run away![83]

In other words, this is the great danger. Thus it is vital to investigate thoroughly with a subtle and discerning mind. Do this in conjunction with the right external conditions—the instructions from your guru—and the right internal ones—such as having a collection of merit and having purified yourself. If you are able to identify the object of refutation correctly, arguments such as one of the logical statements concerning interdependent origination will crumble the mountain of your grasping at true existence. The criterion of having identified this object correctly is that you will realize emptiness without any difficulty.

Changkya Roelpai Dorje said:

> You do not have to search for it: The thing, O seeker, is you.

In other words, you do not have to look far afield to find emptiness; the thing abides together with you, the seeker. Thus, meditate continuously for months or years solely on the identification of the object to be refuted!

THE SECOND KEY POINT: DETERMINING THE FULL SET OF POSSIBILITIES (418)

As we have just heard above, a correct mental image borne of firsthand experience of the object to be refuted may appear clearly to the mind's eye. If such an "I"—the thing being instinctively grasped at—were in fact established by its nature, it would necessarily be established as being either one with or different from the basis of imputation: the aggregates. There is no third possibility other than these two. In general, if a phenomenon exists, it must necessarily be singular or plural. If this is the full set of possibilities for a category, and if something is proved for the whole category, then when an instance of that category exists truly, it must necessarily be either truly singular or truly plural. It is quite certain that this covers all cases; it therefore also applies to such an "I," which can only be either the same as the aggregates or separate from them.

The key point of this is it should lead you to the certainty that, "If it is neither of these two, it cannot exist." You must meditate on this key point not merely for a day or two but until you gain unshakable conviction in it.

THE THIRD KEY POINT: DETERMINING THAT THEY ARE NOT TRULY THE SAME (419)

Begin by bringing to mind the mode of existence of the thing to be refuted. Apply this to the way the self and the aggregates appear: if they were established as one, they would not appear separately to the mind. They must be one, never divisible into separate components. The reason is that things that have the same entity can appear to the mind as separate from one another, but this discordance between the way they appear and their actual mode of existence is the deceptive way of relative truth. Such would not be acceptable if they were established as true: the way it appears would have to correspond with the way it exists. Consequently, it would be pointless to posit a self. To say "the self's aggregates" would be no different from saying "the aggregates' aggregates" or "the self's self." It would be pointless to make the distinction between "the self" and "the self's aggregates." [Nāgārjuna's] *Root of Wisdom* says:

> When you determine that it is not so
> That the self exists apart from the appropriated [aggregates],
> If the appropriated [aggregates] are the self,
> Your [proposed] self would not exist.

In other words, the flaw in such an argument is that there would be no appropriator, the self, that is different from the five appropriated aggregates. As if this were not enough, it says in *Engaging in the Middle Way:*

> It is not right to argue the appropriator and appropriated are one,
> For then the doer and the deed would be one.

In other words, such an argument is absurd, because the receiver and the thing appropriated would be one. The body and the embodied being would be one; the limbs and the creature with the limbs would be one. Further, if the self and the aggregates were one, then, as it says in *Engaging in the Middle Way:*

> If the aggregates were the self, it follows that,
> As they are many, the self too would be multiple.

In other words, just as there are five aggregates, the self would also be five in number.

Another absurd consequence would be that as there is only one self, one could not accommodate five aggregates—they would have to be one as well. As the self is supposed to be the five aggregates, we have the absurdity that it would be meaningless to talk of conception in the mother's womb. Further, as the "I" and the body are supposed to be the same entity by nature, and the body is cremated after death, becoming ash, we have the absurdity that the "I" is cremated at the same time and also turns to ash. And we have further absurdities: when the "I" goes to its next rebirth, the body would be conceived at the time of conception; or, since that body will *not* be so conceived, the "I" will not be conceived in the next rebirth either; it would not be possible for such a self to be reborn in the formless realm; the self would be matter. If the "I" and the mind were one, it would be impossible for the "I" to feel cold or hunger, because the mind does not get cold or feel hungry. The absurd consequence would be that one could not say "I am cold" or "I am hungry" when one is hot, cold, hungry, thirsty, and so on. If both the body and mind were the "I," it would be pointless to make any distinction between "my body" and "my mind."

Furthermore, if the self and the aggregates were established from their own side as being one thing, then their location, time, and everything about them would have to be the same. So, as it says in the *Root of Wisdom:*

> If the aggregates were the self,
> It would be a thing produced and destroyed.

In other words, just as the aggregates are produced and cease to be, the self would also be produced and cease. Thus, just as the form aggregate has past and future discontinuities and is—in this sense—produced and destroyed, so the self would also have its continuity broken; and the absurd consequence is that it, too, would be produced and destroyed.

If the "I" reborn in one's other rebirths and the aggregates of each past or future rebirth were by nature the same entity, the "I" of the past rebirths and the "I" of this present rebirth would be either the same or different. If these "I"s were the same, one would have to experience in this present rebirth the sufferings of being dumb and stupid that one had in one's past rebirth as an animal. Another consequence is that the animal in that past rebirth would have to experience the happiness that is the lot of a human being. But if the "I" of the previous life were naturally separate from the "I" of future rebirths, then, as it says in *Engaging in the Middle Way:*

> The qualities related to Maitreya and Upagupta
> Are different, and thus not included in the same continuum.
> It is not right to include things having
> Individual characteristics under the one continuity.

In other words, the absurd consequence is that this argument cannot accommodate the clairvoyant power of being able to remember many of one's past lives, because these lives would have to be as separate and naturally unrelated as Maitreya and Upagupta, who have different mindstreams. From the *Root of Wisdom:*

> If [the past "I"] were different,
> Without it, it [the present self] would arise.
> Further: [the past "I"] would remain
> Or be reborn and not die.
>
> Then it would absurdly follow that
> On the annihilation [of the past self], karma would dissipate,
> And the karma done by one being
> Would be inidividually experienced by others, and so on.

That is, the disappearance of karma that had already been committed is one fault in the argument. You may then wonder, "Wouldn't the self of a subsequent rebirth experience [karmic] results even though the self of the past rebirth had been discarded?" If this were so, these absurdities would follow: a person established by his nature would experience the results of karma accumulated by another person, who is also established by his nature. This is tantamount to meeting with something for which the karma has not been committed. And so on.

You have determined that the self and the aggregates are not truly the same when you are convinced that: "There is absolutely no way to establish the self and the five aggregates as being established by nature as one."

THE FOURTH KEY POINT: DETERMINING THAT THEY ARE NOT TRULY DIFFERENT (420)

Now that you are certain they are not the same, you should feel, "All that remains is for the self and the aggregates to be established as separate by nature." If they were shown to be naturally separate then, as it says in the *Root of Wisdom:*

> We cannot accept that the self
> Is different from that appropriated [the aggregates].
> If these were different, it would be rightly perceived
> Without the appropriated. But it is not so perceived.

In other words, when you eliminate the goat and sheep from a group consisting of a sheep, a goat, and a bull; you are able to point to the remaining animal and say, "There's the bull!" You must similarly be able to identify something that is unconnected with the aggregates called the "I," which would be the residue after eliminating each of the five aggregates—form, feeling, recognition, compositional factors, and consciousness. But you do not, in fact, come to identify such a thing.

It says in the *Root of Wisdom:*

> If it were different from the aggregates,
> It would not have the characteristics of the aggregates.

That is, the self would not have the production, cessation, etc., that are the characteristics of conditioned phenomena. Also, although the aggregates are born, age, and die, the self would not be born, age, or die, and so on. Anything that affects the aggregates would neither hurt nor harm the self. These examples contradict common sense, and there are many other contradictions. One would still have a sense of an "I" without its aggregate basis. Previously committed karma would disappear; there would also follow the absurdity that I have already mentioned, of one's meeting with something for which the karma had not been committed, and so on.

The point about this process of determining that the self and the aggregates are not truly different is for you to become convinced that "They are definitely not established as being separate by nature."

Thus, while recalling the way in which the thing you have determined to be the object of refutation appears to you, examine this object by means of the above arguments—that it is neither the same as, nor different from, the aggregates. The sort of conviction you gain, which totally refutes these two, is illustrated as follows. Suppose you have lost a bull and there are only two valleys for it to go to. The mere words, "There is no bull in this valley," would not satisfy you, and you would seek the bull from top, to middle, to bottom of the two valleys. When you do not find it, an involuntary feeling will arise within you that the sought-after bull you had set your mind on is not there. Similarly, this "I"—the object clung to by your instinctive self-grasping—seemed until now like something that could be seen by the eye or touched by the hand. When the vivid thought arises that "It is not there," when it becomes completely empty, when you decidedly determine that it does not exist, you have found the Madhyamaka view.

At this point the sharp-witted, owing to their great familiarity with the subject, feel they have discovered something precious. The dull-witted become afraid because they have suddenly lost a most cherished thing. This, however, does no harm. Once, while Je Rinpoche was giving a discourse on the view in Sera Choeding Hermitage, Sherab Senge realized the view and became afraid, grabbing the collar of his monk's shirt. Je Rinpoche understood what had happened, and this made him happy. "The fellow from Nartang," Je Rinpoche said, "has discovered relative truth on his collar!" There is also a story about Ngulchu Togme Sangpo; when he gave a discourse on the view some of his disciples became terrified.

When [the "I"] becomes completely empty, you may get ideas of "This is emptiness! I have realized it!" In this case, either a negation having further implications or an [outright] affirmation is coming to mind, and you should not be misled. If, instead, you are sure that the "I"—the object of refutation—does not exist, your understanding should have two features. You have the conviction or confidence in the nonexistence by nature of the certainty that the "I," the object of such a refutation, definitely does not exist. And as for what is appearing to you [at the time], there should be a complete emptiness that is the mere negation of there being any establishment of this object of refutation as being true. Retain this certainty without forgetting it and always pursue it. If your retention of this certainty weakens or begins to become unclear, it may not be necessary to rise from your meditative absorption, according to circumstances; [in any case,] resume your analysis by means of the four key points as you did before. On rediscovering this certainty, increase its vividness. Then enter single-pointed absorption while this vividness lasts.

While you are in this meditative absorption, a complete emptiness presents itself to you, resembling space. This emptiness is merely the negation of the establishment of the object of refutation as being something true. This is the way you pursue the "skylike" absorption. At this point, by virtue of refuting the self—the object of refutation—the conventional "I" will be blocked. When you do not find it, however, have no fears that you have fallen into the nihilistic view; you must not tire yourself looking for the conventional "I."

WHEN NOT IN ABSORPTION, HOW TO PURSUE THE ATTITUDE THAT THINGS ARE LIKE AN ILLUSION (421)

After rising from this meditative absorption, when you examine what is left among the remnants of the negation of the object to be refuted—doing this while not in absorption—all that seems to remain is the mere name: "I." This is merely the conventional "I." Always bear in mind the certainty that this is what accumulates virtuous or nonvirtuous karma as if in an illusion, and that on this type of "I" will ripen such black or white karmic results. An illustration: although the illusion of horses or elephants appears to the conjurer, he is certain in his own mind that these horses and elephants do not exist. Thus, while he is sure that their appearance is quite false, he undeniably actually sees the agents and actions, the horses and elephants, coming or going, and so forth. As in our example, the "I"—something imputed as a mere label and not naturally existent—nonetheless accumulates karma and experiences happiness and sorrow although it is not something true. Thus you see you can accommodate the fact that the "I" performs actions through its undeniable interdependent origination; and yet, though it appears to you, it is still empty. Though it is empty, it presents itself to you like an illusion. This is how you train yourself.

REMEMBERING IMPERMANENCE AND DEATH

(SEE PP. 301, 320)

When we seek the view for the first time, it is difficult for us to accept emptiness in our mind's eye because of our great familiarity with clinging to true existence; but later it becomes harder for us to accept the appearance of things.

As Nāgārjuna said:

> The peerless Tathāgata taught this:
> All functional things are empty by nature.
> Therefore functional things are interdependent origination.

In other words, their being empty serves as the reason for the interdependent origination of things; their emptiness implies that they can also appear to you. With interdependent origination serving as a reason, this interdependence of things must also imply their emptiness for you.

The formal logic involving mutual interdependence has great importance. An example: when one cites mutual interdependence as proof that a sprout, for example, does not have true existence, it must refute the way one instinctively grasps at an object—here, the sprout—as if it existed in its own right and were not merely something assumed by virtue of having a name applied to it. Such a refutation goes as follows. If, as we perceive, the sprout were established by its nature, it would not be dependent on other things, such as causes or circumstances, nor would it be something assumed through labeling. It would have to be something isolated. But this is not in fact so. It grows owing to a set of causes and conditions—the seed, water, manure, warmth, moisture, and so on. This proves that it is established in dependence on other things and is their outcome: this is something we can actually observe for ourselves. Thus the sprout is an example of interdependent origination. Such arguments and reasonings concerning interdependent origination refute the extreme view that things are established by their nature as being independent of anything else, or as being self-sufficient. So through appearances we are rid of the extreme view of substantialism. Thus, "interdependent origination implies emptiness."

If the seedling were established by its own nature, no cause or circumstance could alter it in any way: the nature of the seedling would necessarily not change into something else. But because it is not established by its own nature, when it has gone beyond the stage of being a sprout, it will eventually grow into a stalk, and will go through other intervening stages as well, until it is barley and is consumed by humans and animals.

This will lead you to the conviction that the presentation of interdependent origination accommodates all such functionality, and that this *is* "emptiness eliminating nihilism and the empty arising as interdependent origination." Thoughts on these matters may be found in the *Sūtra Requested by Anavatapta,* where it says:

> Anything produced through circumstances is not produced;
> It does not have the nature of production.
> Anything that is an outcome of circumstances is empty.
> He who understands emptiness is rigorous.

In the *Root of Wisdom* we find:

> Since there are no phenomena that exist
> That are not interdependently originated,
> There are no phenomena that exist
> That are not empty.

It says in *Engaging in the Middle Way:*

> [Addressing an opponent:] Because functional things arise dependently,
> [Your] conceptions do not bear scrutiny.
> Thus the logic of interdependent origination
> Cuts through the network of wrong views.

Also Je Tsongkapa says:

> Perceiving [that these two] merely go together—that they are not alternatives
> And that mutual interdependence is undeceptive—
> Destroys all the ways in which you grasp at objects with the mind.
> At this point you perfect your analysis of the view.
>
> You eliminate the extreme of specious substantialism;
> You eliminate the extreme of empty nihilism.
> If you understand how emptiness presents itself as causes and effects,
> Views that grasp extremes will not impress you.

If you gain some certainty into how emptiness and interdependent origination do not contradict each other but rather imply each other, you will understand the mutual interdependence of actions and agents, cause and effect, and so on. You will value emptiness and interdependent origination all the more; you will reject sin and practice virtue; you will have compassion, bodhichitta, and will carry out any advice associated with a practice, thus striving in a practice that lacks neither method nor wisdom. Some people do not do this, and instead take cause and effect to be of value only for beginners, while singling out certain instructions for their disciples to follow. Such teachings without cause and effect are not much different from those of the tīrṭhika hedonist school, the Lokāyatas.

ASCERTAINING THE NONEXISTENCE OF A SELF OF PHENOMENA (422)

This has two sections: (1) ascertaining that conditioned phenomena do not naturally exist; (2) ascertaining that unconditioned phenomena do not naturally exist.

ASCERTAINING THAT CONDITIONED PHENOMENA DO NOT NATURALLY EXIST (423)

The subsections are: (1) the ascertainment that physical things do not naturally exist; (2) the ascertainment that consciousness does not naturally exist; (3) the ascertainment that nonassociated compositional factors do not naturally exist.

ASCERTAINING THAT PHYSICAL THINGS DO NOT NATURALLY EXIST (424)

You should readily apply to other phenomena the certainty you have gained into the fact that, as we saw above, a person is not established by his own nature. In a sūtra it says:

> So apply to all
> The same attitude you have for the self.

[Āryadeva] says in the *Four Hundred Verses:*

The view that holds for one
Is the view that holds for all.
Any emptiness that holds for one
Is an emptiness that holds for all.

So first of all we ascertain that physical things do not naturally exist. The consciousnesses that lie within the mental streams of us ordinary beings have been affected by ignorance, and when physical things and so forth appear to us, their mode of appearance is none other than that of seeming to be established in their own right. This appearance is the way the object to be refuted appears, and we must refute such appearances of their supposedly being established in this way.

All phenomena are examples of interdependent origination, that is, a label is merely put upon some basis of imputation—which itself depends upon other components, each with its own basis of imputation. Take the case of a pot, which we had before. To the consciousnesses of ordinary beings who have not achieved the view, the pot does not appear to be merely a phenomenon imputed on some basis of that imputation. Instead, the basis of imputation and the imputed phenomenon are so inextricably mixed that the pot appears to be something self-apparent and established. This is the way in which the object to be refuted appears. It may appear in this way, but when you pursue the reasoning that the basis of imputation and the phenomenon imputed are separate, you will find that the pot, which instinctively is being held to be true, cannot be established as being the same as the basis of the imputation, which is itself supposed to be established as true. Further, once you apply a process of elimination to the basis of imputation of the pot, what remains does not seem to be a pot that you can point to. Instead, the valid conventional pot appears to you in dependence upon its valid basis of imputation—the set of the mouth, the belly, the base, and so on. You must assume that the pot exists merely as a conventional truth, because the pot cannot be established as something that is itself established as true and separate from the basis of imputation.

So in general, if something exists, it must exist as either single or multiple. Similarly, if it is established as being something true, it can only be single or multiple in a way that can be established as true. If it is neither of these two, it cannot be truly existent. For this reason, pots and so forth cannot be established as being true.

In short, extrapolating from the pot, all phenomena—that is, physical things and so forth—must depend upon their bases of imputation; they are not established as true and self-sufficient. The *Four Hundred Verses* says:

> All these are not independent.
> The self, therefore, does not exist.

A pot is generally something single; but it is not established as being naturally single, for it has to depend upon its many components. Also, a pot and a pillar may be separate, but the two are only *assumed* to be separate. Neither of the two is separate on its own; one can only be assumed to be separate in relation to the other. But the pot and the pillar are not established as being separate on their own part. If they were so established, each of the two would necessarily be separate by itself. This results in the absurdity that each is not a single individual. Hence, although the pot and pillar are separate, since the pot itself is a single individual, both *one* and *separate* are only conceptual inputations and not established in their own right. It says in the *Root of Wisdom:*

> *Other* is *other* in relation to another:
> Without another it could not be *other.*
> If *other* were other than *other,*
> It would be *other* without the other.

ASCERTAINING THAT CONSCIOUSNESS DOES NOT NATURALLY EXIST (425)

The thing we call "consciousness" is a functional phenomenon, an illuminating intelligence that occupies itself with some object. There is a very long list of primary minds and mental factors. For all of these there is a part that experiences the entity and the particulars of the object, and a large number of parts being the past and future moments of the consciousness. Apart from the mere conceptual imputation made upon the basis of imputation—the collection of these parts—consciousness is not in the least established on its own part.

However, this is not how it appears to us; it presents itself to us as something quite independent and self-sufficient that independently engages with its object. It is supposed to be something discoverable apart from its object. This is the way in which the object to be refuted presents itself to us. So if this consciousness were established to exist in the way in which it appears—taking today's consciousness in your own mental stream as our example—it would necessarily be established as being either the same as or separate from its past and future moments in time. If it were established as separate from them, what remains after the elimination of the morning's and the evening's consciousnesses should be "today's consciousness." On the contrary, they are inseparable, hence your consciousness is not established as being truly separate from your past or future consciousness.

As for today's consciousness, if both your consciousness this morning and your consciousness this evening were established as being truly singular, it follows—as these two are multiple—that your consciousness today is also multiple. And, as today's consciousness occurred in the morning, it would follow that this evening's consciousness would also occur in the morning. Or, the evening's consciousness did not occur in the morning, so it must also follow that today's consciousness could not have occurred in the morning either. And so on. Hence your consciousness is not established as truly either one with or separate from its components. You must work along these lines in order to gain conviction that it does not truly exist.

If the three elementary facets of consciousness [the object, the consciousness, and the occupation of the consciousness with the object] were established as being truly one and the same thing, there would be the absurd consequence that the doer and the deed would be one. If they were established as being truly separate, one would have to accept that there can be a knower without anything to be known; or that there can be the act of knowing without there being any knower. Because of these and other absurdities, the three elementary facets of consciousness cannot be established on their part as distinct things.

A "consciousness" or an "intelligence" is something constructed upon a basis of imputation that is merely a set of mutually interdependent things, such as the past and future moments that are the consciousness's numerous components. A "consciousness" is something imputed by a valid conventional cognition. We are able to accommodate all the actions and agents of saṃsāra and nirvāṇa within this sort of consciousness.

ASCERTAINING THAT NONASSOCIATED COMPOSITIONAL FACTORS DO NOT EXIST BY NATURE (426)

Here let us deal with time. A year is established only in the sense that it appears as the mere set of twelve months. However, you should determine for yourself that the way the object to be refuted appears to you is the opposite of this. The year and its basis of imputation—the twelve months—cannot be established as one and the same thing by nature. If they were established like this, it would follow that, just as the basis of imputation exists as twelve months, there should also be twelve years. Another consequence is that, as there is only one year, there would also be only one month. They might be established as being separate by nature; yet if we eliminate the twelve months, there is nothing left that could be identified as "the year," and thus "year" is only a label applied to the basis of imputation—the twelve months—by a valid mental cognition. It is merely something verbal and is definitely not something established.

ASCERTAINING THAT UNCONDITIONED PHENOMENA DO NOT NATURALLY EXIST (427)

Unconditioned phenomena are such things as the two types of cessation [the analytic and the nonanalytic],[84] space, emptiness, etc. They do not come into being through conditioning by causes and circumstances, and so are termed "unconditioned."

Let us take the case of space. The object to be refuted is not covered by the mere adopted convention that "space" is only an absence of obstruction or contact, that is, a negative without any further implications. If space were something that could be established as being characteristically one with its north, south, east, and west sectors, the eastern and western sectors of space would then be identical. If this were so, when the dawn came in the sky of the eastern continent of Videha, it would also be sunrise in the sky over the western continent of Godānīya. If space and its various sectors were established as characteristically different, the sum and its parts would be unrelated, different things. Thus there would necessarily be something that could be identified as space in what remains after the elimination of the components of space—the cardinal and midpoints of the compass, the zenith, and the nadir. Since this is not so, space does not truly exist.

There are those who hold emptiness to be established as true. This is very wrong. It says in a sūtra:

> Better to hold the view that the self is [as solid] as Mount Meru
> Than to hold emptiness as being established as true.

In other words, it is an incorrect position. Even emptiness is divided into many components according to its basis of imputation. There are many components of emptiness, and emptiness covers the whole range of bases of particular emptinesses—no matter how large or small these bases may happen to be. Through analysis you will come to know whether these components can be established as being either the same or different [in relation to that emptiness], or whether an object in question [such as a pot]—that is, the basis of a particular emptiness—is established as being independent [from its emptiness]. The sūtras say:

> If you do not perceive form,
> How could you perceive the suchness of form?

THEN, THE WAY YOU DEVELOP SPECIAL INSIGHT (428)

Although you may already have achieved a fully characterized mental quiescence through the methods involving the nine mental states of single-pointed concentration that I outlined earlier, and your mental quiescence has not suffered degeneration, you will still not have achieved special insight but merely meditative suppleness. Let us take personal selflessness as our example. In addition to mental quiescence, you should perform the four-point analysis already discussed; and by so doing, you should develop a vivid conviction that the "I" is definitely not established by its nature, although that is the way you instinctively grasp at an "I" over and above the five aggregates. If you develop this certainty, focus upon it and hold it without forgetting. Prevent dullness or excitement by means of your vigilance and enter into absorbtion. If the force of your retention weakens and your conviction is on the point of becoming unclear, repeat the four-point analysis and so on in the same vein as above. When you regain a powerful conviction, begin single-pointed meditation on this certainty. This is how you should seek clarity in emptiness. Upon gaining clarity, repeat the four-point analysis and other [forms of analysis not dealt with here] while in a state of stable fixation meditation. This is illustrated by the analogy of the small minnow gliding through an extremely clear lake undisturbed by wind. Here you should familiarize yourself over a long period, making equal use of both [meditative] stability and the wisdom to conceptualize. As stated above, you will achieve nine mental states, after which, by virtue of your analysis, you will be led to a special form of meditative suppleness even greater than that experienced when you achieved mental quiescence. Analytic meditation effortlessly accompanies fixation meditation. When you achieve this level you gain true special insight directed into emptiness. Your mental quiescence has now been coupled with this special insight.

DAY 23

Kyabje Pabongka Rinpoche gave a short talk to set our motivations. He quoted Je Tsongkapa, the great Dharmarāja:

> When you rightly understand these points
> Of the three fundamentals of the path,
> Take up solitude and develop the strength of your perseverance;
> You will soon achieve the eternal hope, my child.

He restated the headings we covered yesterday and then continued:

HOW TO TRAIN IN THE UNCOMMON PART OF THE PATH, THE VAJRAYĀNA (429)

As I have already told you, when you have gained some experience of renunciation by means of the small and medium scopes, you should then try to experience bodhichitta through the great scope. Should you succeed, then work toward gaining conviction in the view of emptiness, after which you must enter the secret tantras. But if you start practicing tantra without this sort of preparation, it will not act as the means for your liberation or lead you to complete, peerless enlightenment. There is a great risk that tantra will prove profitless for you, and as dangerous as riding an unbroken horse is for a small child. If you gain insight from the three fundamentals of the path and then enter the secret tantras, you are certain to avail yourself of their unique rapidity.

The secret tantras are said to be even rarer than the buddhas. Through this path you can gain the state of the no-more-learner's unification within your short life in these degenerate times. You should therefore most certainly train in this path. But it is not sufficient to take only a few minor initiations into Hayagriva, Vajrapāṇi, and so on, merely in order to rid yourself of some temporary circumstance. You should receive the four initiations purely and properly—that is, in the maṇḍala of a tutelary deity such as Heruka, Yamāntaka, or Guhyasamāja, and from a qualified vajra master. These four initiations are sure to implant seeds of the four kāyas within you. And it would be very meaningful to keep whatever vows you have taken during the initiation, by safeguarding them as you would your very eyes, and then practicing what you are taught in profound discourses on the two stages. Then your practice will encompass the whole teaching.

The whole path of both sūtra and tantra becomes fully comprehensible when you know the steps in this path properly. The path begins with devoting yourself to a spiritual guide and culminates in the unification of the no-more-learner. However, when there are many disciples who have not been initiated into the highest tantras, the usual practice is to discuss how to train in the Vajrayāna by giving little more than the headings of this subject.

HOW TO TRAIN IN THE FOUR WAYS OF GATHERING DISCIPLES IN ORDER TO RIPEN THE MINDSTREAMS OF OTHERS (430)

In [Maitreya's] *Ornament to the Sūtras* we find:

> I declare these to be: acting generously, so that they will take teachings;
> Speaking sweetly so that they will follow you;
> Working for their benefit;
> And practicing what you preach.

Bodhisattvas wish to work for the benefit of other beings, and they do this by ripening the mindstreams of others through the four ways. You must also work to benefit sentient beings by means of these four.

The first is as follows. Ordinary beings are easily attracted by gifts of material things; so, in order to gradually turn them to the path, you first present them with gifts. Such an action pleases them, and they will join in your circle.

The second is speaking sweetly to the people drawn to you. Your conversations should conform to the accepted normalities, and more importantly, you should tell them of the Dharma in ways suited to their intelligence and aspirations.

The third is to work for your disciples' benefit by teaching them the path of the holy Dharma according to their level of intelligence, thus bringing them to train in its stages.

The fourth is to practice what you preach, by putting into practice the things you have told them.

I shall end this discussion here. Now I will discuss the heading I set aside a few days ago.

DEVELOPING BODHICHITTA THROUGH THE RITUAL OF TAKING VOWS (362)

Here there are two headings: (1) how to acquire the vows you have not yet taken; (2) how to keep them from degenerating once you have acquired them.

HOW TO ACQUIRE THE VOWS YOU HAVE NOT YET TAKEN (431)

Although we call this "developing bodhichitta by means of a ceremony," you will receive these vows only if you experience development of bodhichitta, no matter how sketchy that may be. It is useless to merely repeat the verbal formulas without any feeling. Still, just taking the vows without having any such insight will instill in you an instinct for bodhichitta, so you should take this seriously. Those who have developed some experience and do their best to carry out the visualizations, etc., tomorrow and take the vows sincerely will receive their bodhichitta vows through karmically potent beings. The bodhichitta they develop will go from strength to strength and become very firm.

There are three types of ceremony used to take these bodhichitta vows. The shortest of these has no introductory section. The medium form has both preparatory and main sections, but both sections are carried out on the same day. The longest form has one day set aside for the preparation and another for the main section. We will observe the last of these three types.

The practice is that one must teach the common part of the lamrim in full before giving bodhichitta vows when these are being conferred after any initiations, discourses, oral transmissions, etc., not preceded by a discourse on the lamrim. However, this is not the case here because we are giving the vow in conjunction with a lamrim teaching, and there is no need to add anything more as I have already dealt with [the lamrim] at great length. So I can dispense with any long introductions. Those who conduct the ceremony conferring bodhichitta vows in the future must carry out the ceremony in these different ways, according to whether it is being given in connection with a discourse on the lamrim or not.

He then discussed in detail how to arrange the offerings for the preparatory rites section of tomorrow's ceremony. He also briefly discussed how we should make a number of maṇḍala offerings, make petitions after the maṇḍala offerings, and set our motivation in preparation. Then he continued:

You must devote as much time tonight and tomorrow as you can to reviewing the visualizations [to be performed during the ceremony]. Tomorrow we will be inviting our gurus, the victorious ones, and their children to witness our development of bodhichitta; so we need to sweep the place and lay out offerings. It would not be right to invite a universal emperor to a pauper's hut or to a dirty, dusty place littered with filth. So you should give the area a good sweep at the end of this preparatory session, making sure you do not harm insects on the ground, and so on. Sprinkle scented water to settle the dust, and strew the dais with flowers. You should also deck the master's throne with flowers and precious ornaments. Atiśha once said that the Tibetans' offerings are inferior, so they do not develop bodhichitta. So make this offering a good one. Though they say you should give one sixth of your possessions, you should in any case lay out so many offerings that it will astonish your friends.

You should build up your accumulation [of merit], purify obscurations, safeguard yourself from hindrances, etc., so that you will develop bodhichitta tomorrow during the main ceremony. They say that tomorrow morning you should read the *Translated Word of Buddha,* or if this is not possible, settle for the *Avataṃsaka Sūtra,* etc.[85] We could not manage these in the time available, but those of you who are fast readers could go through the *Eight-Thousand-Verse Perfection of Wisdom Sūtra* or the *Sūtra on the Fortunate Eon.* At the start of the main ceremony, we should perform a threefold offering: offering water and ritual cakes [to the hungry ghosts] and offering ritual cakes to the elementals.

Worldly people celebrate the events of this life with parties. They make a big fuss over the New Year—which after all only means that the sands of time have run out a little more. So why should we not rejoice? We are going to develop unexcelled bodhichitta, enter the Mahāyāna, and become children of the victorious ones. Wear new clothes tomorrow. The ordained should wear both their plain and saffron shawls, and so on. Have a bath, wear clean clothes, and each of you bring something as a token offering for your taking of the bodhichitta vows. This is something you will find in Buddha's biography. As you make your way here, do not regard this place as something ordinary. Instead, visualize it as a four-gated palace. In these four gateways stand the four mahārājas of the cardinal points, guarded by hundreds of thousands of their vassals and retinue. All these are surrounded by the gods who uphold virtue. They are also present to receive the vows. There are murals on the four walls of the palace depicting the deeds our Teacher performed in times gone by when he was a bodhisattva treading the path. Visualize that these things [on the walls] are now actually happening; rejoice and make prayers when you see them.

In the second session, after the guru is seated, you must accumulate merit and purify obscurations, for these acts will serve as the basis for your development of bodhichitta. We will be performing the long version of the preparatory rite. Take the visualization for accumulating the collections and purifying the obscurations seriously. Imagine the guru is actually Bhagavān Śhākyamuni. As the guru introduces topics, imagine the visualization for each topic clearly.

In general, the aspiration form of bodhichitta is the mere wish to achieve buddhahood for the sake of all sentient beings. The involvement form of bodhichitta is the desire to train in the tasks that follow development of bodhichitta. The former is illustrated by someone planning to go to India; the latter by the man who has already set off on the road. There are two ways of performing the ceremony for bodhichitta vows. One is to take the aspiration and involvement parts separately. This is taken from [Asaṅga's] *Bodhisattva Levels.* The other is to take the two forms together, which is found in [Śhāntideva's] *Engaging in the Deeds of Bodhisattvas.* It makes no difference which of these two you do, but some people say one is according to the Madhyamaka system and the other is supposed to be Chittamātrin. However, the ways these two systems treat the development of bodhichitta do not conflict. Our system has it that the former tradition was formulated for those who can only develop bodhichitta and are not [yet] able to train in the bodhisattva deeds. The latter was formulated for those who are able to do both. Tomorrow I shall give the aspiration and involvement forms together.

We offered a maṇḍala in thanksgiving and recited the Lamrim Prayer. *Then Kyabje Pabongka led us three times in the verse:*

May I develop any qualities of the supreme and precious
bodhichitta
I have not already developed.
May it increase, not degenerate,
And go from strength to strength.

Then we recited once "May all sentient beings, who were my parents, be happy..." followed by "May my glorious guru's life be long..." once. At the conclusion of the day's session we recited "All the victorious ones...."

DAY 24

The early part of the day was devoted to a reading of sūtras, dedication of the ritual cakes, etc. Here follows an account of the second part of the day.

Kyabje Pabongka Rinpoche took his seat on the throne. We then performed a long version of the preparatory rite that included a long section on the external offerings and so on. While we offered the maṇḍala to request the bodhisattva vows, each of us held in our hands our small offerings for generating the bodhichitta. After the offering of the maṇḍala, these token offerings were passed along the audience and made into a pile in front of the guru. Rinpoche quoted lines such as those of Je Tsongkapa, the great Dharmarāja of the three realms:

> Development of bodhichitta is the path of the Supreme Vehicle…

He discussed yet again the benefits of bodhichitta as before. He then began:

Train the mind and inspire it with the [lamrim topics] in their order, beginning with the difficulty of finding the optimum human rebirth. When visualizing a topic, imagine you are surrounded by all sentient beings, but with all the beings of the six realms visualized in human form. All male sentient beings appear on your right as your father; all female beings are to your left and appear as your aged mother. Your guru, visualized in the form of Śhākyamuni Buddha, is surrounded by the thousand buddhas of this fortunate eon, and so on.

In the presence of the invited gurus, victorious ones, and their children, we took refuge while kneeling on our right knees. We repeated this verse three times with Kyabje Pabongka Rinpoche:

Until enlightenment, I take refuge
In the Buddha, Dharma, and Supreme Assembly.
With the merit I earn through generosity and so on,
May I gain buddhahood for the sake of all beings.

We then pledged ourselves to the aspiration form of bodhichitta by reciting three times:

I wish to gain enlightenment to free
All beings from the terrors of existence and cessation.
Now that I have formed this intention, until I achieve buddhahood
I shall not forsake it, even at the cost of my life.

Next came the part where we actually took both vows—the aspiration and involvement forms of bodhichitta, simultaneously. He repeated the following verse three times. In it, we first petitioned the invited beings and then took the vows:

O gurus, victors, and your children!
I beseech you, listen to me!
Just as the tathāgatas of old
Developed the wish to be enlightened
And then progressed through
The trainings of a bodhisattva,
So I, too, develop bodhichitta
For the sake of beings
And will progressively train myself
In the bodhisattva trainings.

This was followed by a verse we recited once to express our happiness at taking the vows:

Now my life has proved fruitful:
I have gained an excellent human existence;
Today I have been born into the Buddha race,
I have become a child of the buddhas.

Kyabje Rinpoche then read out some verses that spoke of keeping the vows and explained their meaning, to encourage us. We disciples then recited them after him. Then he addressed his disciples:

If [during the ceremony] we developed bodhichitta, the ground of the vast numbers of buddhafields found in the ten directions, the thrones of the resident buddhas there, and all else trembled. The retinues of these buddhas asked the reason for this, and they were told, "These things all happened by virtue of this: in the snowy country of Tibet, at the lonely place of Chuzang Hermitage, in the presence of a lama named Taenzin Trinlae Gyatso, his disciple so-and-so developed supreme bodhichitta." It is said that they pray that your bodhichitta does not degenerate and that you will complete the tasks of a bodhisattva.

Then Pabongka Rinpoche took as many of the objects we had brought as he could manage. The attendants took the rest. He continued:

We have now received immeasurable root virtues from both teaching and listening to the lamrim. Just consider the root merits we gain from developing bodhichitta! In order that our accumulated root virtues may not disappear [over time], we will entrust them to our venerable protector, Maitreya. When he comes to this continent, displaying his supreme nirmāṇakāya form and performing the deeds of a buddha, we shall be among the followers of this victorious one through the power of these root merits. We shall enjoy the nectar of his speech and receive from him the prediction of our own peerless enlightenment. Thus we shall dedicate our merits to this end. At the end of the third repetition of the verses of dedication, I will raise your offerings into the air. You must all feel that these offerings are your root virtues in the form of the eight auspicious signs, the seven signs of regal power, etc. Feel that they land all around Protector Maitreya in Tuṣhita, that he says "These root merits please me!" and that he prays for you.

He then led us in the following two verses, which we recited three times:

> When the powerful sun of Maitreya
> Rises over the hills of Bodhgaya,

May it open the lotus of my intellect;
May swarms of fortunate ones be satisfied.

Followed by:

Then may Maitreya, the Victor, be so pleased
That he places his right hand on my head,
Predicting my supreme enlightenment.
Soon may I gain buddhahood for the sake of all beings.

At the third repetition, he raised the offerings into the air.

HOW TO KEEP YOUR VOWS FROM DEGENERATING ONCE YOU HAVE ACQUIRED THEM (432)

There are two sets of advice: (1) advice related to the aspiration [form of the bodhisattva vows]; (2) advice related to the involvement form.

ADVICE RELATED TO THE ASPIRATION FORM OF BODHICHITTA (433)

(1) Advice on creating the cause for keeping the bodhichitta you have developed from degenerating during this present life; (2) advice on creating the causes never to be separated from bodhichitta in your remaining rebirths.

ADVICE ON CREATING THE CAUSE FOR KEEPING THE BODHICHITTA YOU HAVE DEVELOPED FROM DEGENERATING IN THIS LIFE (434)

There are four items, as follows:

RECALLING THE BENEFITS OF DEVELOPING BODHICHITTA (435)

RETAKING THE VOWS THREE TIMES EACH DAY AND THREE TIMES EACH NIGHT SO THAT YOU DO NOT LOSE THE BODHICHITTA YOU HAVE ALREADY DEVELOPED AND INCREASE IT AS WELL (436)

PREVENTING YOUR DEVELOPMENT OF BAD THOUGHTS, SUCH AS FEELING WHEN ANOTHER WRONGS YOU, "I SHALL NOT WORK FOR HIS SAKE" (437)

BUILDING YOUR ACCUMULATIONS IN ORDER TO INCREASE THE BODHICHITTA YOU HAVE ALREADY DEVELOPED (438)

ADVICE ON CREATING THE CAUSES NEVER TO BE SEPARATED FROM BODHICHITTA IN YOUR REMAINING REBIRTHS (439)

There are two subsections:

FOUR ACTIONS [PRODUCING] BLACK [KARMIC RESULTS] TO BE ABANDONED (440)

These are:

TRYING TO DUPE YOUR GURU, ABBOT, ORDINATION MASTER, ETC., WITH LIES (441)

FEELING DISTRESS WHEN OTHERS DO SOMETHING VIRTUOUS (442)

SAYING UNPLEASANT THINGS TO BODHISATTVAS OUT OF HOSTILITY (443)

ACTING DECEITFULLY, WITHOUT ANY ALTRUISM (444)

FOUR ACTIONS [PRODUCING] WHITE [KARMIC RESULTS] TO BE CULTIVATED (445)

These are:

VIGILANTLY ABANDONING DELIBERATE LIES (446)

KEEPING HONEST INTENTIONS TOWARD SENTIENT BEINGS AND NOT DECEIVING THEM (447)

DEVELOPING THE ATTITUDE THAT BODHISATTVAS ARE TEACHERS AND GIVING THEM DUE PRAISE (448)

CAUSING THE SENTIENT BEINGS WHO ARE MATURING UNDER YOUR CARE TO UPHOLD BODHICHITTA (449)

THE ADVICE RELATED TO THE INVOLVEMENT FORM OF BODHICHITTA (450)

Here Kyabje Pabongka Rinpoche spoke in detail about the necessity for studying how to keep one's bodhisattva vows properly and how not to sully any of the eighteen main vows or forty-six minor vows. Then he continued:

As was said:

> Though I have taught you the means to liberation,
> Know that your own liberation depends on you.

Practice whatever you can, so that my teachings will not have been in vain. Just as traders, etc., load their horses, mules, and the rest within the carrying capacity of these animals, each of you, whether of excellent, middling, or inferior mind, must at least practice within your capacities. But, above all, make bodhichitta your main practice. You must pursue any of the other meditation subjects in the knowledge that they will assist your bodhichitta.

First you should devote yourself properly to a spiritual guide and put into practice the instructions he gives you. Then develop the wish to extract some essence from your optimum human rebirth. Should you not extract that essence now, it is certain that after death—for this rebirth will not last much longer—you will not be able to choose where you will be reborn. If you are reborn in the lower realms, you will suffer intolerably. You must therefore seek some protection and some means of saving yourself from this.

If, perchance, through your exertions in those methods, you are not reborn in the lower realms, the upper realms also have their sufferings, and after such a rebirth you will be reborn yet again in the lower realms. Contemplate this in detail and you will surely want to be liberated from cyclic existence.

But it is not sufficient for you alone to be liberated, because all sentient beings are nothing less than your kind parents. Not only is it contemptible to thoughtlessly desert them, but also it is not enough that you alone should be liberated from saṃsāra. Thus it is fitting that you enter the Mahāyāna now, because you will have to enter it sooner or later in any case. The only gateway to the Mahāyāna is the development of bodhichitta; so you must work hard at some means of developing this. If you manage to experience effortless bodhichitta, you will then, left to yourself, be able to endure for a long while the hardships associated with working for the sake of sentient beings. However, you would find it most unbearable that in the meantime these beings, your aged mothers, were being tortured by suffering. This is the special type of bodhichitta, and it will make you want to enter the secret tantric path, the supreme of all the yānas. Thus you will receive the four initiations from a fully qualified vajra master in order to be ripened. And in this way you will actually come to attain an approximation of the unification, a coupling together of clear light and the illusory body. To ripen yourself even further [to obtain the actual unification], you must meditate on the generation stage and so on. Through these you will be certain to achieve the state of the unification of the no-more-learner in your one short lifetime in this degenerate age.

In order to achieve this, before the actual stage of the unification you must have achieved the approximation of the unification: the clear light and the pure and impure stages of the illusory body. But to be mature enough to do this, you must definitely have progressed fully in the coarser levels of the generation-stage maturation, and you must have preceded this by obtaining the four pure initiations that will definitely implant the seeds of the four kāyas in you. But in order to become the exceptional vessel or candidate fit enough to receive these, you must have purified your mindstream beforehand with the common path, bodhichitta. Thus you must have received the causes for generating this bodhichitta: so much compassion that you cannot bear all sentient beings to suffer agonies and so forth. The foundation for developing compassion is your inability to bear the general and specific sufferings of saṃsāra that you yourself have to undergo. This should move you to renounce saṃsāra.

But before this you must have developed fear and dread of the sufferings of the lower realms. And how could you develop any of these without having first contemplated the law of cause and effect and the uncertainty of when you will die? You must develop these things. The sole cause for even thinking of beginning on such a path is contemplating how difficult it is to gain an optimum human rebirth—something entirely meaningful. And to develop all these things, you must have devoted yourself properly, in both thought and deed, to a virtuous spiritual guide.

Thus you should not reach for the higher levels right away. You should train your mind by experiencing the progression [of the path], beginning with devotion to a spiritual guide. "Experiencing the progression of the path" means the warm feeling that: "If I study this particular meditation topic for a while, I will develop it in my mindstream." Then, starting at the beginning and moving onward, commence at the starting point of the lamrim—proper devotion to a spiritual guide. Try to develop some contrived insight into each meditation topic. Train by practicing retrospection meditation on your already-developed insights; and for those topics into which you are yet to develop insight, train trying to develop experience into them as well.

In this life we have met with these stainless teachings in both sūtra and tantra, which are completely error free. With such an opportunity, what a pity if you do not develop even an instinct for the secret tantras! Why shouldn't you manage at least review meditation into the generation and completion stages of [the tantra of a] tutelary deity such as Guhyasamāja, Heruka, or Yamāntaka? Be a person who does review meditations on all the teachings. This would make a practice that integrates everything into the one sitting.

When you have managed to develop contrived insight into the topics up to bodhichitta, you should then go straight back to the beginning again and gain uncontrived insight into each of these topics. This way of working through the path is like traveling along a street more than once in the same direction. First develop insight into the topics leading up to bodhichitta in this manner, and then, in addition, work hard at the two stages of the path in the secret tantras. If you do this you will develop in your mindstream the extraordinary realizations described in tantras and in the masterworks of great adepts. And just like Ensapa the victorious one and his followers, you too will very soon be able to make manifest the state of Vajradhara, unification, during your short lifetime in this degenerate age.

Now we should pray that we will lead all six types of beings, who extend to the very boundaries of space itself, to the state of peerless buddhahood, and that we will pacify their individual sufferings; and for that reason we will develop bodhichitta and engage in the peerless tasks of a child of the victorious ones. Thus I want us to recite the final prayer from *Engaging in the Deeds of Bodhisattvas.* This was not the practice of my own precious lama, but it seems to have been something done by the past occupants of the Gandaen throne and their followers. This is reason enough to revive the practice. I ask you to recite these verses without any distraction.

He then led us in the dedication prayer from that great work Engaging in the Deeds of Bodhisattvas. *We offered a maṇḍala in thanksgiving for having received the teachings and made further prayers, verses of auspiciousness, etc. With the foregoing, he conferred the kindness [of teaching] the noble tradition of the path and stages to enlightenment, the heart of the whole doctrine, which will not disappear even at the end of time, dispelling the darkness of the three realms and illuminating them ever brighter.*

COLOPHON BY TRIJANG RINPOCHE

And so I say:

O foremost in the Tathāgata's teachings! Holder of the vajra!
With the sword of love, you destroy worldly existence.
The breadth of your mind was limitless.
You furthered the teachings—
The best of the Victor's good works.
You awaken all beings from their benighted sleep.
Like a moon marked with the ultimate seals
Of emptiness and compassion,
Whose spring tide filled an ever-blissful scenic lake,
Your light caused the lotus of my mind to open fully;
O lord of all Buddha families, return
And once again become my crowning jewel!

O protector, your very words,
Precious one hundred thousand times,
Quenched the desire for
The world or selfish peace.
Here are my scribblings—a strong-box of your instructions;
May the fortunate hold your words to be most precious in their
hearts.

You display Tsongkapa's multilevel doctrine,
You embody the refutation of those against omniscience;
Through the peerless glory of your realizations and teachings,

You led us through the Supreme Vehicle according to the level of
our wits.

All the Sage's scriptures are supreme, a jewel for us embodied
beings;
The mind that realizes these supreme instructions
Regards whatever appears as the revelation of the guru;
This practice is a path pleasing to the victors.

At the defeat of the demons four, the melodious beating of the
victory drum—
The Sage's unmistaken sayings on his profound thought!
May this publication flourish to confer both purposes
And lead many to this hard-to-come-by path.

In the vast lake of stainless deeds,
May the essence of the path, the realm of knowing oneself, mature.
What other path is so clear to beings
Than the meaning of birthless, cessationless, selfless interdependence?

The wish-granting jewel cannot compare with this hard-to-find
rebirth.
Do not wallow in the sick show of these appearances.
If realizing ultimate happiness,
Your eternal goal, has come into view,
Who would practice anything other than this path supreme?

Therefore, people desiring liberation would not presume
To think some spurious path supreme.
They would depend solely on the innermost essence
Of an instruction that is complete,
Content that all their hopes will be answered.

By my effort: a stock of merit that fills the River Ganges,
A string of moon-lustrous pearls long enough to encircle the
universe!
Through interdependent origination—that infinite miracle, that
great wonder—

May the calming moon of the Victor's stainless teaching,
Like a crest jewel worn by gods and men,
Wax gloriously and shine on the fortunate jasmine blossoms.
May this moon long remove the torments of the three realms.

Long live the noble Gelug line,
A lotus lake of perfect yellow flowers,
Door to unending waves of teaching and practice,
Infinite store of complete clarity.

Taenzin Gyatso[86] is a lord of Mount Meru, towering over the peaks of existence and of [selfish] peace;
The omniscience, love, and power of all the victors make up the atoms of your mountain.
May you never waver for hundreds of eons!
May your good works shine like the earrings of the gods of sun and moon.
O glorious Lhasa, city of eternal happiness,
Spread your canopy of gathering, perfect spring clouds
In the sky of merit over our land
And rain down nectars of happiness and benefit.

May we never be without you, supremely kind guru,
And always hold you to the precious drop residing in our crowns.
May we, through proper reliance on you, travel the supreme path
Carried by a wondrous, powerful garuḍa!

In short, may I perfect the tasks of the perfections
For all beings, who fill all of space;
May I attain the ten powers under the Bodhi tree
And soon gain glorious vajra enlightenment.

Pabongka Dorje Chang, master of all lineages, is a unique embodiment and distillation of the omniscience, love, power, and good works of all the victorious ones of the three times and their children. His inconceivably skillful deeds, motivated by his love, turned dullards such as myself into beings fortunate enough to practice the Supreme Vehicle. This was the incomparable kindness of our guru, whose ordination name I shall now give, in view of my purpose: Jampa Taenzin Trinlae Gyatso Paelzangpo. He gave this teaching at the request of Yangdzom Tsering, wife of the master of the Lhalu Gatsel estate, an aristocrat but a lady of unequaled faith. She made this request in order to increase the root merits of two departed members of the blood, Jigme Namgyael and Puntsog Rabgyae. It was given in the Iron-Bird Year of the fifteenth sixty-year cycle [1921] in the debate courtyard of Chuzang Hermitage in Nyangtraen. It brought together three teachings concerning the stages of the path to enlightenment: the concise teaching called the *Swift Path,* and two lineages that developed from *Mañjuśhrī's Own Words*—one from the Central Province and one from the south. It also included a section on the seven-point mind training. He gave this informal but profound teaching out of his supreme kindness.

Although I am but an inconsequential upstart, I had the good fortune to attend this profound and extensive teaching and to enjoy the nectar it contained. Dagyab Dongkong Rinpoche from Ratoe took rough notes every day, and by his request, Pabongka Dorje Chang edited them. However, Pabongka Rinpoche was able to revise the book only as far as number four of the preparatory rites: "Petitions to the Merit Field." Because Pabongka Rinpoche's good works for the sake of others were as extensive as space itself, he left the book in an unfinished state. It fell to me to complete it. I was most happy to complete the work of my kind guru, who was like a father to me.

Time and again I was urged by the lamas and incarnate lamas who had received his oral discourses and who upheld the valid teachings, as well as by many well-versed and realized geshes from all over Tibet. So I added details to the original draft from his other lamrim teachings given at various other times. I thoroughly researched the book to bring it to a high standard, etc. However, I was plagued by constant interruptions, and since I could not devote enough time to it, this task, which is my offering of accomplishment of my precious lama's oral teachings, took a long time to complete.

Pabongka Rinpoche's secretary, Gelong Lozang Dorje, was Ānanda's equal in remembering oral teachings. He edited the book at his leisure, putting everything into its proper place, and suggesting where the various headings should go. He helped me over a long period and gave his time selflessly. I, too, went over the text when I had any time to spare. I corrected the minor slips that were not fair renderings of our guru's speech; I also added some further instructions, not recorded in my notes, from the oral tradition that I could reproduce with certainty, and so on.

I have taken great pains in editing this book in the hope of it acting as an intermediary for my supremely kind guru and that this will prove worthwhile for all. My guru had looked after me since I was seven or eight years old, and I—though lowly and base—have been sustained by the power of his supreme blessings, which he gave out of his compassion. I have no Dharma, I am lazy, and what I tell others contradicts what I do myself—I, Lozang Yeshe Taenzin Gyatso, also named Gandaen Trijang Tulku, tutor to His Holiness the Dalai Lama. I completed this book on Saturday, the fifteenth day of the tenth month of the Fire-Bird Year of the sixteenth calendar cycle [1957], in the constellation of Rohiṇī. This is a most virtuous day to have completed this work.

By this, long may the precious teachings of the stages of the path to enlightenment stay with us! May they flourish and spread in all directions, for all time!

Oṃ svasti!
Oṃ ye dharmā hetuprabhavā hetun teṣhān tathāgato hyavadat,
teśhāñchayo nirodha evaṃ vādī mahāśhramaṇaḥ ye svāhā!

APPENDIXES

1. OUTLINE OF THE TEXT

PART TWO: THE PREPARATORY RITES

PART THREE: THE FOUNDATIONS OF THE PATH

PART FOUR: THE SMALL SCOPE

PART FIVE: THE MEDIUM SCOPE

PART SIX: THE GREAT SCOPE

2. THE LINEAGE OF THESE TEACHINGS

Guru Śhākyamuni Buddha

Lineage of Extensive Deeds	*Lineage of Profound View*
Maitreya	Mañjuśhrī
Asaṅga	Nāgārjuna
Vasubandhu	Chandrakīrti
Vimuktisena	Vidyakokila the elder
Vimuktisenagomin	Vidyakokila the younger (Avadhutipa)
Paranasena	
Vinītasena	
Vairochana	
Haribhadra	
Kusali	
Ratnasena	
Suvarṇadvipa	

Atiśha

Dromtoenpa

Lamrim Lineage	*Classical Lineage*	*Instruction Lineage*
Goenpawa	Potowa	Chaen Ngawa
Nëuzurpa	Sharawa	Tsultrimbar
Tagmapa	Chilbupa	Zhoenue Oe
Namkha Senge	Lhalung Wangchug	Gyergompa

Namkha Gyaelpo	Goenpo Rinpoche	Sangyae Oen
Senge Zangpo	Zangchenpa	Namkha Gyaelpo
Gyalsae Zangpo	Tsonawa	Senge Zangpo
Namkha Gyaeltsaen	Moendrapa	Gyaelsae Zangpo
	Choekyab Zangpo	Namkha Gyaeltsaen

Gelugpa Lineage

Tsongkapa
Jampael Gyatso
Kaedrub Rinpoche
Basoje
Choekyi Dorje
Gyaelwa Ensapa
Sangyae Yeshe
Lozang Choekyi Gyaeltsaen (First Paṇchen Lama)
Koenchog Gyaeltsaen
Lozang Yeshe (Second Paṇchen Lama)
Purchog Ngagwang Jampa
Lozang Nyaendrag
Yoentaen Tayae
Taenpa Rabgyae
Lodroe Zangpo
Lozang Gyatso
Jinpa Gyatso
Taenzin Kaedrub
Lozang Lhuendrub Gyatso
Jampa Taenzin Trinlae Gyatso (Pabongka Rinpoche)
Lozang Yeshe Taenzin Gyatso (Trijang Rinpoche)

3. THE THREE FUNDAMENTALS OF THE PATH

Homage to the venerable gurus.

I shall explain, as best I can,
The import of the essence
Of all the victors' scriptures,
The path praised by holy victors
And their children—the gateway
For the fortunates wanting liberation.

Those unattached to worldly happiness who,
Yearning to give meaning to their optimum rebirth,
Follow a path pleasing to the victors,
O fortunate ones! Listen with clear minds.

Without pure renunciation, there is no way
To still the yearning for the happy fruits
Of this ocean of existence;
And because all embodied beings
Thirst after existence,
They are utterly bound.
Thus, from the first, seek renunciation.

The optimum human rebirth
Is difficult to acquire.
This life does not last long.
Familiarize your mind with these things
And turn away from this life's trivia.

If you contemplate over and over
The undeceptive laws of cause and effect
And saṃsāra's sufferings,
You will turn away from your next lives' trivia.

After such meditations, when you do not long
For the splendors of saṃsāra for even a moment,
When your thoughts day and night
Always yearn for liberation,
You have developed renunciation.

But, if not conjoined with pure bodhichitta,
Even renunciation is not cause
For the choice bliss of highest enlightenment.
Thus the discerning develop supreme bodhichitta.

Swept away by the stream of the four strong currents,
Bound by the fetters of hard-to-stop actions,
Trapped in the iron mesh of self-grasping,
Smothered in the blackness of ignorance,

They are endlessly born and reborn to the world
And continuously tortured by the three sufferings.
Such is the condition of our mothers;
Contemplate this situation,
And develop supreme bodhichitta.

Despite acquaintance with renunciation and bodhichitta,
If you do not have the wisdom that understands the way things exist,
You cannot eradicate the roots of existence.
Thus, work hard at the means of realizing the interdependence of things.

He who sees that for all phenomena in saṃsāra and nīrvāṇa
The law of cause and effect is inevitable
And has righted his perception
Is on the path that gladdens the buddhas.

The appearance that things are mutually interdependent
Is no illusion; but there are those
Who understand emptiness to be something
Devoid of this appearance.
As long as these two
Seem separate to you, you will never
Realize the thoughts of the Great One.

The mere perception [that these two]
Go together—that they are not alternatives,
And that mutual interdependence is undeceptive—
Will destroy all the ways in which you grasp at objects
With the mind. At this point you perfect
Your analysis of the view.

You eliminate the extreme of specious substantialism;
You eliminate the extreme of empty nihilism.
If you understand how emptiness presents itself as causes and effects,
Views that grasp extremes will not impress you.

When you rightly understand these points
Of the three fundamentals of the path,
Take up solitude and develop
The strength of your perseverance;
You will soon achieve the eternal hope, my child.

The learned monk Lozang Dragpa [Je Tsongkhapa] gave the above advice to Ngawang Dragpa, an official at Tsako.

4. AN ORNAMENT FOR THE THROATS OF THE FORTUNATE

A Preparatory Rite in Convenient Sections for Recitation for the Swift Path Concise Teaching of the Lamrim *by Jampael Lhuendrub of Dagpo.*

Before the guru inseparable from Buddha and Vajradhara
I prostrate myself and take refuge for all time.
Out of your great love, take care of me.

This brings together the instructions of the great Gyaelwa Ensapa on the recitations to be performed as the six-part rite to precede lamrim [meditation]. The layout is as follows:

THE FIRST [RITE]: CLEANING YOUR ROOM AND ARRANGING THE SYMBOLS OF ENLIGHTENED BODY, SPEECH, AND MIND

THE SECOND [RITE]: OBTAINING OFFERINGS HONESTLY AND ARRANGING THEM BEAUTIFULLY

THE THIRD [RITE]: ADOPTING THE EIGHT-FEATURED SITTING POSTURE OF VAIROCHANA ON A COMFORTABLE SEAT AND THEN TAKING REFUGE AND DEVELOPING BODHICHITTA IN AN ESPECIALLY VIRTUOUS FRAME OF MIND

First, you visualize the objects of refuge:

In space directly before me is a broad, wide, and precious throne supported by eight huge lions. On it is a seat [built up of] a multicolored lotus, a moon and a sun maṇḍala. [There sits a figure] who is by nature my precious root guru, in the aspect of the Victor Śhākyamuni. His body is like burnished gold; his head has the crown protrusion. He has one face, two hands—his right makes the earth-touching gesture, his left makes the meditative absorption gesture while holding a begging bowl full of nectar. He wears saffron-colored robes. He is adorned and made brilliant by the marks and signs; he is of the nature of light and sits amid a mass of light generated from his body. His two legs are crossed in the vajra posture.

He is surrounded by my personal and lineage gurus, tutelary deities, and the buddhas, bodhisattvas, ḍākas, ḍākinīs, and Dharma protectors, who form a group around him. Before each of these, on magnificent thrones, rests the Dharma that each of them orally transmitted, in the aspect of loose-leaf books having the nature of light.

The figures of this merit field show that they are pleased with me; for my part, I have great faith in them when I remember their qualities and kindness.

Since beginningless time, I and all sentient beings, who have been my mothers, have been born into saṃsāra and for a long while, up until now, have experienced the very many different sufferings of saṃsāra in general, and those of the three lower realms in particular. Even now, it is hard to understand the extent and depth of that suffering. But [now] I have gained something special that is difficult to achieve, and once achieved is most beneficial: the optimum human rebirth. It is difficult to meet with the precious teachings of the Buddha. Now that I have met with these teachings, if I do not achieve pure and complete buddhahood, the best form of liberation from all the sufferings of saṃsāra, I must again experience the whole range of sufferings that saṃsāra in general involves and, more importantly, the sufferings of the three lower realms. The power to protect me from these sufferings resides in the guru and the Three Jewels. So for the sake of all sentient beings, my former mothers, I shall achieve complete buddhahood. I therefore take refuge in the guru and the Three Jewels.

With these thoughts, [recite this formula] three times or however many times you are able:

I take refuge in the guru.
I take refuge in the Buddha.
I take refuge in the Dharma.
I take refuge in the Saṅgha.

Repeat [this verse] three times for the development of bodhichitta:

Until enlightenment, I take refuge
In Buddha, Dharma, and the Supreme Assembly.
With the merit I earn through generosity and so on,
May I gain buddhahood for the sake of all beings.

Recite the following three or more times, so that meditation on the four immeasurables thoroughly suffuses your mental continum:

How welcome it would be if all sentient beings remained in a state of equanimity: free of feelings of intimacy or distance, attachment, or hostility. May they come to this state. I will bring them to this state. May I be blessed by my gurus and deities to have the power to do this!

How welcome it would be if all sentient beings possessed happiness and its causes. May they come to have them. I will make them have them. May I be blessed by my gurus and deities to have the power to do this!

How welcome it would be if all sentient beings were free of suffering and its causes. May they come to be free of them. I will make them free of them. May I be blessed by my gurus and deities to have the power to do this!

How welcome it would be if all sentient beings were never separated from the holy bliss of high rebirth and liberation. May they come to have these. I will make them have these. May I be blessed by my gurus and deities to have the power to do this!

With the following, generate especially [strong] bodhichitta:

For the sake of all sentient beings, who have all been my mother, I will do anything to quickly, quickly obtain the precious state of pure and complete buddhahood. Therefore I shall enter meditation on the teachings of the stages of the path to enlightenment—the door to the profound path of guru deity yoga.

May the ground everywhere
Have no pebbles and so forth,
Be as flat as the palm of one's hand,
Have the nature of lapis lazuli
Yet remain soft.

May the offerings of humans and the gods,
Both real and those emanated by the mind,
And peerless offering-clouds of Samantabhadra
Pervade the whole of the element of space.

Say three times:

Oṃ namo bhagavate, vajra sara pramardane tathagātaya, arhate samyaksaṃ buddhaya, tadyathā, oṃ vajre vajre, mahā vajre, mahā tejra vajre, mahā vidya vajre, mahā bodhichitta vajre, mahā bodhi maṇḍopa samkramaṇa vajre, sarva karma āvaraṇa vishodhana vajre svāhā.

Bless the offering substances by saying these words of the power of truth:

By the truth of the Three Jewels; by the great might of the blessings of all the buddhas and bodhisattvas, along with their might from completing the two accumulations; by the power of the purity and inconceivability of the dharmadhātu [sphere of truth], may everything become suchness.

THE FOURTH [RITE]: VISUALIZING THE MERIT FIELD

Of the two traditions, we will proceed according to the Guru Pūjā *because this is easy to recite.*

Visualization of the merit field:

In space, the broad road used by the gods,
Seen as bliss and void combined,
At the center of overlapping banks of cloud
Of Samantabhadra's offerings,
Stands a wish-granting tree
Bedecked with leaves, flowers, and fruit.
At its summit is a precious throne
Ablaze with five colors of light;
On this rests a huge lotus
With sun and moon discs.
On these sits my root guru
Who is thrice kind to me.

He is by nature all buddhas;
In aspect, a saffron-robed monk,
With one face, two hands, and radiant smile.
His right hand makes the Dharma-teaching mudrā;
The left, the gesture of meditative absorption,
While holding a nectar-filled begging bowl.
He wears the three bright-saffron Dharma robes;
On his head is a yellow pandit's hat.
At his heart are Śhākyamuni and blue Vajradhara
Of one face, two hands, holding bell and vajra.
Vajradhara sits in union with Dhatvīśhvarī;
They experience bliss and void combined;
They wear precious ornaments and robes of celestial silks.

My guru has the marks and signs
And blazes forth thousands of light rays;
A five-colored rainbow encircles him.
He sits in vajra posture; his pure aggregates
Are the five dhyāni buddhas;
His four constituents, the four consorts;
His senses, veins, muscles, and joints
Are actually bodhisattvas; his pores
Are twenty-one thousand arhats;
His limbs—powerful wrathful ones.
The light rays from his body are direction protectors.
Indra, Brahmā, and other gods
Throw themselves at his feet. Around him sit:
My own lamas, a profusion of tutelary gods,
Their maṇḍalas, their attendant gods,
The buddhas and bodhisattvas,
Ḍākas and the protectors of the teachings.
All their three doors are marked by the three vajras.
Hooked rays of light spread out from their *hūṃ* letters,
Bringing back wisdom beings from their natural abodes,
Who indistinguishably merge and stabilize.

[Invocation]

The protectors of each and every sentient being,
Gods who conquer mighty Māra and his hordes,
You who perfectly know all things—
O bhagavān buddhas and your train,
Please come here. *Ja hūṃ baṃ hoḥ:*
You become inseparable
From the commitment beings.

Generation of the bath house:

Here is a perfumed bath house;
With clear and brilliant crystal floor;
With radiant, exquisite pillars
Made of precious substances;
Adorned with a canopy of dazzling pearls.

Carry out the washing:

Just after [Buddha's] birth,
The gods washed his body;
So I also wash with celestial waters
The bodies of the sugatas.
Oṃ sarva tathāgata abhiṣhekata samaya shrīye āḥ hūṃ

Body born of ten million virtues and excellences,
Speech that fulfills the hopes of infinite beings,
Mind that sees all knowables as they are:
I wash the body of Śhākyamuni-Vajradhara.
Oṃ sarva tathāgata abiṣhekata samaya shrīye āḥ hūṃ

I wash the bodies of the Lineage of Extensive Deeds.
I wash the bodies of the Lineage of Profound View.
I wash the bodies of the Lineage of Consecrated Practices.
I wash the bodies of the gurus of my lineage.
Oṃ sarva tathāgata abhiṣhekata samaya shrīye āḥ hūṃ

I wash the bodies of the buddhas, our teachers.
I wash the body of the holy Dharma, our protector.
I wash the bodies of the Saṅgha, our saviors.
I wash the bodies of the Three Jewels, our refuge.
Oṃ sarva tathāgata abhiṣhekata samaya shrīye āḥ hūṃ

Wipe their bodies:

I wipe their bodies with peerless cloth—
Clean and steeped in choice perfume.
Oṃ hūṃ trāṃ hrīḥ āḥ kāya viśhodhanaye svāhā

Anoint their bodies:

I anoint the dazzling bodies of the sages—
As dazzling as burnished, refined gold—
With the choicest fragrances
The billion worlds have to offer.

Offer garments:

Out of my unceasing faith,
I offer celestial robes—soft, light,
Diaphanous—to you who have achieved
The indestructible vajra body.
May I, too, gain the vajra body.

Offer ornaments:

Because the victors are naturally adorned
With the marks and signs,
They have no need of other ornaments;
But I offer the best of jewels and ornaments
So that all beings may obtain
A body with these self-same marks.

The request for them to resume their places:

Because the bhagavāns love
All beings and myself
I ask you to remain
Through your magic powers
As long as I still make offerings to you.

THE FIFTH [RITE]: OFFERING THE SEVEN-LIMBED PRAYER AND A WORLD MAṆḌALA—PRACTICES THAT CONTAIN ALL THE KEY POINTS FOR ACCUMULATING MERIT AND SELF-PURIFICATION

Body born of ten million virtues and excellences,
Speech that fulfills the hopes of infinite beings,
Mind that sees all knowables as they are:
Homage to the head of the Śhākya tribe.

The great compassion of Vajradhara,
The supreme perception of Tilopa and Nāropa,
The supreme glory of Ḍoṃbhīpa and Atiśha:
Homage to the Lineage of Consecrated Practices.

Maitreya, Asaṅga, Vasubhandu, Vimuktisena,
Paranasena, Vinītasena, Dharmakīrti,
Haribhadra, both Kusalis, Suvarṇadvīpa:
Homage to the Lineage of Extensive Deeds.

Mañjuśhrī, who destroyed existence and nonexistence,
Nāgārjuna, Chandrakīrti, the first Vidyakokila,
And other children of the Ārya [Nāgārjuna] who pursued the Buddha's meaning: Homage to the Lineage of Profound View.

Atiśha, holder of supreme instruction on theory and practice,
Lord Drom, grandfather of the Kadampa teachings,
The four yogis, the three brothers, and the rest:
Homage to the Kadampa gurus.

Tsongkapa, who revived the forerunners' tradition in the Land of Snows,
Gyaeltsab Je, great logician, powerful siddha,
Kaedrub Je, lord of sūtra and tantra teachings:
Homage to the Lineage of the Father and his Children.

Vajradhara, embodiment of all three refuges,
Who takes the form of spiritual guides
In order to subdue any disciple,
Who confers common and supreme siddhis:
Homage to my kind gurus.

O eyes through which we see the whole of vast scripture,
Supreme doorways to lead the fortunate to liberation,
Users of skillful means to lovingly protect:
Homage to illuminating spiritual guides.

Guhyasamāja, blissful Heruka,
Most glorious Yamāntaka and the rest,
Protectors of the four wheels of countless tantras:
Homage to the host of tutelary deities.

Marvelous merits from harmonious prayers,
Deeds that never can be rivalled,
Deeds fulfilled in this one fortunate eon:
Homage to the thousand buddhas.

Sunāman, Ratna, Suvarṇabhadra, Aśhoka,
Dharmakīrti, Abhijña, Bhaiṣhajyarāja, Śhākyamuni,
Who have fulfilled the gist of vastest prayers:
Homage to the eight sugatas.

Perfection of Wisdom, the mother of the victors,
Who destroys the seeds of all dark sorrow,
Who removes suffering by its deepest roots:
Homage to the Dharma of the three vehicles.

Mañjuśhrī, Vajrapāṇi, Avalokiteśhvara,
Kṣhitagarbhā, Sarvanivaranaviṣhkaṃbhi,

Ākāśhagarbha, Maitreya, Samantabhadra:
Homage to the eight main princes.

Those who have meditated on the profound twelve links,
Who by themselves reached pratyekabuddha wisdom
And took it to heart in isolation:
Homage to the noble pratyekabuddhas.

Those who heard the Sage's words,
Who held aloft the doctrine's banner,
Aṅgaja, Ajita, Vanavasin,
Kālika, Vajrīputra, Śhrībhadra,
Kanakavatsa, Kanakabharadvāja,
Ārya Bakula, Rāhula,
Chūḍapanthaka, Piṇḍolabharadvāja,
Panthaka, Nāgasena, Gopaka, and Abheda:
Homage to the elders and their retinue.

You who look down from holy Kechari,
Powerful ones who have clairvoyance and work miracles,
You look upon practitioners as a mother sees her son:
Homage to the three divisions of ḍākinīs.

In times long past, when the Blessed One was here,
You protected and, as a mother on her child,
Smiled upon those who practiced properly:
Homage to the Dharma protectors and defenders.

Dhṛitarāṣhṭra, Virūḍhaka,
Virūpākṣha and Vaiśhravaṇa,
You control your retinues and guard the four gates:
Homage to the four mahārājās.

To all those worthy of homage,
I prostrate myself in supreme faith,
With as many bodies
As the atoms in the world.

Homage to the youthful Ārya Mañjuśhrī.
To all the tathāgatas of the three times—those lions among men—
To be found in the ten directions of the universe:
With cleansed body, speech, and mind,
I pay homage to each and every one of you.

With this powerful prayer of noble deeds,
I prostrate before all the victors:
I imagine I have as many bodies
As there are atoms in the world.

On each atom there are as many buddhas
As [the universe] has atoms; and those buddhas
Sit among bodhisattvas. So too do I believe
That all victors fill the expanse of all phenomena.

I sing of the qualities of all the victors
With an inexhaustible ocean of praise,
With a great ocean of every melodious sound.
Thus I praise all sugatas.

I offer the victorious ones
Exquisite flowers, choice garlands,
The clash of cymbals, the best
Of lotions, of parasols,
Of oil lamps and choice incense.

I offer the victorious ones
Exquisite robes, the best of fragrances,
Mounds of incense powders high as Meru—
A sublime array of matchless things.

All this peerless, expansive offering
I imagine for all the victors.
To all the victors I pay this homage,
Making this offering by the power
Of my faith in noble deeds.

Offer the maṇḍala with the following:

Oṃ vajra bhūmi āḥ hūṃ: the most powerful golden base. *Oṃ vajra rekhe āḥ hūṃ:* an iron mountain chain completely surrounds it. In the center—Meru, king of mountains. To the east, the continent of Videha. To the south, Jambudvīpa. To the west, Godānīya. To the north, Kuru. Then east, the minor continents of Deha and Videha; south, Chāmara and Aparachāmara; west, Śhāthā and Uttaramantriṇa; north, Kuru and Kaurava. jewel-mountains, wish-granting trees, wish-granting cows, unploughed wild crops. The precious wheel, precious jewel, precious concubine, precious minister, precious elephant, precious horse, precious general. The great treasure vase. Goddesses of beauty, garlands, songs, dance, flowers, incense, light, perfume. The sun and moon; the precious parasol and banner of absolute victory. In the center: all the magnificent wealth of gods and humans. All this I present to my kind root guru and the holy gurus of his lineage, together with great Lama Lozang Tubwang Dorje Chang, the deities and their trains. For the sake of all beings, please compassionately accept these things. Take them and bless me.

I offer this base, anointed with perfume,
Strewn with flowers, adorned by Mount Meru,
The continents, sun, and moon—
All visualized into a buddhafield.
May all beings enjoy this pure land.

I offer my body, speech, and mind and those of other beings,
Our pleasures, our root virtues from all three times;
I mentally offer a precious maṇḍala,
And the mass of Samantabhadra's offerings,
To my gurus, deities and Three Jewels.
Take them out of your compassion; please bless me.
Idaṃ guru ratna maṇḍalakaṃ niryātayāmi

You may also recite the Confession of Transgressions Sūtra *if you wish to do things more elaborately.*

The mantra to multiply virtue:

Oṃ sambhara sambhara vimanasara mahājapa hūṃ. Oṃ smara smara vimanaskara mahājapa hūṃ.

The Confession of Transgressions Sūtra:

Homage to our Teacher, the Bhagavān, the Tathāgata, the Completely Enlightened One, the Glorious Victor—Śhākyamuni.
Homage to Tathāgata Who Vanquishes through Vajra Essence [Vajramaṇḍapramardin].
Homage to Tathāgata Emanator of Precious Light Rays [Ratnarchi].
Homage to Tathāgata King of the Powerful Nāgas [Geyarāja].
Homage to Tathāgata Tribe of Heroes [Vorasena].
Homage to Tathāgata Glorious Happiness [Voranandin].
Homage to Tathāgata Precious Fire [Ratnāgni].
Homage to Tathāgata Precious Moonlight [Ratnachandraprabha].
Homage to Tathāgata Meaningful to Behold [Amoghadarshin].
Homage to Tathāgata Precious Moon [Ratnachandra].
Homage to Tathāgata Stainless [Vimala].
Homage to Tathāgata Glorious Generosity [Śhrīdatta].
Homage to Tathāgata Purity [Brahmā].
Homage to Tathāgata Bestowed by Purity [Brahmādatta].
Homage to Tathāgata Water God [Varuṇa].
Homage to Tathāgata God of the Water God [Varuṇadeva].
Homage to Tathāgata Gloriously Noble [Śhrībhadra].
Homage to Tathāgata Glorious Sandalwood [Chandanashrī].
Homage to Tathāgata Infinite Brilliance [Anantejas].
Homage to Tathāgata Glorious Light [Prabhasaśhrī].
Homage to Tathāgata Glory of Having No Sorrow [Ashokaśhrī].
Homage to Tathāgata Man of No Clinging [Nārāyaṇa].
Homage to Tathāgata Glorious Flower [Kusumaśhrī].
Homage to Tathāgata Directly Knowing through the Play of Purity's Light Rays [Brahmājyotirvikroḍhitābhijña].
Homage to Tathāgata Directly Knowing through the Play of the Lotus's Light Rays [Padmajyotirvikroḍhitābhijña].
Homage to Tathāgata Glorious Wealth [Danaśhrī].
Homage to Tathāgata Glorious Remembrance [Smṛitiśhrī].

Homage to Tathāgata Most Renowned for Glorious Purity [Brahmāśhrīsuparikīrti].
Homage to Tathāgata King of the Victory Banner that Flies above Indra [Indraketudhvajarāja].
Homage to Tathāgata Glory of Most Complete Dominance [Suvikrāntaśhrī].
Homage to Tathāgata Most Complete Victory in Battle [Yuddhajaya].
Homage to Tathāgata Glory of Having Reached Complete Dominance [Vikrāntagāmiśhrī].
Homage to Tathāgata Glorious Pattern of Light Everywhere [Samantāvabhāsavyuhaśhrī].
Homage to the Tathāgata Complete Dominance through the Precious Lotus [Ratnapadmavikrāmin].
Homage to Tathāgata, the Arhat, the Completely Enlightened Precious One who Sits on a Lotus—King of the Lord of Mountains [Śhailendrarāja].

These and all the tathāgatas, arhats, completely enlightened ones, and bhagavāns to be found in all the worlds in [all] ten directions—all the living bhagavān buddhas in existence—please heed me:

In this rebirth, and in all my rebirth states since beginningless time on the wheel of saṃsāra, I have committed, encouraged others to do, and rejoiced over sinful actions. I have stolen offerings made to stūpas, to the Saṅgha, to the Saṅgha of the ten directions; I have encouraged others to do these; I have rejoiced over such actions. I have committed the five heinous crimes, encouraged others to do them, and rejoiced over such crimes. I have fulfilled the complete karmic process for the ten nonvirtues; I have encouraged others to do this; I have rejoiced when others did this. Obscured by every sort of karmic obscuration, I have been hell beings, and I have been born in animal states, in the realms of hungry ghosts, in remote regions, as barbarians, as long-lived gods, as [humans] with defective sense organs, as people upholding wrong views, and as people who did not rejoice over the coming of a Buddha. Whatever my karmic obscurations may be, I confess them all, admit them all, reveal them all, uncover them all before the bhagavān buddhas, who have primal wisdom, the eyes [of compassion], who have power, valid cognition, and see with their omniscience. In future I will cut myself off from such actions and will refrain from them.

All the bhagavān buddhas, please heed me:

I may have root virtues from practicing generosity in this rebirth and in my other rebirths states in saṃsāra since beginningless time—even of giving a single scrap of food to beings who have been reborn in animal states. I may have root virtues from safeguarding my ethics; I may have root virtues from practicing celibacy; I may have root virtues from ripening sentient beings; I may have root virtues from developing the wish for supreme enlightenment; I may have root virtues from supreme primal wisdom. All the root virtues I may have, I gather them together, bring them together. I gather them together and dedicate them to the supreme, the highest, the higher-than-high, the supreme of supremes. I dedicate them to my supreme, perfect, complete enlightenment. Just as the bhagavān buddhas of the past dedicated their root virtues, and just as the bhagavān buddhas yet to come will dedicate their root virtues, and just as the bhagavān buddhas still alive at present dedicate their root virtues, so I dedicate mine. I confess each and every sin. I rejoice over all merit. I plead with all the buddhas and petition them: may I gain holiest and supreme primal wisdom. I fold my hands to all the present victorious ones still alive and supreme among humans, to all victorious ones of the past, and to all of time yet to come; may I come under your protection.

(Colophon: so ends the Mahāyāna Sūtra entitled the *Three Noble Heaps.*)

The General Confession:

Alas! All the buddhas abiding in the ten directions, such as Guru Vajra - dhara, all the bodhisattvas, and the Saṅgha: please heed me. I, *[say your name]* by name, in all my [past] lives in beginningless saṃsāra until now, being under the power of the delusions of attachment, hostility, and benighted ignorance, have committed the ten nonvirtues with my body, speech, and mind. I have committed the five major heinous crimes, the five minor heinous crimes; I have broken my pratimokṣha vows, my bodhisattva vows, my secret tantra vows. I have shown disrespect to my father and mother, and to my abbot, ordination master, and celibate companions. I have done actions harmful to the Three Jewels; I have abandoned the holy Dharma; I have disparaged the Ārya Saṅgha; I have done things harmful to sentient beings, and so on—I have performed a set of nonvirtues, encouraged others to do these, rejoiced when others did these, and so forth. In brief, whatever my set of grave misdeeds may consist of, whatever causes [it may contain] to prevent my gaining high rebirth or liberation and make me take rebirth in saṃsāra or the lower realms, all these I confess, admit, do not conceal, and reveal before all the buddhas living in the ten directions, such as Guru Vajradhara, and the bodhisattvas; in the future I shall refrain from doing these; as I have confessed and expiated these, may I reach happiness and remain there; this would not have happened had I not confessed and expiated them.

If you are going to perform only a short version, recite:

Under the power of attachment, hostility,
And benighted ignorance, I have sinned
With my body, speech, and mind.
I confess all these individually.

I rejoice over all merits
Of the victors of the ten directions.
Of their children, pratyekabuddhas,
Still-learners and no-more-learners,
And every other being.

O lamps to worlds in the ten directions,
You who achieved nonattachment
And the level of enlightened buddhas,
I beseech you, O protectors:
Turn the supreme wheel!

To those who, to common appearance,
Intend to go to their nīrvāṇa,
With folded hands I plead:
Stay for as many eons
As there are atoms in this world
To help and bring happiness to all beings.

What little virtue I acquired
From homage, offerings, confession,
Rejoicing, requests, and petitions,
I dedicate it all to my enlightenment.

At this point make a long maṇḍala offering. Then, request the three great aims:

I take refuge in the guru and the Three Precious Jewels. Please bless my mindstream. Please bless us so that I and all sentient beings, beings who were once my mothers, stop having any sort of wrong thoughts—from having disrespect for our spiritual guides to our grasping at dualistic signs in the self. Please bless us so that we easily develop every sort of right thought—from having respect for our spiritual guides, and so on. Please, bless us and pacify all our external and internal hindrances.

THE SIXTH [RITE]: FURTHER PETITIONS, WHICH FOLLOW THE ORAL INSTRUCTIONS, MADE IN ORDER TO BE SURE YOUR MINDSTREAM HAS BEEN SUFFICIENTLY IMBUED BY YOUR MEDITATIONS

My precious root guru, take your place
On the lotus and moon-disc on my crown;
Care for me out of great compassion,
And confer the siddhis of body, speech, and mind.

Our Teacher, the Bhagavān—the peerless savior,
Maitreya the invincible—the Victor's holy regent,
Ārya Asaṅga—predicted by the Victorious One:
I make petition to three buddhas and bodhisattvas.

Vasubhandu—crest jewel of Jambudvīpa's scholars,
Ārya Vimuktisena—who found the middle path,
Vimuktisenagomin—who still commands faith:
I make petition to three friends of beings.

Paranasena—who achieved a most wondrous state,
Vinītasena—who trained his mind in profound paths,
Vairochana—treasured for his powerful deeds:
I make petition to the three who opened the eyes of the world.

Haribhadra—who spread the path of perfecting wisdom,
Kusali—who held all the Victor's instructions
Ratnasena—who cared for all with love:
I make petition to three captains of beings.

Suvarṇadvīpa—whose mind had bodhichitta,
Dīpaṃkāra Atiśha—who held the forerunners' tradition,
Dromtoenpa—who made clear the noble path:
I make petition to three backbones of the teachings.

Śhākyamuni—peerless exponent, supreme savior,
Mañjuśhrī—who embodies the omniscience of the victors,
Nāgārjuna—most exalted ārya to see profound meaning:
I make petition to the three crest jewels of philosophers.

Chandrakīrti—who clarified the ārya's thoughts,
Vidyakokila—Chandrakīrti's best disciple,
Vidyakokila the younger—a true victors' child:
I make petition to three powerful intellects.

Dipaṃkāra Atiśha—who rightly perceived the depth
Of mutual dependence and upheld the forerunners' way,
And Dromtoenpa—who clarified the noble path:
I make petition to two jewels of Jambudvīpa.

Goenpawa—that splendid, powerful yogi,
Nëuzurpa—profound single-pointed concentration,
Tagmapa—who upheld all branches of vinaya:
I make petition to three lamps lighting these remote regions.

Namkha Senge—who practiced with great diligence,
Namkha Gyaelpo—who was blessed by the holy ones,
Senge Zangpo—who gave up the eight worldly concerns:
And I make petition to Gyaelsae Zangpo.

Who with bodhichitta saw all beings as his child,
Who was blessed and cared for by the god of gods,
Who was supreme guide for beings in degenerate times:
I make petition to Namkha Gyaeltsaen.

Geshe Potowa—the Victor's regent,
Sharawa—whose wisdom has no equal.

Chaekawa—lineage holder of bodhichitta:
I make petition to three who answer the hopes of beings.

Chilbupa—bodhisattva, lord over transmissions and insights,
Lhalung Wangchug—great scholar steeped in scripture,
Goenpo Rinpoche—protector of beings in all three realms:
I make petition to three great elders.

Zangchenpa—whose ethics were stainless,
Tsonawa—who upheld the hundred thousand sections of vinaya.
Moendrapa—who perfected vast metaphysics;
I make petition to three great saviors of beings.

Lord of vast and profound Dharmas,
Who protected all fortunate beings,
Whose noble works spread the teachings:
I make petition to a glorious guru [Choekyab Zangpo].

Tsultrimbar—great prince of adepts,
Zhoenue Oe—who cultivated his spiritual guide,
Gyergompa—whose mind trained in the Supreme Vehicle's path:
I make petition to three children of the victors.

Sangyaeb Oen—treasure of wondrous qualities,
Namkha Gyaelpo—blessed by the saints,
Senge Zangpo—who gave up eight worldly concerns:
And I make petition to Gyaelsae Zangpo.

Who with bodhichitta saw all beings as his son,
Who was blessed and cared for by the god of gods,
Who was supreme guide for beings in degenerate times:
I make petition to Namkha Gyaeltsaen.

Avalokiteśhvara—great treasure of right-perceiving compassion,
Mañjuśhrī—master of stainless omniscience,
Tsongkapa—crest jewel of scholars in the Land of Snows:
I make petition at Lozang Dragpa's feet.

Jampael Gyatso—great prince of adepts,
Kaedrub Rinpoche—the sun of philosophers and adepts,
Basoje—who held a store of secret instruction:
I make petition to three peerless gurus.

Choekyi Dorje—who attained unification,
Gyaelwa Ensapa—who achieved the three kāyas,
Sangyae Yeshe—who held both transmissions and insights:
I make petition to three great scholar-adepts.

Lozang Choekyi Gyaeltsaen—who held the victory banner of the teachings,
Koenchog Gyaeltsaen—his closest disciple,
Lozang Yeshe—who shone light on the noble path:
I make petition to three venerable lamas.

Ngagwang Jampa—who spread Śhākyamuni's teachings,
Lozang Nyaendrag—considered his closest disciple,
Yoentaen Tayae—who had infinite good qualities:
I make petition to three kind gurus.

Taenpa Rabgyae—who spread Lozang Yeshe's teachings,
Lodroe Zangpo—who worked for all beings' liberation,
Lozang Gyatso—skilled in the right way to teach:
I make petition to three unequalled gurus.

To my supremely kind root guru:
Peerless one, who upheld both teachings and practices,
Who conveyed both transmissions and insights
To four types of receptive fortunates:
With great reverence of body, speech, and mind, I make petition.

He who studied much, who extended
The maṇḍala of oral instruction
And revealed hidden practices of the two stages:
I make petition to Taenzin Kaedrub.

Kindest incarnate lama, whose body
Contained all past, present, and future refuge;
Whose speech taught with Mañjuśhrī's eloquence;
Whose mind was an ocean of spontaneous wisdom
In the three high trainings and cause and effect:
I make petition to Lozang Lhuendrub Gyatso.

[My venerable lama, skilled in all fields,
Whose mind was devoted to the āryas' jewels—
Right love and so on—
Who wore the robes of the four vast good works.
I make petition to Jampa Taenzin Trinlae.

Lozang Yeshe Taenzin Gyatso,
Who embodied the primal wisdom
Of all the noble victors;
O foremost in their stainless teachings,
O protector who emanated
A vast profusion of maṇḍalas.
I make petition to my kind guru.]

You are eyes for seeing into all vast teachings,
You are the best gate taking fortunates to liberation,
You, motivated by love, used skillful means:
I make petition to these spiritual guides, givers of light.

After making this petition most strongly, recite [*Tsongkapa's* Basis of All Good Qualities].

Most kind one, basis of all good qualities,
Proper devotion to you is the root of the path.
Bless me to see this and,
With much effort and respect, to depend on you.

Such a free, wholesome rebirth I shall get only once.
I know it is difficult to receive but most beneficial.
Bless me to give rise to the uninterrupted thought
Wishing both night and day to extract its essence.

Life and body are like foam moving on water.
They will soon be destroyed. I am reminded of death,
And that after death, my body is like a shadow,
And I shall follow black and white karmic results.

Bless me to gain strong conviction
And abandon my host of misdeeds,
Even down to the subtlest of the subtle,
To accomplish every virtue
And to always be scrupulous.

Analyze it: discontent is the door to all suffering.
The magnificence of the world is untrustworthy.
Bless me so that I understand the disadvantages
And develop yearning for the bliss of liberation.

Recalling those most pure thoughts:
Recollection, vigilance, and great scruple;
Bless me to undertake the essence of the practice,
The root of the doctrine—the pratimokṣha vows.

Just as I have fallen into worldly feelings,
So too have all beings, once my mothers;
Bless me to see this, train in supreme bodhichitta,
And take responsibility for freeing these beings.

Yet mere development of bodhichitta while not meditating
On the three types of ethics will not accomplish enlightenment.
Bless me to see this well, and to train
With strong endeavor in the vows of the victors' children.

Pacify my distraction to wrong objects
And may I properly engage in right things;
Bless me to be pacified and soon develop in my stream
Combined mental quiescence and special insight.

May I train in the common path and become a fitting vessel,
Then bless me to become fortunate

To easily take the vows that are the entrance
To the supreme of all the vehicles, the Vajrayāna.

The basis of achieving the two kinds of siddhis
Is said to be keeping one's commitments;
Bless me to hold these with genuine conviction
And keep them as I would my life.

Then may I strive to realize all points
In the essence of the tantras: the two stages.
Bless me that I never waver from performing
The four-session yoga and accomplish the holy teachings.

Long live the spiritual guides who teach this wholesome path
And the companions who practice well.
Bless them so that inner and outer hindrances
May be completely stilled.

In all my lives may I be inseparable from my pure guru,
May I enjoy the glories of the Dharma,
May I consummate the qualities of the levels and paths,
And may I soon achieve the state of Vajradhara.

Think over the meaning of the words as you recite them.

The dissolution of the merit field:

My precious root guru, take your place
On the lotus and moon-disc on my crown;
Care for me out of great compassion,
And confer the siddhis of body, speech, and mind.

The guru moves to the crown of your head, and you perform a brief seven-limbed prayer and maṇḍala offering:

Body born of ten million virtues and excellences,
Speech that fulfills the hopes of infinite beings,

Mind that sees all knowables as they are:
Homage to the head of the Śhākya clan.

The supreme teacher: the precious Buddha,
The supreme protector: the precious holy Dharma,
The supreme savior: the precious Saṅgha:
Homage to you who comprise all refuge.

I make every offering, both real and imagined.
I confess every sin and transgression
Acquired from the beginningless past.
I rejoice in the virtue of all ārya beings.
Remain [with us] till saṃsāra is emptied.
Turn the wheel of Dharma for beings.
I dedicate my own virtue and that of others to enlightenment.

To the guru, tutelary deities, and the Three Jewels,
I offer the four continents, Mount Meru, the sun and moon,
These precious seven in a jeweled maṇḍala,
And a mass of Samantabhadra's offerings.
Out of your compassion, be pleased and bless me.

Make this petition bound to the one guru:

My most divine guru, lord of the four kāyas,
I make petition to you: Śhākyamuni-Vajradhara.
My divine guru, lord of unimpeded dharmakāya,
I make petition to you: Śhākyamuni-Vajradhara.
My divine guru, lord of blissful saṃbhogakāya,
I make petition to you: Śhākyamuni-Vajradhara.
My divine guru, lord of sundry nirmāṇakāya,
I make petition to you: Śhākyamuni-Vajradhara.
My divine guru, embodiment of all gurus,
I make petition to you: Śhākyamuni-Vajradhara.
My divine guru, embodiment of all deities,
I make petition to you: Śhākyamuni-Vajradhara.
My divine guru, embodiment of all buddhas,
I make petition to you: Śhākyamuni-Vajradhara.

My divine guru, embodiment of all Dharma,
I make petition to you: Śhākyamuni-Vajradhara.
My divine guru, embodiment of all Saṅgha,
I make petition to you: Śhākyamuni-Vajradhara.
My divine guru, embodiment of all ḍākas,
I make petition to you: Śhākyamuni-Vajradhara.
My divine guru, embodiment of all dharmapalas,
I make petition to you: Śhākyamuni-Vajradhara.
My divine guru, embodiment of all refuge,
I make petition to you: Śhākyamuni-Vajradhara.

Visualize the guru on your crown as Śhākyamuni and recite:

Homage to Śhākyamuni, guru and Victorious One.
I make offerings to you. I take refuge in you.

Oṃ muni muni mahāmuniye svāhā.

Then, after repeating this name mantra as many times as you can manage, continue [with prayers of dedication and auspiciousness]:

By this virtue, may I soon
Become a guru-buddha
So that I may lead every single being
To that very level.

[The Lamrim Prayer]

By the two accumulations I have amassed
With much effort over a great time,
Which fill a vastness like the sky,
May I become a victor, a powerful one,
A leader of beings—for those whose mental eyes
Are closed by ignorance.

From now on in all my lives
May Mañjuśhrī lovingly care for me.

May I find the supreme path of all the teachings,
Practice it, and please all the victors.

Using whatever I have realized of the points of the path,
May I dispel the mental darkness of beings
Through powerful love and honest skillful means;
May I long uphold the victor's doctrine.

In any place the precious teachings have not reached,
Or where they have since declined,
May I, moved by great compassion,
Shed light upon these beneficial treasures.

By the amazing good works of the victors and their children
And the excellent practice of enlightenment's path in stages,
May the minds of liberation seekers be enriched
And the victors' deeds long be continued.

May all be made conducive for practicing the wholesome path;
May the unconducive be dispelled.
In all their lives, may all
Humans and nonhumans not be cut off
From the pure path praised by the victors.

Whenever the preparatory rites of the Supreme Vehicle
Are properly practiced with [much] effort,
May the powerful always proclaim it,
And may an ocean of auspiciousness pervade all directions.

[Reciting] these words with a strong aspiration, dedicate the root virutes you have acquired toward [fulfilling] the wishes of your own and others' prayers.

Kaendaen Rabgyae, the retired head of Bangrim Choede Monastery, out of much faith, perseverance, and discernment said, "I would like a convenient recitation for the preparatory rites for the concise teaching on the stages of the path to enlightenment, the Swift Path Leading to Omniscience.*" He made this request most urgently, and I have composed this for my own daily practice and with the great altruistic hope that it would benefit others with the same level of fortune as myself. I, who am called Jampael Lhuendrub, and who will always be passing himself off as a leader [of disciples] until the end of time, based this on the instructions from the oral lineage of that peerlessly kind child of the buddhas and lamp of the Kadampa teachings, Kyabje Kaelzang Taenzin, and his two foremost disciples. May the confidential lineages of Mañjuśhrī the protector not die out but become a victory banner for the precious teachings.*

Sarva maṅgalaṃ

May all be good!

5. THE SEVEN-POINT MIND TRAINING

Oṃ svasti.

[Homage to the Great Compassion]

Though there are many ways to teach the Mahāyāna mind training instruction, Geshe Chaekawa formulated the tradition of the seven points. The seven are: (1) teaching the preliminaries on which this Dharma depends; (2) training in bodhichitta, the foundation; (3) converting unfortunate circumstances into a path to enlightenment; (4) teaching a practice to be applied to your whole life; (5) the criteria of having trained the mind; (6) the commitments of the mind-training practice; (7) pieces of advice for the mind-training practice.

(1) TEACHING THE PRELIMINARIES ON WHICH THIS DHARMA DEPENDS

First train in the preliminaries.

There are three of these: meditation on: (1) the difficulty of gaining the optimum human rebirth; (2) death and impermanence; (3) the drawbacks of saṃsāra.

(2) TRAINING THE MIND IN BODHICHITTA, THE FOUNDATION

This has two subdivisions: (1) the ultimate; (2) the relative.

ULTIMATE BODHICHITTA

This has three subdivisions: (1) the preliminaries; (2) the meditation session; (3) between sessions.

THE PRELIMINARIES

(1) Taking refuge and developing bodhichitta; (2) requests; (3) offering the seven-limb prayer; (4) assuming correct posture; (5) taking twenty-one calm breaths.

THE MEDITATION SESSION

Think all phenomena are like a dream.
Examine with the basis of unproduced knowing.
Even the antidote will liberate to its ground.
Sit within the nature of the basis of all.

BETWEEN SESSIONS

Between sessions, be as a person in a dream.

MEDITATION ON RELATIVE BODHICHITTA

This has two sections: (1) during the meditative absorption; (2) between sessions.

DURING MEDITATIVE ABSORPTION

Train alternately in taking and giving.
Mount these two on the energy winds.

BETWEEN SESSIONS

Three subjects, three poisons, and three root virtues.
In your everyday life,
Train yourself with verses
To stimulate remembrance.
Build up your taking by starting with yourself.

(3) CONVERTING UNFORTUNATE CIRCUMSTANCES INTO A PATH TO ENLIGHTENMENT

When the universe is full of sin,
Turn these unfortunate conditions
Into the path to enlightenment!

This has two parts: (1) through thought; (2) through action.

THROUGH THOUGHT

There are two subsections: (1) the relative; (2) the ultimate.

THE RELATIVE

Put the blame on one thing alone.
Meditate on the greater kindness of all.

THE ULTIMATE

Regard all deceptive appearances
As being the four kāyas.
This is the unexcelled
Safekeeping of emptiness.

THROUGH ACTION

The supreme means has four actions.
Immediately apply your practice
To whatever you encounter.

(4) TEACHING A PRACTICE TO BE APPLIED YOUR WHOLE LIFE

The brief essence of instruction
Is the five powers. Practice them!
The Mahāyāna instruction on transference
Concerns the five powers.
Cherish this activity!

(5) THE CRITERIA OF HAVING TRAINED THE MIND

All Dharma comes within one thought.
Uphold the chief of the two witnesses.
Always cultivate mental happiness.
You have mastered it
If you are capable
While distracted.

(6) THE COMMITMENTS OF THE MIND-TRAINING PRACTICE

Always keep to three general points.
Change your aspirations,
But preserve your old manner.
Do not mention others' withered limbs.
Do not think of others at all.
Purify the greatest delusion first.
Abandon all hopes of a result.
Abandon food with poison in it.
Treat [delusion] unfairly.
Don't go wild over insults.
Do not wait in ambush.
Do not attack weak spots
Do not put the load of a dzo on an ox.
Do not run a race.
Don't let the spell go awry.
Don't let the god become a devil.
Don't look for happiness in unhappiness.

(7) PIECES OF ADVICE FOR THE MIND-TRAINING PRACTICE

All yogas are practiced through the one.
Apply the one thing for all distress.
Two actions for first and last.
Patience, if either two happen!
Guard the two as you would your life.
Train in three ascetic practices.
Acquire the causes for the three main things.
Meditate that the three not degenerate.
Do not leave the three idle.
Be impartial to subjects, regard them as pure;
Be versed in the profound and pervasive,
And hold everything dear.
Always meditate when in difficulties.
Don't be dependent on other circumstances.
From today, practice the main thing.
Don't misunderstand.

Don't be too hopeful.
Do not train intermittently.
Be liberated through the two:
Conceptualization and analysis.
Don't get arrogant.
Don't be spiteful.
Don't be changeable.
Don't wish for thanks.

Keep this advice well.

The five degenerations are rampant
But change them to the path to enlightenment.

(That is, practice patience, aspiration, tasting [emptiness], compassion, friendliness, and rejoicing.)

(The source of this instruction:)

This instruction, the essence of nectar,
Comes in a lineage from Suvarṇadvīpa.

(That great and powerful yogi, Chaekawa, having trained his mind well in this instruction, said:)

I have awakened happiness
Through my mind training.
I have much cause to respect it.
All talk of suffering is quite dead.
I now offer this instruction
For subduing self-cherishing.
Now I can die without regrets.

[This version of the root text, in both its length and order, is based on the teachings of Togme Rinpoche, that child of the victorious ones.]

Maṅgalaṃ

NOTES

1 Although Pabongka Rinpoche's audience consisted of lamas, geshes, ordinary monks and nuns, and laypeople, he more often than not addressed himself to the front rows of learned geshes and lamas while teaching.

2 "Modify our behavior" is a gloss of the Tibetan expression *blang dor,* which literally means "engage-abandon," i.e., engage in what is to be practiced and give up what is to be abandoned.

3 The four continents referred to are those according to Buddhist cosmology, which describes each world system (there are a billion of them in total) as a flat disc with an iron fence at its perimeter. Inside there are oceans, and at the center a huge mountain, called Meru, surrounded by seven golden mountain chains and four continents, each with its own two subcontinents, one on either side. Mount Meru has four levels above the ocean water and four below.

4 There are ten levels of development for bodhisattvas—beings who have determined to become enlightened for the sake of all sentient beings. The pure levels are the eighth, ninth, and tenth. From the eighth level onward, the bodhisattva has reached the irreversible stages, and enlightenment is guaranteed. This is described in greater detail in Day 12, p. 369.

5 Of the four main schools of Tibetan Buddhism—Nyingma, Sakya, Kagyu, and Gelug—Pabongka Rinpoche was a great lama of the Gelug tradition. The forerunners of this tradition were the Kadampas, practitioners of the teachings of Atiśha. In fact, both the Kagyu and the Gelug school derive from the Kadampas, and the Gelugpas are sometimes referred to as the neo-Kadampas. This evolution is briefly indicated in Day 6 during the explanation of how the three groups of Kadampas in the merit-field visualization come down through Je Rinpoche to the one group of Gelug teachers (see also appendix 2, *The Lineage of These Teachings,* pp. 694–95).

6 The numbers in the original are confused. The Tibetan actually says "a population of thirty-five thousand," but this would be too small for one hundred thousand households. Amchok Rinpoche suggested the number of 3,500,000.

7 Alaka Chattopadhyaya's *Atīśa and Tibet* (Calcutta: R.D. Press, 1967) identifies this as modern Dhaka, Bangladesh.

8 See note 6.

9 There are five Mahāyāna paths of mental development to enlightenment. The first four—the paths of accumulation, preparation, seeing, and meditation—are those of still-learning; the last is the path of no-more-learning, or enlightenment. Each of the first four are further subdivided into four, and the patience level is the third of the subdivisions of the path of preparation. For a more detailed description see *The Tibetan Tradition of Mental Development,* Geshe Dhargyey (Dharamsala, India: LTWA, 1985).

10 There are eight kinds of *pratimokṣha,* or individual liberation, vows: those of laymen and laywomen *(upāsaka* and *upāsikā),* fast-day vows *(upavāsa),* male and female novice vows *(śhrāmaṇera* and *śhrāmaṇerikā),* probationary nun vows *(śikṣamāṇā),* and fully ordained monk and nun vows *(bhikṣhu* and *bhikṣhuṇī).* Canonical sources generally refer to seven vows, leaving off the fast-day vows.

11 These are the middle way *(madhyamaka),* valid cognition *(pramāṇa),* metaphysics *(abhidharma),* the perfection of wisdom *(prajñāpāramitā),* and discipline *(vinaya).*

12 According to Tibetan medicine, three humors govern the condition of sentient beings: wind, bile, and phlegm. When they are in balance, health is maintained, but the smallest imbalance produces disease (see Day 10, p. 313).

13 Literally, one *dre,* which is roughly a pound and a quarter to a pound and a half.

14 Tibetan medicines are often called by the name of the principal ingredient followed by a number to indicate how many ingredients there are in total.

15 Markers consisting of small rocks, straw standing in a jug, or clay *tsatsa* images are usually placed outside a retreat room to mark the boundary of the retreat, unless it is being conducted within a monastery; in this case it is not possible to place a marker on the true retreat boundary, so it is placed on the window sill of the hut instead. For a lamrim retreat, these are visualized as the four mahārājas, guardians of the four cardinal directions of each world system, to ward off interferences. When only one marker is used, it is visualized as Vaiśhravaṇa, protector of the east and also of ethics and material wealth.

16 All Tibetan translations of Buddhist scriptures begin with the words "In Sanskrit" followed by the original Sanskrit title; this guarantees their authenticity.

17 "From" indicates the usual order of guru, buddhas, deities, bodhisattvas, guardians, Dharma protectors.

18 Traditional Tibetan-style books.

19 Tibetans do not underline important passages in books. Instead they either stick a patch of colored paper at the beginning of a passage or paint red or yellow wash over the words to be emphasized. As there was no readily available glue in Tibet, the lazy would pick some of the film off their teeth and use that.

20 *Brul gtor* are *torma* offerings made to expiate misuse of funds allocated to the Saṅgha.

21 Although foreseeing that it would cost him his life, the bodhisattva Supuṣhpachandra happily went to the land of King Viradatta to spread the Dharma. After leading many beings to happiness, he was killed by the king in a fit of jealous rage. Later the king deeply regretted his action and enshrined the bodhisattva's relics in a stūpa. But it was too late; nothing could bring the teacher back to life.

22 The bodhisattva Samantabhadra is renowned for his extensive offerings to the buddhas. In practice, there are two ways of visualizing the great profusion of Samantabhadra offerings: according to sūtra and according to tantra. Sūtra offerings are the offering of everything good and sumptuous amid five-colored rays of light. The tantric offering is one of bliss and emptiness combined.

23 The full formulation is "All phenomena are selfless, all compounded things are impermanent, all contaminated things are suffering, only nirvāṇa is peace."

24 Asaṅga spent years trying to gain the vision of Maitreya. When he was on the verge of giving up he saw outside his cave visions of Maitreya under different guises demonstrating patience, such as a man trying to wear down a stone with a feather. Asaṅga took heart from these, and was inspired not to give up his meditations. Chandragomin saw a vision of Avalokiteśhvara as a disease-ridden mongrel bitch: on

recognizing the bodhisattva, Chandragomin carried the bitch lovingly on his shoulders to display her to all sundry.

25 Anāthapiṇḍika's daughter (see p. 112). She was married off to a foreign king and so had to live far away from central India. In her misery she prayed to the Buddha, and one morning, in answer to her prayer, he flew to her along with his retinue of śhrāvakas (see also Day 9, p. 266).

26 This prayer is also known as Samantabhadra's prayer.

27 Most of the traditions of Tibetan Buddhism recommend a preliminary *(ngoendro)* retreat to be performed before receiving teachings or going into a long deity retreat. This includes at least reciting the refuge and bodhichitta formulas, making mandala offerings, prostrating, and reciting the mantra of Vajrasattva along with the visualization, one hundred thousand times each. The Gelug tradition places emphasis on continually performing these methods of purification and accumulation of merit rather than at one specific time alone.

28 A monk actually only breaks a minor vow when he puts his lower robe on crookedly, but there is also a major tantric vow of never disregarding one's pratimokṣha vows, so by breaking one he also breaks the other.

29 Pabongka is referring to Yeshe Gyaeltsaen's commentary called *Meaningful to Behold.*

30 One messenger had a great deal of finest-grade barley flour, the other had a small amount of low-grade black barley flour. The second guilefully suggested that they mix their flour together. The first messenger consented then later complained. But it was too late, for by then the two grades of flour were already mixed, and the second messenger had eaten more than his fair share.

31 This is the ability to produce wealth magically.

32 The words "Dharma" *(chos)* in the first line, "protected" *(skyab)* in the second line, and "noble" *(bzang)* in the third line together inscribe the name of the guru being petitioned.

33 Since Atiśha combined the lineages of both the profound and extensive teachings, there are two identical groups of the Classical Tradition gurus. One is placed in front of the Extensive Deeds gurus, the other in front of those of the Profound View. This means there are also two identical sets of each of the other two Kadampa traditions. Many religious paintings adopt a symmetrical arrangement: the Classical Lineage innermost, the Instruction Lineage outermost.

34 Two more verses of praise to Pabongka and Trijang Rinpoche respectively are included at this point in the full lamrim lineage lamas prayer. These can be found in the full version of the preliminary rite *An Ornament for the Throats of the Fortunate,* (see pp. 699–725).

35 In Tibetan, the incorrect version is given as *sgrib bral chos sku'i bdag nyid bla ma lhag pa'i lha.* The intention is that the *bdag nyid,* an extra honorific, should be left out.

36 The Tibetan word for meditation, *sgom,* is the causative/transitive form of the word for "familiar."

37 Asaṅga spent only a single morning in Tuṣhita receiving teachings from Maitreya, but when he returned to earth, he found that fifty years had passed.

38 Gyaeltsab Rinpoche was already a great scholar before becoming a disciple of Je Tsongkapa and originally sought out this famous teacher with the intention of defeating him in debate. When he eventually found Tsongkapa, the master was teaching a great crowd. Undeterred, Gyaeltsab walked up the steps to the throne

with his hat and backpack on while Je Tsongkapa moved over slightly to let him sit down. As the teachings progressed, Gyaeltsab first took off his hat, then his pack, and finally descended the stairs, made three prostrations, and sat down. This eventually proved to be a good omen: before Tsongkapa died, he gave his robe and crown to Gyaeltsab and appointed him successor to the Gandaen throne—the highest position in the Gelug school.

39 In this short paragraph, Pabongka lists many of the figures in the transmission of the Buddha's teachings in both India and Tibet. The seven patriarchs of the teachings were the successors of Guru Śhākyamuni Buddha entrusted with the responsibility of upholding and spreading his doctrine. The eighty mahāsiddhas were accomplished tantric yogis in the Lineage of Consecrated Practices. The six jewels of India were the great pandits Nāgārjuna, Asaṅga, Āryadeva, Vasubandhu, Dignaga, and Dharmakīrti; the two supreme ones were the vinaya masters Gunaprabha and Śhākyaprabha.

40 An expanded version of the *Guru Pūjā* that includes elements from the sixty-two-deity Heruka tantra.

41 According to an indigenous legend, the Tibetan race stemmed from a monkey-faced ogress and a large white ape. The ape was actually an emanation of Avalokiteśhvara and practiced intensive meditational austerities in a cave for years while the ogress wailed and moaned outside, longing to mate with him. Finally, he gave in, and the Tibetans were the result. From him they received their kindheartedness, and from her their suspicious, stubborn, miserly, and lustful nature.

42 The other four are a sea monster, a child, an antelope, and an elephant.

43 Geshe Baen was one of a large group of monks receiving offerings of curd in a temple. Baen Gung-gyael could see he was going to be one of the last to be served. He caught himself becoming jealous of those who had already received some and therefore refused his share when it came, yelling to everyone's astonishment, "I'm a thief!"

44 There are several versions of this story. According to Geshe Ngawang Dhargyay, the man was so carried away by his daydreams that he failed to notice a rat gnawing through the rope holding up a sack of barley flour. The rope broke, the sack hit him on the head, and he died.

45 Udayī was a monk at the time of Buddha who, since he lacked realizations, was frequently doing things with unfortunate repercussions. To curb and restrain such behavior, Buddha established the vinaya code of conduct—rules of discipline intended as guidelines to train and protect the minds of his followers.

46 Being female is considered a less advantageous birth, since women usually meet with far more impediments to practicing Dharma than men. This is dealt with in more detail in Day 13, p. 415.

47 According to Amchok Rinpoche, lay Tibetans believe that this most famous statue in the main temple of Lhasa contains a wish-granting jewel that circulates throughout its body. If you put your head on the statue's knee while the jewel happens to be there, your wish will be granted.

48 Buddhist ideas of human evolution are explained in Vasubandhu's *Treasury of Metaphysics* as follows. When a world system is undergoing destruction, most of the beings in it are either reborn upward in the same world system till they reach the fourth dhyāna plane of the form realm or the higher formless realm—for it is only these upper reaches that do not get destroyed—or they are reborn in some other

world system. After the destruction, when the world system begins to re-form, virtually all the beings who migrated upward will begin to descend again. Many eons later, some beings will have reached such low levels of existence that they begin living on the Southern Continent on the earth's surface. These humans have immeasurable lifespans. Each succeeding human generation on this continent has a shorter lifespan until, one minor eon later, it is only ten years. Over the next minor eon, the human lifespan increases at twice the previous rate, reaching a peak of 80,000 years in the middle of this second minor eon and then dropping back to ten years at its end. This cycle is repeated seventeen more times, after which another whole minor eon passes until lifespans reach immeasurable length once more. Then upward migration begins anew.

49 These are mentioned in passing. The full list is: (1) ignoring this life and devoting oneself wholeheartedly to the Dharma; (2) being prepared to become a pauper; (3) being prepared to die a pauper; (4) being prepared to die alone with no one to take care of one's body; (5) being determined to practice Dharma regardless of reputation; (6) being determined to keep all vows purely; (7) being determined to avoid discouragement; (8) being prepared to be an outcast; (9) accepting the lowest status; (10) attaining exalted buddhahood as the natural result of successful practice.

50 The practice of *taking the essence* or *chuelaen* is a tantric form of fasting used by yogis in order to remain in retreat for long periods of time without needing to rely on gross food. The common practice is to eat one or more pills a day, made from things like flower petals, minerals, or even blessed relics. In this way, the successful yogi can be sustained for years and actually become physically and mentally healthier.

51 "Firm and hard" is the definition of the earth, or solid, element.

52 One conceit of Sanskrit literature is that sandalwood cools anything it touches; Gośhīrṣha sandalwood (snake's heart sandalwood) is supposed to be the best at doing this.

53 The Tibetan name for this hell is *achu*. This is actually the word Tibetans use when they are cold, so I have given the English equivalent sound "Brrr." The Sanskrit word is *Huhuva*.

54 Indra's palace sits in the center of the perfectly flat, lapis-lazuli surface on top of Mount Meru. His reflection can be seen from any vantage point on top of the mountain. This region is called the Realm of the Thirty-three Gods because Indra has a company of thirty-three minor gods who help him reign.

55 This mantra is recited during the visualization of unfocused emptiness that precedes generation of the visualization of a deity. It means "I am the nature (or entity) of the purity of all phenomena."

56 The full title of the text is *A Clear Mirror Elucidating the Truth About Several Monks' Noon Meal.*

57 This was the first book in Tibet and is shrouded in myth. It was supposed to have fallen out of the sky. The *Hundred-Thousand-Verse Perfection of Wisdom Sūtra,* however, is one of the most sacred and revered scriptures and is often put on altars for veneration.

58 The six types are those of the six realms: the hells, hungry ghosts, animals, humans, demigods, and gods. These become five when the demigods are counted among the gods instead of being classified separately.

59 These four are rebirth from a womb, from an egg, from heat and moisture, or miraculously. The last is actually said to be the most common since it includes the rebirths in the hells.

60 The story of Āchārya Manu appears in Yongdzin Yeshe Gyaeltsaen's eighteenth-century commentary on the *Seven-Point Mind Training.*

61 The eight types of suffering are those experienced in the human realm: birth, aging, illness, death, separation from the beautiful, meeting with the ugly, seeking the things we desire but not finding them, and possessing mental and physical aggregates, which are in the very nature of suffering. The six types of suffering are those of saṃsāra in general: no certainty, no satisfaction, repeatedly leaving bodies, repeatedly taking rebirth, moving from high to low, and having no friends. The three types of suffering are the suffering of suffering, the suffering of change, and the suffering that pervades all conditioned phenomena.

62 During an initiation, a vase is placed on the crown of the initiate's head, and he visualizes that waters or nectars overflow the vase, pass into his body through the fontanelle, and then fill his entire body. In this case, Gungtang Rinpoche is describing old people as having received the waters of the death initiation, which have filled their bodies and dribble from their mouths and noses.

63 Mount Meru is half submerged under the ocean. The cube-shaped mountain has eight ledges on its sides, and four of them are underwater.

64 Although this second heading is mentioned, Pabongka never actually explains the secondary delusions, and so it does not appear in the outline in the appendix. A full discussion of the mind and mental factors can be found in *Mind in Tibetan Buddhism* by Lati Rinbochay, translated and edited by Elizabeth Napper (Ithaca, NY: Snow Lion, 1986).

65 The water vapor is the steam of pride. Only the haughty give off this steam, not the humble. The snow in the ravines below lasts longer than the quick-melting snow on the exposed parts of the mountain.

66 This complex topic is explained at great length in the first chapter of Vasubandhu's *Treasury of Metaphysics.*

67 These are some non-Buddhist techniques for developing mental quiescence. The fires referred to are lit next to the meditator's body, one in each of the four cardinal directions, with the sun overhead being counted as the fifth. The meditator is supposed to ignore the extreme heat and discomfort.

68 This term presumably has a broader, more metaphysical meaning, since it is difficult to see how the "becoming" link could be an action of speech.

69 This story appears in Day 14, p. 431.

70 Once a crippled child slipped and rolled down a hill, landing by fantastic coincidence on the back of a *kiang,* the Tibetan wild ass. The kiang ran away, but the child hung on grimly. Everyone yelled to him to let go, but the child shouted back, "A cripple like me will get to ride a kiang only once. Now is the time to enjoy it!"

71 These can be found in Maitreya's *Ornament to Realization.*

72 Hastikovapa made the mistake of first teaching ultimate bodhichitta, the wisdom of emptiness, to a king, who then had the mahāsiddha executed before he had a chance to give the rest of the teaching on conventional bodhichitta, compassion.

73 The practice of *choed* or "cutting off" is a wrathful or forceful method of developing bodhichitta that was passed on to the Tibetan girl Machig Labdroen in a vision of Padampa Sangyae. An important feature of choed is the *kusali* offering that involves the practitioner visualizing his body being chopped up, put into a skullcup, transformed into nectar, and offered to all sentient beings—particularly enemies and

malevolent beings. Regular practitioners of choed were easily recognized in Tibet by their large damaru drum, called a *changdeu,* and human thighbone trumpet, called a *kangling.* Successful practice depends upon the depth of one's realization of the three fundamentals—renunciation, compassion, and recognition of the illusory nature of the body and all other phenomena. With these qualifications one could happily go to a cemetery or other place frequented by evil spirits, invoke them, and offer one's body.

74 Maitrīyogi saw a dog being hit on the leg by a stone. He took on the suffering and found a bruise on his arm.

75 The mantra syllables *hik* and *phaṭ* are used in the tantric transference *(powa)* practice when the practitioner ejects his consciousness from the body at the time of death.

76 These are actually the four major precepts of a monk. They are not listed here.

77 The story resembles Aesop's fable, *The Tortoise and the Hare.* Here the louse wins the race, while the flea uses up all his energy in leaping about.

78 This is another of the many life stories of Guru Śhākyamuni Buddha while he was a bodhisattva cited throughout this book. In this case, the ṛiṣhi's arms and legs were cruelly chopped off by a jealous king, but the ṛiṣhi remained calm and composed.

79 The names of two classes of meter in traditional Sanskrit poetry.

80 The ten sciences include the five major sciences of crafts, medicine, grammar, logic, and religion/philosophy and the five minor sciences of poetry, semantics, prosody, performing arts, and astronomy/astrology.

81 Amchok Rinpoche explained that Lozang Namgyael was suffering from *soglung,* or "depression" as Westerners may call it. This happens when one overdoes meditational practices; the energy winds in the body can get out of balance, the mind starts to go round in circles, and one experiences all the symptoms of stress. To avoid this happening, it is important not to be overambitious in meditation.

82 Referring to Chandrakīrti's sevenfold reasoning. This and other means for determining emptiness are described in Jeffrey Hopkins' *Meditation on Emptiness* (Boston: Wisdom, 1983).

83 The "Mother" is the mother of all buddhas, the perfection of wisdom *(prajñāpāramitā).*

84 The analytic cessation is achieved only during the paths of seeing and meditation while in meditative absorption. A nonanalytic cessation is when something does not happen or a thing is not produced simply because all the necessary causes are not present.

85 *The Translated Word of Buddha* consists of one hundred and eight volumes, the *Avataṃsaka Sūtra* of six. Since this is obviously too much for an individual to recite, the usual method is for a group of people to read different parts aloud at the same time. In this way a couple of thousand people can cover the whole set in a morning.

86 Although most of this poem is a praise to Kyabje Pabongka Rinpoche—also called "Jampa Taenzin Trinlae Gyatso" or "Dechen Nyingpo"—this verse is actually referring to the Fourteenth Dalai Lama, to whom Trijang Rinpoche was tutor.

GLOSSARY

NOTE

This glossary is arranged in three parts.

In the first, all the Sanskrit and Tibetan names and words that appear throughout the book have been listed in the phonetic form that I have used in this translation and in English alphabetical order, along with their Sanskrit and Tibetan transliterations. This will enable readers to check back from the Sanskrit words used in this translation to the original Tibetan.

The second glossary is intended more for those with some knowledge of Tibetan. Here, these same words and names appear, but this time the transliterated form of the original Tibetan comes first, in Tibetan alphabetical order, followed by the English and Sanskrit versions used in this book. This should be particularly helpful for people translating lamrim teachings from the Tibetan who are unfamiliar with the more widely known Sanskrit names of important Buddhist figures.

Finally, there is a glossary of English terms along with the original Sanskrit and Tibetan where appropriate. This will show how I have chosen to translate certain technical terms, and provides a useful cross reference as well.

Note: A star before a Sanskrit word or name indicates either that the Sanskrit is conjectural or that the word is authentic but its equivalence with the Tibetan name has not been proved.

I. SANSKRIT AND TIBETAN NAMES AND WORDS WITH THEIR ENGLISH SPELLING

English	*Sanskrit*	*Tibetan*
Abhīrati	Abhīrati	mNgon dga'
Āchārya	Āchārya	sLob dpon
Āchārya Manu	Āchārya Manu	Atsara Manu
Ādarśha	Ādarśha	Kun mthong
Agnibhu	Agnibhu	Me skyes
Airāvaṇa	Airāvaṇa	Sa la rab brtan
Airāvaṇa	Airāvaṇa	Sa srung gi bu
Ajātaśhatru	Ajātaśhatru	Ma skyes dgra/ mThong ldan
Ājñatakauṇḍinya	Ājñatakauṇḍinya	Kun shes ko'u di n.ya
Ākāśhagarbha	Ākāśhagarbha	Nam mkha' snying po/Nam snying
Akṣhapāda	Akṣhapāda	rKang mig
Akṣhobhya	Akṣhobhya	Mi bskyod pa
Amdo	—	A mdo
Amé Jangchub Rinchen	—	A mes byang chub rin chen
Amitābha	Amitābha	'Od dpag med
Amoghadarśhī	Amoghadarśhī	mThong ba don yod
Amoghasiddhi	Amoghasiddhi	Don grub
Ānanda	Ānanda	Kun dga' bo
Anantatejas	Anantatejas	gZi brjid mtha' yas
Anāthapiṇḍaḍa	Anāthapiṇḍaḍa	mGon med zas sbyin
Anavatapta	Anavatapta	Ma dros pa

Ange Nyama Paeldarbum	—	Ang ge nya ma dpal dar 'bum
Aṅgulimālā	Aṅgulimālā	Sor mo'i phreng can
Aparachāmara	Aparachāmara	rNga yab gzhan
Aranemi	Aranemi	rTsibs kyi mu khyud
arhat	arhat	dGra bcom pa
Artso (the Eighteen Mendicants of)	—	Ar tsho (ban de bco brgyad)
Āryadeva	Āryadeva	'Phags pa lha
Āryaśhūra	Āryaśhūra	'Phags pa dpa' bo
Asaṅga	Asaṅga	Thogs med
Asaṅgavyava('s jester)	—	Asangghabyaba('i atsara)
Aśhoka	Aśhoka	Mya ngan med
Aśhokaśhrī	Aśhokaśhrī	Mya ngan med pa'i dpal
Aśhvajit	Aśhvajit	rTa thul
Atar	—	A thar
Āṭavaka	Āṭavaka	'Brog gnas
Atiśha	Atiśha	Jo bo rje
Avadhūtipa	Avadhūtipa	Awadhutipa
Avalokitavrata	Avalokitavrata	sPyan ras gzigs brtul shugs
Avalokiteśhvara	Avalokiteśhvara	sPyan ras gzigs
Avataṃsaka Sūtra	Avataṃsakasūtra	mDo phal po che
Baen Gung-gyael	—	'Ban gung rgyal
Bangrim Choede	—	Bang rim chos sde
Bardo	—	bar do
Basoje	—	Ba so rje
Benares	Vāraṇāsi	Wāraṇāsi
Bengal	Bhaṅgal	Bhaṃgal
Bhagavān	Bhagavān	bCom ldan 'das
Bhaita	—	Bhaita
Bhāvaviveka	Bhāvaviveka	Legs ldan 'byed
bhikṣhu	bhikṣhu	dge slong
Bimbisāra	Bimbisāra	gZugs can snying po
Bodha	Bodha	rTogs ldan
Bodhgaya	Bodhagāya	rDo rje gdan

Bodhibhadra	Bodhibhadra	Byang chub bzang po
bodhichitta	bodhichitta	byang chub sems
bodhisattva	bodhisattva	Byang chub sems dpa'
Boen	—	Bon
Boenpo	—	Bon po
Brahmā	Brahmā	Tshangs pa
Brahmādata	Brahmādata	Tshangs pas byin
Brahmajyotivi-krodhitābhijña	Brahmajyotivi-krodhitābhijña	Tashangs pa'i 'od zer rnam par rol pas mngon par mkhyen pa
Brahman	Brahman	bram ze/bram ze'i khye'u
Brahmāśhrīsupari-kīrti	Brahmāśhrīsupari-kīrti	Tshangs dpal shin tu yongs grags
Brahmāvihāra	Brahmāvihāra	Tshangs pa'i gnas
Buddha	Buddha	Sangs rgyas
Buddhajñāna	Buddhajñāna	Sangs rgyas ye shes
Buddhapālita	Buddhapālita	Sangs rgyas bskyangs
Butoen	—	Bu ston
Cha	—	Phywa
Chaekawa	—	'Chad kha wa
Chaen Ngawa	—	sPyan snga ba
Chag the translator	—	Chag lo
Chagtrichog	—	Phyag khri mchog
Chakrasaṃvara	Chakrasaṃvara	'Khor lo sdom pa
Chāmara	Chāmara	rNga yab
champaka	champaka	tsampaka
Chanakya	Chanakya	Tsanakya
Chandanaśhrī	Chandanaśhrī	Tsan dan dpal
Chandra	Chandra	Zla ba
Chandragarbha	Chandragarbha	Zla ba'i snying po
Chandragomin	Chandragomin	Tsandragomin
Chandrakīrti	Chandrakīrti	Zla ba grags pa
Chandraprabha	Chandraprabha	Zla 'od
Changkya Roelpai Dorje	—	lCang skya rol pa'i rdo rje
Chilbupa	—	sPyil bu pa

Chim Jampaelyang	—	mChims 'jam dpal byangs
Chittamātrin	Chittamātrin	Sems tsam pa
choed	—	gcod
Choegyael	—	Chos rgyal
Choekyab Zangpo	—	Chos skyab bzang po/ Chos skyobs bzang po
Choekyi Dorje	—	Chos kyi rdo rje
Choekyi Oezer	—	Chos kyi 'od zer
Choglae Namgyael of Bodong	—	Bo dong phyogs las rnam rgylal
Chūḍapanthaka	Chūḍapanthaka	Lam chung pa
Chunda	Chunda	Tsunda
Chushur	—	Chu shur
Chuzang Hermitage	—	Chu bzang ri khrod
Chuzang Lama Yeshe Gyatso	—	Chu bzang bla ma Ye shes rgya mtsho
Da Oe Rinchen	—	Zla 'od rin chen
Dagpo	—	Dwags po
ḍāka	ḍāka	mkha' 'gro
ḍākinī	ḍākinī	mkha' 'gro ma
Danaśhrī	Danaśhrī	Nor dpal
Dawa Dragpa	—	Zla ba grags pa
Deha	Deha	Lus
Dentoen Kyergangpa	—	Den ston skyer sgang pa/dBon ston skyer sgang pa
Derge	—	sDe dge
Devadatta	Devadatta	lHas byin
Dhanapāla	Dhanapāla	Nor skyong
dhāraṇī	dhāraṇī	gzungs
dharmadhātu	dharmadhātu	chos dbyings
dharmakāya	—	chos sku
Dharmakīrti	Dharmakīrti	Chos kyi grags pa
Dharmarāja	Dharmarāja	Chos rgyal
Dharmarakṣhita	Dharmarakṣhita	Dharmārakṣhita
Dharmodgata	Dharmodgata	Chos 'phags

Dhatvīśhvarī	Dhatvīśhvarī	dByings phyug ma
Dingri	—	Ding ri
Dīpaṃkara Śhrījñāna	Dīpaṃkara Śhrījñāna	dPal mar me mdzad ye shes
Dokham	—	mDo khams
Doelpa	—	Dol pa
Ḍoṃbhīpa	Ḍoṃbhīpa	Ḍoṃbhi
Doshul	—	rDo shul
Dragor	—	Gra 'or
Drangri	—	'Brang ri
dravidian	—	mi nag po
dre	—	Bre
Drepung	—	'Bras phungs
Drimé Tengka	—	Dri med steng kha
Drogoen Choepag	—	'Gro mgon chos 'phags
Drogoen Rinpoche	—	'Gro mgon rin po che
Drom Loding	—	'Brom lo lding
Dromtoenpa	—	'Brom ston pa bre
drona	drona	bre
Drubchog Lozang Namgyael	—	Grub mchong blo bzang rnam rgyal
Drubkang Geleg Gyatso	—	sGrub khang dge legs rgya mtsho
Drugpa Kuenleg	—	'Brug pa kun legs
Drungpa	—	Brung pa
Duḥkhitaka	*Duḥkhitaka	sDug bsngal 'gyur
Durāgata	Durāgata	Nyes 'ong
dūrva	dūrva	dur ba
dzogchen	—	rdzogs chen
Dzogchen Paelge	—	rDzogs chen dpal dge
Dzungaria	—	Jun gar
Elapatra Nāga	Elapatranāga	Klu E la'i 'dab ma
elephant-headed Ana	—	A wa glang mgo
Epa	—	E pa
Fifth Dalai Lama	—	lNga pa chen po
Ganaśhava	Ganaśhava	Ga na sha ba

Gaṇḍaka	Gaṇḍaka	Yid 'ong ldan
Gandaen Trijang Tulku	—	dGa' ldan khrid byang sprul sku
Gaṇeśha	Gaṇeśha	gDong drug
Ganges	Ganga	Gangga
gañjira	gañjira	ganydzira
Garlog	—	Gar log
garuḍa	garuḍa	khyung/nam mkha' lding
Gaura	*Gaura	Ser skya
Gauraśhānti	*Gauraśhānti	Ser skya zhi ba
Gautama	Gautama	Go'u tam
Gelugpa	—	dGe lugs pa
Genduen Drub	—	dGe 'dun grub
Genduen Jamyang	—	dGe 'dun 'jam dbyangs
Genduen Taenzin Gyatso	—	dGe 'dun bstan 'dzin rgya mtsho
Gesar Ling	—	Gling ge sar
geshe	—	dge bshes
Godānīya	Godānīya	Ba lang spyod
Goekar	—	rGod dkar
Goenpawa	—	dGon pa ba
Goenpo Rinpoche	—	mGon po rin po che
Goetsang	—	rGod tshang
Golog Arig	—	mGo log a rig
Gomang	—	sGo mang
Gompa Rabsael	—	sGom pa rab gsal/ Bla chen po
Gośhīrṣha	Gośhīrṣha	Goshīrsha
Gungtang	—	Gung thang
Gungtang	—	Gung thang 'jam dpal dbyangs
Guhyasamāja	Guhyasamāja	gSang ba'i 'dus pa
guru	guru	bla ma
Gushri Kaelzang	—	Kaushri bskal bzang
Gyaelsae Zangpo	—	rGyal sras bzang po
Gyaeltsab Rinpoche	—	rGyal tshab rin po che

Gyaeltsaen Zangpo	—	rGyal mtshan bzang po
Gyaelwa Doendrub	—	rGyal ba don grub
Gyaelwa Ensapa	—	rGyal ba dben sa pa
Gyaelwang Choeje	—	rGyal dbang chos rje
Gyamaba	—	rGya ma ba
Gyatsoen Senge	—	rGya brtson seng ge
Gyer Drowai Goenpo	—	dGyer 'gro ba'i mgon po
Gyergompa	—	Gyer sgom pa
Gyuetoe	—	rGyud stod
Halakṛiṣhṇa	*Halakṛiṣhṇa	Hala nag po
Haribhadra	Haribhadra	Seng ge bzang po
Hāritī	Hāritī	'Phrog ma
Hastikovapa	*Hastikovapa	Glang po'i ko ba pa
Hayagrīva	Hayagrīva	rTa mgrin
Heruka	Heruka	bDe mchog/Heruka
Hevajra	Hevajra	dGyes pa rdo rje/ Kye rdo rje/Kyai rdo rje
Himalayas	himavat	Ri bo gangs can
Hīnayāna	hīnayāna	theg dman
Indra	Indra	brGya byin
Indraketudhva-jarāja	Indraketudhva-jarāja	dBang po'i tog gi rgyal mtshan gyi rgyal po
Īśhvara	Īśhvara	dBang phyug
Jadrael	—	Bya bral
Jain	Jaina	gCer bu ba
Jalandharī	Jalandharī	Dzalandharapa
Jambudvīpa	Jambudvīpa	'Dzam bu gling
Jampa Choedaen	—	Byams pa chos ldan
Jampa Taenzin Trinlae Gyatso	—	Byams pa bstan 'dzin 'phrin las rgya mtsho
Jampael Gyatso	—	'Jam dpal rgya mtsho
Jampael Lhuendrub	—	'Jam dpal lhun grub
Jamyang Shaypa	—	'Jam dbyangs bzhad pa
Jangchub Oe	—	(lHa btson) Byang chub 'od
Jangchub Rinchen	—	Byang chub rin chen

Jangchub Togme	—	Byang chub thogs med
Jangsem Retrengwa	—	Byang sems rwa sgreng ba
Jayulwa	—	Bya yul ba
Je Rinpoche	—	rJe rin po che
Je Sherab Gyatso	—	rJe shes rab rgya mtsho
Jetavana Grove	Jetavana	rGyal byed kyi 'tshal
Jetsun Jampa Taenzin Trinlae Gyatso	—	rJe btsun byams pa bstan 'dzin 'phrin las rgya mtsho (dpal bzang po)
Jinpa Gyatso	—	sByin pa rgya mtsho
Jitāri	Jitāri	Dzetāri
Jīvaka Kumarabhṛita	Jīvaka Kumarabhṛita	'Tsho byed gzhon nu
Jñānaguhyavajra	Jñānaguhyavajra	Ye shes gsang ba'i rdo rje
Jñānottara	Jñānottara	Ye shes bla ma
Jonangpa	Jonangpa	Jo nang pa
Kachen Namkha Dorje	—	dKa' chen ram mkha' rdo rje
Kachoe Taendar	—	mKha' spyod bstan dar
Kadam	—	bKa' gdams
Kadampa	—	bKa' gdams pa
Kaedrub Rinpoche	—	mKhas grub rin po che
Kaelzang Gyatso (the Seventh Dalai Lama)	—	(rGyal mchog) bsKal bzang rhua mtsho
Kaelzang Taenzin	—	sKal bzang bstan 'dzin
Kagyuepa	—	bKa' brgyud pa
Kakang	—	Ka khang
Kālachakra	Kālachakra	Dus 'khor
Kālayamāri	Kālayamāri	dGra nag
Kalmāṣhapada	Kalmāṣhapada	rKang khra
Kalyāṇaśhrī	Kalyāṇaśhrī	dGe ba'i dpal
Kamaba	—	Ka ma ba
Kāmadeva	Deviputramāra	bDud dga' rab dbang phyug
Kamlungpa	—	Khams lung pa
Kanakamuni	Kanakamuni	gSer thub
Kanakavatsa	Kanakavatsa	gSer be'u

Kapilanāgara	Kapilanāgara	Grong khyer ser skya
Karag Gomchung	—	Kha rag sgom chung/Kha rag pa
Kardo Lozang Gomchung	—	mKhar rdo blo bzang sgom chung
Karmayama	Karmayama	Las (kyi) gshin rje
Kaśhi	Kaśhi	Kashi
Kashmir	Kashmīra	Kha chen
Kāśhyapa	Kāśhyapa	'Od srung
Kātyāyana	Kātyāyana	Katyayana
Kaurava	Kaurava	sGra mi snyan gyi zla
Kawa Śhākya Wangchug	—	Ka ba shākya dbang phyug
Ketsang Jamyang (Moenlam)	—	sKed tshang 'jam dbyangs (smon lam)
Kham	—	Khams
Khampa	—	Khams pa
Khaṇḍakapāla	Khaṇḍakapāla	Khaṇḍakapāla
Khaṇḍakāri	Khaṇḍakāri	sKul byed
Koenchog Gyaeltsaen	—	dKon mchog rgyal mtshan
Kokalika	Kokalika	Kokalika
Kongpo	—	Kong po
Koṭikarṇa	Koṭikarṇa	rNa ba bye ri
Krakuchchanda	Krakuchchhanda	'Khor ba 'jig
Kṛikin	Kṛikin	Kṛi kri
Kṛiṣhṇāchārya	Kṛiṣhṇāchārya	Nag po spyod pa
Kṛiṣhṇagiri	Kṛiṣhṇagiri	Ri nag po
Kṣhāntivadin	Kṣhāntivadin	bZod par smra ba
Kṣhatriya	Kṣhatriya	rGyal rigs
Kṣhitigarbha	Kṣhitigarbha	Sa'i snying po
Kubjottarā	Kubjottarā	sGur mchog
Kuenleg	—	Kun legs
Kumāra Maṇibhadra	Kumāramaṇibhadra	gZhon nu nor bzang
Kuru	Kuru	sGra mi snyan
Kurukullejñāna	Kurukullejñāna	Myur mdzad ye shes

Kusali	Kusali	Kusāli
kuśha	kuśha	rtswa mchog/kusha
Kuśhinagarī	Kuśhinagarī	rTswa mchog drong khyer
Kusumaśhrī	Kusumaśhrī	Me tog dpal
Kutoenpa	—	Khu ston pa
Kuzhu	—	sKu zhabs
Kyicha	—	lHa sar gtsang chu
Kyimo Dzatreng	—	sKyi mo rdza 'phreng
Kyirong	—	sKyid rong/sKyid grong
Kyungpo Lhaepa	—	Khyung po lhas pa
Labdroen	—	Lab sgron
Lakṣhmī	*Lakṣhmī	dPal mo
Lama Dampa	—	Bla ma dam pa
Lamrim Choeding	—	Lam rim chos sdings
Langdarma	—	Glang dar ma
Langkor	—	Glang 'khor
Langri Tangpa	—	Glang ri thang pa
Legdaen Sherab	—	Legs ldan shes rab
Lhading	—	lHa sdings
Lhalama	—	lHa bla ma
Lhalu Gatsel	—	Lha glu dga' tshal
Lhalung Wangchug	—	lHa lung dbang phyug
Lhazang Khan	—	rGyal po lHa bzang
Lhazowa	—	lHa bzo wa
Lhodrag	—	lHo brag
Lingraepa	—	Gling ras pa
Lodroe Gyaeltsaen	—	Blo gros rgyal mtshan
Lodroe Zangpo	—	Blo gros bzang po
Lokāyata	Lokāyata	rGyang 'phen pa
Longdoel Lama Rinpoche	—	Klong rdol bla ma rin po che
Lozang Choekyi Gyaeltsaen (Lozang Choegyaen)	—	Blo bzang chos kyi rgyal mtshan (Blo bzang chos rgyan)
Lozang Choepel	—	Blo bzang chos 'phel

Lozang Doendaen	—	Blo bzang don ldan
Lozang Dorje	—	Blo bzang rdo rje
Lozang Dragpa	—	Blo bzang grags pa
Lozang Gyatso	—	Blo bzang rgyal ba
Lozang Jinpa	—	Blo bzang sbyin pa
Lozang Kaetsuen	—	Blo bzang mkhas btsun
Lozang Lhuendrub (Trinlae) Gyatso	—	Blo bzang lhun grub ('phrin las) rgya mtsho
Lozang Namgyael	—	Blo bzang rnam rgyal
Lozang Nyaendrag	—	Blo bzang snyan grags
Lozang Yeshe	—	Blo bzang ye shes
Lozang Yeshe Taenzin Gyatso	—	Blo bzang ye shes bstan 'dzin rgya mtsho
Mābhvātā	Mābhvātā	Nga las nus
Machig Labdroen	—	Ma gcig lab sgron
Madhyamaka	Madhyamaka	dBu ma
Mādhyamika	Mādhyamika	dBu ma pa
Magadha	Magadha	Yul dbus
Mahābala	Mahābala	Mahābala
mahābrahmā	mahābrahmā	tshangs pa chen po
Mahākāla	Mahākāla	mGon po
mahāmudrā	mahāmudrā	phyag rgya chen po
Mahāpanthaka	Mahāpanthaka	Lam chen pa
mahārāja	mahārāja	rgyal chen
Mahāratnachūḍa	Mahāratnachūḍa	gTsug na rin chen
Mahardhikā	Mahardhikā	mThu mo che
Mahāsaṃgika	Mahāsaṃgika	Phal chen sde
Mahāsattva	Mahāsattva	sNying stobs chen po skye ba
mahātma	mahātma	bdag nyid chen po
Mahāyogi	Mahāyogi	rNal 'byor pa chen po
Maitrakanyaka	Maitrakanyaka	mdza' bo'i bu mo
Maitreya	Maitreya	Byams pa
Maitrīyogi	Maitrīyogi	byams pa'i rnal 'byor
Maitrobala	Maitrobala	byams pa'i stobs
Mākandika	Mākandika	Ma dus

Malabar	Malaya	Malaya
Māmakī	Māmakī	Māmakī
Mānavagaura	*Mānavagaura	Shed bu ser skya
Mangyul	—	Mang yul
Mañjughoṣha	Mañjughoṣha	'Jam (dpal) dbyangs
Mañjuśhrī	Mañjuśhrī	'Jam dpal dbyangs
Mañjuśhrīmitra	Mañjuśhrīmitra	'Jam dpal bshes gnyen
Mañjuvajra	Mañjuvajra	'Jam dpal rdo rje
māra	māra	bdud
Marpa of Lhodrag	—	lHo brag Mar pa
Maudgalyāyana	Maudgalyāyana	Maung gal bu
Mayi Cha	—	rMa yi phya
Milarepa	—	Mi la ras pa
Mitrayogi	Mitrayogi	Mitradzoki
Moendrapa	—	Mon grwa pa
Moendro Choedrag	—	sMon 'gro chos grags
Moenlam Paelwa	—	sMon lam dpal ba
Mogul	—	sTag gzig
Mount Meru	Meru	Ri rab lhun po
Mṛigāradhara	Mṛigāradhara	Ri dwags 'dzin
Munīndra	Munīndra	Thub dbang
nāga	nāga	klu
Nāgabodhi	Nāgabodhi	Klu byang
Nāgārjuna	Nāgārjuna	Klu sgrub
Nāgeśhvararāja	Nāgeśhvararāja	Klu dbang gi rgyal po
Nagtso	—	Nag tsho
Nālandā	Nālandā	Nālendra
Namkha Gyaelpo	—	Nam mkha' rgyal po
Namkha Gyaeltsaen	—	Nam mkha' rgyal mtshan/Lho brag grub chen
Namkha Senge	—	Nam (mkha') seng ge
Nanda	Nanda	gCung dGa' bo/dGa' bo
Nandaka	Nandaka	dGa' byed
Nārāyaṇa	Nārāyaṇa	Sred med kyi bu

Nāro Boenchung	—	Nāro bon chung
Nāropa	Nāropa	Nāropa/Nāro
Nartang	—	sNar thang
Nepal	—	Bal po rdzong/Bal yul
Neuzurpa	—	sNe'u zur pa
Ngagwang Chogdaen	—	Ngag dbang mchog ldan
Ngagwang Dragpa	—	Ngag dbang grags pa
Ngagwang Jampa	—	Ngag dbang byams pa
Ngagwang Norbu	—	Ngag dbang nor bu
Ngagwang Tutob	—	Ngag dbang mthu stobs
Ngari	—	mNga' ris
Ngulchu Dharmavajra	—	Ngul chu yab sras
Ngulchu Togme Sangpo	—	dNgul chu thogs med bzang po
ngulkar	—	dngul skar
nirmāṇakāya	nirmāṇakāya	sPrul sku
Nyaentoenpa	—	gNyan ston pa
Nyagmo	—	Nyag mo
Nyagrodhikā	Nyagrodhikā	Nyagrodha'i grong khyer
Nyingma	—	rNying ma
Nyugrumpa	—	sNyug rum pa
Oekar	—	'Od dkar
Oelga Choelung	—	'Ol dga' chos lung
Oen Gyaelsae	—	'On rgyal sras
Pabongka	—	Pha bong kha
Padampa Sangyae	—	Pha dam pa sangs rgyay
Padmajyoti-vikroḍitābhijña	Padmajyoti-vikroḍitābhijña	Padma'i 'od zer rnam par rol pas mngon par mkhyen pa
Padmaka	Padmaka	Padma can
Padmasaṃbhava	Padmasaṃbhava	Padma 'byung gnas/ Guru rin po che/ sLob dpon rin po che
Paeldaen Yeshe	—	dPal ldan ye shes
Paenpo	—	'Phan po
Paṇchen (Lama)	—	Paṇ chen (Rin po che)

Pangkong	—	sPang skong
Panthaka	Panthaka	Lam pa
Paramavarṇa	*Paramavarṇa	Kha dog dam pa
Paranasena	Paranasena	mChog gi sde
Paryāsannakama	Paryāsannakama	gTogs 'dod
Pehar	—	Pe har
pig-headed yakṣha	—	Yag sha phag mgo
Potala	—	Po to la
Potowa	—	Po to ba
Prabhāketu	Prabhāketu	'Od kyi tog
Prabhāsaśhrī	Prabhāsaśhrī	'Od dpal
Prabhāvatī	Prabhāvatī	dPal mo 'od zer can
Prachaṇḍālī	Prachaṇḍālī	Rab gtum ma
Prakāśha	Prakāśha	Rab rgyas
Prakṛiti	Prakṛiti	sNying stobs chen po
Pramudita	Pramudita	Rab dga'
Praṇidhānamati	*Praṇidhānamati	sMon lam blo gros
Prāsaṅgika	Prāsaṅgika	Thal 'gyur pa
Prasenajit	Prasenajit	gSal rgyal
pratyekabuddha	pratyekabuddha	rang rgyal/rang sangs rgyas
Priyabhadra	*Priyabhadra	sNyan pa bzang ldan
Puchungwa	—	Phu chung ba
Puentsog Gyatso	—	Phun tshogs rgya mtsho
Puhreng	—	Pu hreng
Purāṇa	Purāṇa	rDzogs byed
Purchog Ngagwang Jampa	—	Phur lcog ngag dbang byams pa/Bla ma byams pa rin po che
Pūrṇa	Pūrṇa	Gang po
Radreng	—	Rwa sgreng
Raechungpa	—	Ras chung pa
Raelpa Chaen	—	Ral pa can
Rāhula	Rāhula	sGra gcan 'dzin
Rāhulagupta	Rāhulagupta	Rāhulagupta/sGra gcan 'dzin sbas

Rajgir	Rājagṛiha	rGyal po'i khab
rākṣha	rākṣha	srin po
Ratnachandra	Ratnachandra	Rin chen zla ba
Ratnachandraprabha	Ratnachandraprabha	Rin chen zla 'od
Ratnāgni	Ratnāgni	Rin chen me
Ratnākaraśhānti/Śhāntipa	Ratnākaraśhānti	Ratna a ka/Shāntipa
Ratnapadmavikrāmin	Ratnapadmavikrāmin	Rin po che dang padma lab rab tu bzhugs pa ri dbang gi rgyal po
Ratnarchi	Ratnarchi	Rin po che 'od 'phro
Ratnasaṃbhava	Ratnasaṃbhava	Rin 'byung
Ratnasena	Ratnasena	dGe ba can
Rāvaṇa	*Rāvaṇa	sGra sgrog
Rego Āchārya	—	Re sgo a tsa ra
rig pa	—	rig pa
Rinchen Pel	—	Rin chen 'phel
Rinchen Zangpo	—	Rin chen bzang po
ṛiṣhi	ṛiṣhi	drang srong
Rohiṇī	Rohiṇī	sNar ma
Rohita	Rohita	Rohita
Rong	—	Rong
Rongpa Gargewa	—	Rong pa mgar dge ba
Rudra	Rudra	Drag po
Sadāprarudita	Sadāprarudita	rTag tu ngu
Saelshe	—	gSal shes
Sagama	Sagama	Sagama
Sāgarmati	Sāgarmati	Blo gros rgya mtsho
Sakya	—	Sa skya
Sakya Paṇḍita	—	Sa skya paṇḍita
Samandrarāja	*Samandrarāja	rGya mtsho'i dul
Samantabhadra	Samantabhadra	Kun tu bzang po
Samantāvabhā-savyuhaśhrī	Samantāvabhā-savyuhaśhrī	Kun nas snang ba bkod pa'i dpal
saṃbhogakāya	saṃbhogakāya	longs sku
Sāṃkhya	Sāṃkhya	Grangs can pa
saṃsāra	saṃsāra	'khor ba

sang	—	srang
Saṅgharakṣhita	Saṅgharakṣhita	dGe 'dun 'tsho
Sangpuba	—	gSang phu ba
Sangyae Gompa	—	Sangs rgyas sgom pa
Sangyae Gytaso	—	Sangs rgyas rgya mtsho
Sangyae Oen	—	Sangs rgyas dbon
Sangyae Oentoen	—	Sangs rgyas dbon ston
Sangyae Yeshe	—	Sangs rgyas ye shes
Senge Zangpo	—	Seng ge bzang po
Sera	—	Se ra
Sera Je	—	Se ra rje
Sera Mae	—	Se ra smad
Seto Kaeldaen	—	Se mtho skal ldan
Setsuen	—	Se btsun
Śhailendrarāja	Śhailendrarāja	Ri dbang gi rgyal po
Śhakti	Śhakti	mDung thung can
Śhākya	Śhākya	Shākya
Śhākyamuni	Śhākyamuni	Shākya thub pa
śhālā	śhālā	sāla
Śhālmala	Śhālmala	Shalmali
Śhambhala	Śhambhala	Shambhala
Śhaṃkara	Śhaṃkara	bDe byed
Shangpa Rinpoche	—	Shangs pa rin po che
Śhāntarakṣhita	Śhāntarakṣhita	mKhan chen bodhi sattwa/Zhi 'tsho
Śhāntendra	Śhāntendra	dBang po zhi
Śhāntideva	Śhāntideva	Zhi ba lha
Śhāntipa/Ratnākaraśhānti	Ratnākaraśhānti	Shāntipa/Ratna a ka
Sharawa	—	Sha ra ba
Śhāriputra	Śhāriputra	Shāri'i bu
Śhāthā	Śhāthā	g.Yo ldan
Shenrab	—	gShen rabs
Sherab Senge	—	Shes rab seng ge
Śhīlarākṣha	Śhīlarākṣha	Tshul khrims srung ba
Śhīva	Śhīva	dBang phyug

śhrāvaka	śhrāvaka	nyan thos
Śhrāvastī	Śhrāvastī	mNyan yod
Śhrībhadra	Śhrībhadra	dPal bzang
Śhrīdatta	Śhrīdatta	dPal sbyin
Śhrīgupta	Śhrīgupta	dPal sbas
Śhrījāta	*Śhrījāta	dPal skyes
Śhrīmān	*Śhrīmān	dPal ldan
Śhrīprabhā	Śhrīprabhā	dPal mo 'od zer can
Śhrīsena	Śhrīsena	dPal gyi sde
Śhuddhodana	Śhuddhodana	Zas gtsang ma
Śhuklā	*Śhuklā	dKar mo
Śhyāmavatī	Śhyāmavatī	sNgo bsangs ma
Siddhārtha	Siddhārtha	gZhon nu don grub
Smṛitiśhrī	Smṛitiśhrī	Dran pa'i dpal
Soenam Gyatso, the (Third) Dalai Lama	—	rGyal dbang bSod nams rgya mtsho
Songtsaen Gampo	—	Srong btsan sgam po
Sthirā	*Sthirā	gnas pa'i grong khyer
Subahu	Subahu	dPung bzang
Subhadra	Subhadra	Rab bzang
Subhūti	Subhūti	Rab 'byor
Sudāsaputra	Sudāsaputra	Sudāsa'i bu
Sugata	Sugata	bDe gshegs
Sukhāvatī	Sukhāvatī	bDe ba can
Sumagadhā	Sumagadhā	Magadha bzang mo
Sumati	Sumati	Blo bzang
Sumatikīrti	Sumatikīrti	Blo bzang grags pa
Supuṣhpa Chandra	Supuṣhpa Chandra	Me tog zla mdzes
Sūrata	Sūrata	Des pa
Supraṇihita	*Supraṇihita	Legs smon
Suvarṇabhāsottama	Suvarṇabhāsottama	gSer 'od dam pa
Suvarṇadvīpa	Suvarṇadvīpa	gSer gling
Suvarṇadvīpi	Suvarṇadvīpi	gSer gling pa
Suvarṇavasu	*Suvarṇavasu	gSer dbyig

Suvikrāntaśhrī	Suvikrāntaśhrī	Shin tu rnam par ngon pa'i dpal
Svāgata	Svāgata	Legs 'ong
Svātantrika	Svātantrika	Rang rgyud pa
swastika	svasatika	g.yung drung
Taenpa Gyatso	—	bsTan pa rgya mtsho
Taenpa Rabgyae	—	bsTan pa rab rgyas
Taenpai Droenme	—	bsTan pa'i sgron me
Taenzin Gyatso	—	bsTan 'dzin rgya mtsho
Taenzin Kaedrub	—	bsTan 'dzin mkhas grub
Tagmapa	—	Thag ma pa
Tagtsang Lotsawa	—	sTag tshang Lotsāwa
Tanag	—	rTa nag
Tapugpa	—	rTa phug pa
Tārā	Tārā	sGrol ma
Tashikyil	—	bKra shis 'khyil
Tashi Lhuenpo	—	bKra shis lhun po
Tathāgata	Tathāgata	De bzhin gshegs pa
Tilopa	Tilopa	Telo
tīrṭhika	tīrṭhika	mu stegs pa
Toelekor	—	Thod le kor
Toelungpa	—	sTod lung pa
Toepur	—	sTod phur
Togme Sangpo	—	Thogs med bzang po/dNgul chu rgyal sras
Tridagpo Tsepel	—	Khri dwags po tshe 'phel
Trisong Detsaen	—	Khrid srong lde btsan
Trizam Bridge	—	Khri zam zam kha
Tsang	—	gTsang
Tsangpa Gyarae	—	gTsang pa rgya ras
tsatsa	—	tsa tstsha/sā tstsha
Tsechogling	—	Tshe mchog gling
Tsonawa	—	mTsho sna wa
Tsultrim	—	Tshul khrims
Tsultrimbar	—	Tshul khrims 'bar

Tsultrim Gyaelwa	—	Tshul khrims rgyal ba
Tubtaen Rabgyae	—	Thub bstan rab rgyas
tue	—	thud
Tukaen Dharmavajra	—	Thu'u bkwan Dharmabadzra
Tuṣhita	Tuṣhita	dGa' ldan
Udayana	Udayana	Shar pa
Udayī	Udayī	'Char kha
Udbhaṭasiddhasvāmin	Udbhaṭasiddhasvāmin	Tho btsun grub rje
Ugra	Ugra	dGra shul can
Umapa	—	dBu ma pa
Upadhāna	*Upadhāna	Legs pa'i skar ma
Upagupta	Upagupta	Nyer sbas
upāsaka	upāsaka	dge bsnyen
urṇa	urṇa	mdzod spu
Uruvilvākāśhyapa	Uruvilvākāśhyapa	lTeng rgyas 'od srungs
uṣhṇīṣha	uṣhṇīṣha	gtsug tor
Utpalavarṇā	Utpalavarṇā	Utpala'i mdog can
Utrayana	Utrayana	Utrayana
Uttara	Uttara	Chu smad skyes
Uttaramantriṇa	Uttaramantriṇa	Lam mchog 'gro
Vachigira	Vachigira	Batsigira
Vaibhāṣhika	Vaibhāṣhika	Bye brag smra ba
Vairochana	Vairochana	rNam snang
Vairochana (Haribhadra's teacher)	Vairochana	sNang mdzed
Vaiśhravaṇa	Vaiśhravaṇa	rNam thos sras
Vajradhara	Vajradhara	rDo rje 'chang
Vajrahṛidaya	Vajrahṛidaya	rDo rje snying po/ rDo rje snying po rgyan
Vajramaṇḍapra-mardin	Vajramaṇḍapra-mardin	rDo rje snying po rab tu 'joms pa
Vajrapāṇi	Vajrapāṇi	Phyag na rdo rje
Vajrarūpa	Vajrarūpa	gZugs kyi rdo rje
Vajravarāhī	Vajravarāhī	rDo rje phag mo
Vajrī	Vajrī	rdo rje ma

Vararuchi	Vararuchi	mChog sred
Varuṇa	Varuṇa	Chu lha
Varuṇadeva	Varuṇadeva	Chu lha'i lha
Vasubandhu	Vasubandhu	dByig gnyen
Vedas	Veda	Rig byed
Vegadhārin	Vegadhārin	Shugs 'chang
Vibhudatta	*Vibhudatta	sGur chung
Videha	Videha	Lus 'phag po/Lus 'phags
Vidyākokila	Vidyākokila	Rig pa'i khu byug
Vidyākokila the younger	—	Rig pa'i khu byug gnyis pa
Vikramapura	Vikramapura	Bikāmapuri
Vikramśhīla	Vikramśhīla	Brikamalashīla
Vikrantāntagā-miśhrī	Vikrantāntagā-miśhrī	rNam par gnon pa'i gshegs pa'i dpal
Vimala	Vimala	Dri ma med pa
Vimuktisena	Vimuktisena	rNam grol sde
Vimuktisenagomin	Vimuktisenagomin	bTsun pa rnam grol sde
viṇā	viṇā	pi waṃ
Vinītasena	Vinītasena	Dul ba'i sde
Vipaśhyin	Vipaśhyin	rNam gzigs
Virūḍhaka	Virūḍhaka	'Phags skyes po
Viṣhṇu	Viṣhṇu	Khyab 'jug
Voranandin	Voranandin	dPal dgyes
Vorasena	Vorasena	dPa' bo'i sde
Vyāpaka	Vyāpaka	Khyab byed
Vyilingalita	Vyilingalita	Byi ling ga li ta
yak	—	g.yag
yakṣhinī	yakṣhinī	gnod sbyin
Yama	Yama	gShin rje
Yamāntaka	Yamāntaka	gShin rje gshed/ 'Jigs byed
Yardrog	—	Yar 'brog
Yerpa	—	Yer pa
Yeshe Gyaeltsaen	—	Ye shes rgyal mtshan
Yeshe Gyatso	—	Ye shes rgya mtsho

Yeshe Oe	—	Ye shes 'od
Yoentaen Tayae	—	Yon tan mtha' yas
yojana	yojana	dpag tshad
Yuddhajaya	Yuddhajaya	g.yul las shin tu rnam par rgyal ba
Yungtoenpa	—	g.Yung ston pa
Yungwai Pur	—	Yung ba'i phur
Zangchenpa	—	Zangs chen pa
Zhangpa Rinpoche	—	Zhang Rin po che
Zhangtreng Kaber Chung	—	Zhang 'phreng ka ber chung
Zhangtsuen Yerpa	—	Zhang btsun yer pa
zho	—	zho
Zhoenue Oe	—	gZhon nu'od/Bya yul ba

2. TIBETAN TRANSLITERATIONS OF TIBETAN AND SANSKRIT NAMES AND WORDS

Tibetan	*English*	*Sanskrit*
Ka khang	Kakang	—
Katyayana	Kātyāyana	Kātyāyana
Ka ba shākya dbang phyug	Kawa śhākya Wangchug	—
Ka ma ba	Kamaba	—
Kashi	Kaśhi	Kaśhi
Kun dga' bo	Ānanda	Ānanda
Kun tu bzang po	Samantabhadra	Samantabhadra
Kun mthong	Ādarśha	Ādarśha
Kun nas snang ba bkod pa'i dpal	Samantāvabhā-savyuhaśhrī	Samantāvabhā-savyuhaśhrī
Kun legs	Kuenleg	—
Kun shes ko'u di n.ya	Ājñatakauṇḍinya	Ājñatakauṇḍinya
Kusāli	Kusali	Kusali
Kokalika	Kokalika	Kokalika
Kong po	Kongpo	—
Kaushri bskal bzang	Gushri Kaelzang	—
Kye rdo rje/dGyes pa rdo rje/Kyai rdo rje	Hevajra	Hevajra
Kṛi kri	Kṛikin	Kṛikin
klu	nāga	nāga
Klu sgrub	Nāgārjuna	Nāgārjuna
Klu byang	Nāgabodhi	Nāgabodhi
Klu dbang gi rgyal po	Nāgeśhvararāja	Nāgeśhvararāja

Klu E la'i 'dab ma	Elapatra Nāga	Elapatranāga
Klong rdol bla ma rin po che	Longdoel Lama Rinpoche	—
dKa' chen ram mkha' rdo rje	Kachen Namkha Dorge	—
dKar mo	Śhuklā	*Śhuklā
dKon mchog rgyal mtshan	Koenchog Gyaeltsaen	—
bKa' brgyud pa	Kagyuepa	—
bKa' gdams	Kadam	—
bKa' gdams pa	Kadampa	—
bKra shis 'khyil	Tashikyil	—
bKra shis lhun po	Tashi Lhuenpo	—
rKang khra	Kalmāṣhapada	Kalmāṣhapada
rKang mig	Akṣhapāda	Akṣhapāda
sKal bzang bstan 'dzin	Kaelzang Taenzin	—
sKu zhabs	Kuzhu	—
sKul byed	Khaṇḍakāri	Khaṇḍakāri
sKed tshang 'jam dbyangs (smon lam)	Ketsang Jamyang (Moenlam)	—
sKyi mo rdza 'phreng	Kyimo Dzatreng	—
sKyid rong/sKyid grong	Kyirong	—
(rGyal mchog) bsKal bzang rhua mtsho	Kaelzang Gyatso (the Seventh Dalai Lama)	—
Kha chen	Kashmir	Kashmīra
Kha dog dam pa	Paramavarṇa	*Paramavarṇa
Kha rag sgom chung/Kha rag pa	Karag Gomchung	—
Khaṇḍakapāla	Khaṇḍakapāla	Khaṇḍakapāla
Khams	Kham	—
Khams pa	Khampa	—
Khams lung pa	Kamlungpa	—
Khu ston pa	Kutoenpa	—
Khyab 'jug	Viṣhṇu	Viṣhṇu
Khyab byed	Vyāpaka	Vyāpaka
khyung/nam mkha' lding	garuḍa	garuḍa
Khyung po lhas pa	Kyungpo Lhaepa	—
Khri dwags po tshe 'phel	Tridagpo Tsepel	—
Khri zam zam kha	Trizam Bridge	—

Khrid srong lde btsan	Trisong Detsaen	—
mKhan chen bodhisattwa/ Zhi 'tsho	Śhāntarakṣhita	Śhāntarakṣhita
mkha' 'gro	ḍāka	ḍāka
mkha' 'gro ma	ḍākinī	ḍākinī
mKha' spyod bstan dar	Kachoe Taendar	—
mKhar rdo blo bzang sgom chung	Kardo Lozang Gomchung	—
mKhas grub rin po che	Kaedrub Rinpoche	—
'khor ba	saṃsāra	saṃsāra
Khor ba 'jig	Krakuchchenda	Krakuchchanda
'Khor lo sdom pa	Chakrasaṃvara	Chakrasaṃvara
Ga na sha ba	Ganashava	Ganashava
Gangga	Ganges	Ganga
Gang po	Pūrṇa	Pūrṇa
ganydzira	gañjira	gañjira
Gar log	Garlog	—
Gung thang	Gungtang	—
Gung thang 'jam dpal dbyangs	Gungtang	—
Guru Rin po che/Padma 'byung gnas/sLob dpon rin po che	Padmasaṃbhāva	Padmasaṃbhāva
Goshīrsha	Gośhīrṣha	Gośhīrṣha
Go'u tam	Gautama	Gautama
Gyer sgom pa	Gyergompa	—
Gra 'or	Dragor	—
Grangs can pa	Sāṃkhya	Sāṃkhya
Grub mchong blo bzang rnam rgyal	Drubchog Lozang Namgyael	—
Grong khyer ser skya	Kapilangara	Kapilangara
Glang 'khor	Langkor	—
Glang dar ma	Langdarma	—
Glang po'i ko ba pa	Hastikovapa	*Hastikovapa
Glang ri thang pa	Langri Tangpa	—
Gling ge sar	Gesar Ling	—
Gling ras pa	Lingraepa	—

dGa' ldan	Tuṣhita	Tuṣhita
dGa' ldan khrid byang sprul sku	Gandaen Trijang Tulku	—
dGa' byed	Nandaka	Nandaka
dge bsnyen	upāsaka	upāsaka
dGe 'dun grub	Genduen Drub	
dGe 'dun 'jam dbyangs	Genduen Jamyang	—
dGe 'dun bstan 'dzin rgya mtsho	Genduen Taenzin Gyatso	—
dGe 'dun 'tsho	Saṅgharakṣhita	Saṅgharakṣhita
dGe ba can	Ratnasena	Ratnasena
dGe ba'i dpal	Kalyāṇaśhrī	Kalyāṇaśhrī
dGe lugs pa	Gelugpa	—
dge bshes	geshe	—
dge slong	bhikṣhu	bhikṣhu
dGon pa ba	Goenpawa	—
dGyer 'gro ba'i mgon po	Gyer Drowai Goenpo	—
dGyes pa rdo rje/ Kye rdo rje/Kyai rdo rje	Hevajra	Hevajra
dGra bcom pa	arhat	arhat
dGra nag	Kālayamāri	Kālayamāri
dGra shul can	Ugra	Ugra
mGo log a rig	Golog Arig	—
mGon po	Mahākāla	Mahākāla
mGon po rin po che	Goenpo Rinpoche	—
mGon med zas sbyin	Anāthapiṇḍaḍa	Anāthapiṇḍaḍa
'Gro mgon chos 'phags	Drogoen Choepag	—
'Gro mgon rin po che	Droegoen Rinpoche	—
rGod dkar	Goekar	—
rGod tshang	Goetsang	—
rGya brtson seng ge	Gyatsoen Senge	—
rGya ma ba	Gyamaba	—
rGya mtsho'i dul	Samandrarāja	Samandrarāja
rGyang 'phen pa	Lokāyata	Lokāyata
rgyal chen	mahārāja	mahārāja
(rGyal mchog) bsKal bzang rgya mtsho	Kaelzang Gyatso (the Seventh Dalai Lama)	—

rGyal po lHa bzang	Lhazang Khan	—
rGyal po'i khab	Rajgir	Rājagṛiha
rGyal ba dben sa pa	Gyaelwa Ensapa	—
rGyal ba don grub	Gyaelwa Doendrub	
rGyal byed kyi 'tshal	Jetavana Grove	Jetavana
rGyal dbang chos rje	Gyaelwang Choeje	—
rGyal dbang bSod nams rgya mtsho	Soenam Gyatso, the (Third) Dalai Lama	—
rGyal tshab rin po che	Gyaltsab Rinpoche	—
rGyal mtshan bzang po	Gyaeltsaen Zangpo	—
rGyal rigs	Kṣhatriya	Kṣhatriya
rGyal sras bzang po	Gyaelsae Zangpo	—
rGyud stod	Gyuetoe	—
sGur chung	Vibhudatta	*Vibhudatta
sGur mchog	Kubjottarā	Kubjottarā
sGo mang	Gomang	—
sGom pa rab gsal/Bla chen po	Gompa Rabsael	—
sGra sgrog	Rāvaṇa	*Rāvaṇa
sGra gcan 'dzin	Rāhula	Rāhula
sGra gcan 'dzin sbas/Rāhulagupta	Rāhulagupta	Rāhulagupta
sGra mi snyan	Kuru	Kuru
sGra mi snyan gyi zla	Kaurava	Kaurava
sGrub khang dge legs rgya mtsho	Drubkang Geleg Gyatso	—
sGrol ma	Tārā	Tārā
brGya byin	Indra	Indra
Nga las nus	Mābhvātā	Mābhvātā
Ngag dbang grags pa	Ngagwang Dragpa	—
Ngag dbang mchog ldan	Ngagwang Chogdaen	—
Ngag dbang mthu stobs	Ngagwang Tutob	—
Ngag dbang nor bu	Ngagwang Norbu	—
Ngag dbang byams pa	Ngagwang Jampa	—
dngul skar	ngulkar	—
dNgul chu yab sras	Ngulchu Dharmavajra	—
dNgul chu thogs med bzang po	Ngulchu Togme Sangpo	—

mNga' ris	Ngari	—
mNgon dga'	Abhīrati	Abhīrati
rNga yab	Chāmara	Chāmara
rNga yab gzhan	Aparachāmara	Aparachāmara
lNga pa chen po	Fifth Dalai Lama	—
sNgo bsangs ma	Śhyāmavatī	Śhyāmavatī
gCung dGa' bo/dGa' bo	Nanda	Nanda
gCer bu ba	Jain	Jaina
gcod	choed	—
bCom ldan 'das	Bhagavān	Bhagavān
lCang skya rol pa'i rdo rje	Changkya Roelpai Dorje	—
Chag lo	Chag the translator	—
Chu smad skyes	Uttara	Uttara
Chu bzang bla ma Ye shes rgya mtsho	Chuzang Lama Yeshe Gyatso	—
Chu bzang ri khrod	Chuzang Hermitage	—
Chu shur	Chushur	—
Chu lha	Varuṇa	Varuṇa
Chu lha'i lha	Varuṇadeva	Varuṇadeva
Chos kyi grags pa	Dharmakīrti	Dharmakīrti
Chos kyi rdo rje	Choekyi Dorje	—
Chos kyi 'od zer	Choekyi Oezer	—
chos sku	dharmakāya	—
Chos skyab bzang po/ Chos skyobs bzang po	Choekyab Zangpo	—
Chos rgyal	Choegyael	—
Chos rgyal	Dharmarāja	Dharmarāja
Chos 'phags	Dharmodgata	Dharmodgata
chos dbyings	dharmadhātu	dharmadhātu
mChims 'jam dpal byangs	Chim Jampaelyang	—
mChog gi sde	Paranasena	Paranasena
mChog sred	Vararuchi	Vararuchi
'Chad kha wa	Chaekawa	—
'Char kha	Udayī	Udayī
Jun gar	Dzungaria	—

Jo nang pa	Jonangpa	Jonangpa
Jo bo rje	Atiśha	Atiśha
’Jam dpal rgya mtsho	Jampael Gyatso	—
’Jam dpal rdo rje	Mañjuvajra	Mañjuvajra
’Jam dpal dbyangs	Mañjuśhrī	Mañjuśhrī
’Jam dpal bshes gnyen	Mañjuśhrīmitra	Mañjuśhrīmitra
’Jam dpal lhun grub	Jampael Lhuendrub	—
’Jam dbyangs bzhad pa	Jamyang Shaypa	—
rJe btsun byams pa bstan ’dzin ’phrin las rgya mtsho	Jetsun Jampa Taenzin Trinlae Gyatso	—
rJe rin po che	Je Rinpoche	—
rJe shes rab rgya mtsho	Je Sherab Gyatso	—
Nyag mo	Nyagmo	—
nyan thos	śhrāvaka	śhrāvaka
Nyer sbas	Upagupta	Upagupta
gNyan ston pa	Nyaentoenpa	—
mNyan yod	Śhrāvastī	Śhrāvastī
rNying ma	Nyingma	—
sNyan pa bzang ldan	Priyabhadra	*Priyabhadra
sNying stobs chen po	Prakṛiti	Prakṛiti
sNying stobs chen po skye ba	Mahāsattva	Mahāsattva
sNyug rum pa	Nyugrumpa	—
Telo	Tilopa	Tilopa
gTogs ’dod	Paryāsannakama	Paryāsannakama
rTa mgrin	Hayagrīva	Hayagrīva
rTa thul	Aśhvajit	Aśhvajit
rTa nag	Tanag	—
rTa phug pa	Tapugpa	—
rTag tu ngu	Sadāprarudita	Sadāprarudita
rTogs ldan	Bodha	Bodha
rTod phur	Toepur	—
lTeng rgyas ’od srungs	Uruvilvākāśhyapa	Uruvilvākāśhyapa
sTag tshang Lotsāwa	Tagtsang Lotsawa	—
sTag gzig	Mogul	—
sTod lung pa	Toelungpa	—

bsTan pa rgya mtsho	Taenpa Gyatso	—
bsTan pa rab rgyas	Taenpa Rabgyae	—
bsTan pa'i sgron me	Taenpai Droenme	—
bsTan 'dzin mkhas grub	Taenzin Kaedrub	—
bsTan 'dzin rgya mtsho	Taenzin Gyatso	—
Thag ma pa	Tagmapa	—
Thal 'gyur pa	Prāsaṅgika	Prāsaṅgika
thud	tue	—
Thub dbang	Munīndra	Munīndra
Thub bstan rab rgyas	Tubtaen Rabgyae	—
Thu'u bkwan Dharmabadzra	Tukaen Dharmavajra	—
Tho btsun grub rje	Udbhaṭasiddhasvāmin	Udbhaṭasiddha-svāmin
Thogs med	Asaṅga	Asaṅga
Thogs med bzang po/ dNgul chu rgyal sras	Togme Sangpo	—
Thod le kor	Toelekor	—
mThu mo che	Mahardhikā	Mahardhikā
mThong ldan/Ma skyes dgra	Ajātaśhatru	Ajātaśhatru
mThong ba don yod	Amoghadarśhī	Amoghadarśhī
theg dman	Hīnayāna	hīnayāna
Dwags po	Dagpo	—
Ding ri	Dingri	—
dur ba	dūrva	dūrva
Dul ba'i sde	Vinītasena	Vinītasena
Dus 'khor	Kālachakra	Kālachakra
De bzhin gshegs pa	Tathāgata	Tathāgata
Den ston skyer sgang pa/ dBon ston skyer sgang pa	Dentoen Kyergangpa	—
Des pa	Sūrata	Sūrata
Don grub	Amoghasiddha	Amoghasiddha
Ḍoṃbhi	Ḍoṃbhīpa	Ḍoṃbhīpa
Dol pa	Doelpa	—
Drag po	Rudra	Rudra
drang srong	ṛiṣhi	ṛiṣhi
Dran pa'i dpal	Smṛitiśhrī	Smṛitiśhrī

Dri ma med pa	Vimala	Vimala
Dri med steng kha	Drimé Tengka	—
Dharmārakṣhita	Dharmarakṣhita	Dharmarakṣhita
gDong drug	Gaṇeśha	Gaṇeśha
bdag nyid chen po	mahātma	mahātma
bdud	māra	māra
bDud dga' rab dbang phyug	Kāmadeva	Deviputramāra
bDe ba can	Sukhāvatī	Sukhāvatī
bDe byed	Śhaṃkara	Śhaṃkara
bDe gshegs	Sugata	Sugata
bDe mchog/Heruka	Heruka	Heruka
mDung thung can	Śhakti	Śhakti
mDo khams	Dokham	—
mDo phal po che	*Avataṃsaka Sūtra*	Avataṃsakasūtra
rDo rje 'chang	Vajradhara	Vajradhara
rDo rje snying po/ rDo rje snying po rgyan	Vajrahṛidaya	Vajrahṛidaya
rDo rje snying po rab tu 'joms pa	Vajramaṇḍapra-mardin	Vajramaṇḍapra-mardin
rDo rje gdan	Bodhgaya	Bodhagāya
rDo rje phag mo	Vajravarāhī	Vajravarāhī
rdo rje ma	Vajrī	Vajrī
rDo shul	Doshul	—
sDug bsngal 'gyur	Duḥkhitaka	*Duḥkhitaka
sDe dge	Derge	—
Nāropa/Nāro	Nāropa	Nāropa
Nāro bon chung	Nāro Boenchung	—
Nālendra	Nālandā	Nālandā
Nag po spyod pa	Kṛiṣhṇāchārya	Kṛiṣhṇāchārya
Nag tsho	Nagtso	—
Nam mkha' rgyal po	Namkha Gyaelpo	—
Nam mkha' rgyal mtshan/ Lho brag grub chen	Namkha Gyaeltsaen	—
Nam mkha' snying po/ Nam snying	Ākāśhagarbha	Ākāśhagarbha
Nam mkha' lding/khyung	garuḍa	garuḍa

Nam (mkha') seng ge	Namkha Senge	—
Nam snying/Nam mkha' snying po	Ākāśhagarbha	Ākāśhagarbha
Nor skyong	Dhanapāla	Dhanapāla
Nor dpal	Danaśhrī	Danaśhrī
Nyagrodha'i grong khyer	Nyagrodhikā	Nyagrodhikā
gnas pa'i grong khyer	Sthirā	*Sthirā
gnod sbyin	yakṣhinī	yakṣhinī
rNa ba bye ri	Koṭikarṇa	Koṭikarṇa
rNam grol sde	Vimuktisena	Vimuktisena
rNam thos sras	Vaiśhravaṇa	Vaiśhravaṇa
rNam snang	Vairochana	Vairochana
rNam par gnon pa'i gshegs pa'i dpal	Vikrantāntagā-miśhrī	Vikrantāntagā-miśhrī
rNam gzigs	Vipaśhyin	Vipaśhyin
rNal 'byor pa chen po	Mahāyogi	Mahāyogi
sNang mdzad (Haribhadra's teacher)	Vairochana	Vairochana
sNar thang	Nartang	—
sNar ma	Rohiṇī	Rohiṇī
sNe'u zur pa	Neuzurpa	—
Padma can	Padmaka	Padmaka
Padma 'byung gnas/ Guru Rin po che/ sLob dpon rin po che	Padmasaṃbhāva	Padmasaṃbhāva
Padma'i 'od zer rnam par rol pas mngon par mkhyen pa	Padmajyoti-vikroḍitābhijña	Padmajyoti-vikroḍitābhijña
Paṇ chen (Rin po che)	Paṇchen (Lama)	—
pi waṃ	viṇā	viṇā
Pu hreng	Puhreng	—
Pe har	Pehar	—
Po to la	Potala	—
Po to ba	Potowa	—
dPa' bo'i sde	Vorasena	Vorasena
dpag tshad	yojana	yojana
dPal skyes	Śhrījāta	*Śhrījāta
dPal gyi sde	Śhrīsena	Śhrīsena

dPal dgyes	Voranandin	Voranandin
dPal ldan	Śhrīmān	*Śhrīmān
dPal ldan ye shes	Paeldaen Yeshe	—
dPal sbas	Śhrīgupta	Śhrīgupta
dPal sbyin	Śhrīdatta	Śhrīdatta
dPal mar me mdzad ye shes	Dīpaṃkara Śhrījñāna	Dīpaṃkara Śhrījñāna
dPal mo	Lakṣhmī	*Lakṣhmī
dPal mo 'od zer can	Prabhāvatī	Prabhāvatī
dPal bzang	Śhrībhadra	Śhrībhadra
dPung bzang	Subahu	Subahu
sPang skong	Pangkong	—
sPyan snga ba	Chaen Ngawa	—
sPyan ras gzigs	Avalokiteśhvara	Avalokiteśhvara
sPyan ras gzigs brtul shugs	Avalokitavrata	Avalokitavrata
sPyil bu pa	Chilbupa	—
sprul sku	nirmāṇakāya	nirmāṇakāya
Pha dam pa sangs rgyay	Padampa Sangyae	—
Pha bong kha	Pabongka	—
Phal chen sde	Mahāsaṃgika	Mahāsaṃgika
Phu chung ba	Puchungwa	—
Phun tshogs rgya mtsho	Puentsog Gyatso	—
Phur lcog ngag dbang byams pa/Bla ma byams pa rin po che	Purchog Ngagwang Jampa	—
Phywa	Cha	—
Phyag khri mchog	Chagtrichog	—
phyag rgya chen po	mahāmudrā	mahāmudrā
Phyag na rdo rje	Vajrapāṇi	Vajrapāṇi
'Phags skyes po	Virūḍhaka	Virūḍhaka
'Phags pa dpa' bo	Āryaśhūra	Āryaśhūra
'Phags pa lha	Āryadeva	Āryadeva
'Phan po	Paenpo	—
'Phrog ma	Hārītī	Hārītī
Batsigira	Vachigira	Vachigira
Ba lang spyod	Godānīya	Godānīya

Ba so rje	Basoje	—
Bang ri chos sde	Bangrim Choede	—
bar do	bardo	—
Bal po rdzong/Bal yul	Nepal	—
Bikāmapuri	Vikramapura	Vikramapura
Bu ston	Butoen	—
Bo dong phyogs las rnam rgyal	Choglae Namgyael of Bodong	—
Bon	Boen	—
Bon po	Boenpo	—
Bya bral	Jadrael	—
Byang chub thogs med	Jangchub Togme	—
Byang chub bzang po	Bodhibhadra	Bodhibhadra
Byang chub rin chen	Jangchub Rinchen	—
byang chub sems dpa'	bodhisattva	bodhisattva
Byang sems rwa sgreng ba	Jangsem Retrengwa	—
Byams pa	Maitreya	Maitreya
Byams pa chos ldan	Jampa Choedaen	—
Byams pa bstan 'dzin 'phrin las rgya mtsho	Jampa Taenzin Trinlae Gyatso	—
Byams pa'i stobs	Maitrobala	Maitrobala
Byams pa'i rnal 'byor	Maitrīyogi	Maitrīyogi
Byi ling ga li ta	Vyilingalita	Vyilingalita
Bye brag smra ba	Vaibhāṣhika	Vaibhāṣhika
bram ze/bram ze'i khye'u	Brahman	Brahman
Brikamalashīla	Vikramśhīla	Vikramśhīla
bre	drona/dre	drona
Bla chen po/sGom pa rab gsal	Gompa Rabsael	—
bla ma	guru	guru
Bla ma dam pa	Lama Dampa	—
Bla ma byams pa rin po che/ Phur lcog ngag dbang byams pa	Purchog Ngagwang Jampa	—
Blo gros rgya mtsho	Sāgarmati	Sāgarmati
Blo gros rgyal mtshan	Lodroe Gyaeltsaen	—
Blo gros bzang po	Lodroe Zangpo	—
Blo bzang	Sumati	Sumati

Blo bzang mkhas btsun	Lozang Kaetsuen	—
Blo bzang grags pa	Lozang Dragpa	—
Blo bzang grags pa	Sumatikīrti	Sumatikīrti
Blo bzang rgyal ba	Lozang Gyatso	—
Blo bzang chos kyi rgyal mtshan	Lozang Choekyi Gyaeltsaen	—
Blo bzang chos rgyan	Lozang Choegyaen	—
Blo bzang chos 'phel	Lozang Choepel	—
Blo bzang snyan grags	Lozang Nyaendrag	—
Blo bzang don ldan	Lozang Doendaen	—
Blo bzang rdo rje	Lozang Dorje	—
Blo bzang rnam rgyal	Lozang Namgyael	—
Blo bzang sbyin pa	Lozang Jinpa	—
Blo bzang ye shes	Lozang Yeshe	—
Blo bzang ye shes bstan 'dzin rgya mtsho	Lozang Yeshe Taenzin Gyatso	—
Blo bzang lhun grub ('phrin las) rgya mtsho	Lozang Lhuendrug (Trinlae) Gyatso	—
Brung pa	Drungpa	—
Bhaṃgal	Bengal	Bhaṅgal
dBang po zhi	Śhāntendra	Śhāntendra
dBang po'i tog gi rgyal mtshan gyi rgyal po	Indraketudhva-jarāja	Indraketudhva-jarāja
dBang phyug	Īśhvara	Īśhvara
dBang phyug	Śhīva	Śhīva
dBu ma	Madhyamaka	Madhyamaka
dBu ma pa	Mādhyamika	Mādhyamika
dBu ma pa	Umapa	—
Den ston skyer sgang pa/ dBon ston skyer sgang pa	Dentoen Kyergangpa	—
dByig gnyen	Vasubandhu	Vasubandhu
dByings phyug ma	Dhatvīśhvarī	Dhatvīśhvarī
'Ban gung rgyal	Baen Gung-gyael	—
'Brang ri	Drangri	—
'Bras phungs	Drepung	—
'Brug pa kun legs	Drugpa Kuenleg	—

’Brog gnas	Āṭavaka	Āṭavaka
’Brom ston pa	Dromtoenpa	—
’Brom lo lding	Drom Loding	—
sByin pa rgya mtsho	Jinpa Gyatso	—
Ma skyes dgra/mThong ldan	Ajātaśhatru	Ajātaśhatru
Magadha bzang mo	Sumagadhā	Sumagadhā
Ma gcig lab sgron	Machig Labdroen	—
Ma dus	Mākandika	Mākandika
Ma dros pa	Anavatapta	Anavatapta
Māmakī	Māmakī	Māmakī
ma rig pa	ma rig pa	—
Malaya	Malabar	Malaya
Mahabala	Mahābala	Mahābala
Mang yul	Mangyul	—
Mi bskyod pa	Akṣhobhya	Akṣhobhya
Mitradzoki	Maitrijyoki	Maitrijyoki
Mi nag po	Dravidian	—
Mid la ras pa	Milarepa	—
Mu stegs pa	tīrṭhika	tīrṭhika
Me skyes	Agnibhu	Agnibhu
Me tog dpal	Kusumaśhrī	Kusumaśhrī
Me tog zla mdzes	Supuṣhpa Chandra	Supuṣhpa Chandra
Mon grwa pa	Moendrapa	—
Maung gal bu	Maudgalyāyana	Maudgalyāyana
Mya ngan med	Aśhoka	Aśhoka
Mya ngan med pa’i dpal	Aśhokaśhrī	Aśhokaśhrī
Myur mdzad ye shes	Kurukullejñāna	Kurukullejñāna
rMa yi phya	Mayi Cha	—
sMon lam dpal ba	Moenlam Paelwa	—
sMon lam blo gros	Praṇidhānamati	*Praṇidhānamati
Tsan dan dpal	Chandanaśhrī	Chandanaśhrī
Tsanakya	Chanakya	Chanakya
Tsandragomin	Chandragomin	Chandragomin
tsampaka	champaka	champaka
Tsunda	Chunda	Chunda

gTsang	Tsang	—
gTsang pa rgya ras	Tsangpa Gyarae	—
gtsug tor	uṣhṇīṣha	uṣhṇīṣha
gTsug na rin chen	Mahāratnachūḍa	Mahāratnachūḍa
bTsun pa rnam grol sde	Vimuktisenagomin	Vimuktisena-gomin
rtswa mchog/kusha	kuśha	kuśha
rTswa mchog drong khyer	Kuśhīnagarī	Kuśhīnagarī
rTsibs kyi mu khyud	Aranemi	Arenemi
Tshangs pa	Brahmā	Brahmā
tshangs pa chen po	mahābrahmā	mahābrahmā
Tshangs pa'i gnas	Brahmāvihāra	Brahmāvihāra
Tashangs pa'i 'od zer rnam par rol pas mngon par mkhyen pa	Brahmajyotivi-kroḍhitābhijña	Brahmajyotivi-kroḍhitābhijña
Tshangs pas byin	Brahmādatta	Brahmādatta
Tshangs dpal shin tu yongs grags	Brahmāśhrīsupari-kīrti	Brahmāśhrī-supari-kīrti
Tshul khrims	Tsultrim	—
Tshul khrims rgyal ba	Tsultrim Gyaelwa	—
Tshul khrims 'bar	Tsultrimbar	—
Tshul khrims srung ba	Śhīlarākṣha	Śhīlarākṣha
Tshe mchog gling	Tsechogling	—
mTsho sna wa	Tsonawa	—
'Tsho byed gzhon nu	Jīvaka Kumarabhṛita	Jīvaka Kumarabhṛita
Dzalandharapa	Jalandharī	Jalandharī
Dzetāri	Jitāri	Jitāri
mdza' bo'i bu mo	Maitrakanyaka	Maitrakanyaka
mdzod spu	urṇa	urṇa
'Dzam bu gling	Jambudvīpa	Jambudvīpa
rdzogs chen	dzogchen	—
rDzogs chen dpal dge	Dzogchen Paelge	—
rDzogs byed	Purāṇa	Purāṇa
Wāraṇāsi	Benares	Vāraṇāsi
Zhang 'phreng ka ber chung	Zhangtreng Kaber Chung	—

Zhang btsun yer pa	Zhangtsuen Yerpa	—
Zhang Rin po che	Zhangpa Rinpoche	—
Zhi ba lha	Śhāntideva	Śhāntideva
Zhi tsho/mKhan chen bodhisattwa	Śhāntarakṣhita	Śhāntarakṣhita
zho	zho	—
gZhon nu don grub	Siddhārtha	Siddhārtha
gZhon nu nor bzang	Kumāra Maṇibhadra	Kumāra-maṇibhadra
gZhon nu'od/Bya yul ba	Zhoenue Oe	—
Zangs chen pa	Zangchenpa	—
Zas gtsang ma	Śhuddhodana	Śhuddhodana
Zla ba	Chandra	Chandra
Zla ba grags pa	Chandrakīrti	Chandrakīrti
Zla ba grags pa	Dawa Dragpa	—
Zla ba'i snying po	Chandragarbha	Chandragarbha
Zla 'od	Chandraprabha	Chandraprabha
Zla 'od rin chen	Da Oe Rinchen	—
gZi brjid mtha' yas	Anantatejas	Anantatejas
gZugs kyi rdo rje	Vajrarūpa	Vajrarūpa
gZugs can snying po	Bimbasara	Bimbasara
bZod par smra ba	Kṣhāntivadin	Kṣhāntivadin
'Od kyi tog	Prabhāketu	Prabhāketu
'Od dkar	Oekar	—
'Ol dga' chos lung	Oelga Choelung	—
'On rgyal sras	Oen Gyaelsae	—
'Od dpag med	Amitābha	Amitābha
'Od dpal	Prabhāsaśhrī	Prabhāsaśhrī
'Od srung	Kāśhyapa	Kāśhyapa
yag sha phag mgo	pig-headed yakṣha	—
Yar 'brog	Yardrog	—
Yid 'ong ldan	Gaṇḍaka	Gaṇḍaka
Yung ba'i phur	Yungwai Pur	—
Yul dbus	Magadha	Magadha
Ye shes rgya mtsho	Yeshe Gyatso	—

Ye shes rgyal mtshan	Yeshe Gyaeltsaen	—
Ye shes bla ma	Jñānottara	Jñānottara
Ye shes 'od	Yeshe Oe	—
Ye shes gsang ba'i rdo rje	Jñānaguhyavajra	Jñānaguhyavajra
Yer pa	Yerpa	—
Yon tan mtha' yas	Yoentaen Tayae	—
g.yag	yak	—
g.Yung ston pa	Yungtoenpa	—
g.yung drung	swastika	svasatika
g.yul las shin tu rnam par rgyal ba	Yuddhajaya	Yuddhajaya
g.Yo ldan	Śhāthā	Śhāthā
Rwa sgreng	Radreng	—
rang rgyal/rang sangs rgyas	pratyekabuddha	pratyekabuddha
Rang rgyud pa	Svātantrika	Svātantrika
Ratna a ka/Shāntipa	Ratnākaraśhānti/Śhāntipa	Ratnākaraśhānti
Rab dga'	Pramudita	Pramudita
Rab rgyas	Prakāśha	Prakāśha
Rab gtum ma	Prachaṇḍālī	Prachaṇḍālī
Rab 'byor	Subhūti	Subhūti
Rab bzang	Subhadra	Subhadra
Ral pa can	Raelpa Chaen	—
Ras chung pa	Raechungpa	—
Rāhulagupta/sGra gcan 'dzin sbas	Rāhulagupta	Rāhulagupta
Ri dwags 'dzin	Mṛigāradhara	Mṛigāradhara
Ri nag po	Kṛiṣhṇagiri	Kṛiṣhṇagiri
Ri bo gangs can	Himalayas	himavat
Ri dbang gi rgyal po	Śhailendrarāja	Śhailendrarāja
Ri rab lhun po	Mount Meru	Meru
rig pa	rig pa	—
Rig pa'i khu byug	Vidyākokila	Vidyākokila
Rig pa'i khu byug gnyis pa	Vidyākokila the younger	—
Rin chen 'phel	Rinchen Pel	—
Rin chen me	Ratnāgni	Ratnāgni

Rin chen bzang po	Rinchen Zangpo	—
Rin chen zla ba	Ratnachandra	Ratnachandra
Rin chen zla 'od	Ratnachandraprabha	Ratnachan draprabha
Rin po che dang padma lab rab tu bzhugs pa ri dbang gi rgyal po	Ratnapadmavikrāmin	Ratnapadma-vikrāmin
Rin po che 'od 'phro	Ratnarchi	Ratnarchi
Rin 'byung	Ratnasaṃbhava	Ratnasaṃbhava
Re sgo a tsa ra	Rego Āchārya	—
Rong	Rong	—
Rong pa mgar dge ba	Rongpa Gargewa	—
Rohita	Rohita	Rohita
Lab sgron	Labdroen	—
Lam chung pa	Chūḍapanthaka	Chūḍapanthaka
Lam chen pa	Mahāpanthaka	Mahāpanthaka
Lam mchog 'gro	Uttaramantriṇa	Uttaramantriṇa
Lam pa	Panthaka	Panthaka
Lam rim chos sdings	Lamrim Choeding	—
Las (kyi) gshin rje	Karmayama	Karmayama
Lus	Deha	Deha
Lus 'phag po/Lus 'phags	Videha	Videha
Legs ldan 'byed	Bhāvaviveka	Bhāvaviveka
Legs ldan shes rab	Legdaen Sherab	—
Legs pa'i skar ma	Upadhāna	*Upadhāna
Legs smon	Supraṇihita	*Supraṇihita
Legs 'ong	Svāgata	Svāgata
longs sku	saṃbhogakāya	saṃbhogakāya
Shākya	Śhākya	Śhākya
Shākya thub pa	Śhākyamuni	Śhākyamuni
Sha ra ba	Sharawa	—
Shāri'i bu	Śhāriputra	Śhāriputra
Shangs pa rin po che	Shangpa Rinpoche	—
Shāntipa/Ratna a ka	Śhāntipa	Ratnākaraśhānti
Shambhala	Śhambhala	Śhambhala
Shar pa	Udayana	Udayana

Shalmali	Śhālmala	Śhālmala
Shin tu rnam par ngon pa'i dpal	Suvikrāntaśhrī	Suvikrāntaśhrī
Shugs 'chang	Vegadhārin	Vegadhārin
Shed bu ser skya	Mānavagaura	*Mānavagaura
Shes rab seng ge	Sherab Senge	—
gShin rje	Yama	Yama
gShin rje gshed/'Jigs byed	Yamāntaka	Yamāntaka
gShen rabs	Shenrab	—
Sa skya	Sakya	—
Sa skya paṇḍita	Sakya Paṇḍit	—
Sagama	Sagama	Sagama
sāla	śhālā	śhālā
Sa la rab brtan	Airāvaṇa	Airāvaṇa
Sa srung gi bu	Airāvaṇa	Airāvaṇa
Sangs rgyas	Buddha	Buddha
Sangs rgyas bskyangs	Buddhapālita	Buddhapālita
Sangs rgyas rgya mtsho	Sangyae Gytaso	—
Sangs rgyas sgom pa	Sangyae Gompa	—
Sangs rgyas dbon	Sangyae Oen	—
Sangs rgyas dbon ston	Sangyae Oentoen	—
Sangs rgyas ye shes	Buddhajñāna	Buddhajñāna
Sangs rgyas ye shes	Sangyae Yeshe	—
Sa'i snying po	Kṣhitigarbha	Kṣhitigarbha
Sudāsa'i bu	Sudāsaputra	Sudāsaputra
Se mtho skal ldan	Seto Kaeldaen	—
Se btsun	Setsuen	—
Se ra	Sera	—
Se ra rje	Sera Je	—
Se ra smad	Sera Mae	—
Seng ge bzang po	Haribhadra	Haribhadra
Seng ge bzang po	Senge Zangpo	—
Sems tsam pa	Chittamātrin	Chittamātrin
Ser skya	Gaura	*Gaura
Ser skya zhi ba	Gauraśhānti	*Gauraśhānti
Sor mo'i phreng can	Aṅgulimālā	Aṅgulimālā

slob dpon	āchārya	āchārya
sLob dpon rin po che/ Padma 'byung gnas/ Guru Rin po che	Padmasaṃbhava	Padmasaṃbhava
srang	sang	—
srin po	rākṣha	rākṣha
Sred med kyi bu	Nārāyaṇa	Nārāyaṇa
Srong btsan sgam po	Songtsaen Gampo	—
gSang phu ba	Sangpuba	—
gSang ba'i 'dus pa	Guhyasamāja	Guhyasamāja
gSal rgyal	Prasenajit	Prasenajit
gSal shes	Saelshe	—
gSer gling	Suvarṇadvīpa	Suvarṇadvīpa
gSer gling pa	Suvarṇadvīpi	Suvarṇadvīpi
gSer thub	Kanakamuni	Kanakamuni
gSer be'u	Kanakavatsa	Kanakavatsa
gSer dbyig	Suvarṇavasu	*Suvarṇavasu
gSer 'od dam pa	Suvarṇabhāsottama	Suvarṇabhā-sottama
Hala nag po	Halakṛiṣhṇa	*Halakṛiṣhṇa
Heruka/bDe mchog	Heruka	Heruka
lHa glu dga' tshal	Lhalu Gatsel	—
lHa sdings	Lhading	—
lHa bla ma	Lhalama	—
(lHa btson) Byang chub 'od	Jangchub Oe	—
lHa bzo wa	Lhazowa	—
lHa lung dbang phyug	Lhalung Wangchug	—
lHa sar gtsang chu	Kyicha	—
lHas byin	Devadatta	Devadatta
lHo brag	Lhodrag	—
lHo brag Mar pa	Marpa of Lhodrag	—
A thar	Atar	—
A mdo	Amdo	—
A mes byang chub rinchen	Amé Jangchub Rinchen	—
Atsara Manu	Āchārya Manu	Āchārya Manu
A wa glang mgo	elephant-headed Ana	—

Awadhutipa	Avadhūtipa	Avadhūtipa
Asangghabyaba('i atsara)	Asaṅgavyava('s jester)	—
Ang ge nya ma dpal dar 'bum	Ange Nyama Paeldarbum	—
Ar tsho (ban de bco brgyad)	Artso (the Eighteen Mendicants of)	—
Utpala'i mdog can	Utpalavarṇā	Utpalavarṇā
Utrayana	Utrayana	Utrayana
E pa	Epa	—

3. ENGLISH TERMS WITH THEIR SANSKRIT AND TIBETAN EQUIVALENTS

English	*Sanskrit*	*Tibetan*
absurdity/absurd consequence	—	'gal ba
access level	sāmantaka	nyer bsdogs
accumulate	saṃchaya	bsag pa
accumulation	gaṇa	tshogs
action/deed	karma	las
action tantra	kriyā tantra	bya rgyud
activation	—	gsos 'debs
adept	siddha	grub pa/grub thob
adjustment/readjustment	abhisaṃskāra	'du byed pa
advantages/benefits	upakāra/guṇa	phan yon
affecting the mindstream	—	rgyud bslad pa
afflicted	upādāna	nyer len
aggregate	skandha	phung po
all-embracing	—	rgya che chung mnyams pa'i
altruism	—	lhag bsam
amelioration rites	—	bskang gso
analysis	vichāra	dpyod pa
analytic meditation	—	dpyad sgom
anger	pratigha	khong khro
anger/wrath/forceful	krodha	khro ba
anthology of spells	—	be'u bum

arhat	arhan/arhat	dgra bcom pa
arrogance	garvīta	kheng pa
ārya	ārya	'phags pa
ascetic practice/asceticism	tapasyā	dka'spyod/dka' thub
aspect	ākāra	rnam pa
aspiration/wish	chhanda	'dun pa
Assemble-and-be-crushed	saṃghāta	bsdud 'joms
assert	upagachchhati	khas lang
atom	aṇu	rdul
attachment/desire/lust	rāga	'dod chags
attitude/recognition	saṃjñā	'du shes
auspicious gesture	*pratītyasamut-pādagranya	rten 'brel bsgrigs pa
authentic/valid cognition	pramāṇa	tshad ma
bad company	—	grogs ngan
bane	doṣha	nyes pa
barbarian	mlechchha/turuṣhka	kla klo
basis of imputation	—	gdags gzhi
becoming	bhava	srid pa
becoming discplined	damana	dul ba byed pa
becoming pacified	śhamana	zhi bar byed pa
becoming single-pointed	ekotīkaraṇa	rtse gcig tu byed pa
becoming very pacified	vyupaśhama	nye bar zhi bar byed pa
begging bowl	piṇḍapātra	lhung bzed
beginner	ādikarmika	las dang po ba
being	gati	'gro ba
being on one's best behavior	—	mi 'dod bzhin du nan gyis slong ba
belief/trustworthy	—	yid ches
benefit/advantage	upakāra/guṇa	phan yon
benighted ignorance	moha	gti mug
billion worlds	—	'jig rten stong gsum
Black Line	kālasūtra	thig nag

blessing/consecration	adhiṣhṭhāna	byin labs
bliss/happiness/comfort	sukha	bde ba
bodhichitta	bodhichitta	byang chub sems
bodhisattva	bodhisattva	byang chub sems dpa'
body consciousness	kāyavijñāna	lus kyi rnam shes
body-sense faculty	kāyendriya	lus kyi dbang po
bolster	—	grogs su 'khyer ba
border/retreat	sīmā	mtshams
Buddhist	—	nang pa
by virtue of the laws of probability	—	srid pa'i dbang du byas
candidate	—	rten
careless/reckless	pramāda	bag med pa
caste/race/family	gotra	rigs
cause	hetu	rgyu
celibacy	brahmacharyā	tshangs spyod
cessation	nirodha	'gog pa
cherish	—	gces 'dzin
chess	śhalāka	mig mang
choice	—	'dam ga
chowrie	chāmara	rnga yab
churl	bāla	byis pa
clairvoyance	abhijñā	mngon par shes pa
clarity of the image	—	gsal cha
Classical Tradition	—	gzhung pa pa
clinging	upādāna	len pa
cold hells	—	grang dmyal
color	varṇa	kha dog
comfort/bliss/happiness	sukha	bde ba
commitments	samāya	dam tshigs
compassion	karuṇā	snying rje
completing karma	—	rdzogs byed kyi las
completion stage	niṣhpannakrama	rdzogs rim

compositional factor	saṃskāra	’du byed
concentration being	*samādhisattva	ting nge ’dzin sems dpa’
conceptual thoughts/preconceptions	vikalpa	rnam rtog
concise discourse	—	dmar khrid
conclusive	sādhana	sgrub byed
concomitant	—	mtshungs ldan
concubine	—	btsun mo
conditioned phenomenon	saṃskṛita	’dus byas
confession/expiation	deśhana	bshags pa
congruous to	—	dang mthun pa
congruous with the cause	niṣhyanda	rgyu mthun
consciousness	vijñāna	shes pa/rnams shes
consequence	prasaṅga	thal ’gyur
consistent	—	’gal med du
constituent/sense element	dhātu	khams
contact	sparśha	reg pa
contaminated/defiled	sāsrava	zag bcad
contaminated action	sāsravakarma	zag bcad kyi las
contemplation	chintā	bsam pa
context/short-term	avasara	gnas skabs
Continual Resurrection	saṅjīvana	yang sos
contrived/forced	kṛitrima	bcos ma
conventional truth	saṃvṛitisatya	kun rdzob bden pa
correct view/perfect view	samyakdṛiṣhṭi	yang dag pa’i lta ba
covetousness	lobha	brnab sems
craving	tṛiṣhṇa	sred pa
creating a schism	bhedaka	dbyen byed pa
creature	amānuṣha	mi ma yin
crown protusion/uṣhṇīṣha	uṣhṇīṣha	gtsug tor
cyclic existence	saṃsāra	’khor ba
death	maraṇa	’chi ba

decay	—	rgad pa
deceipt	śhāṭhya	g.yo ba
deceipt with respect to the object being offered	—	rgyu'i g.yo
declared prohibition	—	bcas pa'i kha na ma tho ba
dedication	pariṇāma	bsngo ba
deed/action	karma	las
defiled/contaminated	sāsrava	zag bcad
definitive	nītārtha	nges don
degenerate age/degenerate time	kali/kalki	snyigs dus
deity yoga	*devayoga	lha'i rnal 'byor
deleterious	—	ngan len
deluded mind	kleśhāvaraṇa	nyon yid
delusion	kleśha	nyon mongs
demands of society	saṃsarga	'du 'dzi
demigod	asura	lha ma yin
demon	māra	bdud
denial	—	skur 'debs
desire/attachment/lust	rāga	'dod chags
desire realm	kāmadhātu	'dod khams
determination	kṣhipta	'phen pa
development of bodhichitta	chittotpāda	sems bskyed
devotion	paryupāsati	bsten
dhyāna concentration	dhyāna	bsam gtan
direct cognition	pratyakṣha	mngon sum
direction/side	pakṣha	phyogs
discipline	vinaya	'dul ba
discourse	—	khrid
disparage	abhibhava/avakṣhā	brnyas smod
distinguishing feature	charyātantra	khyad chos
distraction	vikṣhepa	g.yeng ba
doubt	vichikitsā	the tshom
dullness	laya	bying ba
ear consciousness	śhrotravijñāna	rna ba'i rnam shes

ear-sense faculty	śhrotrendriya	rna ba'i dbang po
earth/level	bhūmi	sa
effect/result/fruit/product	phala	'bras bu
effort	vyāyāma	rtsol ba
elder	sthavira	gnas brtan
element/constituent	dhātu	khams
elemental	bhūta	'byung po
elements	—	'byung ba (bzhi)
emanation	prapañcha/nirmāṇa	sprul pa
emanation body	nirmāṇakāya	sprul sku
emptiness	śhūnyatā	stong pa nyid
endowment/inheritance	samṛiddhi	'byor ba
energy channel	nāḍī	rtsa
energy wind	prāṇa	rlung
engaging the mind/ fixing the mind	chittastāpanā	sems 'job pa
enjoyment body	saṃbhogakāya	longs sku
enlightenment	bodhi	byang chub/sangs rgya
entity	bhāva	ngo bo
environmental results	adhipatiphalam	bdag 'bras
eon	kalpa	bskal pa
eon of darkness	—	mun bskal
eon of illumination	—	sgron bskal
equanimity	upekṣhā	btang snyoms
essence of the tathāgatas	tathāgatagarbhā	de bzhin gshegs pa'i snying po
established as being self-contained/established as existing in isolation	—	tshugs thub tu grub pa
established as being true	satyasat	bden par grub pa
established by its characteristics	svalakṣhaṇasiddhi	rang gi mtshan nyid kyis grub pa
established by its nature	svabhāvasiddhi	rang bzhin gyis grub pa
established from its own side	*svarūpasiddhi	rang gi ngos nas grub pa

established in dependence upon	apekṣhyasamutpāda	lots nas grub pa
established by its entity	*svabhāvatāsiddhi	ngo bo nyid kyis grub pa
established upon an object	—	yul gyi steng nas grub pa
established upon the object of imputation	—	btags yul gyi steng nas grub pa
eternal hope(s)	—	gtan gyi 'dun ma
ethics	śhīla	tshul khrims
Even Hotter	pratāpana	rab tu tsha ba
ever-present mental factors	sarvatraga	kun 'gro
exaggeration	samāropa	sgro 'dogs
excitement	auddhatya	rgod pa
exerting pressure on others	naiṣhpeṣhikatva	thob kyis 'jal ba
exist truly	satyasat	bden par yod pa
existent	sat	yod pa
expiation/confession	deśhana	bshags pa
Extensive Deeds Lineage	charyātantra	(rgya che ba'i) spyod brgyud
extreme	anta	mtha'
extreme of nihilism	uchchhedānta	chad mtha'
extremely obscure	*atyarthaparokṣha	shin tu lkog gyur
eye consciousness	chakṣhurvijñāna	mig gi rnam shes
eye faculty	chakṣhurindriya	mig gi dbang po
eye sense	charkṣhrāyatana	mig gi skye mched
fabrications	prapañcha	spros pa
faculty	indriya	dbang po
faith	śhraddhā	dad pa
familiarity	abhyāsa	goms/goms 'dris
family/race/cast	gotra	rigs
fault	doṣha	skyon
feature	—	khyad chos
feeling	vedanā	tshor ba
Fiery Trench	kulūlakarsu	me ma mur gyi 'obs
final step	nigama	mjug

First Buddhist Convocation	—	bka' bsdu dang po
first five disciples	—	'khor lnga sde
first-hand mental image	arthasāmānya	don spyi
fitness/meditative suppleness	prasrabdhi	shin sbyangs
fixated absorption	samādhāna	mnyam par 'jog pa
fixation meditation	—	'jog sgom
fixation with some continuity	saṃstāpanā	rgyun du 'jog pa
fixed	—	nges pa
fixing the mind/engaging the mind	chittastāpanā	sems 'jog pa
flattery	—	kha gsag
forced/contrived	kṛitrima	bcos ma
forced fixation	balavāhana	sgrim ste 'jug pa
forceful/wrath/anger	krodha	khro ba
forgetting the instruction	avavādasammoṣha	gdams ngag br jed pa
form/physical/visible form	rūpa	gzugs
form realm	rūpadhātu	gzugs khams
formal discourse	—	bshad khrid
formal logic/logic/reasoning	yukti	rigs pa
formal logic statement	hetu	gtan tshigs
formless realm	ārūpadhātu	gzugs med khams
framework	—	rkang grangs
freedom	bhīna	rang dbang
fruit/result/product/effect	phala	'bras bu
full set of possiblities	vyapta	khyab pa
functional thing/thing	bhāva	dngos po
fundamental/main/principal	pradhana	gtso bo
future lives	āyatyām	tshe phyi ma
general	samudāya	spyi
generation stage	utpattikrama	bskyed rim
generosity	dāna	sbyin pa
gentian	—	spang
genuine/unforced	*akṛitrima	bcos min

giving in order to receive	—	rnyed pas rnyed pa tshol ba
goal	—	thob bya
gods	deva	lha
good fixation	upasthāpanā	nye bar 'jog pa
good fortune/ level of good fortune	bhāga	skal pa
good works	karma/samudāchāra	'phrin las
gossip/idle gossip	pralāpa/bhinnalāpa	ngag 'khyel
grasping at the self	ātmagrāha	bdag tu 'dzin pa
great compassion	mahākaruṇā	snying rje chen po
great lamentation	mahāraurave	ngu 'bod chen po
great scope	*mahāpuruṣha	skyes bu chen po
grogginess/mental fog	styāna	rmugs pa
guise	nṛitya/nāṭa	gar
hallucination	—	snang ba
happiness/comfort/bliss	sukha	bde ba
harmful intent	vyāpāda	gnod sems
harmonious	—	gzhi mthun yod pa
heading	—	sa bcad
hedonist	lokāyata	rgyang 'phen pa
heinous crime	*ānantaryakarma	mtshams med kyi las
hell	naraka	dmyal ba
hermitage	parvata/kandara	ri khrod
hidden texts	—	gter ma
high training	śhikṣhā	bslab pa
highest yoga tantra	anuttarayoga-tantra	bla med rnal 'byor kyi rgyud
hindering spirits	vighna	bgegs
holy being/saint	satpuruṣha	skyes bu dam pa
holy man/sage	ṛiṣhi	drang srong
honestly	*aśhāṭhya	g.yo med
hostility	dveṣha	zhe sdang
Hotter	tapana	tsha ba

house arrest	—	bzang btson
hungry ghost	preta	yi dwags
I	ahaṃ	nga
ignorance	avidyā	ma rig pa
illusion	māyā	sgyu
image retention	muṣhṭibandha	'dzin stangs
immutable karma	*achalakarma	mi g.yo ba'i las
impermanence	anitya	mi rtag pa
imputed	parikalpita	kun btags
in the mind's eye	—	yid yul du 'char ba
inauspicious gesture	—	rten 'brel 'phyug pa
independent	—	rang rkya ba
Indonesia	suvarṇadvīpa	gser gling
inference	anumāna	rjes dpag
inferential valid cognition	anumānapramāṇa	rjes dpag tshad ma
informal discourse	—	nyams khrid
inheritance/endowment	samṛiddhi	'byor ba
initation	anujñā	rjes gnang
innate/instinctive/simultaneous	sahaja	lhan skyes
insight/religious experiences	—	nyams
inspiration	—	dbug dbyung
instinct/latency	vāsanā	bags chags
instruction	upadeśha	gdam ngag/gdams pa/man ngag
Instruction Lineage	—	man ngag pa
instrument of virtue	—	dge ba'i snod
insulting words	pāruṣhya	tshig rtsub
intention	chintā	bsam pa
intention/true thinking	saṃdhi	dgongs pa
interchange of self and others	—	bdag bzhan brje ba
interdependent origination	pratītyasamutpāda	rten 'byung
internalization of a meditation topic	—	dmigs rnam

interpretive	neyārtha	drang don
interrupted fixation	sachchhidravāhana	bar du chad cing 'jug pa
intractable/unyielding to the Dharma	—	chos dred
invovlement form of bodhichitta	—	'jug sems
iron staff	khakkhara	'khar gsil
jealousy	īrṣhyā	phrag dog
jurisdiction	gochara	spyod yul
karmic links	saṃyoga	rten 'brel
karmic process	*karmamārga	las lam
karmic ripening	vipāka	rnam smin
karmic traces	—	lag rjes
karmically potent beings/ special merit field	—	zhing khyad par can
key	marma	gnad
killing	prāṇātipāta	srog gcod
kindheartedness	—	sems bzang po
kindness	prasāda	bka' drin
knowables	jñeya	shes bya
knowledge-bearers	vidyādhara	rig 'dzin
label	—	btags
lack of benightedness	amoha	gti mug med pa
lack of faith	āśhraddhya	ma dad pa
lack of focus	skuraṇa	spro ba
lack of vigilance	asaṃprajanya	shes bzhin ma yin pa
lamrim tradition	—	lam rim pa
latency/instinct	vāsanā	bags chags
laziness	kausīdya	le lo
leaving a rebirth	—	tshe 'pho ba
level/earth	bhūmi	sa
level of good fortune/ good fortune	bhāga	skal pa
lineage discourse	—	khrid rgyun
liberation	mokṣha	thar pa

lifespan	āyu	tshe
life story	vimokṣha	rnam thar
lineage guru	gurusaṃpradāya	bla brgyud
listening/study	śhruta	thos pa
locomotive energy winds	ṅāyakaprāṇa	'dren pa'irlung
logic/reasoning/formal logic	yukti	rigs pa
love	maitri	byams pa
love through the force of attraction	—	yid 'ong byams pa
luminescence phase	—	mched
lust/desire/attachment	rāga	'dod chags
main/fundamental/principal	pradhāna	gtso bo
main part (of a teaching)	mūla/vastu	dngos gzhi
major empowerment	abhiṣheka	dbang
mandatory	anāgamya	mi lcogs med pa
mark	lakṣhaṇa	mtshan
material things	āmiśha	zang zing
matter	kanthā	bem po
meditation device	ālambana	dmigs rten
meditation session	prahara	thun
meditation topic	ālambanapratyaya	dmigs skor
meditative absorption	samāhita	mnyam bzhag
meditative suppleness/fitness	prasrabdhi	shin sbyangs
medium scope	madhyamapuruṣha	skyes bu 'bring ba
memory/recollection/remembrance	smṛiti	dran pa
mental consciousness	manovijñāna	yid kyi rnam shes
mental continuum/mental stream/lineage	saṃtāna	rgyud
mental factor	chaitta	sems byung
mental fog/grogginess	styāna	rmugs pa
mental process	manaskāra	yid byed
mental quiescence	śhamatha	zhi gnas
mental stream/mental continuum	saṃtāna	gyud
merely imputed	prajñaptimātra	btags tsam

merit	puṇya	bsod nams
merit field	—	tshogs zhing
metaphysics	abhidharma	chos mngon pa
method/means	upāya	thabs
Middle Way	mādhyamika	dbu ma
mind	chitta	sems
mind-stopped trance	—	'gog pa ('i snyoms 'jug)
mindstream	saṃtāna	gyud
mind training	—	blo sbyong
misdeed	duśhcharyā	nyes spyod
miserliness	mātsarya	ser sna
modifying behavior	heyopādeya	blang dor
monastic debate/thesis	pratijñā	dam bca'
monk	bhikṣhu	dge slong
monsoon retreat	vārṣhika	dbyar gnas
motive	samutpāda/samutthāna	kun slong
moved to renounce	udvignamānasa	yid 'byung
mysteries	guhya	gsang ba
natural prohibition	—	rang bzhin gyi kha na ma tho ba
naure	prakṛiti	rang bzhin
negative/refutation	pratiṣhedha	dgag pa
negative with further implications	paryudāsaprati-ṣhedha	ma yin dgag
negative without further implications	prasjyaprati-ṣhedha	med dgag
neutral	avyākṛita	lung ma bstan
never-returner	anāgāmin	phyir mi 'ong ba
no-more-learning, path of	aśaikṣamārga	mi slob lam
nonadjustment	anabhisaṃskāra	'du mi byed pa
non-associated compositional factor	viprayuktasaṃskāra	ldan min 'du byed
nonattachment	alobha	ma chags pa
non-Buddhists	—	phyi rol pa
nonexistent	asat	med pa

nonvirtuous	akuśhala	mi dge ba
nose consciousness	ghrāṇavijñāna	sna'i rnam shes
nose faculty	ghrāṇendriya	sna'i dbang po
notion of happiness	—	bde bar rlom pa
novice	śhramaṇera	dge tshul
obscuration to liberation	kleśhāvaraṇa	nyon sgrib
obscuration to omniscience	jñeyāvaraṇa	shes grib
obscure	parokṣha	lkog gyur
observation of the conscious workings of the mind	—	sems ngo lta ba
Occasional Hells	prādeśhikanaraka	nyi tshe ba'i dmyal ba
omniscience	sarvākārajñāna	rnam mkhyen
once-returner	āgāmin	phyir 'ong ba
optimum human rebirth	—	dal 'byor
oral transmission/transmission	āgama	lung
ordained	pravrajita	rab byung
ordinary being	pṛithagjana	so so skye bo
our Teacher (Buddha)	praṇeta	ston pa
pagoda	—	rgya phibs
palace	prāsāda	pho brang
patchy fixation	avasthāpanā	slan te 'jog pa
path	mārga	lam
path of accumulation	saṃbhāramārga	tshogs lam
path of meditation	bhāvanāmārga	sgom lam
path of no more learning	aśhaikṣhamārga	mi slob lam
path of preparation	prayogamārga	sbyor lam
path of seeing	darśhanamārga	mthong lam
pathetic	ārtta	nyam thag pa
patience	kṣhānti	bzod pa
peak	mūrdhan	rtse mo
perfect view/correct view	samyakdṛiṣhṭi	yang dag pa'i lta ba
perfection	pāramitā	phar rol tu phyin pa

Perfection Vehicle	pāramitāyāna	phar phyin theg pa
performance tantra	charyātantra	spyod rgyud
performing rituals in peoples' homes	—	grong chog
permanent	nitya	rtag pa
perserverence/persistence	vīrya	brtson 'grus
person	puruṣha	skyes bu
person/personality	pudgala/puruṣha	gang zag
personal self	pudgalātman	gang zag gi bdag
pervade	vyāpta	khyab
perverted dharma	—	log chos
petition	adhyeśhaṇa	gsol ba 'debs
phantom	saṃsthānika	dbyibs can
phenomenon/dharma	dharma	chos
physical/form/visible form	rūpa	gzugs
physical body	rūpakāya	gzugs khams
physical rebirth	śharīra	rten/lus rten
pitfall	atyaya	nyes pa
Plain of Razor-sharp Knives	kṣhurapūrṇasthalam	spu gris gtams pa'i thang
platform	pariṣhaṇḍa	bang rim
possibility	—	mu
potency	bāla/śhakti	nus pa
practical teaching	—	myong khrid
prayer	praṇidhāna	smon lam
precipitating karma	—	'phen byed kyi las
preconceptions/conceptual thoughts	vikalpanā	rnam rtog
preparatory rites	—	sbyor chos
prerequisite	gaṇa	tshogs
pride	māna	nga rgyal
priest	parivrājaka	kun tu rgyu
primal wisdom	jñāna	ye shes
primal wisdom body	jñānakāya	ye shes chos sku
principal/fundamental/main	pradhāna	gtso bo

product/result/fruit/effect	phala	’bras bu
profiting from a sale	—	blus zos pa
Profound View Lineage	gambhīratantra	(zab mo) lta brgyud
profusion	megha	sprin
prohibition	avadya	kha na ma tho ba
proper devotion	—	bsten tshul
prophecies	vyākaraṇa	lung bstan
prostration/homage	abhivandana/namaḥ	phyag ’tshal
purification	dhauta viśhodhāna	sbyang ba
pursuing a practice	—	nyams len skyong
Putrid Swamp	kuṇapa	ro myags kyi ’dam
qualities	guṇa	yon tan
race/cast/family	gotra	rigs
reality/suchness	tathatā	de bzhin nyid/de kho na nyid
reasoning/logic	yukti	rigs pa
rebirth into the world	—	’jig rten
reckless/careless	pramāda	bag med pa
recognition/attitudes	saṃjñā	’du shes
recollection/memory/remembrance	smṛiti	dran pa
refutation/negative	pratiṣhedha	dgag pa
regret	kaukṛitya	’gyod pa
rejoicing	anumodana	rjes su yid rang
religious experiences/insight	—	nyams/nyams chung
remembrance/memory/recollection	smṛiti	dran pa
remote lands	prānta	mtha’ ’khob
renunciation	niḥsaraṇa	nges ’byung
reptiles	mahoraga/urogati	lto ’phye
repudiation	duśhaṇa	sun ’byin
respect	ādara/bhakti	gus pa
respect/to regard/visualization	adhimokṣha	mos pa
responsibility	bhāra	khur po

restraint	saṃvara	sdam pa
result/fruit/product/effect	phala	'bras bu
retreat/border	sīmā	mtshams
retrospection meditation	—	(b)shar sgom
right perception	nikhalamba	dmigs med
rigorous	apramāda	bag yod pa
ripen	vipāka	rnam smin
root delusion	mūlakleśha	rtsa nyon
royal duties	rājya	rgyal srid
sage	muni	thub pa
sage/holy man	ṛiṣhi	drang srong
saint/holy being	satpuruṣha	skyes bu dam pa
scrupulous	apramāda	bag yod pa
second-hand mental image	śhabdasāmānya	sgra spyi
secondary delusion	upakleśha	nye nyon
secret tantras	guptavāda/guhyamantra	gsang sngags
seed	bīja	sa bon
self	ātman	bdag
self of phenomena	dharmātman	chos kyi bdag
self-evident thing	—	ling nge ba
selflessness	nairātmya	bdag med
selflessness of phenomena	dharmanairātmya	chos kyi bdag med
selflessness of the person	pudgalanairātmya	gang zag gi bdag med
sense	āyataṅa	skye mched
sense element/element/constituent	dhātu	khams
sentient being	sattva	sems can
shame	apatrāpya	khrel yod pa
shameless	anapatrāpya	khrel med pa
shameless/without shyness/	āhrīkya	ngo tsha med pa
shape	saṃsthāna	dbyibs
short-term/context	avasara	gnas skabs
side/direction	pakṣha	phyogs
signs	anuvyañjana	dpe (byad)

simultaneously operating condition	sahāripratyaya	lhan cig byed rkyen
sin	pāpa	sdig pa
single-pointed concentration	samādhi	ting nge 'dzin
sleep	middha	gnyid
small scope	*mṛidupuruṣha	skye bo chung ba
smell	gandha	dri
sound	śhabda	sgra
space/sky	ākāśha	nam mkha'
special insight	vipaśhyanā	lhag mthong
special merit field/ karmically potent beings	—	zhing khyad par can
specific	viśheṣha	bye brag
sphere of truth	dharmadhātu	chos dbyings
spirit	graha	gdon
spiritual guide	mitra	bshes gnyen
spontaneous fixation	anābhogovāhana	lhun grub tu 'jug pa
stability of the image	—	gnas cha
stealing	adattādāna	ma sbyin pa len pa
still-learning, [path of]	śaikṣamārga	slob pa lam
stranger	—	bar ma
stream-enterer	śhrotāpanna	rgyun zhugs pa
study/listening	śhruta	thos pa
stūpa	stūpa	mchod rten
subject	viṣhaya	yul
subsidiary cause/ condition/circumstance	pratyaya	rkyen
substance/substantial	dravya	rdzas
subtantialism	*satanta	yod mtha'
suchness/reality	tathatā	de bzhin nyid/de kho na nyid
suffering	duḥkha	sdug bsngal
summoning up (a mental state)	—	gsal thebs
superficial renunciation	—	nge 'byung sna thung

surrounding hells	pratyekanaraka	nye 'khor ba'i dmyal ba
symbols of enlightened body, speech, and mind	—	rten gsum
synonym	ekārtha	don gcig
take on responsiblity	—	khur du kyer ba
tangible result	—	mthong chos
taste	rasa	ro
ten levels	daśhabhūmi	sa bcu
tenet	siddhānta	grub mtha'
that on which the mind focuses/ that to which the attention is directed/visualization	ālambana	dmigs pa/dmigs yul
thesis/monastic debate	pratijñā	dam bca'
thing/functional thing	bhāva	dngos po
thing to be negated	pratiṣhedhya	dgag bya
thought	chetanā	sems pa
three refuges	triśharaṇa	skyabs gsum
threshold level	—	chung rim
threshold phase	—	thob
throwing karma	—	'phan byed kyi las
to common appearances	—	tshul bstan
tongue consciousness	jihvāvijñāna	lce'i rnam shes
tongue faculty	jihvendriya	lce'i bang po
touch/physical sensations	spraṣhṭavya	reg bya
trance	samāpatti	snyoms 'jug
transference	—	'pho ba
transmission/oral transmission	āgama	lung
transworldly	lokottara	'jig rten las 'das pa
trauma of birth from the womb	—	mngal grib
trivia	—	snang/snang shas
true existence	satyasat	bden par yod pa
true thinking/intention	saṃdhi	dgongs pa
truth	satya	bden pa
tutelary deity	iṣhṭadevatā	yi dam
tutor	—	yongs 'dzin

Two Forerunners	mahāratha	shing rta chen mo
two ounces	pala	srang
ultimate	paramārtha	don dam pa
ultimate truth	paramārthasiddhi	don dam bden pa
unconditioned phenomenon	asaṃskṛitadharma	'dus ma byas kyi chos
Uncrossable Torrent	vaitarāṇi	'gyur byed kyi chu klung rab med
under the power of others	paratantra	gzhan dbang
understanding all beings to be your mothers	—	mar shes
unfocusing	—	'phro ba
unforced/genuine	*akṛitrima	bcos min
unification	yuganaddha	zung 'jug
uninterrupted fixation	niśhchhidravāhana	chad pa med par 'jug pa
uninterrupted path	ānantaryamārga	bar chad med lam
universal emperor	chakravartinrāja	'khor lo bsgyur ba'i rgyal po
unrealistic thinking	—	tshul bzhin ma yin pa'i yid la byed pa
unyielding to the Dharma/intractable	—	chos dred
valid cognition/authentic	pramāṇa	tshad ma
vehicle	yāna	theg pa
victor/victorious one	jina	rgyal ba
view	dṛiṣhṭi	lta ba
view that equates the self with the perishable	satkāyadṛiṣhṭi	'jig tshogs lta ba
vigilance	samprajanya	shes bzhin
virtue	śhubha	dge ba
visible form/physical/form	rūpa	gzugs
visualization/respect/to regard	adhimokṣha	mos pa
visualization/that on which the mind focuses/that to which the attention is directed	ālambana	dmigs pa/dmigs yul
vows	saṃvara	sdom pa

wisdom	prajñā	shes rab
wish/aspiration	chhanda	'dun pa
wish-granting jewel	chintāmaṇi	yid bzhin nor bu
without aversion	adveṣha	zhe sdang med pa
Without Respite	avīchi	mnar med
without shyness/ shameless	āhrīkya	ngo tsha med pa
world/world system	loka/martyaloka	'jig rten
wrath/anger/forceful	krodha	khro ba
wrong livelihood	mithyājīvit	log 'tsho
wrong view	mithyādṛiṣhṭi	log pa'i lta ba
yearning	prārthana	don gnyer ba
yeti	tarkṣhu	dred
yoga tantra	yogatantra	rnal 'byor rgyud

BIBLIOGRAPHY

Note

The following abbreviations are used:

P: *The Tibetan Tripitaka.*
Peking edition, edited by Dr. Daisetz T. Suzuki, Suzuki Research Foundation, Tokyo, 1962.

T: *A Complete Catalogue of the Tibetan Buddhist Canons.*
Tohoku Imperial University, 1934.

Blo sbyong brgya rtsa:
Sems dpa' chen po dkon mchog rgyal mtshan gyis phyogs bsgrigs mdzad pa'i blo sbyong brgya rtsa dang dkar chag gdung sel zla ba bcas.
Shes rig par khang, Dharamsala, 1973.

Bla ma'i rnal 'byor:
Bla ma'i rnal 'byor dang yi dam khag gi bdag bskyed sogs zhal 'don gces btus.
Shes rig par khang, Dharamsala, reprinted 1979.

1. SŪTRAS AND TANTRAS CITED

Ākāśhagarbha's Confession
Nam snying gi bshags pa
P322 vol. 7, T641
Ārya ākāśhagarbha aṣhṭottarashataka nāma dhāraṇ mantra sahita
'Phags pa nam mkha'i snying po'i mtshan brgya rtsa brgyad pa gzungs sngags dang cad pa

Ākāśhagarbha's Sūtra
P926 vol. 36
Ārya ākāshagarbha nāma mahāyāna sūtra
'Phags pa nam mkha'i snying po shes bya ba theg pa chen po'i mdo

Avataṃsaka Sūtra
P761 vols. 25–26, T44
Buddhāvataṃsaka nāma mahā vaipulya sūtra
Sangs rgyas phal po che shes bya ba shin tu rgyas pa chen po'i mdo
Cleary, Thomas. *The Flower Ornament Scripture,* vols. 1–3, Boston: Shambhala Publications, 1986.

✓*Confession of Transgressions Sūtra*
lTung bshags
(See *Sūtra of the Three Noble Heaps)*

Eight-Thousand-Verse Perfection of Wisdom Sūtra
P734 vol. 21, T10
Ārya aṣhṭasāhasrikā prajñāpāramitā
'Phags pa shes rab kyi pha rol tu phyin pa brgyad stong pa
Conze, Edward. *Aṣṭasāhasrikā Prajñāpāramitā.* Bolinas, CA: Four Seasons, 1962.

General Confession
Phyi bshags

Great Play Sūtra
P763 vol. 63, T95
Ārya lalitavistara nāma mahāyāna sūtra
'Phags pa rgya cher rol pa shes bya ba thegs pa chen po'i mdo

Great Sūtra on Buddha's Nirvāṇa
P788 vol. 31, T120
Ārya mahāparinirvāṇa nāma mahāyāna sūtra
'Phags pa yongs su mya ngan las 'das pa chen po'i mdo

Guhyasamāja Root Tantra
P81 vol. 3, T442
Sarva tathāgata kāya vach chitta rahasya guhyasamāja nāma mahākalpa rāja
De bzhin gshegs pa thams cad kyi sku gsung thugs kyi gsang chen gsang ba 'dus pa zhes bya ba brtag pa'i gyal po chen po

Heart [of Wisdom] Sūtra
Shes rab snying po
P160 vol. 6
Bhagavatī prajñāpāramitā hṛidaya sūtra
bCom ldan 'das ma shes rab kyi pha rol tu phin pa'i snying po'i mdo
Conze, Edward. *Buddhist Wisdom Books.* New York: Harper & Row, 1972.

Heruka Tantra
P10 vol. 2
Śhrī mahā saṃvarodaya tantra rāja nāma
dPal bde mchog 'byung ba shes bya ba'i rgyud kyi rgyal po chen po

Hevajra Tantra
P10 vol. 1, T417
Hevajra tantra rāja nāma
Kye'i rdo rje shes bya ba rgyud kyi rgyal po
Snellgrove, David L. *Hevajra Tantra.* London: Oxford, 1959.

Instruction Given to the King Sūtra
P887 vol. 35, T214, T215, T221
Ārya rājāvavādaka nāma mahāyāna sūtra
'Phags pa rgyal po la gdams pa shes bya ba theg pa chen po'i mdo

Kālachakra Tantra
P4 vol. 1
Parama ādibuddhoddhrita śhrī kālachakra nāma tantra rāja

mChog gi dang po'i sang rgyas las byung ba rgyud kyi rgyal po dpal dus kyi 'khor lo shes bya ba

King of Single-Pointed Concentration Sūtra
P795 vols. 31–32, T4010
Ārya sarva dharma svabhāva samatā vipañchita samādhi rāja nāma mahāyāna sūtra
'Phags pa chos thams cad kyi rang bshin mnyam pa nyid mam par spros pa ting nge 'dzin gyi rgyal po shes bya ba theg pa chen po'i mdo
Partial translation in: Regamey, K. *Three Chapters from the Samādhirājasutra.* Warsaw: 1958.

Lamp on the Three Jewels Sūtra
dKon mchog sgron me'i mdo
(Not in P or T)

Laying Out of Stalks Sūtra
P761 vols. 60–61 no. 45, T44
lDong po mkod pa'i (or sometimes *rgyan pa'i*) *mdo*

Living Tree Sūtra
mDo ljon shing
(Not in P)

Mañjuśhrī Root Tantra
P162 vol. 6, T543
Ārya mañjuśhrī mūla tantra
'Phags pa 'jam dpal gyi rtsa ba'i gyud

Meeting of Father and Son Sūtra
P760 vol. 23 no. 16, T44
Ārya pitāputra samāgama nāma mahāyāna sūtra
'Phags pa yab dang sras mjal ba shes bya ba theg pa chen po'i mdo

One Hundred Thousand Verses Perfection of Wisdom Sūtra
P730 vols. 12–18, T8
Śhatasāhasrikā prajñāpāramitā
Shes rab kyi pha rol tu phyin pa stong phrag brgya pa
Conze, Edward. *The Large Sūtra on Perfect Wisdom.* Berkeley: University of California, 1975.

Perfection of Wisdom Sūtras
P730 to 759 vols. 12–21, T8–43
Prajñāpāramitā sūtra
Shes rab kyi pha rol tu phyin pa'i mdo

Plea for Altruism sūtra
P760 vol. 24 no. 25, T69
Ārya adhyaśhaya samchodana nāma mahāyāna sūtra
'Phags pa lhag pa'i bsam pa bskul pa shes bya ba thegs pa chen po'i mdo

Pratimokṣha Sūtra
P1031 vol. 42, T2
Pratimokṣha Sūtra
So sor thar pa'i mdo

Prayer of Maitreya
P717 vol. 9, also P1040 vol. 45, T1096
(No Sanskrit title given)
'Phags pa byams pa'i smon lam

Rice Seedlings Sūtra
P876 vol. 34, T210
Ārya śhāhstamba nāma mahāyāna sūtra
'Phags pa sā lu'i ljang ba shes bya ba theg pa chen po'i mdo

Royal Prayer of Noble Deeds
(Not listed in P), T1095
Samantabhadra charyā praṇidhāna rāja
Kun du bzang po spyod pa'i smon lam gyi rgyal po

Short Perfection of Wisdom Sūtra
P735 vol. 49, T13
Ārya prajñāpāramitā gāthā
'Phags pa sher rab kyi pha rol tu phyin pa sdud pa tshigs su bcad pa

Śhrīkhasama Tantra
P31 vol. 3
Śhrīkhasama tantra rāja nāma
dPal nam mkha' dang mnyam pa'i rgyud kyi rgyal po shes bya ba

Spell of Kaṇḍakāri
sKul byed kyi gzungs
(Not listed in P or T)

Sūtra Delivered to the Monks
P968 vol. 39, T302
Bhikṣhu prareju sūtra nāma
dGe slong la rab tu gces pa'i mdo shes bya ba

Sūtra for Nanda on Entering the Womb
P760 vol. 52 no. 13, T58

Ārya āyuṣhman nanda garbhāvakrānti nirdeśha nāma mahāyāna sūtra
'Phags pa tshe dang ldan pa dga' bo mnyal du jug pa bstan pa shes ba theg pa chen poi mdo

✓ *Sūtra of the Three Noble Heaps*
P950 vol. 38, T284
Ārya triskandhaka nāma mahāyāna sūtra
'Phags pa phung po gsum pa zhes bya ba theg pa chen po'i mdo

Sūtra on Having Much Remembrance
P953 vol. 37–38, (not in T)
Ārya saddharmānusmṛiti upasthāna
'Phags pa dam pa'i chos dran pa nye bar gshag pa

Sūtra on Having Pure Ethics
P969 vol. 39, T303
Śhīla saṃyukta sūtra
Tshul khrims yang dag par ldan pa'i mdo

Sūtra on Maitreya's Life Story
Byams pa'i rnam par thar pa'i mdo
P751 vol. 21, T35
Maitrī sūtra
Byams pa'i mdo

Sūtra on the Factors Contributing to Death
Chi ba'i rkyen mdo
(Not in P or T)

Sūtra on the Fortunate Eon
P762 vol. 27, T94
Ārya bhadrakalpikā nāma mahāyāna sūtra
'Phags pa bskal pa bzang po pa shes bya ba theg pa chen po'i mdo

Sūtras on the Layout of the Pure Fields
Dag shing gi dkod pa('i) mdo
(e.g., P760 vol. 23 no. 15, (not in T)
Ārya mañjuśhrī buddhakṣhetra guṇavyūha nāma mahāyāna sūtra
'Phags pa yams dpal gyi sangs rgyas kyi shing gi yon tan bkod pa shes bya ba theg pa chen po'i mdo)

Sūtra on the Inconceivable [Mysteries]
P760 vol. 22 no. 3, T47
Ārya tathāgata achintya guhya nirdeśha nāma mahāyāna sūtra

'Phags pa de bzhin gshegs pa'i gsang ba bsam gyis mi khyab pa bstan pa shes bya ba theg pa chen po'i mdo

Sūtra on the Jurisdiction of Utterly Pure Endeavor
sPyod yul yongs su dag pa'i mdo
(Not listed in P or T)

Sūtras on the Recollection of the Three Jewels
dKon mchog rjes su dran gyi mdo
P5433 vol. 103, T279
Āryabuddhānusmṛiti
'Phags pa sangs rgyas rjes su dran pa
P5434 vol. 103, T280
Dharmānusmṛiti
Chos rjes su dran pa
P5435 vol. 103, T281
Saṇghānusmṛiti
dGe 'dun rje su dran pa

Sūtra on the Ten Stages
P761 vols. 25–26, (not in T)
Daśhabhūmika sūtra
mDo sde sa bcu pa
Honda, M. "An Annotated Translation of the 'Daśabhūmika.'" *Studies in Southeast and Central Asia,* ed. by D. Sinor. Śatapiṭaka Series 74. New Delhi: 1968, pp. 115–276.

Sūtra on the Wise and Foolish
P1008 vol. 40, T341
(No Sanskrit title)
mDzangs blun zhe bya ba'i mdo
Frye, Stanley. *Sutra of the Wise and the Foolish (mdo bdzaṅs blun)* (sic.) or *The Ocean of Narratives (üliger-ün dalia dalai), trans. from the Mongolian.* Dharamsala: LTWA, 1981.

Sūtra Requested by Anavatapta
P823 vol. 33, T156
Ārya anavatapta nāga rāja paripṛichchhā nāma mahāyāna sūtra
'Phags pa klu'i rgyal po ma dros pas zhus pa shes bya ba theg pa chen po'i mdo

Sūtra Requested by Brahmā
P825 vol. 33, T158
Ārya brahmā paripṛichchhā nāma mahāyāna sūtra
'Phags pa tshangs pas zhus pa shes bya ba theg pa chen po'i mdo

Sūtra Requested by Sāgaramati
P819 vol. 33, T152
Ārya sāgaramati paripṛichchha nāma mahāyāna sūtra
'Phags pa blo gros rgya mtshos zhus pa shes bya ba theg pa chen po'i mdo

Sūtra Requested by Ugra
P760 vol. 23 no. 19, T63
Ārya gṛihapati ugra panipṛichchhā nāma mahāyāna sūtra
'Phags pa khyim bdag drag shul can gyis zhus pa shes bya ba theg pa chen po'i mdo

Sūtra Weaving Everything Together
P893 vol. 35, T227
Ārya sarva vaidalya saṃgraha nāma mahāyāna sūtra
'Phags pa rnam par 'thag pa cad bsdus shes bya ba theg pa char po'i mdo

Suvarṇabhālsottama's Confession Sūtra
gSer 'od dam pa'i bshags mdo
P175 vol. 7, T556
Ārya suvarṇaprabhāsottama sūtrendrarāja nāma mahāyāna sūtra
'Phags pa gser 'od dam pa mdo sde'i dbang poi rgyal po shes bya ba theg pa chen po'i mdo
(Chapter 4 of this sūtra is called "rMi lam na bshags pa" ["Expiation During Dreams"].)

Tantra Requested by Subāhu
P428 vol. 9, T805
Ārya subāhu paripṛichchhā nāma tantra
'Phags pa dpung bzang gis shus pa shes bya ba'i rgyud

Ten Wheels of Kṣhitigarbha Sūtra
(Not in P), T239
Daśhachakra kṣhitigarbha nāma mahāyāna sūtra
'Dus pa chen po las sa'i snying po'i 'khor lo bcu pa zhes bya ba theg pa chen po'i mdo

Translated Word of Buddha
'Ka' 'gyur
P1 to P1055 vol. 1 to 45

Transmission of the Vinaya
P1030–55 vol. 41–45, T1–7
Vinayāgama
'Dul ba lung
(This name refers to the vinaya section of the *Translated Word of Buddha.*)

Vajra Victory Banner Sūtra
rDo rje rgyal mtshan gyi mdo
(Not in P or T)

Vajrapāṇi Initiation Tantra
Lag na rdo rje dbang bskur ba'i rgyud
(Not in P)

Vinaya
'Dul ba
(This name refers to sections of both the *Translated Word of Buddha* and the translated commentaries, i.e., P103–55 vols. 41–45 and P5605–49 vols. 120–27, T1–7, and the relevant commentaries.)

White Lotus of Compassion Sūtra
P779 vol. 29, T111
Ārya mahākaruṇā puṇḍarīka nāma mahāyāna sūtra
'Phags pa snying rje chen po'i padma dkar po shes bya ba theg pa chen po'i mdo

White Lotus Sūtra
P781 vol. 30, T113
Saddharma puṇḍarīka nāma mahāyāna sūtra
Dam pa'i chos padma dkar po shes bya ba theg pa chen po'i mdo

2. SANSKRIT AND TIBETAN TREATISES CITED

Amdo Zharmar Genduen Taenzin Gyatso *(A mdo Zhwa dmar dge 'dun bstan 'dzin rgya mtsho)* (1852–1910)

Red Hat Lamrim

Zhwa dmar lam rim

Reprinted in *Two Instructions on the Lamrim Teachings, the Lam rim myur lam and the Lam rim bde lam of the bKra shis llhum po tradition by rGyal rong Chos mdzad blo bzang thogs med and A mdo Zhwa dmar dge 'dun bstan 'dzin rgya mtsho,* New Delhi: Ngagwang Sopa, 1979.

Āryadeva *('Phags pa lha)*

Four Hundred Verses

P5246 vol. 95, T3846

Chatuḥśhataka śhāstra kārikā nāma

bsTan bcos bzhi brgya pa shes bya'i tshig le'ur byas pa

Asaṅga *(Thogs med),* (fourth century)

Bodhisattva Levels

P5538 vol. 110, T4037

Yogacharyābhūmau Bodhisattvabhūmi

rNal 'byor spyod pa'i sa las byang chub sems dpai sa

Compendium of Metaphysics, A

P5550 vol. 112, T4049

Abhidharma samuchchhaya

Chos mngon pa kun las btus pa

Five Texts on the Levels

P5536–43 vols. 109–11, T4036–42

(1) *The Stages to the Yogacharyā*

Yogacharyābhūmi

rNal 'byor spyod pa'i sa

(2) *To Fully Define the Stages of the Yogacharyā*
Yogacharyābhūmi nirṇaya saṃgraha
rNal 'byor spyod pa'i sa rnam par gtan la dbab pa bsdu ba
(3) *The Short Basics of the Stages of the Yogacharyā* (also called *The Bodhisattva Levels* (q.v.))
Yogacharyābhūmau vastu saṃgraha
rNal 'byor spyod pa'i sa las gzhi bsdu ba
(4) *A Short Enumeration of the Stages of the Yogacharyā*
Yogacharyābhūmau parayāya saṃgraha
rNal 'byor spyod pa'i sa las rnam grang bsdu ba
(5) *A Short Exposition of the Yogacharyā*
Yogacharyābhūmau vivaraṇa saṃgraha
rNal 'byor spyod pa'i sa las rnam par shad pa bsdu pa
Śhrāvaka Levels
P5537 vol. 110, T4036
Yogacharyābhūmau shrāvaka bhūmi
rNal 'byor spyod pa'i nyan thos la yi sa

Aśhvaghoṣha *(rTa dbyangs)* also called Āryaśhūra *('Phags pa dpa' bo)*
✓ *Fifty Verses on the Guru*
P4544 vol. 81, T3721
Gurupañchāśhikā
bLa ma Inga bcu pa
Fifty Verses of Guru Devotion. Dharamsala: LTWA, 1975.
Jātaka Tales
P5650 Vol. 128, T4150
Jātakamāla
sKyes rabs kyi rgyud
The Jātakamālā, or Garland of Birth Stories of Āryaśhūra. Reprinted, Delhi: Motilal Barnarsidass, 1971.

Atiśha (c. 982–1054)
Atiśha's Own Commentary to the "Lamp on the Path"
P5344 vol. 103, T3948
Bodhipathapradīpa pañjikā nāma
Byang chub lam gyi sgron ma'i dka'grel shes bya ba
✓• *Lamp on the Path to Enlightenment*
P5378 vol. 103, T3947, T4465
Bodhipathapradīpa
Byang chub lam gyi sgron ma
Sherburne, Richard. *A Lamp for the Path and Commentary.* London: Allen and Unwin, 1983

Root of Wisdom
P5222 vol. 94, T3191
Prajñā hṛidaya vyākhyā
Shes rab snying po'i rnam par bshad pa

Avalokitavrata *(sPyan ras gzigs brtul shugs)*
Commentary to "The Lamp of Wisdom," A
P5259 vols. 96–97, T3859
Prajñāpradīpa ṭīkā
Shes rab sgron me'i rgya cher 'grel ba

Bhāvaviveka *(Legs ldan 'byed)*
Heart of the Middle Way
P5255 vol. 96, T3855
Madhyamaka hṛidaya kārikā
dBu ma'i snying po'i tshig le'ur byas pa
Lamp of Wisdom
P5255 vol. 96, T3853
Prajñā pradīpa mūla madhyamaka vṛitti
dBu ma'i rtsa ba'i 'grel pa shes rab sgron ma

Buddhapālita *(Sangs rgyas bskyangs)*
Pursuit of Buddhahood
P5242 vol. 95, T3842
Buddhapālitā mūla madhyamaka vṛitti
dBu ma rtsa 'grel pa buddhapālita

Chaekawa, Geshe *(dGe bshes 'chad kha ba)*
Seven-Point Mind Training
Theg pa chen po'i gdams ngag blo sbyong don bdun ma'i rtsa ba
Reissued in woodblocks by Kamtrul Rinpoche *(Khams sprul rin po che).*
bKra shis rdzong, undated.

Chandragomin *(Tsandragomin)*
Letter to a Disciple, A
P5683 vol. 129, T4183, T4497
Shiṣhyallekha
Slob ma la springs pa'i spring yig

Chandrakīrti *(Zla ba grags pa),* (c. 600–650)
Engaging in the Middle Way
P5261 vol. 98, T3861
Madhyamakāvatāra kārikā nāma
dBu ma la jug pa shes bya ba'i tshig le'ur byas pa

Huntington, C.W. with Geshe Namgyal Wangchen. *The Emptiness of Emptiness.* Honolulu: University of Hawaii Press, 1989.

Seventy Verses on Taking Refuge
P5366 vol. 103, P5478 vol. 103
Triśharaṇagamana saptati
sKyabs 'gro bdun cu pa

Changkya Ngagwang Lozang Choedaen *(lCang skya Ngag bdang blo bzang chos ldan),* (1642–1714)
Vajra Garland
rDo rje phreng ba
'Phreng be dang kyi ya nas bshadpa'i dkyil 'khor zhe lnga'i ras bris kyi dkyil 'khor du dbang bskur ba'i ngag 'don gyi chog sgrigs blo gsalmgul rgyan nor bu'i 'phreng ba

Chim Jampaelyang *(mChims 'jams dpal dbyangs)*
Commentary to Vasubhandu's "Treasury of Metaphysics"
mChims mdzod

Dagpo Rinpoche *(Dwags po rin po che)*
Verses on the Maṇḍala
Maṇḍāl tshigs bcad ma

DALAI LAMAS

First Dalai Lama, Genduen Drub *(dGe 'dun grub),* (1391–1474)
Collected Works of the First Dalai Lama
Reprinted Gangtok: Dodrup Lama Sangye, 19– (sic.)

✓• Third Dalai Lama, Soenam Gyatso *(bSod nams rgya mtsho),* (1543–88)
Essence of Refined Gold
Lam rim gser zhun ma
Dalai Lama III. *The Essence of Refined Gold.* Translated by Glenn H. Mullin. Ithaca, Snow Lion Publications, 1983.

Fifth Dalai Lama, Ngagwang Lozang Gyatso *(Ngag dbang blo bzang rgya mtsho),* (1617–82)
Mañjuśhrī's Own Words
Lam rim jams dpal zhal lung
(In volume 12 of his *Collected Works*)

Seventh Dalai Lama, Kaelzang Gyatso *(bsKal bzang rgya mtsho),* (1708–57)
Collected Works of Kaelzang Gyatso
Reprinted Gangtok: Dodrup Sangye, 1975–

Dharmakīrti *(Chos grags),* (seventh century)
Commentary on Valid Cognition, A
P5709 vol. 103, T4201
Pramāṇavarttika kārikā
Tshad ma rnam 'grel gyi tshig le'ur byas pa

Dharmarakṣhita
✓ *Poisons Conquered by the Peacock's Mind Training*
Blo sbyong rma bya dug 'joms
Included in *Blo sbyong brgya rtsa*
✓ *Wheel of [Sharp] Weapons*
Blo sbyong mtshon cha 'kor lo
Included in *Blo sbyong brgya rtsa*
Dhargye, Geshe et al. *The Wheel of Sharp Weapons.* Dharamsala: LTWA, 1976.

Dharmattrāta *(Chos skyob)*
Sayings of the Buddha
P992 vol. 39, T4099, T326
Udānavarga
Ched du brjod pa'i tshoms
Rockhill, W. Woodville. *Udānavarga: A Collection of Verses From the Buddhist Canon.* New Delhi: D.K. Publishers' Distributers, 1982.
Sparham, Gareth. *The Tibetan Dhammapada.* London: Wisdom Publications, 1986.
Sayings of the Buddha on Impermanence
Mi rtag pa'i tshoms
(First chapter of the above)

Doelpa Sherab Gyatso *(Dol pa rog shes rab rgya mtsho,* also known as *Dol pa dMar zhur pa),* (1059–1131)
Blue Compendium
Be'u bum sngon po

Drolungpa *(Gro lung pa)*
Stages of the Teachings
bsTan rim

Gungtang Rinpoche *(Gung thang rin po che),* (1762–1823)
Collected Works of Gung thang dkon mchog bstan pa'i sgron me
Reprinted by Ngawang Gelek Demo, New Delhi, 1972–

✓ Jampael Lhuendrub *('Jam dpal lhun grub)*
An Ornament for the Throats of the Fortunate (A Convenient Recitation, a Preparatory Rite for the "Swift Path" Concise Teaching of the Lamrim)
(Byang chub lam gyi rim pa'i dmar khrid myur lam gyi sngon 'gro'i ngag 'don gyi rim pa khyer bde bklag chog) bskal bzang mgrin rgyan

Kamalagupta *(mNga' bdag lha ye shes rgyal mtshan)*
Ornament to the Vajrahṛidaya Tantra
P86 vol. 3, T451
Śhrī vajrahṛidayālaṃkāra tantra nāma
dPal rdo rje snying po rgyan gyi rgyud ces bya ba

Ketsang Jamyang *(sKed tshang jam dbyangs)*
Ketsang's Lamrim
sKed tshang lam rim
Prayer of Ketsang Jamyang
sKed tshang 'jam dbyangs smon lam

✓ Langri Tangpa *(Glang ri thang pa)*, (1054–1123)
Mind Training in Eight Verses
Blo sbyong tshig rkang brgyad ma lo rgyus dang bcad pa
Included in *Blo sbyong brgya rtsa* (This is an expanded version of the text, and includes various anecdotes.)
Rabten, Geshe & Dhargyey, Geshe. *Advice from a Spiritual Friend.* London: Wisdom Publications, 1986.

Maitreya *(Byams pa)*
Distinguishing Between the Extremes and the Middle Way
P5522 vol. 108, T4021
Madhyānta vibhaṅga
dBus dang mtha' rnam par byed pa
(See Maitreya's *Five Treatises*)
Stcherbatsky, Theodore. *Madhyānta-Vibhanga.* Calcutta: Indian Studies Past and Present, 1971.
Five Treatises
P5521 to 5525 vol. 108, T4020–24
(1) *Ornament to the Mahāyāna Sūtras* (v.i.)
(2) *Distinguishing Between the Extremes and the Middle Way* (v.s.)
(3) *Ornament to Realization* (v.i.)
(4) *Verses on Distinguishing Between Phenomena and Their True Nature*
Dharma dharmatā vibhaṅga kārikā
Chos dang chos nyid rnam par 'byed pa'i tshig le'ur byas pa
(5) *Sublime Continuum of the Great Vehicle* (v.i.)

Ornament to Realization
P5184 vol. 88
Abhisamayālaṃkāra
mNgon par rtogs pa'i rgyan
(See Maitreya's *Five Treatises*)
Conze, Edward. *Abhisamayālaṅkāra.* Serie Orientale Roma VI. Rome: Is.M.E.O., July 1954.
Ornament to the Sūtras, An
P5521 vol. 108
Mahāyāna sūtrālaṃkāra kārikā
Theg pa chen po'i mdo sde'i rgyan gyi tshig le'ur byas pa
(See Maitreya's *Five Treatises*)
Sublime Continuum of the Great Vehicle
P5525 vol. 108
Uttaratantra
Mahāyānottaratantra śhāstra
Theg pa chen po rgyud bla ma'i bstan bcos
(See Maitreya's *Five Treatises*)
Obermiller, E. "Sublime Science of the Great Vehicle to Salvation." *Acta Orientalia,* XI, ii, iii, and iv.

Mātṛicheṭa *(Ma khol)*
One Hundred and Fifty Verses of Praise
P2038 vol. 46
Śhatapañchā śhatika nama stotra
Adhyarddha shataka nāma stotra
bsTod pa brgya lnga bcu pa
Praise to the Praiseworthy
P2038 vol. 46
Varṅanārha varṇana
bsNgags 'os bsngags bstod

Milarepa *(Mi la ras pa),* (1040–1123)
Collected by Tsangnyoen Heruka *(gTsang smyon Heruka),* (1452–1507)
Songs of Milarepa
rJe btsun mi la ras pa'i rnam thar rgyas par phye ba mgur 'bum
Chang, Garma C. *The Hundred Thousand Songs of Milarepa.* Boulder: Shambhala, 1977.

Nāgārjuna *(Klu sgrub)*
Nāgārjuna's Letter
P5409 vol. 103, T4182, T4496
Suhṛillekha

bShes pa'i spring yig

Tharchin, Geshe Lobsang *(dGe bshes Blo bzang mthar phyin)*, and Engle, Artemus B. *Nāgārjuna's Letter.* Dharamsala: LTWA, 1982.

Praise in Similes

P2011 vol. 46

dPe la bstod pa

Nirupama stava

dPe med par bstod pa

Precious Garland

P5658 vol. 129, T4158

Rāja parikathā ratnāvalī

rGyal po la gtam bya ba rin po che phreng ba

Hopkins, Jeffrey & Rimpoche, Lati. *The Precious Garland and the Song of the Four Mindfulnesses.* London: George Allen & Unwin, 1975.

Six Logic Treatises

P5224–27 vol. 95 and 5658 vol. 129, T3824–28, T4158

(1) *Root of the Middle Way*

Prajñā nāma mūla madhyamaka kārikā

dBu ma tsa ba tshig le'ur byas pa shes rab ces bya ba

(2) *Sixty Stanzas on Reasoning*

Yuktiṣhaṣhṭikā kārikā nāma

Rigs pa drug cu pa'i tshig le'ur byas pa shes bya ba

Lindtner, C. *Master of Wisdom: Writings of the Buddhist Master Nāgārjuna.* Berkeley: Dharma Publishing, 1986.

(3) *Thorough Investigation, A*

Vaidalya sūtra nama

Shib mo rnam par 'thag pa shes bya ba'i mdo

Ibid.

(4) *Seventy Stanzas on Emptiness*

Śhūnyatā saptati kārikā nāma

sTong pa nyid bdun cu pa'i tshig le'ur byas pa shes bya ba

Ibid.

(5) *Refutation of Objections, A*

Vigraha vyāvartanī kārikā nāma

rTsod pa bzlog pa'i tshig le'ur byas pa shes bya ba

(6) *Precious Garland* (v.s.)

Namkha Pael *(Nam mkha' dpal)*

Rays of the Sun Mind Training

Blo sbyong nyi ma'i 'od zer

Reprinted by Kyabje Ling Rinpoche's staff *(sKyabs rje gling bla grwang).* New Delhi, 1975.

Ngagwang Dragpa *(Ngag dbang grags pa)*
Pith of Excellent Scripture
Legs gsung nying khu

Ngulchu Dharmabhadra *(dNgul chu Dharmabhadra)* (1772–1850)
Collected Works of Ngulchu Dharmabhadra
Reprinted, New Delhi: Champa Oser, 1973–1980.

PANCHEN LAMAS

First Paṇchen Lama, Lozang Choekyi Gyaeltsaen *(Blo bzang chos kyi rgyal mtshan)*, (1569–1662)
Gelugpa Mahāmudrā
dGe ldan bka' brgyud rin po che'i phyag chen rtsa ba rgyal ba'i gzhung lam
Woodblock reprint, Gangtok, 1978
Petitions for the Bardo: Petitions Made to Be Freed from the Perilous Road of the Bardo
Bar do 'phrang sgrol gyi gsol 'debs
Reprinted in a book entitled: *lTung bshags, spyi bshags, gtso rgyal ma, bzang spyod, byams smon, spyod jug, thog mtha' ma, bde smon, ji srid ma, byams ba'i sku gzugs, bde chen lhun grub, bar do'i gsol 'debs, blo bzang rgyal bstan ma, rje rin po che'i bstan pa dang mjal ba'i smon lam bcas bzhugs so.* Gangtok, 1978(?).
Melodious Laughter of Lozang Dragpa, Answers to "Questions on the Whitest Altruism of All"
Dris lan blo bzang bzhad pa'i sgra dbyangs
✓ • *Easy Path Lamrim*
Lam rim bde lam
(In volume 4 of his *Collected Works*)
✓ • *Guru Pūjā*
Zab lam bla ma mchod pa'i cho ga bde stong dbyer med ma dang, tshogs mchod bcad
Reprinted in *Bla ma'i rnal 'byor*
Berzin, Alexander et al. *The Guru Pūjā.* Dharamsala: LTWA, 1981.

Second Paṇchen Lama, Lozang Yeshe *(Paṇ chen blo bzang ye shes)*, (1663–1737)
Swift Path Lamrim
Lam rim myur lam
Collected Works of Lozang Yeshe
Paṇ chen blo bzang ye shes kyi gsung 'bum
Reprinted by bKra shis lhun po Monastery, New Delhi, 1981–.

Potowa, Geshe *(dGe bshes Po to ba)*, (1027–1105)
Analogies
dPe chos rin chen spungs pa
Reprinted, together with commentary by Kyabje Ling Rinpoche, tutor to H.H. the Fourteenth Dalai Lama *(Yongs 'dzin gling rin po che)*, by Mongolian Lama Guru Deva at the Pleasure of Elegant Sayings Printing Press, Tibetan Monastery, Sarnath, Varanasi, U.P., 1965.

Purchog Ngagwang Jampa *(Phur bu lcog ngag dbang byams pa)*, (1682–1763)
Collected Works of Purchog Ngagwang Jampa
Reprinted by Ngagwang Sopa, New Delhi, 1973–75.

Shāntideva *(Zhi ba lha)*, (c. 700)
Compendium of Instruction, A
P5272 vol. 102, T3940
Shikṣhā samuchchhaya kārikā
bsLab pa kun las btus pa'i tshig le'ur byas pa
Bendall, C. and Rouse, W.H.D. *Śikṣā Samuccaya.* Repr. Delhi: Motilal Banarsidass, 1971.
✓ • *Engaging in the Deeds of Bodhisattvas*
Bodhisattvacharyāvatāra
P5272 vol. 99, T3871
Byang chub sems dpa'i spyod pa la 'jug pa
Batchelor, Stephen. *A Guide to the Bodhisattva's Way of Life.* Dharamsala: LTWA, 1979.

Trijang Rinpoche, Kyabje *(Kyabs rje khrid byang rin po che)*, (1901–81)
Liberation in the Palm of Your Hand
A Profound, Completely Unmistaken Instruction for Conferring Liberation in the Palm of Your Hand, Pith of the Thoughts of the Unequalled King of the Dharma [Tsongkapa], the Written Record of a Concise Discourse on the Stages of the Path to Enlightenment, Pith of All Scripture, Essence of the Nectar of Instructions.
rNam sgrol lag bcangs su gtod pa'i man ngag zab mo tshang la ma nor ba mtshungs med chos kyi rgyal po'i thugs bcud byang chub lam gyi rim pa'i n yams khrid kyi zin bris gsung rab kun gyi bcud bsdus gdams ngag bdud rtsi'i snying po
Undated woodblocks published in India by *dGa' ldan shar rtse grwa tshang.*

Tsechogling Rinpoche Yeshe Gyaeltsaen *(Tshe mchog gling rin po che ye shes rgyal mtshan)*, (1713–93)
Collected Works of Tsechogling Yeshe Gyaeltsaen

Tshe mchog gling yongs 'dzin Ye shes rgyal mtshan gyi gsung 'bum
Reprinted by Tibet House, New Delhi, 1974.

Tsongkapa *(Tsong kha pa),* (1357–1419)
✔● *Basis of All Good Qualities*
Yon tan bzhi gyur ma
Also reprinted in *Bla ma'i mal 'byor*
✔● *Brief Essence of Eloquence*
(See also *In Praise of Interdependent Origination*)
P6016 vol. 153
*Sangs rgyas bcom ldan 'das…la zab mo rten cing 'brel bar 'byung ba gsung ba'i
sgo nas bstod pa legs par bshad pai snying po shes bya ba*
Included in vol. 2 of the Guru Deva edition, in the *Miscellanea (thor bu)*
13a4–16a3.
Translated as: "Praise for Relativity" in Thurman, Robert A.F., ed. *The
Life and Teachings of Tsong Khapa.* Dharamsala: LTWA, 1982.
Collected Works of Tsongkapa
P6001 to 6210 vols. 152 to 161
rGyal ba tsong kha pa chen po'i bka' 'bum
Also reprinted by Lama Guru Deva as *rJe'i gsung 'bum* in "poti"-style
complete edition of photo reproductions from the Lhasa edition, with
additional dedication prayers especially composed by Kyabje Trijang
Rinpoche, undated.
Great Stages of the Path
P6001 vol. 152
Lam rim chen mo
Translation of the sections on special insight: Napper, Elizabeth. *Depen-
dent-Arising and Emptiness.* Wisdom: Boston, 1989.
✔● *In Praise of Interdependent Origination*
rTen 'brel bstod pa
(See *Brief Essence of Eloquence*)
✔ *Lamrim Prayer*
dGe rtsa rnams ring 'bad ma
The dedication prayers at the end of *Great Stages of the Path*
Medium Stages of the Path
P6002 vol. 152
Lam rim chung ba
Translation of the special insight section, as "The Middle Length Tran-
scendent Insight" in Thurman, Robert A.F., ed. *The Life and Teachings of
Tsong Khapa.* Dharamsala: LTWA, 1982.
Questions on the Whitest Altruism of All
P6070 vol. 153

dGe sbyor gyi gnad kyi dri ba snyan bskul lhag bsam rab dkar shes bya ba

✓• *Songs from Experience,* or *Small Stages of the Path*

nyams mgur (or *Lam rim bsdus don*)

Included in vol. 2 of the Guru Deva edition, in the *Miscellanea (thor bu)* 55b1–58a2.

Translated as "Lines of Experience" in Thurman, Robert A.F., ed. *The Life and Teachings of Tsong Khapa.* Dharamsala: LTWA, 1982.

✓• *Three Fundamentals of the Path*

P6087 vol. 153

Lam gyi gtso bo rnam gsum

Included in vol. 2 of the Guru Deva edition, in the *Miscellanea (thor bu)* 193b5–194b5

• Translation as the "Three Principal Paths" in Tsongkapa, *Principal Teachings of Buddhism.* Howell, NJ: MSTP, 1988.

Also translated as "Three Principles of the Path" in Thurman, Robert A.F., ed. *The Life and Teachings of Tsong Khapa.* Dharamsala: LTWA, 1982.

✓• *Rosary of Supreme Healing Ambrosia*

P6068 vol. 153

Lho brag mkhan chen phyag rdor ba la zhu lan sman mchog bdud rtsi'i phreng ba

Translated as "Supremely Healing Nectar Garland" in Thurman, Robert A.F., ed. *The Life and Teachings of Tsong Khapa.* Dharamsala: LTWA, 1982.

Attributed to Tsongkapa

Verses on the True One

bDen pa po'i le'u

Tukaen Dharmavajra *(Thu'u bkwan dharma badzra),* (1737–1802)

Mirror on Eloquence

Grub mtha' thams cad kyi khungs dang 'dod tshul ston pa legs bshad shel gyi me long. Sarnath: "Chhos Je Lama," 1963.

Udbhaṭasiddhasvāmin *(mtho btsun grub rje)*

Supreme Praise

P5476 vol. 103, T1109

Viśheṣha stava

Khyad par du 'phags par bstod pa

Vararuchi, Ācharyā *(Slob dpon mchog sred)*

One Hundred Verses

P5824 vol. 144, T4332

Ārya koṣha nāma

Tshig su bcad pa brgya pa

Vasubandhu *(dByig gnyen),* (fourth century)
Instruction for the Multitudes
P5422 vol. 103, T4166, T4509
Sambhāra parikathā
Tshogs gyi gtam
Treasury of Metaphysics, A
P5590 vol. 115, T4089
Abhidharmakoṣha kārikā
Chos mngon pa'i mdzod kyi tshig le'ur byas pa

Yeshe Tsoendrue *(Ye shes brtson 'grus)*
Essence of Nectar Lamrim
Byang chub lam gyi rim pa'i gdams pa zab mo rnams tshigs su bcad pa'i sgo nas nyams su len tshul dam chos bdud rtsi'i snying po. Woodblock, Buxa: Thar 'dod gling, no date.
Rabten, Geshe *(dGe bshes rab bsten). The Essential Nectar, Meditations on the Buddhist Path.* Editing and verse translation by Martin Willson. London: Wisdom Publications, 1984.

WORKS CITED WHOSE AUTHOR IS NOT KNOWN

Book of the Kadampas
bKa'gdams glegs bam
Reprinted by the Buddhist Temple, Varanasi, U.P., 1973.
Clear Mirror, A
gSal ba'i me long
Btsun pa dang ra lug glang gsum 'bel gtam byas pa'i tsul du dris pa'i yi ge btsun 'ga zhig gi gung tsigs kyi de nyid gsal ba'i me long, found in vol. 2 of the *Collected Works.* Leh, Ladakh: S.W. Tashigangpa, 495–527.
Commentary on the Difficult Points of the Kṛiṣhṇayamarī Tantra
dGra nag gi dka' 'grel
Compassionate Refuge
sKyabs thugs rje ma
Golden Rays Mind Training
Blo sbyong gser'od
(Same as *The Rays of the Sun Mind Training*?)
Great Discussion of the Particulars
Mahāvibhāṣha
Phye brag bshad mdzod chen mo
(Never translated into Tibetan)

History of the Kadampas
dKa'gdams chos 'byung
History of the Kadampas
dKa' gdams bu chos
(volume 2 of the *Book of the Kadampas*)
✓ *Hundreds of Gods of Tuṣhita*
dGa' ldan lha brgya'i ma
Inseparable Bliss and Void Pūjā
Bla ma mchod bde stong dbyer med ma
(Not listed in P or T)
Miraculous Book of the Gelugpas
dGa' ldan sprul pa'i glegs bam
One Hundred Biographies
rTogs brjod brgya pa
One Hundred Ritual Cakes Ceremony
gTor ma brgya rtsa
[Genre. Many authors, including Je Rinpoche, have composed such works; e.g., a Sakyapa version: *gTor ma brgya rtsa'i mam par bshad pa dang dkar cha bzhi'imam bshad* by Choe Namgyael, the abbot of Tanag Tubtaen *(Chos mam rgyal, rta nag thub bstan mkhan po)*. Gangtok: Sherab Gyaltsen, 1979.]
One Hundred Verses on Karma
P1007 vol. 39, T340
Karmaśhataka
Las brgya tham pa
Also known as *One Hundred Verses [on Karma] from the Sūtras (mDo sde las brgya pa)*
Purification of the Six Types of Sentient Beings and Their Abodes
Rigs drug gnas sbyong
Seal of Pankong
dPangs skong phyag brgya
(Undated private reprint by Geshe Ngagwang Nyima *(Ngag dbang nyi ma)* and Choeje Rabtaen *(Chos rje rab brtan)*.)
Shaking Out the Contents of Saṃsāra
'Khor ba dong sprugs
Sūtra for Classifying Karma
P1005 vol. 3959, T4484
Karma vibhaṅga
Las mam par 'byed pa
Summary of Precious Good Qualities
Yon tan rin po che sdud pa

Systematized Vinaya
P1032 vol. 42–43, T3
Vinaya vibhaṅga
'Dul ba mam par 'byed pa
White Naga Anthology
Klu 'bum dkar mo

3. OTHER WORKS

Chattopadhyaya, Alaka. *Atīśa and Tibet.* Calcutta: R.D. Press, 1967.

Conze, Edward. *Abhisamayālaṅkāra.* Serie Orientale Roma VI. Rome: Is.M.E.O., July 1954.

———. *Aṣṭasāhasrikā Prajñāpāramitā.* Bolinas: Four Seasons, 1962.

———. *The Large Sūtra on Perfect Wisdom.* Berkeley: University of California, 1975.

———. *The Short Prajñāpāramitā. Texts.* London: Luzac, 1973.

Dagyab, L.S. *Tibetan Dictionary.* Dharamsala: 1966.

———. *Buddhist Symbols.* Boston: Wisdom Publications, 2000.

Dalai Lama III, Sonam Gyatso. *Essence of Refined Gold.* With commentary by H.H. the Dalai Lama XIV. Ed. and trans. by Glenn Mullin. Ithaca: Snow Lion Publications, 1982.

Dalai Lama XIV, Tenzin Gyatso. *The Buddhism of Tibet and The Key to the Middle Way.* Trans. by Jeffrey Hopkins and Lati Rinpoche. London: George Allen and Unwin, 1975.

———. *Essence of the Heart Sutra.* Trans. and ed. by Thupten Jinpa. Boston: Wisdom Publications, 2002.

———. *Kindness, Clarity, and Insight.* Trans. by Jeffrey Hopkins. Ithaca: Snow Lion Publications, 1984.

———. *Opening the Eye of New Awareness.* Trans. by Donald S. Lopez, with Jeffrey Hopkins. Boston: Wisdom Publications, 1985 (Reprint, 1999).

———. *Path to Bliss.* Trans. by Thupten Jinpa, ed. by Christine Cox. Ithaca: Snow Lion Publications, 1991.

———. *Practicing Wisdom: The Perfection of Shantideva's Bodhisattva Way.* Trans. and ed. by Thupten Jinpa. Boston: Wisdom Publications, 2005.

———. *The World of Tibetan Buddhism: An Overview of Its Philosophy and Practice.* Trans. and ed. by Thupten Jinpa. Boston: Wisdom Publications, 1995.

Das, Sarat Chandra. *A Tibetan-English Dictionary with Sanskrit Synonyms.* New Delhi: Motilal Banarsidass, 1976.

Dhargyey, Geshe Ngawang. *Anthology of Well-Spoken Advice,* vol. 1. Ed. by Alexander Berzin based on oral translations by Sharpa Tulku. Dharamsala: LTWA, 1983.

———. *The Tibetan Tradition of Mental Development.* Dharamsala: LTWA, 1985.

Frye, Stanley, trans. *Sūtra of the Wise and the Foolish.* Dharamsala: LTWA, 1981.

Gomo Tulku. *Becoming a Child of the Buddhas: A Simple Clarification of the "Root Verses of Seven Point Mind Training."* Trans. and ed. by Joan Nicell. Boston: Wisdom Publications, 1998.

Guenther, Herbert V., trans. and annotated. *The Jewel Ornament of Liberation,* by sGam po pa. Berkeley: Shambhala, 1971.

Guenther, Herbert V., and Leslie S. Kawamura. *Mind in Buddhist Psychology.* Emeryville: Dharma, 1975.

Hopkins, Jeffrey. *Meditation on Emptiness.* Boston: Wisdom Publications, 1983 (Reprint, 1996).

———. *The Tantric Distinction.* Boston: Wisdom Publications, 1984 (Reprint, 1999).

Klein, Anne C. *Knowledge and Liberation.* Ithaca: Snow Lion Publications, 1986.

Lati Rinbochay. *Mind in Tibetan Buddhism.* Trans. by Elizabeth Napper. Ithaca: Snow Lion Publications, 1986.

✓ • McDonald, Kathleen. *How to Meditate.* Boston: Wisdom Publications, 1986 (Revised, 2006).

Mullin, Glenn H., and Michael Richards, ed. *Meditations on the Lower Tantras.* Dharamsala: LTWA, 1983.

Murti, T.R.V. *The Central Philosophy of Buddhism.* London: George Allen and Unwin, 1955.

Napper, Elizabeth. *Dependent-Arising and Emptiness.* Boston: Wisdom Publications, 1989 (Reprint, 2003).

Obermiller, E. *History of Buddhism* by Bu-ston. Suzuki Reprint Series, 1931.

Pabongka Rinpoche. *Liberation in Our Hands* (3 volumes). Trans. by Geshe Lobsang Tharchin with Artemus B. Engle. Howell, N.J.: Mahāyāna Sūtra and Tantra Press, 1990–2001.

Rabten, Geshe. *Echoes of Voidness.* Trans. by Stephen Batchelor. London: Wisdom Publications, 1983.

• ✓———. *The Essential Nectar.* Ed. and verse trans. by Martin Willson. London: Wisdom Publications, 1984.

———. *The Preliminary Practices of Tibetan Buddhism.* Trans. by Gonsar Tulku. Dharamsala: LTWA, 1982.

Rabten, Geshe, and Geshe Dhargyey. *Advice from a Spiritual Friend.* Trans. by Brian Beresford. London: Wisdom Publications, 1984.

Regamey, K. Three Chapters from the *Samādhirājasūtra.* Warsaw: Warsaw Society of Arts and Letters, 1938.

Ruegg, David S. *The Literature of the Madhayamaka School of Philosophy in India.* Wiesbaden: Otto Harrasowitz, 1981.

Roerich, George N. *The Blue Annals.* Delhi: Motilal Banarsidass, 1976.

Shakabpa, Tsepon W.D. *Tibet: A Political History.* New York: Potala Publications, 1974.

Shāntideva. *The Bodhicaryāvatāra.* Trans. by Kate Crosby and Andrew Skilton. Birmingham, U.K.: Windhorse Publications, 2002 (1995).

———. *A Guide to the Bodhisattva Way of Life.* Trans. by Vesna A. Wallace and B. Alan Wallace. Ithaca: Snow Lion Publications, 1997.

———. *A Guide to the Bodhisattva's Way of Life.* Trans. by Stephen Batchelor. Dharamsala: LTWA, 1982.

———. *Śikṣā Samuccaya.* Trans. by C. Bendall and W.H.D. Rouse. Delhi: Motilal Banarsidass, 1971.

———. *The Way of the Bodhisattva.* Trans. by the Padmakara Translation Group. Boston: Shambhala Publications, 1997.

Sherburne, Richard, trans. *A Lamp for the Path and Commentary of Atiśha.* London: George Allen and Unwin, 1983.

Snellgrove, David L., and Hugh Richardson. *A Cultural History of Tibet.* New York: Praeger, 1968.

Sopa, Geshe Lhundub. *Peacock in the Poison Grove.* Ed. by Michael Sweet and Leonard Zwilling. Boston, Wisdom Publications, 2001.

———. *Stages of the Path to Enlightenment, Volume 1: The Preliminary Practices.* Ed. by David Patt and Beth Newman. Boston: Wisdom Publications, 2003.

———. *Stages of the Path to Enlightenment, Volume 2: Karma.* Ed. by David Patt. Boston: Wisdom Publications, 2005.

Sopa, Geshe Lhundup, and Jeffrey Hopkins. *Cutting Through Appearances: The Practice and Theory of Tibetan Buddhism.* Ithaca: Snow Lion, 1989.

Sparham, Gareth. *The Tibetan Dhammapada.* London: Wisdom Publications, 1986.

Speyer, J.S., trans. *The Jātakamālā, or Garland of Birth-Stories, of Aryaśhura.* Delhi: Motilal Barnarsidass, 1971.

Stcherbatsky, Theodore. *Buddhist Logic.* New York: Dover, 1962.

———. *Madhyānta-Vibhanga.* Calcutta: Indian Studies Past and Present, 1971.

Tāranātha. *History of Buddhism in India.* Trans. by Lama Chimpa and Alaka Chattopadhyaya. Calcutta: Bagchi, 1980.

———. *The Seven Instruction Lineages.* Trans. by David Templeman. Dharamsala: LTWA, 1983.

Tatz, Dr. Mark. *Chandragomin's Twenty Verses on the Bodhisattva Vow and Its Commentary.* Dharamsala: LTWA, 1982.

Tharchin, Geshe Lobsang, and Artemus B. Engle, trans. *Nāgārjuna's Letter.* Dharamsala: LTWA, 1982.

Thurman, Robert A.F., ed. *The Life and Teachings of Tsong Khapa.* Dharamsala: LTWA, 1982.

Tsongkapa. *The Principal Teachings of Buddhism (with a commentary by Pabongka Rinpoche).* Trans. by Geshe Lobsang Tharchin with Michael Roach. Howell, N.J.: Mahāyāna Sūtra and Tantra Press, 1988.

Tsongkhapa. *The Fulfillment of All Hopes: Guru Devotion in Tibetan Buddhism.* Trans. and ed. by Gareth Sparham. Boston: Wisdom Publications, 1999.

———. *Splendor of an Autumn Moon: The Devotional Verse of Tsongkhapa.* Trans. by Gavin Kilty. Boston: Wisdom Publications, 2001.

Tucci, Giuseppe. *The Religions of Tibet.* Trans. from the German and Italian by Geoffrey Samuel. London: Routledge and Kegan Paul, 1980.

Wallace, B. Alan. *The Attention Revolution.* Boston: Wisdom Publications, 2006.

———. *Tibetan Buddhism from the Ground Up.* Boston: Wisdom Publications, 1994.

Wangyal, Geshe. *The Door of Liberation.* Boston: Wisdom Publications, 2006.

Willson, Martin. *In Praise of Tārā.* London: Wisdom Publications, 1986.

Yangsi Rinpoche. *Practicing the Path: A Commentary on the "Lamrim Chenmo."* Boston: Wisdom Publications, 2003.

Yeshe, Lama Thubten. *Introduction to Tantra.* Ed. by Jonathan Landaw. Boston: Wisdom Publications, 1987 (Revised, 2001).

———. *Becoming Vajrasattva: The Tantric Path of Purification.* Ed. by Nicholas Ribush. Boston: Wisdom Publications, 2004 (1995).

Yeshe, Lama, and Zopa Rinpoche. *Wisdom Energy.* Ed. by Jonathan Landaw with Alexander Berzin. London: Wisdom Publications, 1982 (Reprint, 2000).

Zopa, Lama Thubten. *Transforming Problems into Happiness.* Boston: Wisdom Publications, 2001 (1993).

INDEX

TRANSLATOR'S DEDICATION

By the merit gained from the translation, publication, and reading of this book, may all sentient beings soon reach enlightenment. May there be peace in this world, may there never be nuclear war, and may all beings have the opportunity to practice the Dharma.

PUBLISHER'S ACKNOWLEDGMENT

The publisher gratefully acknowledges the generous help of the Hershey Family Foundation in sponsoring the printing of this book.

ABOUT THE AUTHORS

Pabongka Rinpoche, Jampa Tenzin Trinlae Gyatso (1878–1941), attained his geshe degree at Sera Monastic University, Lhasa. He became a highly influential teacher in Tibet, serving as the root guru of the present Dalai Lama's two tutors and of many other Gelug lamas who have brought the Dharma to the West since they fled Tibet in 1959. *Liberation* captures the essence of Pabongka Rinpoche's fifteen published volumes on all aspects of Buddhism.

Trijang Rinpoche (1901–81) was the foremost student of Pabongka Rinpoche. He was also the Junior Tutor of the Fourteenth Dalai Lama and the root guru of many Gelug lamas now teaching in the West.

Michael Richards (1950–) is an Australian scholar who lived in the Tibetan exile community of Dharamsala for many years and translated this work in consultation with many lamas there.

ABOUT WISDOM

WISDOM PUBLICATIONS is dedicated to offering works relating to and inspired by Buddhist traditions.

To learn more about us or to explore our other books, please visit our website at www.wisdompubs.org. You can subscribe to our e-newsletter or request our print catalog online, or by writing to:

Wisdom Publications
199 Elm Street
Somerville, Massachusetts 02144 USA

You can also contact us at 617-776-7416, or info@wisdompubs.org.

Wisdom is a nonprofit, charitable 501(c)(3) organization, and donations in support of our mission are tax deductible.

Wisdom Publications is affiliated with the Foundation for the Preservation of the Mahayana Tradition (FPMT).